I0824898

50 STATES
500 NATIONAL PARKS

pil

Publications International, Ltd.

Images from Shutterstock.com and Wikimedia Commons

Louis Weber, CEO
Publications International, Ltd.
8140 Lehigh Avenue
Morton Grove, IL 60053

ISBN: 978-1-63938-917-9

Manufactured in China.

8 7 6 5 4 3 2 1

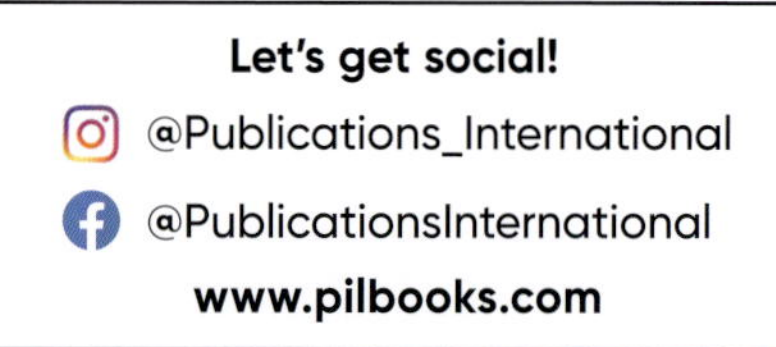

TABLE OF CONTENTS

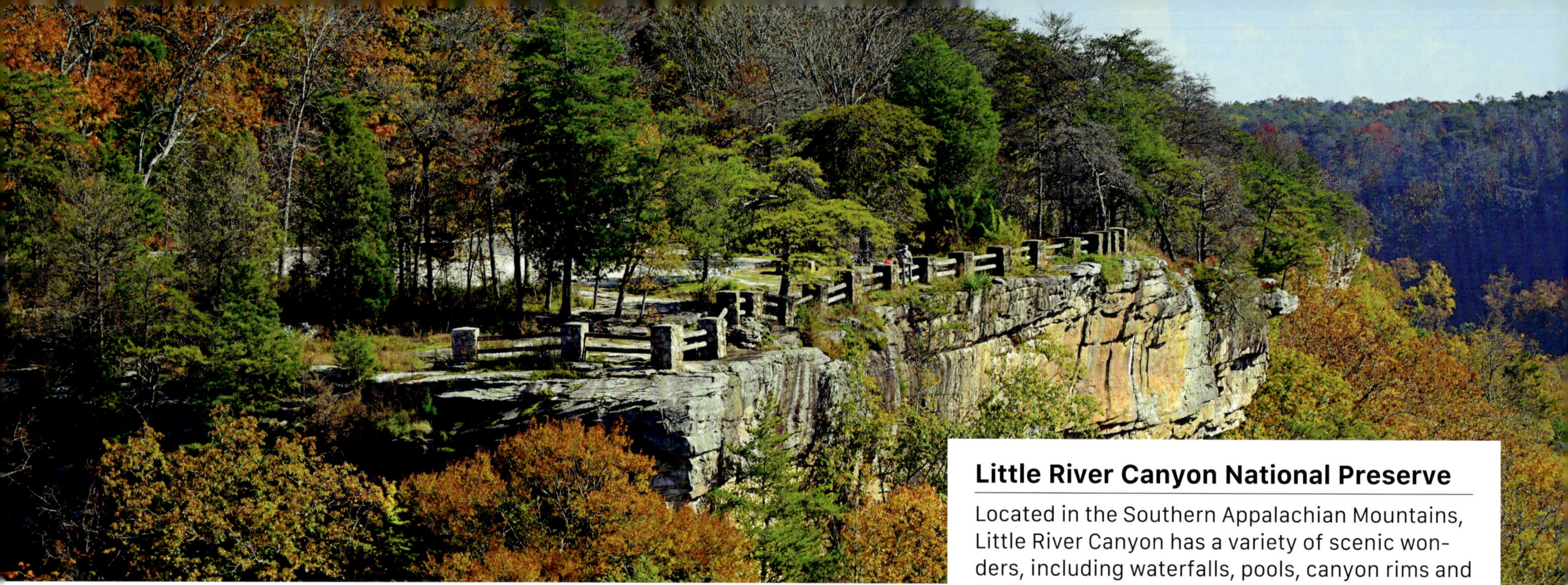

ALABAMA

Little River Canyon National Preserve

Located in the Southern Appalachian Mountains, Little River Canyon has a variety of scenic wonders, including waterfalls, pools, canyon rims and bluffs, forested uplands, sandstone cliffs, and more. Perhaps its most unique feature is that the majority of Little River flows atop Lookout Mountain in northeast Alabama.

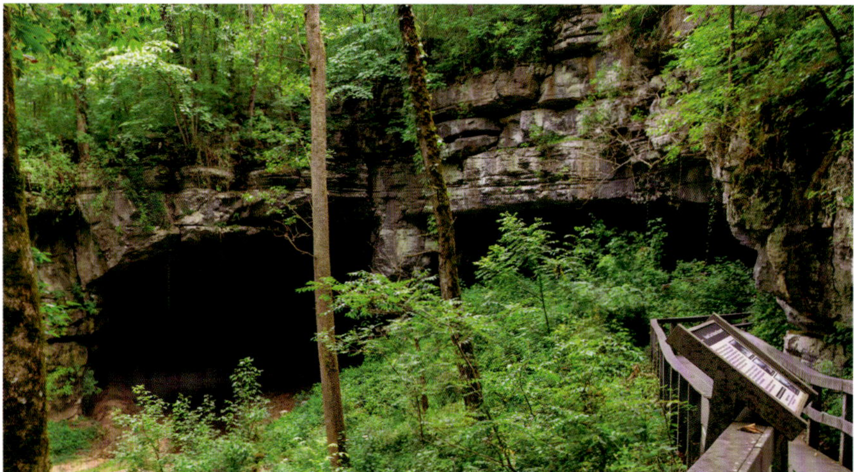

Russell Cave National Monument

In the 1950s, archeologists discovered artifacts going as far back as 10,000 years ago in what is now known as Russell Cave. Boasting one of the most complete records of prehistoric cultures in the Southeast, Russell Cave offers valuable educational opportunities, scenic walking trails, and serves as a station on the North Alabama Birding Trail.

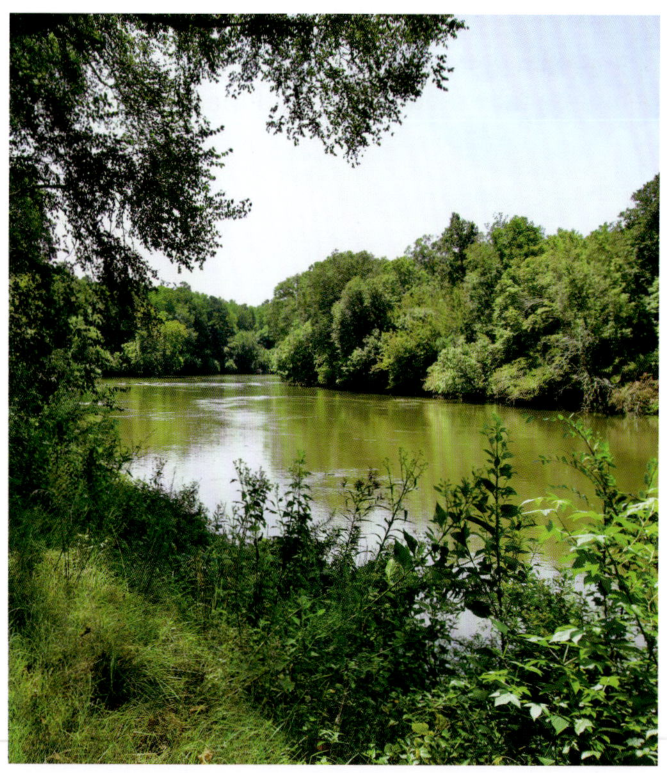

Horseshoe Bend National Military Park

Located in Tallapoosa County, it serves as the site of the penultimate battle of the Creek War on March 27, 1814. The site is a popular location for school field trips, but it also offers nature trails, picnic areas, boating, fishing, and bicycling.

Selma to Montgomery National Historic Trail

This 54-mile National Historic Trail marks the journey of Dr. Martin Luther King, Jr. and nonviolent activists in support of the Voting Rights Act of 1965. Beginning at Mount Zion AME Zion Church in Marion, it winds its way to Montgomery, and is dotted by interpretative centers and signs that mark where participants camped, and where historic moments took place.

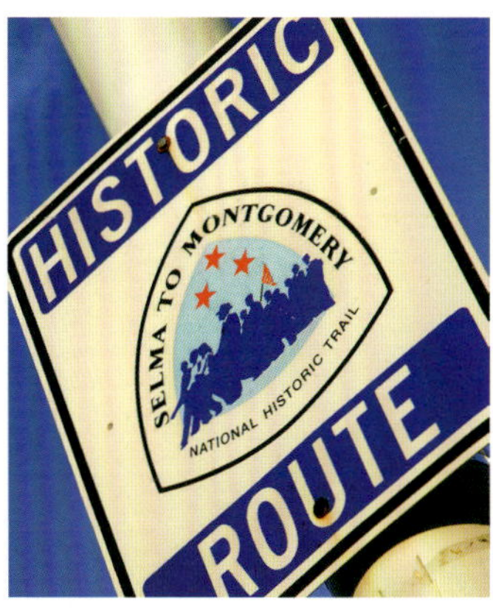

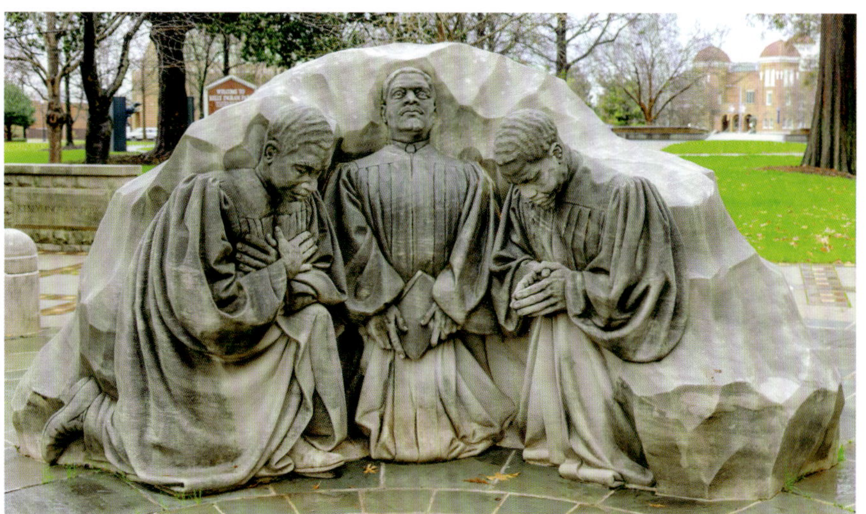

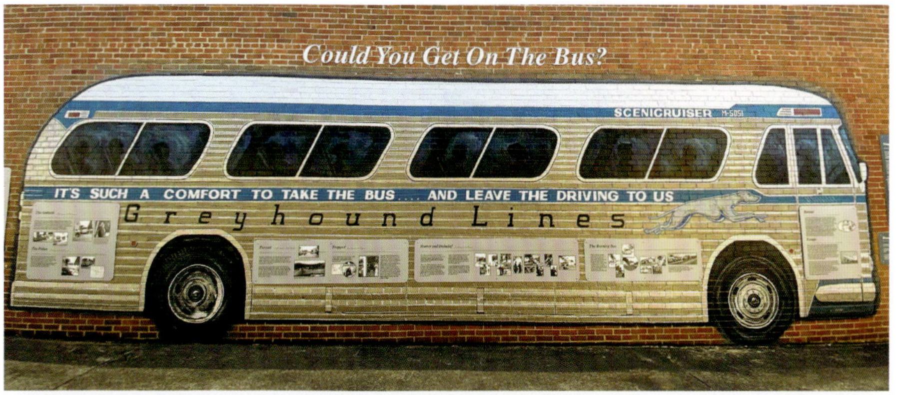

Birmingham Civil Rights National Monument

Dedicated as a national monument in 2017, this national park site in downtown Birmingham contains the Birmingham Civil Rights Institute, A. G. Gaston Motel, 16th Street Baptist Church, Kelly Ingram Park, and much more. The sculpture of praying ministers at Kelly Ingram Park *(see above)* is one of many art installments that depict various events that took place during the campaign for civil rights in 1963.

Freedom Riders National Monument

Located in Anniston, Freedom Riders National Monument seeks to preserve and commemorate the Freedom Riders during the Civil Rights Movement. The first site is of the former Greyhound bus depot where a mob attacked White and Black Freedom Riders who sought to end racial segregation in interstate busing. The site today features a mural *(see above)* and educational panels.

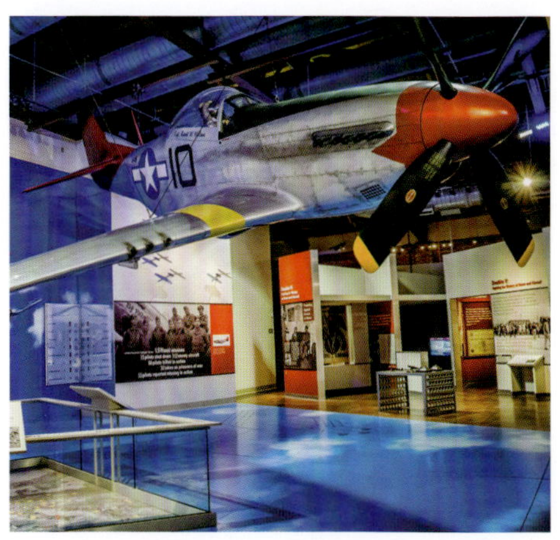

Tuskegee Airmen National Historic Site

This historic site honors the Tuskegee Airmen, a group of primarily African American airmen who fought in WWII. It contains the Hanger #1 Museum and Hanger #2 Museum where you can learn about the famous airmen, the rigors of training, view WWII-era training aircrafts *(see left)*, and more.

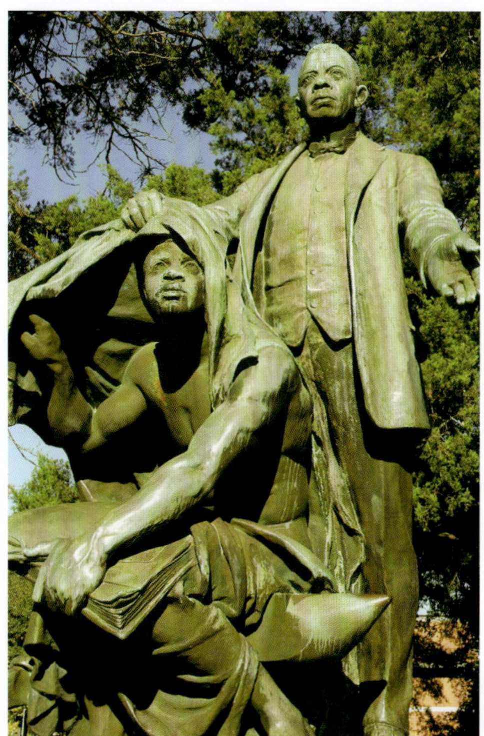

Tuskegee Institute National Historic Site

This site preserves the historic Tuskegee Institute, a college for African Americans founded in 1881. The main features of the site are The Oak—where Booker T. Washington, the institute's first principal *(see left)*, lived—and the George Washington Carver Museum, which housed George Washington Carver's laboratory. Additionally, the site encompasses a 50-acre Historic Campus District that features historic buildings still used by Tuskegee University to this day.

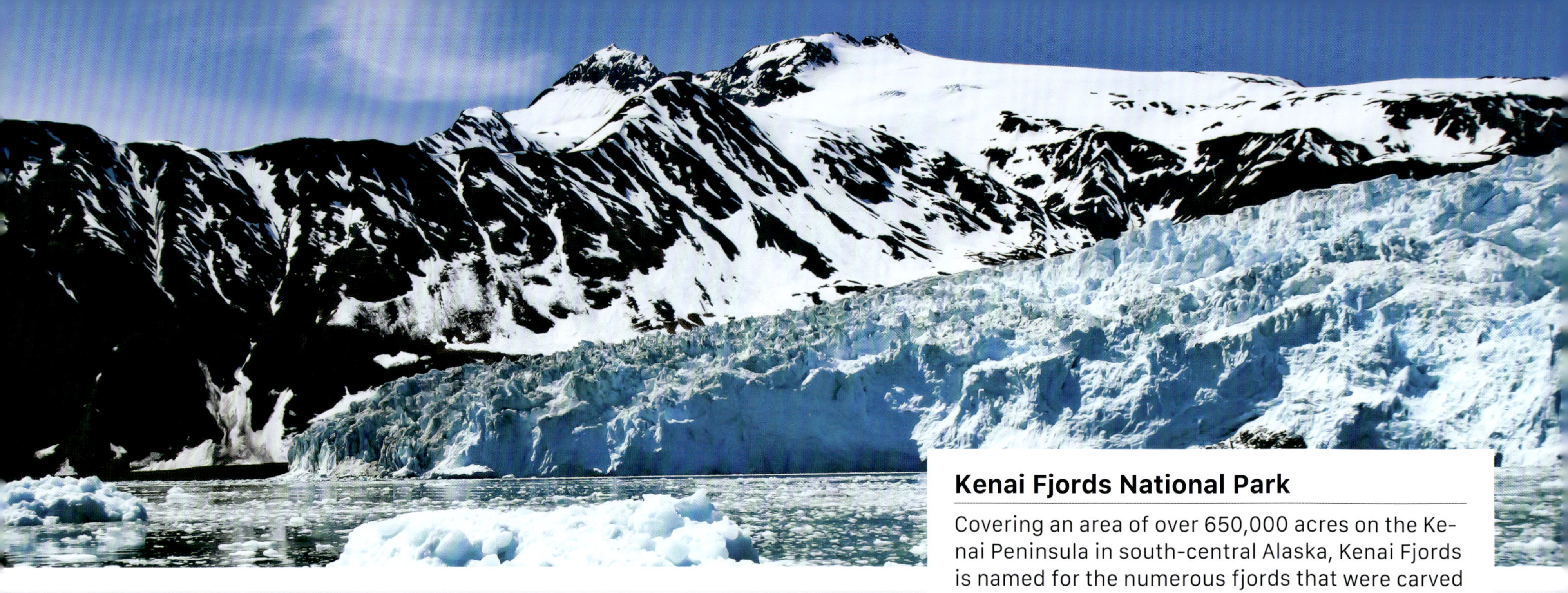

ALASKA

Kenai Fjords National Park

Covering an area of over 650,000 acres on the Kenai Peninsula in south-central Alaska, Kenai Fjords is named for the numerous fjords that were carved by glaciers moving down the mountains. The park includes more than 500 miles of shoreline, with glaciers flowing from Harding Icefield.

Kobuk Valley National Park

With no roads leading into the park, Kobuk Valley National Park requires a chartered air taxi from Nome, Bettes, or Kotzebue to visit. While difficult to enter, it is well-worth the effort with its stunning wetlands, majestic Baird Mountains, and curious sand dunes.

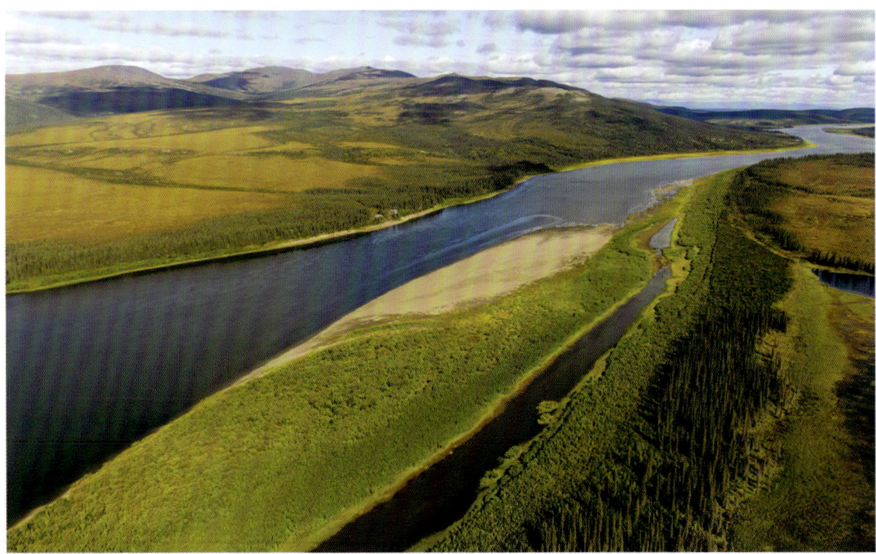

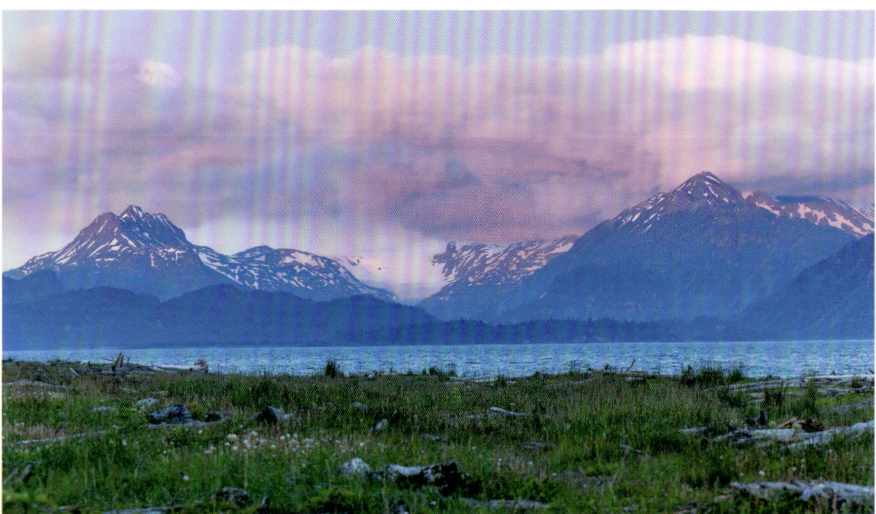

Denali National Park and Preserve

Formally known as Mount McKinley National Park, Denali National Park and Preserve contains the tallest peak in North America. It offers numerous activities in both summer and winter—with hiking and biking, and fishing available in the summer, and skiing, winter biking, and snowshoeing available during the winter months.

Gates of the Arctic National Park and Preserve

Originally planned as a national monument, Gates of the Arctic National Park and Preserve is one of the most remote and pristine national parks in the U.S. Local air taxies provide flightseeing trips, day trips, or overnight camping trips. Due to its sheer remoteness, its hiking and camping is only for the most rugged adventurers.

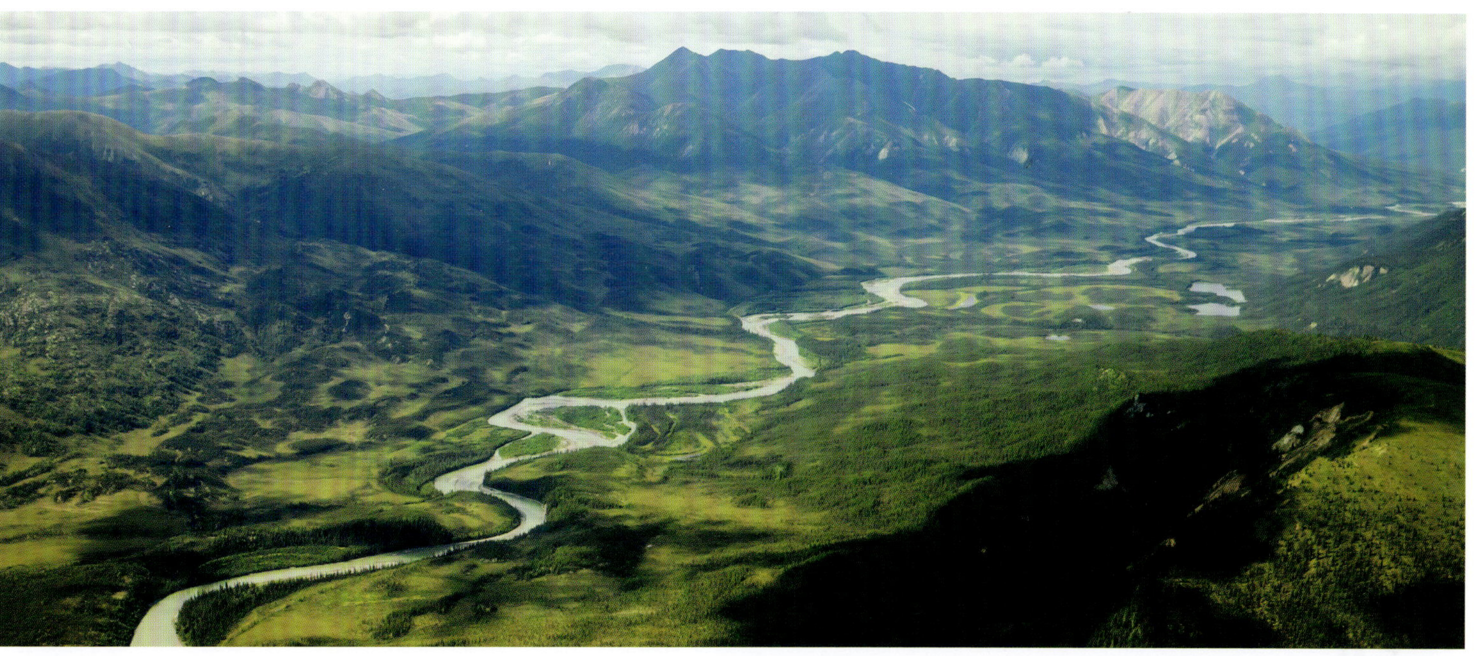

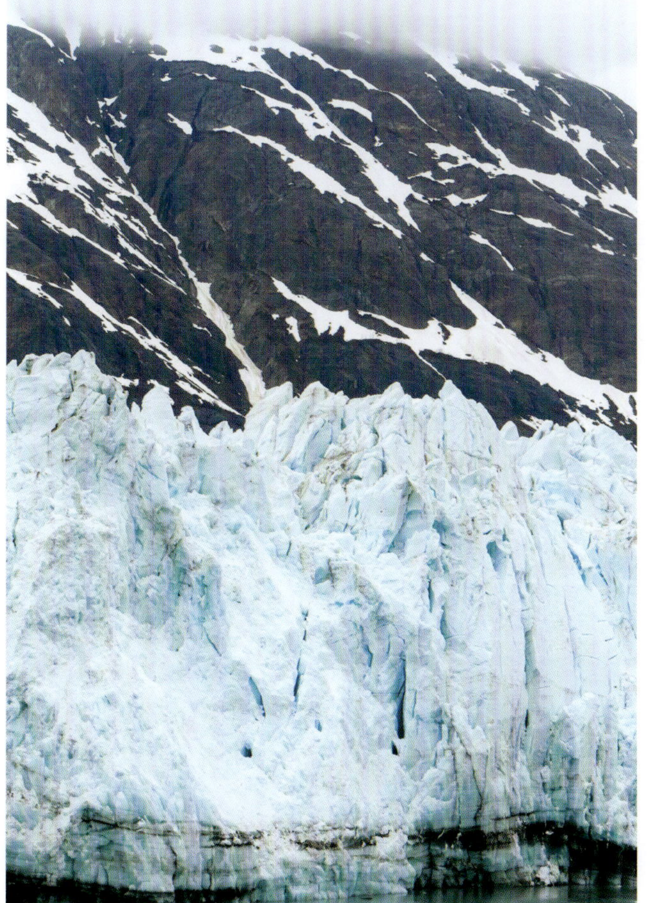

Glacier Bay National Park and Preserve

Glacier Bay is a breathtaking wilderness famous for its glaciers, fjords, and abundant wildlife. It spans over 3.3 million acres of rugged mountains, temperate rainforests, dynamic glaciers, and marine ecosystems. One of the only developed areas, Bartlett Cove has a park lodge, visitor center with exhibits, walk-in campground, and ship and boat boarding area.

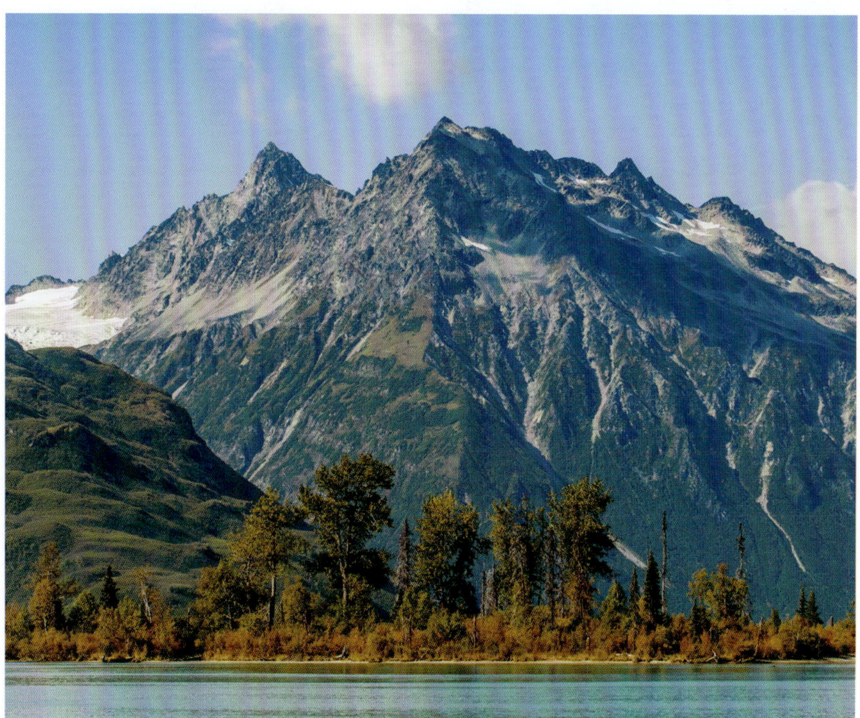

Lake Clark National Park and Preserve

Lake Clark National Park and Preserve is a remote and breathtaking wilderness area known for its diverse landscapes, vibrant ecosystems, and cultural heritage. Spanning over 4 million acres, it offers crystal-clear lakes, towering volcanoes, and a haven for wildlife.

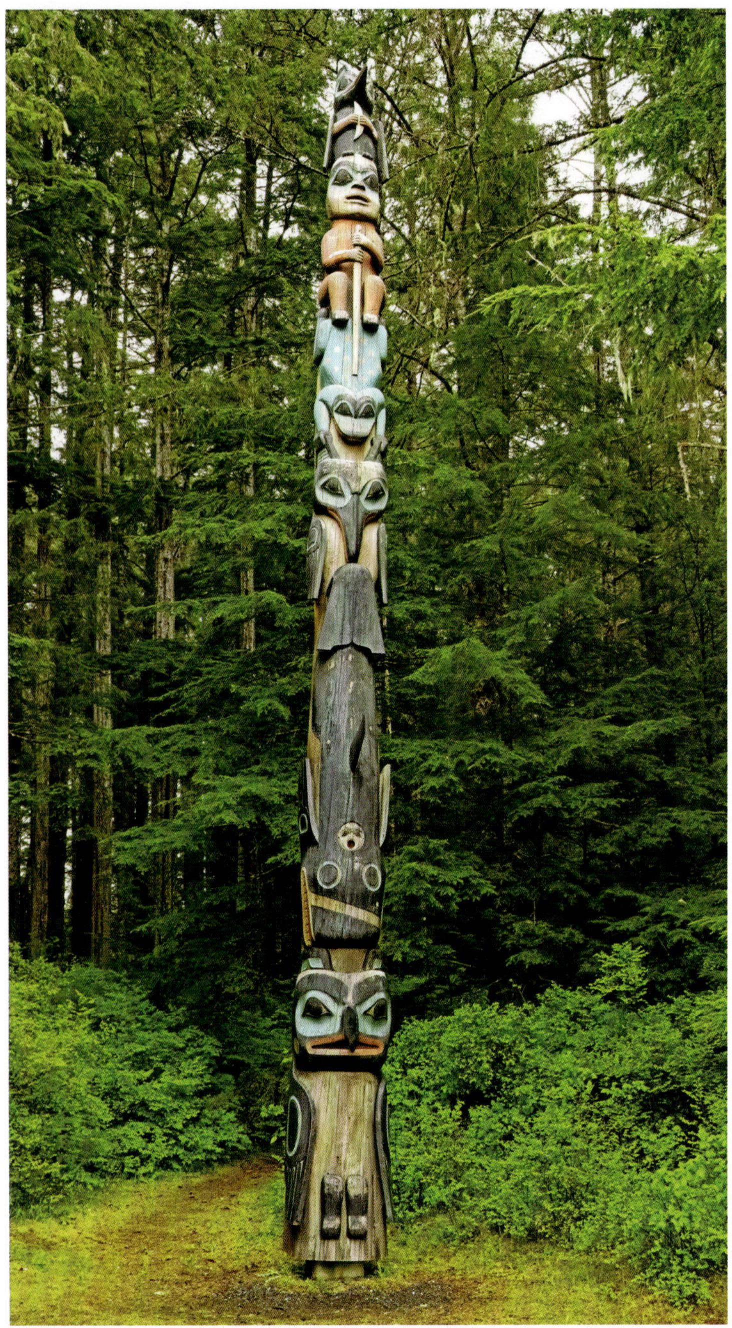

Sitka National Historical Park

Previously known as Indian River Park and Totem Park, Sitka National Historical Park preserves the site of a battle between invading Russian traders and Indigenous Tlingit. Visitors can view the historic Tlingit and Haida totem poles, the restored Russian Bishop's house, and the E. W. Merrill collection of 1,167 glass plate negatives from 20th-century Sitka.

Noatak National Preserve

Noatak National Preserve is believed to be the last unaltered, complete river system in the U.S. As with many Alaskan national parks and preserves, it doesn't have any roads going in or out—visitors will need to travel there by plane, boat, or snowmobile, depending on the season. River float trips are extremely popular, as are camping, hiking, and sport hunting.

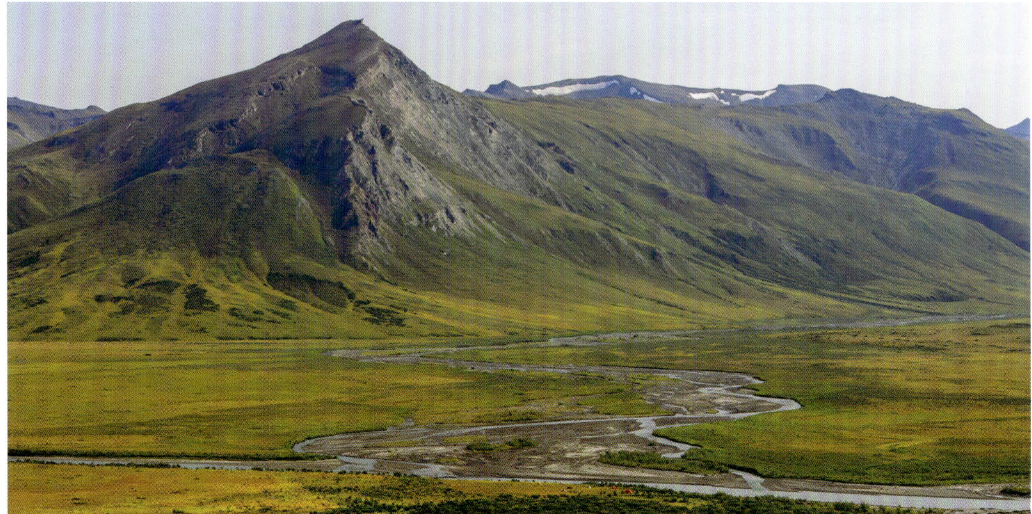

Wrangell – St. Elias National Park and Preserve

Wrangell–St. Elias National Park and Preserve comes at the visitor in waves of superlatives. Wrangell–St. Elias is the largest national park: 20,587 square miles or more than 13 million acres. The park is six times the size of Yellowstone and larger than Switzerland. It has nine of the sixteen highest U.S. mountains—four of them are above 16,000 feet. Wrangell–St. Elias contains the nation's largest glacial system; glaciers cover more than one-quarter of the park.

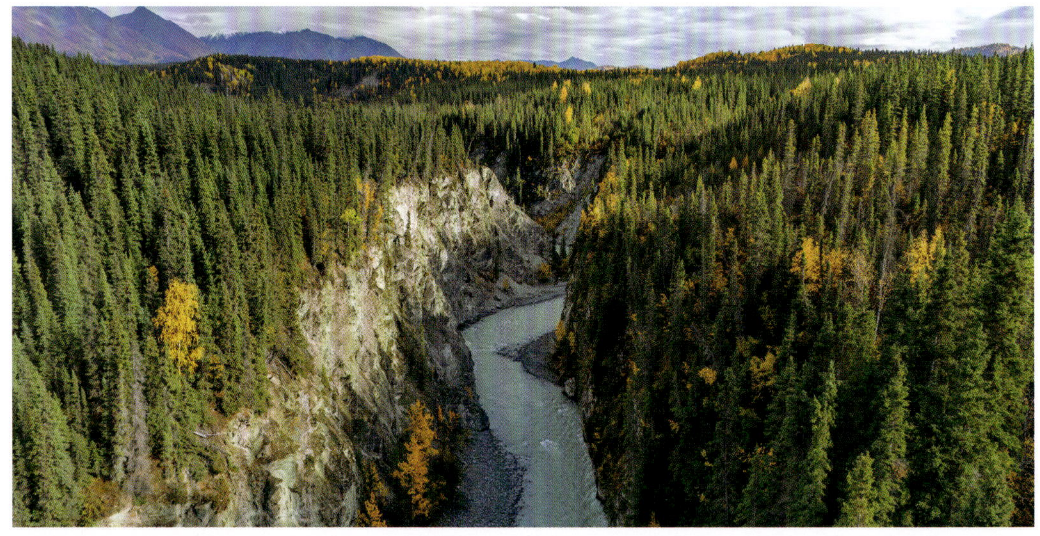

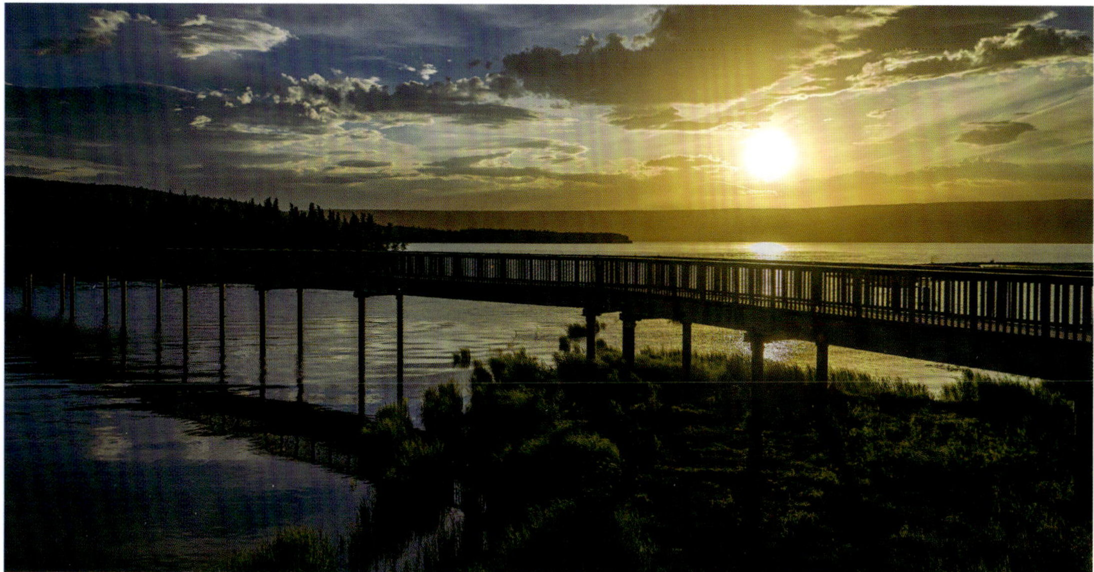

Katmai National Park and Preserve

Katmai National Park and Preserve is notable for the Valley of Ten Thousand Smokes, a valley that's filled with ash flow from the eruption of Novarupta in 1912. Another must-see site is Brooks Camp, a popular destination for bear viewing, sport fishing, beautiful scenery, and facilities that showcase the history of the area.

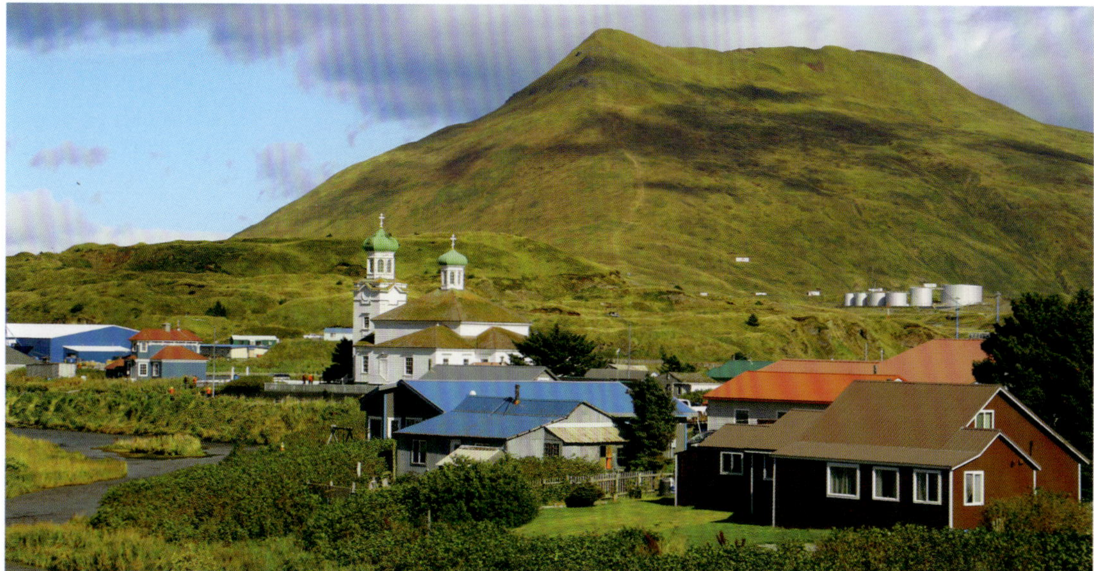

Aleutian Islands World War II National Historic Area

The Aleutian Islands is the location of the only World War II military campaign that was fought on American soil. This National Historic Area exists to honor and preserve Unangax̂ accounts of the war, educating visitors of their harrowing experiences during WWII, their 4,000-year-old culture, and their efforts to seek justice and restitution.

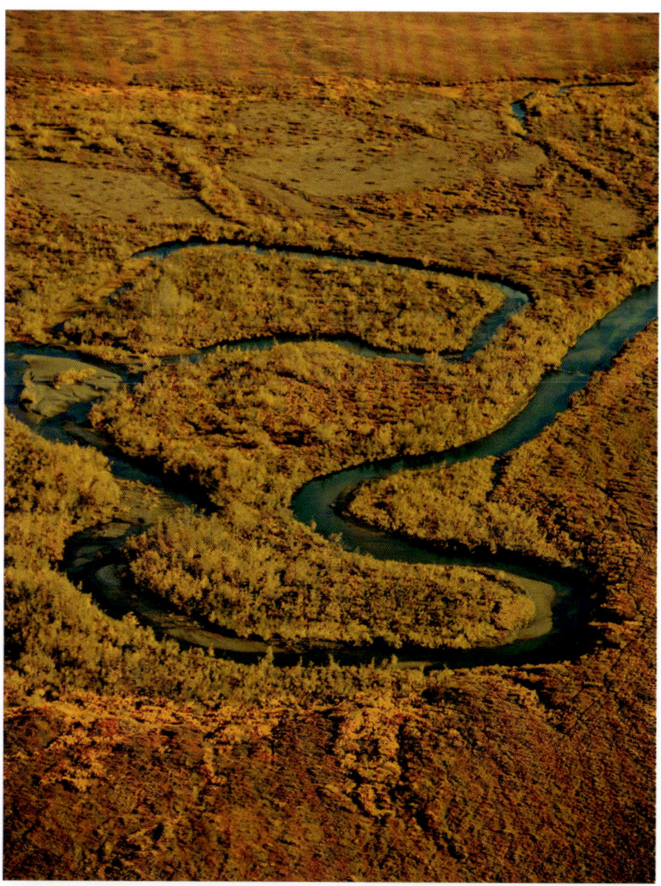

Cape Krusenstern National Monument

Cape Krusenstern National Monument, located in northwestern Alaska along the Chukchi Sea, is a vast and remote area known for its unique archaeological significance, coastal landscapes, and pristine Arctic ecosystems. It covers about 650,000 acres and is part of the Western Arctic National Parklands.

Other Alaska National Parks

- Bering Land Bridge National Preserve
- Yukon–Charley Rivers National Preserve
- Aniakchak National Monument and Preserve
- Klondike Gold Rush National Historical Park
- Goldbelt Tram
- Tracy Arm Fjord

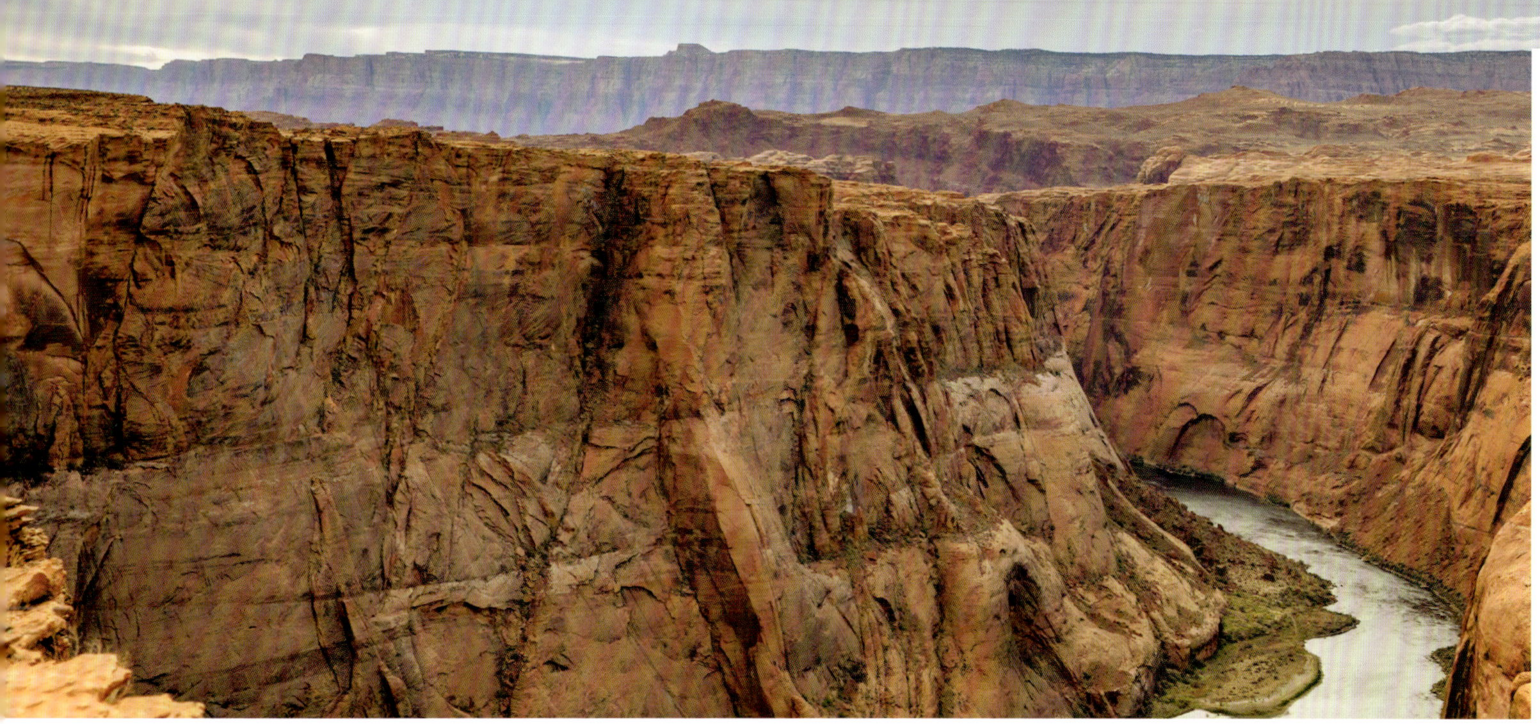

Grand Canyon National Park

Although there is no consensus on the Seven Natural Wonders of the World, the Grand Canyon is on virtually every short list—sometimes the only such landmark in the U.S. More than four million visitors come to see the canyon every year, seeking its beauty beyond compare. Beyond marveling at its striking visage, visitors can enjoy hiking, rafting the Colorado River, mule rides, helicopter or airplane tours, camping, stargazing, and more.

ARIZONA

Petrified Forest National Park

Wander through a desert filled with fossilized trees, painted badlands, and endless stories of Earth's ancient past at Petrified Forest National Park. Visitors can explore the petrified wood, hike picturesque trails, drive the scenic park road, discover ancient petroglyphs etched by Indigenous peoples, learn at the visitors centers, and more.

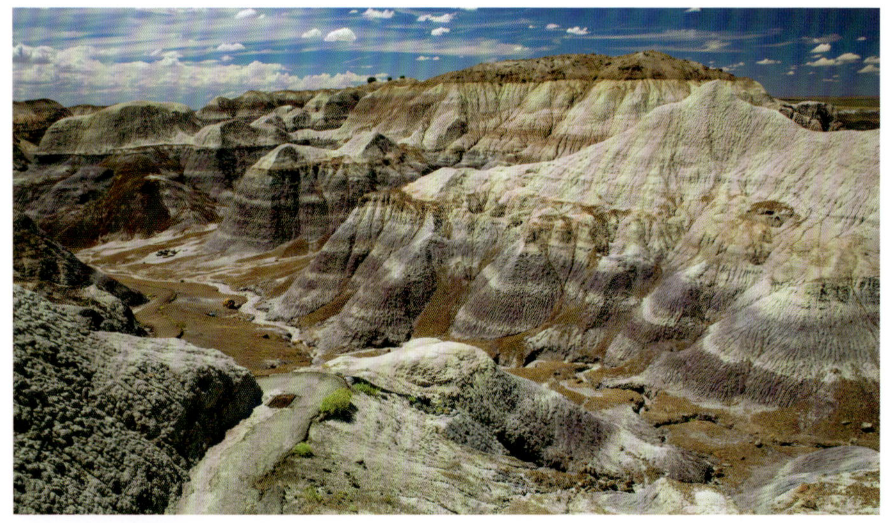

Saguaro National Park

Saguaro National Park, located in southern Arizona, is famous for its amazing landscapes, dominated by towering saguaro cacti *(see right)*, the largest cacti in the U.S. It protects a portion of the Sonoran Desert, showcasing a plethora of desert flora and fauna, and offers breathtaking mountain and desert vistas. Visitors can also enjoy scenic drives, hiking, ranger programs, backpacking and camping, and learning at the Rincon Mountain Visitor Center and the Red Hills Visitor Center.

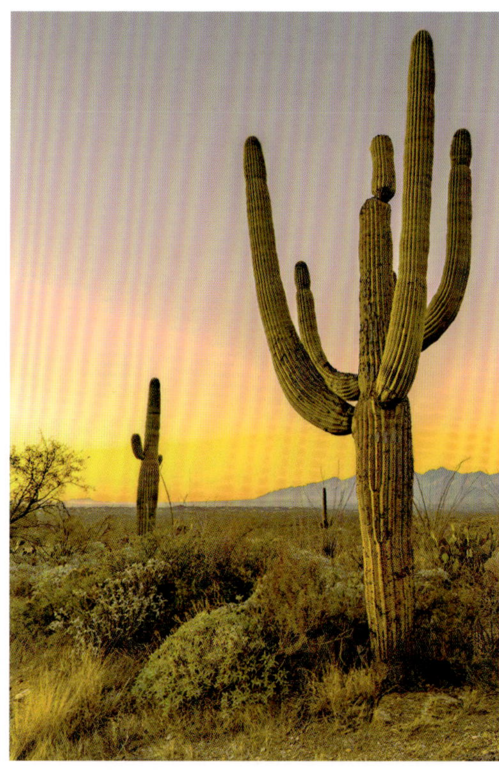

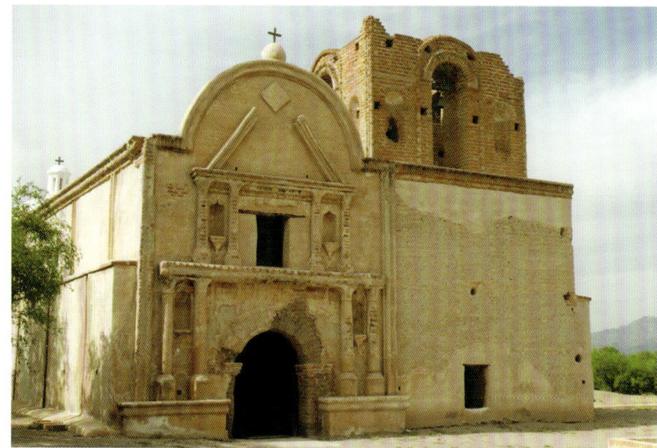

Tumacácori National Historical Park

Tumacácori National Historical Park is celebrated for preserving the history and heritage of Spanish missions in the Southwest U.S. The park features the remains of three missions, including the well-preserved Mission San José de Tumacácori *(see above)*, which dates back to 1691, making it the oldest Jesuit mission in southern Arizona. It showcases a blend of Native American, Spanish, and Mexican cultural influences.

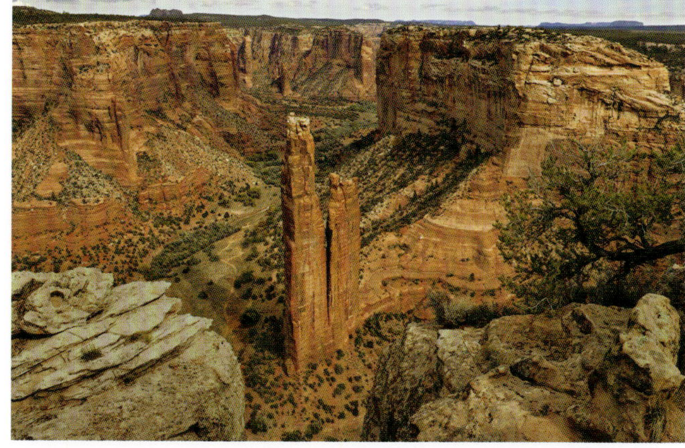

Canyon de Chelly National Monument

Canyon de Chelly National Monument, located in northeastern Arizona within the Navajo Nation, is famous for its stunning red rock canyons, rich Indigenous history, and breathtaking views of ancient cliff dwellings. Its major claim-to-fame is Spider Rock *(see above)*, a sandstone spire that rises 750 feet from the canyon floor.

Casa Grande Ruins National Monument

Casa Grande Ruins National Monument is renowned for its "Big House," an ancient structure built by the Ancestral Sonoran Desert People over 700 years ago in what is known as the Hohokam period. This adobe-style structure, surrounded by remnants of a once-thriving agricultural community, offers a glimpse into the ingenuity of one of the Southwest's earliest cultures.

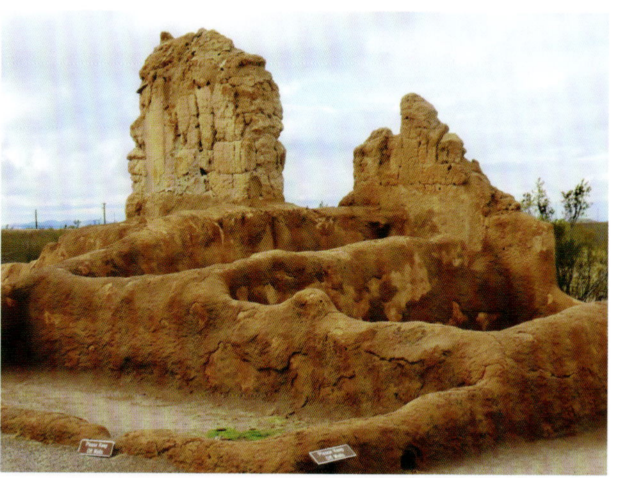

Chiricahua National Monument

Chiricahua National Monument is celebrated for its "Wonderland of Rocks"—a dramatic landscape filled with towering rock spires, balancing rocks *(see left)*, and unique volcanic formations. This geological wonder was created by massive volcanic eruptions millions of years ago and has since become a haven for hikers, wildlife enthusiasts, and history buffs.

Coronado National Memorial

Coronado National Memorial, located in southeastern Arizona near the U.S.-Mexico border, commemorates the first major European expedition into the American Southwest, led by conquistador Francisco Vásquez de Coronado in 1540. Known for its picturesque views of the San Pedro Valley, the memorial celebrates the cultural blending of Indigenous and Spanish traditions, and offers unique natural features, such as caves and diverse ecosystems.

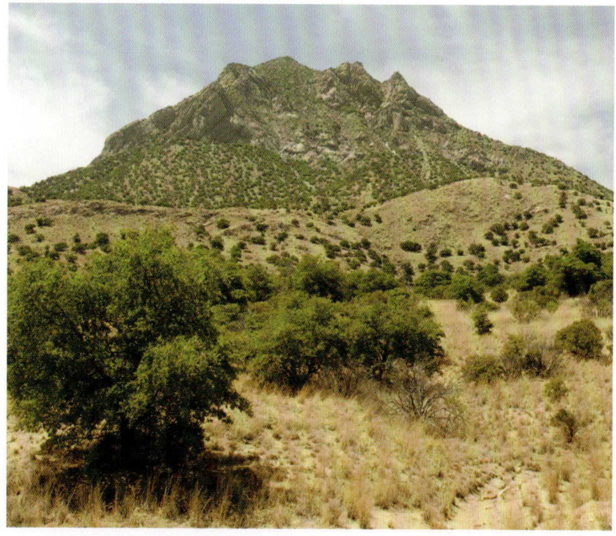

Fort Bowie National Historic Site

Fort Bowie National Historic Site preserves the remnants of a 19th-century military outpost that played a pivotal role in the U.S. Army's campaigns during the Apache Wars. The site commemorates the complex history of the region, including conflicts between the Chiricahua Apache and U.S. settlers, and highlights the cultural significance of key events like the Bascom Affair and the surrender of Apache leader Geronimo.

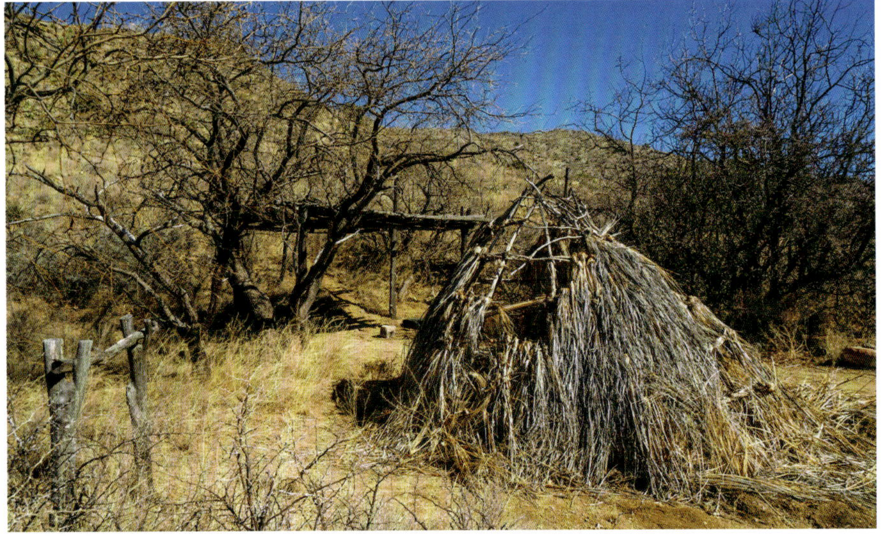

Sunset Crater Volcano National Monument

Sunset Crater Volcano National Monument preserves the site of a volcanic eruption that occurred nearly 1,000 years ago. The eruption, which formed Sunset Crater, left behind a rugged landscape of lava flows, cinder fields, and vibrant red and orange hues that inspired the crater's name. The monument highlights the transformative power of volcanic activity and its impact on the landscape, ecosystems, and human history of the region.

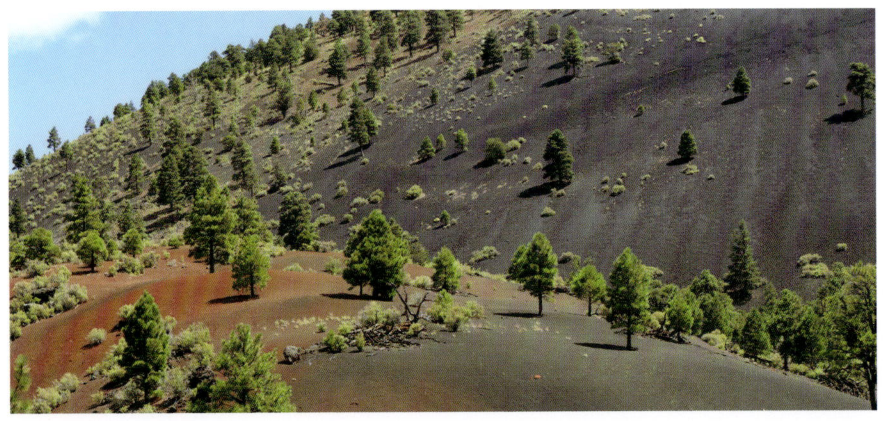

Hubbell Trading Post National Historic Site

Hubbell Trading Post National Historic Site is the oldest continuously operating trading post on the Navajo Nation, established in 1878 by John Lorenzo Hubbell. The site preserves the history of trade between Navajo people and settlers, showcasing the importance of commerce, culture, and art in the region. It is a living historic site where visitors can still experience the atmosphere of a 19th-century trading post.

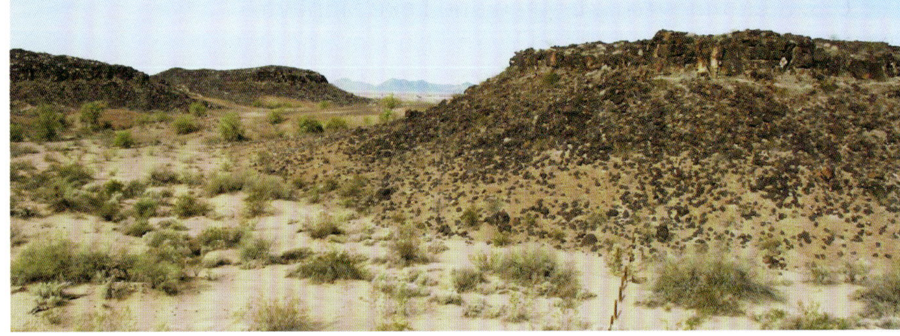

Juan Bautista de Anza National Historic Trail

Juan Bautista de Anza National Historic Trail commemorates the 1,200-mile route taken by Juan Bautista de Anza in 1775–1776, when he led a group of settlers from present-day Sonora, Mexico, to the San Francisco Bay area in California. This historic trail highlights the cultural, historical, and environmental significance of Anza's expedition, which established the first overland route connecting New Spain to Alta California. The trail passes through Arizona, California, and Mexico, offering a blend of history and outdoor adventure.

Montezuma Castle National Monument

Montezuma Castle National Monument is renowned for its remarkably well-preserved prehistoric cliff dwellings. Built by the Sinagua people around 900 years ago, the five-story, 20-room structure is nestled into a limestone cliff 100 feet above the valley floor. Despite its name, it has no connection to Montezuma or the Aztecs. Instead, it serves as a testament to the ingenuity and resilience of the Sinagua culture, offering a glimpse into life in the American Southwest centuries ago.

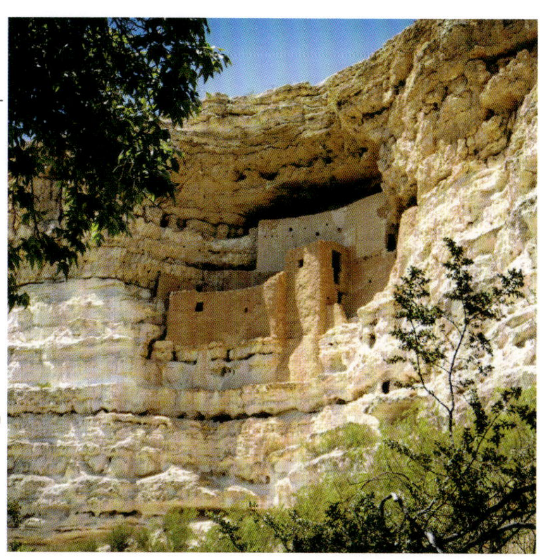

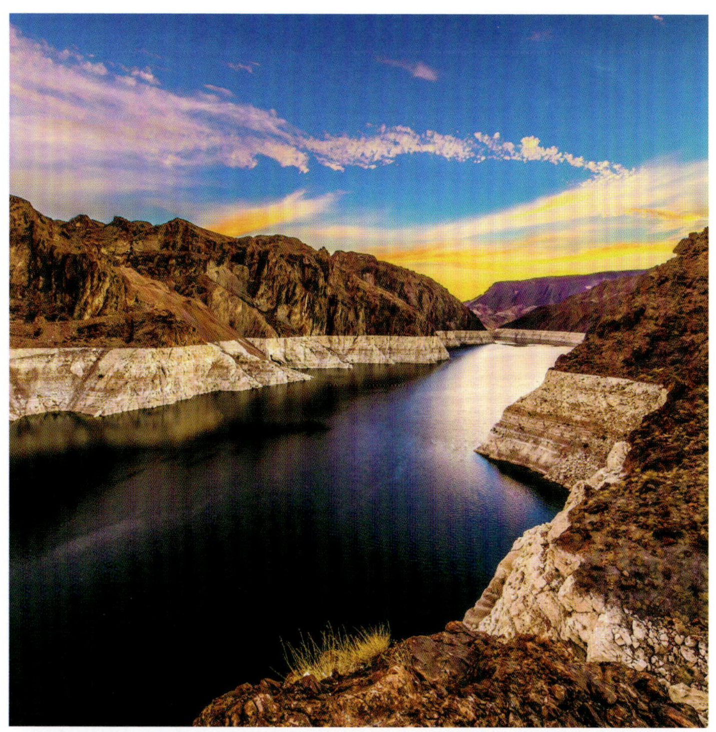

Lake Mead National Recreation Area

Lake Mead National Recreation Area, spanning southern Nevada and northwestern Arizona, is known for being the first designated National Recreation Area in the U.S. It's home to Lake Mead and Lake Mohave, two expansive reservoirs formed by the Hoover and Davis Dams on the Colorado River. Known for its rugged desert landscapes, vast water-based recreational activities, and proximity to the Hoover Dam, it's a haven for outdoor enthusiasts and history buffs alike.

Navajo National Monument

Navajo National Monument, located in northern Arizona near the Navajo Nation, preserves three of the most impressive Ancestral Puebloan cliff dwellings: Betatakin, Keet Seel, and Inscription House. These ancient villages, built into massive sandstone alcoves, date back to the 13th century, and were once home to the Ancestral Puebloans, ancestors of modern-day Hopi and Zuni peoples. The site is also known for its stunning views of the high desert, and its cultural and historical significance to Native peoples.

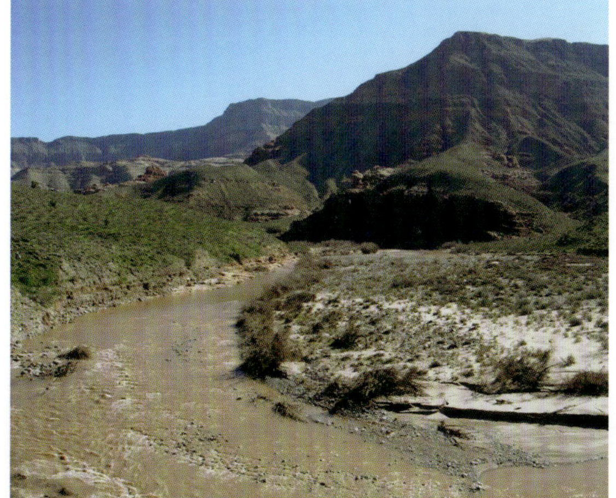

Old Spanish National Historic Trail

The Old Spanish National Historic Trail commemorates the historic trade route used between 1829 and 1848 to connect Santa Fe and Los Angeles. Stretching across six states—New Mexico, Colorado, Utah, Arizona, Nevada, and California—the trail was a crucial link for traders, who transported goods such as wool, horses, and mules. Known as one of the most arduous trade routes in the American Southwest, it highlights the cultural exchange between Spanish, Mexican, Indigenous, and American peoples.

Other Arizona Sites

- Glen Canyon National Recreation Area
- Organ Pipe Cactus National Monument
- Pipe Spring National Monument
- Tonto National Monument
- Tuzigoot National Monument
- Walnut Canyon National Monument
- Wupatki National Monument
- Arizona-Sonora Desert Museum

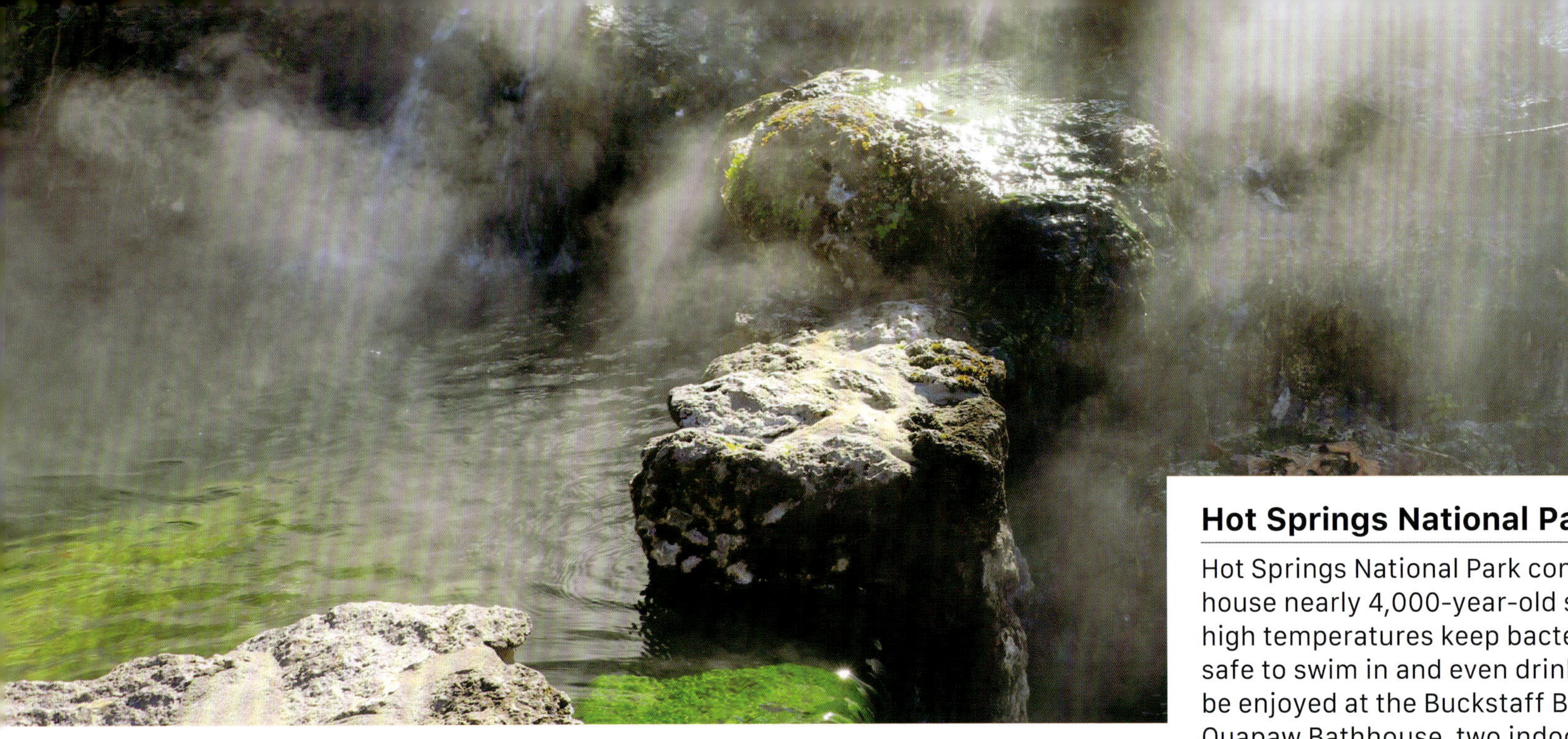

ARKANSAS

Hot Springs National Park

Hot Springs National Park contains springs that house nearly 4,000-year-old spring water. Their high temperatures keep bacteria at bay, making it safe to swim in and even drink. These springs can be enjoyed at the Buckstaff Bathhouse and the Quapaw Bathhouse, two indoor bathhouses that have the natural spring water piped in. While visitors can't submerge in the outdoor springs, they can be visited at various locations in the park.

Pea Ridge National Military Park

Dedicated in 1963 during the centennial of the American Civil War, Pea Ridge was built to preserve the battlefield of the 1862 Battle of Pea Ridge. The park features a visitor center and museum, a driving tour, hiking trails, a section of the pre-war Old Telegraph/Wire Road, the restored Elkhorn Tavern, and some of the best-preserved Civil War battlefields.

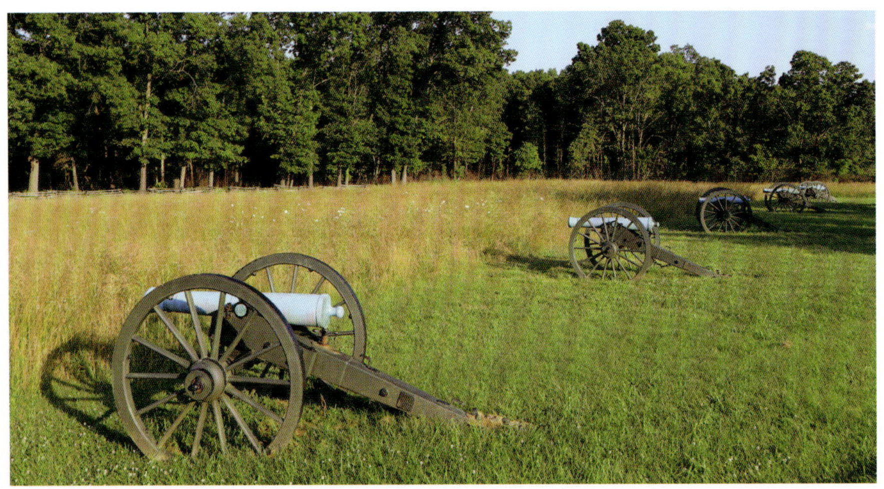

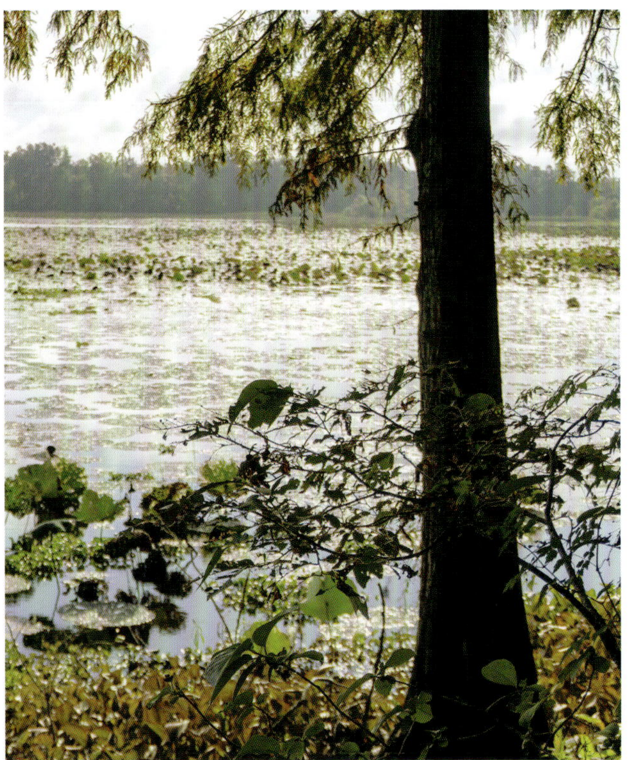

Arkansas Post National Memorial

The site of the trading post known as "Poste de Arkansea" saw its fair share of history over the centuries. It serves as a memorial for the complex history of all of the cultures who inhabited it, including the Quapaw, and the French, Spanish, American, and Confederate militaries.

Buffalo National River

Established in 1972, Buffalo National River is American's first national river. Enjoy many activities such as canoeing, tubing, kayaking, hiking, camping, picnicking, fishing, horseback riding, birding, guided tours, and more.

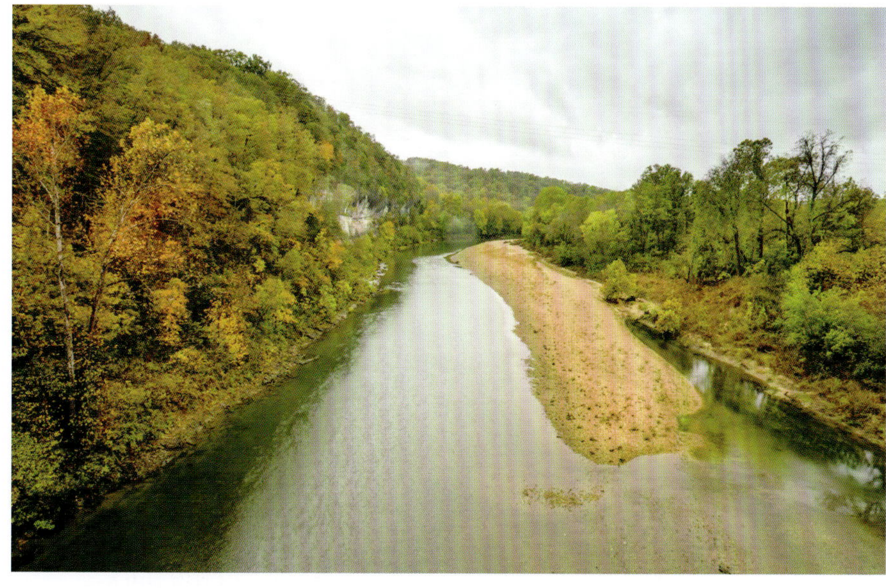

Fort Smith National Historic Site

The original Fort Smith was established by the U.S. in 1817, but was later replaced and operated until 1871. This was the first site of the United States District Court for the Western District of Arkansas, and served as the hub of the town of Fort Smith. The site was designated as a National Historic Landmark in 1961.

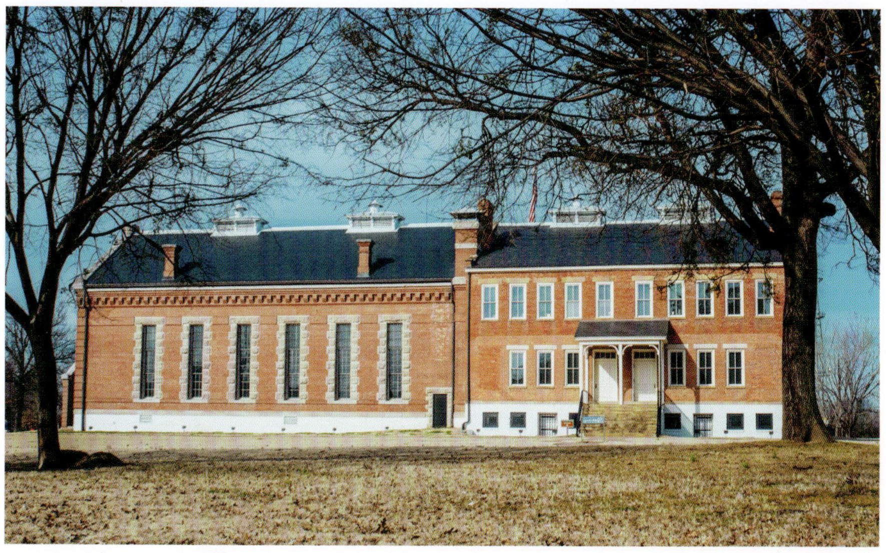

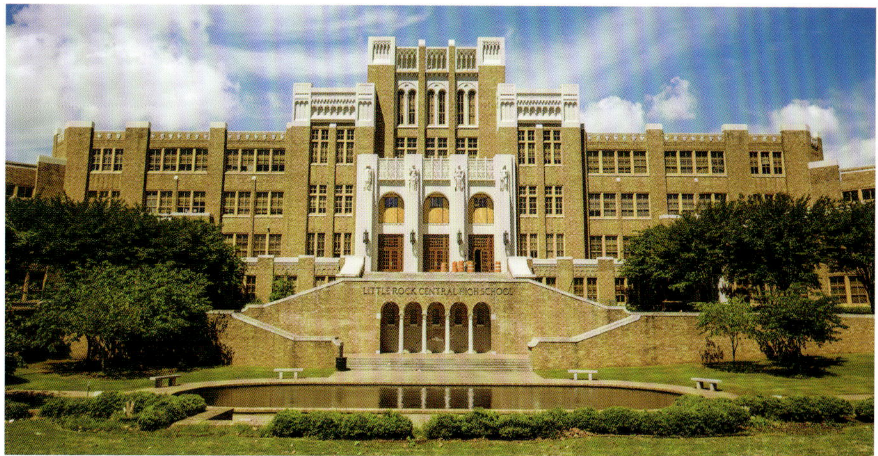

Little Rock Central High School National Historic Site

Learn about the courageous Little Rock Nine and the history of the school's desegregation at the Little Rock Central High School National Historic Site. View exhibits at the park's visitor center, watch the park's interpretive film, and explore the other historic buildings and outdoor activities, including the original Magnolia Mobil Gas Station, which functioned as the media headquarters during the 1957 crisis.

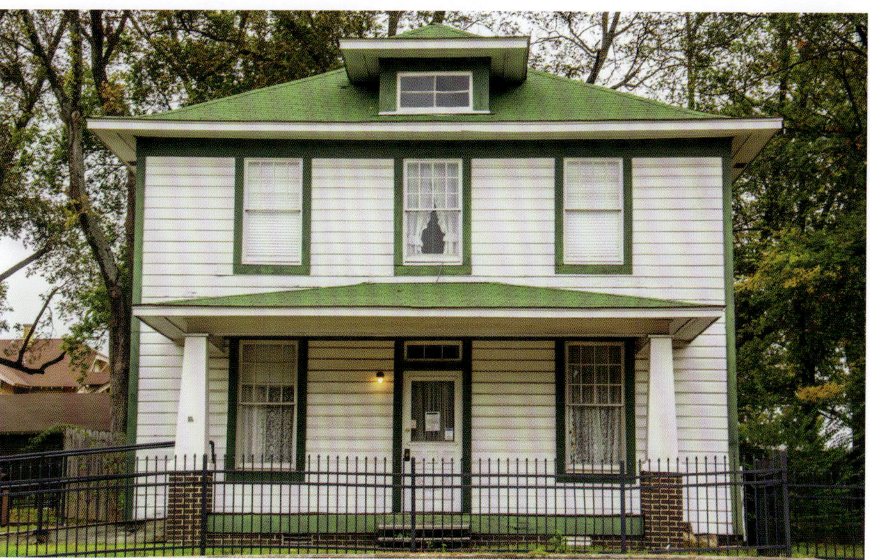

President William Jefferson Clinton Birthplace Home National Historic Site

President William Jefferson Clinton Birthplace Home National Historic Site in Hope, AK, is the birthplace of the 42nd president of the U.S., Bill Clinton. It was established as a national historic site in 2011, and it remains a place where visitors can enjoy guided tours of the house and view memorable moments in President Clinton's life.

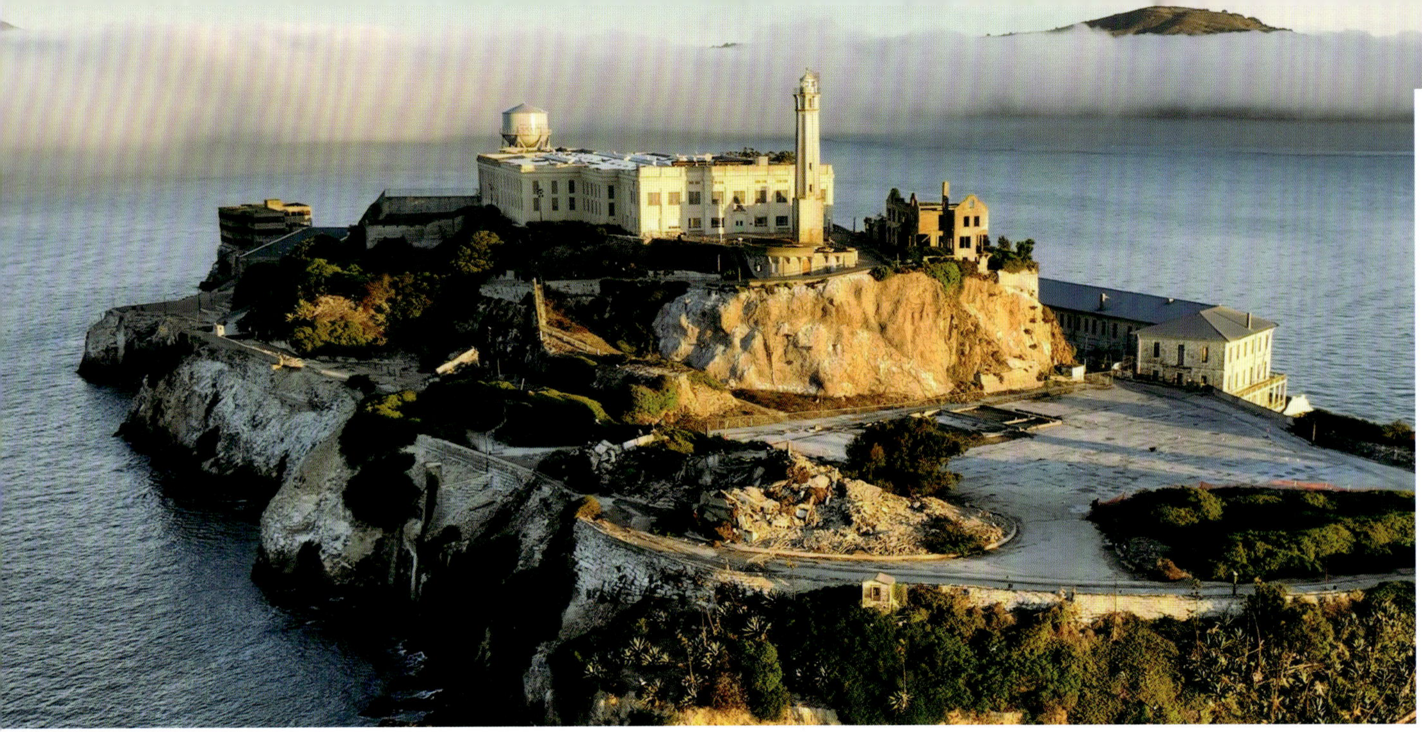

Alcatraz Island

Alcatraz Island, located in the San Francisco Bay, is famous for its history as a maximum-security federal prison that housed some of America's most notorious criminals, including Al Capone and Robert Stroud (the "Birdman of Alcatraz"). Before its time as a prison, the island served as a military fortification and later as a military prison. It's also recognized for its role in the 1969–1971 Native American Occupation, a pivotal event in the American Indian Rights Movement. Today, it's part of the Golden Gate National Recreation Area and is known for its rich history, wildlife, and dramatic views of San Francisco.

CALIFORNIA

Death Valley National Park

Death Valley National Park, located in eastern California and Nevada, is renowned for being the hottest, driest, and lowest National Park in the U.S. Known for its dramatic and otherworldly landscapes, the park features expansive salt flats, rugged mountains, sand dunes, colorful canyons, and unique geological formations. It's home to Badwater Basin, the lowest point in North America at 282 feet below sea level. Death Valley also holds the record for the hottest temperature ever recorded on Earth: 134°F, or 56.7°C, in 1913.

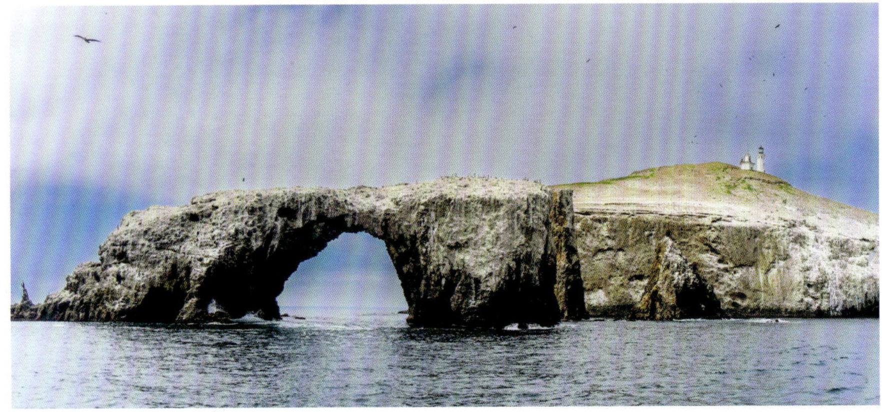

Channel Islands National Park

Channel Islands National Park, located off the coast of Southern California, is a remote and stunning archipelago made up of five islands: Anacapa, Santa Cruz, Santa Rosa, San Miguel, and Santa Barbara. Known as the "Galápagos of North America," the park is famous for its diverse ecosystems, unique plant and animal species found nowhere else on Earth, and pristine natural beauty. The islands offer a tranquil escape for outdoor enthusiasts, as well as a glimpse into the history of Chumash Native Americans.

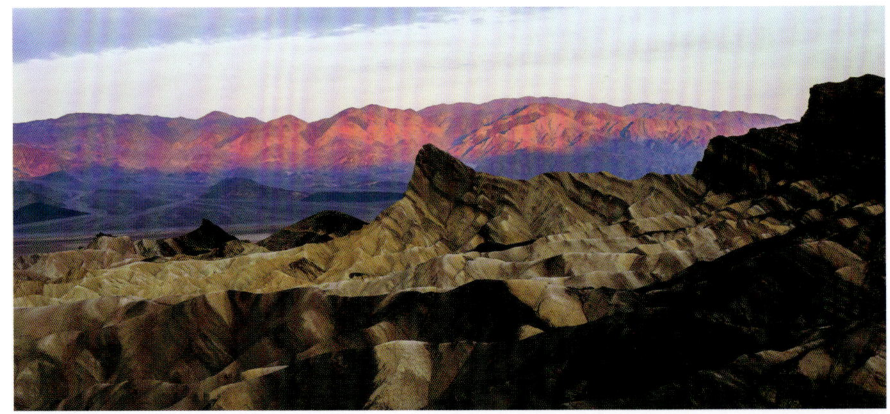

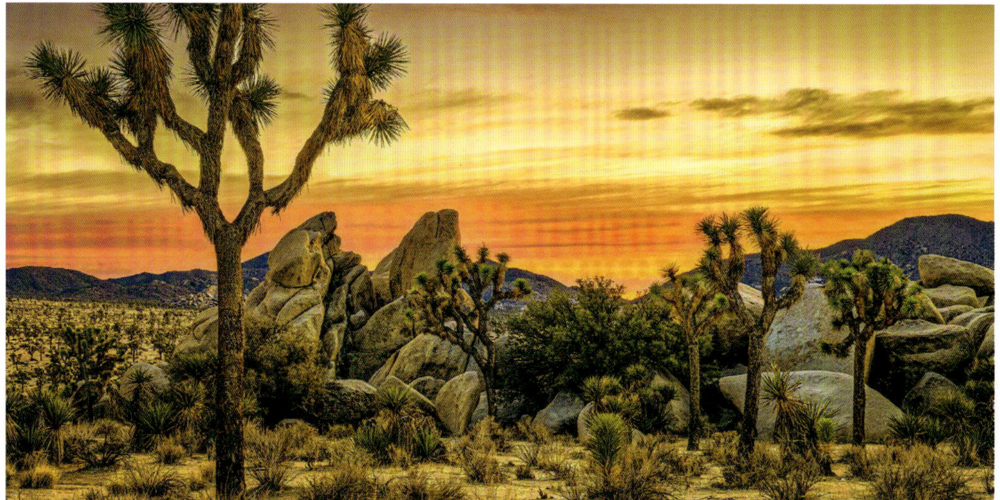

Joshua Tree National Park

Joshua Tree National Park, where the Mojave and Colorado Deserts converge, is known for its unique desert landscapes. It's named after the distinctive Joshua trees, a type of yucca plant with spiky, twisted branches that dot the rugged terrain. Known for its surreal rock formations, wide-open skies, and variety of ecosystems, this park is a haven for outdoor enthusiasts, rock climbers, and stargazers.

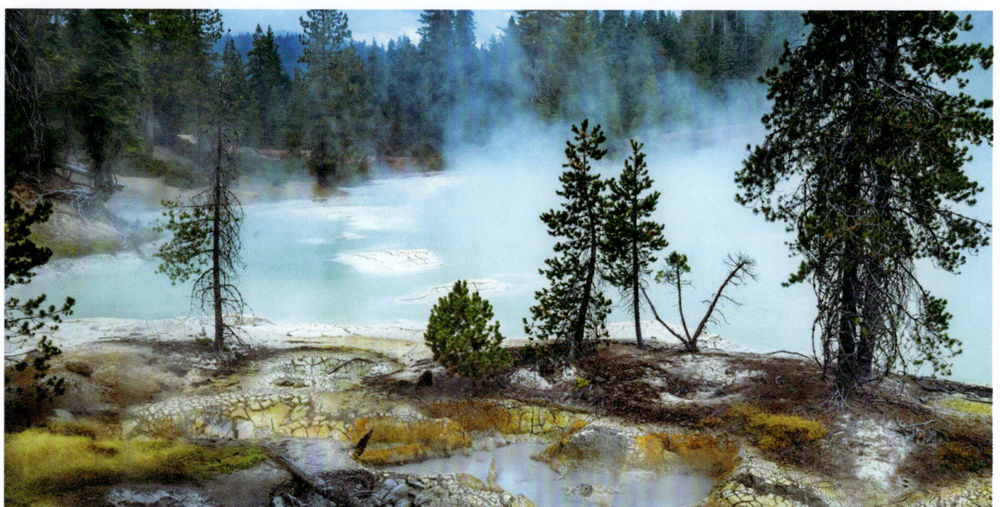

Lassen Volcanic National Park

Lassen Volcanic National Park is renowned for its dramatic volcanic landscapes, geothermal features, and alpine beauty. The park is home to Lassen Peak, one of the largest plug dome volcanoes in the world, and showcases all four types of volcanoes: shield, cinder cone, composite, and plug dome. The park offers a unique blend of geological wonders and serene natural settings, with its steaming fumaroles, bubbling mud pots, and pristine lakes.

Mojave National Preserve

Mojave National Preserve is famous for its vast, unspoiled desert landscapes and striking natural features. Spanning nearly 1.6 million acres, the preserve encompasses towering sand dunes, ancient volcanic cinder cones, sprawling Joshua tree forests, and rugged mountain ranges. Appreciated for its solitude, varied ecosystems, and fascinating geological formations, Mojave offers a peaceful escape into the stark beauty of the desert.

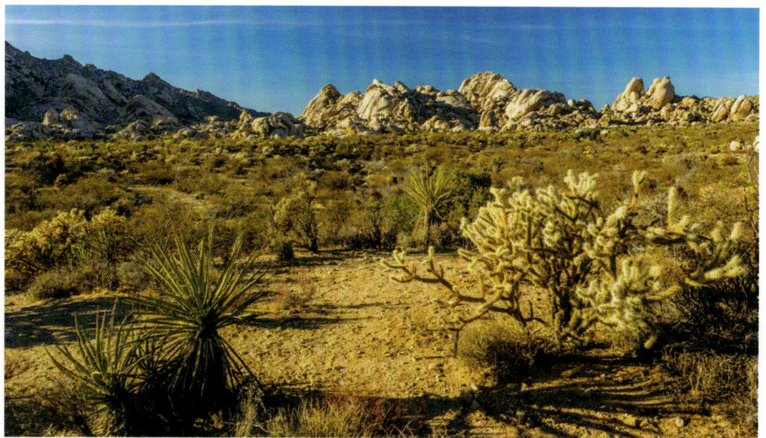

Pinnacles National Park

Pinnacles National Park is celebrated for its unique rock spires, towering volcanic formations, and hidden talus caves. The park's dramatic landscape was shaped by volcanic activity over 23 million years ago and is a haven for rock climbers, hikers, and wildlife enthusiasts. It is also one of the few places in the U.S. where visitors can spot the California condor, an endangered species with a wingspan of nearly 10 feet.

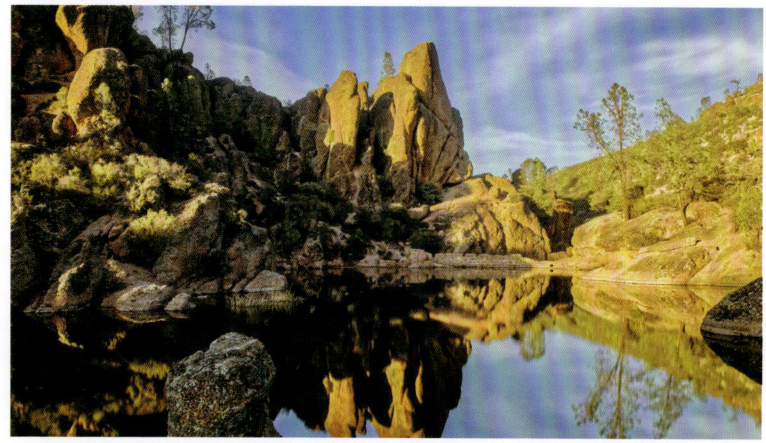

Redwood National and State Parks

Redwood National and State Parks, located in Northern California, are renowned for protecting some of the tallest trees on Earth: the picturesque coast redwoods, *Sequoia sempervirens*. These ancient giants can reach heights of over 350 feet and are part of a varied ecosystem that includes lush fern-filled forests, dramatic coastlines, and beautiful rivers. The park system, a collaboration between the National Park Service and California State Parks, also preserves cultural history, including sites significant to Indigenous peoples.

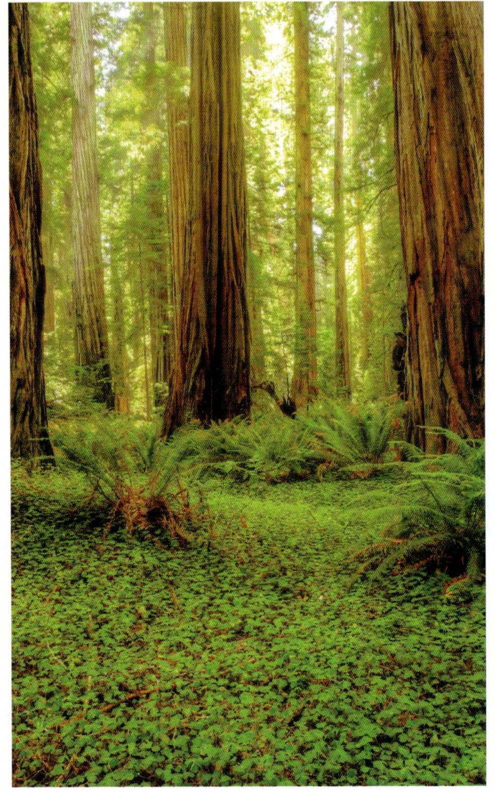

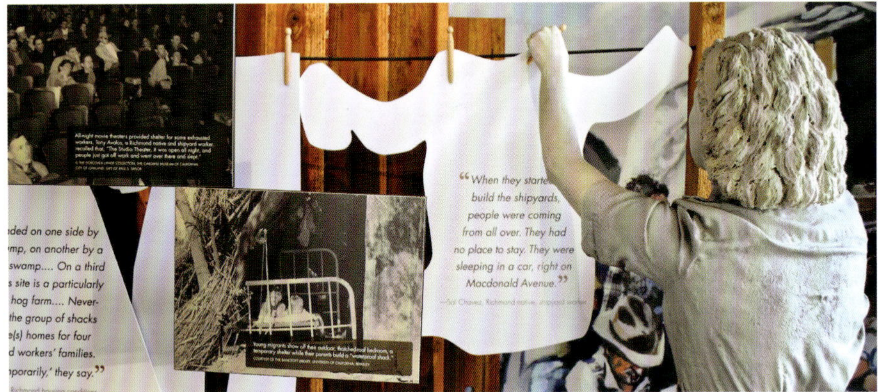

Rosie the Riveter World War II Home Front National Historical Park

Rosie the Riveter World War II Home Front National Historical Park, located in Richmond, California, honors the contributions of American workers—especially women—on the home front during World War II. The park commemorates the iconic Rosie the Riveter symbol, representing the millions of women who entered the workforce to support the war effort. It also preserves sites and stories of wartime industrial production, shipbuilding, and the social changes that reshaped the United States.

San Francisco Maritime National Historical Park

San Francisco Maritime National Historical Park, located in the Fisherman's Wharf district, is a celebration of the city's rich maritime heritage. The park is famous for its fleet of historic ships, preserved and docked at Hyde Street Pier, as well as its museum collections and waterfront locations. Visitors can explore 19th and 20th-century ships, learn about the history of sailing and trade on the West Coast, and immerse themselves in the stories of sailors, dock workers, and coastal communities.

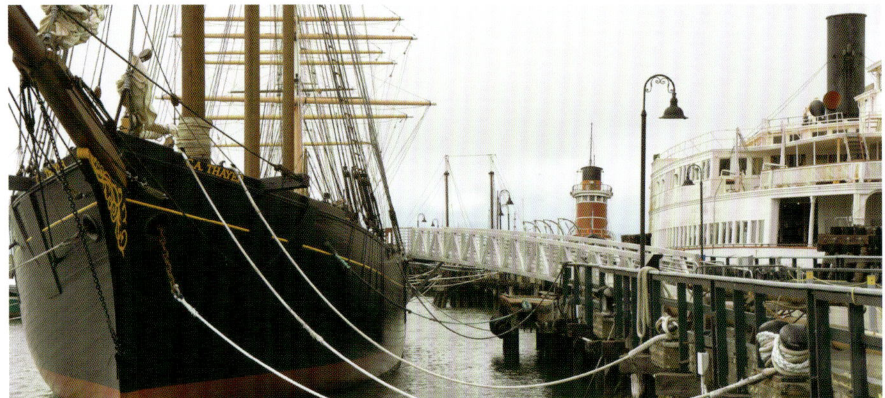

Sequoia and Kings Canyon National Parks

Located side by side in California's southern Sierra Nevada Mountain Range, Sequoia and Kings Canyon National Parks are celebrated for their breathtaking landscapes and giant sequoia trees, including General Sherman, the largest known living single-stem tree on Earth by volume. Sequoia National Park features lush forests, towering peaks, and deep canyons, while Kings Canyon National Park *(see below)* is known for its rugged wilderness, glacially-carved valleys, and roaring rivers. Together, they protect some of the most dramatic and ancient natural wonders in the U.S.

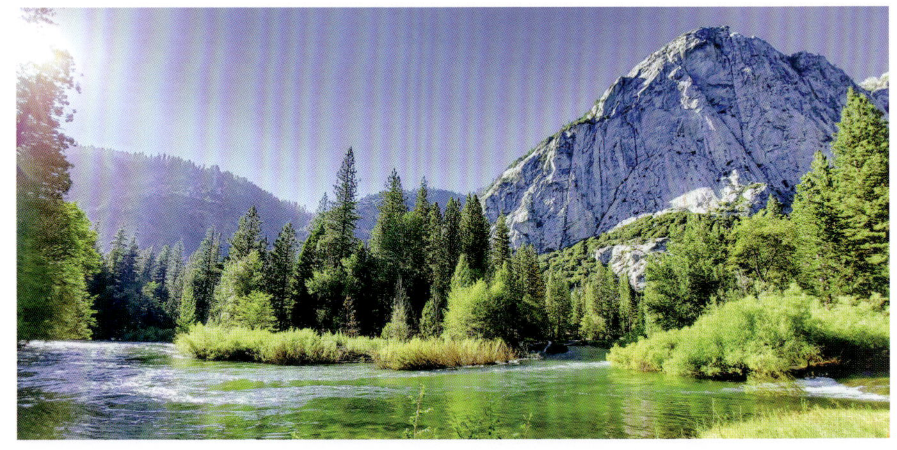

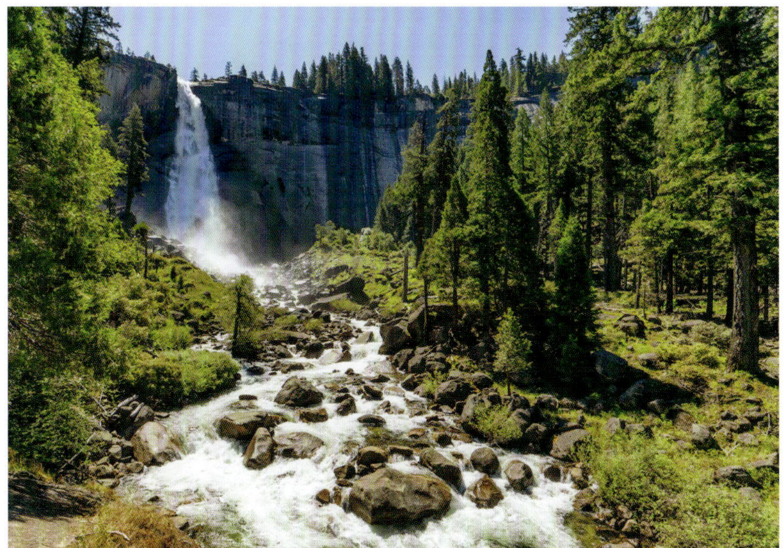

Yosemite National Park

Yosemite National Park, located in California's Sierra Nevada Mountain Range, is world-famous for its stunning granite cliffs, towering waterfalls, ancient sequoias, and sweeping valleys. Inspiring landmarks like El Capitan, Half Dome, and Yosemite Falls draw millions of visitors each year. The park is also known for its diverse ecosystems, pristine wilderness, and its role in inspiring the modern conservation movement, led by naturalist John Muir.

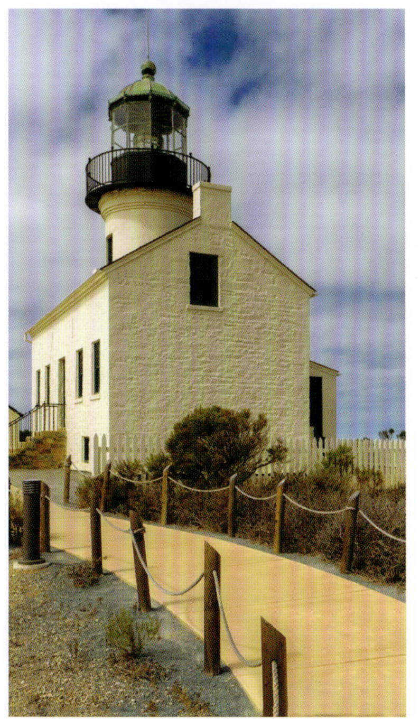

Cabrillo National Monument

Cabrillo National Monument, located at the tip of the Point Loma Peninsula in San Diego, California, commemorates the landing of Juan Rodríguez Cabrillo in 1542, the first European expedition to explore the West Coast of the United States. The site offers breathtaking views of San Diego Harbor, the Pacific Ocean, and the surrounding coastline. It's also known for its tide pools, historic Old Point Loma Lighthouse, and military history exhibits.

Point Reyes National Seashore

Point Reyes National Seashore, located along the rugged California coast north of San Francisco, is known for its breathtaking coastal scenery, varied wildlife, and historic landmarks. This protected area features dramatic cliffs, pristine beaches, lush forests, and rolling grasslands. It's a haven for wildlife viewing, including elephant seals, tule elk, and gray whales during their migration. The seashore is also home to the iconic Point Reyes Lighthouse *(see below)* and a rich maritime and ranching history.

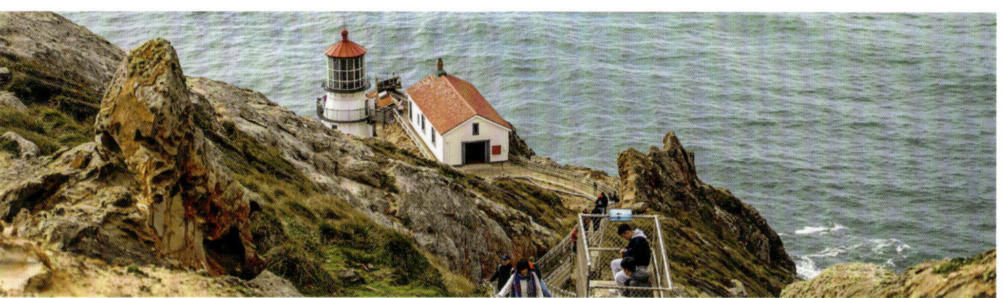

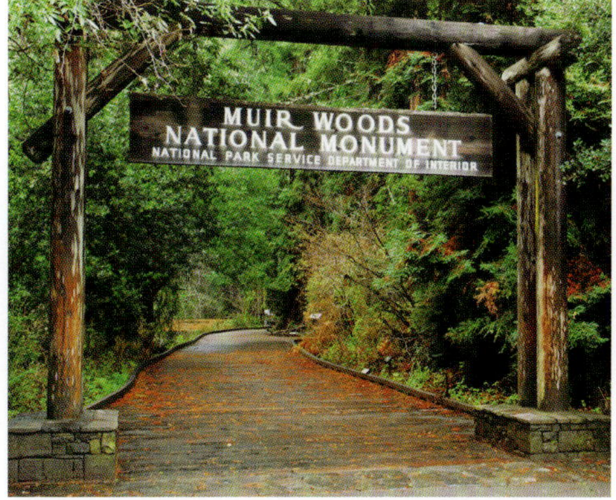

Muir Woods National Monument

Muir Woods National Monument is a respected natural sanctuary famous for its towering old-growth coastal redwood trees, some of which are over 1,000 years old and exceed 250 feed in height. This protected area is part of the Golden Gate National Recreation Area and offers visitors a tranquil escape into nature.

Castle Mountains National Monument

Castle Mountains National Monument, located in the Mojave Desert of California, is distinguished for its rugged, remote beauty, featuring remarkable Joshua tree forests, desert grasslands, and the Castle Peaks, a dramatic series of jagged volcanic spires. Established in 2016, the monument protects diverse ecosystems and cultural sites, including Native American petroglyphs and remnants of old mining towns. It offers solitude and breathtaking vistas in a less-visited corner of the desert.

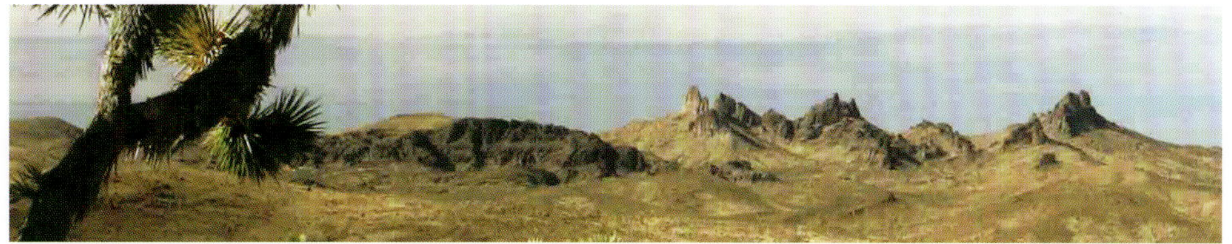

César E. Chávez National Monument

César E. Chávez National Monument honors the life and legacy of César Chávez, a civil rights leader and co-founder of the United Farm Workers (UFW). This site was Chávez's home, the UFW headquarters, and a place where he organized campaigns for labor rights and social justice. The monument preserves his gravesite, historic buildings, and exhibits that highlight the farmworker movement and Chávez's contributions to equality and workers' rights.

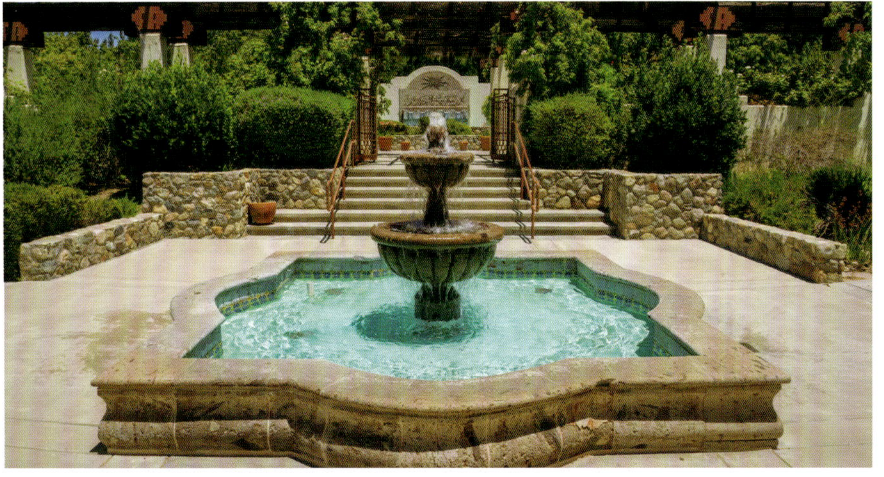

Devils Postpile National Monument

Devils Postpile National Monument is notable for its striking geological formations, particularly the basalt columns that were created by ancient lava flows and glacial activity. The monument also features pristine natural landscapes, including lush meadows, forested trails, and the stunning Rainbow Falls. It's a favorite destination for geology enthusiasts, hikers, and those seeking tranquil wilderness experiences.

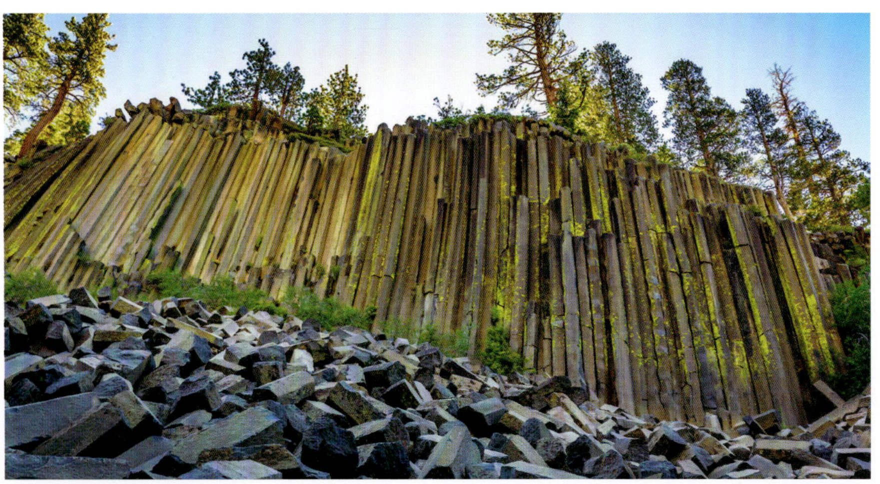

Eugene O'Neill National Historic Site

Eugene O'Neill National Historic Site preserves the home of Eugene O'Neill, the only American playwright to win the Nobel Prize for Literature. Known as Tao House, this was where O'Neill wrote some of his most famous works, including *Long Day's Journey Into Night* and *The Iceman Cometh*. The site reflects O'Neill's retreat from public life and his connection to the natural surroundings that inspired his creative work.

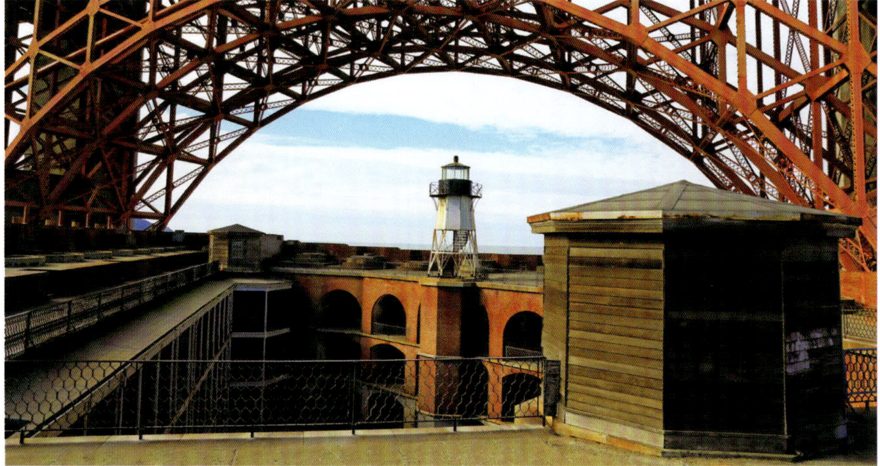

Fort Point National Historic Site

Fort Point National Historic Site, located beneath the southern end of the Golden Gate Bridge in San Francisco, California, is celebrated for its role in coastal defense during the 19th century. Built during the 1850s Gold Rush era, this brick masonry fort was designed to protect the San Francisco Bay from potential attackers. Its striking architecture, rich military history, and breathtaking views of the Golden Gate Bridge and Pacific Ocean make it a fascinating destination.

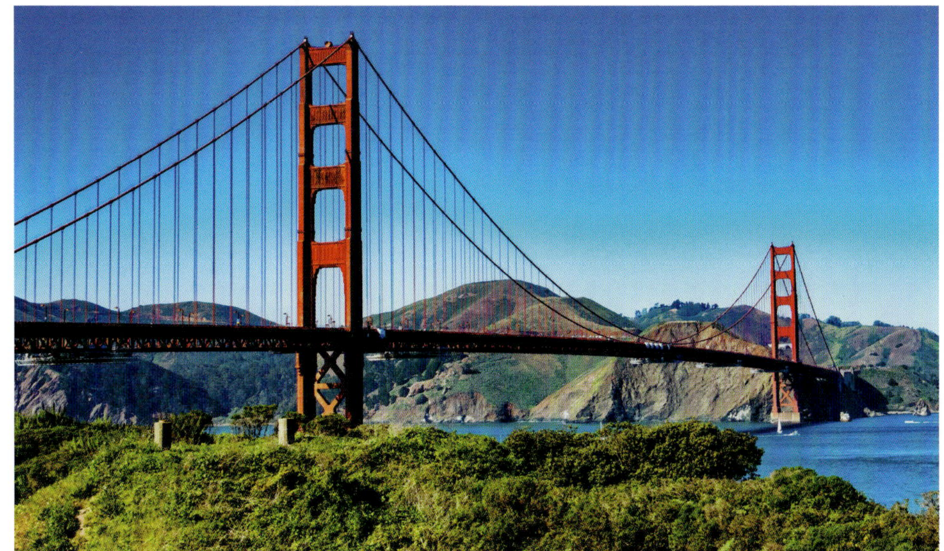

Golden Gate National Recreation Area

Golden Gate National Recreation Area (GGNRA) is one of the largest urban national parks in the world, stretching across 80,000 acres in and around San Francisco, California. It's celebrated for its breathtaking coastal landscapes, historic landmarks, and diverse ecosystems. Iconic sites like Muir Woods National Monument, Alcatraz Island, and the Marin Headlands are part of the park. GGNRA offers a mix of natural beauty, cultural history, and recreational opportunities, making it a favorite for locals and visitors alike.

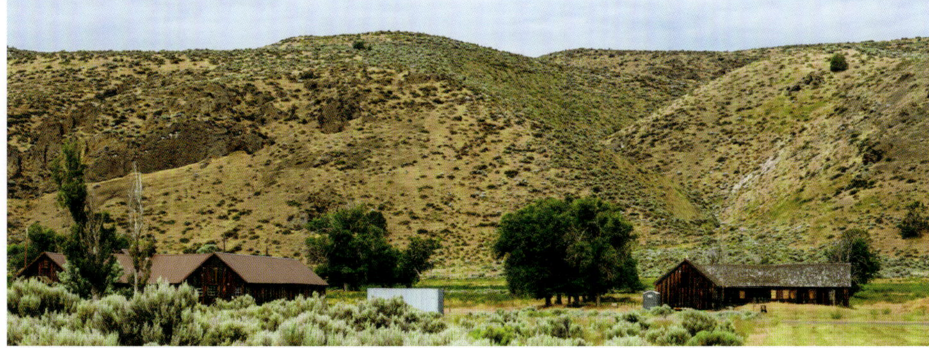

Tule Lake National Monument

Tule Lake National Monument, located in Northern California near the Oregon border, preserves the history of the Japanese American incarceration during World War II. It was the site of the largest and most controversial of the ten internment camps, holding over 18,000 people. The monument also includes landmarks associated with the Modoc War of 1872–1873 and the area's unique volcanic landscape, offering a poignant reminder of civil liberties and resilience during challenging times.

John Muir National Historic Site

John Muir National Historic Site celebrates the life and legacy of John Muir, America's most influential conservationist and the "Father of the National Parks." The site preserves his Victorian home and surrounding orchards, where he lived and wrote many works advocating for wilderness preservation. Muir's efforts were instrumental in establishing national parks like Yosemite and Sequoia.

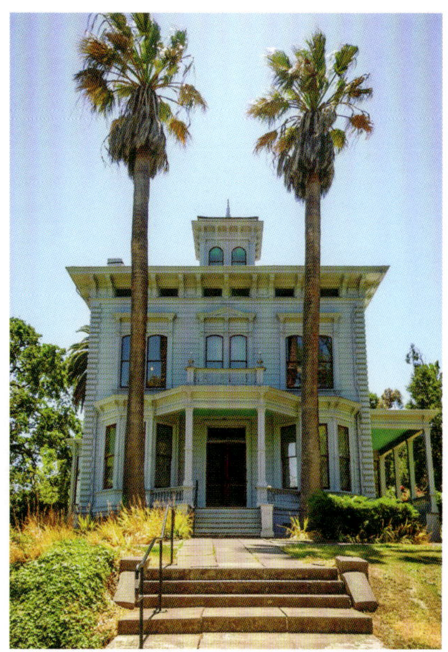

Lava Beds National Monument

Lava Beds National Monument is renowned for its unique volcanic landscape, featuring over 800 lava tube caves, rugged lava fields, and dramatic geology. It also holds deep historical significance as the site of the Modoc War, with preserved battlefields and Native American petroglyphs. The monument offers an incredible blend of geological wonder and cultural history.

Other California Sites

- The California National Historic Trail
- Manzanar National Historic Site
- Port Chicago Naval Magazine National Memorial
- Santa Monica Mountains National Recreation Area
- Whiskeytown National Recreation Area
- The Getty Center & The Getty Villa Museum

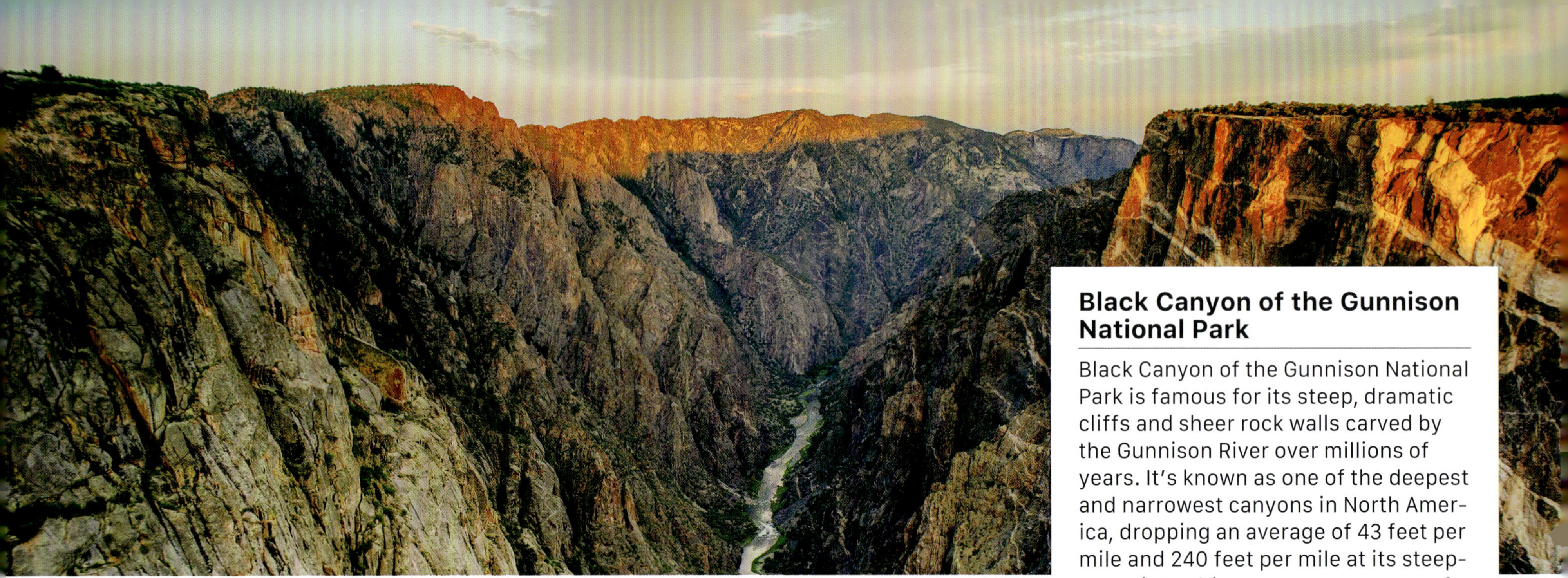

COLORADO

Black Canyon of the Gunnison National Park

Black Canyon of the Gunnison National Park is famous for its steep, dramatic cliffs and sheer rock walls carved by the Gunnison River over millions of years. It's known as one of the deepest and narrowest canyons in North America, dropping an average of 43 feet per mile and 240 feet per mile at its steepest point—this causes some areas of the canyon to receive only 33 minutes of sunlight per day, giving it its "black" appearance.

Great Sand Dunes National Park and Preserve

Great Sand Dunes National Park and Preserve is home to the tallest sand dunes in North America, with some reaching heights of over 750 feet. Set against the stunning backdrop of the Sangre de Cristo Mountains, the park features a unique combination of ecosystems, including sand dunes, alpine forests, wetlands, and grasslands.

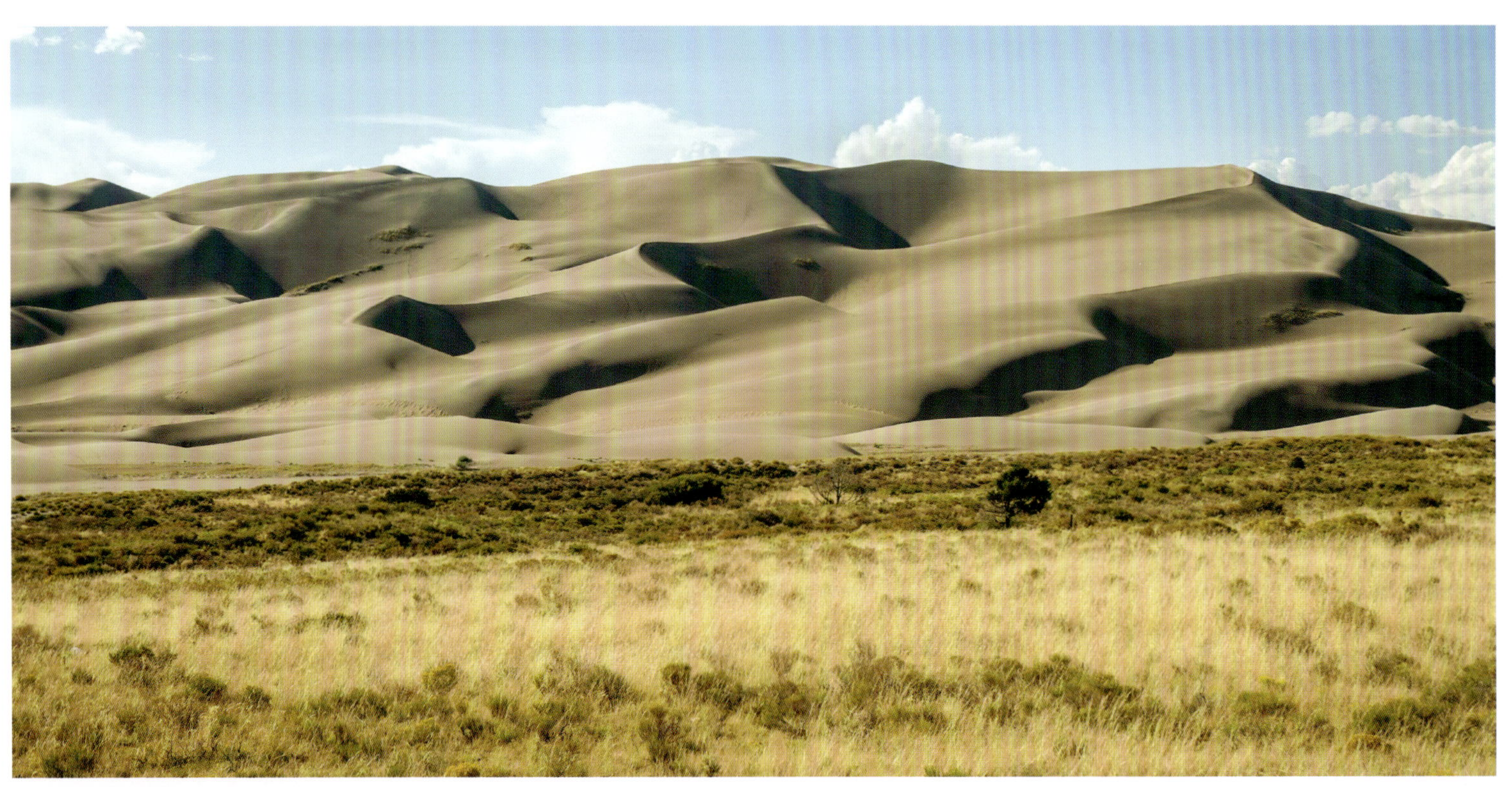

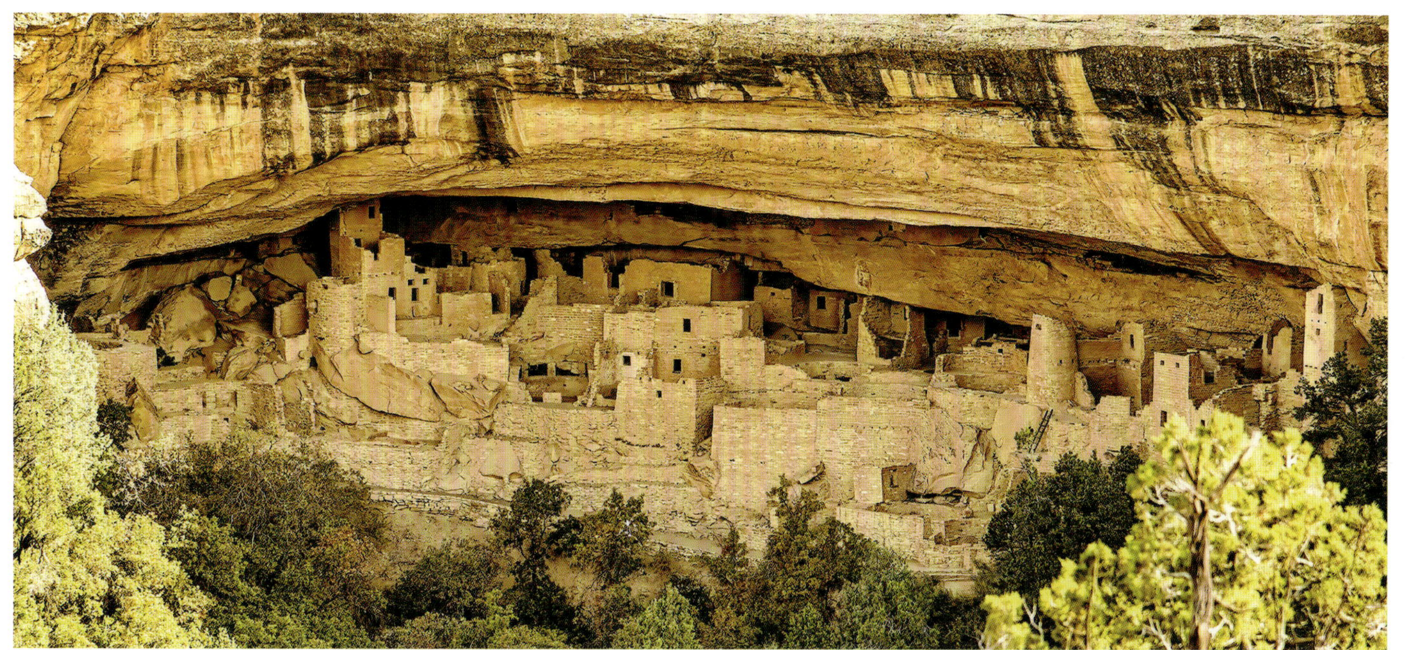

Mesa Verde National Park

Mesa Verde National Park is famous for its exceptionally well-preserved Ancestral Puebloan cliff dwellings. This UNESCO World Heritage Site features over 600 cliff dwellings, including the incredible Cliff Palace *(see left)*, Balcony House, and Long House. The park offers a window into the lives of the Ancestral Puebloans, who inhabited the region from approximately 650 to 1285 CE, and it's celebrated for its archaeological significance and cultural heritage

Amache National Historic Site

Amache National Historic Site preserves the site of the Amache incarceration camp, officially known as the Granada Relocation Center. During World War II, this site was one of ten internment camps where more than 7,000 Japanese Americans were forcibly relocated and incarcerated under Executive Order 9066. The site serves as a solemn reminder of this chapter in U.S. history, emphasizing the importance of civil rights, and the resilience of the Japanese American community.

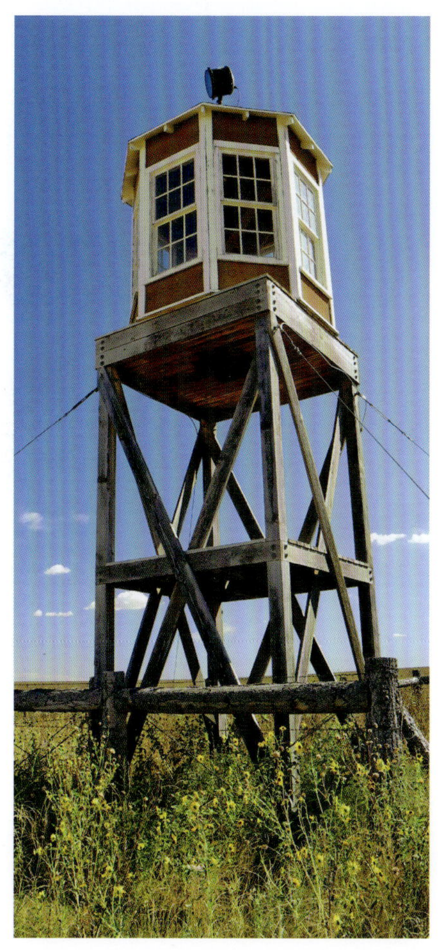

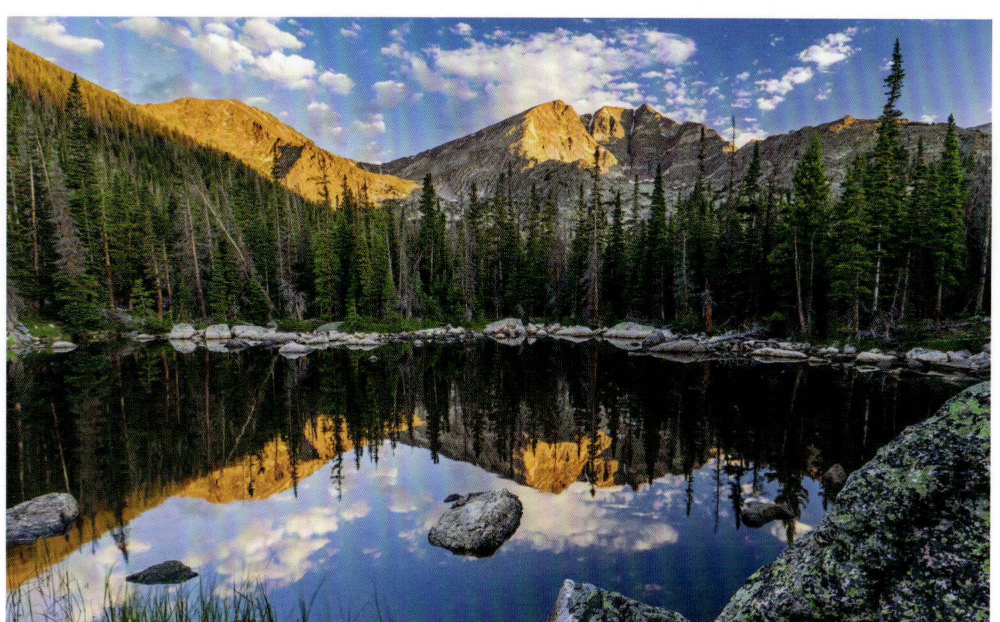

Rocky Mountain National Park

Rocky Mountain National Park is renowned for its towering peaks, alpine lakes, and diverse ecosystems ranging from mountain forests to snowy tundra. The park features 60 mountain peaks exceeding 12,000 feet, including the iconic Longs Peak which stands at 14,259 feet tall. Known for its breathtaking vistas, abundant wildlife, and opportunities for outdoor recreation, it's one of the most popular national parks in the U.S. and offers a quintessential Rocky Mountain experience.

Bent's Old Fort National Historic Site

Bent's Old Fort National Historic Site preserves a reconstructed 1840s adobe fort that served as a vital trading post along the Santa Fe Trail. The fort was a multicultural hub where traders, trappers, Indigenous peoples, and settlers came together to trade goods, primarily bison hides. It played a critical role in the expansion of the American West and offers insights into the interactions between diverse cultures during a transformative period in U.S. history.

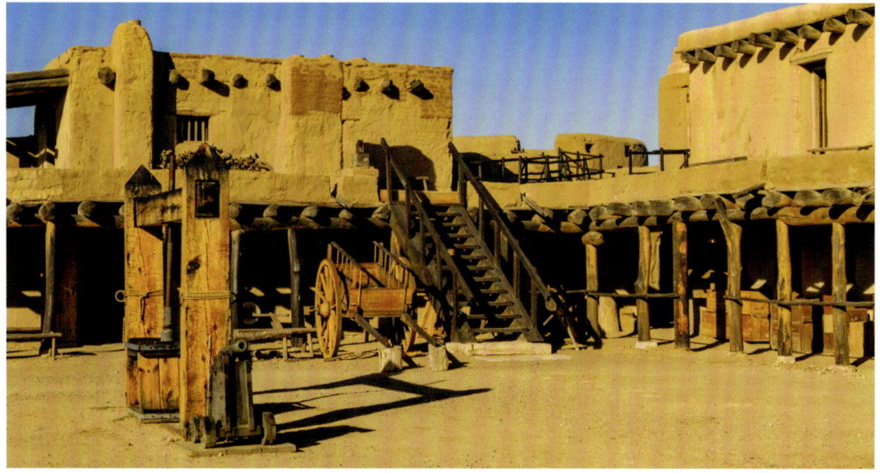

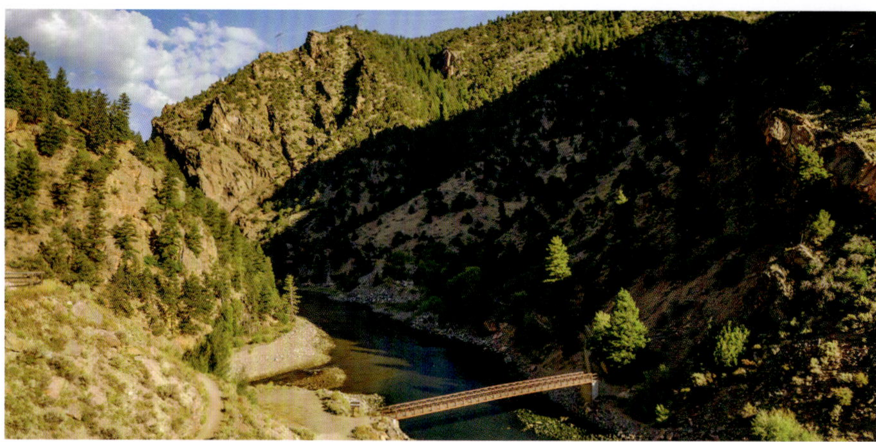

Curecanti National Recreation Area

Curecanti National Recreation Area is known for its stunning reservoirs, dramatic canyon landscapes, and endless opportunities for water-based recreation. Anchored by three reservoirs—Blue Mesa, Morrow Point, and Crystal—along the Gunnison River, the area is a haven for boating, fishing, hiking, and exploring the rugged beauty of Colorado's high desert. It's also a gateway to the nearby Black Canyon of the Gunnison National Park.

Colorado National Monument

Colorado National Monument is famous for its dramatic red rock canyons, towering monoliths, and sweeping desert landscapes. This iconic park features rugged sandstone cliffs carved by millions of years of erosion, offering breathtaking vistas of the Colorado Plateau. Visitors flock to see formations like Independence Monument, Coke Ovens, and Kissing Couple, as well as the abundant wildlife and recreational opportunities.

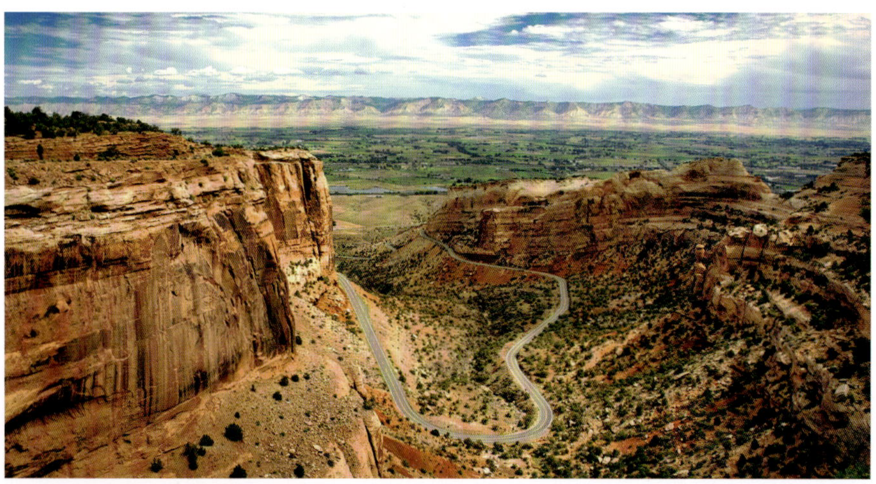

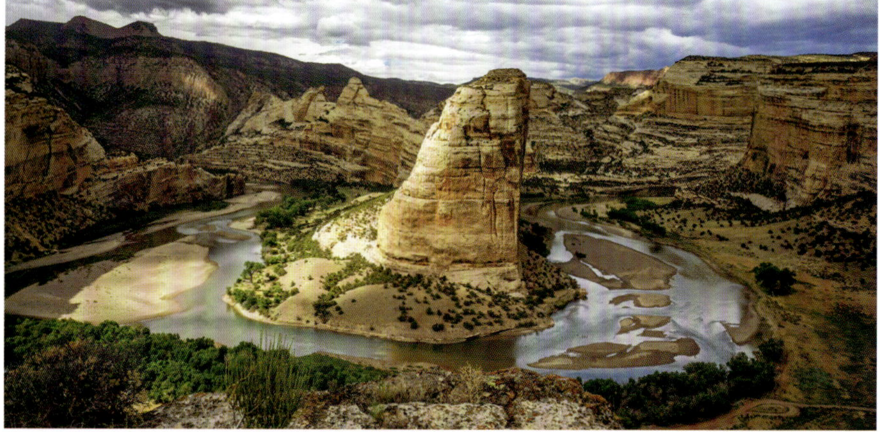

Dinosaur National Monument

Dinosaur National Monument, located on the border of Colorado and Utah, is recognized for its rich fossil beds, striking geological formations, and varied landscapes that range from rugged canyons to desert plains. The monument preserves one of the most significant dinosaur fossil quarries in the world, showcasing prehistoric remains and petroglyphs left by ancient cultures. It also offers incredible opportunities for river rafting, hiking, and wildlife viewing in a uniquely wild setting.

Florissant Fossil Beds National Monument

Florissant Fossil Beds National Monument is distinguished for its exceptionally well-preserved fossils of plants and insects from the Eocene Epoch, around 34 million years ago. The monument also features massive petrified redwood stumps, some over 14 feet wide, that are remnants of ancient forests. It offers a fascinating glimpse into prehistoric ecosystems and the geological processes that preserved them.

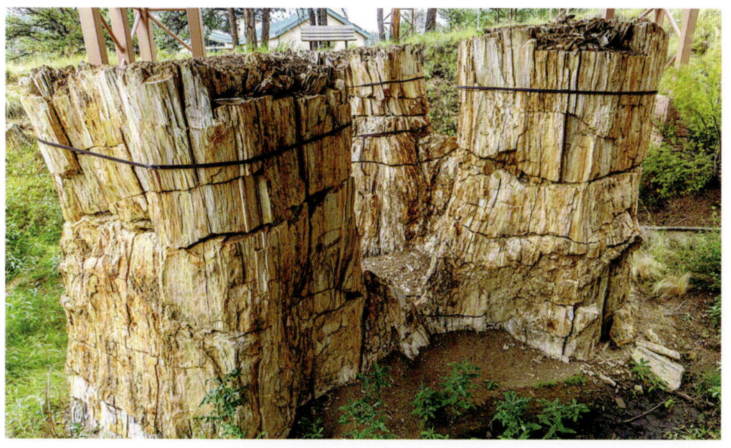

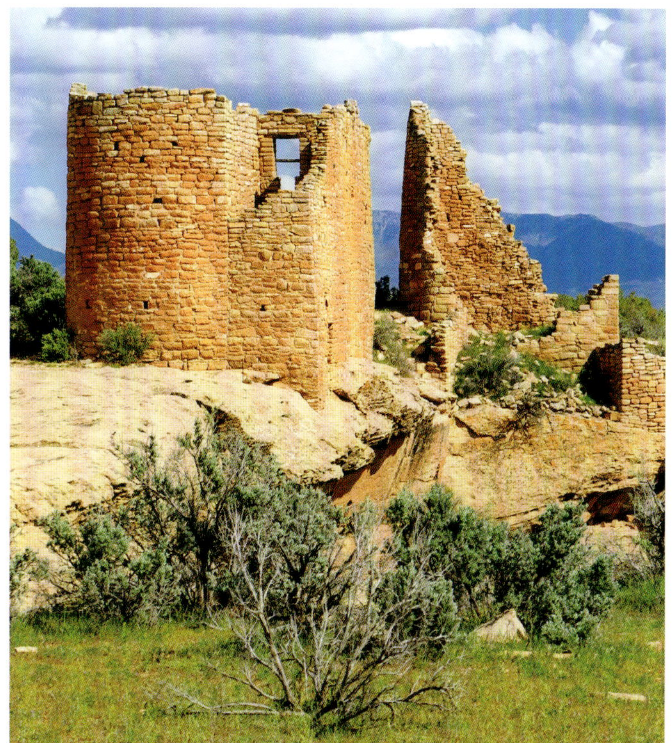

Hovenweep National Monument

Hovenweep National Monument, located on the Colorado-Utah border, is celebrated for its remarkable prehistoric stone structures built by the Ancestral Puebloans over 700 years ago. These unique and well-preserved towers, dwellings, and ceremonial structures sit atop canyon rims and mesas, offering a glimpse into the lives of the people who thrived in this rugged landscape. The area also features beautiful desert scenery and a rich cultural history.

Sand Creek Massacre National Historic Site

Sand Creek Massacre National Historic Site commemorates one of the most tragic events in American history: the Sand Creek Massacre of 1864. On November 29, 1864, U.S. Army soldiers attacked a peaceful encampment of Cheyenne and Arapaho people, killing over 230 men, women, and children. The site serves as a place of reflection, honoring the victims and fostering understanding of this dark chapter in U.S. history.

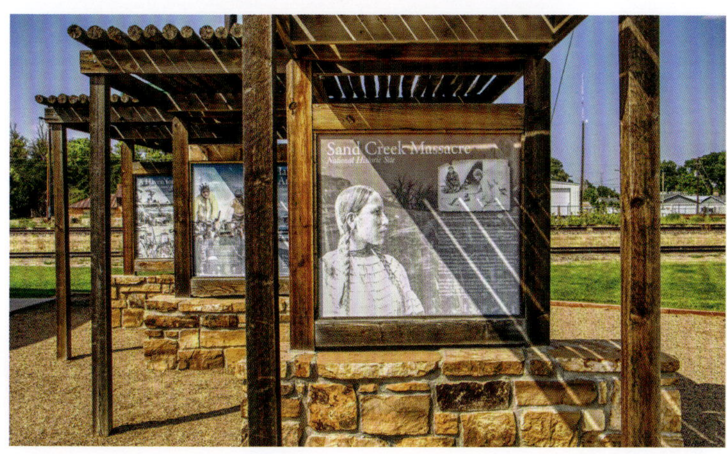

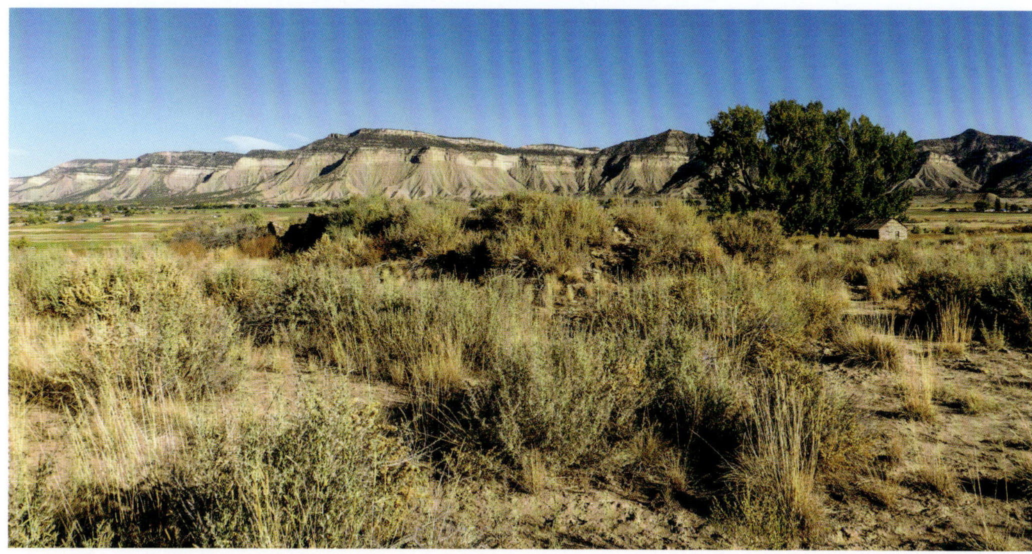

Yucca House National Monument

Yucca House National Monument is an unexcavated Ancestral Puebloan site that dates back over 1,000 years. Once a thriving agricultural community, it's one of the largest archaeological sites in the region and provides insight into the lives of the people who lived in the Mesa Verde area. Its preservation in a natural state offers a rare opportunity to experience an ancient cultural site undisturbed by modern excavation.

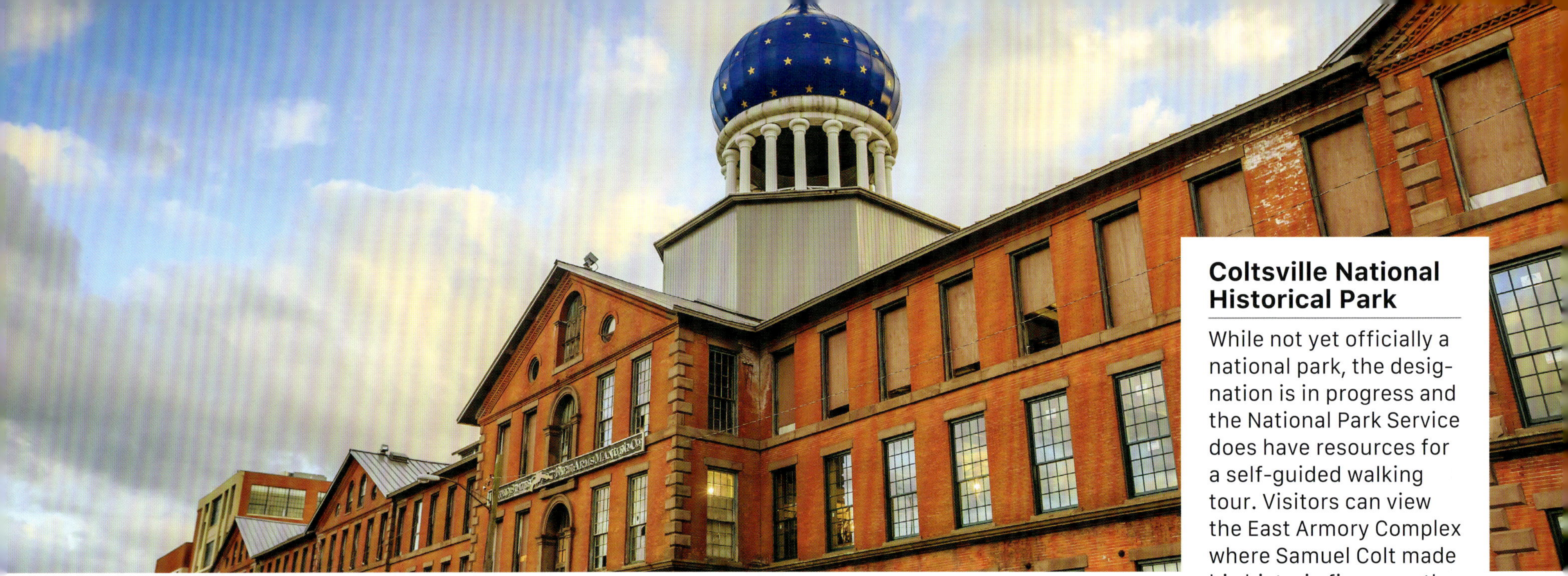

CONNECTICUT

Coltsville National Historical Park

While not yet officially a national park, the designation is in progress and the National Park Service does have resources for a self-guided walking tour. Visitors can view the East Armory Complex where Samuel Colt made his historic firearms, the worker houses, the Samuel Colt Monument, Colt Park, and more.

Washington–Rochambeau Revolutionary Route National Historic Trail

Covering 680 miles and spanning across six states, the Washington–Rochambeau Revolutionary Route is a series of roads that the Continental Army and the Expédition Particulière took during their 14-week march from Newport, RI, to Yorktown, VA. One surviving structure along the trail is an encampment site in Bolton, CT, that Rochambeau's army used while marching to the Battle of Yorktown in 1781.

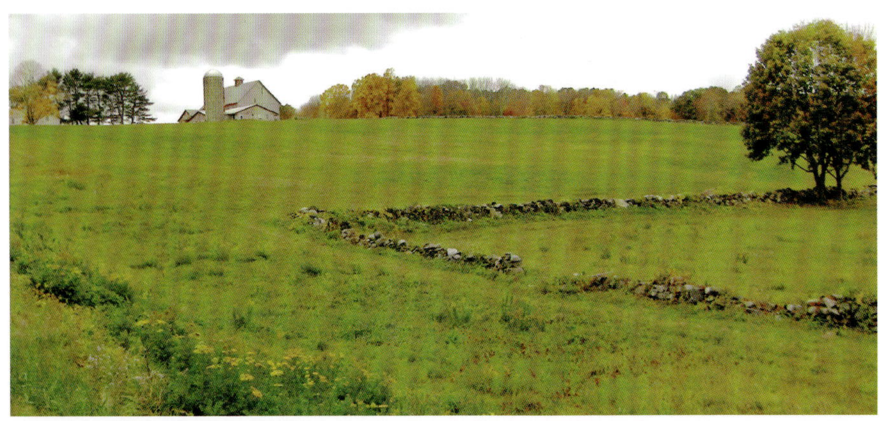

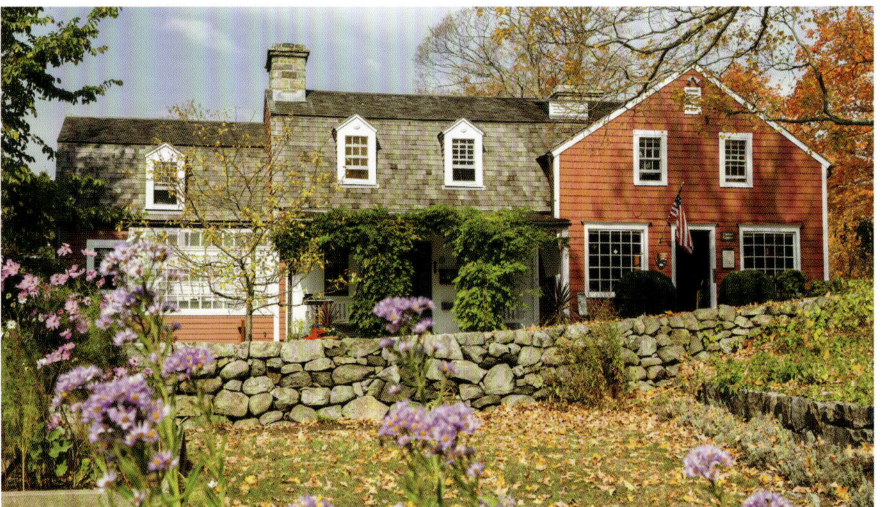

Weir Farm National Historical Park

Located in Ridgefield and Wilton, CT, Weir Farm National Historical Park commemorates the life and work of American impressionist painter J. Alden Weir and the world-class artists who stayed at the site. Attend painting workshops, view objects in the park's collections, tour the Weir House and studios, and more.

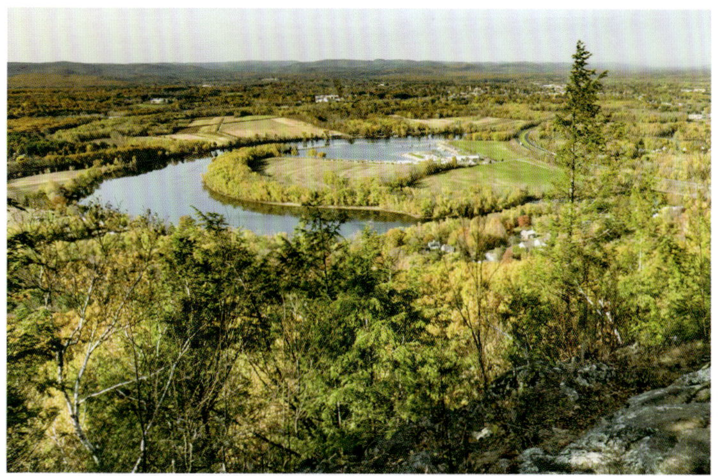

New England National Scenic Trail

Sometimes called the Triple-M Trail, the New England National Scenic Trail system includes most of three single trails: Metacomet-Monadnock Trail, Mattabesett Trail, and Metacomet Trail. At 215 miles long, the route extends through 41 communities from Guilford, Connecticut, through the Pioneer Valley of Massachusetts, to the New Hampshire state border.

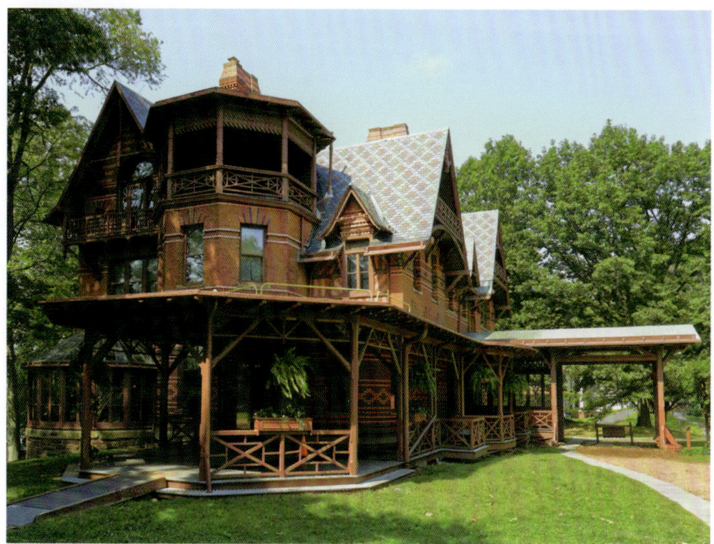

The Mark Twain House & Museum

This eccentric house was built in the American High Gothic style for Samuel Langhorne Clemens (Mark Twain) and his family. Many of Twain's best-known works were written while living here; it now hosts tours and a museum dedicated to the beloved author.

Gillette Castle State Park

Gillette Castle State Park was designed and built by William Gillette, an American actor famous for portraying Sherlock Holmes on stage. Besides being able to tour the castle and its grounds, visitors can visit a museum, hiking trails, picnic areas, and a visitors center.

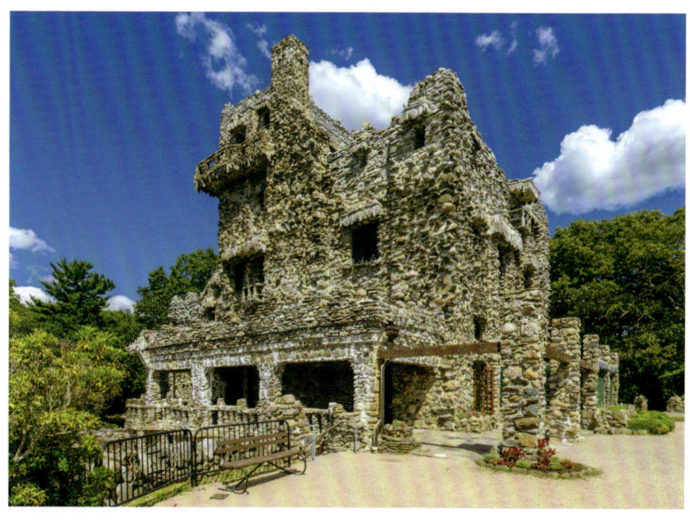

Connecticut's Old State House

Connecticut's Old State House is a historic building that played a significant role in the state's and the nation's early political history. Completed in 1796, it's one of the oldest state houses in the U.S. and served as the center of all three branches of Connecticut state government until 1878. It now serves as a history museum, offering tours all year around.

Mystic Seaport Museum

Founded as the Marine Historical Association, Mystic Seaport Museum is the largest maritime museum in the U.S. Visitors can enjoy the museum and its exhibits, and view four vessels designated as National Historic Landmarks: *Emma C. Berry*, *L. A. Dunton*, *Charles W. Morgan*, and *Sabino*.

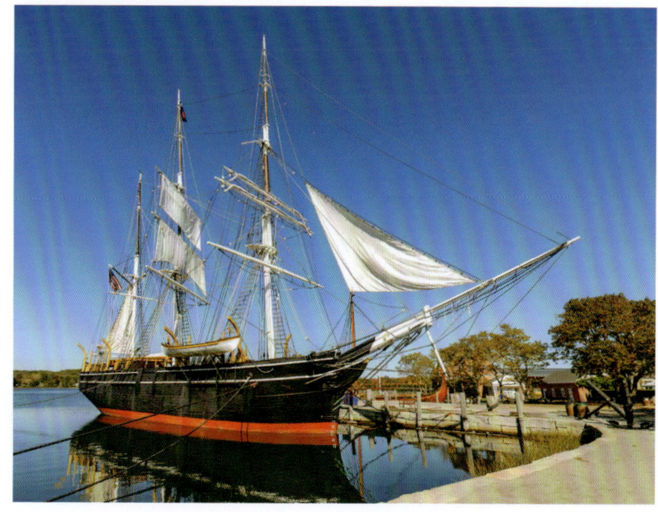

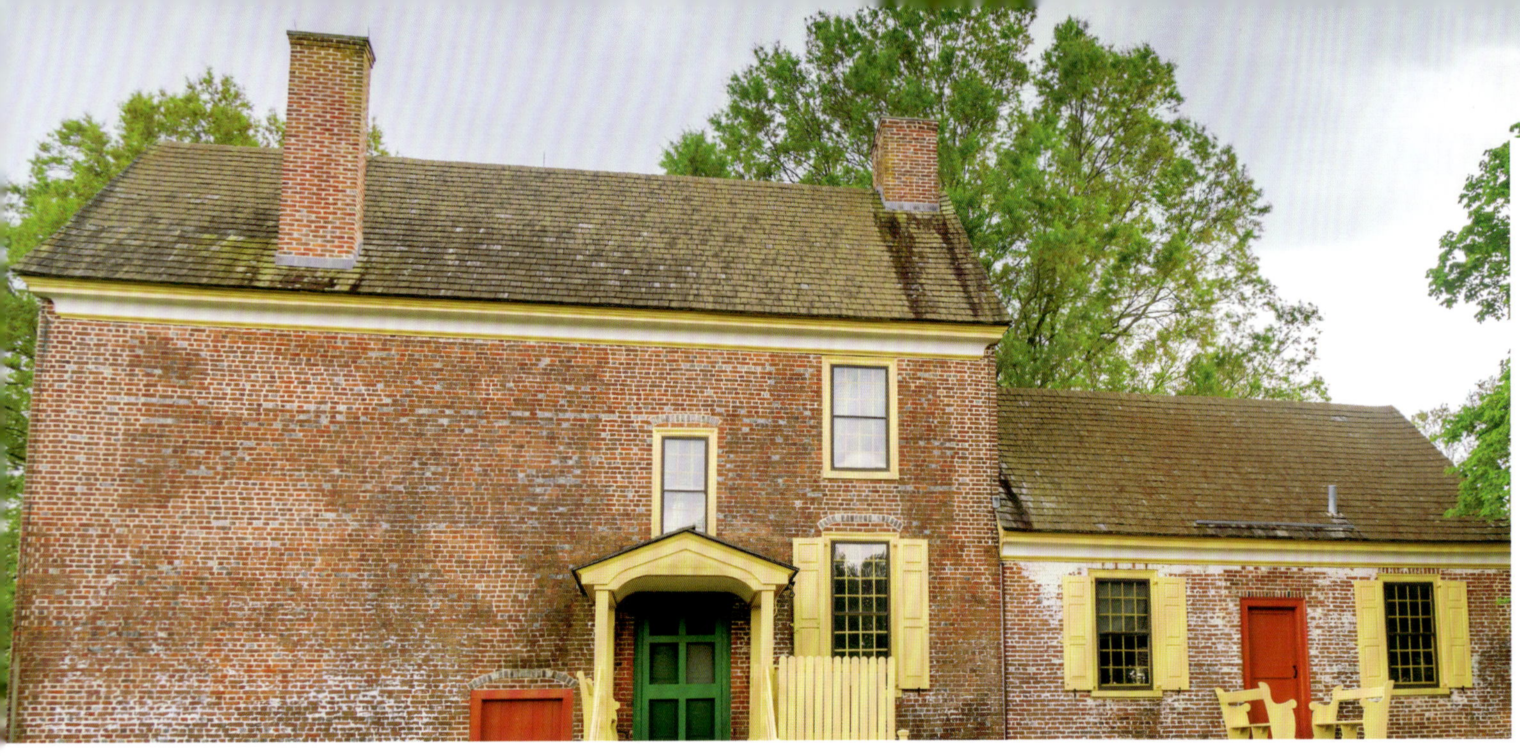

First State National Historical Park

First State National Historical Park consists of seven different sites in Delaware: Beaver Valley, Fort Christina *(see left)*, Old Swedes Church, New Castle Court House, the Dover Green, John Dickinson Plantation, and Ryves Holt House. The park covers the history of Colonial Delaware and the role it played leading up to American Independence. It also tells the story of early Dutch, Swedish, Finnish, and English settlers.

DELAWARE

Captain John Smith Chesapeake National Historic Trail

Captain John Smith Chesapeake National Historic Trail is the first national water trail in the U.S., encompassing over 3,000 miles of waterways throughout the Chesapeake Bay and its tributaries. It follows the routes Captain John Smith explored during his voyages between 1607 and 1609, offering a unique way to experience the history, culture, and ecology of the Chesapeake Bay region.

Amstel House

Also known as the Dr. Finney House, Amstel House is a preserved building in New Castle built in the 1730s. In 1931, concerned citizens worked to protect the house from being torn down, and later formed the New Castle Historical Society. It was added to the National Register of Historic Places in 1977.

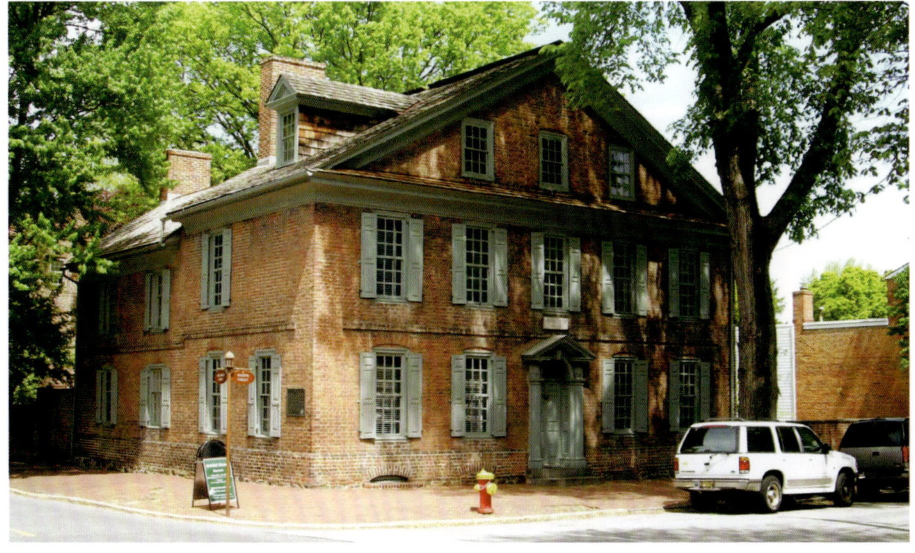

Bridgeville Historical Society Museum

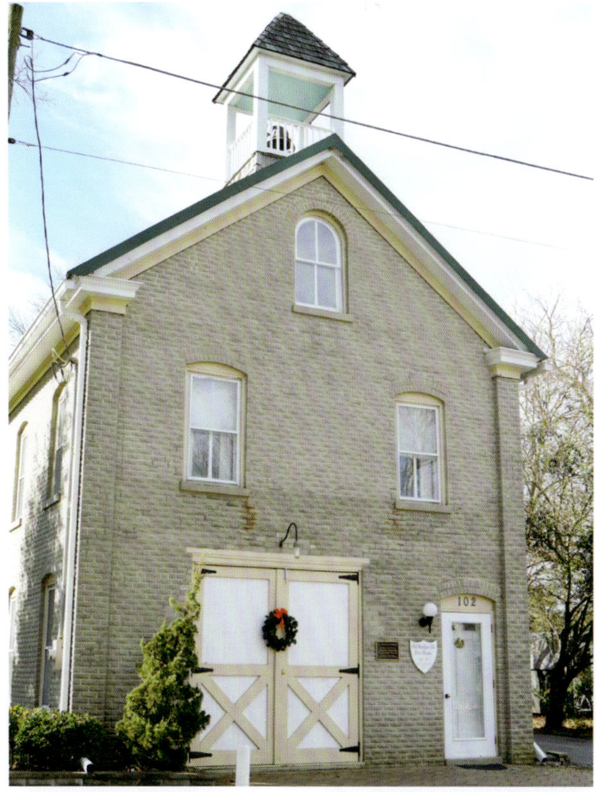

Maintained by the Bridgeville Historical Society and housed in the old Bridgeville fire house, this museum displays historical items, maps, pictures, family, business histories, and more that show off the diversity and richness of Bridgeville, DE, and its surrounding communities.

Gov. William H. Ross House

Also known as The Ross Mansion, this site is a historic home located near Seaford, DE, and maintained by the Seaford Historical Society. The Society operates it as a pre-Civil War period historic house museum, educating visitors on life in Delaware before the Civil War.

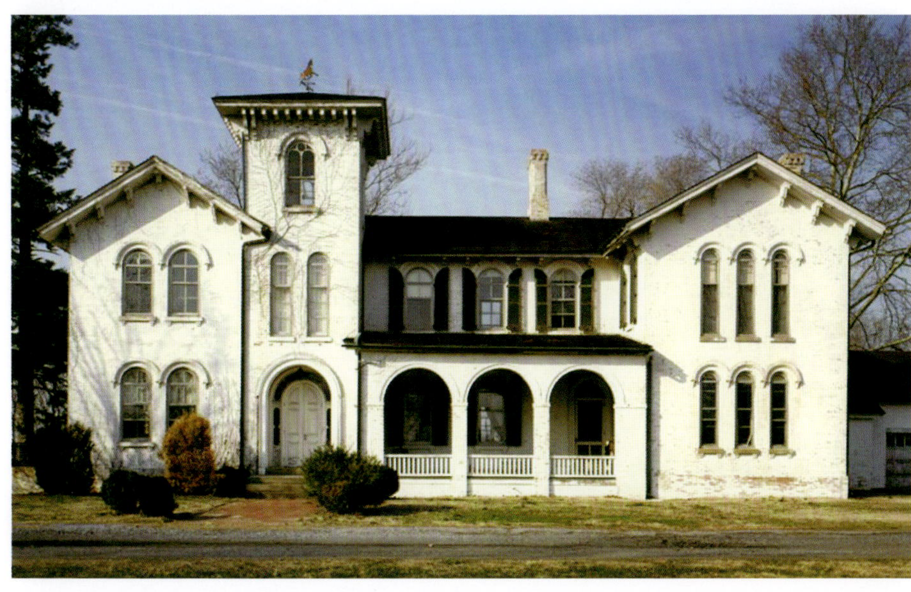

Wilmington and Western Railroad

Wilmington and Western Railroad is a heritage railroad that opened in 1872. Originally built to move goods and passengers between the small towns and mills that lined Delaware's Red Clay Valley, it now functions as a popular tourist attraction that allows visitors to ride 100-year-old trains on over 10 miles of beautiful scenery.

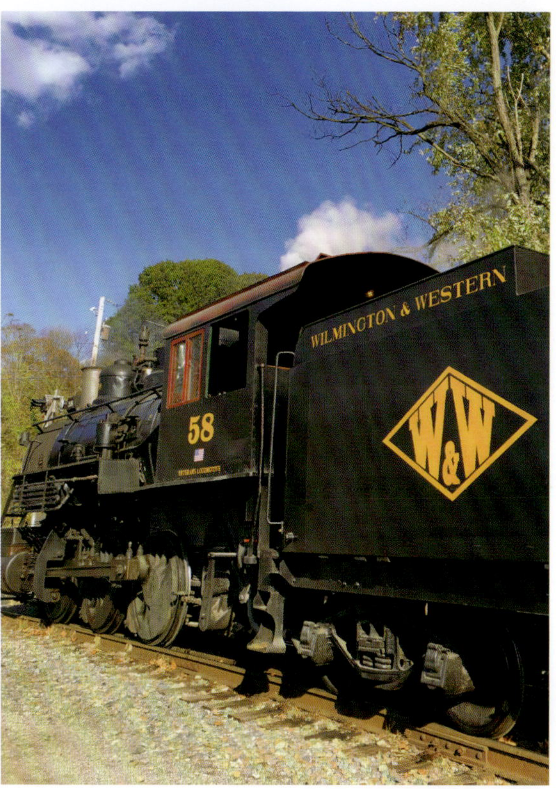

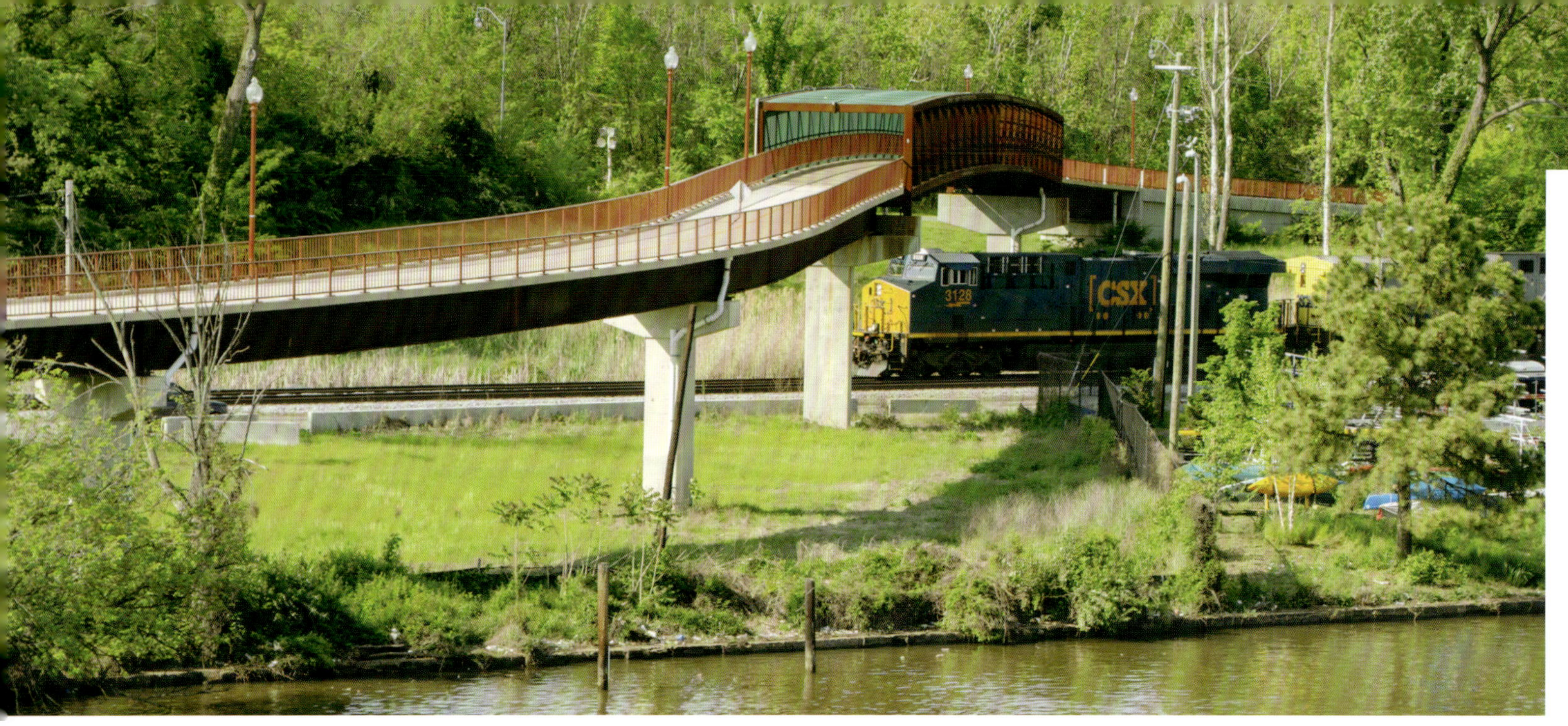

Anacostia Park

Anacostia Park, located along the Anacostia River in Washington, D.C., is one of the city's largest urban parks. Known for its natural beauty, recreational opportunities, and cultural significance, the park offers green space for outdoor activities, events, and wildlife observation. It's a hub for connecting with nature in the heart of the city and provides access to scenic river views and trails.

DISTRICT OF COLUMBIA (WASHINGTON D.C.)

Capitol Hill Parks

Capitol Hill Parks are a collection of small urban green spaces scattered throughout Washington, D.C.'s Capitol Hill neighborhood. Managed by the National Park Service, these parks serve as local gathering spots, offering serene spaces for relaxation, recreation, and community activities. The network of parks includes notable locations like Folger Park, Lincoln Park, and Marion Park, each with unique features and historical significance.

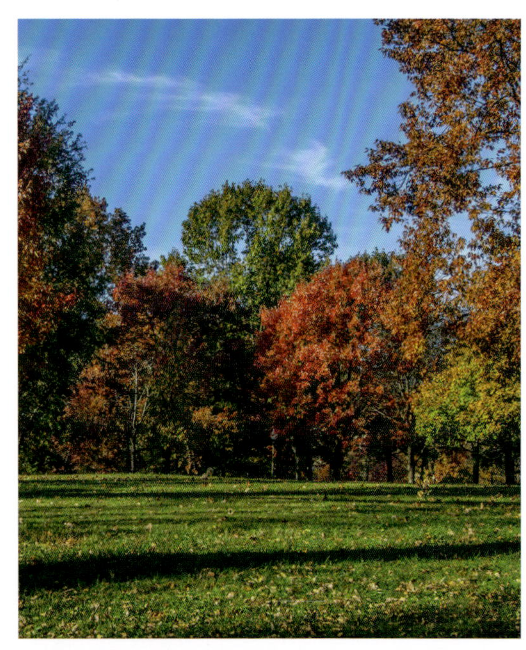

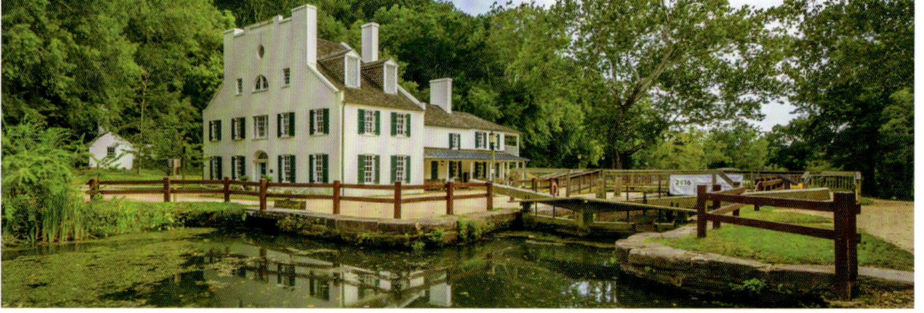

Chesapeake and Ohio Canal National Historical Park

Chesapeake and Ohio (C&O) Canal National Historical Park, stretching 184.5 miles along the Potomac River from Georgetown, D.C., to Cumberland, Maryland, preserves the history and engineering marvel of the C&O Canal. Built between 1828 and 1850, the canal played a vital role in transporting goods during the 19th century. The park is known for its scenic towpath, historic locks, aqueducts, and the natural beauty of the Potomac River Gorge.

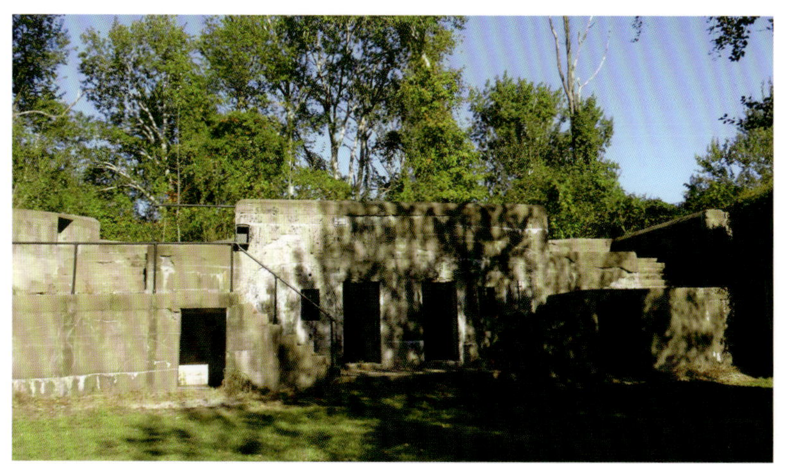

Fort Dupont Park

Fort Dupont Park is a historic site and a large urban green space. Originally one of several Civil War-era forts built to defend the nation's capital, the park is now known for its lush wooded trails, open recreational spaces, and community events. It's a haven for outdoor enthusiasts and a vital cultural hub for the surrounding community.

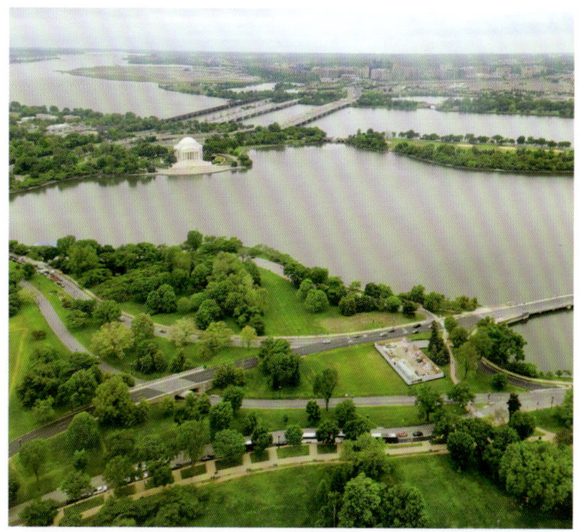

Rock Creek Park

Rock Creek Park, established in 1890, is one of the oldest national parks in the United States. Known for its peaceful natural environment, historic landmarks, and diverse recreational opportunities, the park serves as a green oasis in the heart of the city. Visitors enjoy its wooded trails, historic sites like Peirce Mill, and vibrant wildlife.

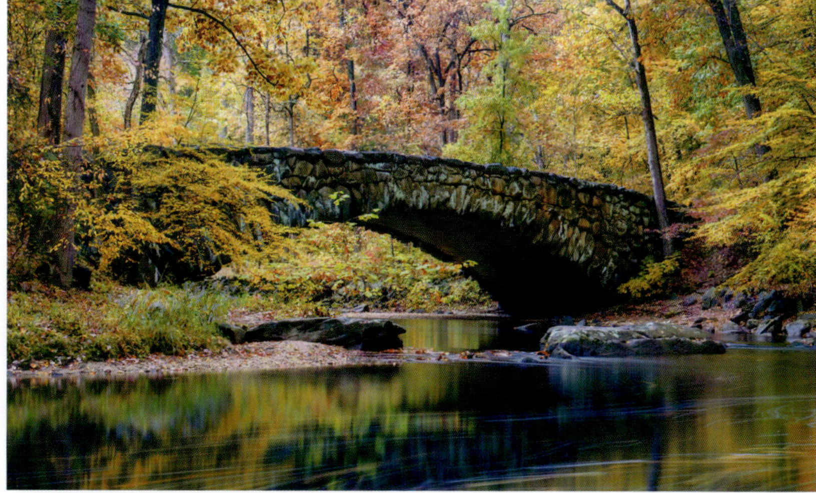

National Mall and Memorial Parks

National Mall and Memorial Parks, often referred to as "America's Front Yard," is a sprawling open space in the heart of Washington, D.C., home to some of the nation's most iconic monuments, memorials, and museums. It honors American history, democracy, and culture, featuring landmarks like the Lincoln Memorial, Washington Monument, Vietnam Veterans Memorial, and Martin Luther King Jr. Memorial. It also hosts significant events and serves as a gathering place for millions of visitors annually.

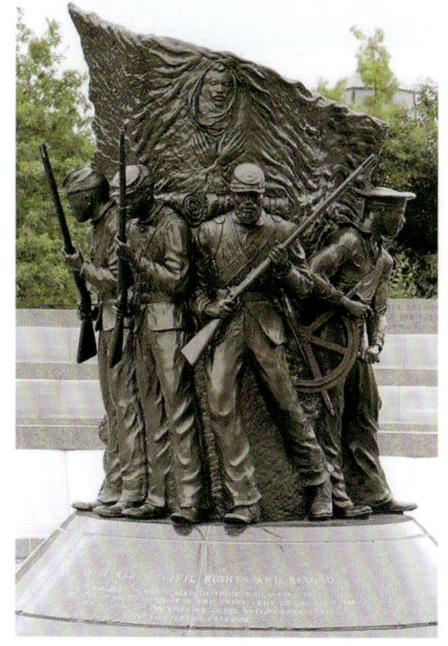

African American Civil War Memorial

The African American Civil War Memorial honors the nearly 210,000 African American soldiers and sailors who served in the Union Army and Navy during the Civil War. It features the Spirit of Freedom statue *(see left)*, a powerful bronze sculpture depicting African American soldiers and families, and a Wall of Honor engraved with the names of those who served. It stands as a testament to their contributions to the war effort, and the fight for freedom and equality.

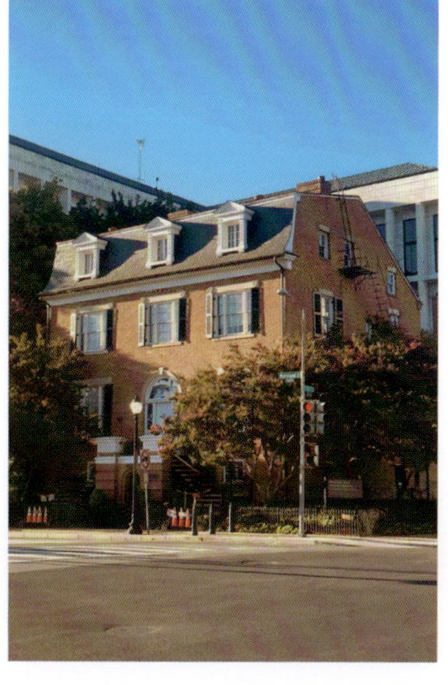

Belmont-Paul Women's Equality National Monument

Belmont-Paul Women's Equality National Monument, located near Capitol Hill in Washington, D.C., is a landmark of the American women's suffrage and equal rights movements. The site was the headquarters of the National Woman's Party, led by suffragist Alice Paul, and served as a hub for advocating women's voting rights and equality. Named after suffrage leaders Alva Belmont and Alice Paul, it preserves the rich history of the fight for women's equality.

Pennsylvania Avenue

Pennsylvania Avenue, often called "America's Main Street," is a historic and symbolic corridor in Washington, D.C., connecting the White House and the U.S. Capitol Building. Known for its political significance and role in national celebrations, parades, and protests, it also features landmarks such as the National Archives Building, National Gallery of Art, and Freedom Plaza. The avenue represents democracy and serves as a stage for historic moments in American history.

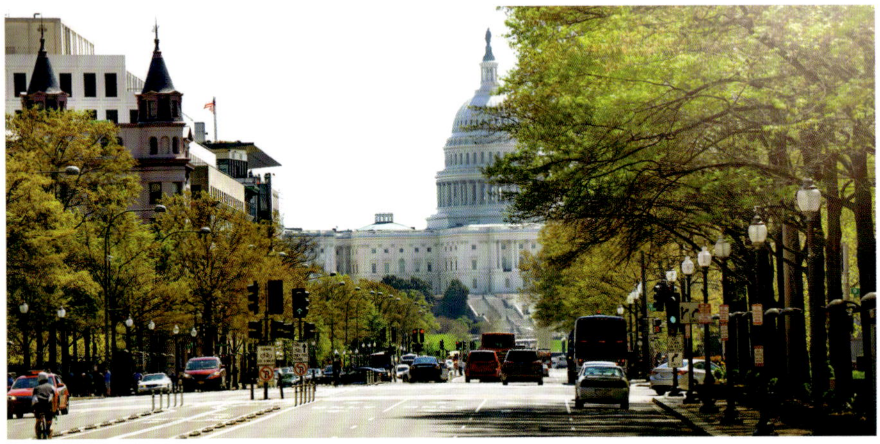

The White House and President's Park

The White House is one of the most iconic symbols of the United States, serving as the official residence and workplace of the President. Surrounded by President's Park, which includes Lafayette Square and the Ellipse, the area is known for its historic significance, beautifully landscaped grounds, and role in American political and cultural history.

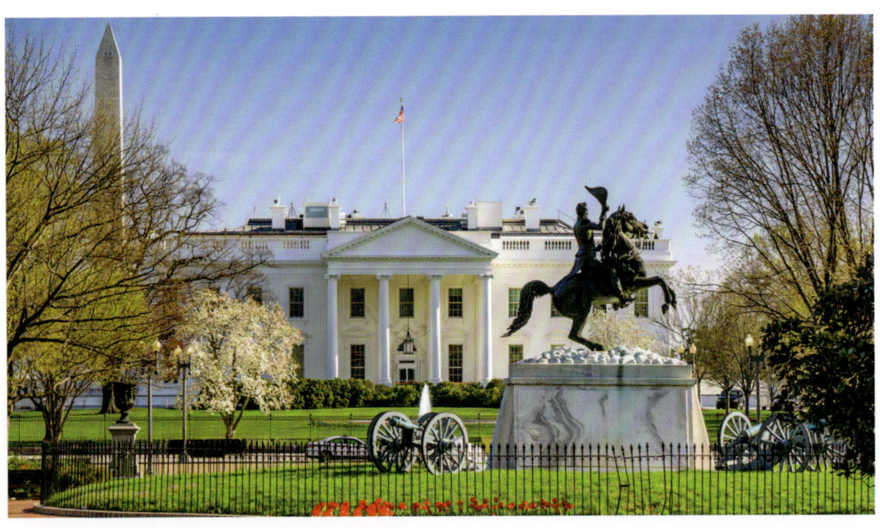

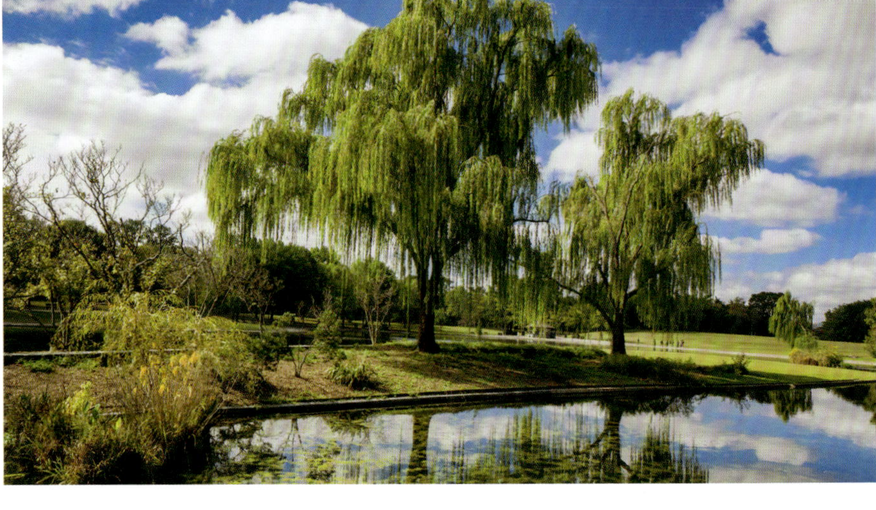

Constitution Gardens

Constitution Gardens, located on the National Mall in Washington, D.C., is a tranquil green space dedicated to celebrating American history and democracy. Known for its picturesque lake and island, the gardens honor the 56 signers of the Declaration of Independence with commemorative stones. It also provides a peaceful retreat amidst the bustling monuments and museums of the National Mall.

Thomas Jefferson Memorial

Jefferson Memorial, located on the Tidal Basin in Washington, D.C., honors Thomas Jefferson, the principal author of the Declaration of Independence and the third President of the United States. This elegant neoclassical structure, inspired by Jefferson's love of classical architecture, features a grand rotunda, a bronze statue of Jefferson, and inscriptions of his most notable writings.

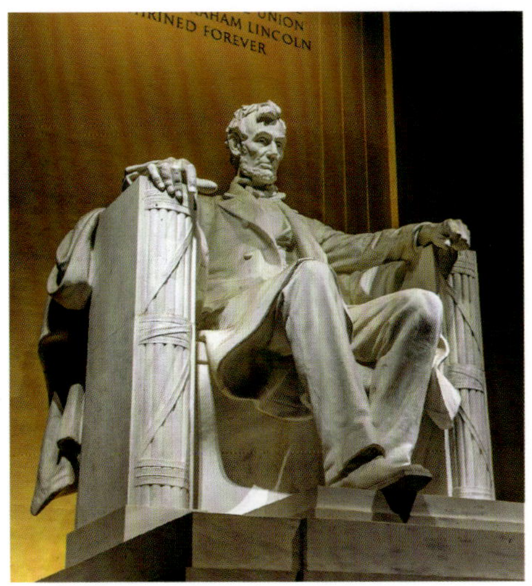

Lincoln Memorial

Lincoln Memorial, located on the western end of the National Mall in Washington, D.C., honors Abraham Lincoln, the 16th President of the United States, who preserved the Union during the Civil War and abolished slavery. Known for its grand Greek Revival architecture, the memorial houses a towering statue of Lincoln and features inscriptions of his Gettysburg Address and Second Inaugural Address.

Frederick Douglass National Historic Site

Frederick Douglass National Historic Site preserves Cedar Hill, the home of Frederick Douglass, one of the most prominent abolitionists, orators, writers, and statesmen in American history. The site offers insights into Douglass's life, his fight for freedom and equality, and his lasting impact on civil rights.

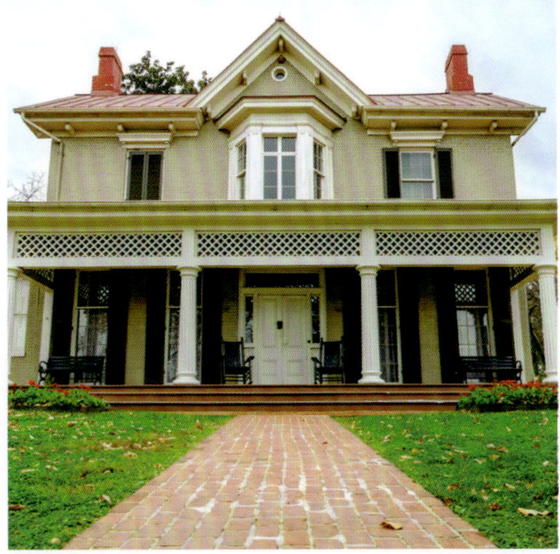

Martin Luther King, Jr. Memorial

Martin Luther King, Jr. Memorial honors the life and legacy of Dr. Martin Luther King, Jr., a leader of the American civil rights movement. The memorial's centerpiece, the "Stone of Hope," *(see left)* features a 30-foot-tall sculpture of Dr. King emerging from a granite block, inspired by his famous words: "Out of the mountain of despair, a stone of hope."

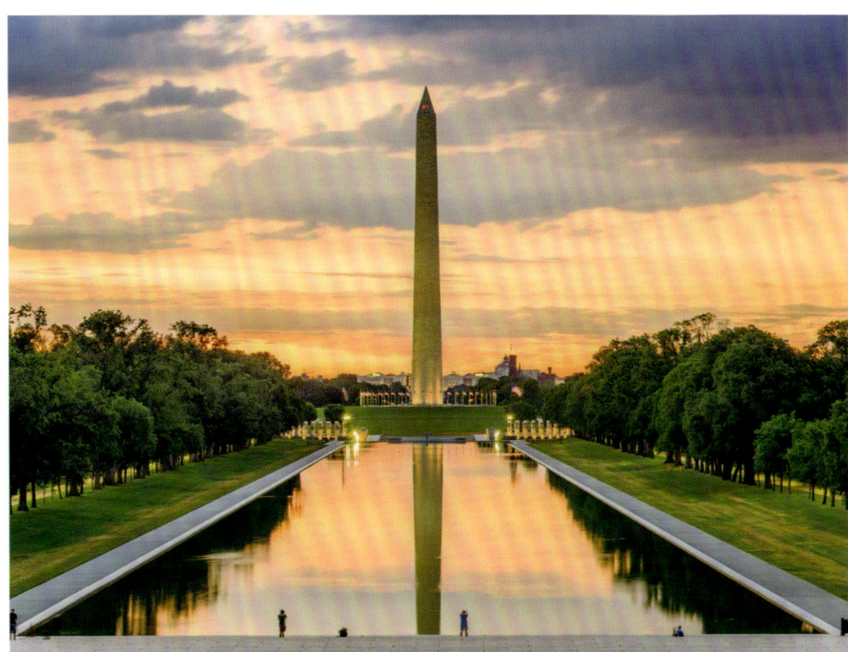

Washington Monument

Washington Monument, located at the center of the National Mall in Washington, D.C., is a towering tribute to George Washington, the first President of the United States and a key figure in the nation's founding. Standing at 555 feet, it's the world's tallest stone structure and obelisk, symbolizing Washington's enduring legacy and the nation's ideals.

Other Washington D.C. National Sites

- Carter G. Woodson Home National Historic Site
- Dwight D. Eisenhower Memorial
- Ford's Theatre
- Franklin Delano Roosevelt Memorial
- Korean War Veterans Memorial
- LBJ Memorial Grove on the Potomac
- Mary McLeod Bethune Council House National Historic Site
- National Capital Parks-East
- Star-Spangled Banner National Historic Trail
- Theodore Roosevelt Island
- Vietnam Veterans Memorial
- World War I & II Memorials

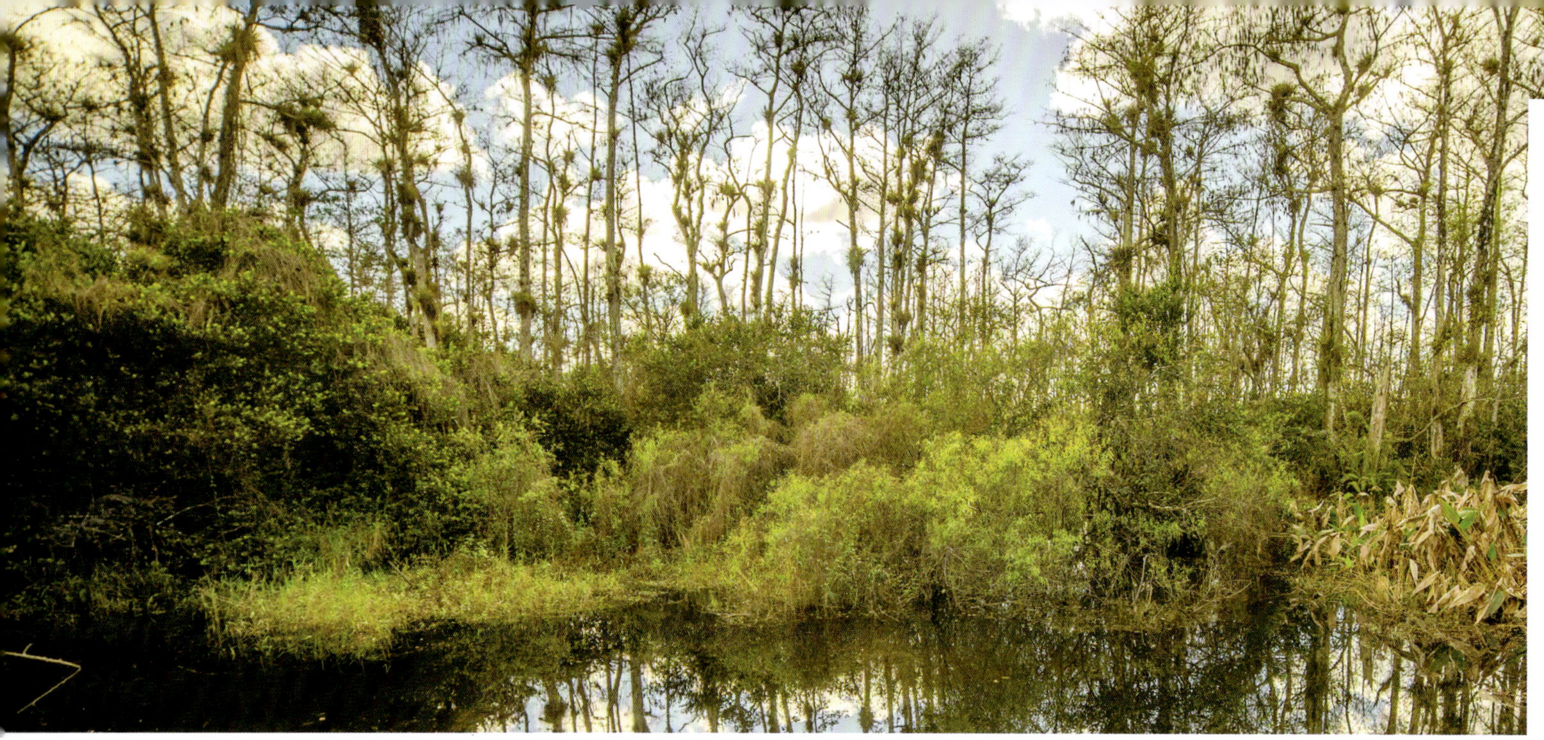

Big Cypress National Preserve

Big Cypress National Preserve is a vast natural area in South Florida, adjacent to Everglades National Park. Spanning over 729,000 acres, it serves as a critical watershed, protecting the diverse ecosystems of the Everglades. It features a mix of swamps, prairies, hardwood hammocks, and pinelands, providing habitats for a variety of wildlife, including alligators, cougars, black bears, and numerous bird species.

FLORIDA

Biscayne National Park

Biscayne National Park, located in southern Florida, is a stunning marine park that protects a unique blend of ecosystems, including coral reefs, mangroves, and the northernmost Florida Keys. Covering over 172,000 acres, the park is 95% water, making it a haven for aquatic adventures and a vital area for marine conservation.

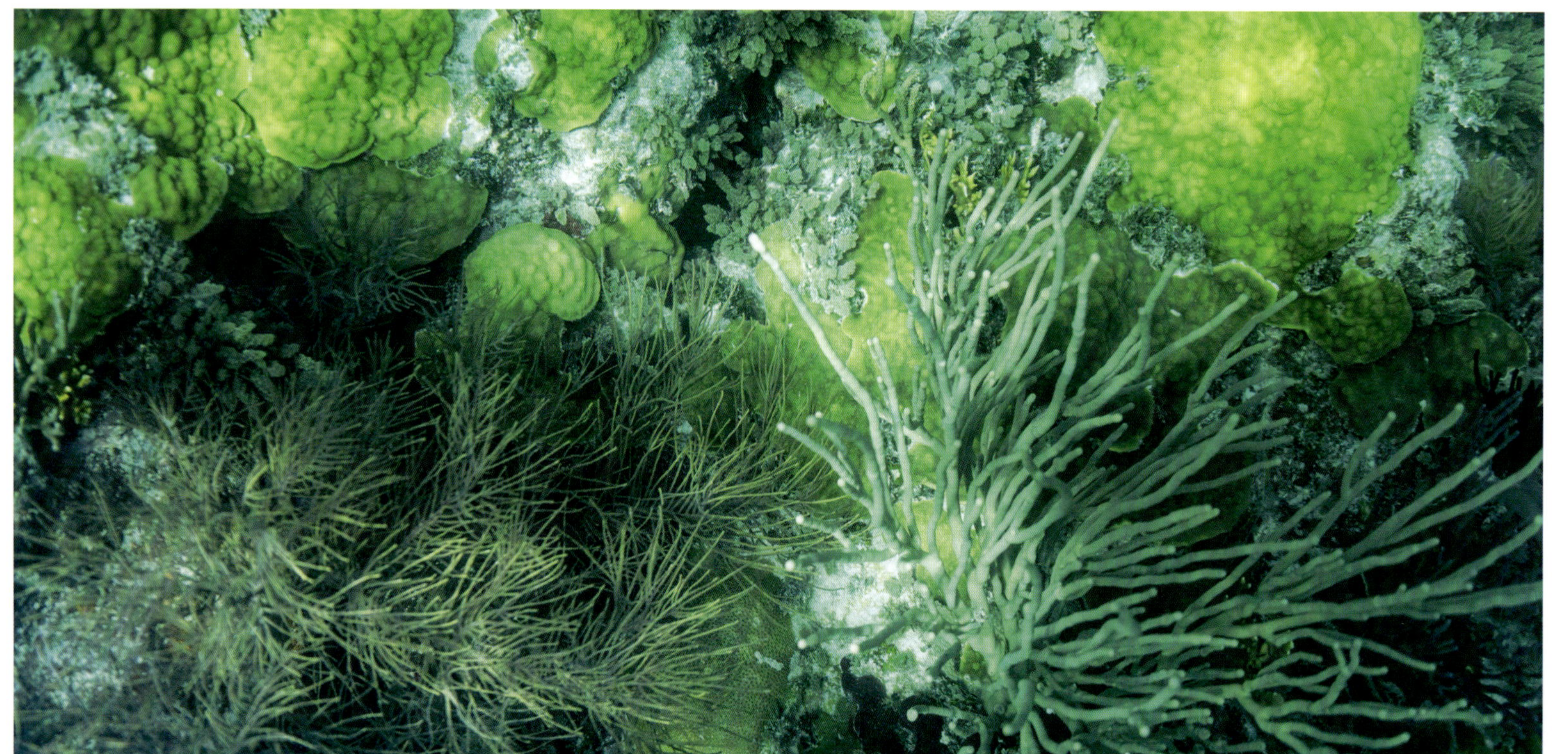

Canaveral National Seashore

Canaveral National Seashore, located on Florida's east coast between New Smyrna Beach and Titusville, is a protected barrier island that offers pristine beaches, varied ecosystems, and a glimpse into Florida's natural and cultural history. This undeveloped stretch of coastline spans 58,000 acres and is managed by the National Park Service. Access to the seashore may be restricted during launch-related activities due to its proximity to the John F. Kennedy Space Center—visitors may get a close view of launches at nearby Playalinda Beach.

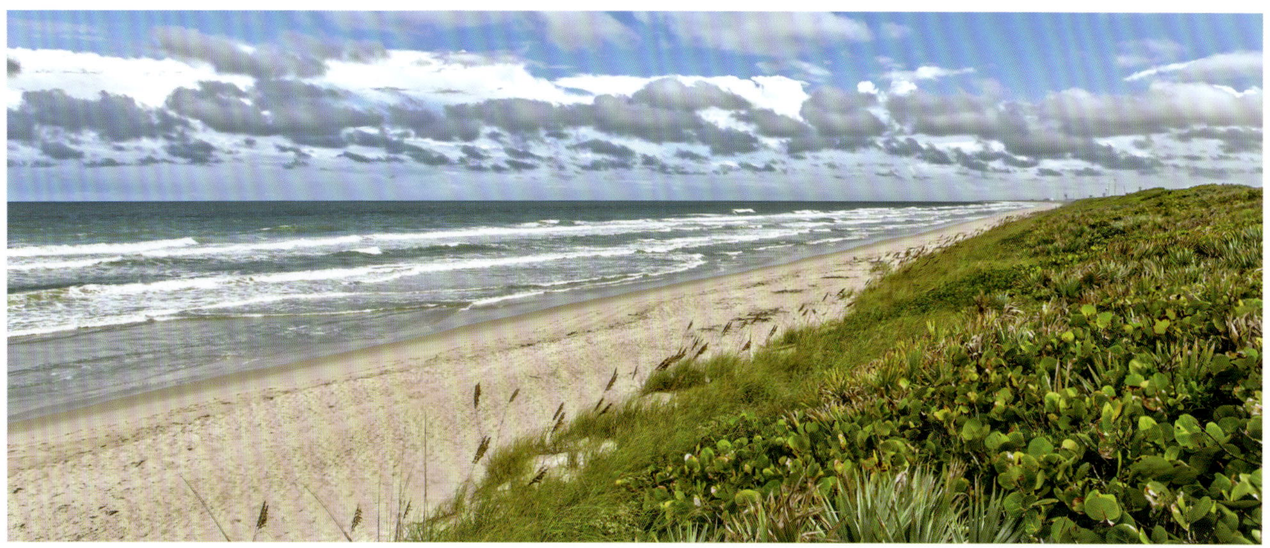

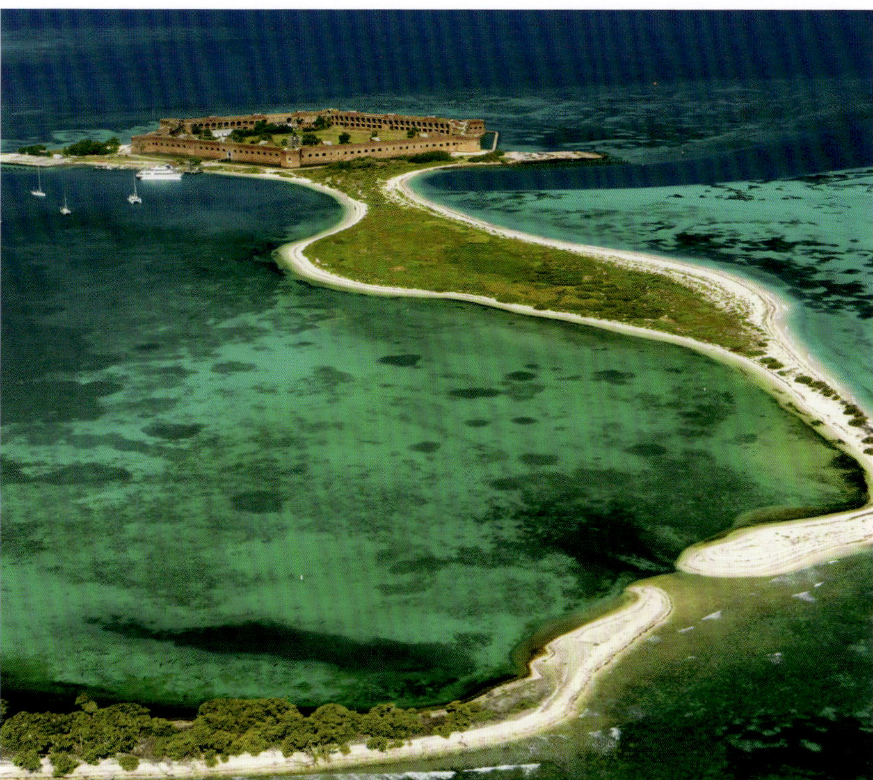

Dry Tortugas National Park

Dry Tortugas National Park, located about 70 miles west of Key West, FL, is a remote and captivating destination renowned for its crystal-clear waters, coral reefs, and historic structures. Accessible only by boat or seaplane, the park encompasses seven small islands and surrounding marine areas, covering roughly 100 square miles.

Everglades National Park

Everglades National Park is the largest subtropical wilderness in the United States and a UNESCO World Heritage Site. Covering over 1.5 million acres, it's a unique ecosystem dominated by slow-moving freshwater, sawgrass marshes, mangroves, and wetlands. The park plays a crucial role in preserving biodiversity and protecting endangered species such as the West Indian manatee, the Florida panther, and the American crocodile.

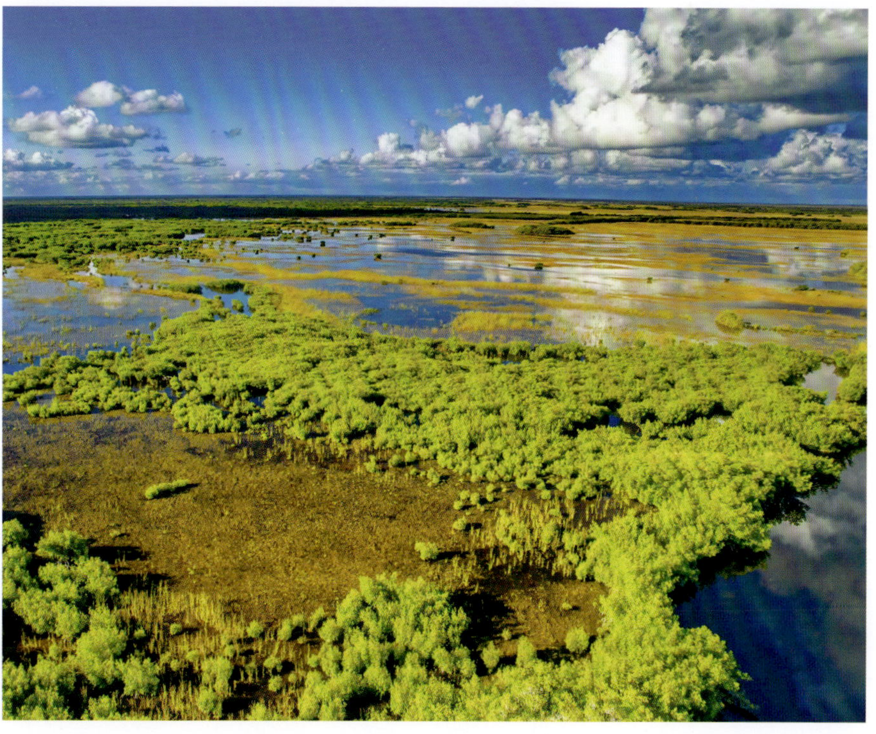

NASA Kennedy Space Center Visitor Complex

Located on Merritt Island, the Kennedy Space Center Visitor Complex features an abundance of attractions related to space exploration. Visitors can view exhibits and displays, historic spacecraft and memorabilia, entertaining and informative shows, and a variety of bus tours of the spaceport. The complex also features daily presentations from veteran NASA astronauts.

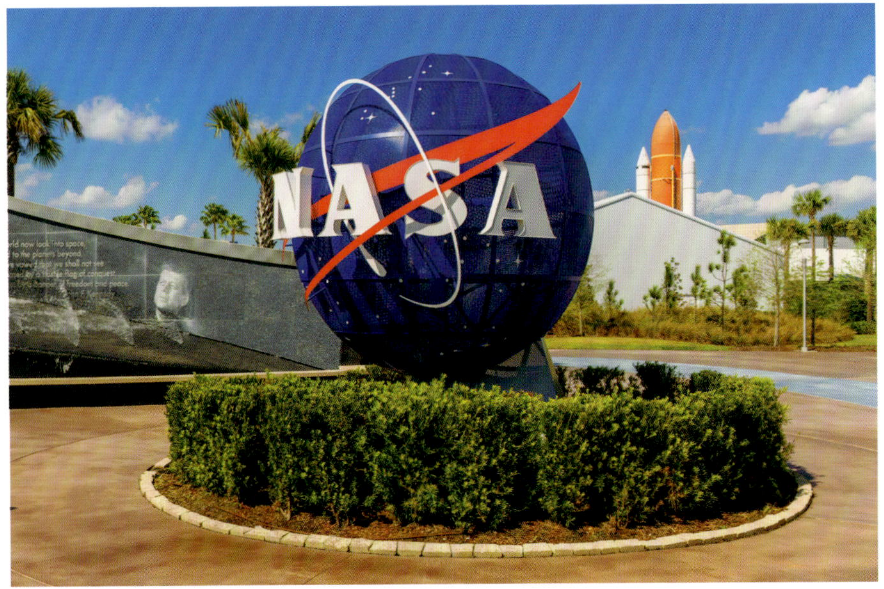

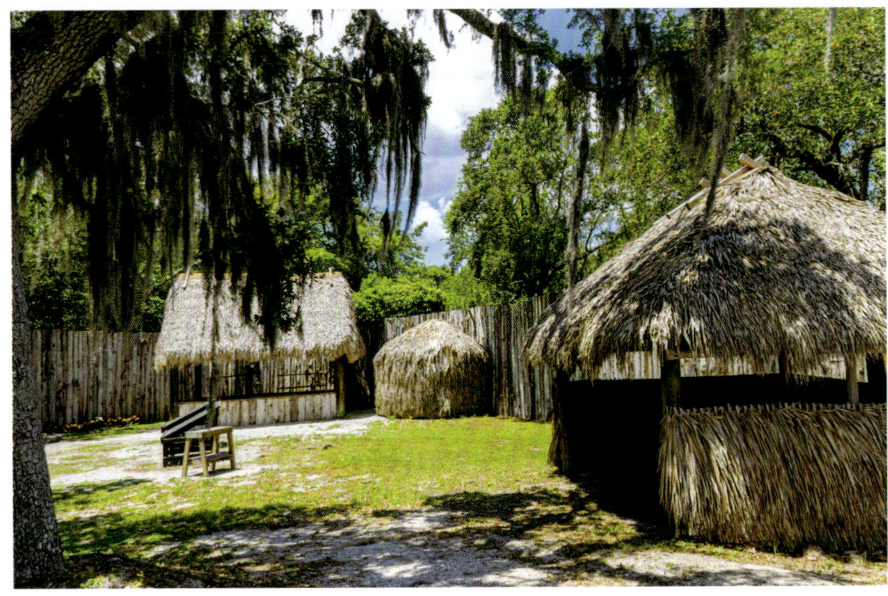

De Soto National Memorial

De Soto National Memorial commemorates the 1539 landing of Spanish explorer and conquistador Hernando de Soto, and his expedition's impact on the Indigenous peoples of the southeastern United States. The site preserves the history of early European exploration and Native American cultures through its visitor center, which contains historic armor, 16th-century weapons, and period artifacts.

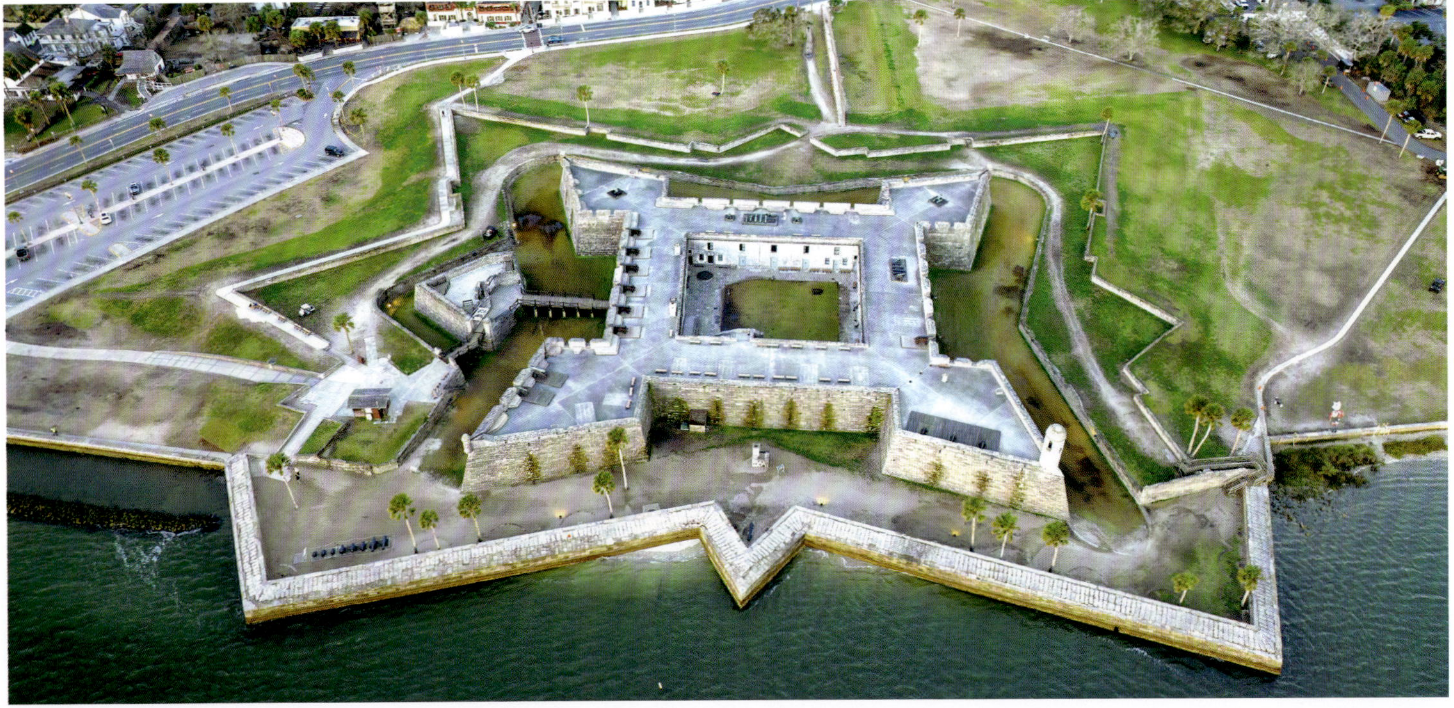

Castillo de San Marcos National Monument

Castillo de San Marcos National Monument is the oldest masonry fort in the continental United States. Built by the Spanish in 1672, it stands as a testament to the colonial history of the region and the strategic importance of Florida in the New World. The fort's coquina walls—a unique limestone made from shell fragments—are both an architectural marvel and a symbol of resilience.

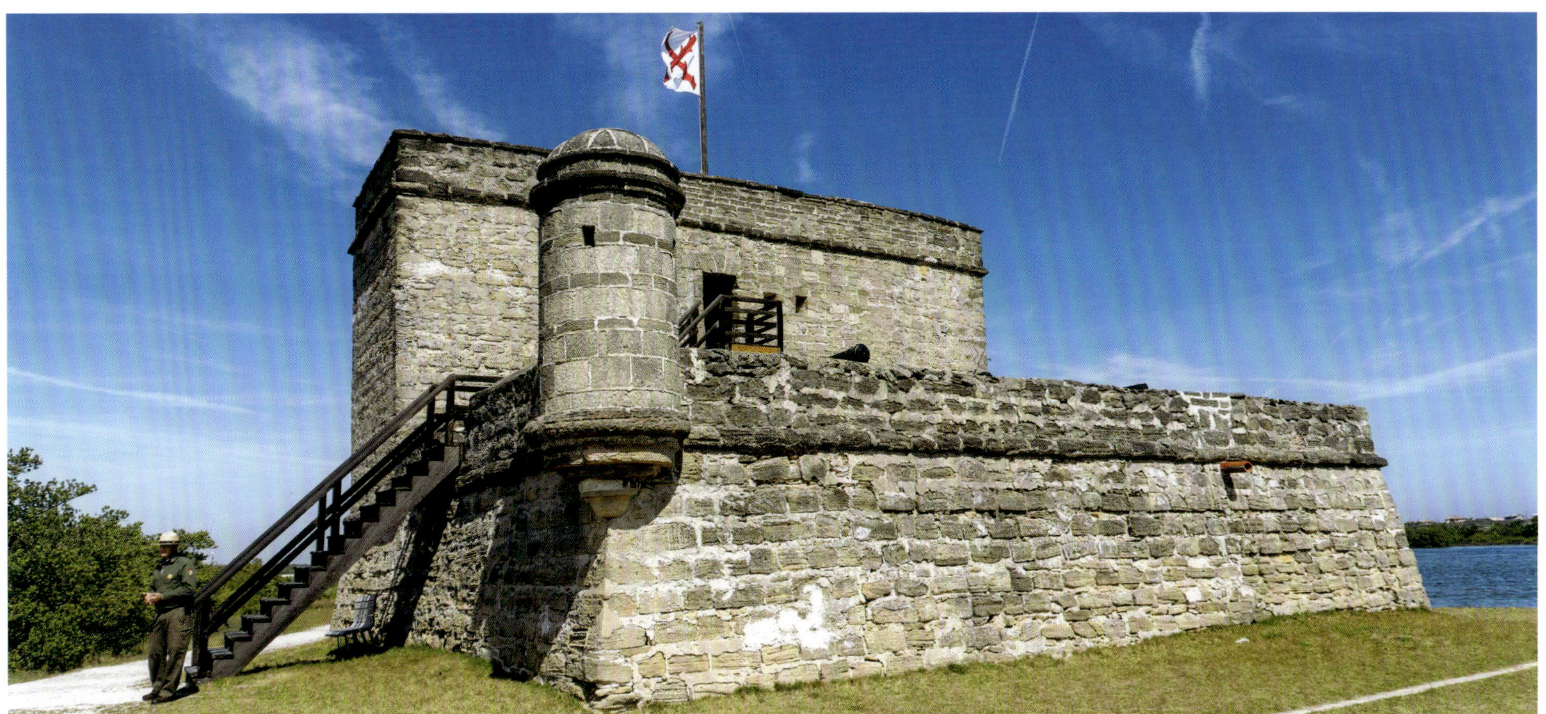

Fort Matanzas National Monument

Fort Matanzas National Monument preserves the historic fort and its surrounding ecosystem. Built by the Spanish in 1742, this small but strategically-vital fort guarded the southern approach to St. Augustine via the Matanzas River, serving as an early warning system against British attacks.

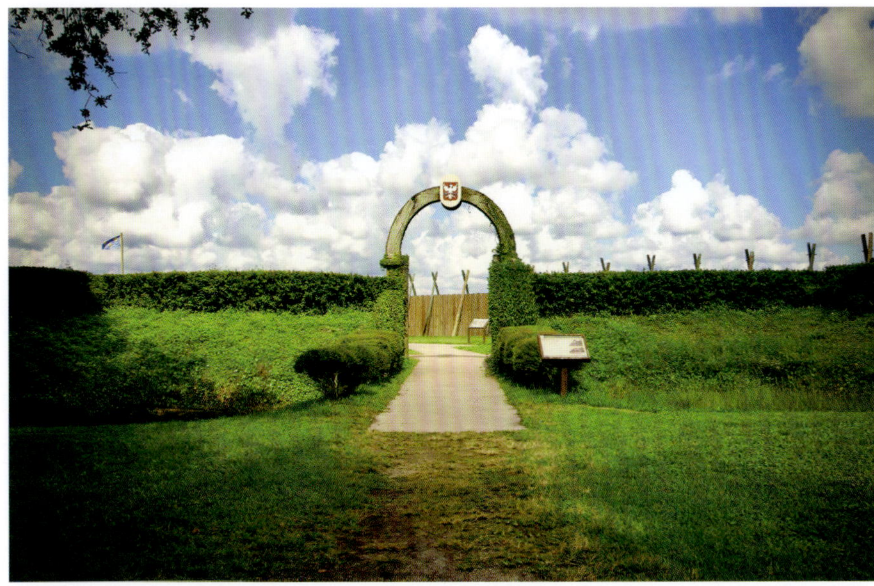

Fort Caroline National Memorial

Fort Caroline National Memorial commemorates the short-lived French settlement of Fort de la Caroline, established in 1564 by Huguenots—a group of Calvinist French Protestants—seeking religious freedom. The memorial highlights the struggles between European powers and the impact on Indigenous peoples during the early colonial period.

Timucuan Ecological and Historic Preserve

Timucuan Ecological and Historic Preserve is a 46,000-acre protected area that blends natural beauty with rich cultural history. Established in 1988, the preserve celebrates the legacy of the Timucua people, early European settlers, and the region's varied ecosystems. The preserve includes Fort Caroline National Memorial, and the Kingsley Plantation, the oldest standing plantation in Florida.

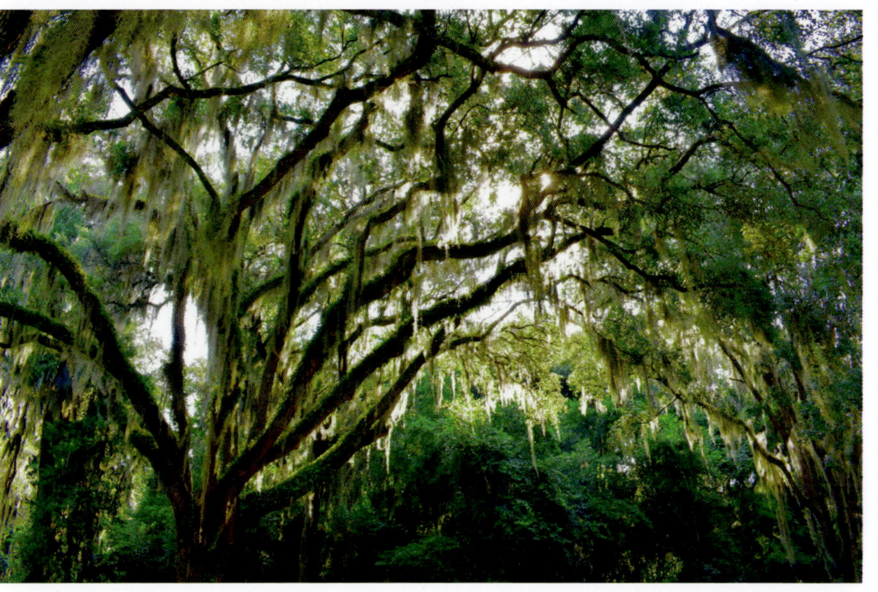

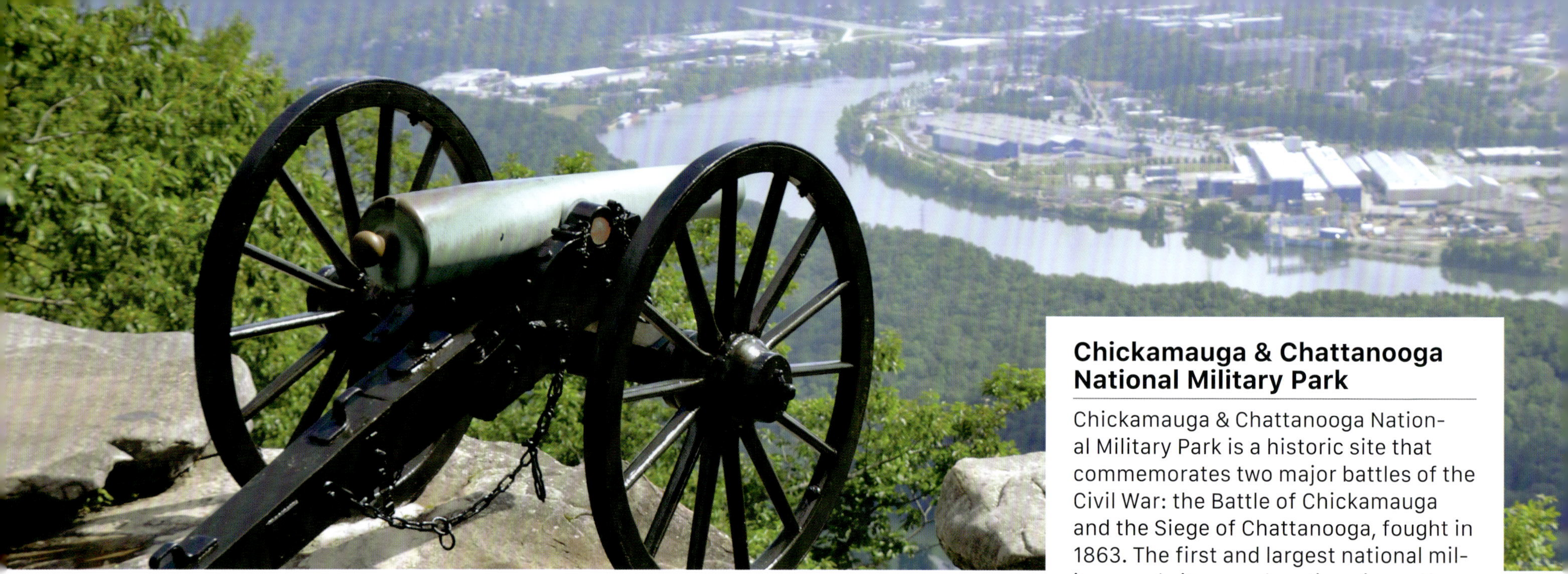

GEORGIA

Chickamauga & Chattanooga National Military Park

Chickamauga & Chattanooga National Military Park is a historic site that commemorates two major battles of the Civil War: the Battle of Chickamauga and the Siege of Chattanooga, fought in 1863. The first and largest national military park, it spans locations in northwest Georgia and southeast Tennessee, preserving the memory of these pivotal events in American history.

Cumberland Island National Seashore

Cumberland Island National Seashore, located off the coast of Georgia, is a pristine and ecologically rich barrier island known for its natural beauty, historical sites, and diverse wildlife. Established in 1972, it's managed by the National Park Service and offers visitors a unique blend of history, recreation, and conservation.

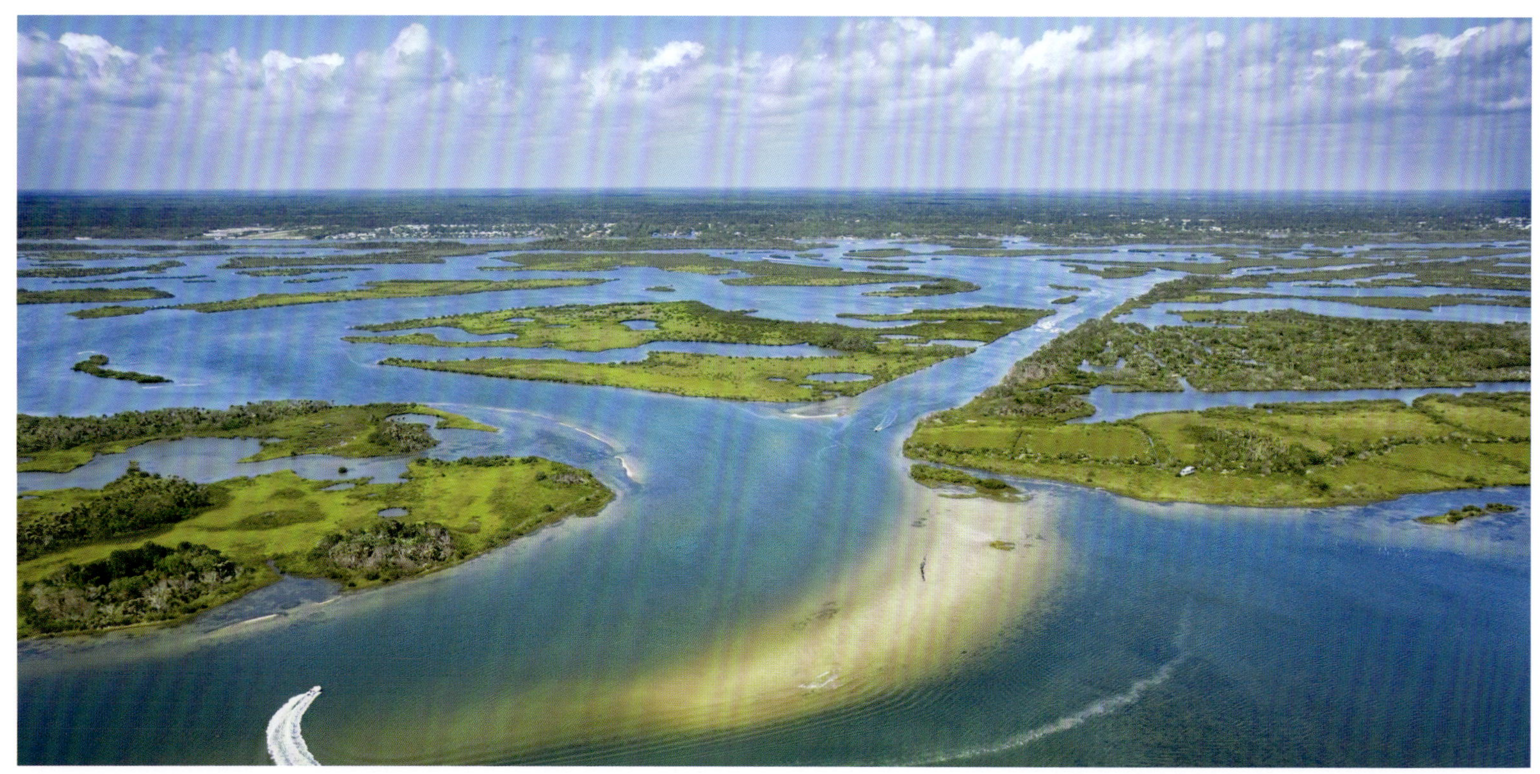

Jimmy Carter National Historical Park

Jimmy Carter National Historical Park, located in Plains, Georgia, honors the life and legacy of Jimmy Carter, the 39th President of the United States. Established in 1987, the park preserves sites associated with Carter's early life, education, political career, and post-presidential contributions to peace and humanitarian causes. Visitors can enjoy guided and self-guided tours, interpretive exhibits and programs about Carter's legacy, and opportunities to explore Plains's small-town charm.

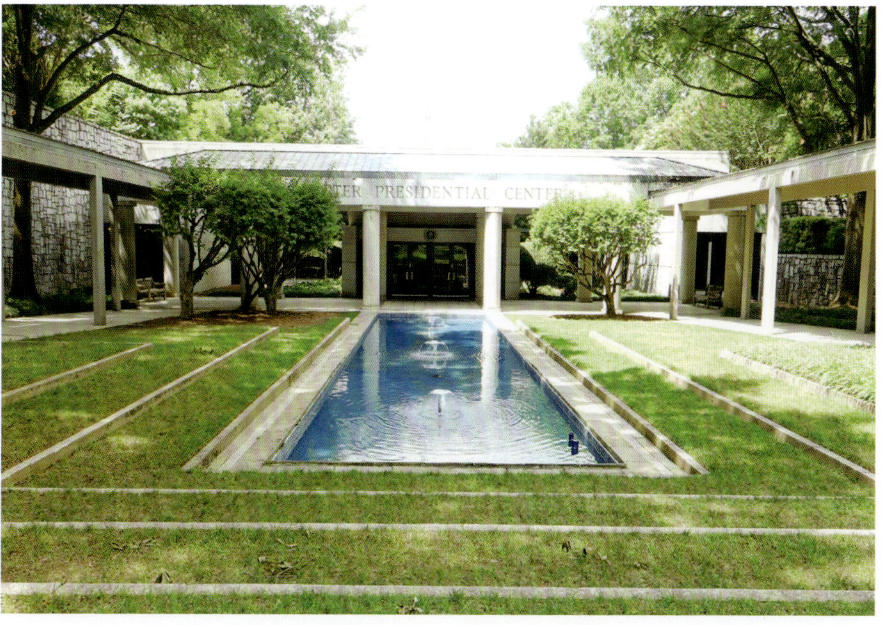

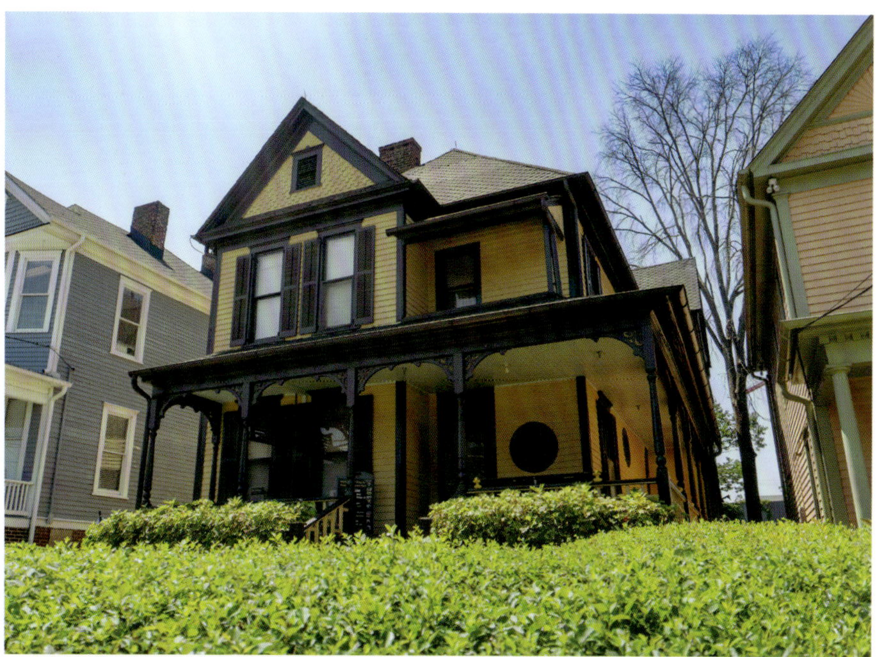

Martin Luther King, Jr. National Historical Park

Martin Luther King, Jr. National Historical Park honors the life, legacy, and civil rights contributions of Dr. Martin Luther King, Jr. This site preserves key locations associated with his upbringing, ministry, and leadership in the American Civil Rights Movement. Visitors can enjoy educational programs and self-guided walking tours through the historic Sweet Auburn District, a hub of African American culture and activism during Dr. King's lifetime.

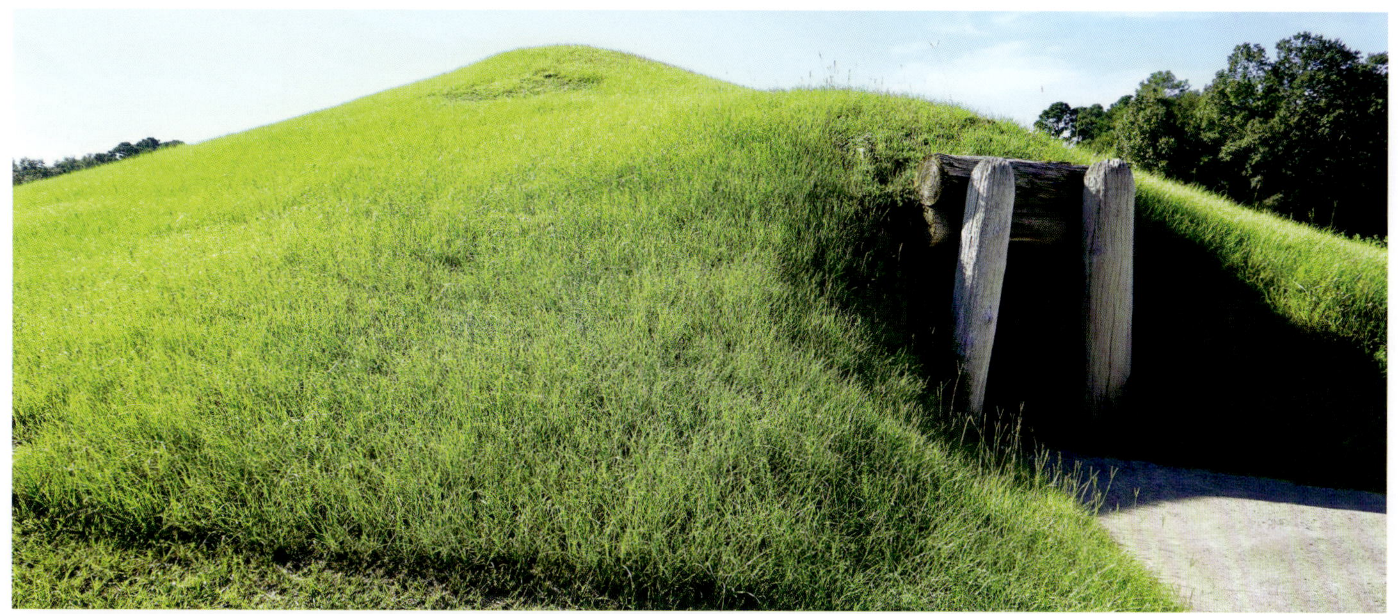

Ocmulgee Mounds National Historical Park

Ocmulgee Mounds National Historical Park is a site of significant cultural and historical importance. It preserves over 17,000 years of continuous human history, focusing on the Native American cultures that thrived in the area. The park highlights ancient earthworks built by the South Appalachian Mississippian people between 900 and 1200 CE, as well as evidence of earlier Paleo-Indian and Woodland cultures.

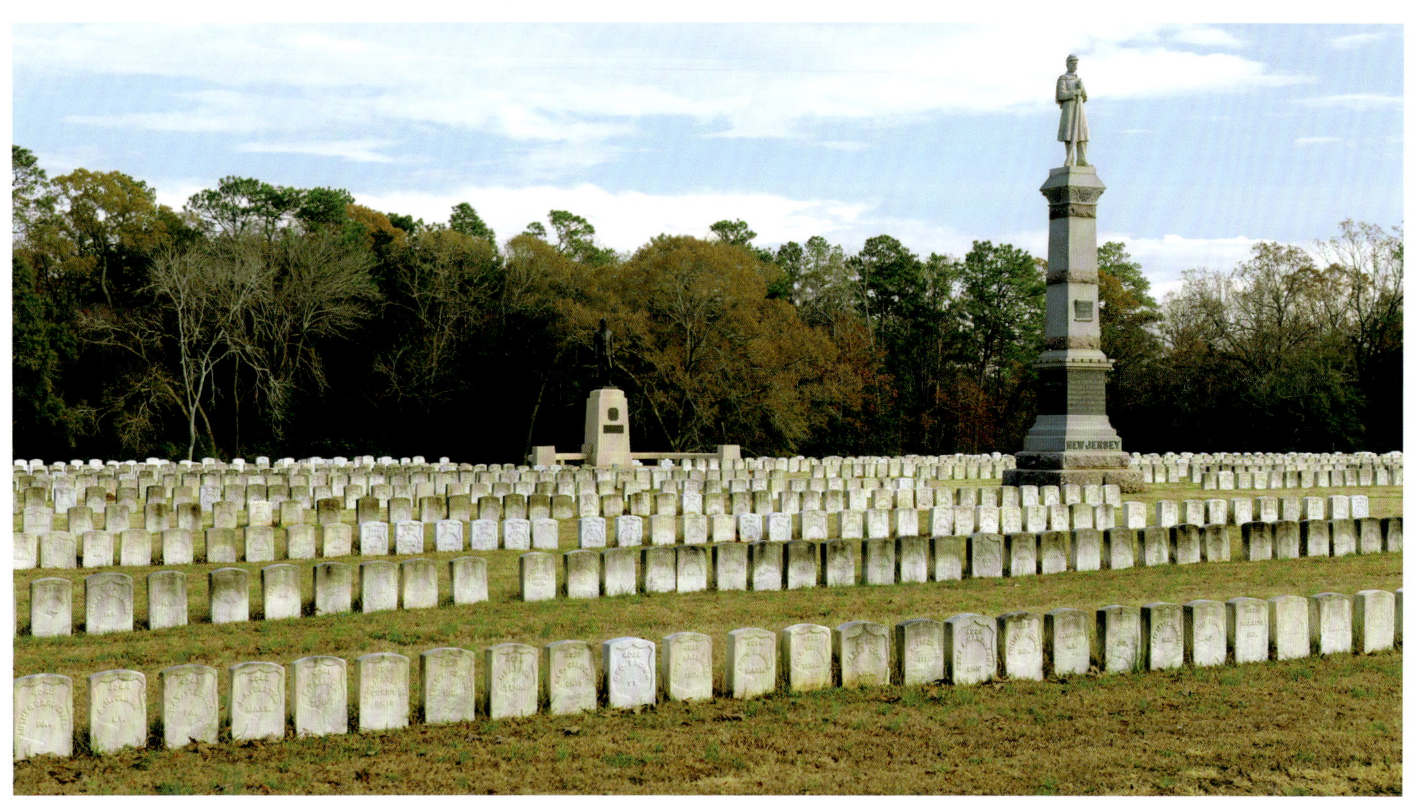

Andersonville National Historic Site

Andersonville National Historic Site serves as a powerful memorial to all American prisoners of war. It preserves the site of the Camp Sumter Military Prison, one of the largest Confederate prisoner-of-war camps during the Civil War, and honors the sacrifices of those who endured the hardships of wartime imprisonment. The prison was overcrowded by four times its capacity, and had an inadequate water supply, inadequate food, and unsanitary conditions. Nearly 13,000 of the 45,000 Union prisoners died due to overcrowding, disease, and malnutrition.

Appalachian National Scenic Trail

The Appalachian National Scenic Trail, also known as the A.T., is one of the longest and most iconic hiking trails in the world. Stretching approximately 2,197 miles, it traverses 14 states from Springer Mountain in Georgia to Mount Katahdin in Maine. The trail offers breathtaking landscapes, rich biodiversity, and a challenging experience for hikers of all skill levels.

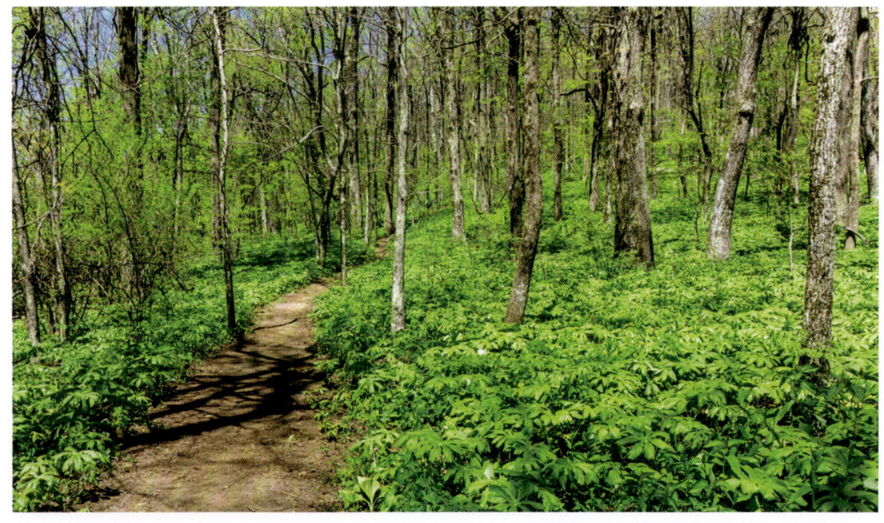

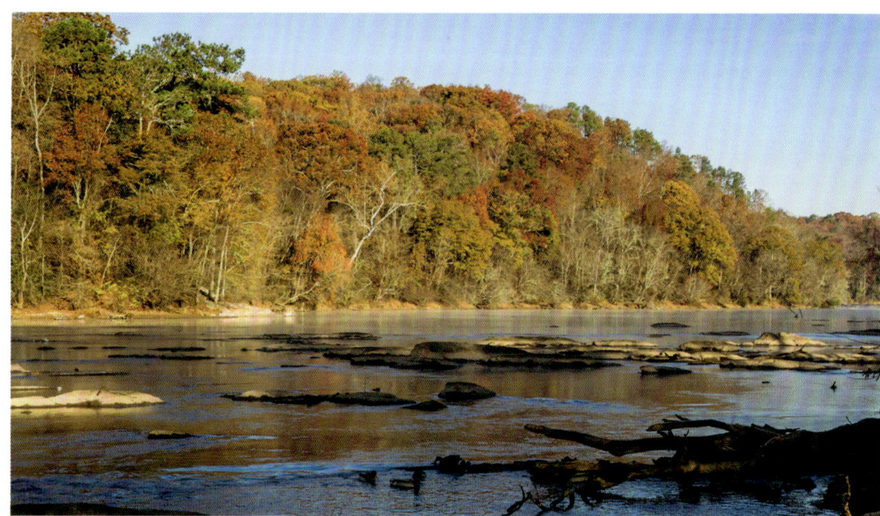

Chattahoochee River National Recreation Area

The Chattahoochee River National Recreation Area is a scenic 48-mile stretch of the Chattahoochee River, located in northern Georgia near Atlanta. Managed by the National Park Service, this area offers a mix of natural beauty, outdoor recreation, and historical significance with its preserved historic sites such as the Marietta Paper Mill ruins, the ruins of Ivy Mill, the Roswell Mill, and more.

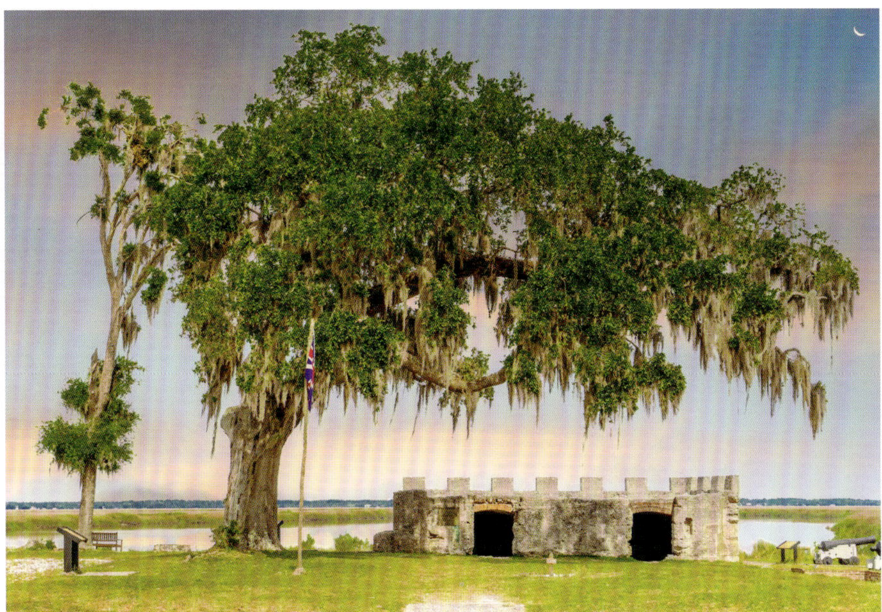

Fort Frederica National Monument

Fort Frederica National Monument is located on St. Simons Island in Georgia and preserves the site of a strategic British colonial fort and town from the 18th century. It was established in 1736 to protect the Georgia colony from Spanish Florida and played a significant role in the 1742 battles of Bloody Marsh and Gully Hole Creek. The site offers a glimpse into early American colonial life and military history.

Fort Pulaski National Monument

Fort Pulaski National Monument is located on Cockspur Island near Savannah, Georgia. This historic site preserves Fort Pulaski, a well-maintained 19th-century coastal defense fortification that played a pivotal role during the Civil War. The fort is a stunning example of star-shaped military architecture and features moats, drawbridges, and walls made of brick and tabby concrete.

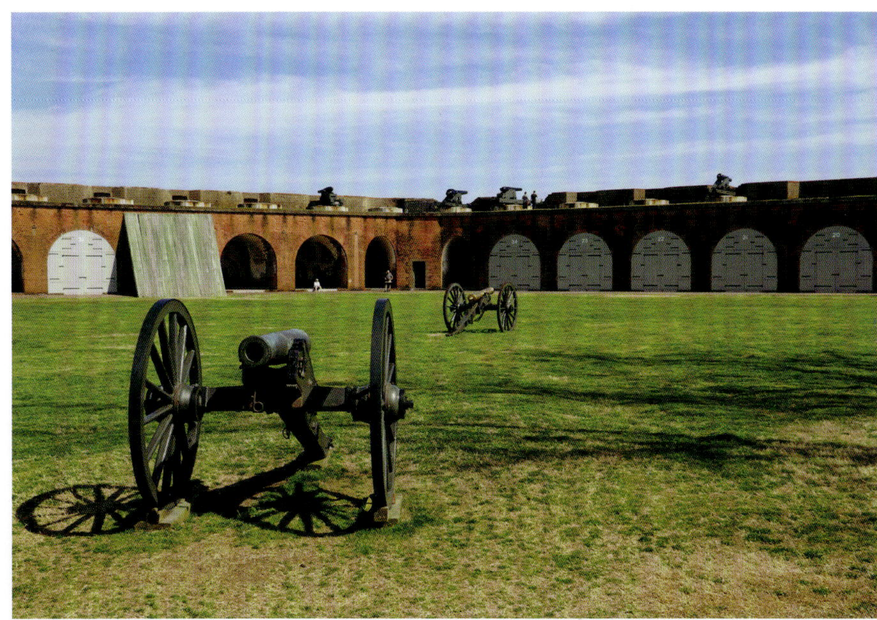

Kennesaw Mountain National Battlefield Park

Kennesaw Mountain National Battlefield Park preserves the site of the Battle of Kennesaw Mountain, a significant conflict during the American Civil War. The battle, fought from June 18 to July 2, 1864, was part of the Union Army's effort to capture the city of Atlanta. The park commemorates both the battle and the broader history of the Civil War in Georgia.

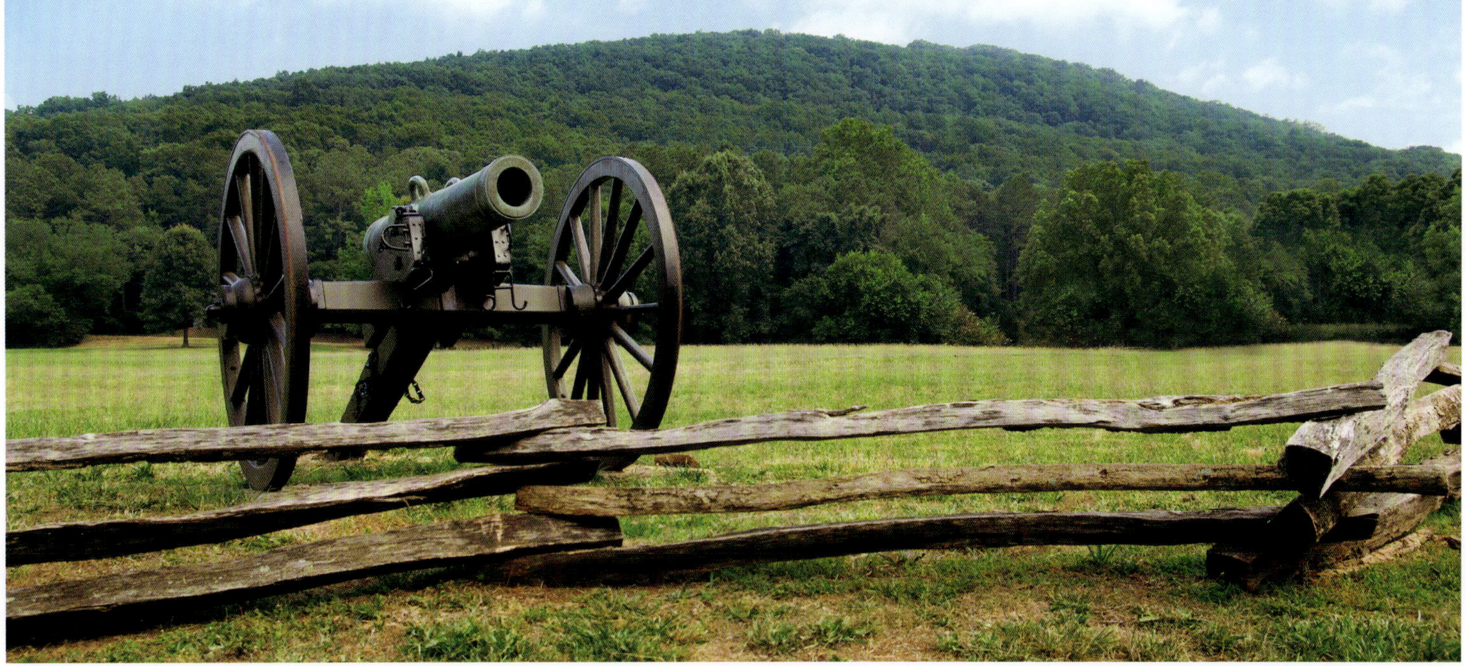

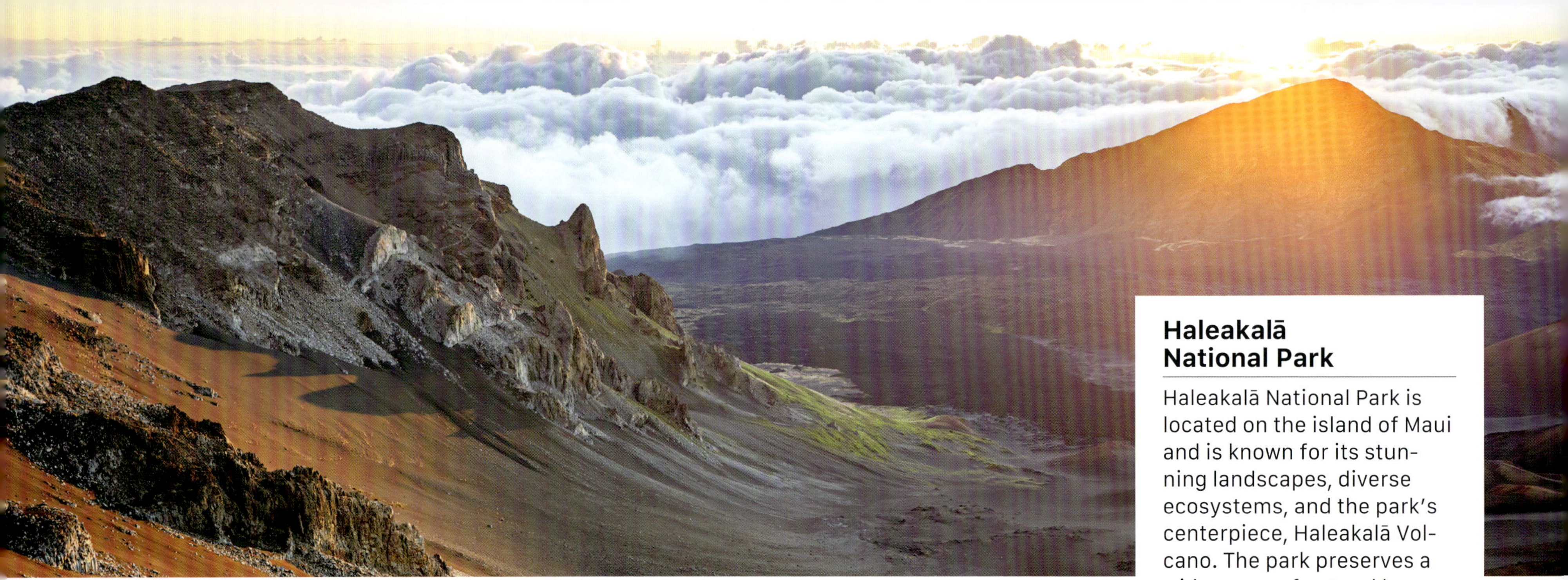

HAWAIʻI

Haleakalā National Park

Haleakalā National Park is located on the island of Maui and is known for its stunning landscapes, diverse ecosystems, and the park's centerpiece, Haleakalā Volcano. The park preserves a wide range of natural beauty, from the crater floor to tropical rainforests and the coastal environments.

Kalaupapa National Historical Park

Kalaupapa National Historical Park is located on the island of Molokai and preserves the history of the Kalaupapa Settlement, a remote community established in the 19th century for individuals affected by Hansen's disease, also known as leprosy. The park honors the stories of those who were forcibly relocated to the settlement, the caregivers, and the efforts to treat and care for those with the disease.

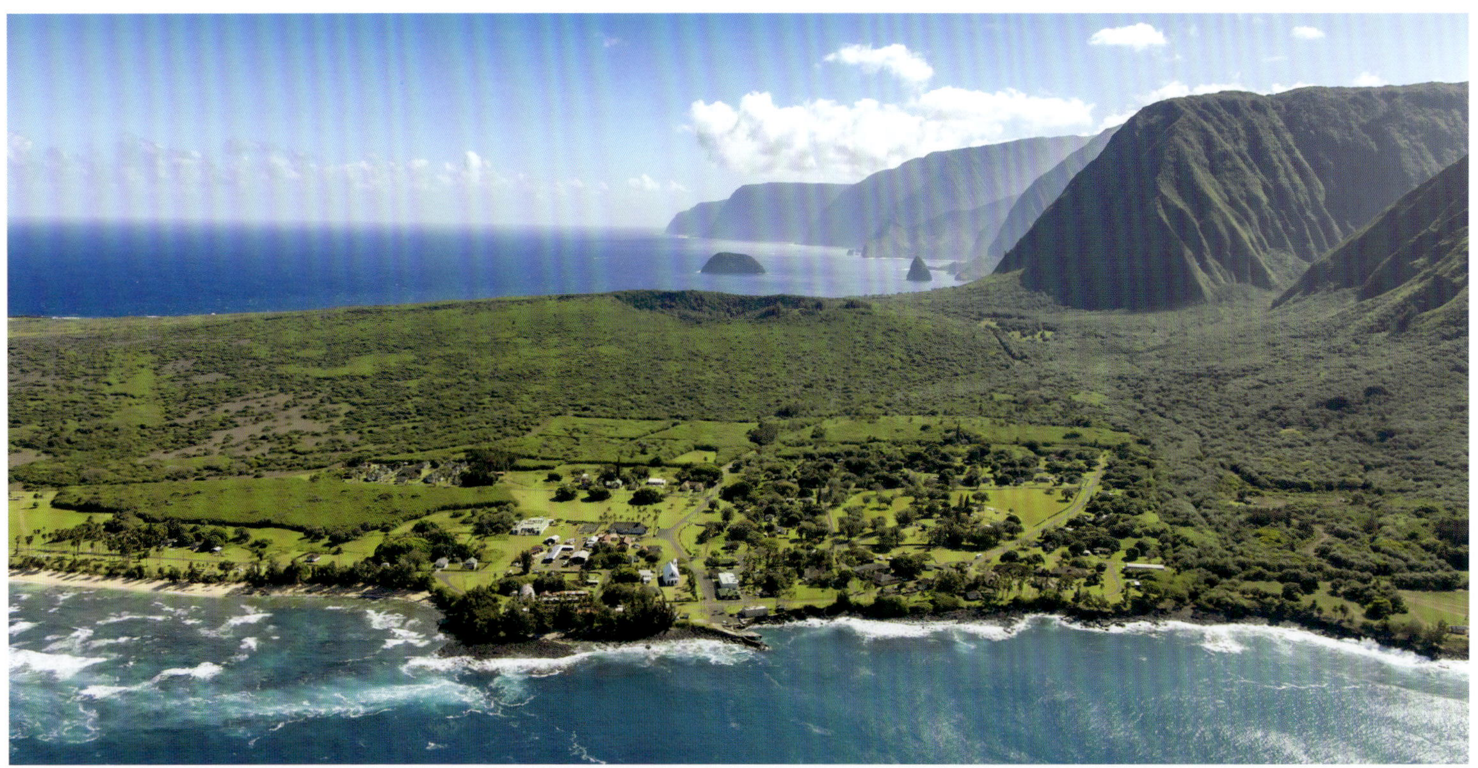

Hawai'i Volcanos National Park

Hawai'i Volcanos National Park is located on the Big Island of Hawai'i and is home to two of the most active volcanoes in the world: Kīlauea and Mauna Loa. The park offers visitors a unique opportunity to explore volcanic landscapes, learn about volcanic processes, and witness the power of nature in one of the most geologically active places on Earth.

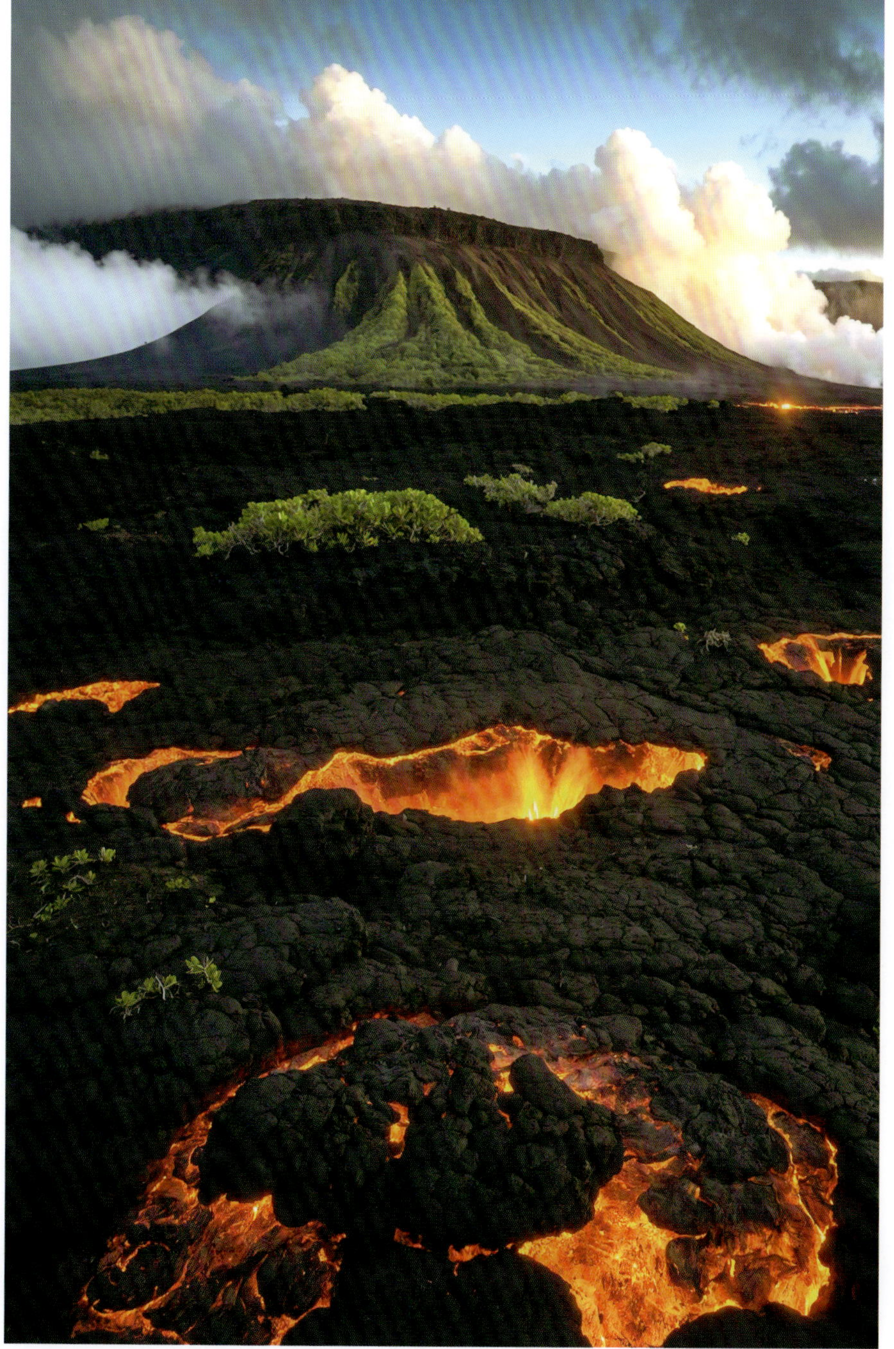

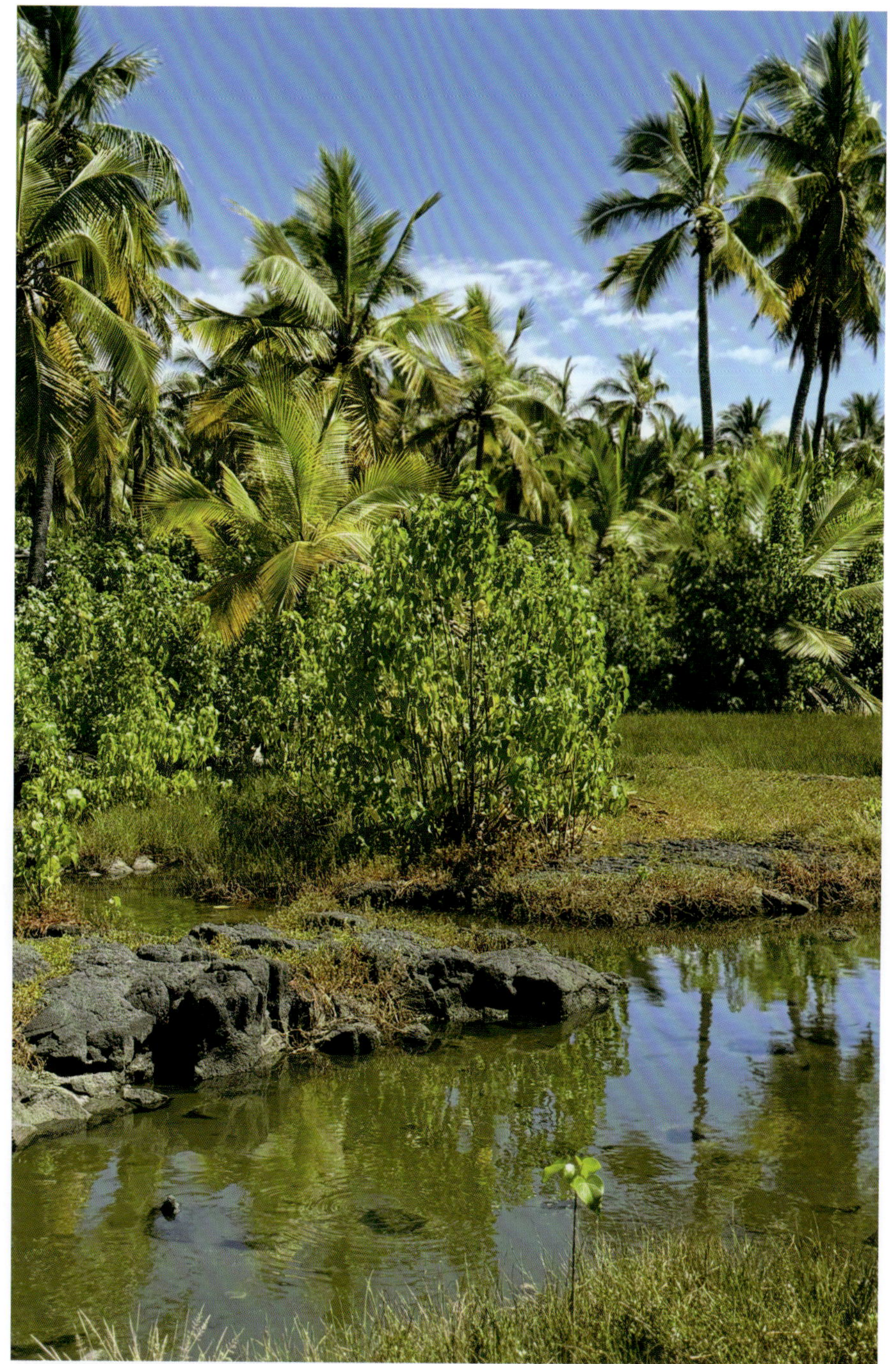

Kaloko-Honokōhau National Historical Park

Kaloko-Honokōhau National Historical Park is located on the west coast of the Big Island of Hawai'i, near the town of Kailua-Kona. This park preserves and interprets the cultural and natural history of the Hawai'ian Islands, particularly focusing on the traditional Hawai'ian lifestyle and the significance of the Kaloko and Honokōhau areas, which were once vibrant fishing and agricultural sites.

Pu'uhonua o Hōnaunau National Historical Park

Pu'uhonua o Hōnaunau National Historical Park is located on the west coast of the Big Island of Hawai'i, near the town of Hōnaunau. The park is an important cultural site that preserves the history of a royal sanctuary and place of refuge for ancient Hawai'ians. The park offers visitors the opportunity to explore Hawai'i's unique traditions, sacred sites, and well-preserved historic structures.

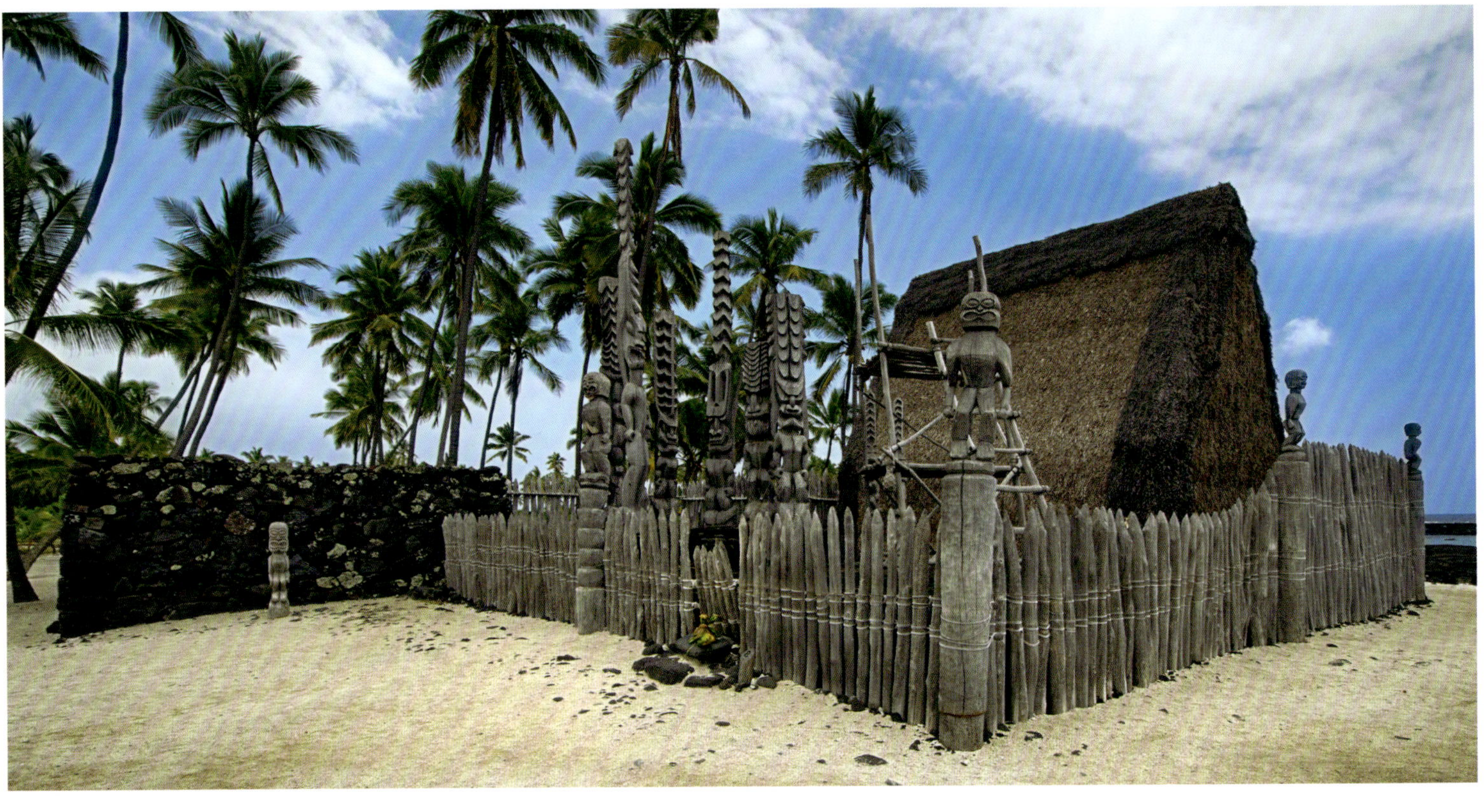

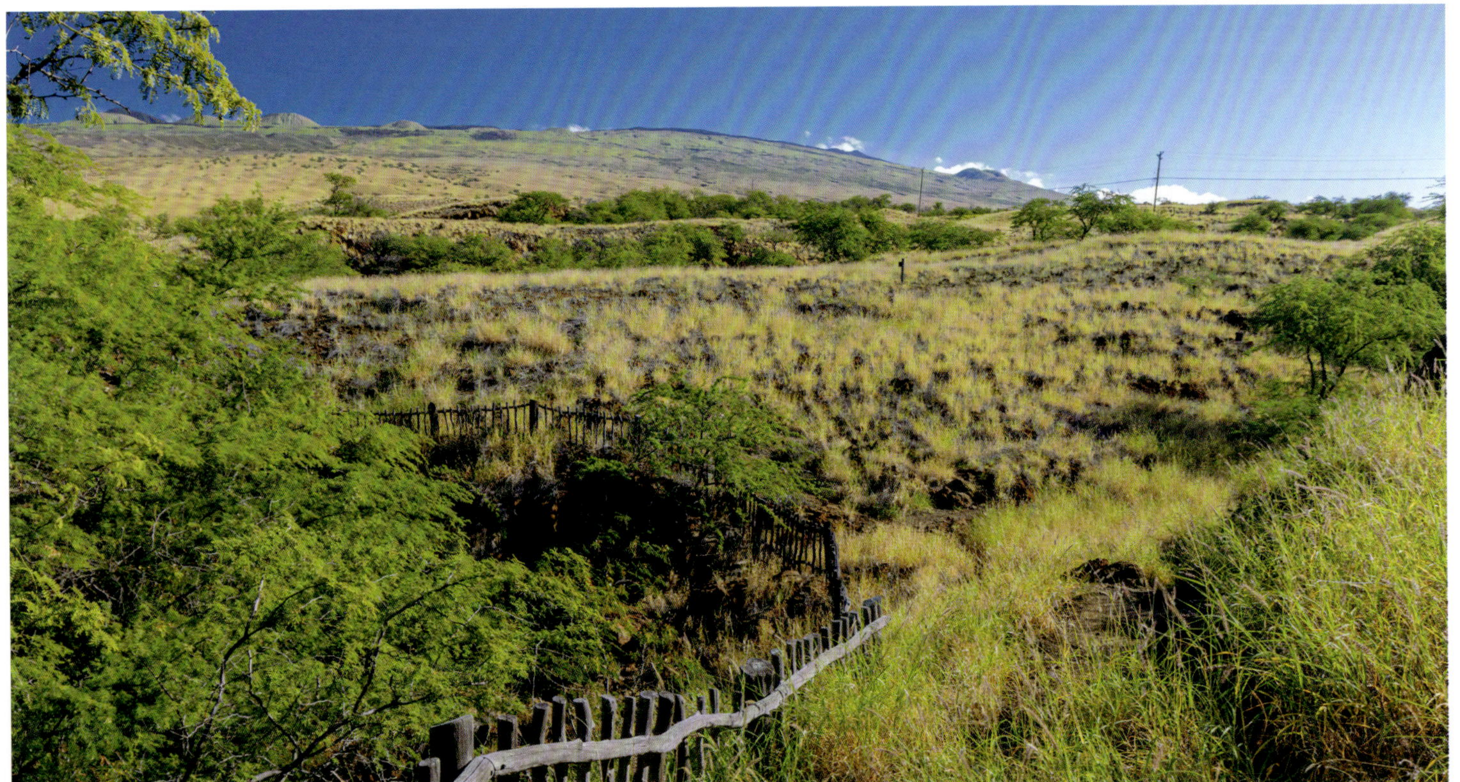

Ala Kahakai National Historic Trail

Ala Kahakai National Historic Trail is a long-distance hiking trail located on the Big Island of Hawai'i. The trail stretches along the island's coastline, passing through some of the most historically significant and culturally rich sites in Hawai'i. This 175-mile trail follows ancient pathways once used by Hawai'ian royalty and commoners for travel, trade, and religious purposes, and it offers a unique opportunity to explore the island's cultural heritage and natural beauty.

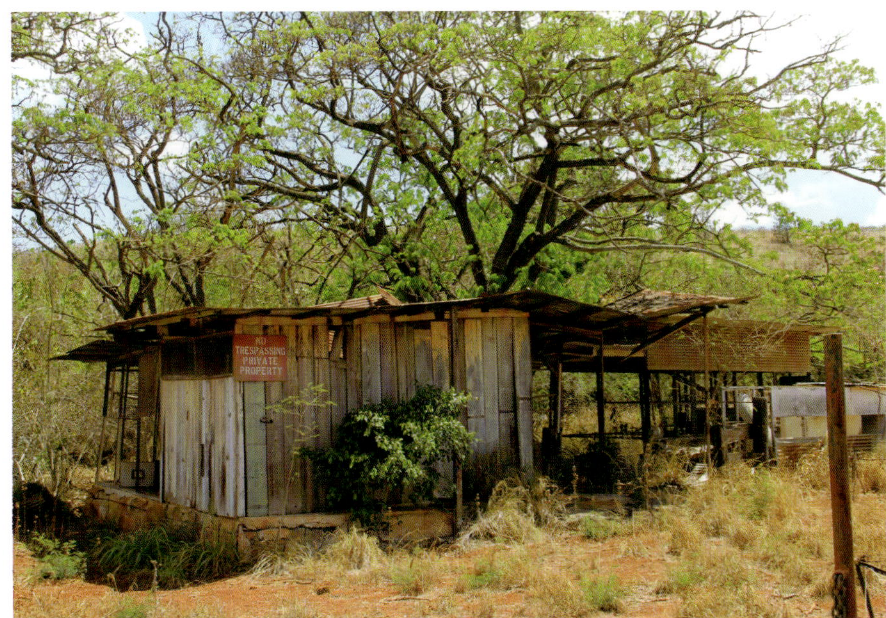

Honouliuli National Historic Site

Honouliuli National Historic Site is located on the west site of Oahu and commemorates the Honouliuli Internment Camp, one of the largest and most significant Japanese American internment camps during World War II. The site honors the history of those who were forcibly detained there, including both Japanese Americans and people of other ethnicities, and sheds light on the dark chapter of American history when civil rights were violated in the name of peceived national security.

Pearl Harbor National Memorial

Pearl Harbor National Memorial is located on the island of Oahu and commemorates the tragic events of December 7, 1941, when the Empire of Japan launched a surprise military attack on the United States naval base at Pearl Harbor. This attack resulted in the loss of over 2,400 American lives and 12 ships, and led to the U.S.'s entry into World War II. The memorial honors those who died in the attack and preserves the historical significance of the event.

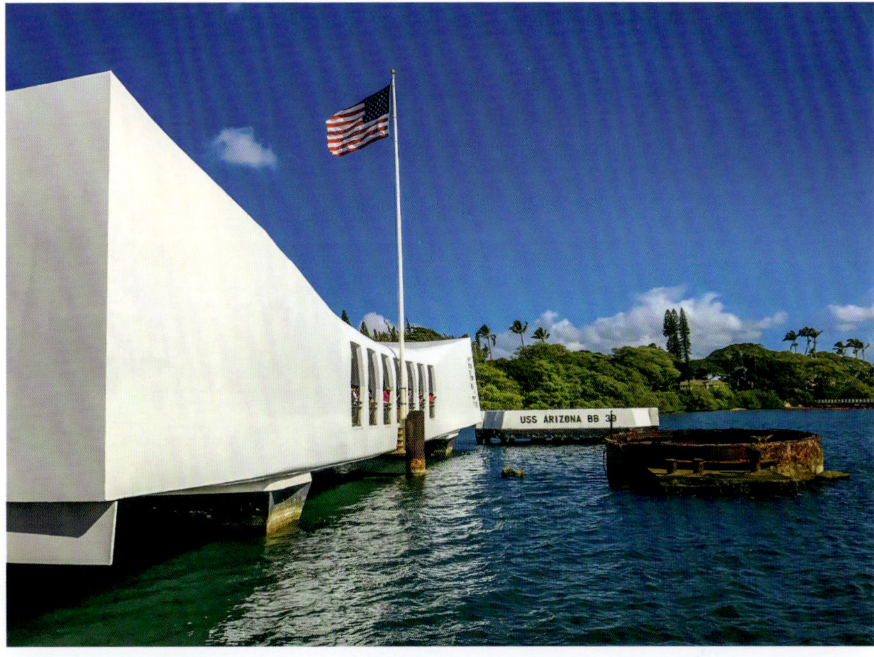

Pu'ukoholā Heiau National Historic Site

Pu'ukoholā Heiau National Historic Site is located on the Big Island of Hawai'i, near the town of Kawaihae. The site conserves Pu'ukoholā Heiau, one of the most significant and well-preserved ancient Hawai'ian temples, and it marks a key location in the unification of the Hawai'ian Islands under King Kamehameha I in 1810. Visitors can view wooden lele (offering towers—*see right*), enjoy educational exhibits at the visitor center, and walk a short hiking trail that offers stunning views of Kawaihae Harbor and the coastline.

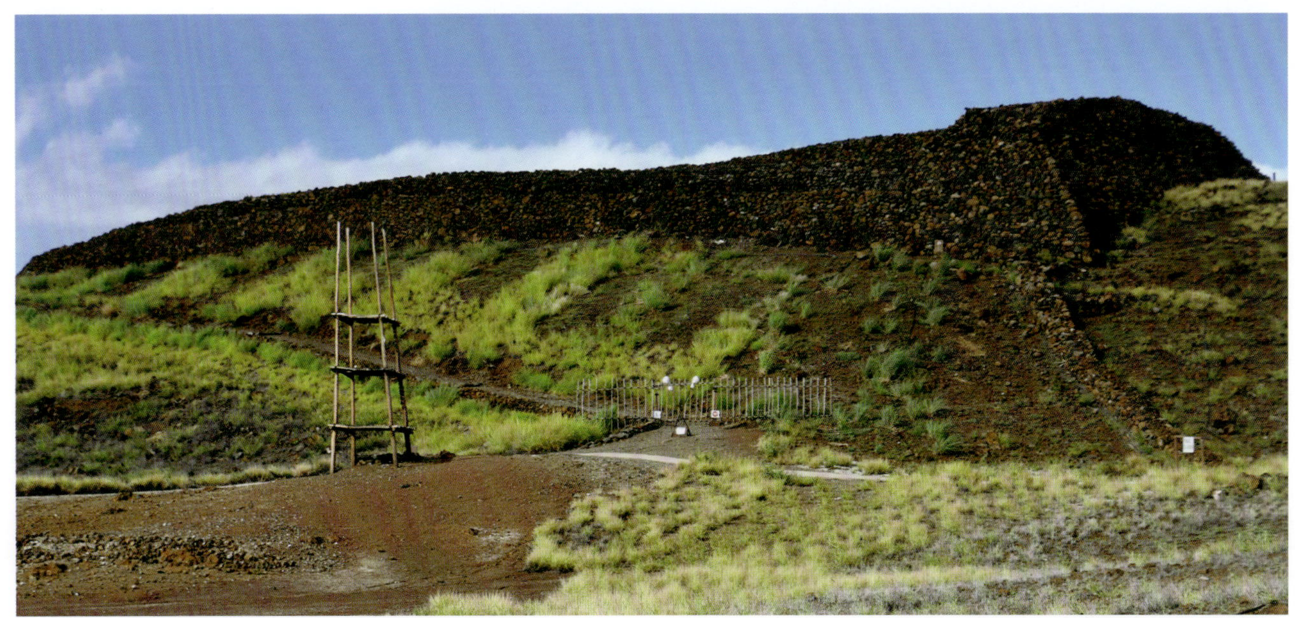

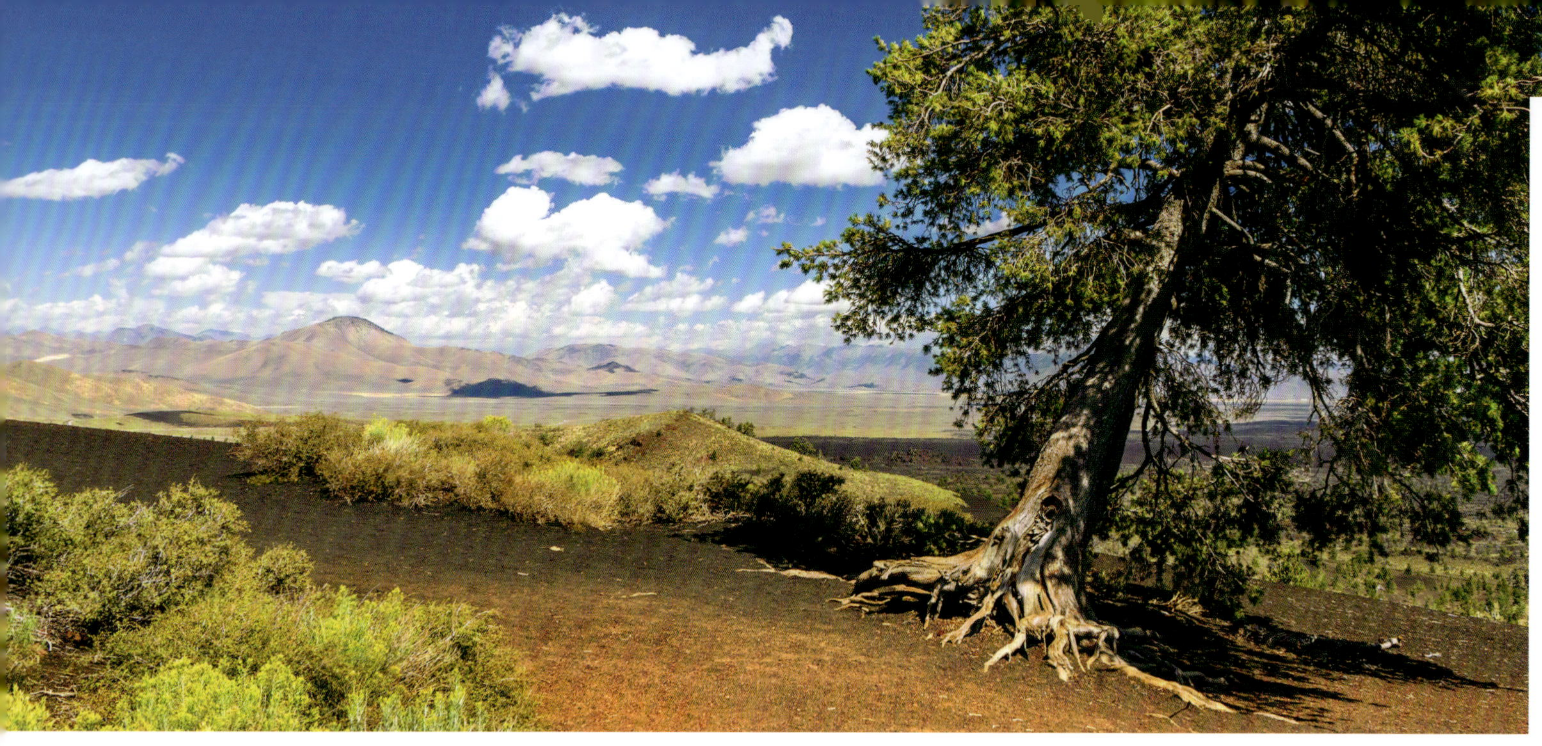

Craters of the Moon National Monument and Preserve

Nestled halfway between Boise, ID, and Yellowstone National Park, Craters of the Moon encompasses three major lava fields and is the largest mostly Holocene-aged basaltic lava field in the contiguous United States. Some popular sites to see are the Robert Limbert Visitor Center, the North Crater Flow Trail, the Devils Orchard Nature Trail, and Inferno Cone *(see left)*.

IDAHO

Nez Perce–Clearwater National Forests

Clearwater National Forest sits on the northern border of Nez Perce National Forest. Both were established in 1908, and they were combined at an administrative level in 2012. Jointly, they cover 4 million acres of land. The forests are filled with wildlife, including wolves, black bears, cougars, and mountain goats. Along with offering recreation, they are also home to fisheries and livestock grazing.

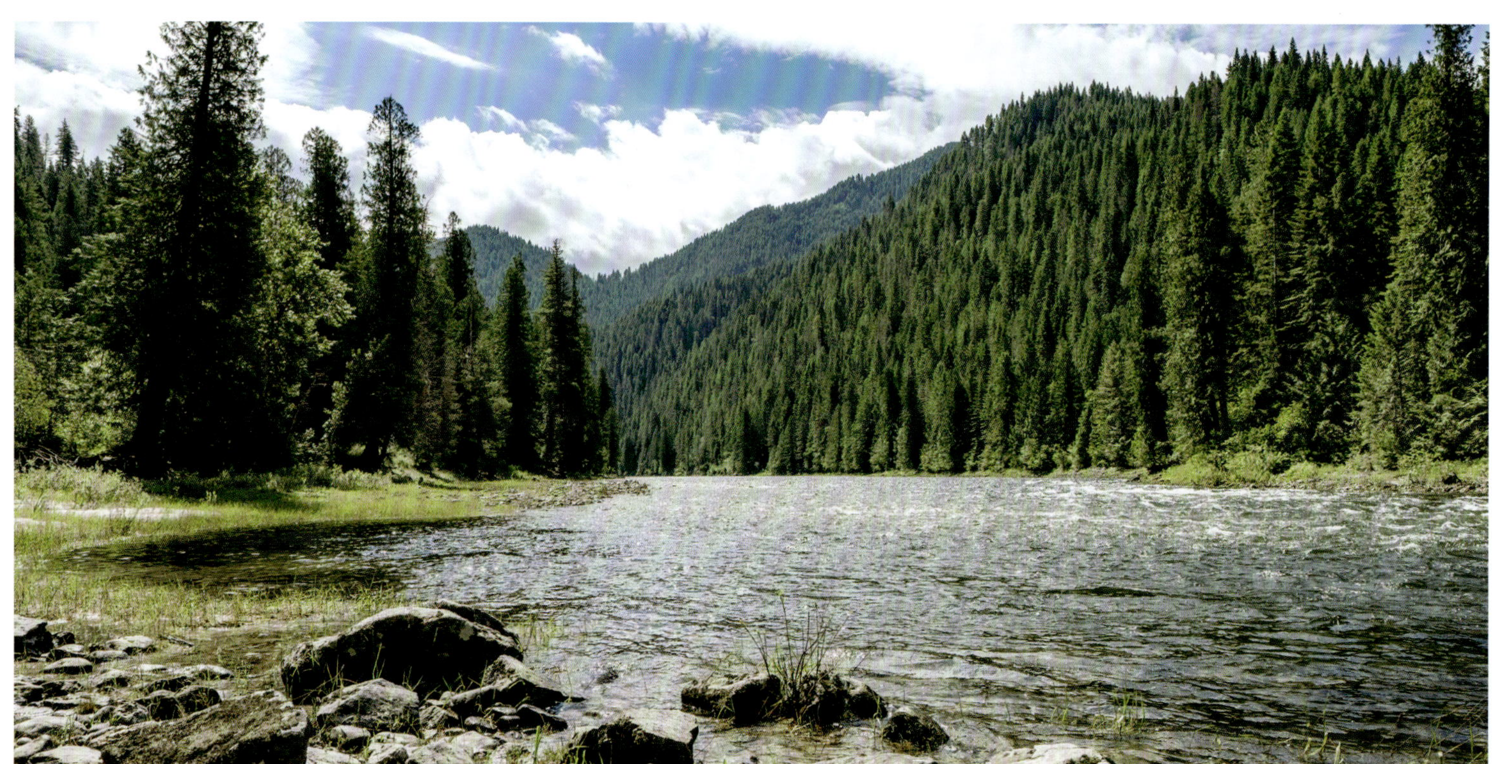

Yellowstone National Park

Yellowstone National Park, established in 1872, is the first national park—not only in the United States, but in the world. Yellowstone is massive, spanning three states: Wyoming (where most of it lies), Montana, and Idaho. It's home to more than half of the world's thermal features, including majestic geysers, brilliantly hued hot pools, and belching mud pots.

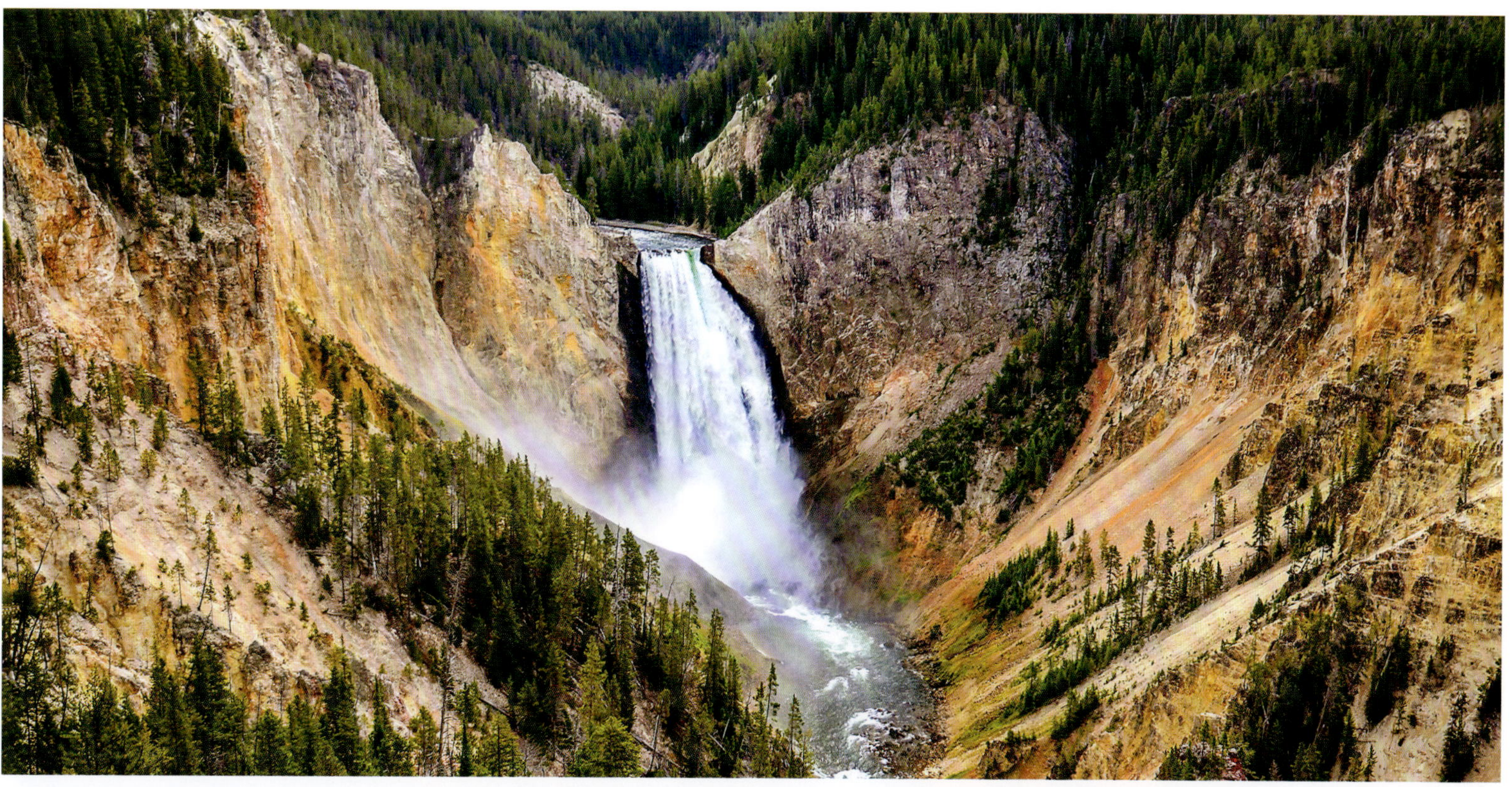

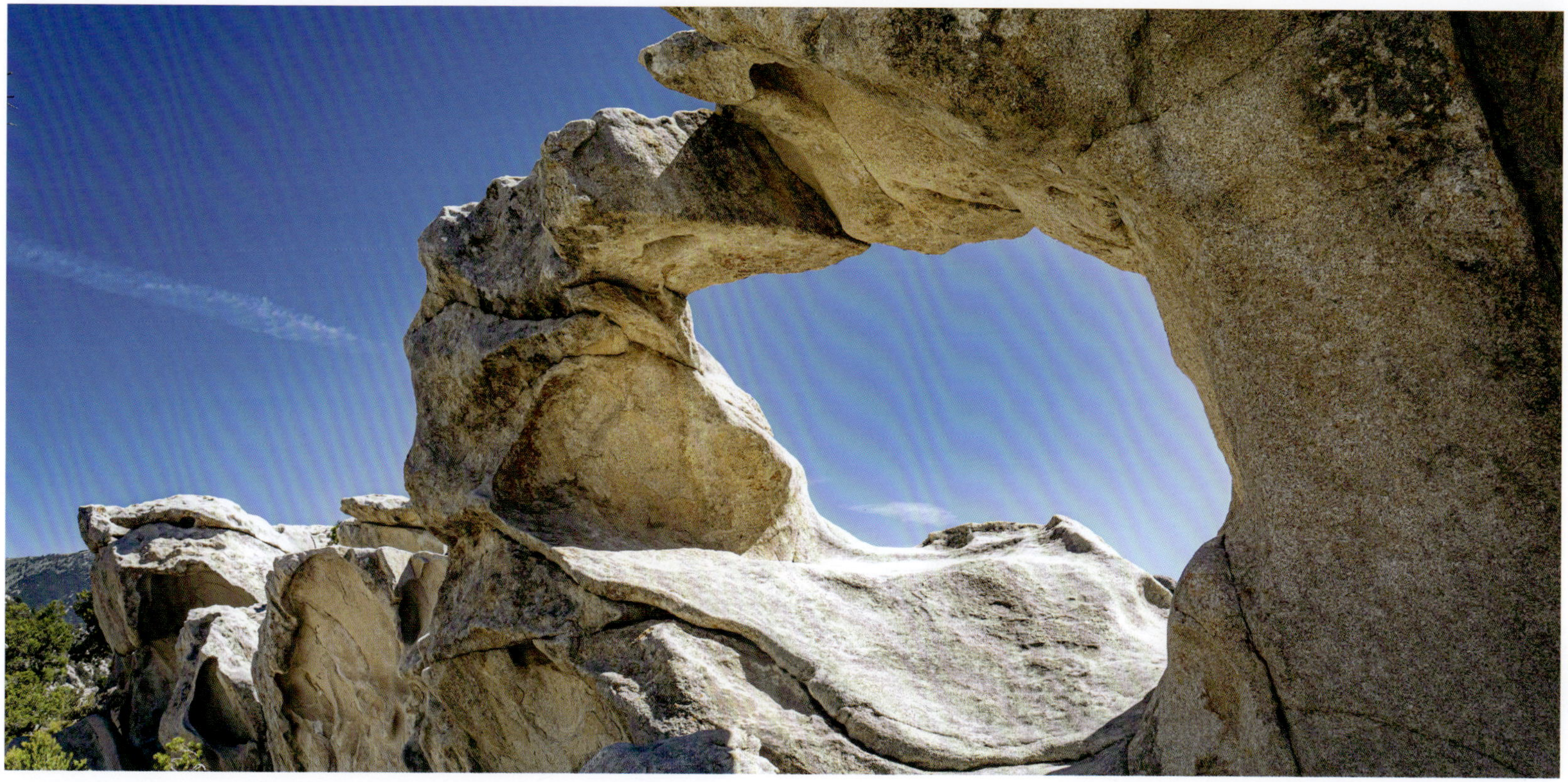

City of Rocks National Reserve

Also known as the "Silent City of Rocks," City of Rocks National Reserve is known for its enormous granite rock formations. It's a popular spot for rock climbing, camping, hiking, opportunities for geologic study, and viewing remnants of the Old West.

Hagerman Fossil Beds National Monument

Hagerman Fossil Beds National Monument is a protected site of one of the richest known fossil deposits in North America, with fossils dating from 3.07 million to 4 million years ago. Visitors can learn about the over 200 species that have been discovered at the Thousand Springs Visitor Center.

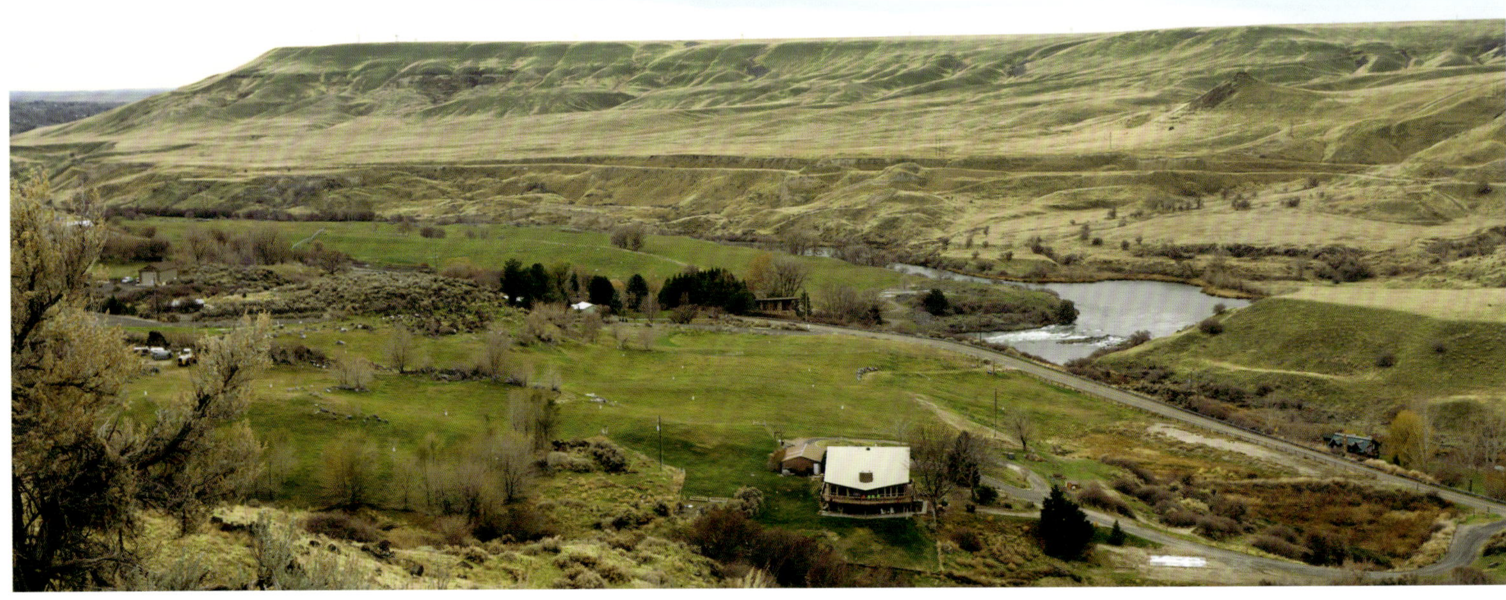

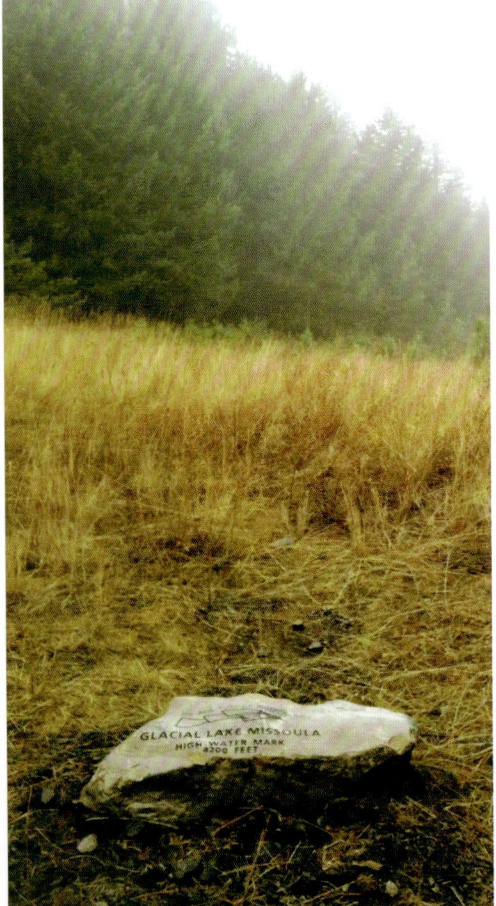

Ice Age Floods National Geologic Trail

Adventurers who follow the Ice Age Floods National Geologic Trail can explore geologic clues and special landscapes made by an ancient ice dam. About 18,000 to 15,000 years ago, an ice dam blocked the Clark Fork River in northern Idaho, creating Glacial Lake Missoula. Eventually, the dam weakened and burst, spewing forth for as much as 600 cubic miles. This repeated several more times throughout history, dotting the landscape with gigantic ravines of volcanic rock, boulders that had been moved hundreds of miles, and high-water lines; several of the latter are marked along the trail *(see left)*.

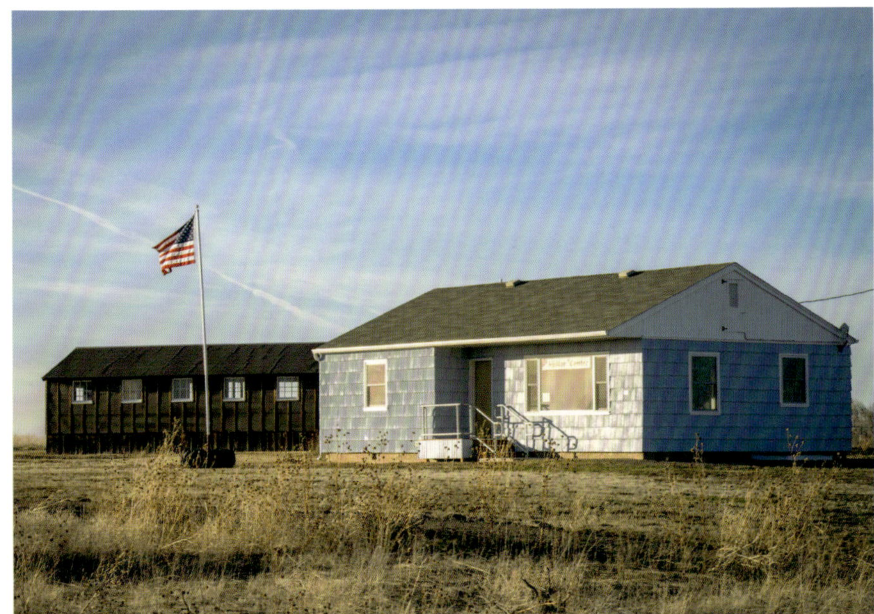

Minidoka National Historic Site

Standing in remembrance to a dark period in American history, the Minidoka National Historic Site was established in 2001 to commemorate the more than 13,000 Japanese Americans who were forcibly removed from their homes and imprisoned at the Minidoka War Relocation Center during World War II. The visitor center is open during the summer and offers visitors information, museum exhibits, a park film, and a small bookstore.

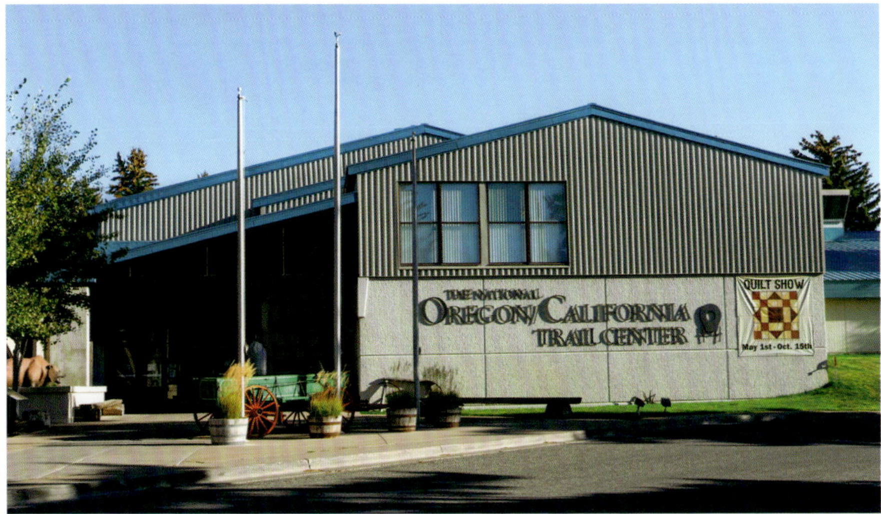

The National Oregon/California Trail Center

Located in Montpelier, Idaho, the National Oregon/California Trail Center is an interactive interpretive center dedicated to the history of the trails that ran through the town in the 1850s. Visitors can immerse themselves in the history of the trail through the accurate and lively actors, and experiences such as visiting a gun shop, riding in a covered wagon, and spending time around the evening wagon train at the Clover Creek Encampment.

Old Idaho Penitentiary Site

After being officially closed as a functional prison in 1973, Old Idaho Penitentiary Site was placed on the National Register of Historic Places. Today, visitors can tour the exhibits in the buildings and cell houses, the Idaho Merci Train boxcar, and the J. Curtis Earl Memorial Exhibit. The old prison has also become a popular site for ghost hunters, with the Travel Channel's *Destination Fear* and *Ghost Adventures* both filming episodes at the prison.

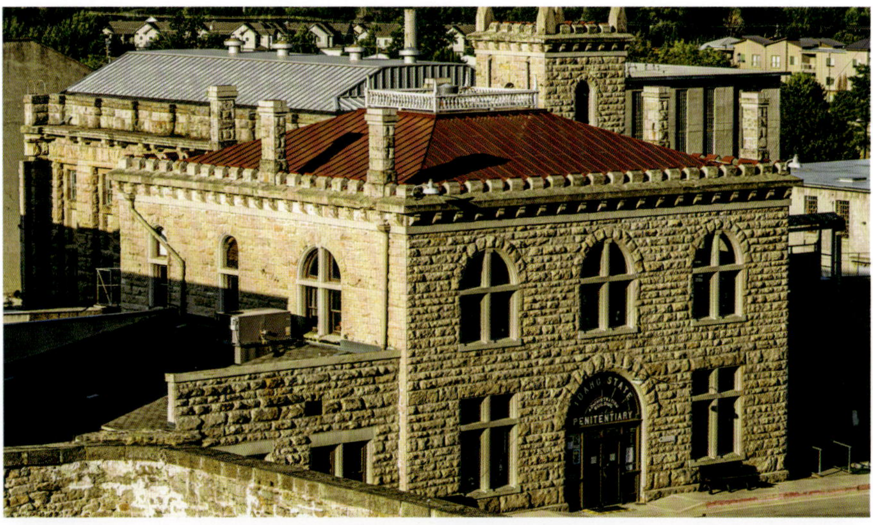

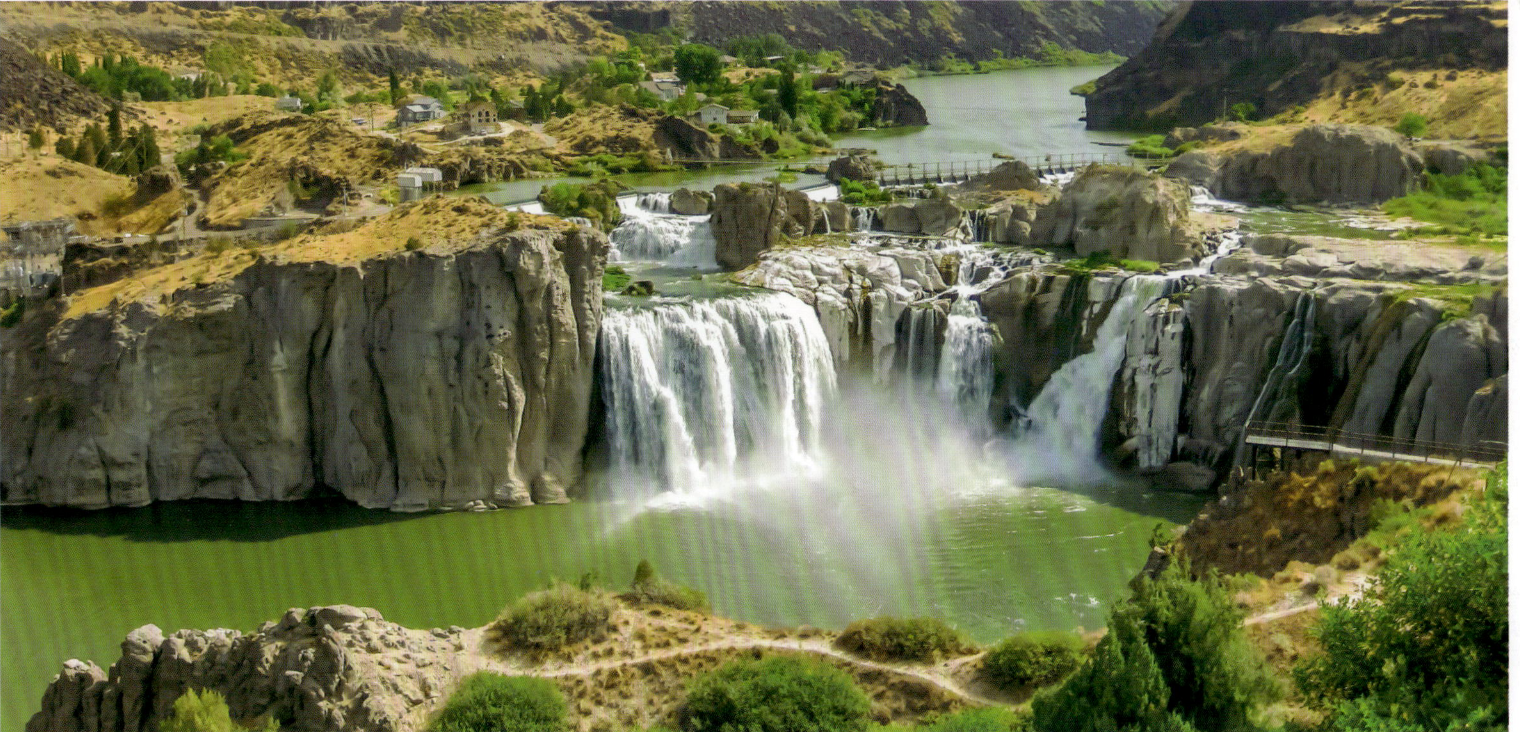

Shoshone Falls

The 212-foot-tall Shoshone Falls is also known as the "Niagara of the West." Shoshone Falls is a few miles northeast of Twin Falls, Idaho, in the Snake River Canyon. It has long served as a tourist attraction—pioneers on the Oregon Trail were known to take a side trip to view the Falls as they traveled to their destination. Visitors today can picnic, hike, and swim in the area.

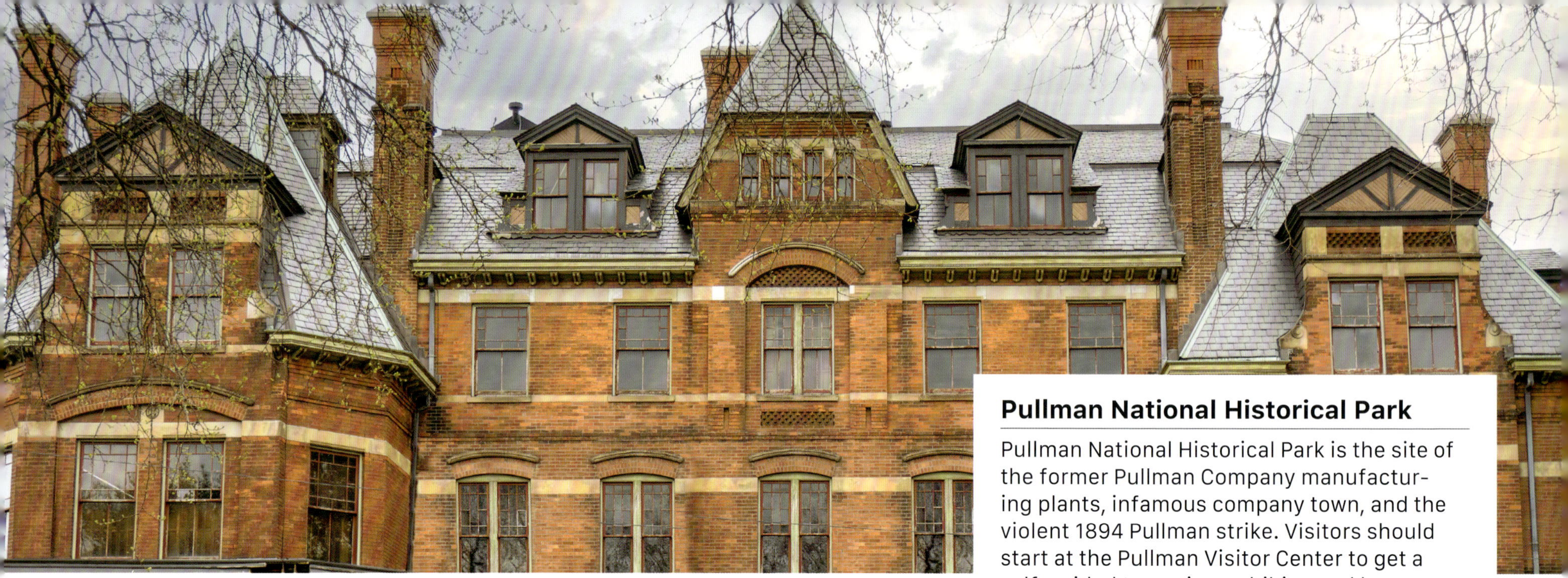

ILLINOIS

Pullman National Historical Park

Pullman National Historical Park is the site of the former Pullman Company manufacturing plants, infamous company town, and the violent 1894 Pullman strike. Visitors should start at the Pullman Visitor Center to get a self-guided tour, view exhibits, and learn more about what is currently being offered. Visitors can explore the administration and factory complex, and the Hotel Florence *(see above)*.

Lincoln Home National Historic Site

Located in Springfield, IL, Lincoln Home National Historic Site preserves the house where President Abraham Lincoln, his wife, Mary Todd Lincoln, and their children lived from 1844 to 1861. The memorial site includes a visitor center and four blocks surrounding the home. These four blocks feature structures restored to their late-1800s appearance, and have two houses—the Dean House and the Arnold House—that are open to the public and feature exhibits.

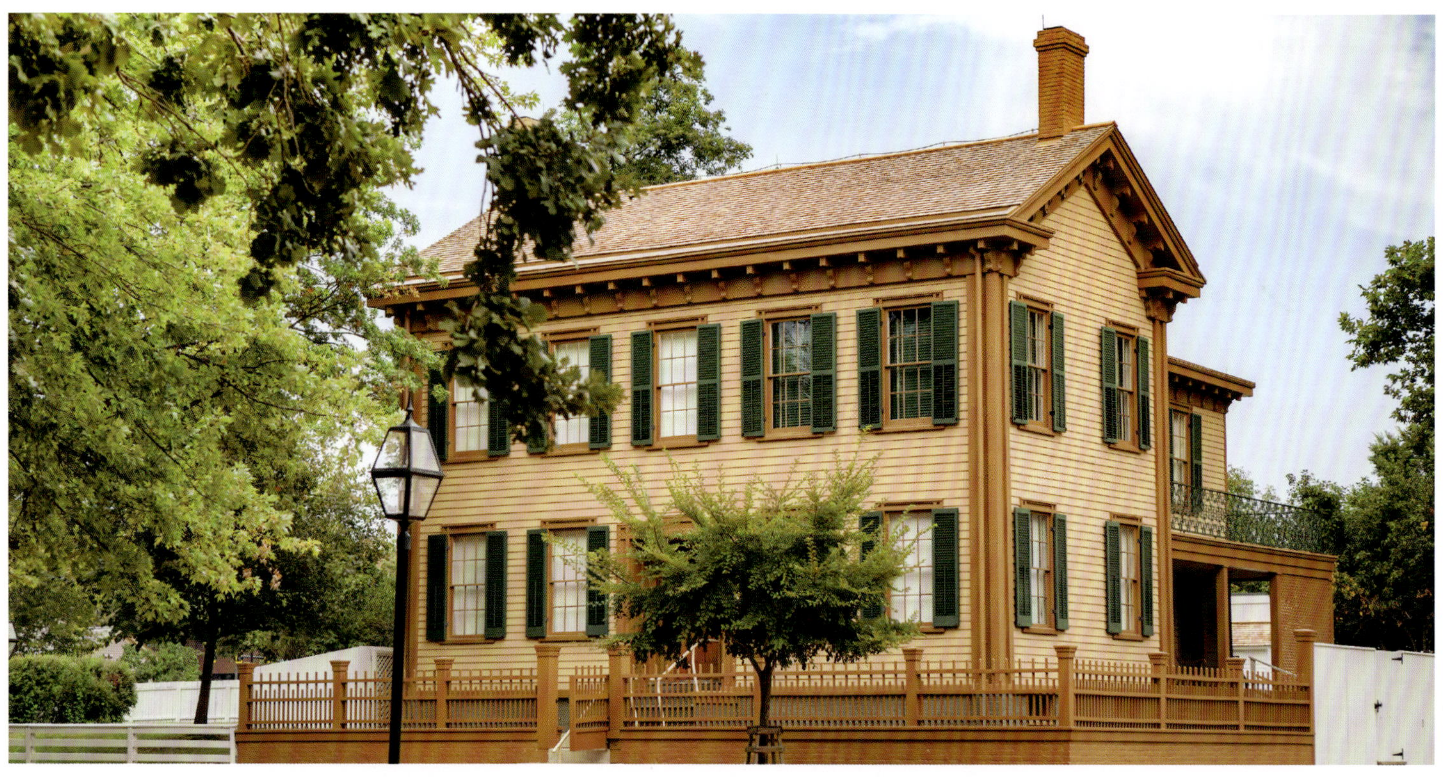

New Philadelphia National Historic Site

This historic site is all that remains of the now-vanished town of New Philadelphia, IL. New Philadelphia was founded in 1836 by a formally enslaved man, Free Frank McWorter, and was the first to be platted and registered by an African American before the American Civil War. The grounds feature an information kiosk, outdoor historical exhibits, a ¼-mile walking trail, gravel streets, and grounds around the Burdick House.

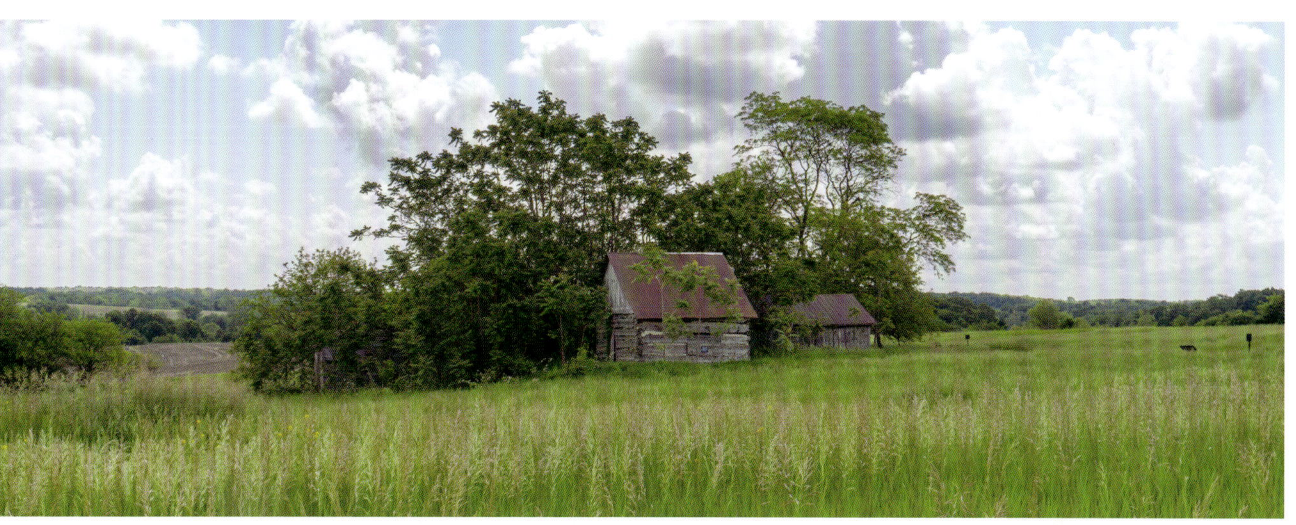

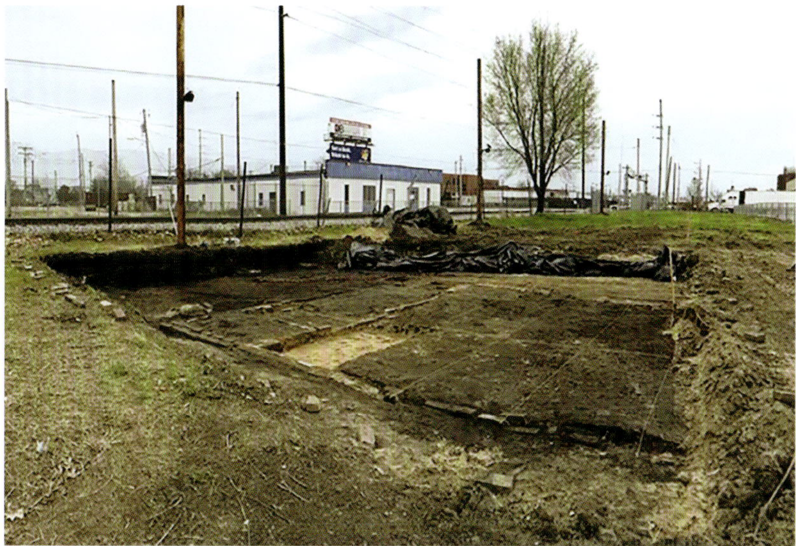

Springfield 1908 Race Riot National Monument

Located in Springfield, IL, this national monument commemorates the Springfield 1908 Race Riots, wherein violent, racist mobs attacked the neighborhoods of Black Americans, murdering rampantly and destroying Black businesses and homes. While nothing remains of this historic neighborhood, archaeologists have been able to find some remains and scars of the riot *(see above)*. Visitors can also take the 1908 Race Riot walking tour from the Springfield Convention & Visitors Bureau, view the Acts of Intolerance monument outside of the Abraham Lincoln Presidential Library and Museum, and visit the 1908 Race Riot Mural at HSHS St. John's Hospital Women & Children's Clinic, which is located near the new national monument.

Field Museum of Natural History

The Field Museum of Natural History in Chicago, IL, is one of the largest and most renowned natural history museums in the world. Founded in 1893, the museum originated from artifacts and exhibits displayed at the World's Columbian Exposition. Highlights of the museum include Sue the T. rex—one of the most complete and best-preserved *Tyrannosaurus rex* skeletons ever discovered—Máximo the Titanosaur, the Grainger Hall of Gems, and much more.

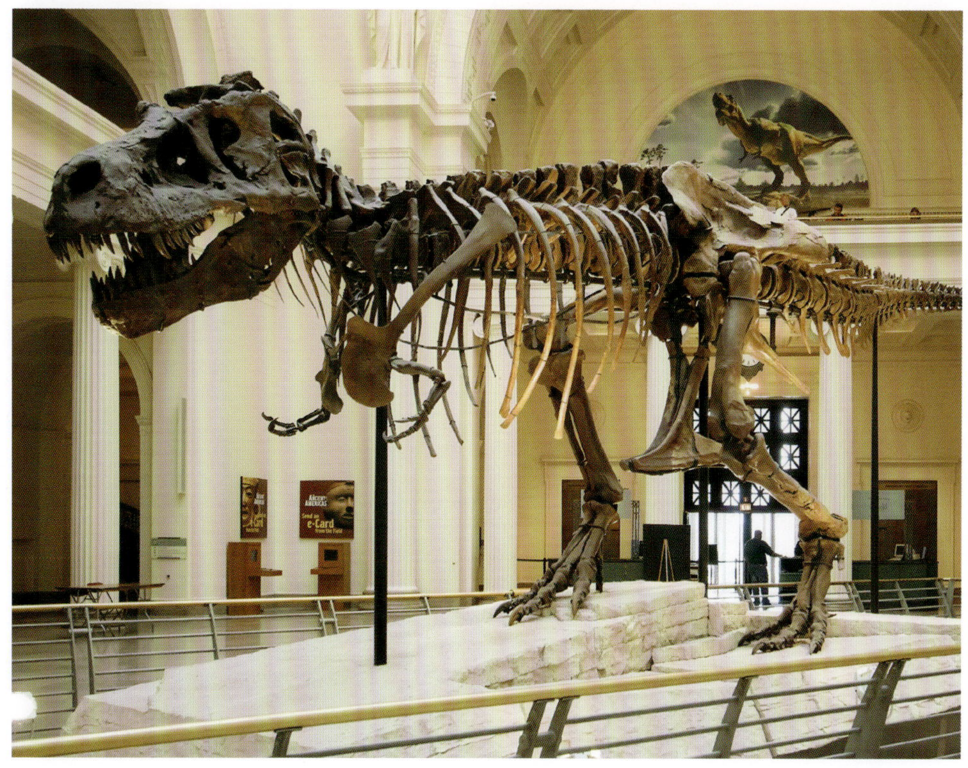

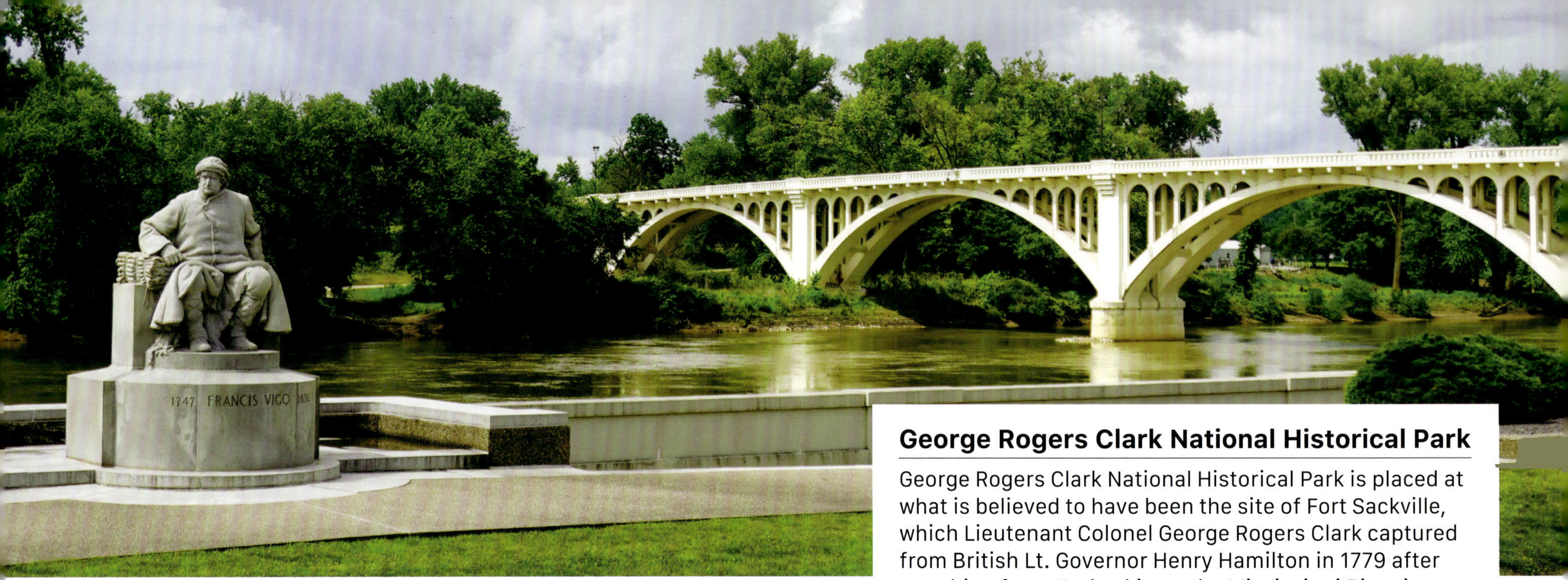

INDIANA

George Rogers Clark National Historical Park

George Rogers Clark National Historical Park is placed at what is believed to have been the site of Fort Sackville, which Lieutenant Colonel George Rogers Clark captured from British Lt. Governor Henry Hamilton in 1779 after marching from Kaskaskia on the Mississippi River in mid-winter. Visitors can view spectacular murals in the memorial building, statues of various important Revolutionary figures, and various other memorials.

Indiana Dunes National Park

Indiana Dunes National Park, located along the southern shore of Lake Michigan, offers a stunning combination of beaches, dunes, wetlands, and diverse ecosystems. Formally a national lakeshore, it was designated a national park in 2019, and it spans over 15,000 acres of natural beauty. The park is known for its unique geography, rich biodiversity, and historical significance.

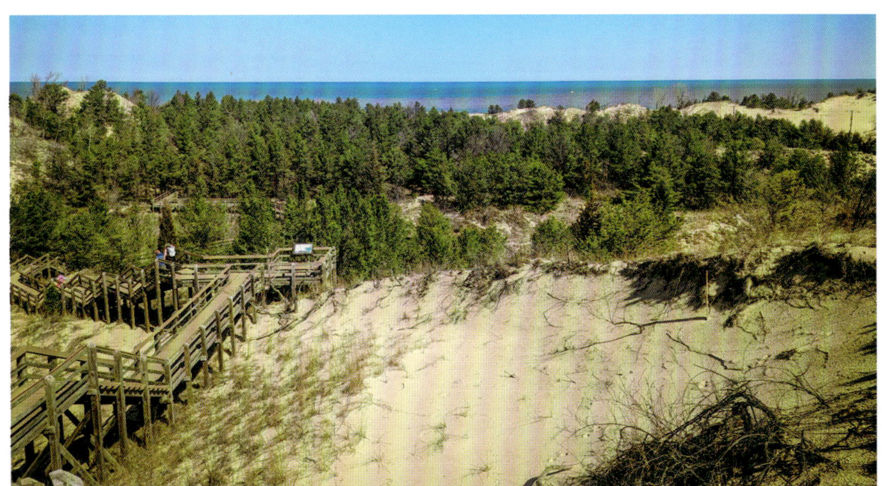

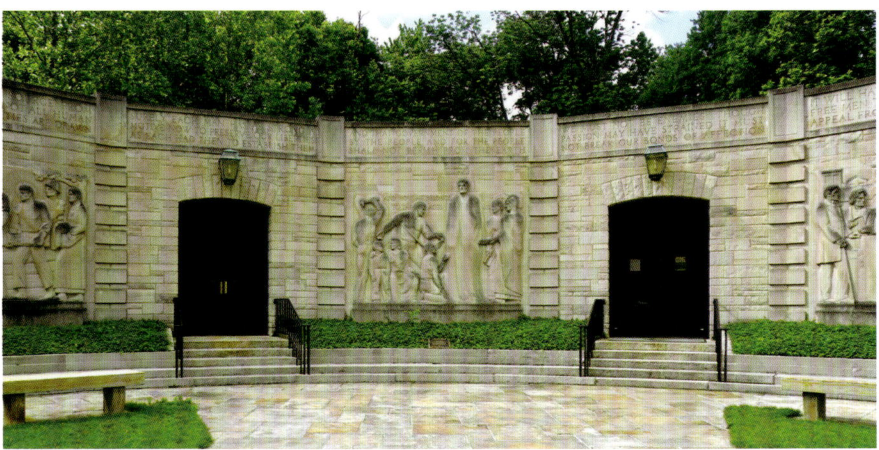

Lincoln Boyhood National Memorial

Lincoln Boyhood National Memorial in Lincoln City, IN, preserves the farm site where Abraham Lincoln lived from 7 years old to 21 years old. The monument commemorates his early life and the influences that shaped him into the person who would become the 16th President of the United States. The site includes historical buildings, a visitor center, and interpretive exhibits that explore Lincoln's childhood experiences and their impact on his leadership.

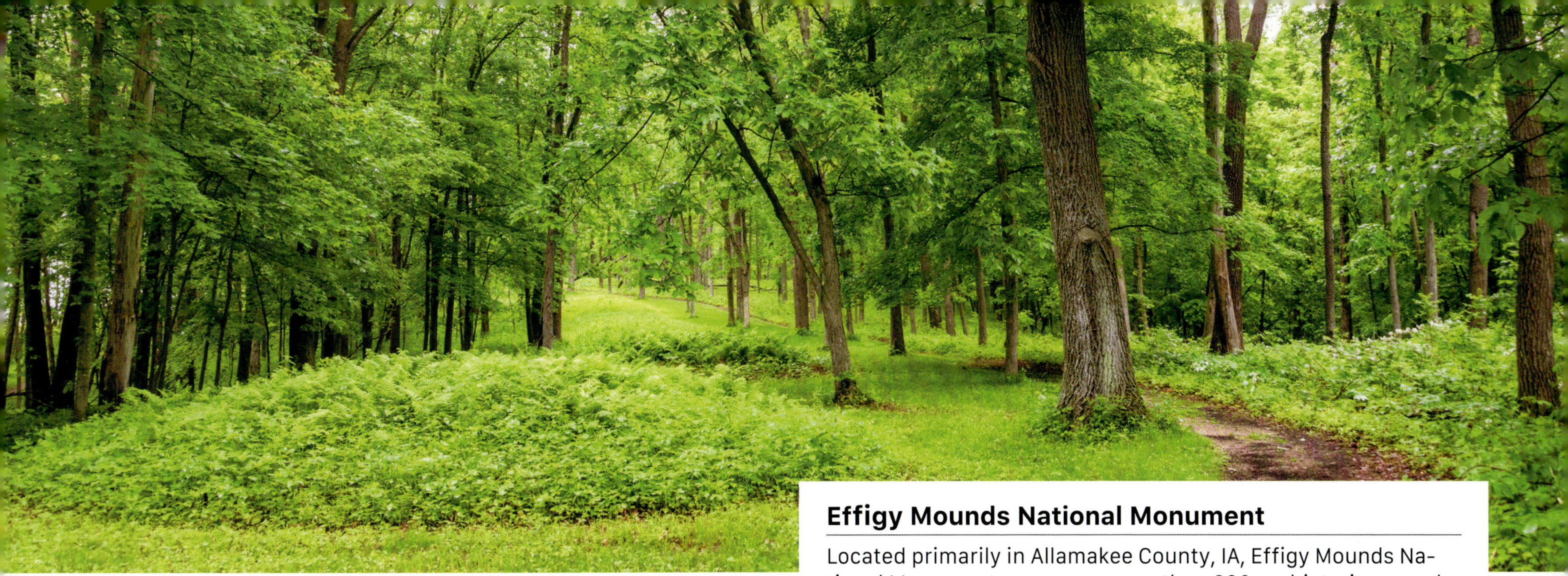

IOWA

Effigy Mounds National Monument

Located primarily in Allamakee County, IA, Effigy Mounds National Monument preserves more than 200 prehistoric mounds built by pre-Columbian Mound Builder cultures. The visitor center offers opportunities for curious minds to learn more about the meanings of the mounds and the people who built them.

Herbert Hoover National Historic Site

Herbert Hoover National Historic Site commemorates the early life of Herbert Hoover, 31st president of the United States. Visitors can see Hoover's birthplace cottage, a blacksmith shop similar to the one his father owned, the first West Branch schoolhouse, and the Quaker meetinghouse that the Hoover family attended. Guests can also visit the Herbert Hoover Presidential Library and Museum to learn about his legacy and view memorabilia.

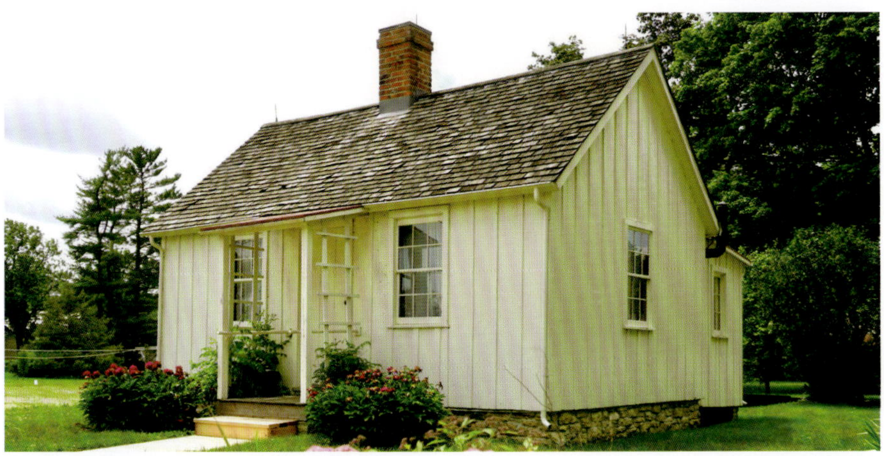

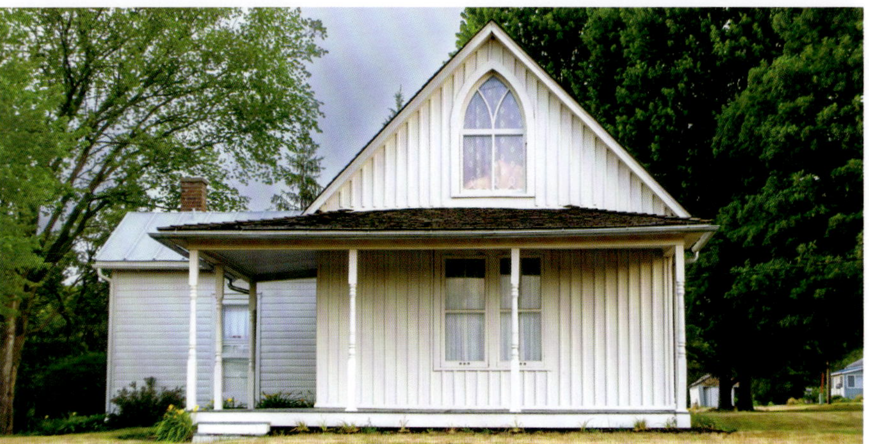

American Gothic House

Also known as the Dibble House, the American Gothic House is located in Eldon, IA. It was designed in the Carpenter Gothic style, and was the backdrop of one of the most recognizable 20th-century paintings, Grant Wood's *American Gothic*. Visitors can tour the first floor of the house, take photos in front of its iconic façade, and visit the adjacent American Gothic House Center, which contains exhibits about the painting, the artist, and the community around the house.

KANSAS

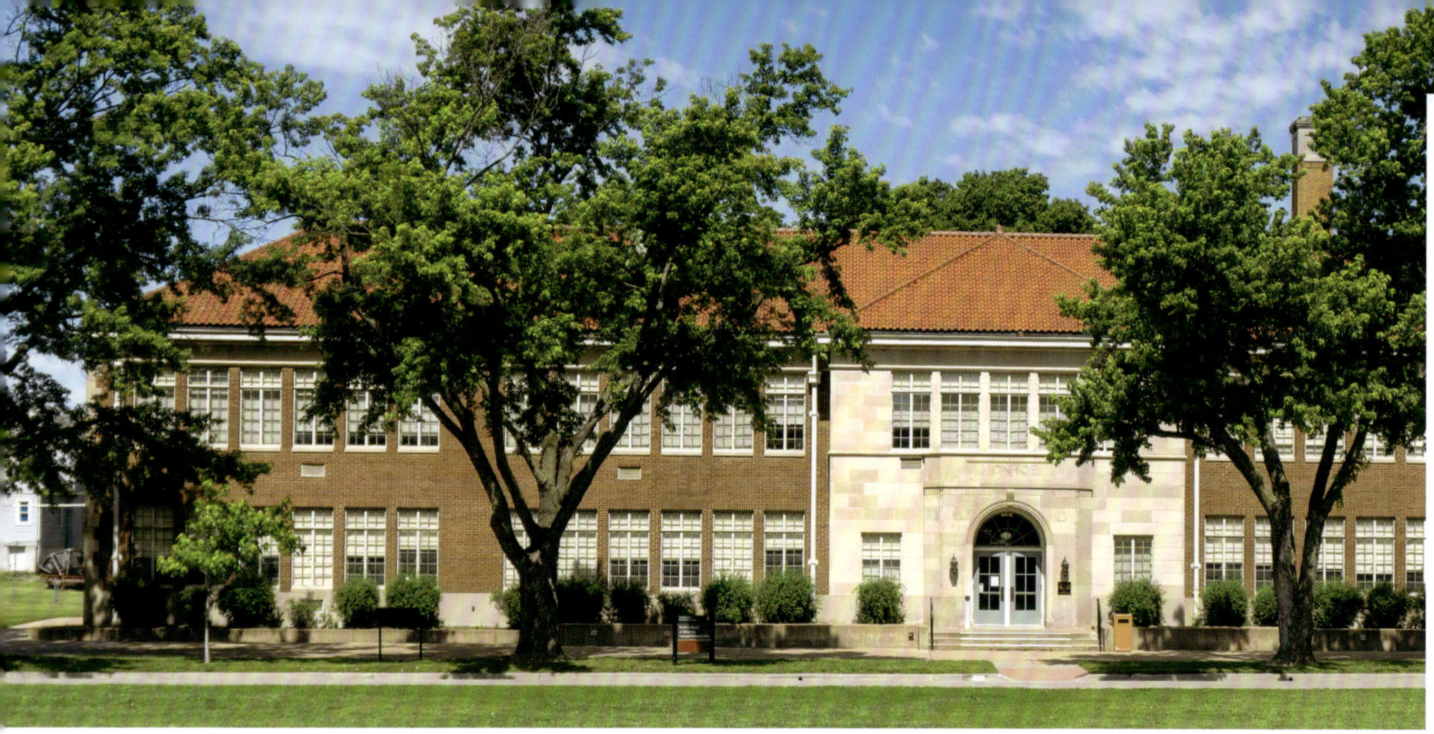

Brown v. Board of Education National Historical Park

Brown v. Board of Education National Historical Park commemorates the U.S. Supreme Court decision that ended racial segregation in public schools on May 17, 1954. Visitors can view the numerous educational exhibits, watch a film on the history of racism and segregation, and view a restored former kindergarten room to see what it was like to attend a segregated Monroe school during the court case. On the site's grounds, visitors can view a historic playground, enjoy Cushinberry Park, and walk or bike the Landon Nature Trail.

Fort Larned National Historic Site

Fort Larned National Historic Site is a complete and authentic army post from the 1860s and '70s, and is considered the best-restored fort from the Indian Wars period. Visitors can enjoy living history, weapons demonstrations, tours of the original sandstone buildings, evidence of wagon ruts along the Santa Fe Trail, and more.

Pony Express National Historic Trail

The Pony Express National Historic Trail commemorates the route used by the Pony Express, a mail delivery service that operated from April 1860 to October 1861. The service, known for its speed and reliability, became a symbol of the spirit of the American West. The trail spans across 2,000 miles from St. Joseph, Missouri, to Sacramento, California.

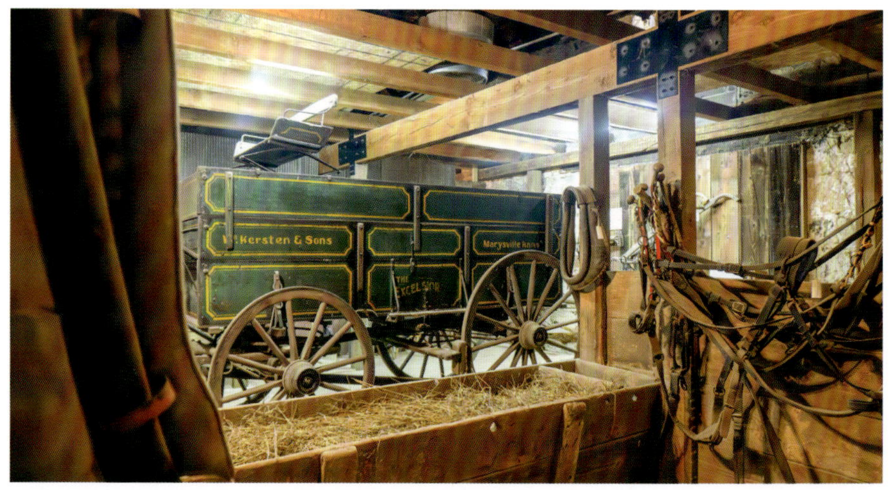

Fort Scott National Historic Site

Fort Scott National Historic Site is a replica of the 1840s military fort that served as an outpost for the U.S. army. The site includes interpretive exhibits, period furnishings, and living history programs that include soldiers running military drills on horseback and artillery demonstrations. While 11 of the structures on the site are original buildings, others are reconstructions built on original foundations.

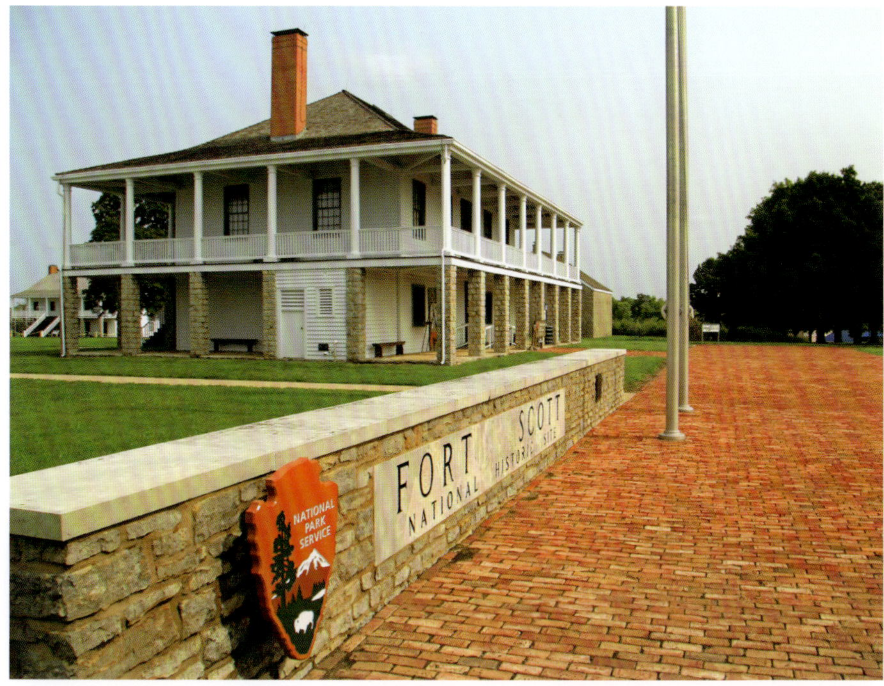

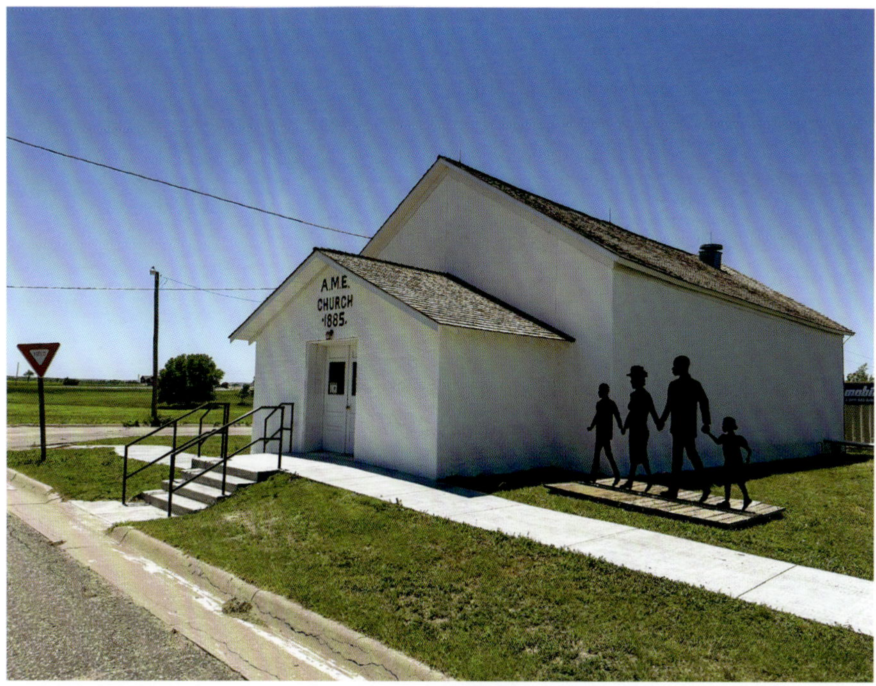

Nicodemus National Historic Site

Nicodemus National Historic Site commemorates the oldest and only remaining Black settlement west of the Mississippi River. It represents the involvement of African Americans in the homesteading movement across the Great Plains as they left Kentucky at the end of the Civil War. Visitors can view historic photos and documents at the visitor center, and see five historic buildings through either a self-guided walking tour, or one guided by a park ranger.

Tallgrass Prairie National Preserve

Tallgrass Prairie National Preserve protects what little remains of the once vast tallgrass prairie ecosystem. With 11,000 acres to explore, visitors can take a tour of the historic buildings, view the park orientation film in the visitor center, go hiking through the prairie, and learn about conservation efforts.

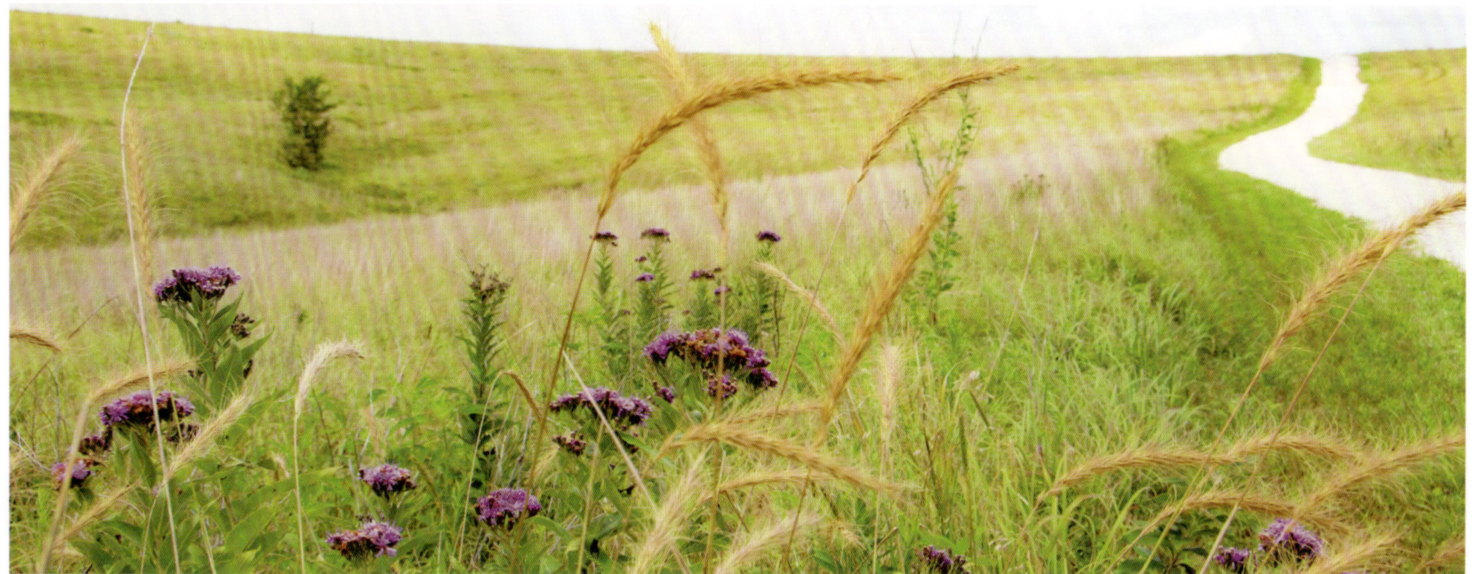

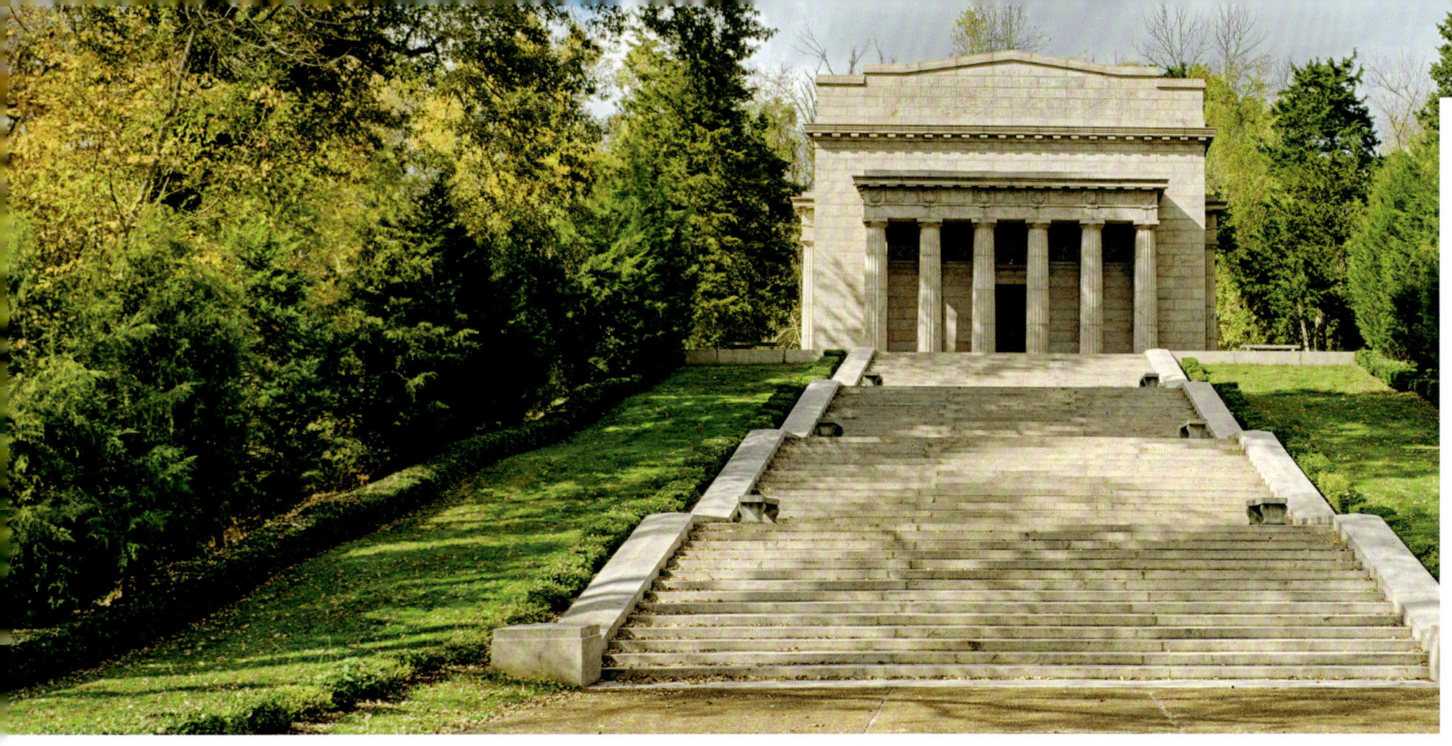

Abraham Lincoln Birthplace National Historical Park

Abraham Lincoln Birthplace National Historical Park commemorates Sinking Spring Farm, the place where the future 16th president was born. Visitors can see the first Lincoln memorial building *(see left)*, which contains the symbolic birth cabin of Abraham Lincoln. They can also visit the Sinking Spring, the site of the Boundary Oak, log cabins near Nancy Lincoln Inn, and the visitor center. Located 10 miles northeast of this site is the Boyhood Home Unit at Knob Creek, the location where Lincoln formed his earliest childhood memories.

KENTUCKY

Cumberland Gap National Historical Park

For thousands of years, Cumberland Gap served as a bridge for people and animals to travel through the Cumberland Mountains. Visitors to the park can follow in their ancient footsteps, explore the Gap Cave with a park guide, enjoy majestic mountain views, and view the historic Hensley Settlement atop Brush Mountain.

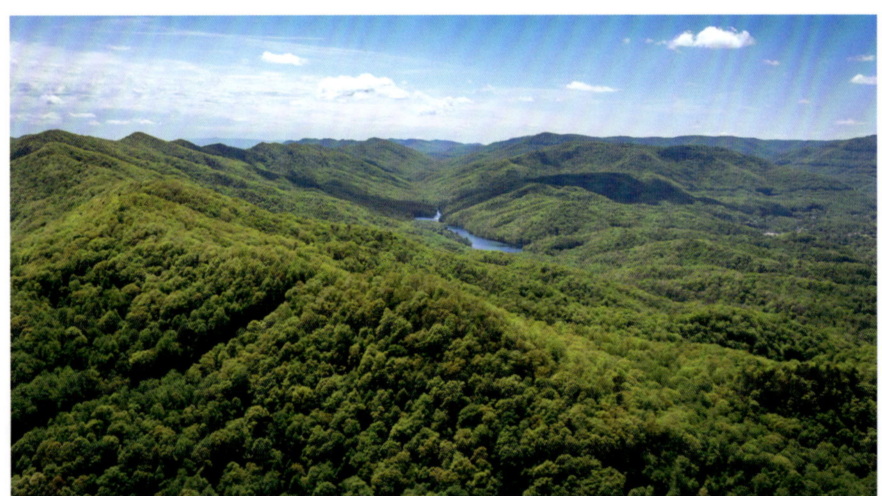

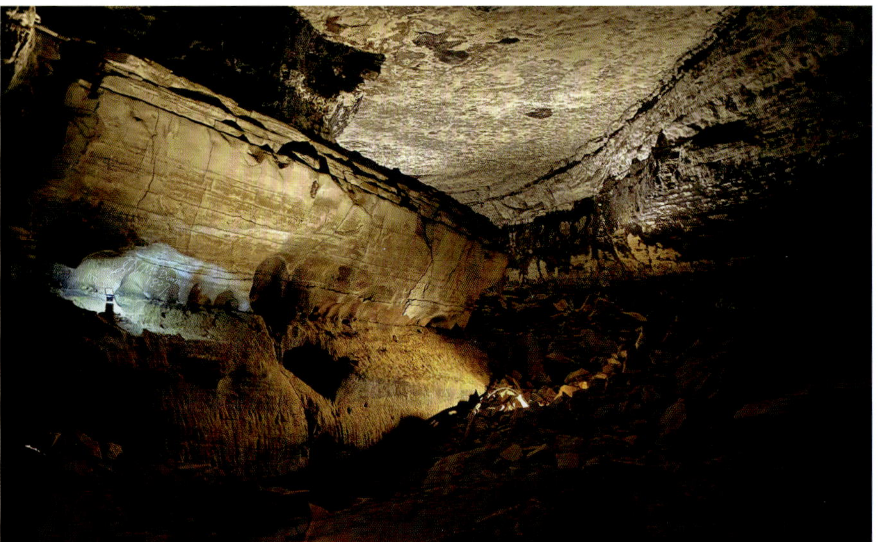

Mammoth Cave National Park

Mammoth Cave National Park is home to the longest cave system in the world *(see above)*, along with river valleys, forests, historic churches and cemeteries, and sinkholes. Visitors can enjoy cave tours and other outdoor recreational activities.

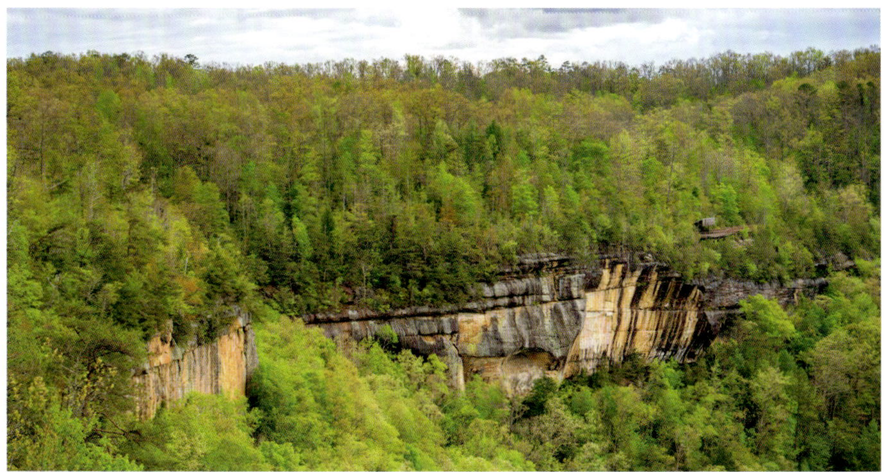

Big South Fork National River & Recreation Area

Big South Fork National River & Recreation Area, located in Tennessee and Kentucky, is a stunning natural area that protects the Big South Fork of the Cumberland River and its tributaries. Spanning over 125,000 acres, it offers a mix of outdoor recreational activities to enjoy, such as hiking, horseback riding, whitewater rafting, and more. Visitors can also see the Blue Heron Mining Community, a coal mining town once owned by the Stearns Coal and Lumber Company.

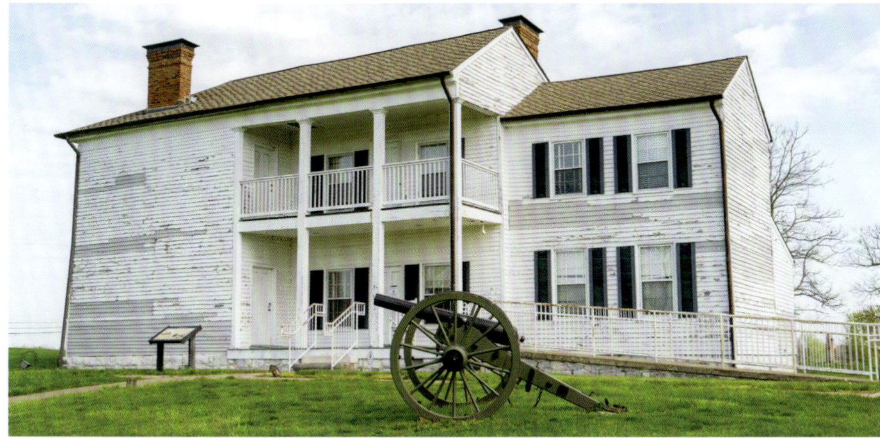

Camp Nelson National Monument

In April of 1863, Camp Nelson was a fortified supply depot for the U.S. Army. Over the next three years, it served as a training center for United States Colored Troops, a refugee camp for their families, a shelter for civilians fleeing the Civil War, and a refuge for enslaved people hoping to secure their freedom. Visitors to the Camp Nelson National Monument can learn about the site's amazing history through ranger tours, the visitor center, museum, reconstructed U.S. Army barracks, and more.

Fort Donelson National Battlefield

Fort Donelson National Battlefield in western Kentucky is a historical site commemorating Fort Heiman, a pivotal Civil War fortification. While still under development, visitors to the Fort Donelson National Battlefield can enjoy interpretive wayside exhibits, historic earthworks, and a small pavilion with exhibits.

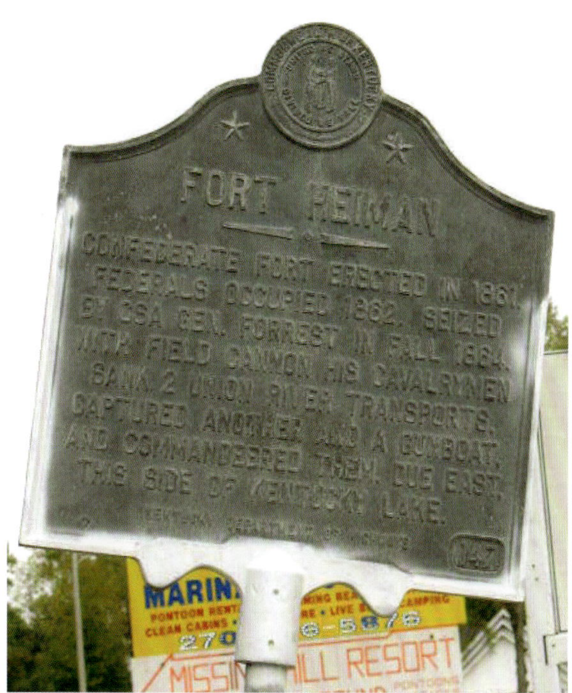

Mill Springs Battlefield National Monument

Mill Springs Battlefield National Monument commemorates one of the first significant early Union victories in the American Civil War. Visitors can learn about the battle and its significance at the visitor center and museum, Zollicoffer Park *(see below)*, Brown-Lanier House, Mill Springs Mill, through a 10-stop driving tour, and more.

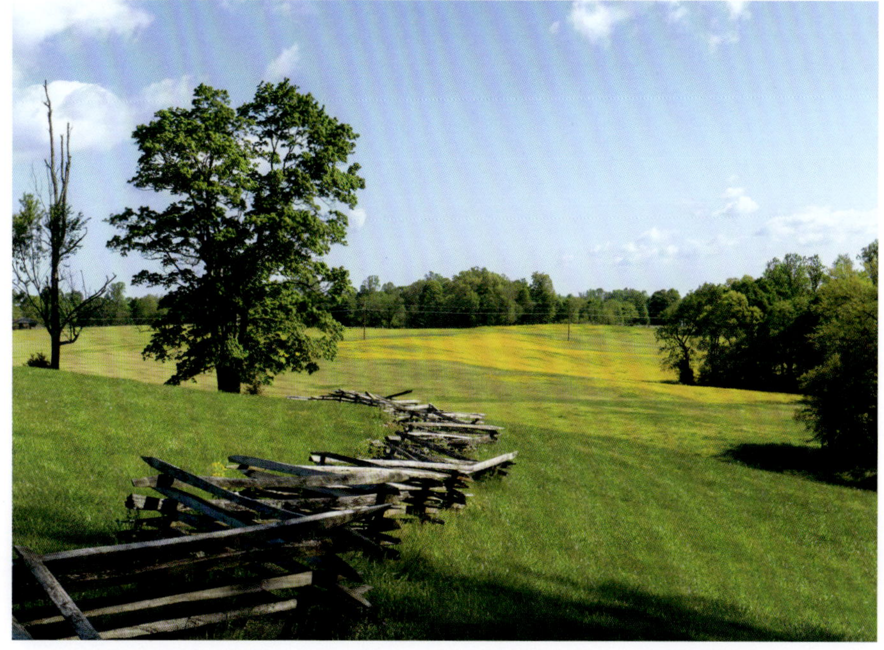

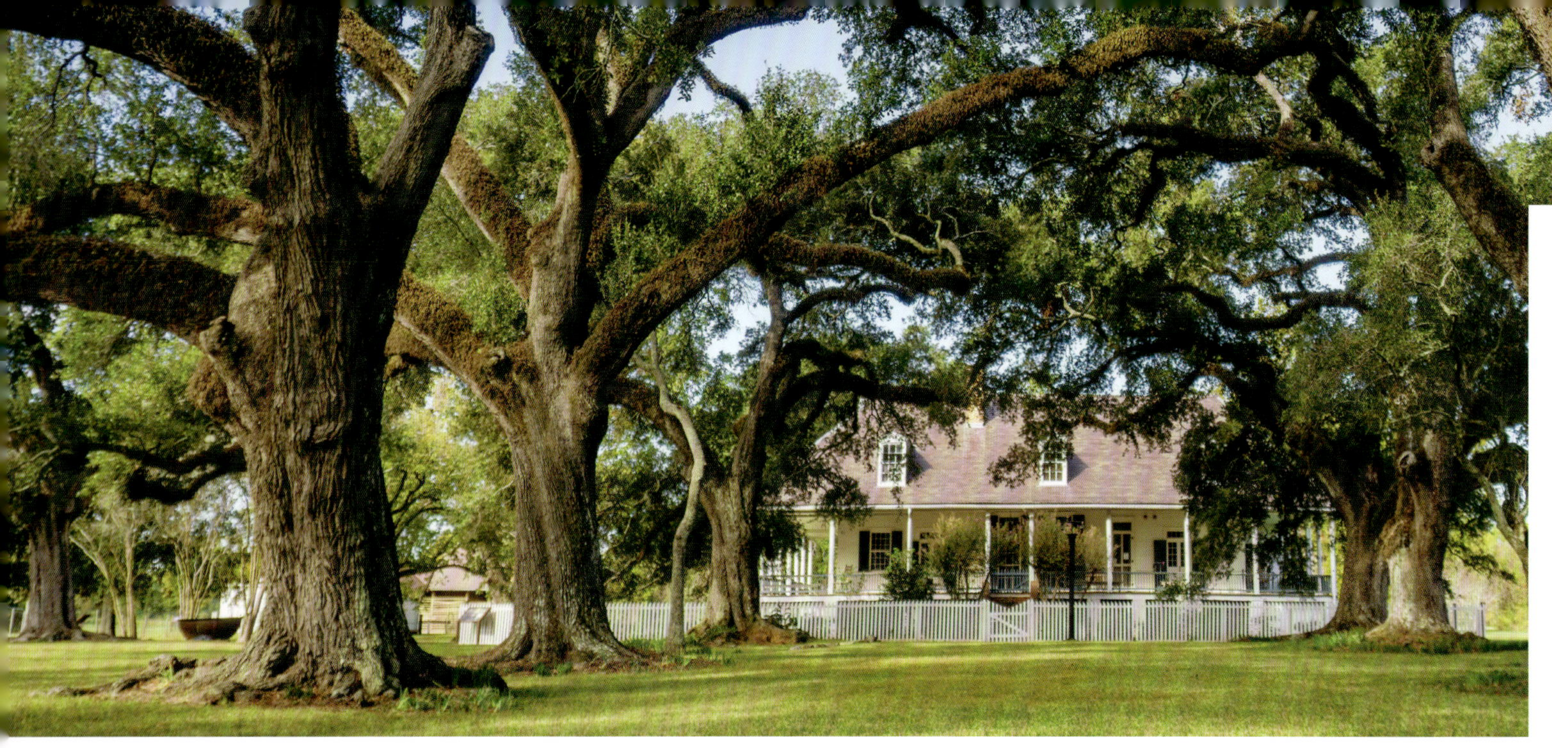

Cane River Creole National Historical Park

Cane River Creole National Historical Park preserves the history and heritage of the Creole culture and its agricultural history in the region. The park spans over 65 acres and consists of several historic sites, including the Oakland *(see left)* and Magnolia Plantations, two of the most intact Creole cotton plantations in the U.S.

LOUISIANA

Jean Lafitte National Historical Park and Preserve

Jean Lafitte National Historic Park and Preserve is composed of six different sites, all miles apart from each other. They consist of the Barataria Preserve, French Quarter Visitor Center, Chalmette Battlefield and Cemetery, Prairie Acadian Cultural Center, and Wetlands Acadian Cultural Center. They each feature a number of historical educational opportunities on the region's vast array of cultural mixes.

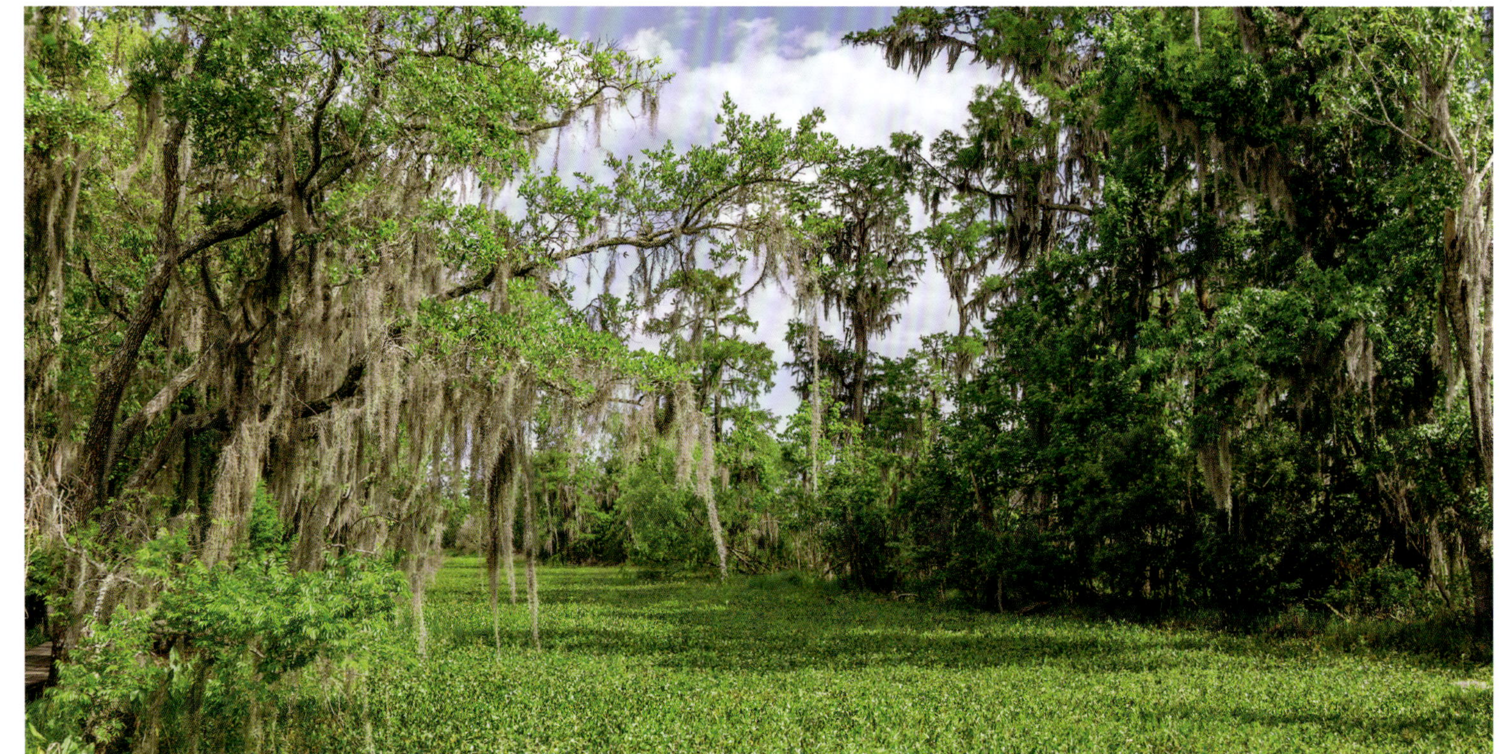

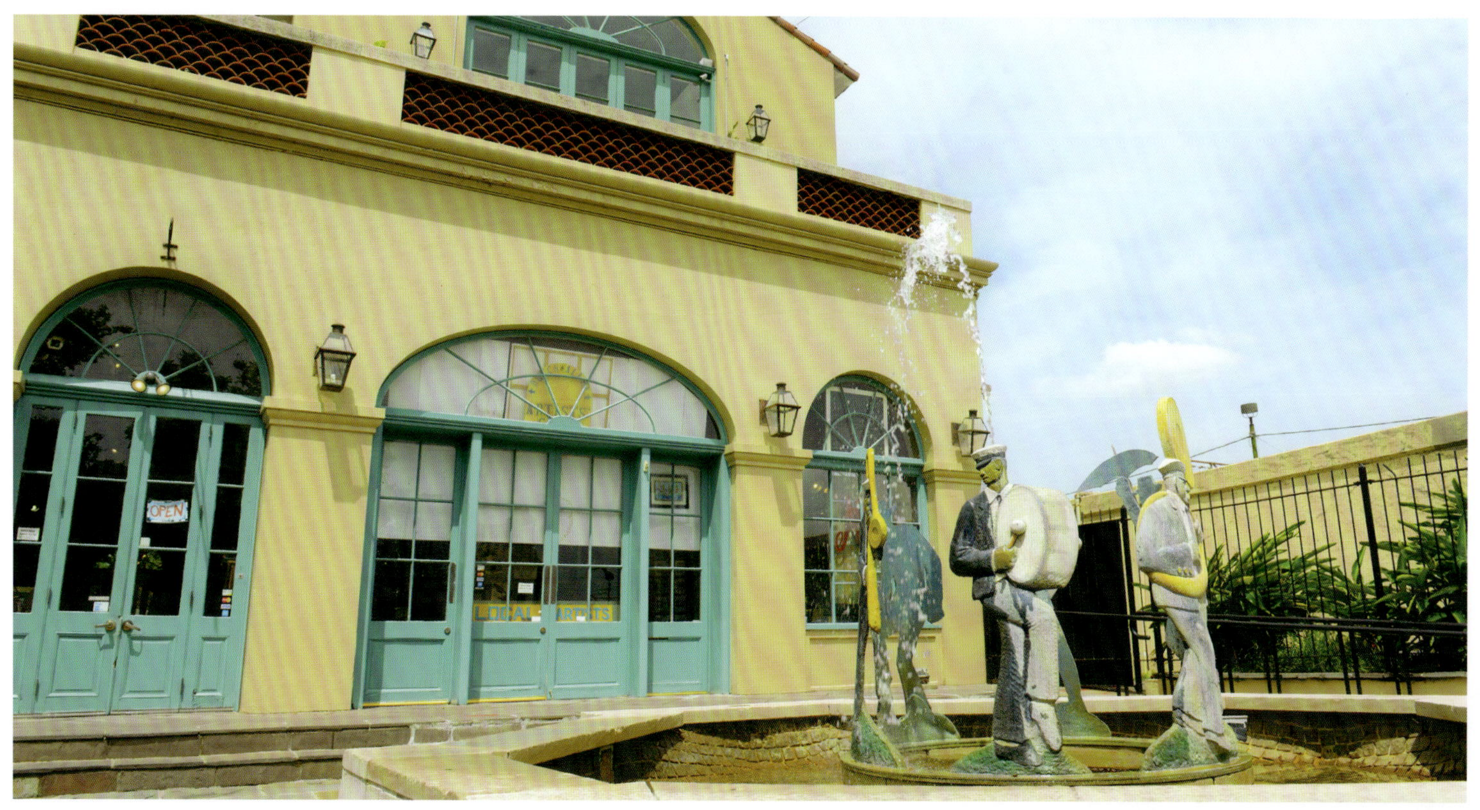

New Orleans Jazz National Historical Park

New Orleans Jazz National Historical Park is located in the heart of New Orleans, LA, and is dedicated to preserving and celebrating the history of jazz music, a genre that was born in the city in the late 19th and early 20th centuries. The park offers a rich cultural experience through exhibits, music programs, and guided tours that highlight the vibrant legacy of jazz in New Orleans, and its influence on American and global music.

Poverty Point National Monument

Poverty Point National Monument, located in northeastern Louisiana near the Mississippi River, is one of the most significant prehistoric archaeological sites in North America. The monument preserves the remains of a vast ancient complex built by Indigenous peoples around 3,500 years ago during the Late Archaic period. The site is known for its massive earthworks, and its role in the development of complex societies long before European contact.

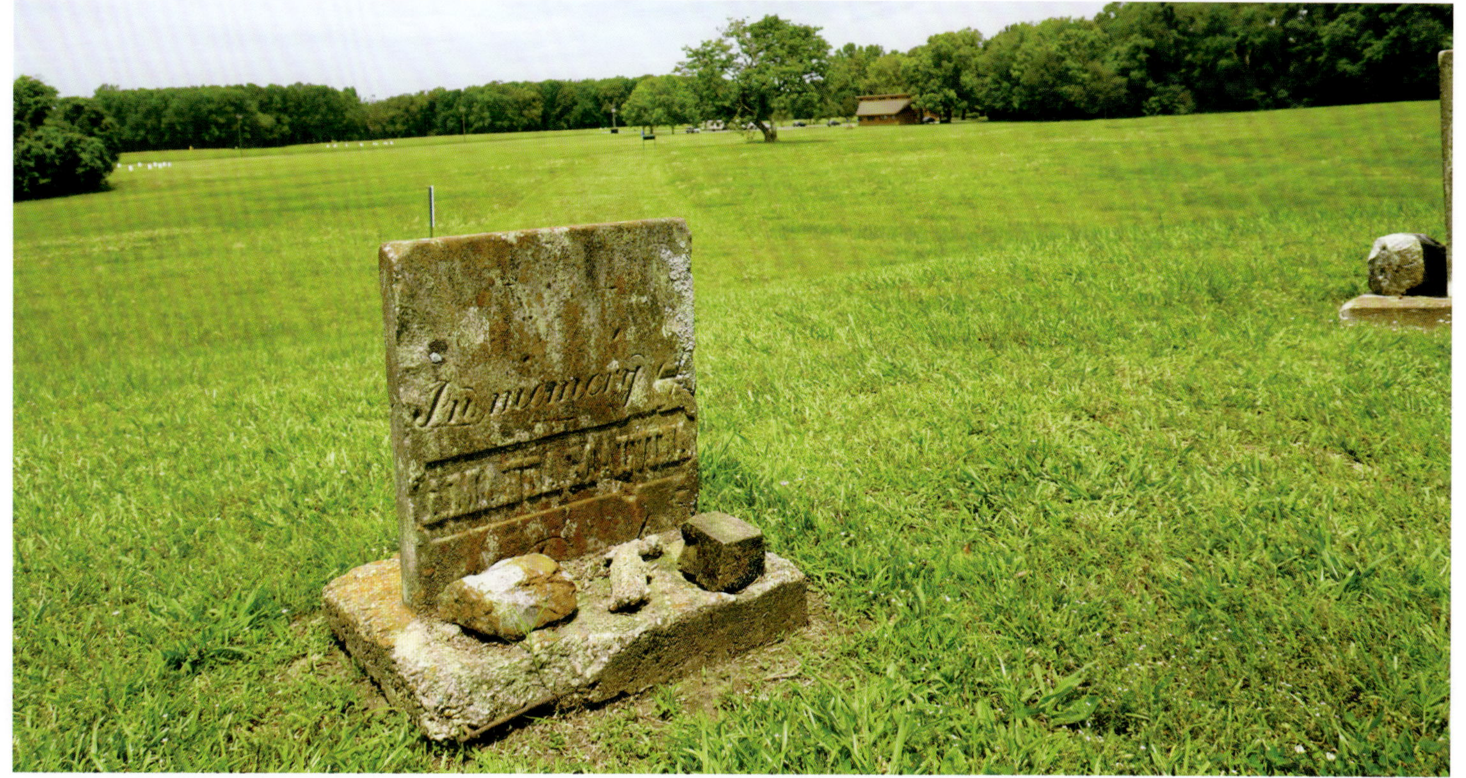

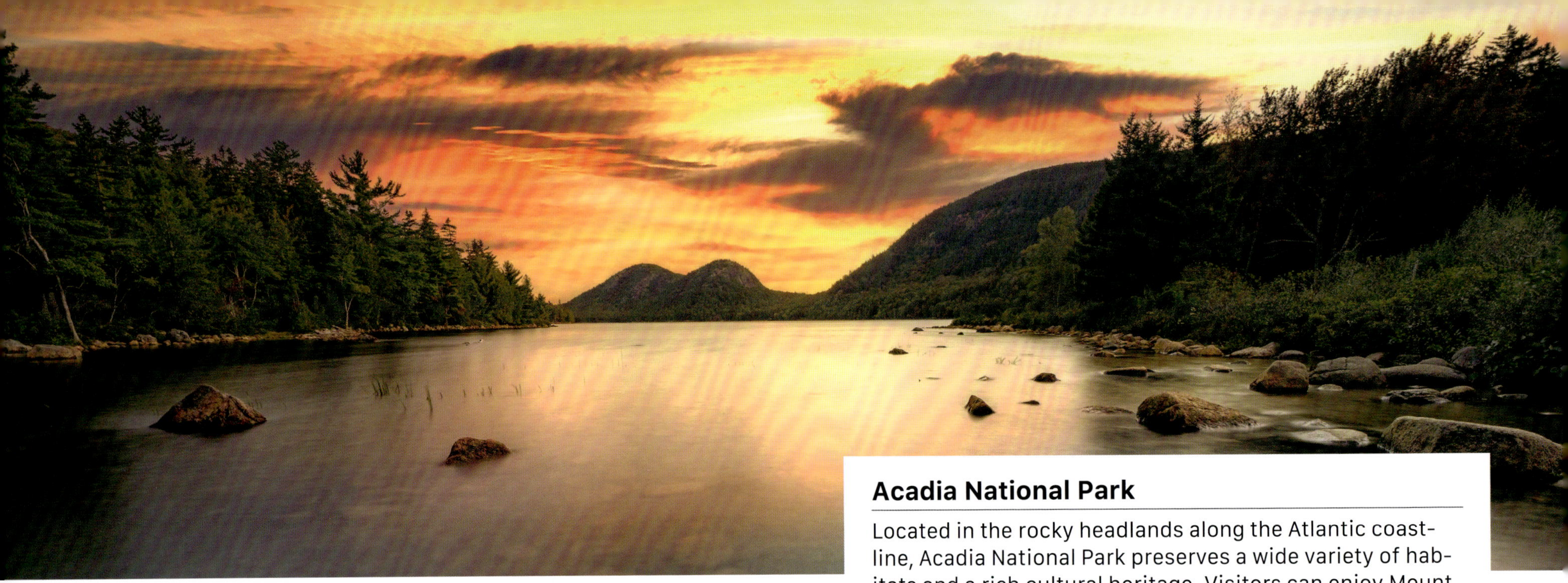

Acadia National Park

Located in the rocky headlands along the Atlantic coastline, Acadia National Park preserves a wide variety of habitats and a rich cultural heritage. Visitors can enjoy Mount Desert Island, Schoodic Peninsula, Isle au Haut, Jordan Pond/Otter Cove, miles and miles of coastline and scenic motor roads, and more than 150 miles of hiking trails.

MAINE

Frances Perkins National Monument

Frances Perkins National Monument commemorates Frances Perkins, a workers' rights advocate, the first woman to hold a presidential cabinet position, and the longest-serving U.S. Secretary of Labor. While she lived in many places during her illustrious life, the Perkins Family Homestead remained a steady place for her to return to—and served as an ideal place for the monument to her legacy. Visitors to the homestead can explore the house and farm buildings, viewing artifacts and documents from several generations of the Perkins family.

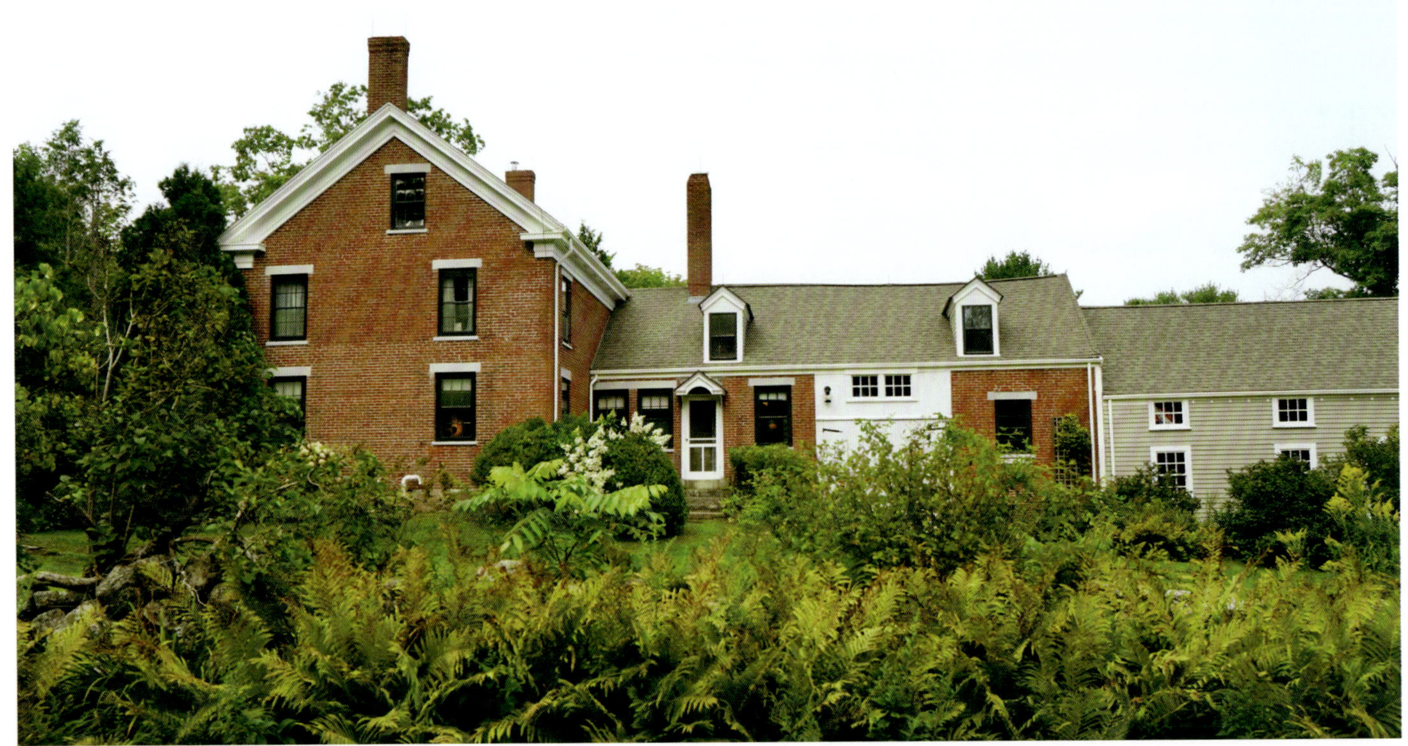

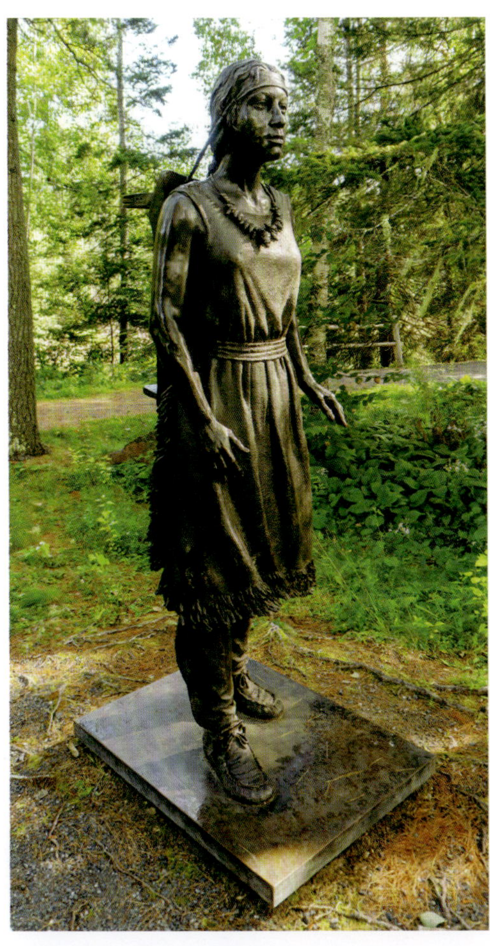

Saint Croix Island International Historic Site

Located in Calais, ME, Saint Croix Island International Historic Site commemorates the French presence there in 1604 and 1605, along with the Passamaquoddy who have taken care of the land for over 15,000 years. Visitors can learn about the original settlement at the interpretive trail shelter and viewpoint, through the informational exhibits at the ranger station, and by exploring the self-guided interpretive trail.

Burnham Tavern

Burnham Tavern is a historic tavern in Machias, ME. Built in 1770, it's one of the oldest surviving buildings in the Machias area. It's known for being used as a meeting place by the local militia during the American Revolutionary War, particularly during the events that led to the 1775 Battle of Machias. During the battle, Burnham Tavern was used as a makeshift hospital for treating the wounded on both sides. Visitors can view artifacts related to the capture of the HMS *Margaretta* at this historic site.

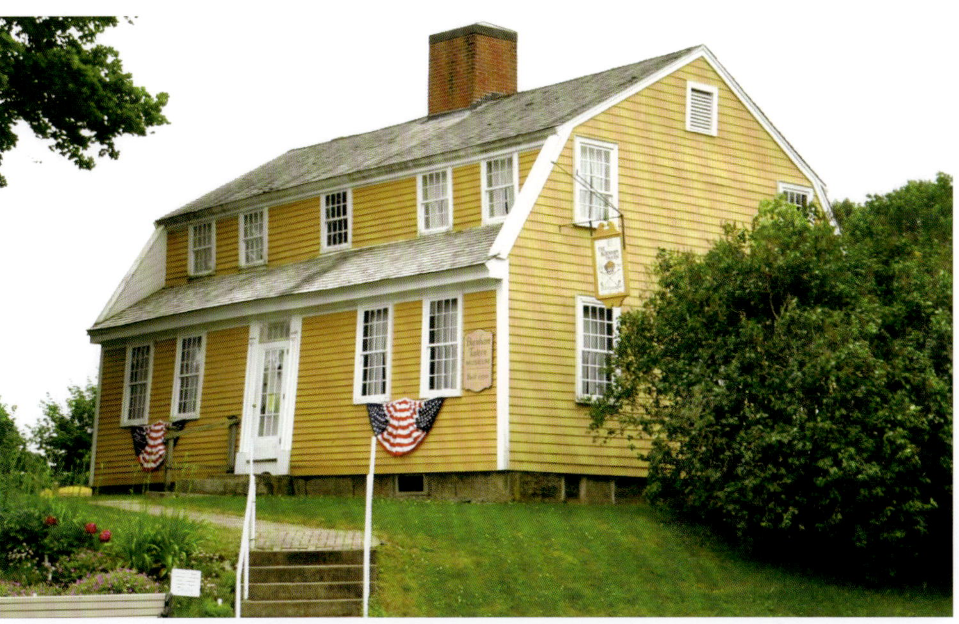

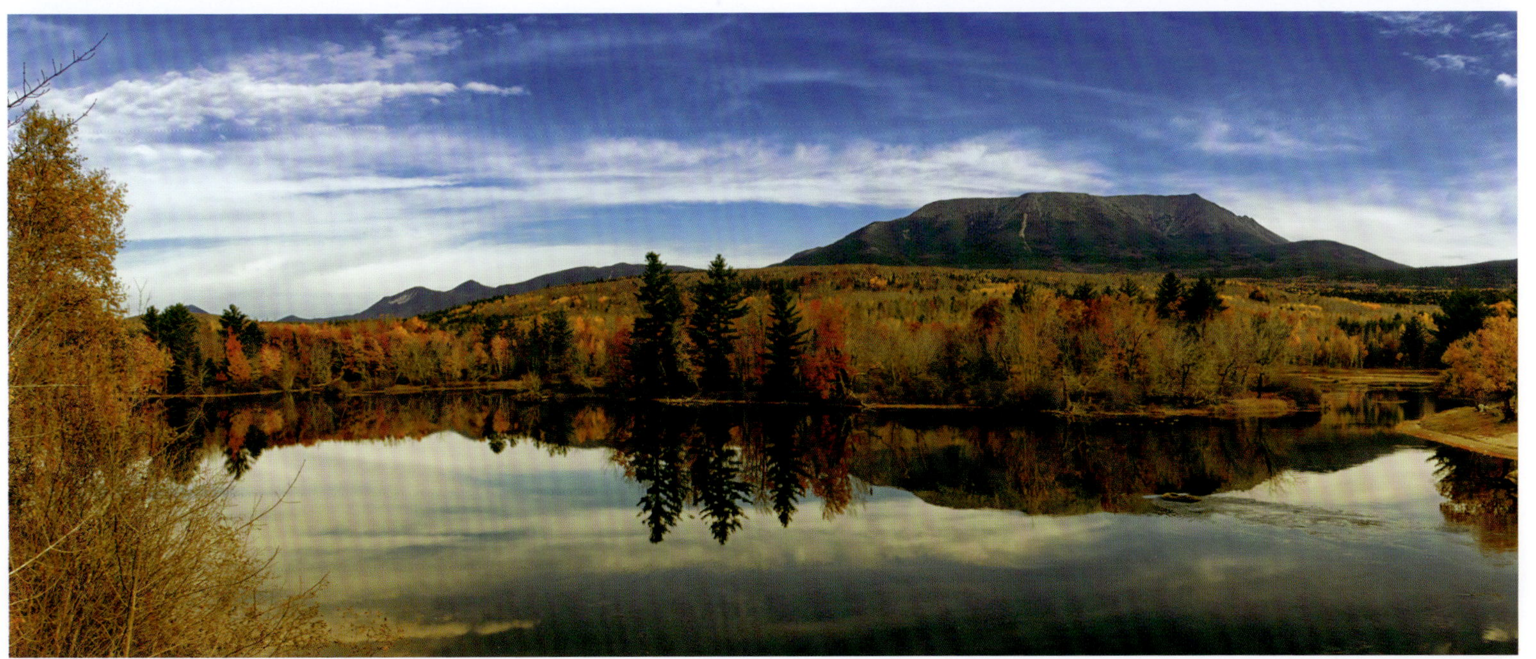

Katahdin Woods and Waters National Monument

Katahdin Woods and Waters National Monument has a variety of outdoor activities and experiences, such as hiking, camping, stargazing, biking, fishing, birding, and much more. Enjoy its spectacular fall colors during September through mid-October.

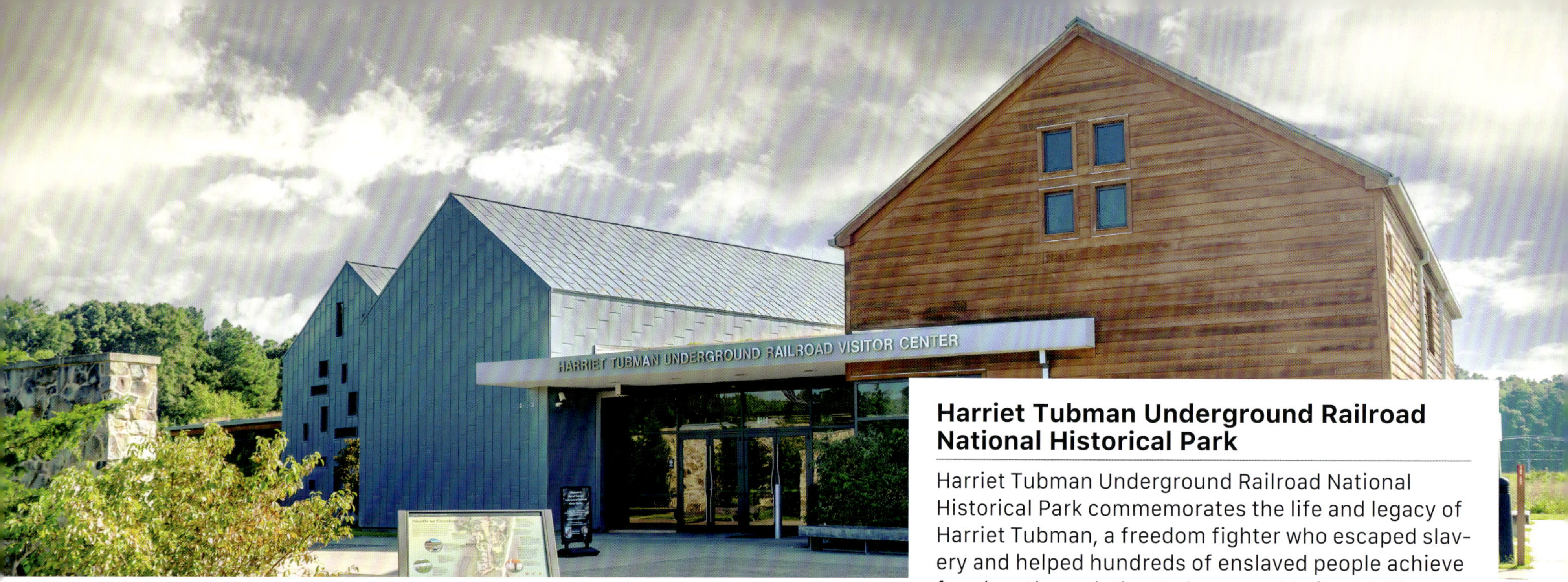

MARYLAND

Harriet Tubman Underground Railroad National Historical Park

Harriet Tubman Underground Railroad National Historical Park commemorates the life and legacy of Harriet Tubman, a freedom fighter who escaped slavery and helped hundreds of enslaved people achieve freedom through the Underground Railroad. The park preserves sites significant to her early life and work as a conductor on the Underground Railroad, as well as the broader story of resistance to slavery.

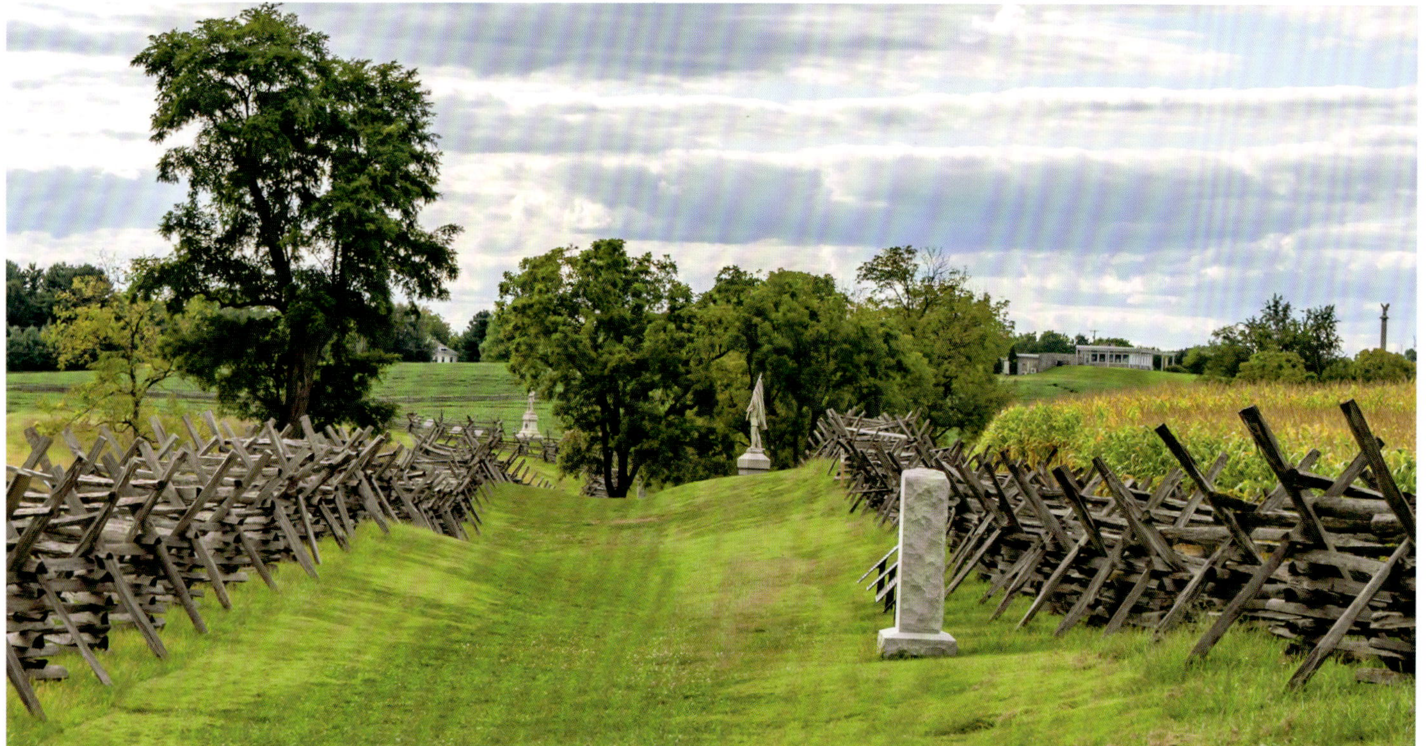

Antietam National Battlefield

Antietam National Battlefield commemorates the site of the Battle of Antietam, the bloodiest single-day battle in American history. This Civil War clash between Union and Confederate forces resulted in an estimated 22,720 casualties. The battle marked a pivotal turning point, leading to President Abraham Lincoln's issuance of the Emancipation Proclamation. The battlefield is preserved as a tribute to the soldiers who fought, and as a space for reflection and education.

Baltimore-Washington Parkway

The Baltimore-Washington Parkway, officially known as the Baltimore-Washington Memorial Parkway, is a scenic, historic roadway that connects the cities of Baltimore, Maryland, and Washington, D.C. Known for its tree-lined vistas and accessibility to landmarks, the parkway is both a functional roadway and a corridor for recreation and nature preservation.

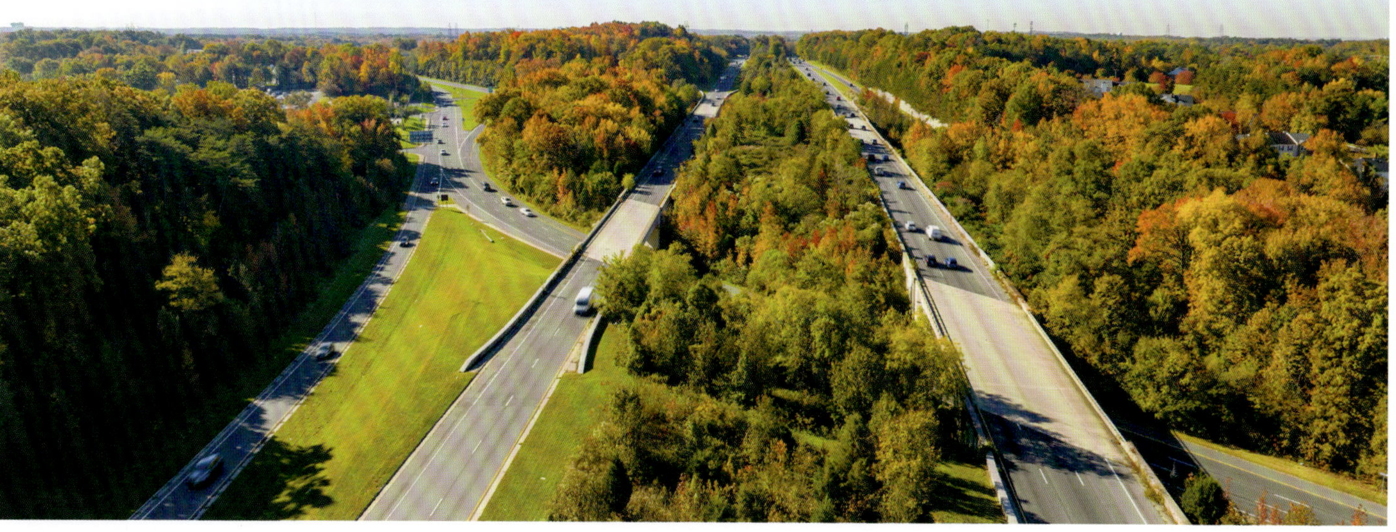

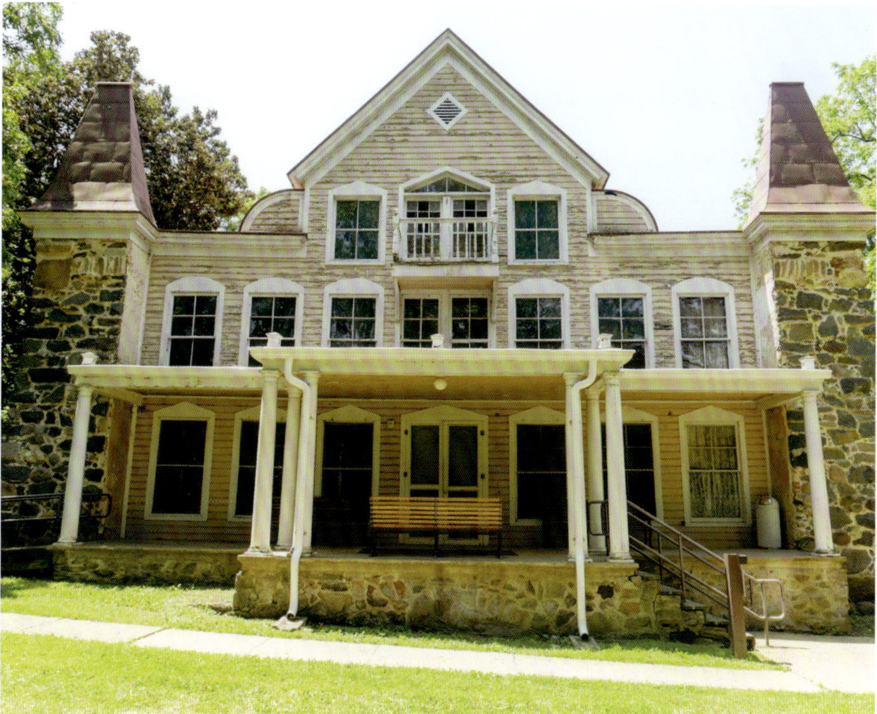

Clara Barton National Historic Site

Clara Barton National Historic Site honors the life and legacy of Clara Barton, founder of the American Red Cross. The site preserves Barton's home *(see above)*, which also served as the first headquarters for the organization. Known as the "Angel of the Battlefield" for her tireless work during the Civil War, Barton dedicated her life to humanitarian efforts, and this site offers insights into her pioneering work in disaster relief and public service.

Fort McHenry National Monument and Historic Shrine

Fort McHenry, located in Baltimore, MD, is best known as the site of the Battle of Baltimore during the War of 1812. The fort's defense against British naval forces inspired Francis Scott Key to write "The Star-Spangled Banner," which became the U.S.'s national anthem. It is both a historic fort and a national shrine, honoring its role in shaping American identity.

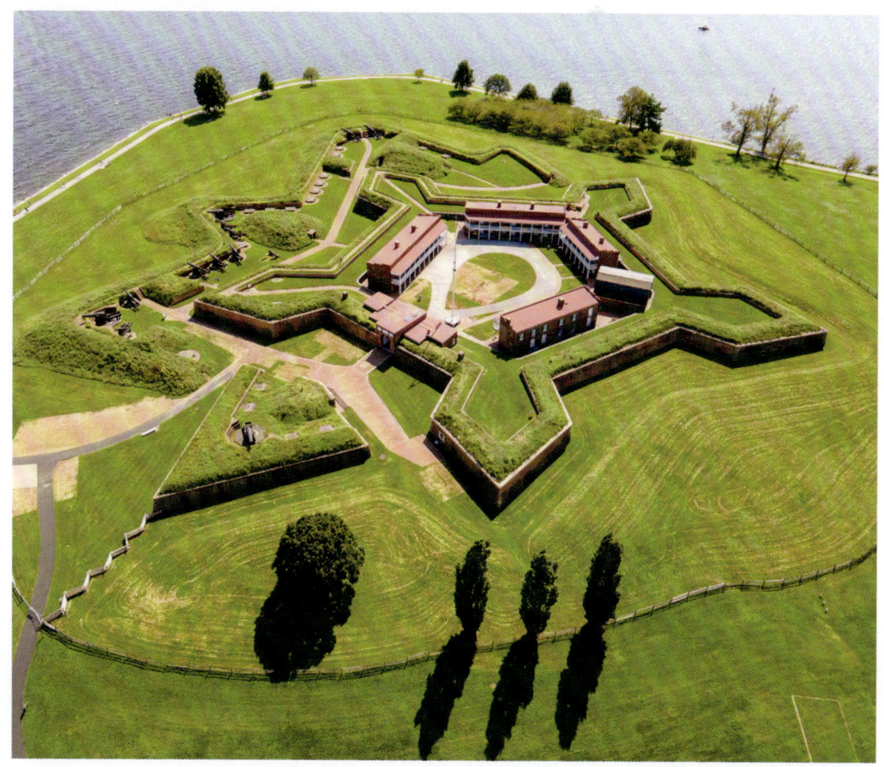

Fort Foote Park

Fort Foote Park, located on the Potomac River, preserves the remains of Fort Foote, a Civil War-era defensive fort built to protect Washington, D.C. Constructed in 1863, the fort featured massive Rodman cannons *(see below)* and was strategically placed to guard against Confederate naval attacks. Today, the park is a peaceful retreat offering a blend of history, scenic views of the Potomac River, and opportunities for outdoor recreation.

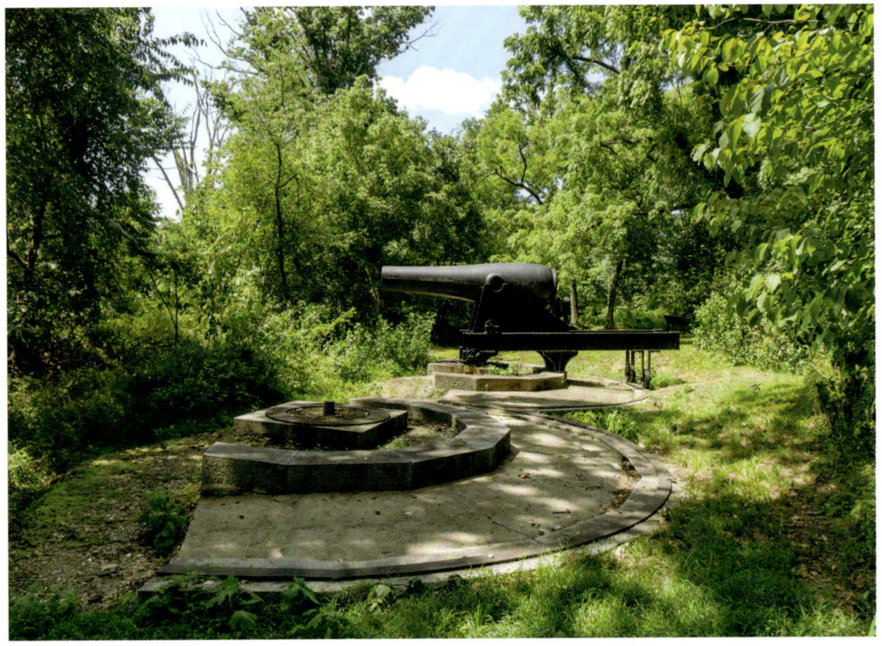

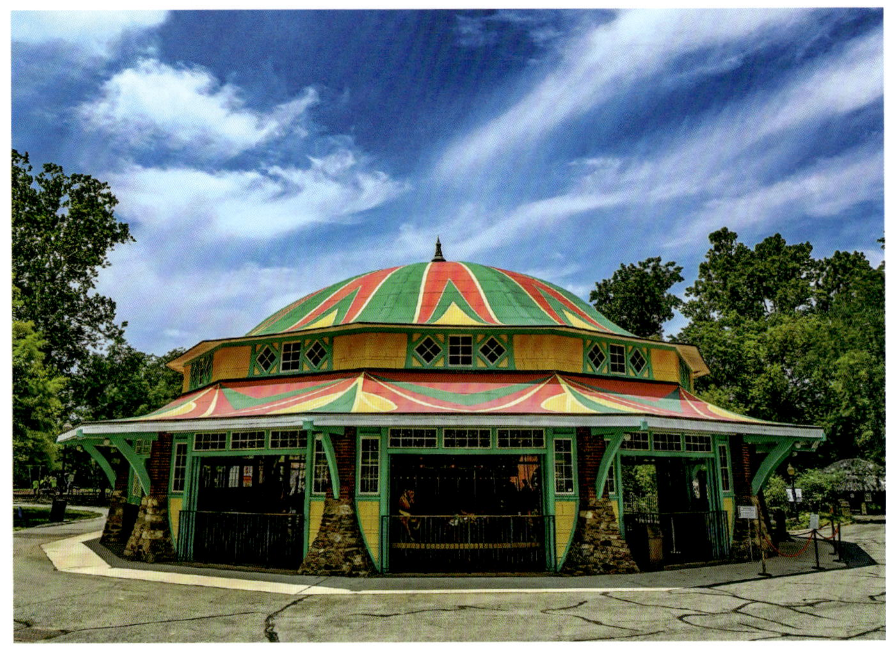

Glen Echo Park

Glen Echo Park is a historic cultural and recreational site that has transformed over the years. Originally founded as a Chautauqua retreat in 1891 and later becoming a popular amusement park, it is now a hub for arts, education, and history. The park is listed on the National Register of Historic Places and features an iconic 1921 Dentzel Carousel *(see above)*, art studios, and performance spaces, making it a lively destination for families, artists, and history enthusiasts.

Fort Washington Park

Fort Washington Park, located on the Maryland side of the Potomac River near Washington, D.C., is best known for its role in defending the nation's capital. Originally built in 1809 and re-built in 1824, this imposing masonry fort served as a key defensive structure through the 19th and early 20th centuries. Today, it preserves over 200 years of military history and offers visitors a mix of historic exploration, beautiful river views, and recreational opportunities.

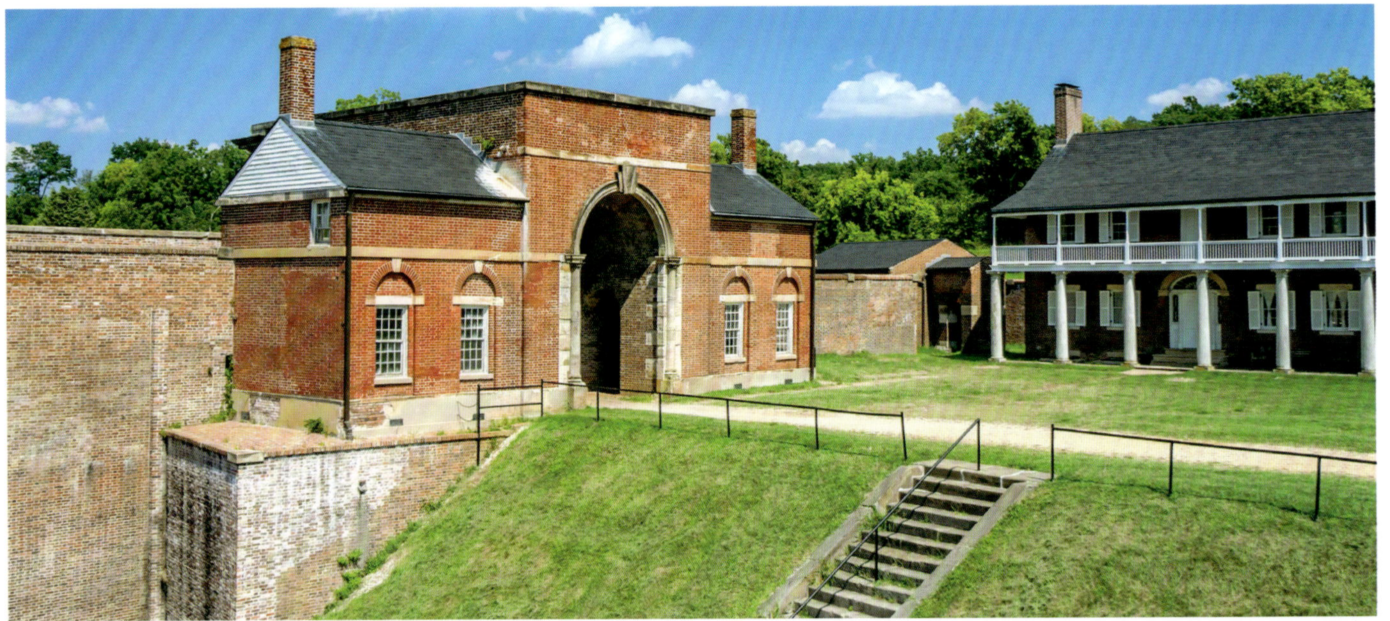

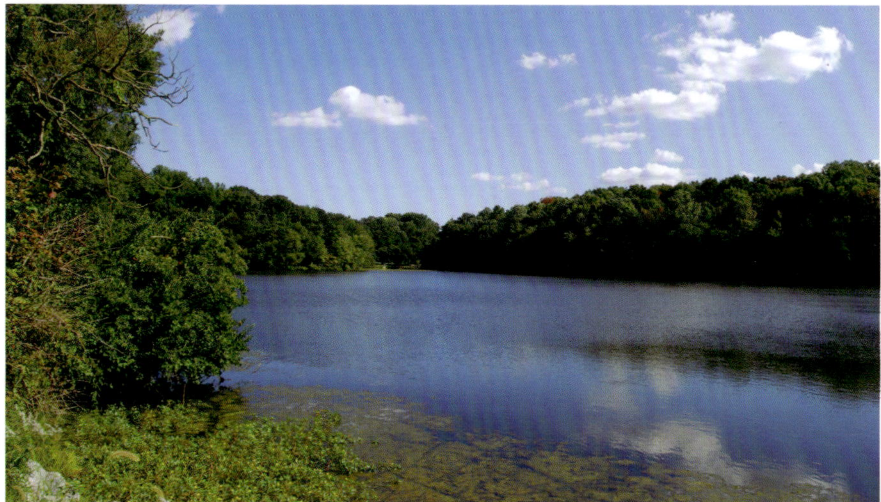

Greenbelt Park

Greenbelt Park is a tranquil natural retreat just outside Washington, D.C. Managed by the National Park Service, it offers a peaceful escape with lush forests, well-maintained trails, and a serene campground. Known for its affordability and proximity to urban areas, the park is a favorite for hikers, picnickers, and nature enthusiasts seeking outdoor activities near the nation's capital.

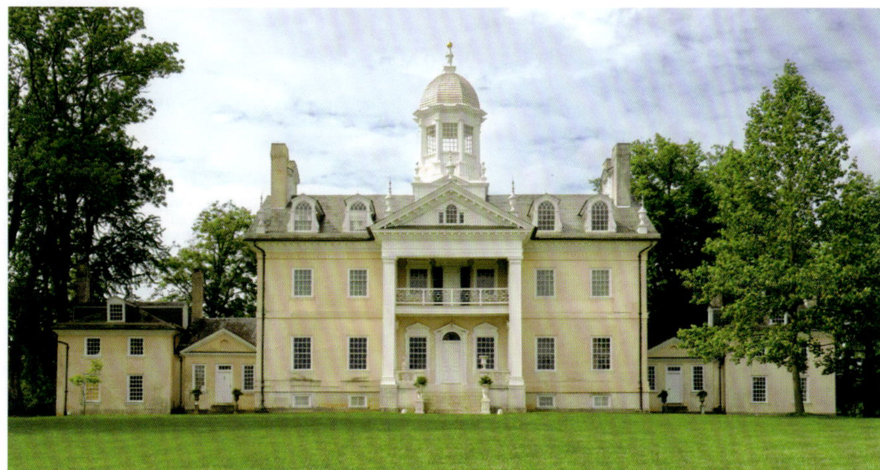

Hampton National Historic Site

Hampton National Historic Site preserves the 18th-century Ridgely estate, which was once one of the largest and most prosperous plantations in the United States. The site provides a glimpse into the lives of the Ridgely family, enslaved individuals, and tenant farmers who lived and worked there. It includes the grand Hampton Mansion, extensive gardens, and historic outbuildings, offering insights into early American wealth, labor, and culture.

Piscataway Park

Piscataway Park, located along the Potomac River in Maryland, is known for its stunning natural landscapes and its historical significance. Established to protect the view from Mount Vernon—the home of George Washington—the park features rolling farmland, wetlands, and wooded areas. It also honors the culture and history of the Piscataway people, a Native American group who originally inhabited the region.

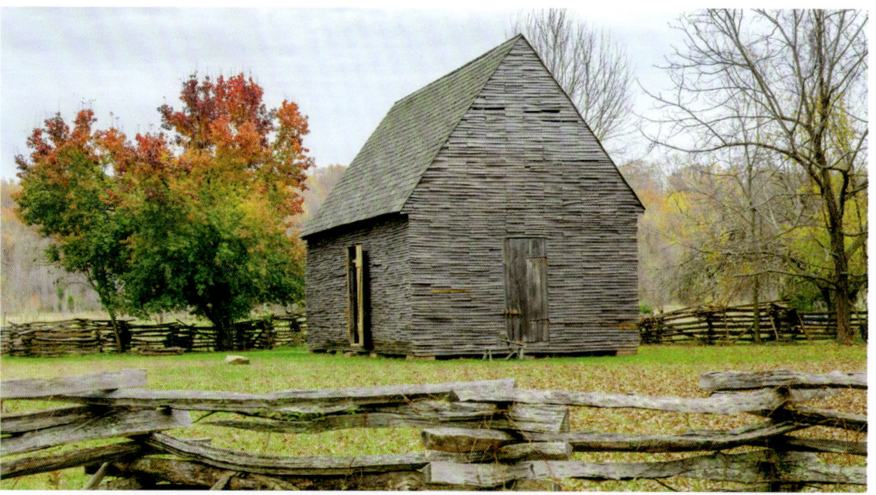

Thomas Stone National Historic Site

Thomas Stone National Historical Site preserves the Habre-de-Venture estate, home of Thomas Stone, one of the 56 signers of the Declaration of Independence. The site highlights Stone's contributions to the founding of the United States and offers insight into 18th-century plantation life, including the roles of enslaved individuals who lived and worked on the property.

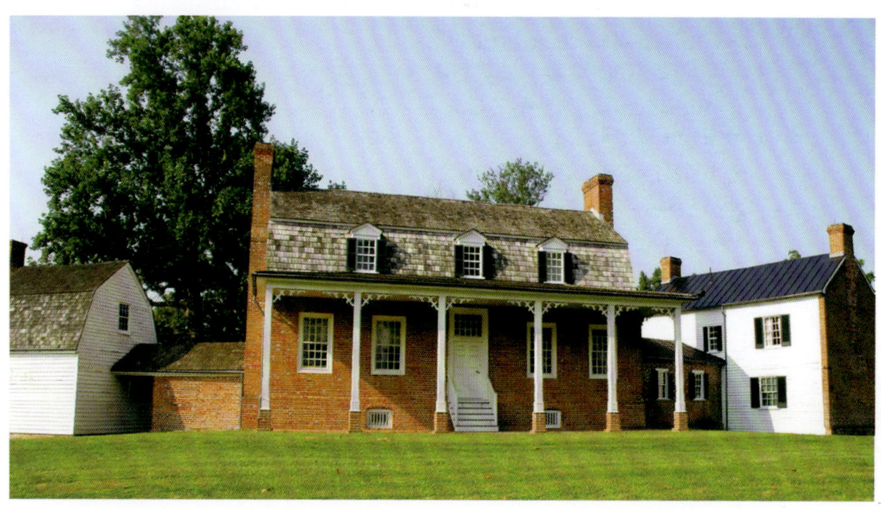

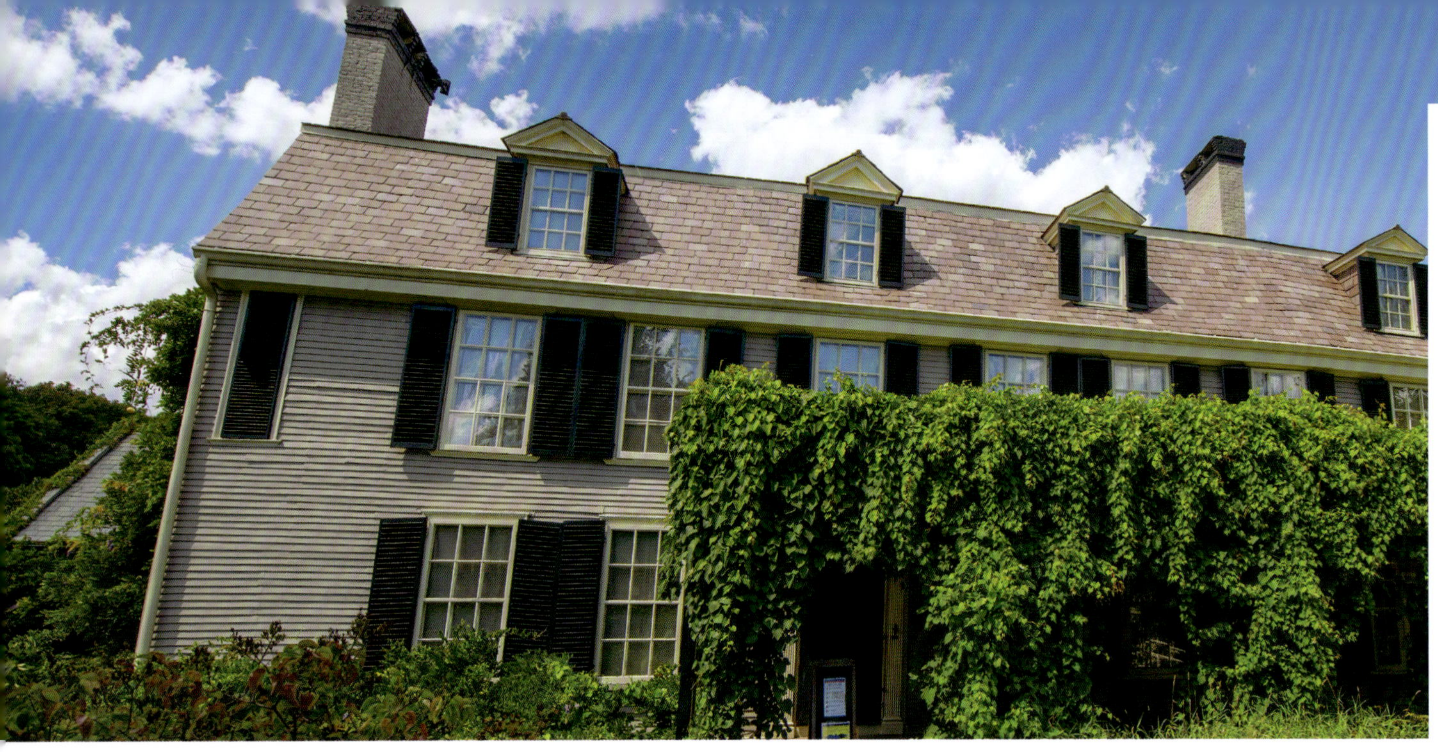

Adams National Historical Park

Formally Adams National Historic Site, Adams National Historical Park preserves the homes of five generations of Adams: U.S. presidents John Adams and John Quincy Adams *(see left)*; Charles Francis Adams, U.S. envoy to Great Britain; and writers and historians Henry Adams and Brooks Adams. The off-site visitors center offers scheduled tours of the houses in season (April to November), and guided tours of the Church of the Presidents. Additionally, the United First Parish Church, where the Adamses worshipped, is open to visitors with a small donation.

MASSACHUSETTS

Boston National Historical Park

Boston National Historical Park showcases Boston's role in the American Revolution and other parts of history. All eight properties are National Historic Landmarks and are connected by the Freedom Trail, a walking tour of downtown Boston. The sites that make up the historical park are Bunker Hill Monument, Bunker Hill Museum, Charlestown Navy Yard, Dorchester Heights, Faneuil Hall *(see right)*, Old North Church, Old South Meeting House, Old State House, and Paul Revere House.

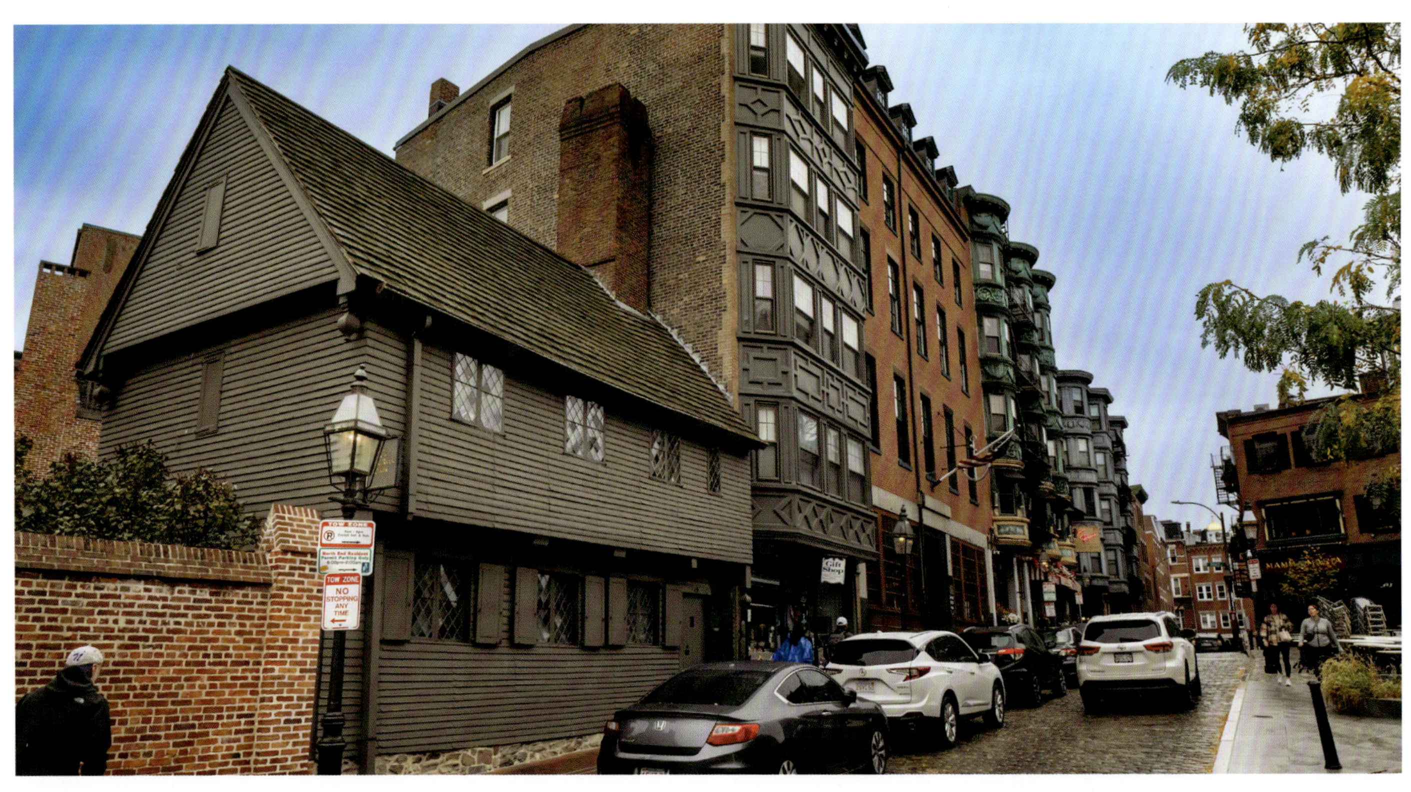

Cape Cod National Seashore

Cape Cod National Seashore consists of 40 miles of pristine, sandy beach, marshes, ponds, and uplands. Visitors can see lighthouses and cultural landscapes, and enjoy outdoor activities like swimming, walking, biking, hunting, fishing, over sand beach driving, and more.

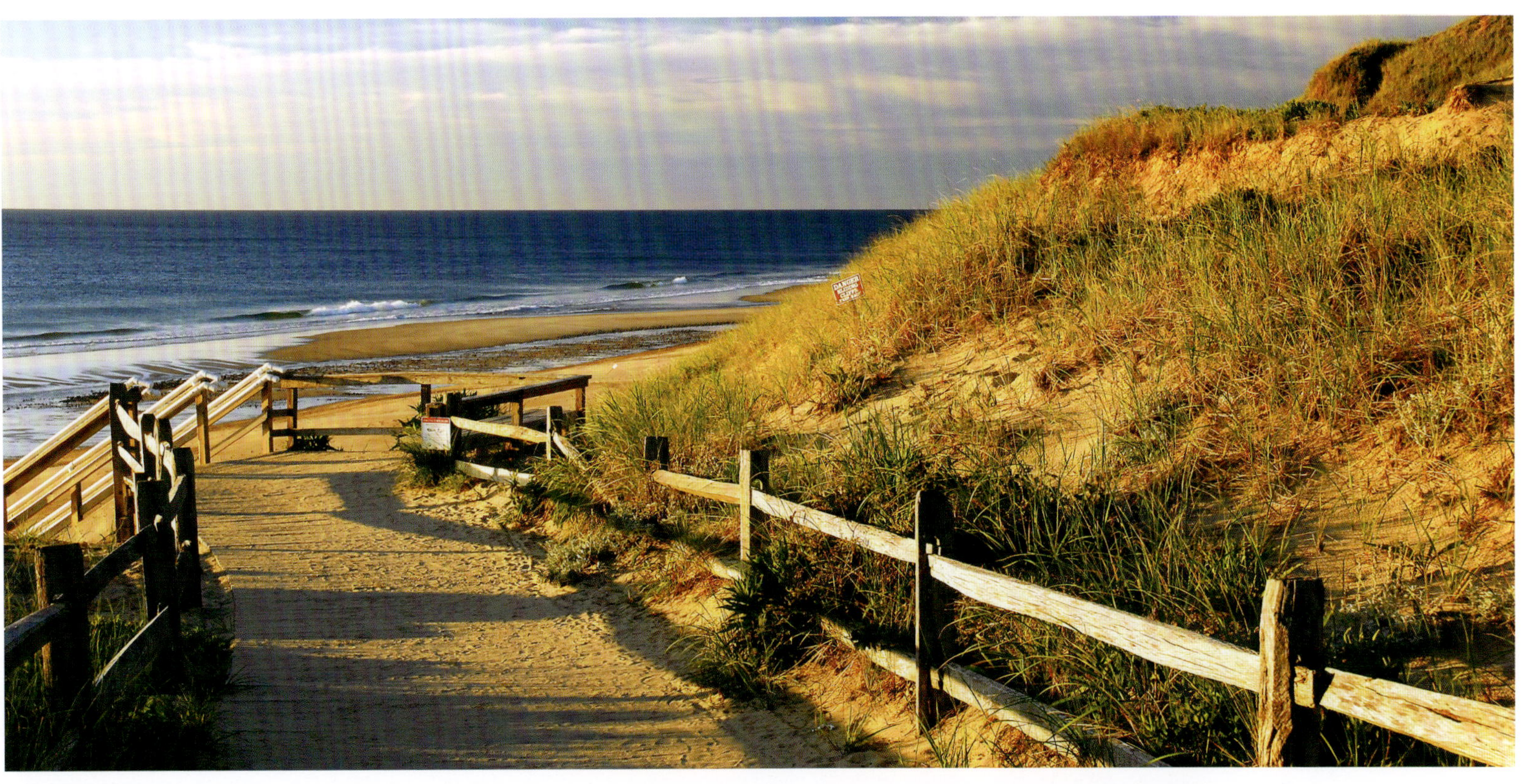

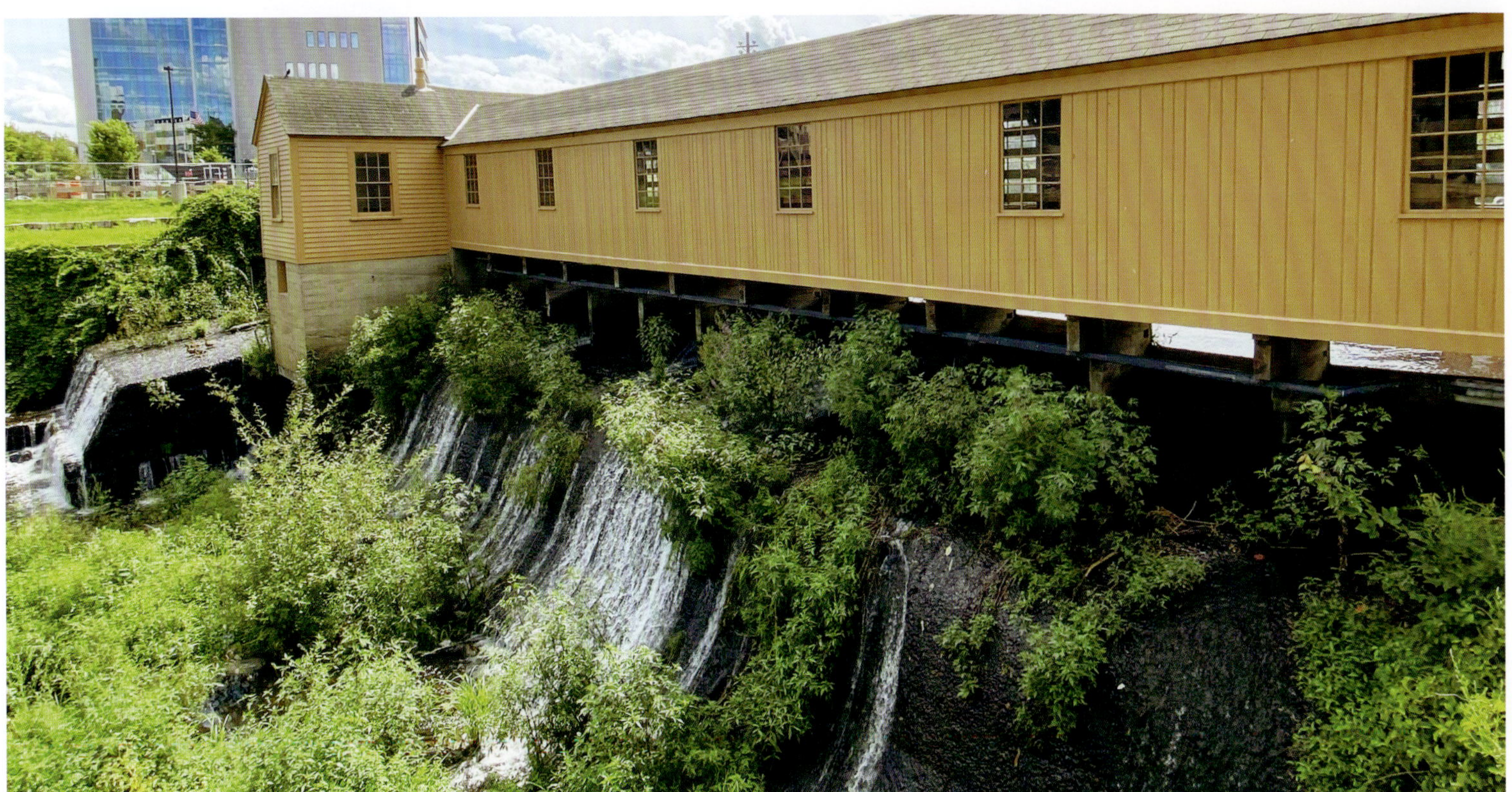

Lowell National Historical Park

Lowell National Historical Park commemorates the era of textile manufacturing in the city of Lowell during the Industrial Revolution. There are a number of notable features in the park, including Boott Cotton Mill and Museum *(see left)*, the Francis Gate, Pawtucket Dam and Gatehouse, Suffolk Mill Turbine and Powerhouse, the Worthen House, National Streetcar Museum, and more.

Minute Man National Historical Park

Minute Man National Historical Park commemorates the opening battle of the American Revolutionary War. Interesting sites include Concord's North Bridge *(see right)*, the "Battle Road Trail" between Lexington and Concord, The Wayside, Barrett's Farm, and Lexington Battle Green. Visitor centers can also be found at the hill overlooking the North Bridge and along Battle Road; films are shown that provide historical accounts of the Lexington-Concord events.

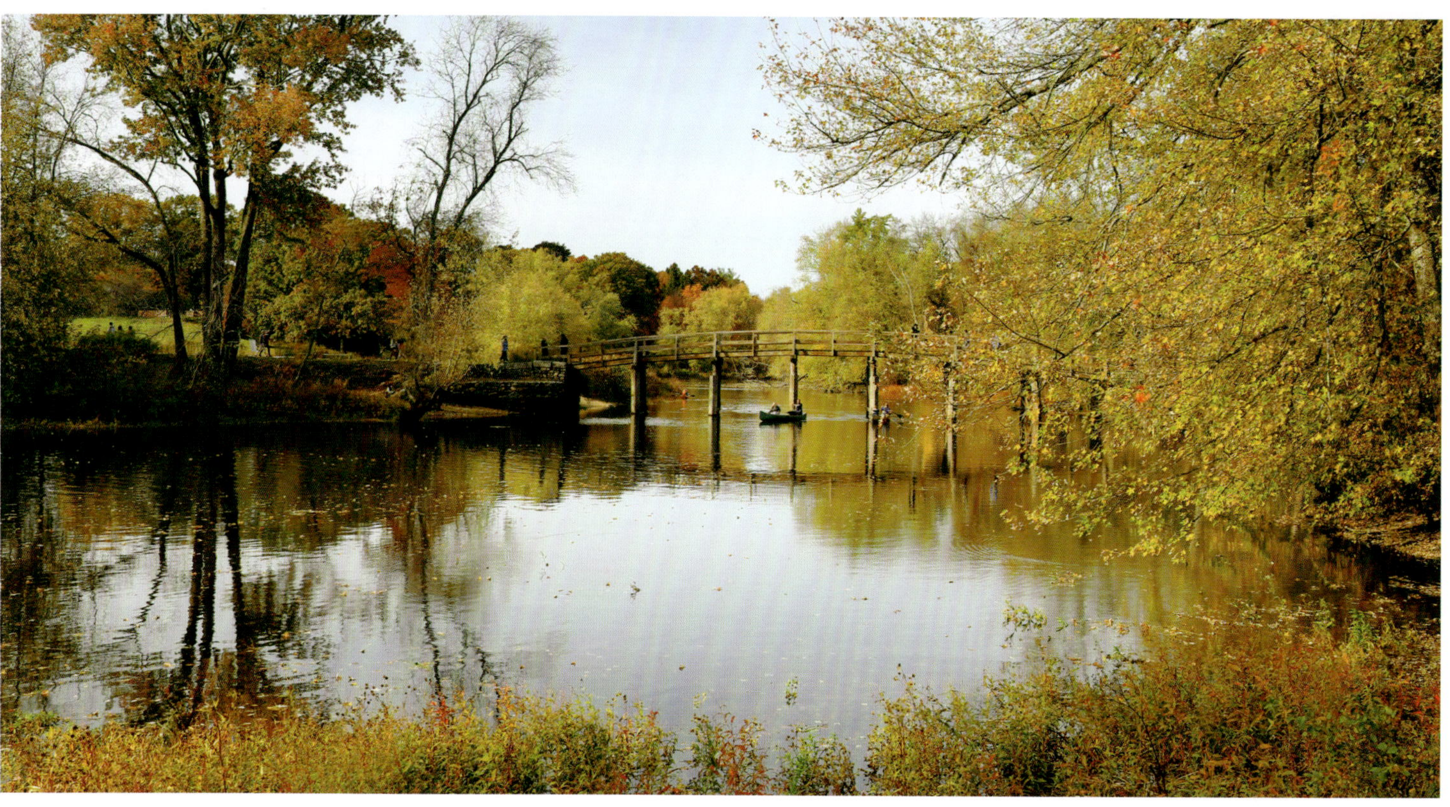

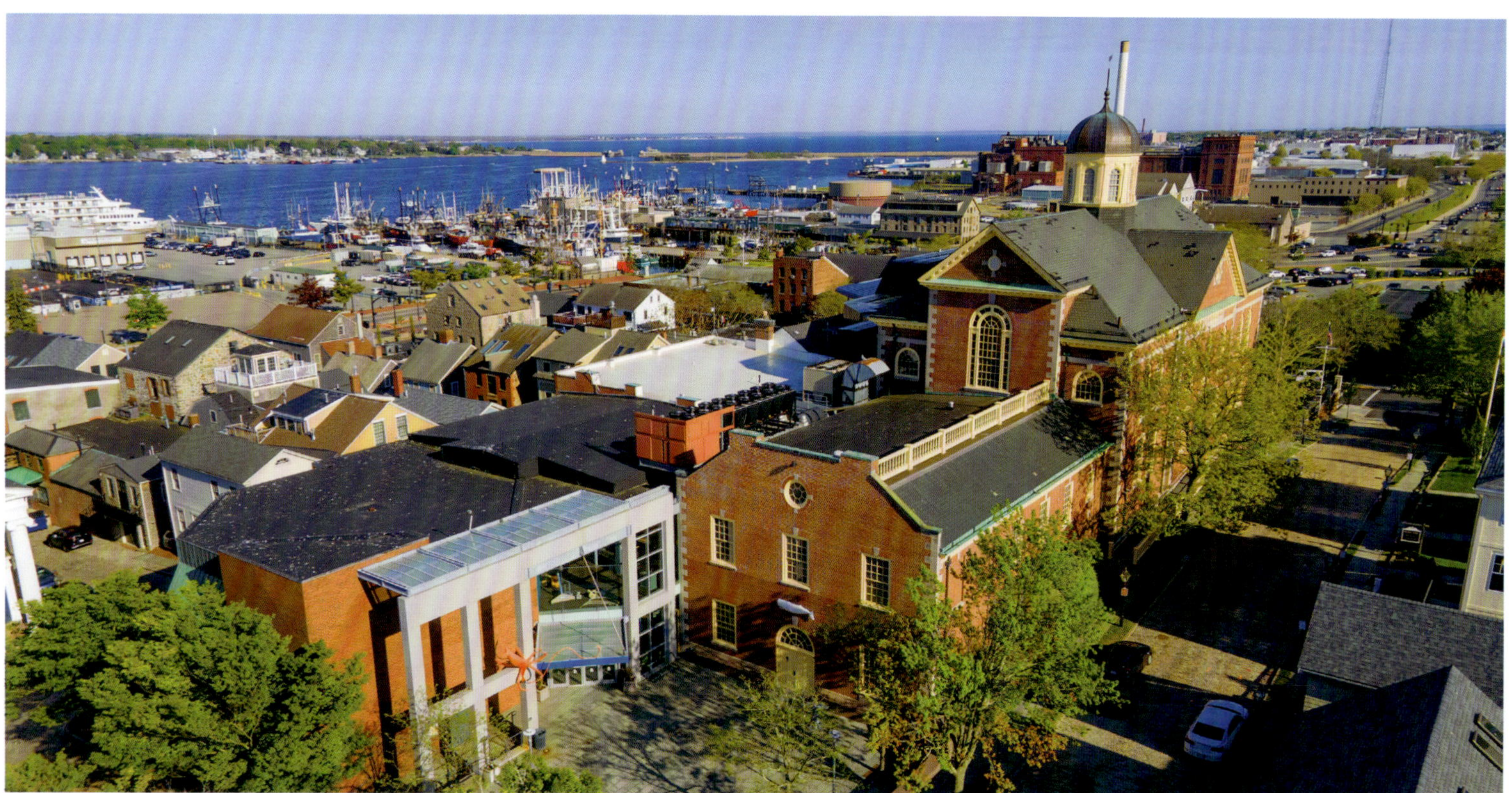

New Bedford Whaling National Historical Park

Comprising 13 city blocks, New Bedford Whaling National Historical Park commemorates the history of whaling in New Bedford, MA. The park includes a visitor center, the New Bedford National Historic Landmark District, the New Bedford Whaling Museum, the Seamen's Bethel, the schooner *Ernestina-Morrissey*, and the Rotch-Jones-Duff House and Garden Museum.

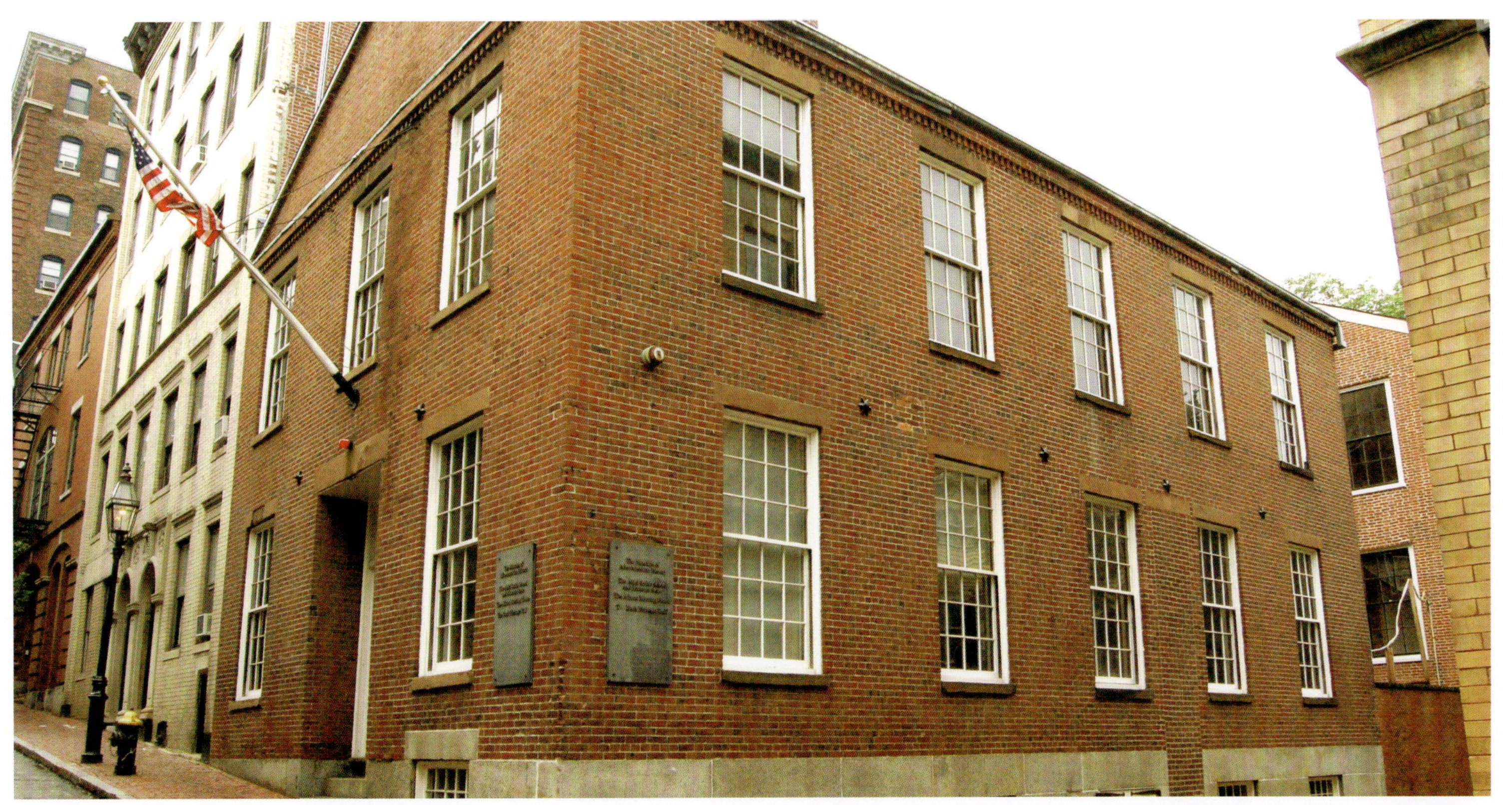

Boston African American National Historic Site

Boston African American National Historical Site commemorates the history of Boston's 19th-century African American community. Visitors can see 15 pre- and post-Civil War structures, including the 1806 African Meeting House, Robert Gould Shaw / 54th Massachusetts Volunteer Regiment Memorial, Abiel Smith School, John Coburn House, Lewis and Harriet Hayden House, and much more.

Boston Harbor Islands National Recreation Area

Boston Harbor Islands National Receration Area is made up of 34 islands and peninsulas. The park includes hiking trails, beaches, the Civil War-era Fort Warren, and Boston Light, the oldest lighthouse station in the U.S. Seasonal ferries can take visitors to Georges Island, Spectacle Island, and Peddocks Island.

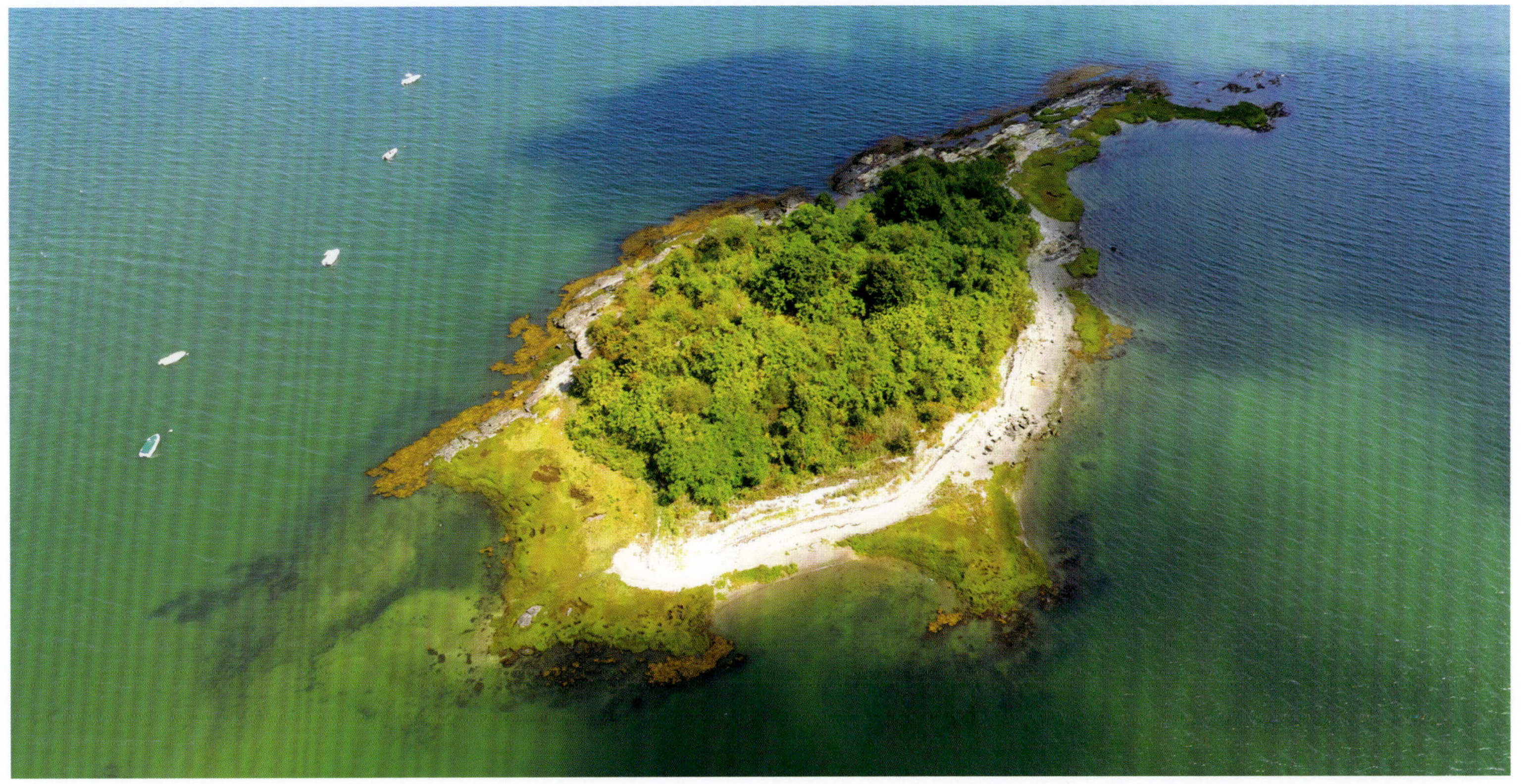

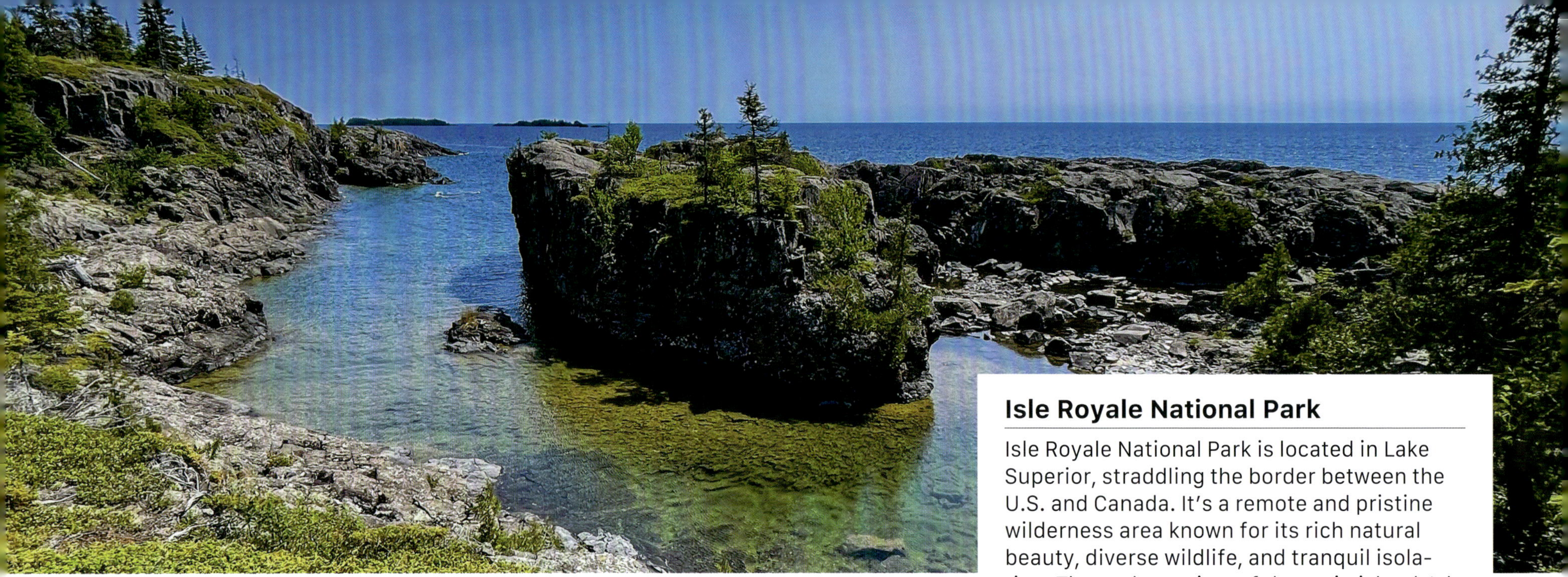

MICHIGAN

Isle Royale National Park

Isle Royale National Park is located in Lake Superior, straddling the border between the U.S. and Canada. It's a remote and pristine wilderness area known for its rich natural beauty, diverse wildlife, and tranquil isolation. The park consists of the main island, Isle Royale, as well as over 400 smaller islands and is accessible only by boat or seaplane—adding to its sense of solitude and adventure.

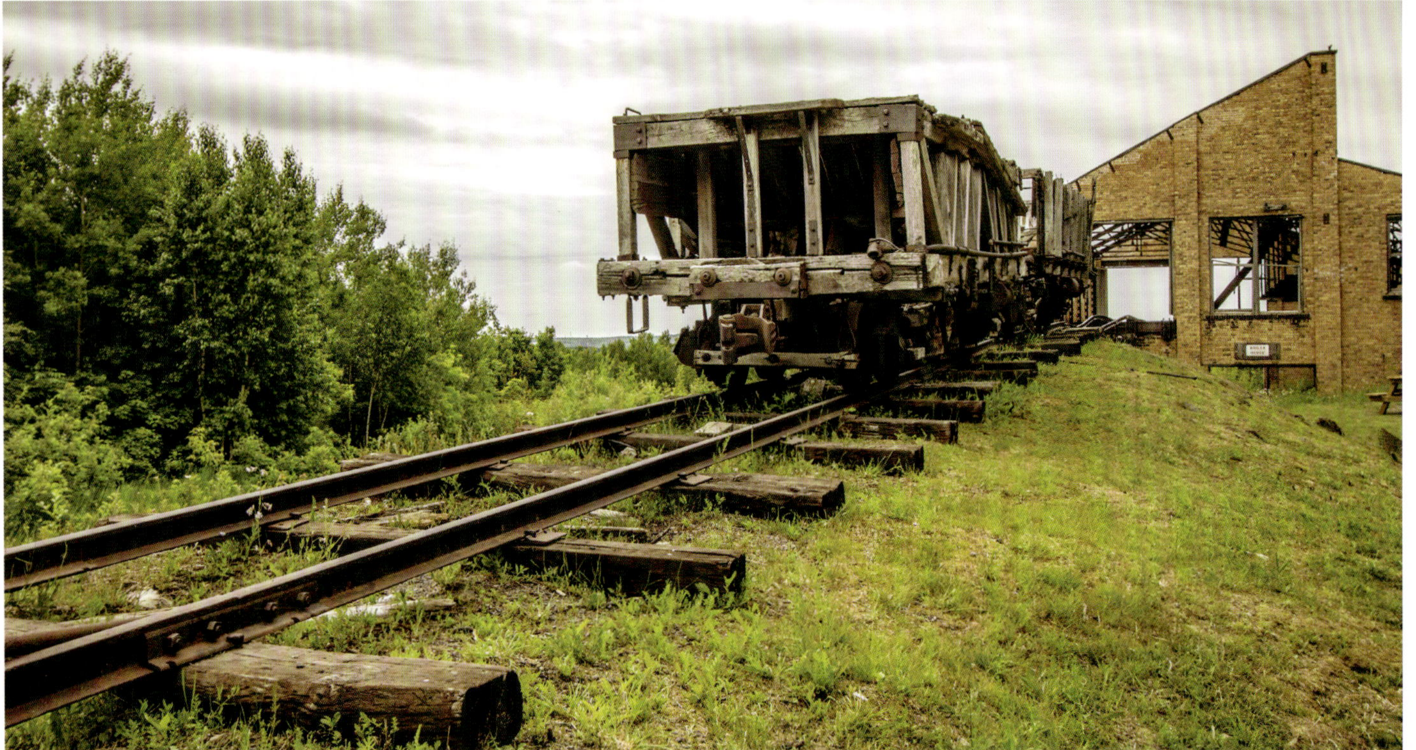

Keweenaw National Historical Park

Keweenaw National Historical Park is located in the Keweenaw Peninsula in the Upper Peninsula of Michigan. The park preserves the history of the copper mining industry that was once the driving force of the local economy and played a significant role in the development of the United States in the 19th and early 20th centuries. The park encompasses both historic mining sites and the cultural heritage of the region, offering visitors a glimpse into the lives of the workers and the impact of the copper boom.

Pictured Rocks National Lakeshore

Pictured Rocks National Lakeshore is located along the southern shore of Lake Superior in Michigan's Upper Peninsula. It's renowned for its dramatic landscapes, including towering sandstone cliffs, unblemished beaches, lush forests, and crystal-clear lakes. The park is named for the vibrant and colorful mineral-streaked cliffs *(see below)* known as the Pictured Rocks, which are one of the most striking features of the area.

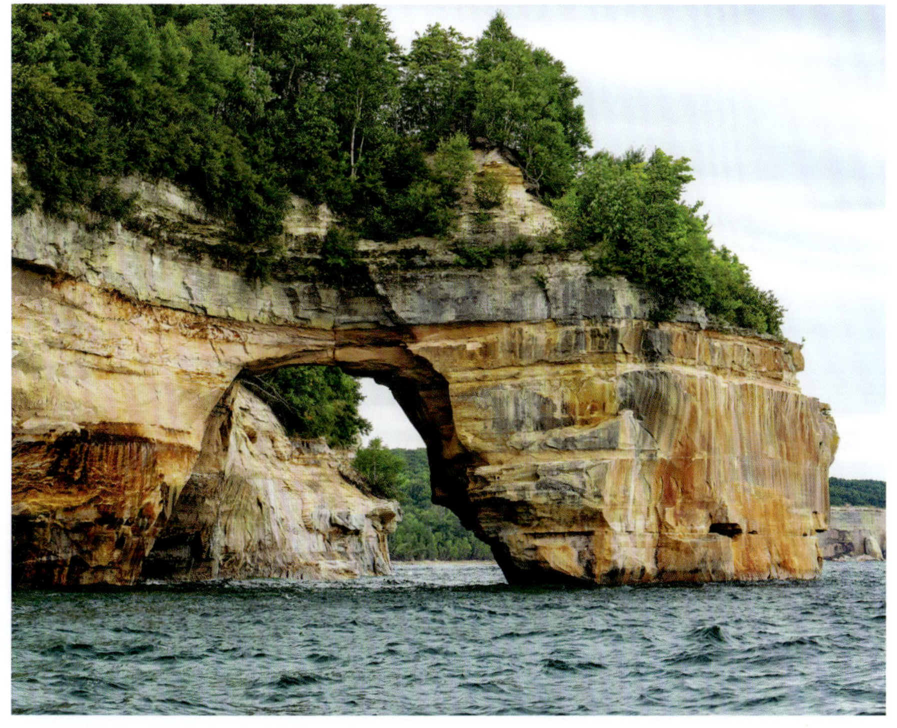

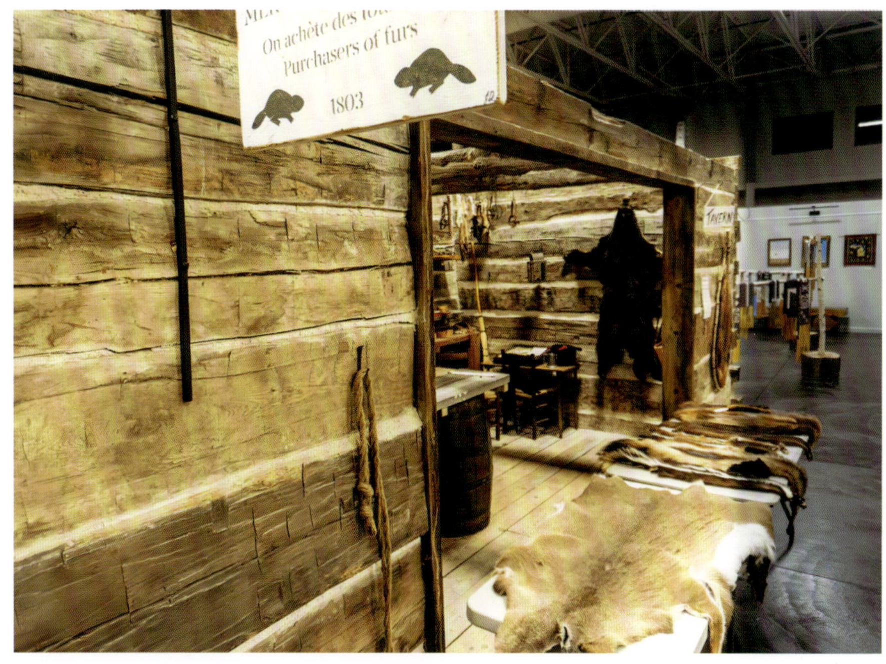

River Raisin National Battlefield Park

River Raisin National Battlefield Park is located in Monroe, MI, along the River Raisin near Lake Erie. The park commemorates the Battle of the River Raisin, which took place during the War of 1812. This battle is often remembered for its intense fighting and the heavy casualties suffered by American forces. The park serves to honor the soldiers and civilians who fought and died during the battle and provides insight into the larger context of the War of 1812. The park features a visitor center that contains maps, artifacts, detailed accounts, exhibits, and interpretive programs.

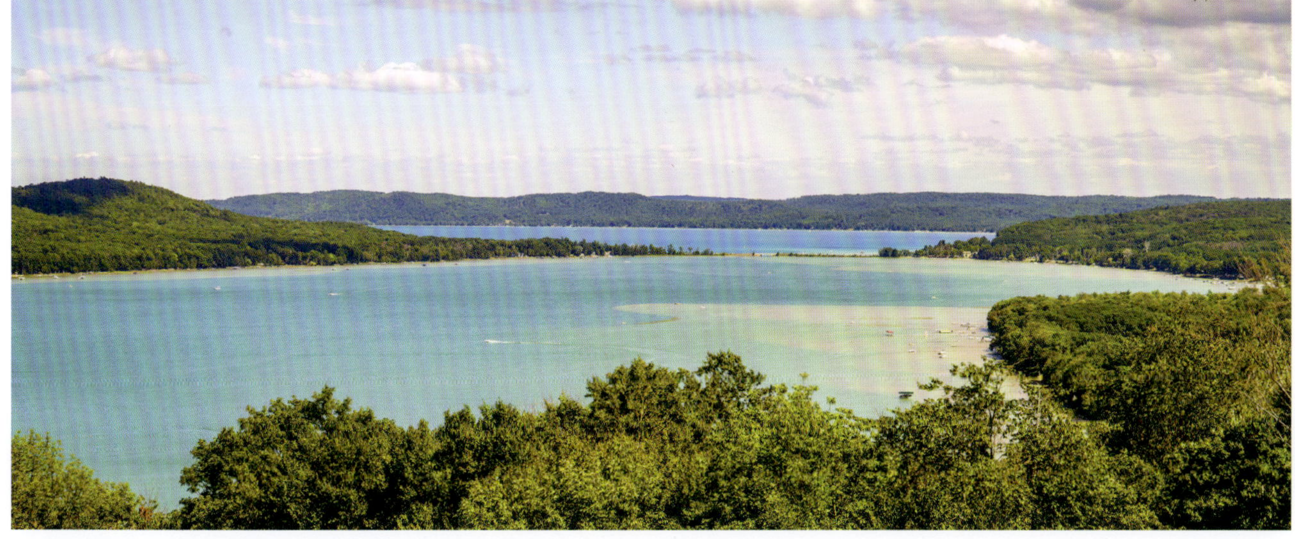

Sleeping Bear Dunes National Lakeshore

Sleeping Bear Dunes National Lakeshore is located along the northwest coast of Michigan's Lower Peninsula, stretching for over 35 miles along the Lake Michigan shoreline. This stunning national lakeshore is known for its dramatic sand dunes, unaltered beaches, verdant forests, radiant lakes, and scenic views. It offers a variety of outdoor activities, from hiking and swimming to wildlife watching and camping, making it a popular destination for nature lovers and adventure seekers.

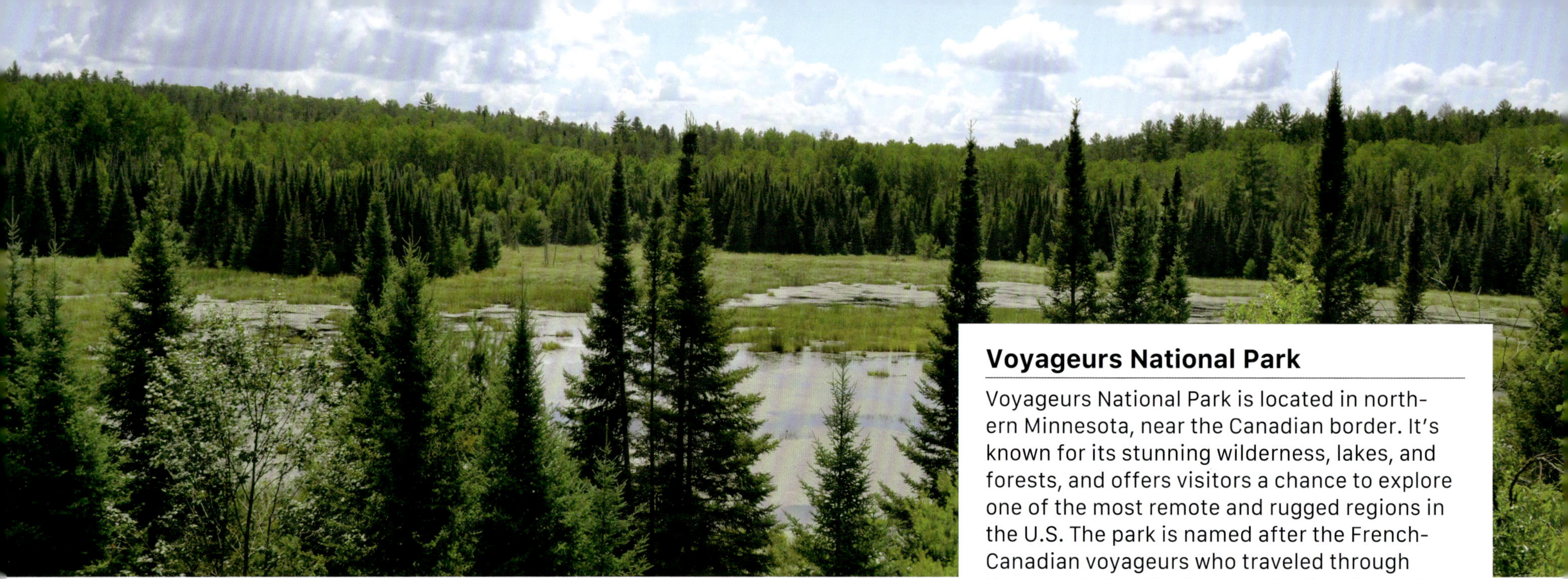

MINNESOTA

Voyageurs National Park

Voyageurs National Park is located in northern Minnesota, near the Canadian border. It's known for its stunning wilderness, lakes, and forests, and offers visitors a chance to explore one of the most remote and rugged regions in the U.S. The park is named after the French-Canadian voyageurs who traveled through the area during the fur trade in the 18th and 19th centuries. Today, it's a haven for outdoor enthusiasts, offering activities like boating, fishing, hiking, wildlife watching, and camping.

Grand Portage National Monument

Grand Portage National Monument is located in northeastern Minnesota, near the shores of Lake Superior. This historic site preserves the legacy of the Grand Portage, a vital fur trade route used by the North West Company in the late 18th and early 19th centuries. The park highlights the cultural and historical significance of the Grand Portage and the Indigenous peoples who lived in the area. Visitors to the park can explore both the natural beauty and the rich history of this important site in American fur trade history.

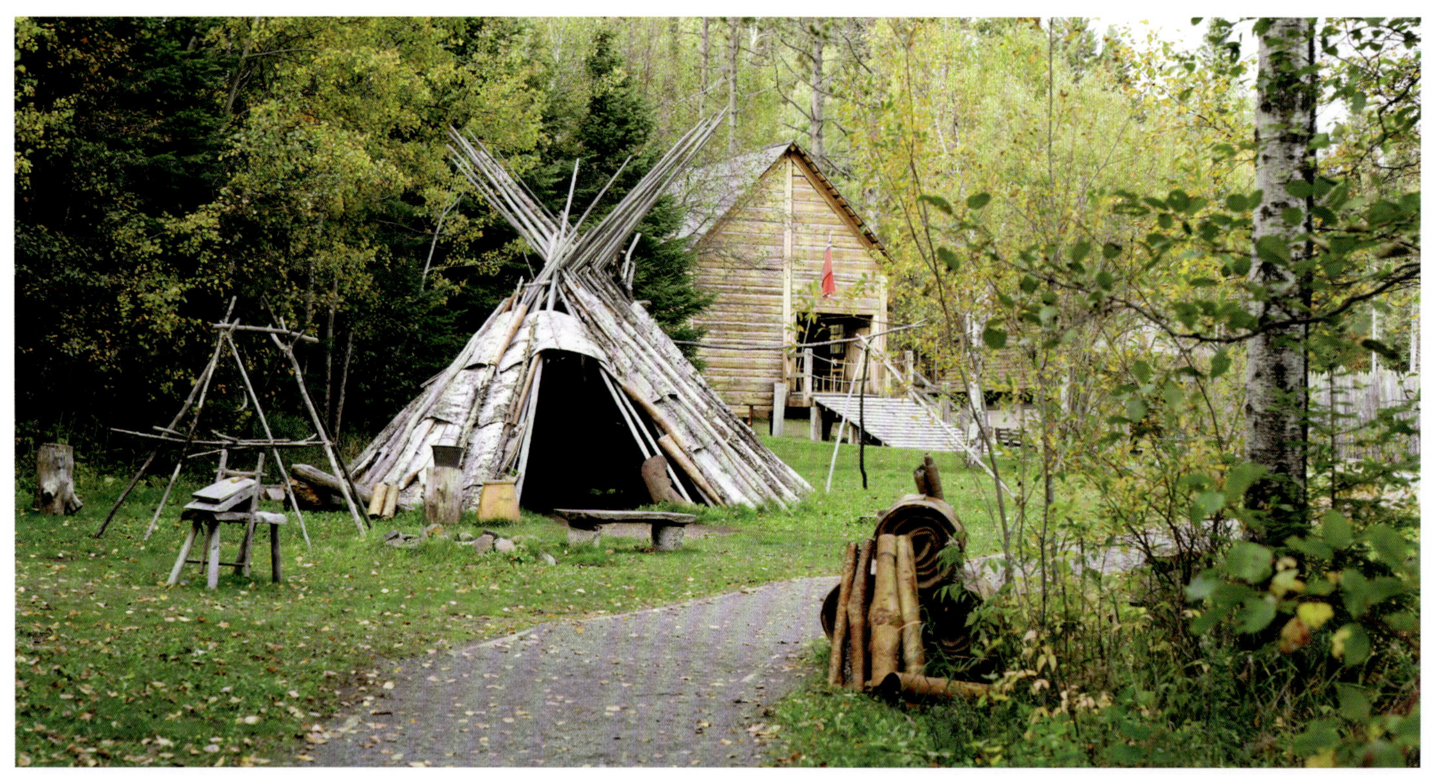

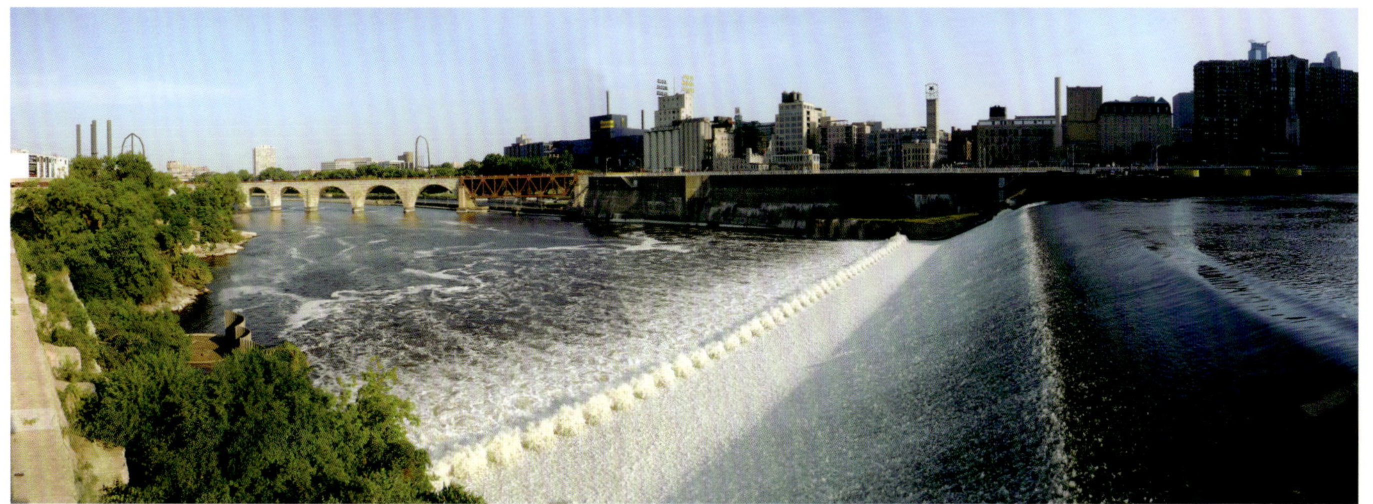

Mississippi National River and Recreation Area

Mississippi National River and Recreation Area lies along a 72-mile stretch of the Mississippi River in the Twin Cities metropolitan area, MN. The park preserves and interprets the natural and cultural history of the Mississippi River, offering recreational opportunities, scenic views, and educational programs that highlight the river's significance in the history of the U.S.

Pipestone National Monument

Pipestone National Monument is renowned for its historical and cultural significance as a source of pipestone, a soft red stone used by Native American tribes for centuries to craft ceremonial pipes and tools. The monument preserves this sacred site, which has been used for quarrying the stone for over 2,000 years, and is a key location for understanding Native American traditions and history.

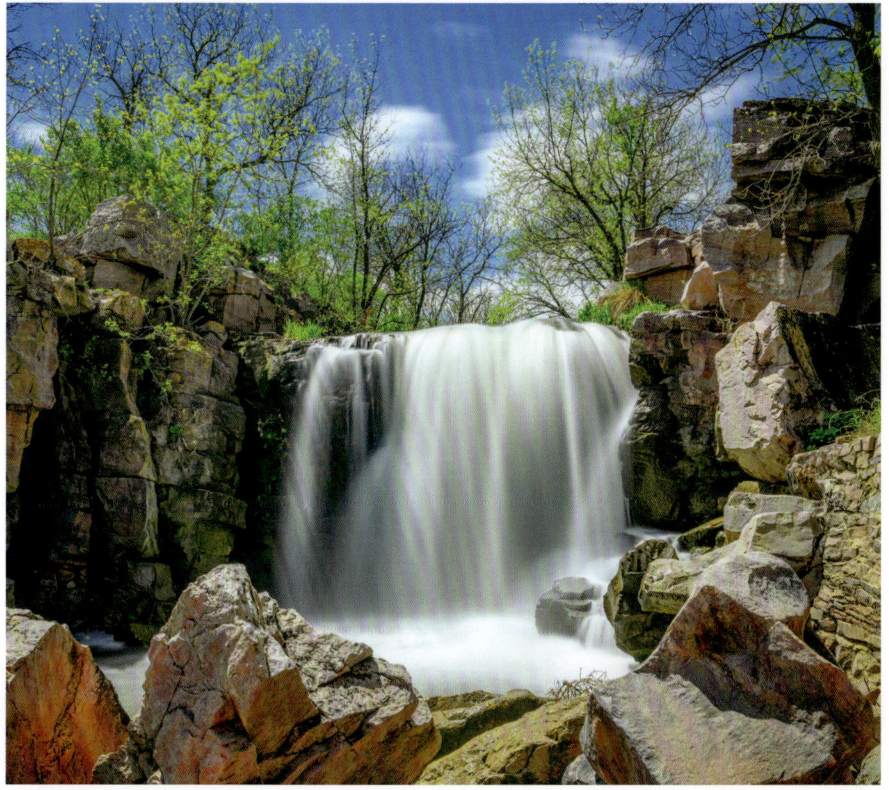

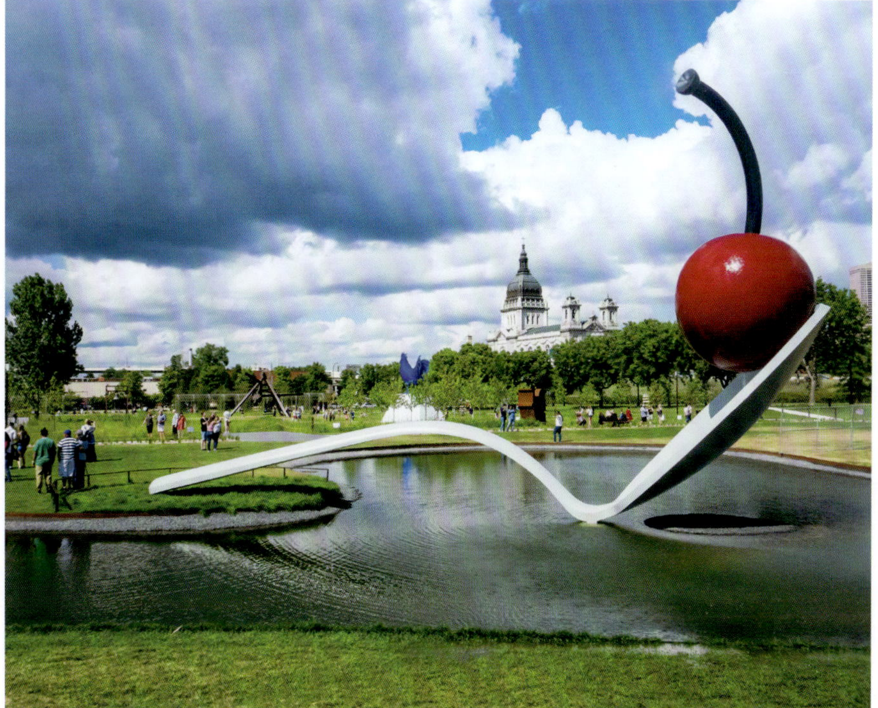

Minneapolis Sculpture Garden

The Minneapolis Sculpture Garden is a famous outdoor art park located near downtown Minneapolis, Minnesota. Operated by the Walker Art Center in collaboration with the Minneapolis Park and Recreation Board, it's one of the largest urban sculpture gardens in the United States, offering a dynamic blend of art, nature, and community space. The garden features over 40 sculptures, representing a wide range of modern and contemporary art styles; rotating exhibits keep the collection fresh and engaging for repeat visitors.

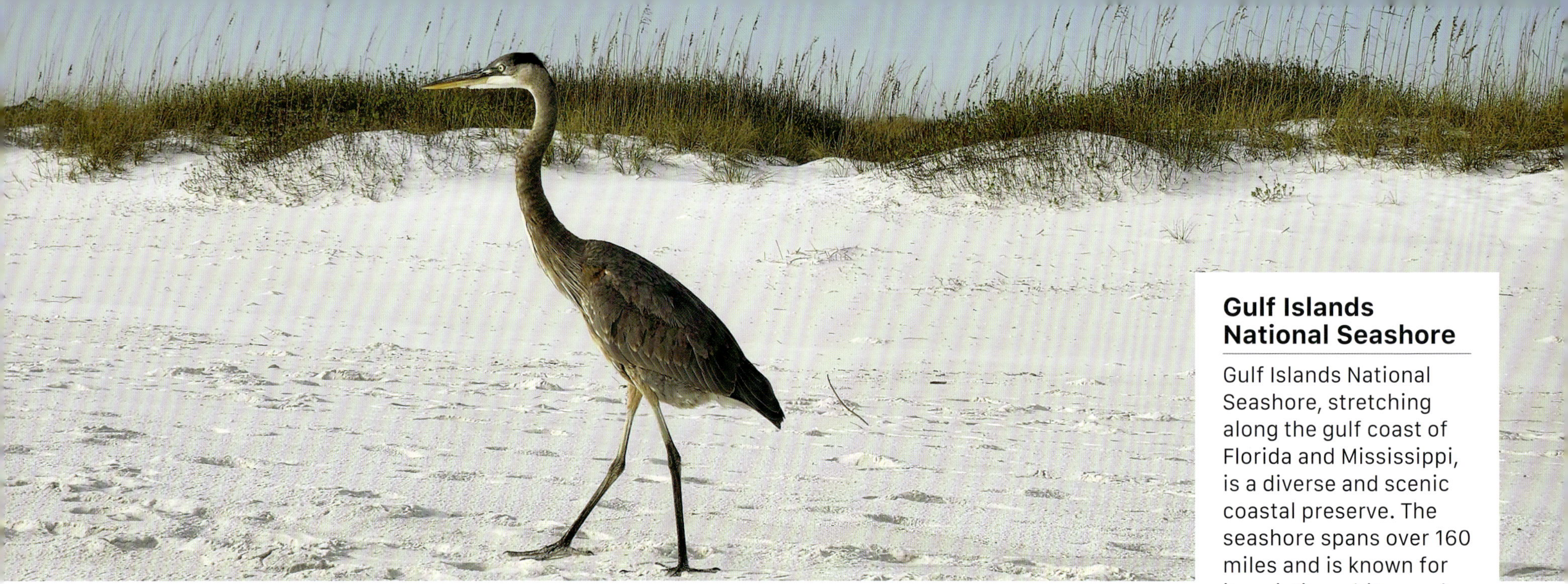

MISSISSIPPI

Gulf Islands National Seashore

Gulf Islands National Seashore, stretching along the gulf coast of Florida and Mississippi, is a diverse and scenic coastal preserve. The seashore spans over 160 miles and is known for its pristine white sand beaches, historic forts, lush coastal marshes, and abundant wildlife.

Natchez National Historical Park

Natchez National Historical Park celebrates the rich cultural history of one of the oldest and most historically-significant towns in the southern U.S. It focuses on the Antebellum South, Native American heritage, African American experiences, and European settlement, and offers visitors a chance to explore Forks of the Road, Fort Rosalie, Melrose *(see below)*, the William Johnson House, and more.

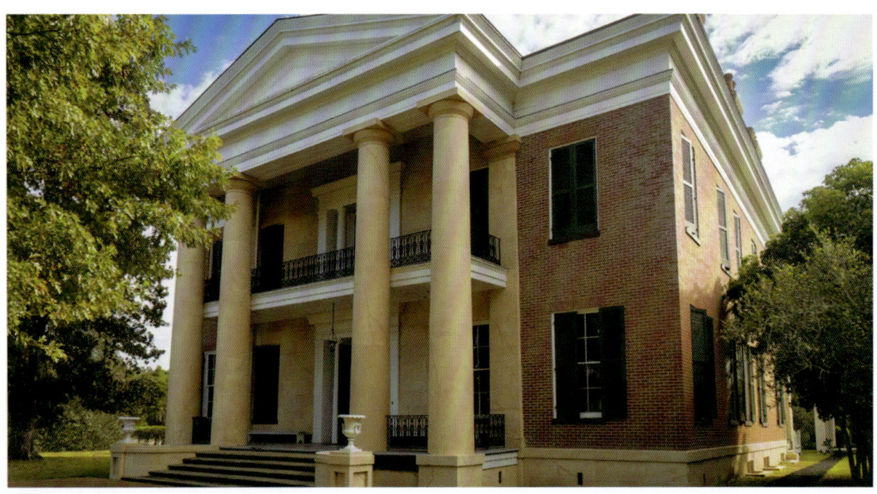

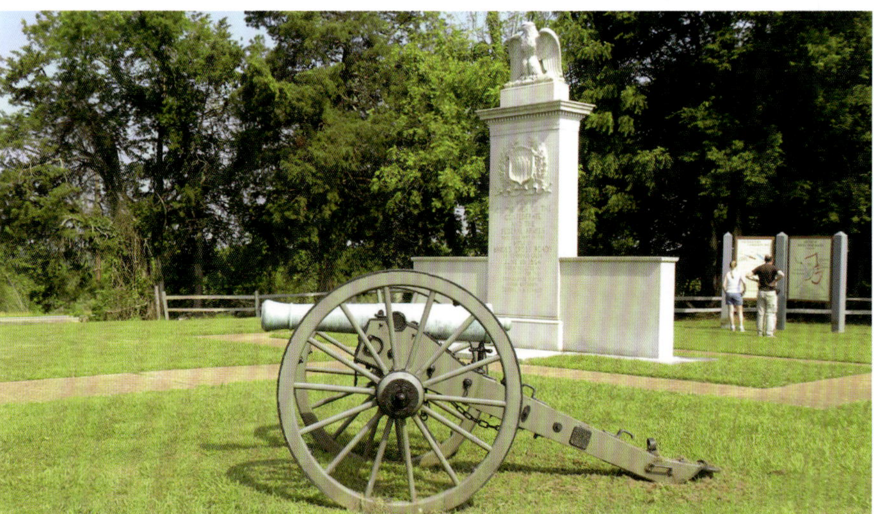

Brices Cross Roads National Battlefield Site

Brices Cross Roads National Battlefield Site is located near Baldwyn, MS, and commemorates the Civil War battle fought on June 10, 1864. The battle was a decisive victory for Confederate forces under Major General Nathan Bedford Forrest, despite being heavily outnumbered by Union forces led by Brigadier General Samuel D. Sturgis.

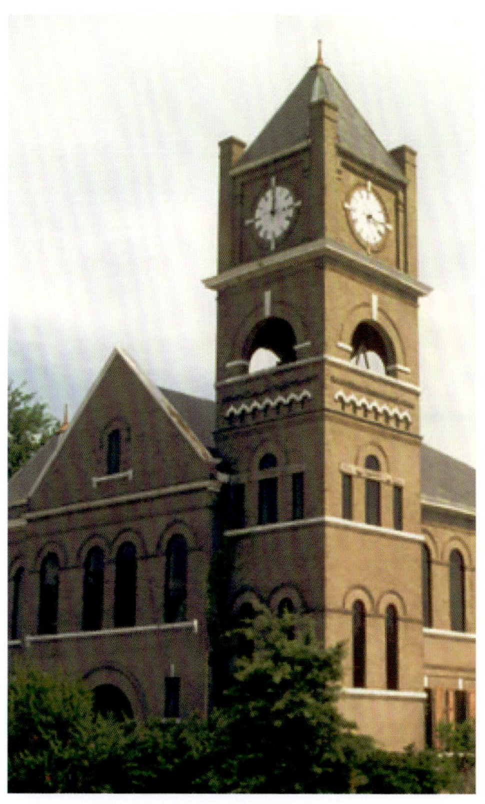

Emmett Till and Mamie Till-Mobley National Monument

Emmett Till and Mamie Till-Mobley National Monument has three sites—one in Illinois and two in Mississippi. The Mississippi units include Graball Landing, where Emmett Till's body was discovered, and Tallahatchie County Courthouse *(see left)*, where the trial of Till's killers took place. Graball Landing features a memorial marker that serves as a solemn reminder of racial violence and injustice. The courthouse serves as an educational site to explore the trial and its profound influence on the Civil Rights Movement.

Medgar and Myrlie Evers Home National Monument

Medgar and Myrlie Evers Home National Monument commemorates the life, legacy, and sacrifices of the civil rights leaders Medgar and Myrlie Evers. This site preserves the family home where they lived, and where Medgar was tragically murdered in 1963.

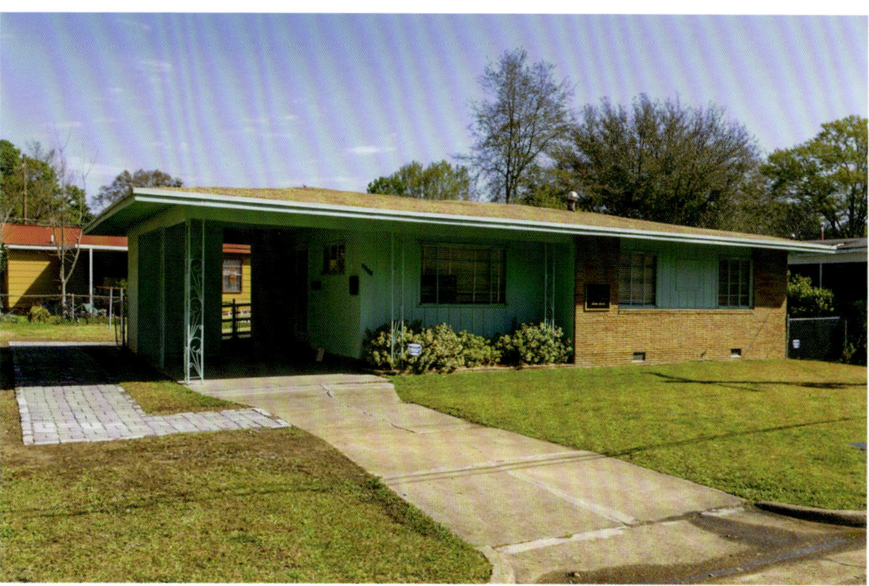

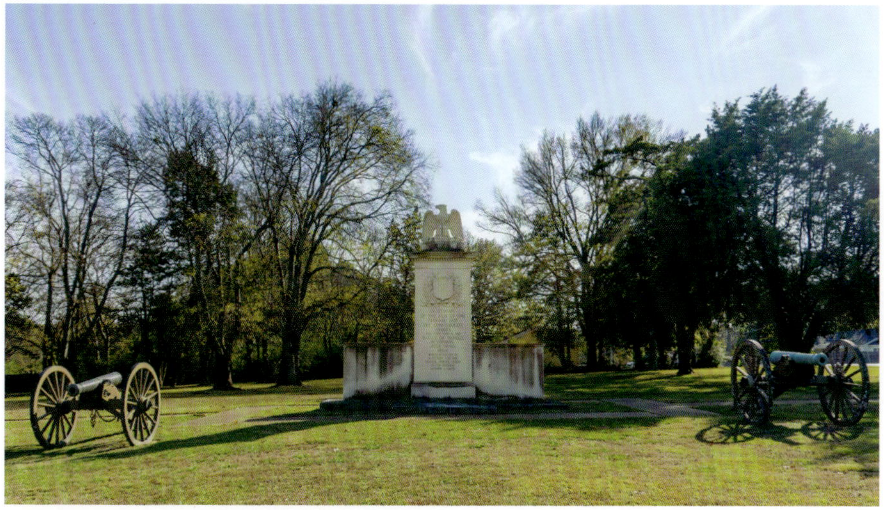

Tupelo National Battlefield

Tupelo National Battlefield is a small, but historically significant, site managed by the National Park Service. It commemorates the Battle of Tupelo, fought on July 14–15, 1864, during the Civil War. This battle saw Union forces under Major General Andrew J. Smith defeat Confederate forces led by Lieutenant General Nathan Bedford Forrest and Major General Stephen D. Lee.

Vicksburg National Military Park

Vicksburg National Military Park preserves the site of the battle that would determine the outcome of the American Civil War—the Siege of Vicksburg in 1863. The military park features a number of monuments and memorials, the Vicksburg National Cemetery, the USS *Cairo* Gunboat and Museum, driving and guided tours, and much more.

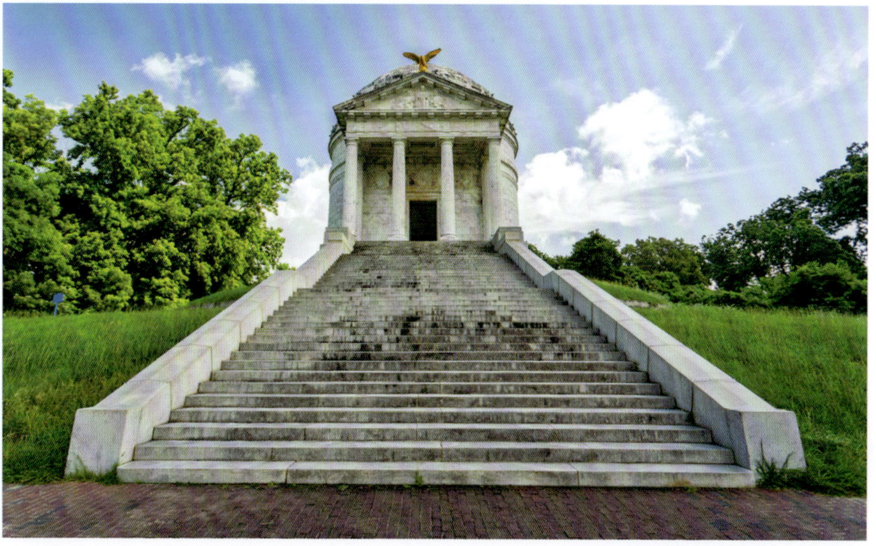

MISSOURI

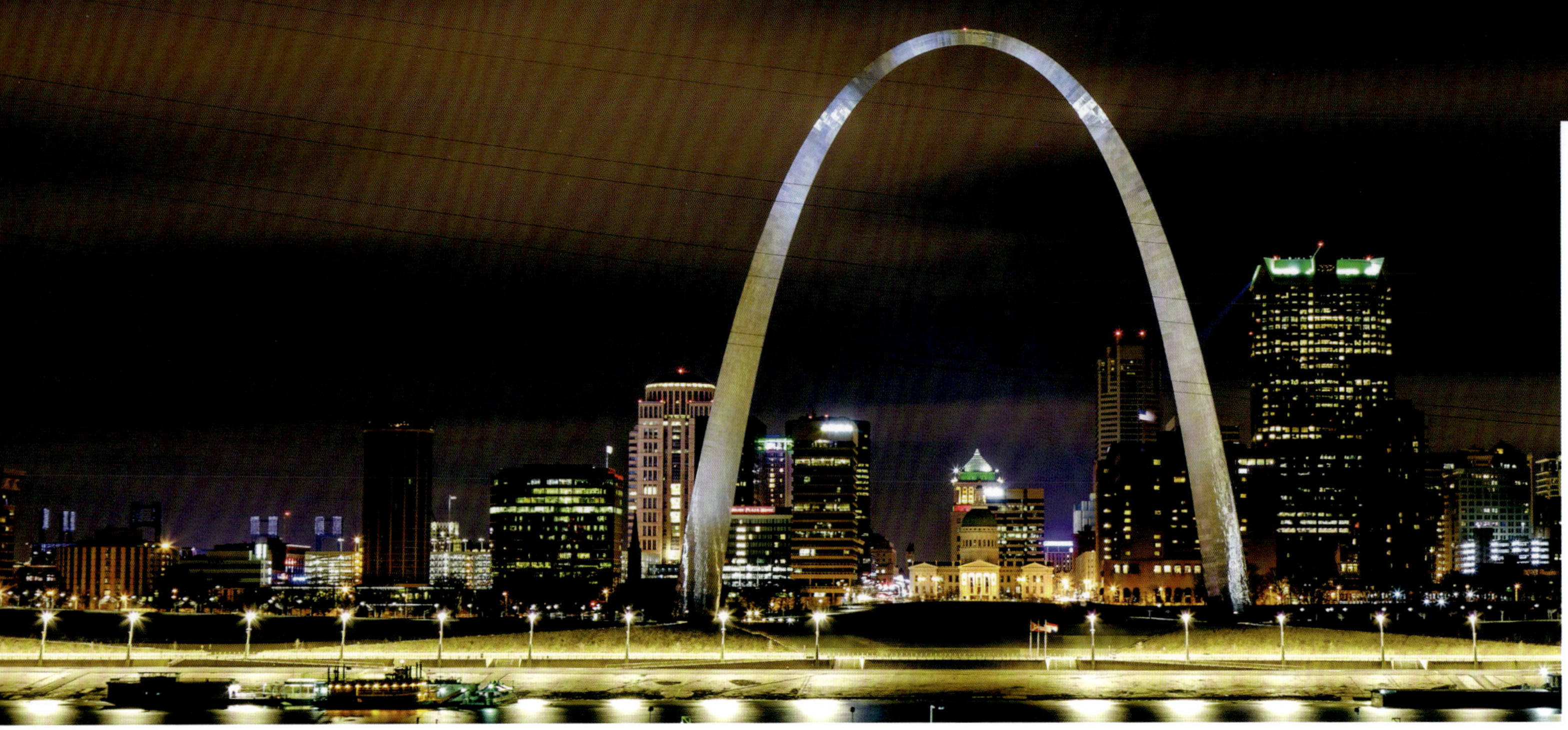

Gateway Arch National Park

Gateway Arch National Park is a prominent and iconic U.S. landmark. The park is home to the Gateway Arch, the world's tallest arch, and is located near the starting point of the Lewis and Clark Expedition. The park encompasses 91 acres and includes historical sites, museums, and scenic views along the Mississippi River.

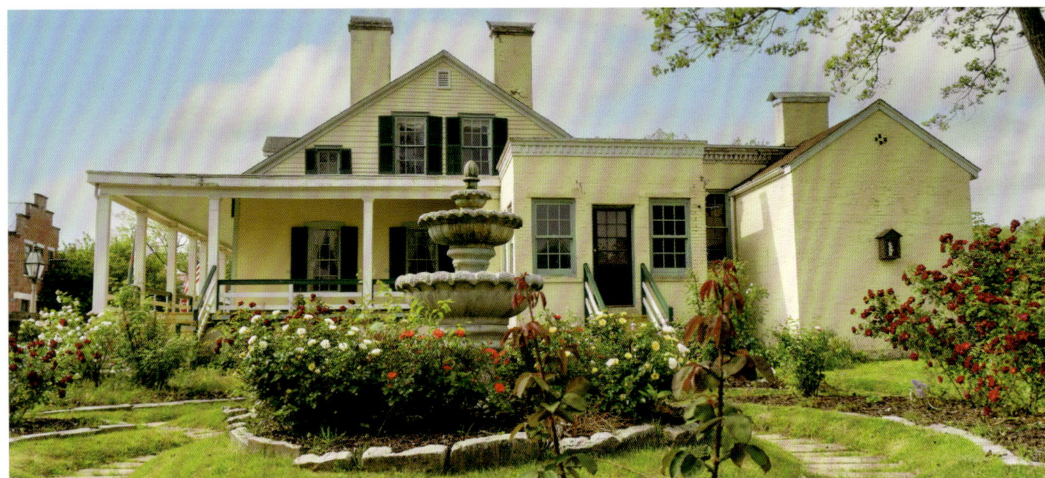

Ste. Geneviève National Historical Park

Ste. Geneviève National Historical Park preserves the history of French colonial America in the Mississippi River Valley. The park was established to protect and interpret the unique history of the area, which played a key role in the expansion of the U.S., and its settlement by French immigrants. The park offers a look into the French colonial architecture, cultural heritage, and the life of early settlers in Missouri.

Butterfield Overland National Historic Trail

The Butterfield Overland National Historic Trail commemorates the mail route that stretched along the southern United States from St. Louis, Missouri, and Memphis, Tennessee, to San Francisco, California. Starting in 1858, stagecoaches left twice a week carrying passengers, freight, and mail.

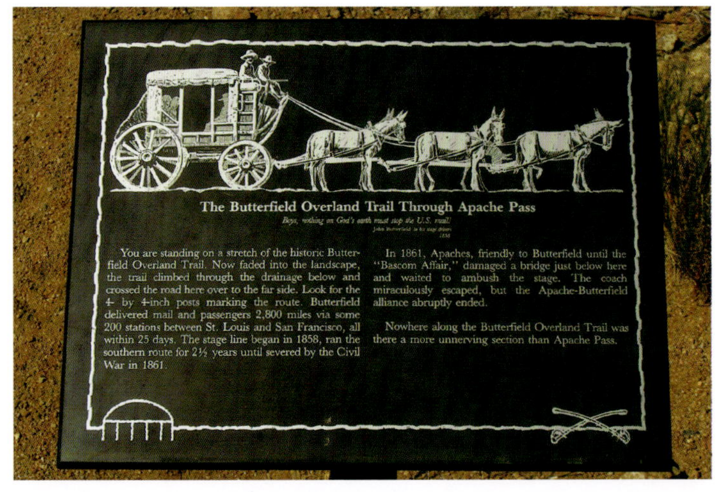

George Washington Carver National Monument

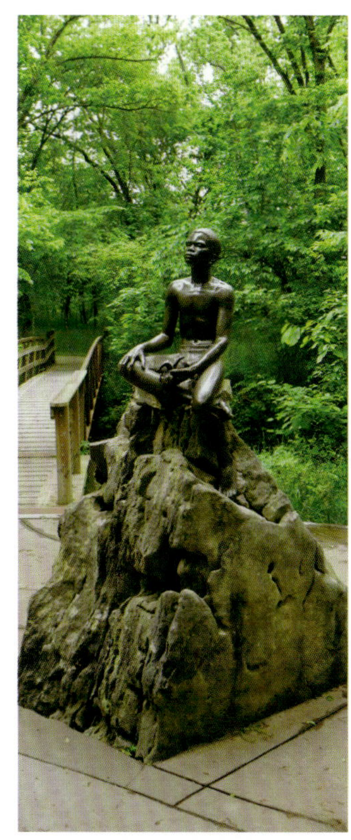

George Washington Carver National Monument preserves the childhood home and legacy of George Washington Carver, an influential African American agricultural scientist, educator, and inventor. Carver is best known for his work with peanuts and other crops, and for promoting sustainable agricultural practices. The park honors his contributions to science, agriculture, and education, as well as his commitment to improving the lives of farmers in the South.

Harry S Truman National Historic Site

Harry S Truman National Historic Site preserves the home and legacy of Harry S. Truman, the 33rd President of the United States. Truman is known for his leadership during the end of World War II, the decision to drop atomic bombs on Japan, the Marshall Plan for rebuilding Europe, and his role in establishing the United Nations and the NATO alliance. The site provides visitors with a glimpse into Truman's life before, during, and after his presidency.

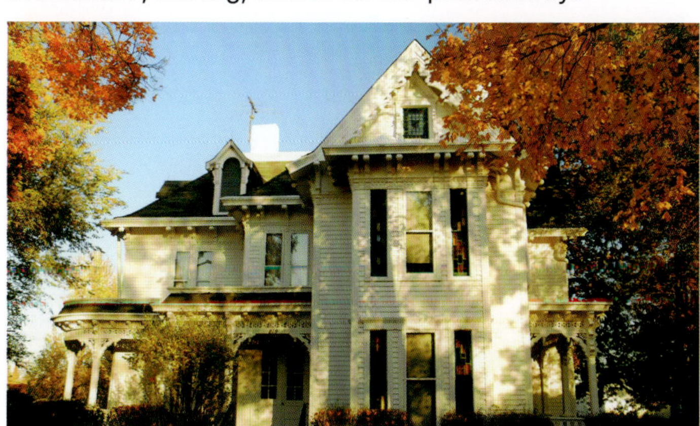

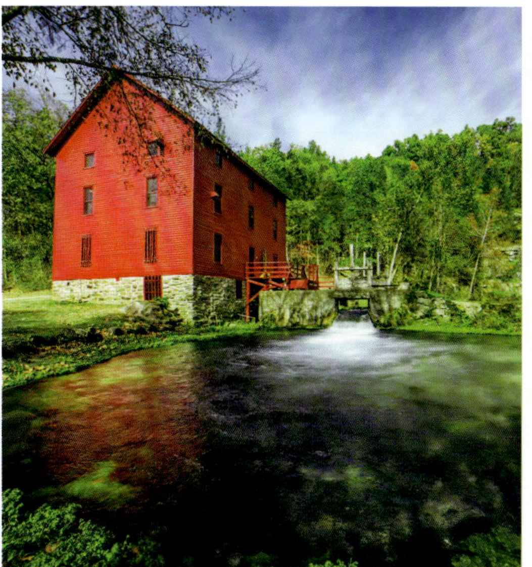

Ozark National Scenic Riverways

Located in the Ozark Highlands of southern Missouri, the Ozark National Scenic Riverways is the first national park to protect a river system. Established in 1964 to preserve the pristine beauty of the Current River and the Jacks Fork River, along with their surrounding natural areas, this park is renowned for its clear-flowing rivers, scenic limestone bluffs, extensive caves, and diverse wildlife, offering visitors a unique opportunity to experience outdoor recreation and natural beauty.

Ulysses S. Grant National Historic Site

Ulysses S. Grant National Historic Site preserves the White Haven estate, the former home of Ulysses S. Grant, the 18th President of the United States and prominent Union general during the American Civil War. The site provides a deeper understanding of Grant's life before, during, and after his presidency, including his military career, leadership, and personal experiences.

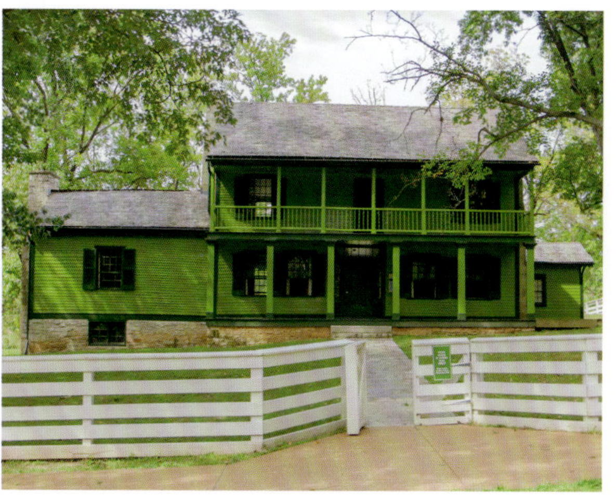

Wilson's Creek National Battlefield

Wilson's Creek National Battlefield is a historic site located near Springfield, MO, that preserves the location of the Battle of Wilson's Creek, a significant early engagement of the American Civil War. The battle, fought on August 10, 1861, was one of the first major conflicts of the war west of the Mississippi River. The site offers visitors a chance to explore the battle's historical significance, the people involved, and its impact on the court of the war.

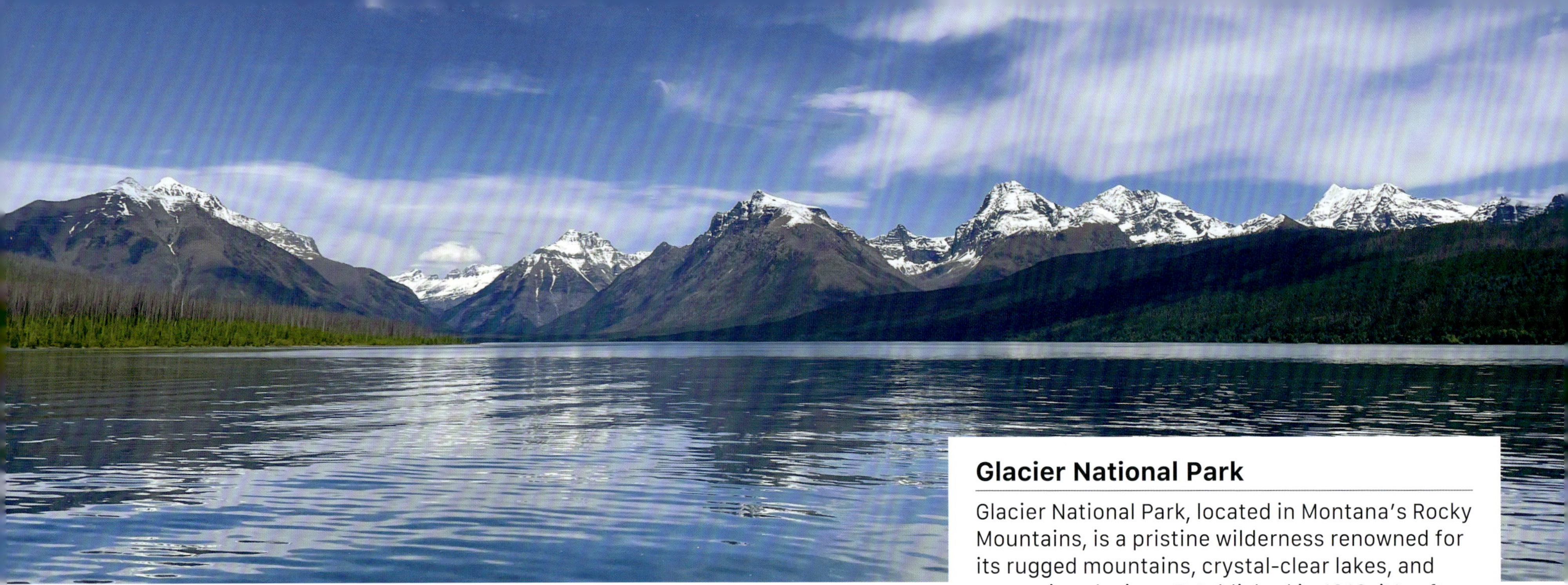

Glacier National Park

Glacier National Park, located in Montana's Rocky Mountains, is a pristine wilderness renowned for its rugged mountains, crystal-clear lakes, and expansive glaciers. Established in 1910, it's often referred to as the "Crown of the Continent Ecosystem" due to its amazing landscapes, diverse ecosystems, and rich history.

MONTANA

Nez Perce National Historical Park

Nez Perce National Historical Park is a unique collection of sites across four states—Idaho, Montana, Oregon, and Washington—that preserves and commemorates the history and culture of the Nimíipuu, or the Nez Perce people. Established in 1965, it honors their enduring legacy, historic events, and connection to the land.

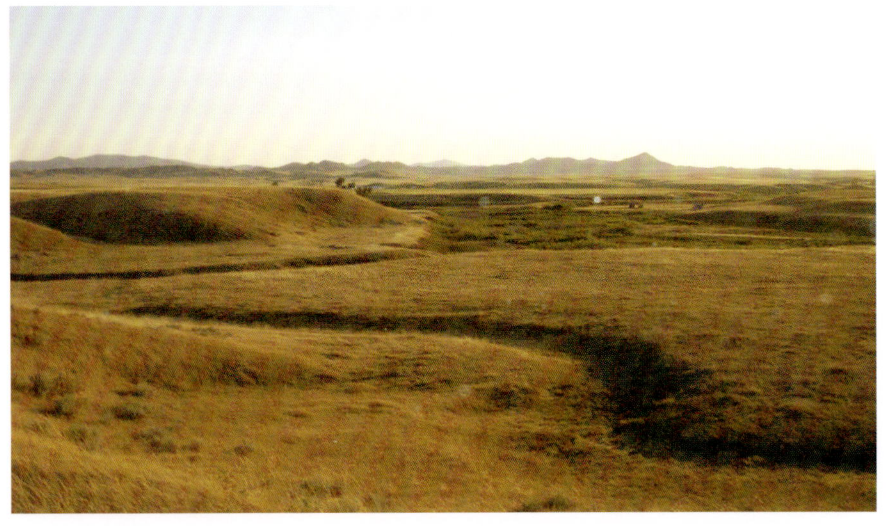

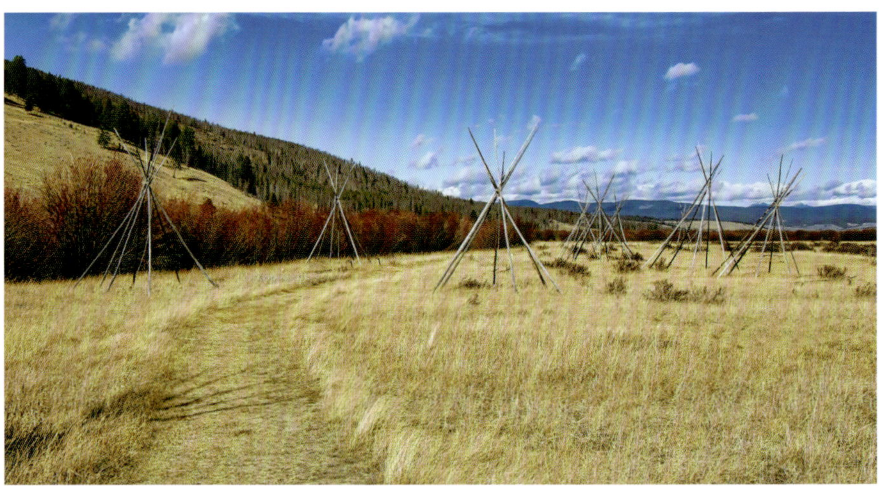

Big Hole National Battlefield

Big Hole National Battlefield is a significant site commemorating a tragic event during the Nez Perce War of 1877 where the U.S. Army launched a surprise attack on approximately 800 fleeing Nez Perce, including women and children. The site honors the bravery and resilience of the Nez Perce people, and reflects the broader struggles of Native American tribes during westward expansion.

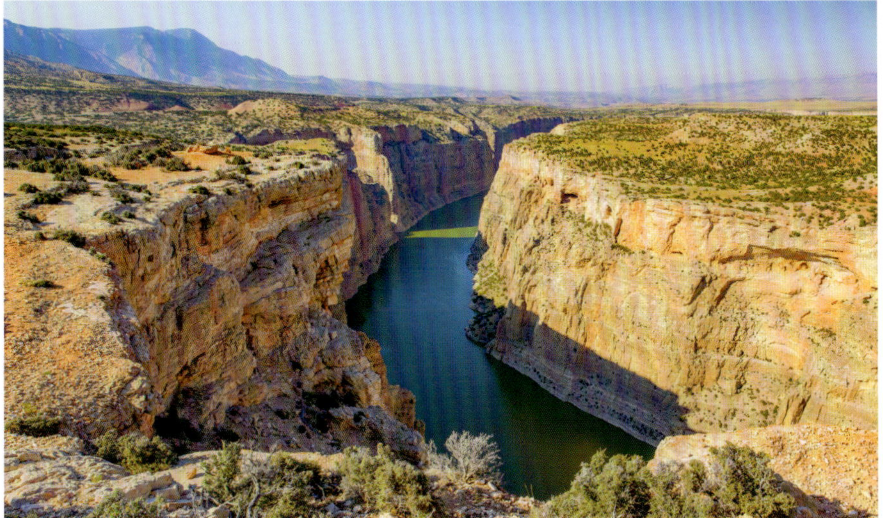

Bighorn Canyon National Recreation Area

Bighorn Canyon National Recreation Area is a stunning landscape of deep canyons, vast reservoirs, and varied wildlife that straddles the border of Montana and Wyoming. Established in 1966, it offers a mix of recreational opportunities and cultural history, making it a unique destination for adventurers and nature enthusiasts alike. Compared to the South District, the northern half is less developed, providing a more remote and tranquil experience.

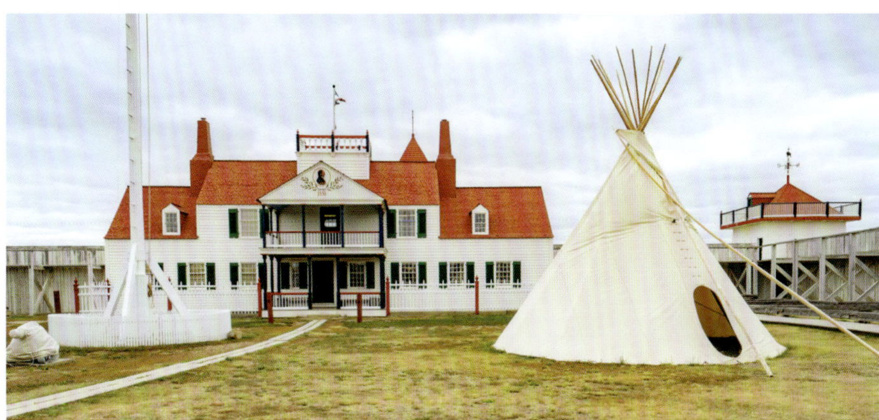

Fort Union Trading Post National Historic Site

Fort Union Trading Post National Historic Site, located near the confluence of the Missouri and Yellowstone Rivers on the North Dakota-Montana border, is a restored 19th-century trading post that highlights the pivotal role of trade in shaping relationships between Native American tribes and European-American traders. It was established in 1828 and became the most significant fur trading post on the Upper Missouri River.

Grant-Kohrs Ranch National Historic Site

Grant-Kohrs National Historic Site preserves the history of the American cattle ranching industry. It offers a glimpse into the life and legacy of cowboys, ranchers, and the open range cattle era, showcasing a working cattle ranch and its historic buildings. Visitors can tour the Grant-Kohrs Ranch House, which has been restored with period furnishings, offering insight into the life of a prosperous ranching family.

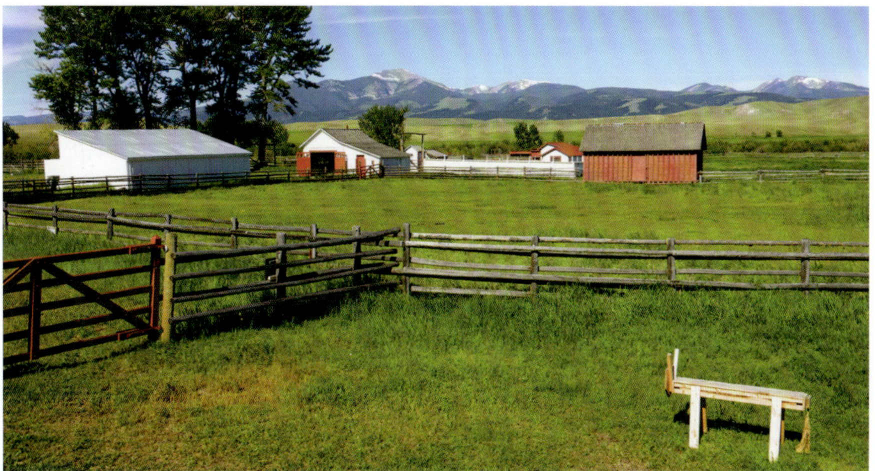

Little Bighorn Battlefield National Monument

Little Bighorn Battlefield National Monument commemorates the famous 1876 battle between the 7th Cavalry Regiment and the combined forces of the Lakota, Northern Cheyenne, and Arapaho tribes. Known historically as Custer's Last Stand, it's a poignant reminder of the clash between Native American cultures and westward expansion.

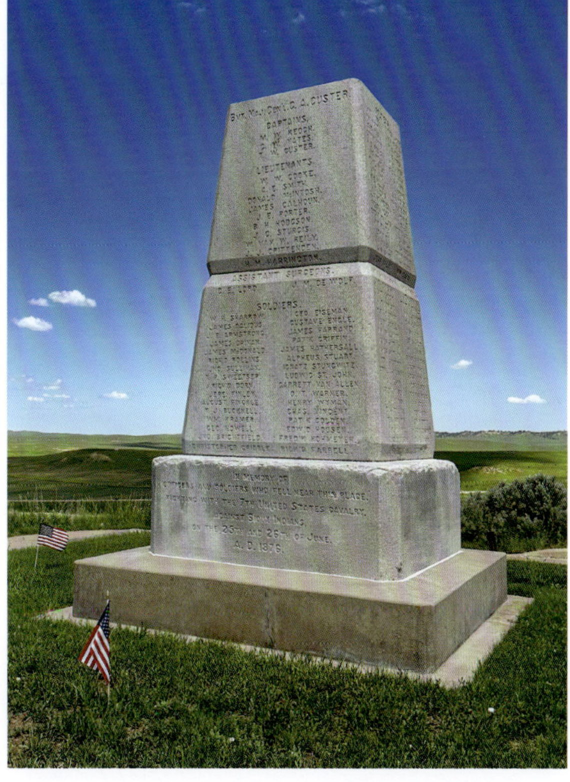

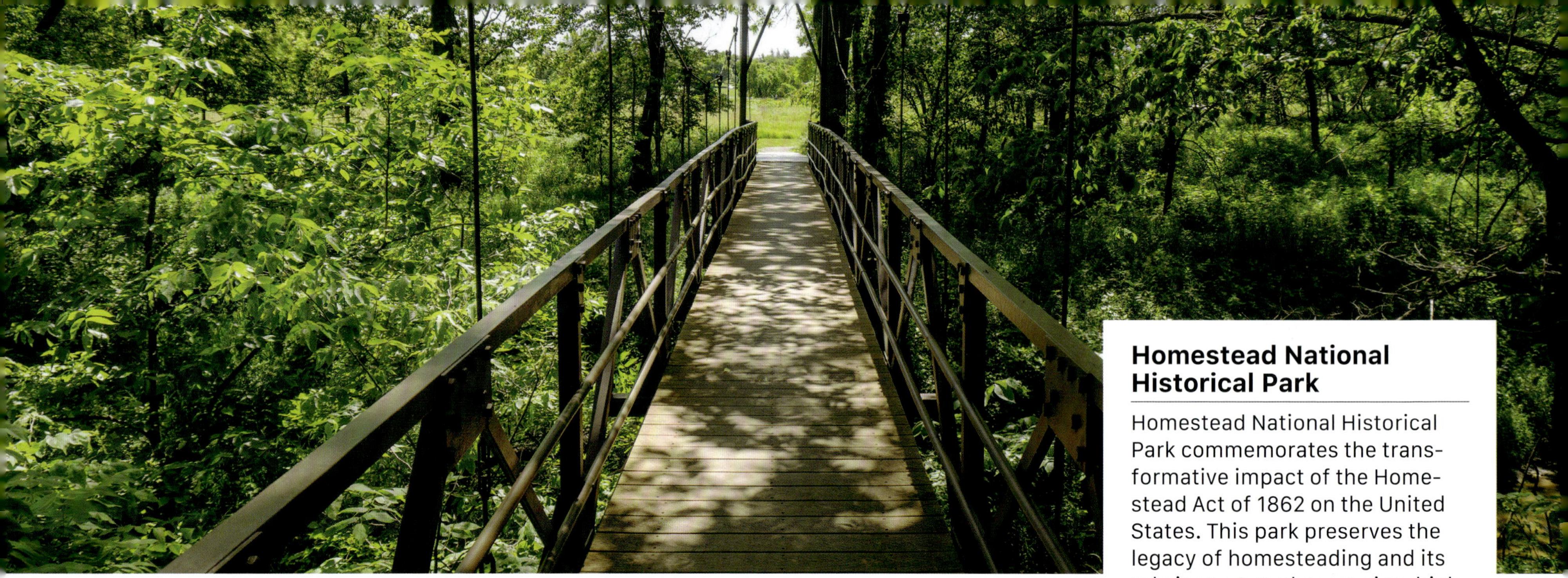

Homestead National Historical Park

Homestead National Historical Park commemorates the transformative impact of the Homestead Act of 1862 on the United States. This park preserves the legacy of homesteading and its role in westward expansion, highlighting the challenges, triumphs, and profound changes it brought to the land and its people.

NEBRASKA

Agate Fossil Beds National Monument

Agate Fossil Beds National Monument is a unique site that combines paleontological discoveries, Native American history, and stunning landscapes. The park preserves ancient Miocene-era fossil beds and serves as a testament to the region's geological and cultural richness.

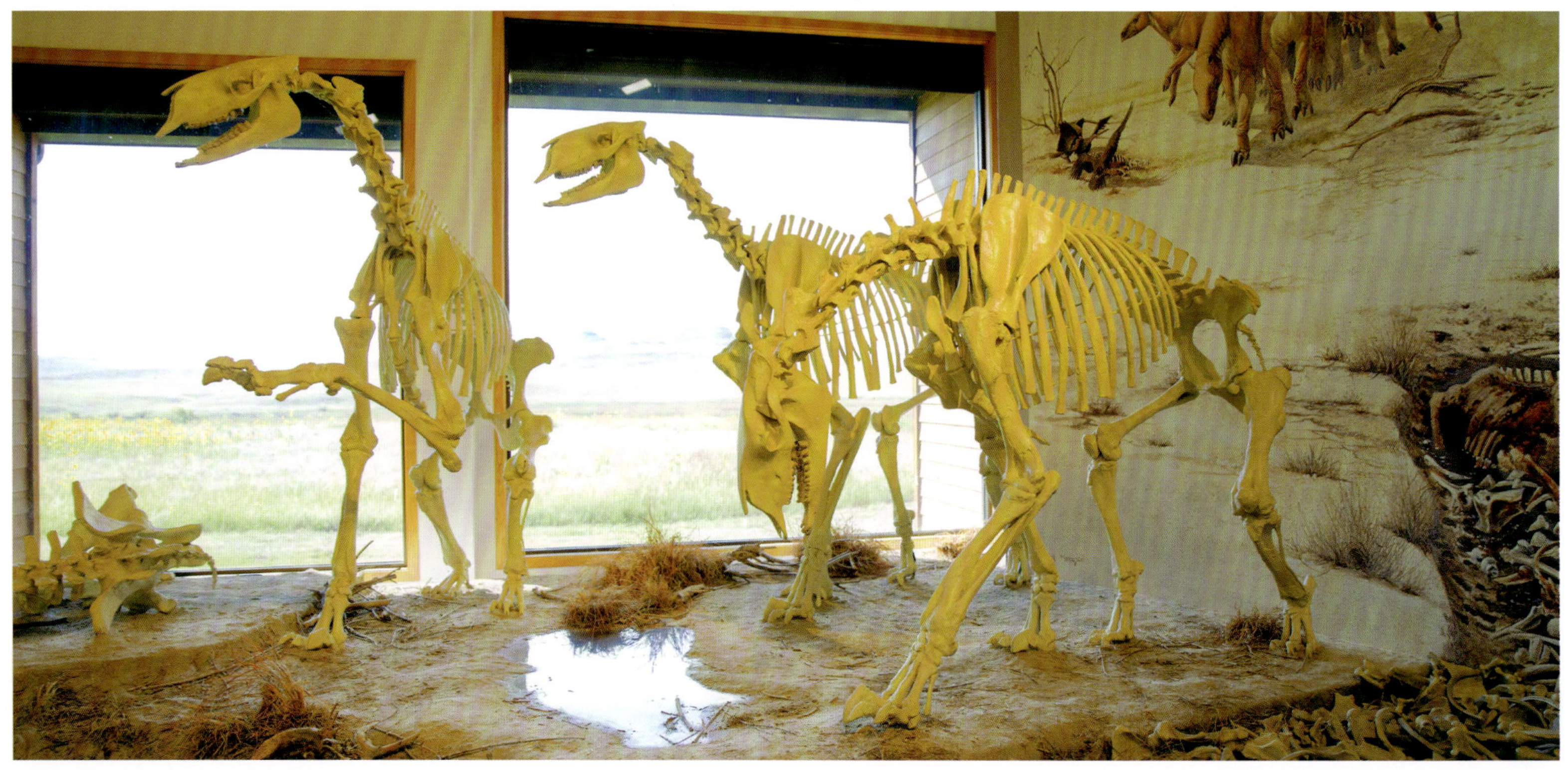

Missouri National Recreational River

Located along the border of Nebraska and South Dakota, the Missouri National Recreational River preserves the free-flowing segments of the Missouri River, offering visitors a glimpse of the river's natural beauty, cultural history, and recreational opportunities. Unlike much of the river that has been dammed or channelized, these stretches retain a more natural, untamed character.

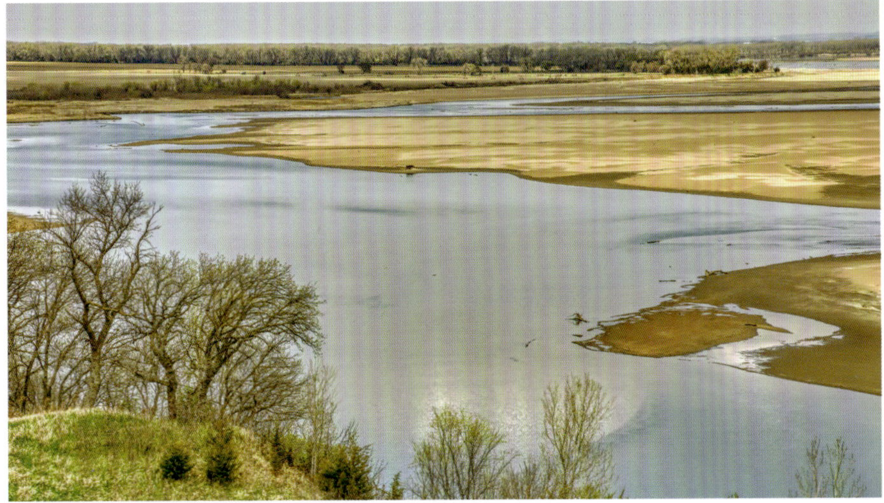

Niobrara National Scenic River

The Niobrara National Scenic River is a 76-mile stretch of river renowned for its breathtaking scenery, varied ecosystems, and recreational opportunities. Designated as a National Scenic River in 1991, it offers a tranquil escape into nature and a chance to experience one of the most biologically diverse regions in the Great Plains.

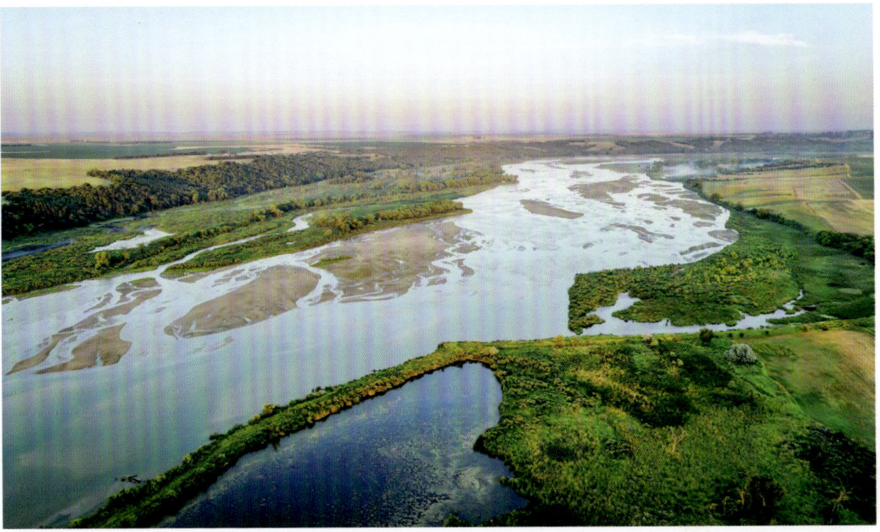

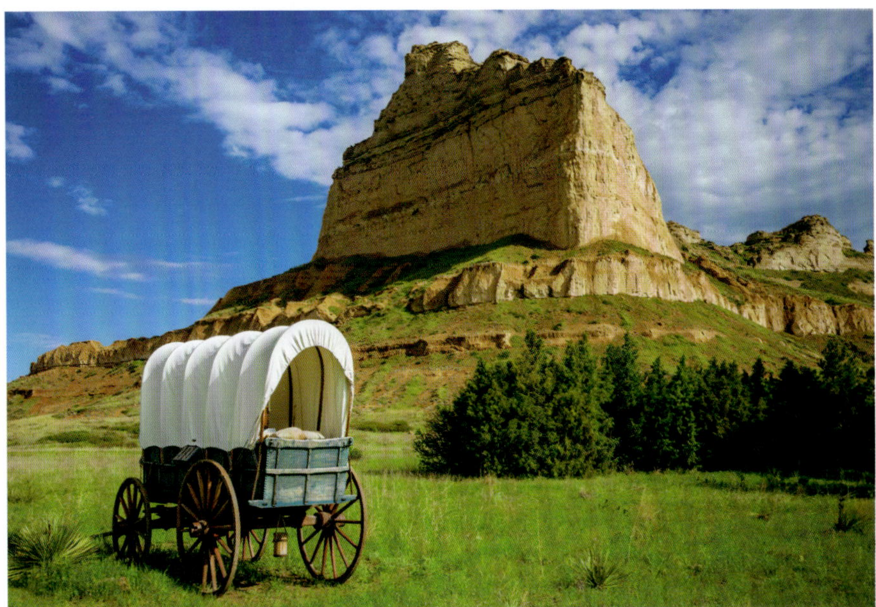

Scotts Bluff National Monument

Scotts Bluff National Monument is a striking natural landmark that has served as a beacon for travelers for thousands of years. Rising over 800 feet above the North Platte River, it was an essential waypoint for Native Americans, fur traders, and pioneers traveling westward on the Oregon, California, and Pony Express Trails.

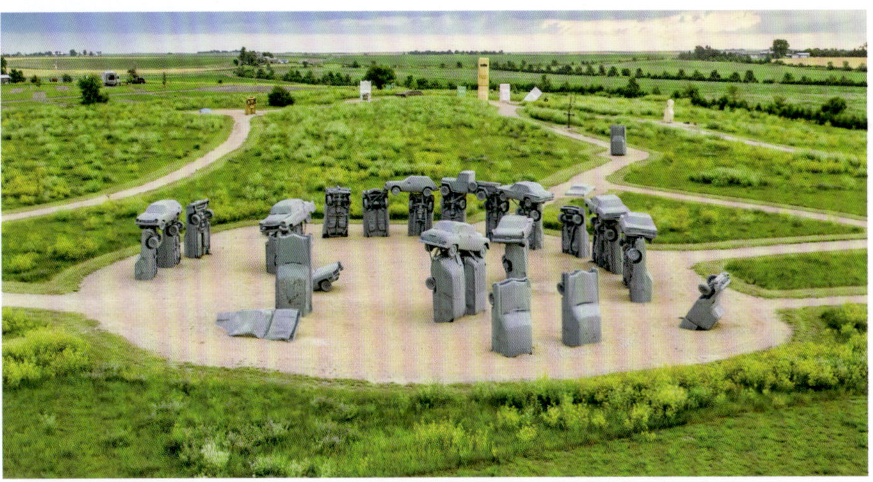

Carhenge

Located near Alliance, NE, Carhenge is a quirky and iconic roadside attraction that reimagines England's Stonehenge using vintage cards. This artistic installation, created by Jim Reinders, draws thousands of visitors each year, offering a playful and unique experience in the Nebraska Sandhills.

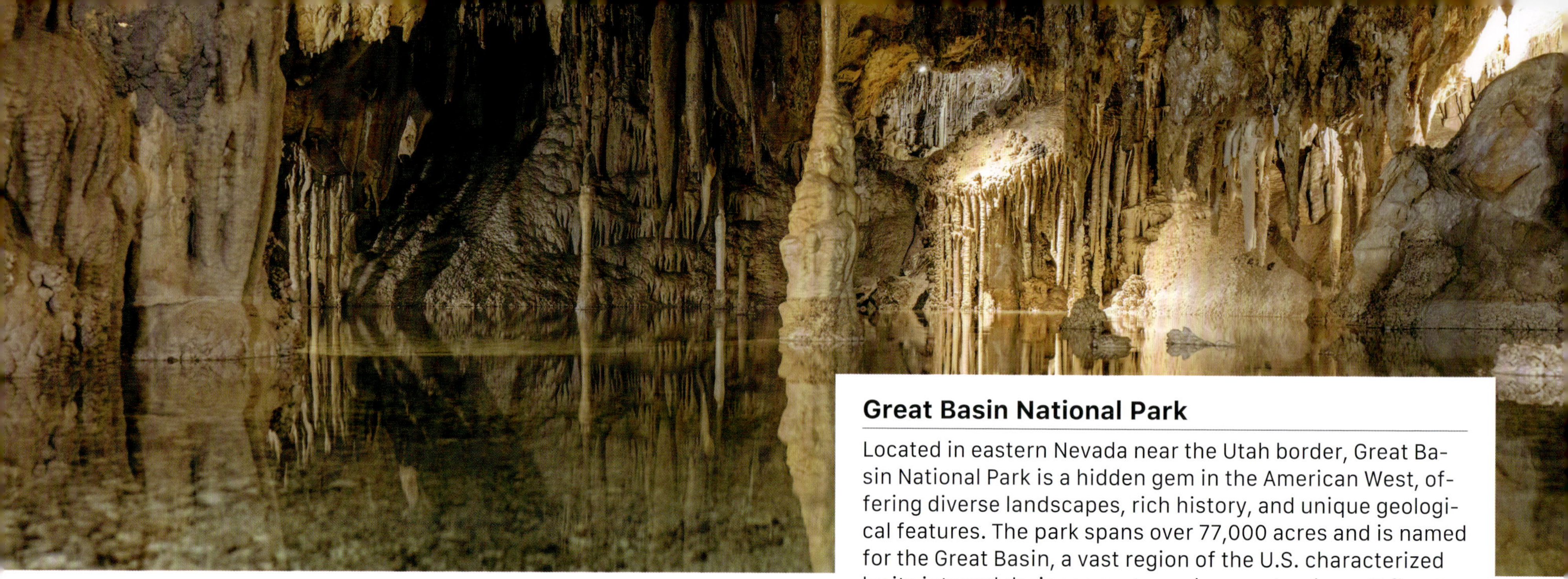

NEVADA

Great Basin National Park

Located in eastern Nevada near the Utah border, Great Basin National Park is a hidden gem in the American West, offering diverse landscapes, rich history, and unique geological features. The park spans over 77,000 acres and is named for the Great Basin, a vast region of the U.S. characterized by its internal drainage system where water doesn't flow to the sea. Visitors can explore the Lehman Caves *(see above)*, a limestone cave system with extraordinary formations, including stalactites, stalagmites, and rare "cave shields."

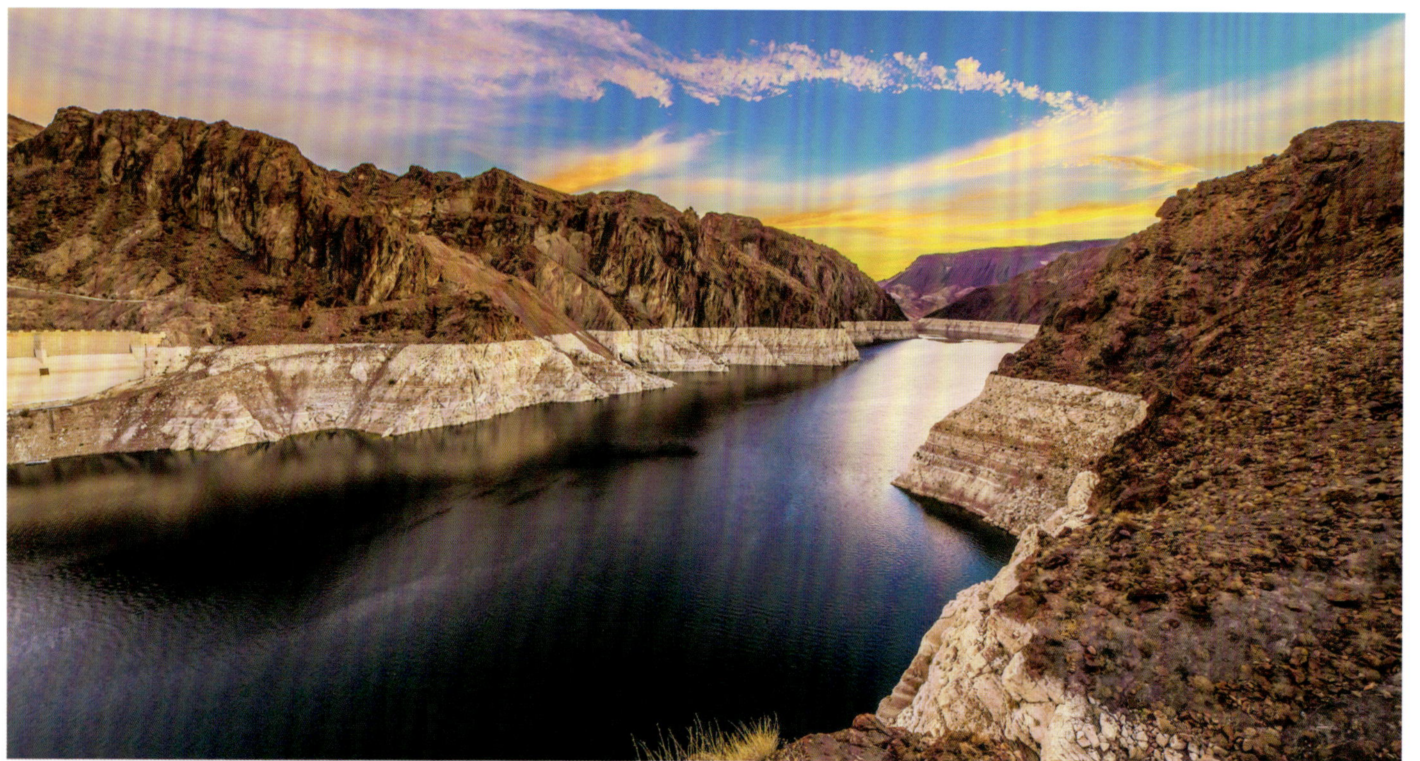

Lake Mead National Recreation Area

Lake Mead National Recreation Area is a vast and breathtaking landscape spanning parts of Nevada and Arizona, centered around Lake Mead—the largest reservoir in the U.S. The park, established in 1964, offers a wide variety of outdoor recreation, dramatic desert landscapes, and rich history, all set against the backdrop of the Colorado River. Visitors can enjoy tours of the Hoover Dam and adventures set in three of the four U.S. desert ecosystems: the Mojave Desert, the Great Basin Desert, and the Sonoran Desert.

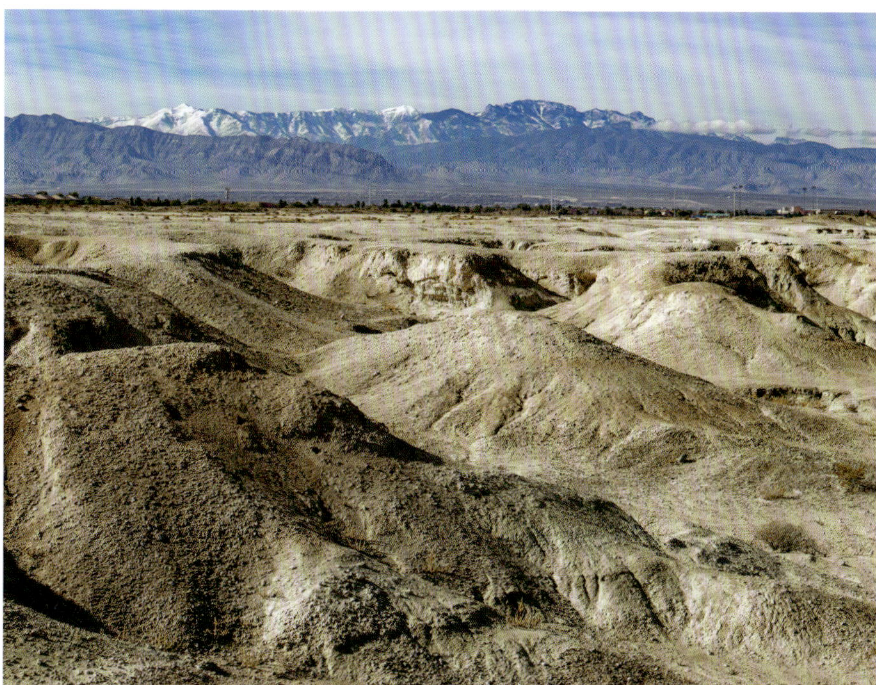

Tule Springs Fossil Beds National Monument

Tule Springs Fossil Beds National Monument protects a rich repository of Pleistocene-era fossils, providing a glimpse into the ancient environment of the region. Species found here include mammoths, saber-toothed cats, giant ground sloths, camels, and bison.

Area 51

Area 51 is a highly classified U.S. Air Force facility located in the Nevada desert, approximately 83 miles north of Las Vegas. Officially known as Groom Lake, it's been the subject of numerous conspiracy theories and rumors, particularly regarding extraterrestrial life and UFOs. While access to Area 51 is rigorously restricted, with no public entry allowed, its endurance in popular culture has resulted in many alien-themed restaurants and gift shops populating the surrounding area.

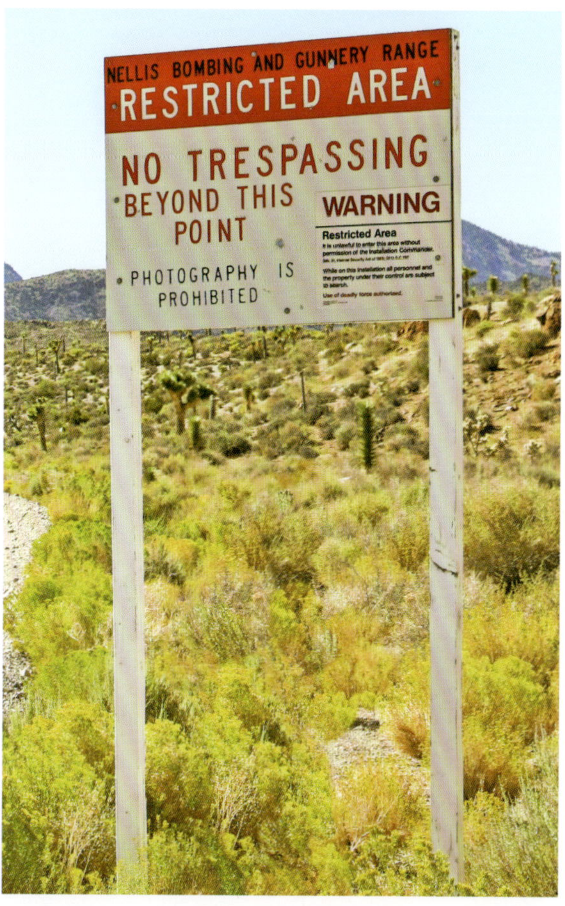

Red Rock Canyon National Conservation Area

Located just 17 miles west of Las Vegas, NV, Red Rock Canyon National Conservation Area is a stunning desert landscape known for its vibrant red sandstone formations, hiking trails, rock climbing opportunities, and varied wildlife. As a National Conservation Area managed by the Bureau of Land Management, it offers visitors a blend of outdoor recreation, geological wonders, and rich history.

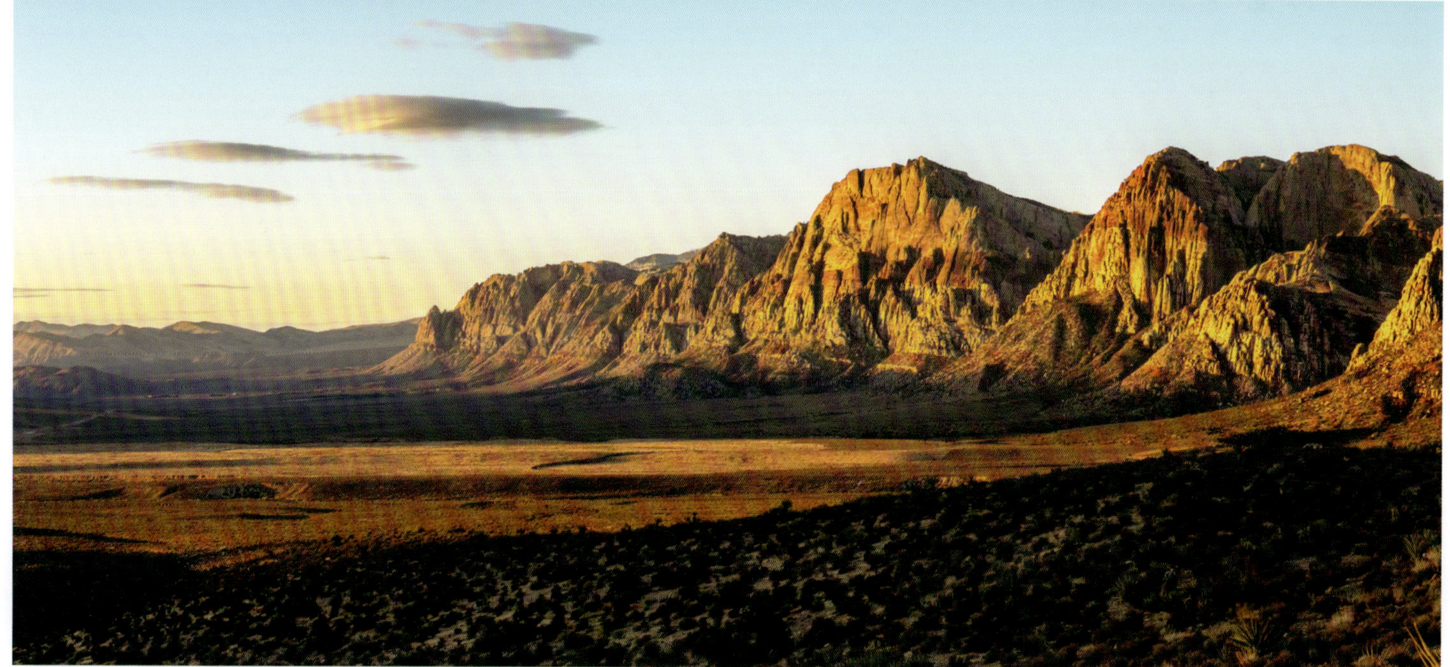

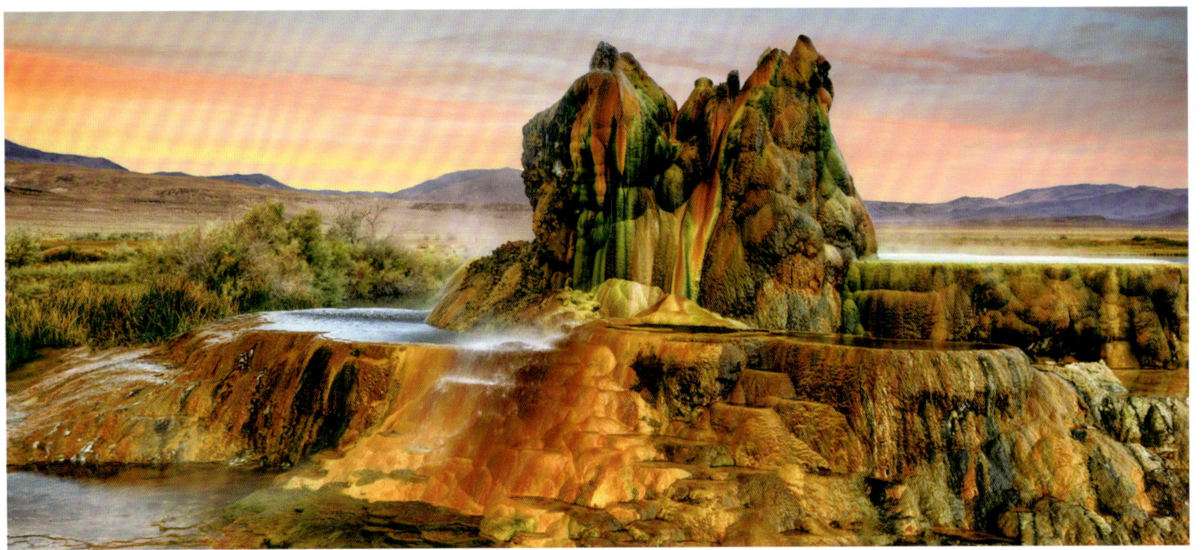

Fly Geyser

Located in Nevada's Black Rock Desert, Fly Geyser is an amazing and colorful geothermal feature that formed accidentally in 1964 during a well drilling. The geyser resulted from water erupting through geothermal pockets and depositing minerals over time, creating a vibrant, cone-shaped structure that continues to grow. The geyser is part of a privately-owned property managed by the nonprofit Friends of Black Rock-High Rock. Guided tours are available, allowing visitors to view the geyser and its surrounding wetlands.

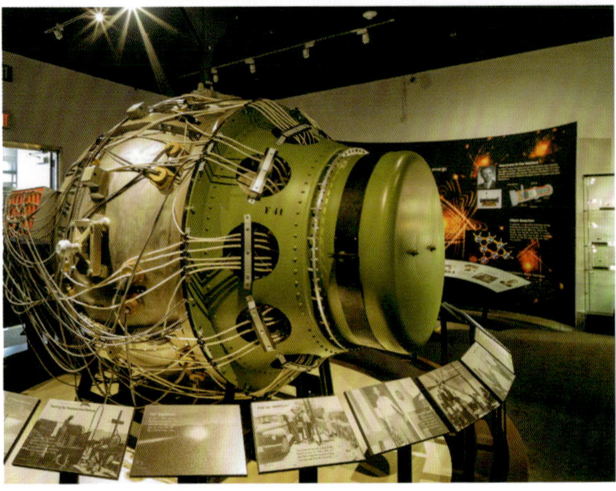

National Atomic Testing Museum

The National Atomic Testing Museum is dedicated to preserving and showcasing the history of nuclear testing, and its impact on science, technology, and world events. Affiliated with the Smithsonian Institution, the museum provides an in-depth look at the U.S. nuclear weapons testing program, particularly at the Nevada Test Site, which operated from 1951 to 1992.

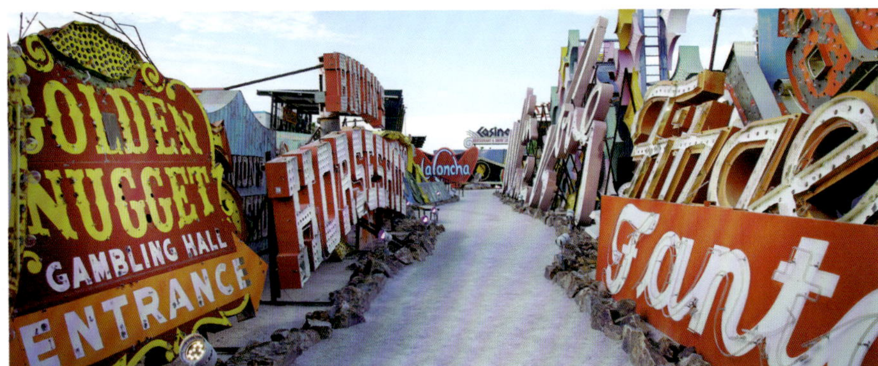

The Neon Museum

The Neon Museum is a unique attraction dedicated to preserving and showcasing Las Vegas's iconic neon signage. Founded in 1996, the museum features an outdoor exhibition called the Neon Boneyard where visitors can view a collection of over 200 historic signs, many of which were once part of famous casinos and hotels. The museum also offers educational programs, exhibits, and guided tours, providing insights into the history of the city and the craftsmanship behind the signs. At night, many of the restored signs are lit up, offering a spectacular display that brings the city's neon legacy to life.

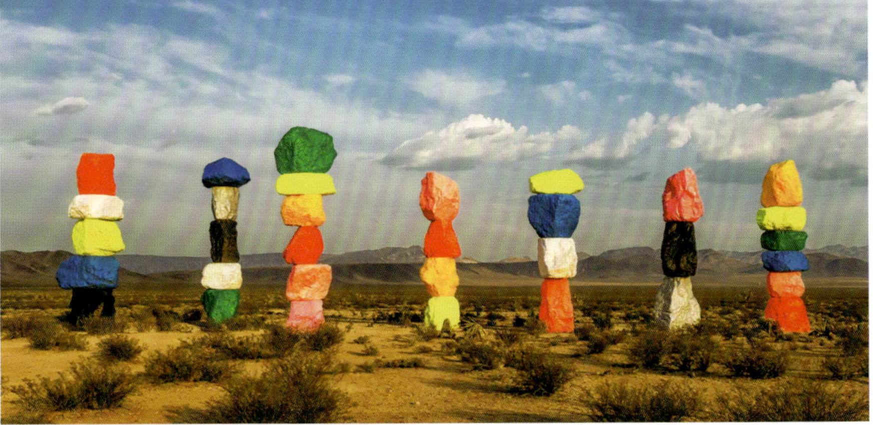

Seven Magic Mountains

Seven Magic Mountains is an intriguing public art installation located just south of Las Vegas in Ivanpah Valley. Created by artist Ugo Rondinone, this vibrant installation consists of seven brightly colored boulders, each standing over 30 feet tall. The installation is set against the backdrop of the Nevada desert, providing a striking contrast between the natural landscape and the bold, artificial colors of the rocks.

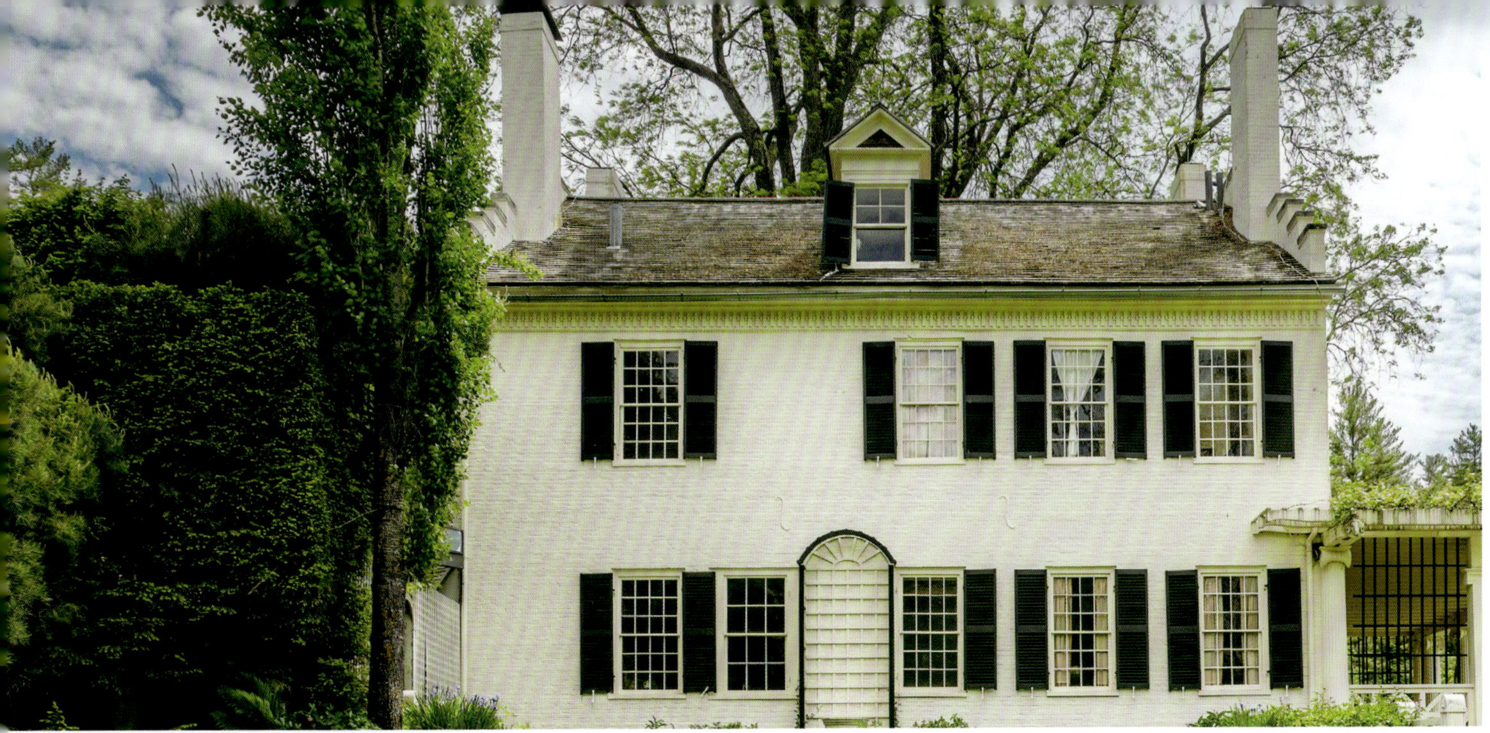

Saint-Gaudens National Historical Park

Saint-Gaudens National Historical Park is dedicated to the life and work of Augustus Saint-Gaudens, one of America's greatest sculptors. The park encompasses the home, studio, and gardens of Saint-Gaudens, offering visitors a chance to explore the creative space where many of his most famous works were conceived. The park is a celebration of his legacy and contributions to American art, and it offers a beautiful setting for those interested in art, history, and nature.

NEW HAMPSHIRE

Kancamagus Highway

The Kancamagus Highway is one of the most scenic drives in the northeastern United States. Spanning 34.5 miles through the White Mountain National Forest, this road offers stunning views of the White Mountains, rivers, and waterfalls. It's especially famous for its vibrant fall foliage, making it a popular destination for nature lovers, photographers, and anyone wanting to experience the beauty of New Hampshire and New England.

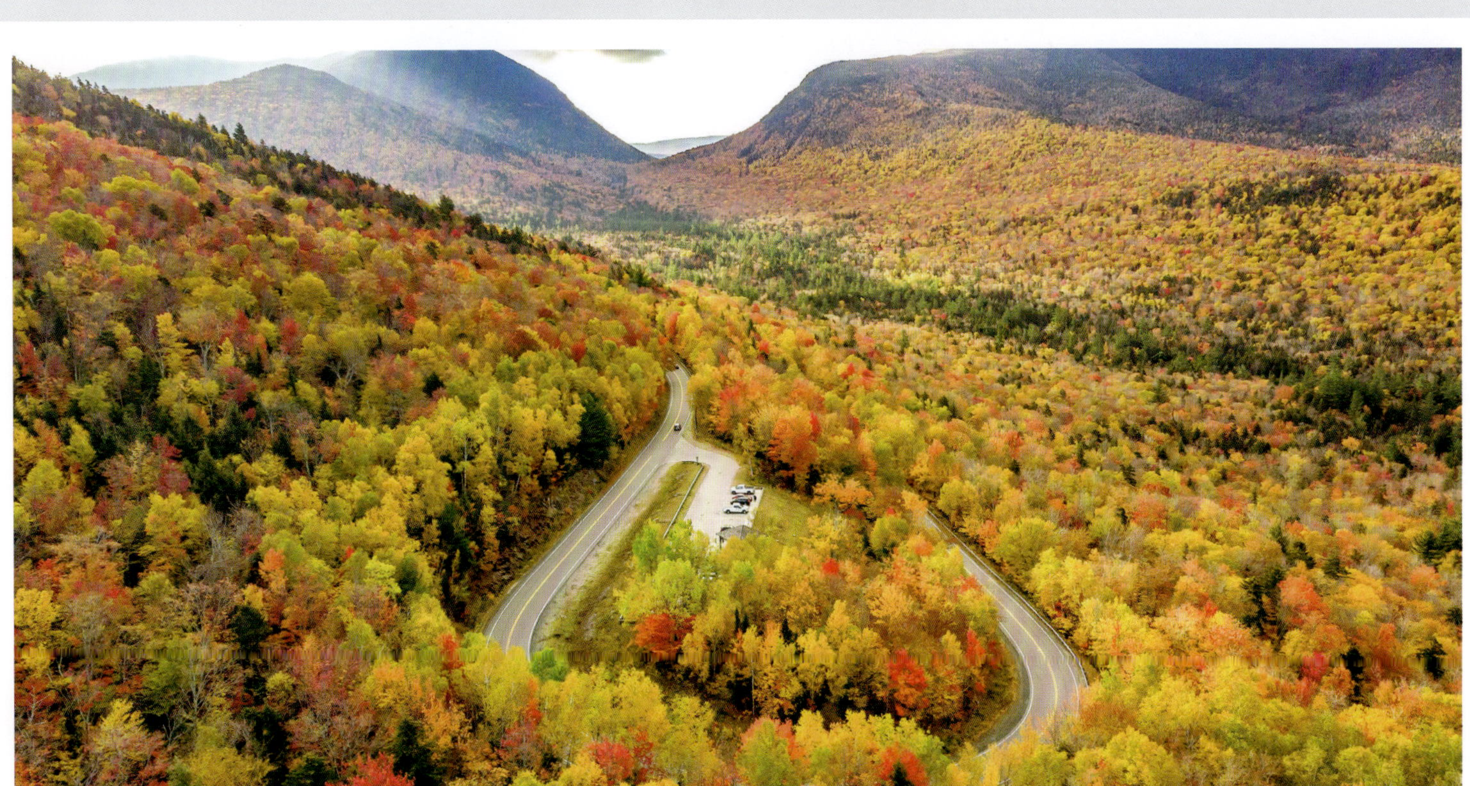

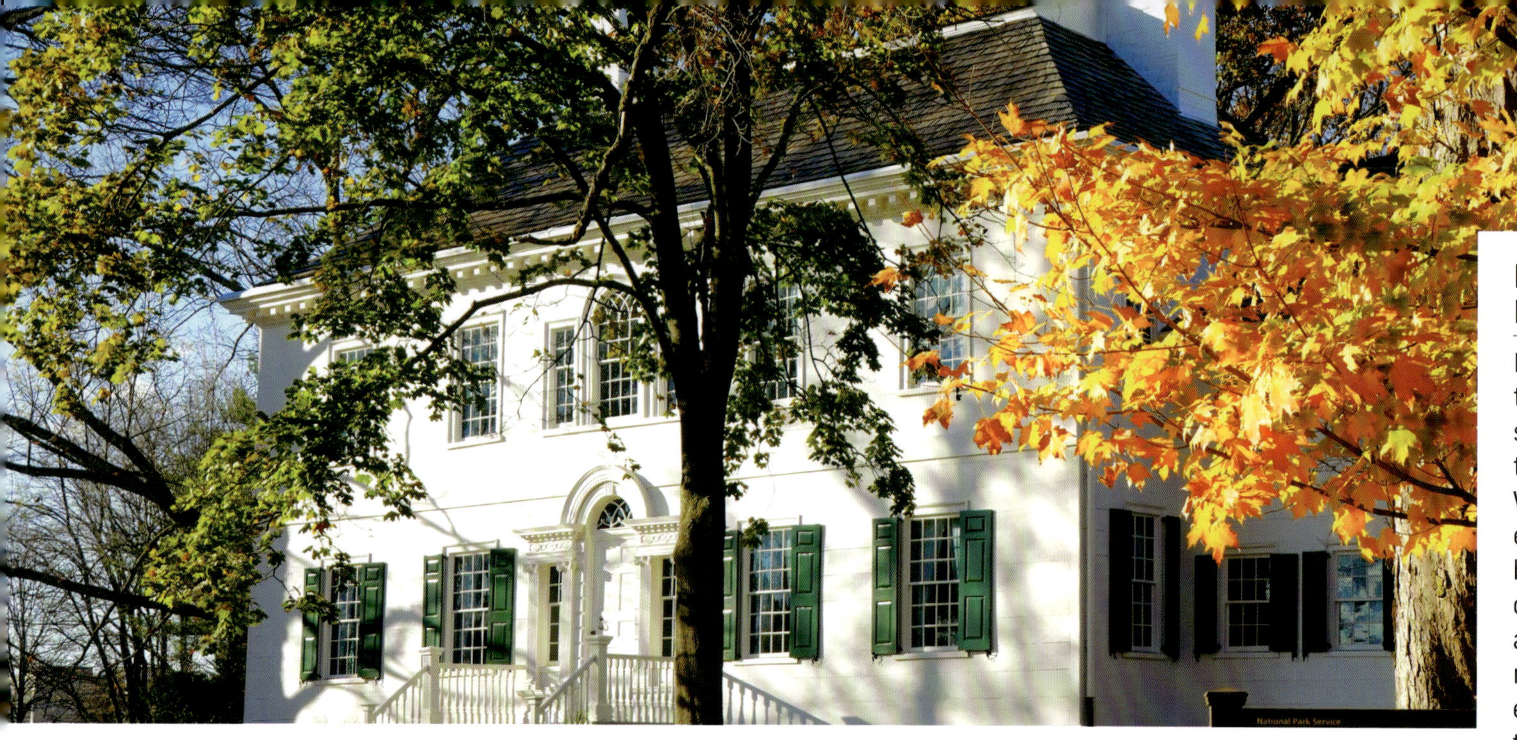

Morristown National Historical Park

Morristown National Historical Park is a significant site preserving the legacy of the American Revolutionary War. It commemorates the events and challenges faced by the Continental Army during the winters of 1777 and 1779–1780 when Morristown served as its winter encampment. Visitors can tour four key sites: Jockey Hollow, Ford Mansion, Fort Nonsense, and Washington's Headquarters Museum.

NEW JERSEY

Paterson Great Falls National Historical Park

Paterson Great Falls National Historical Park is a site of both natural beauty and historical significance. It centers around the Great Falls of the Passaic River, one of the largest waterfalls by volume in the eastern U.S., with a height of 77 feet. The park highlights the role of the falls in America's industrial development.

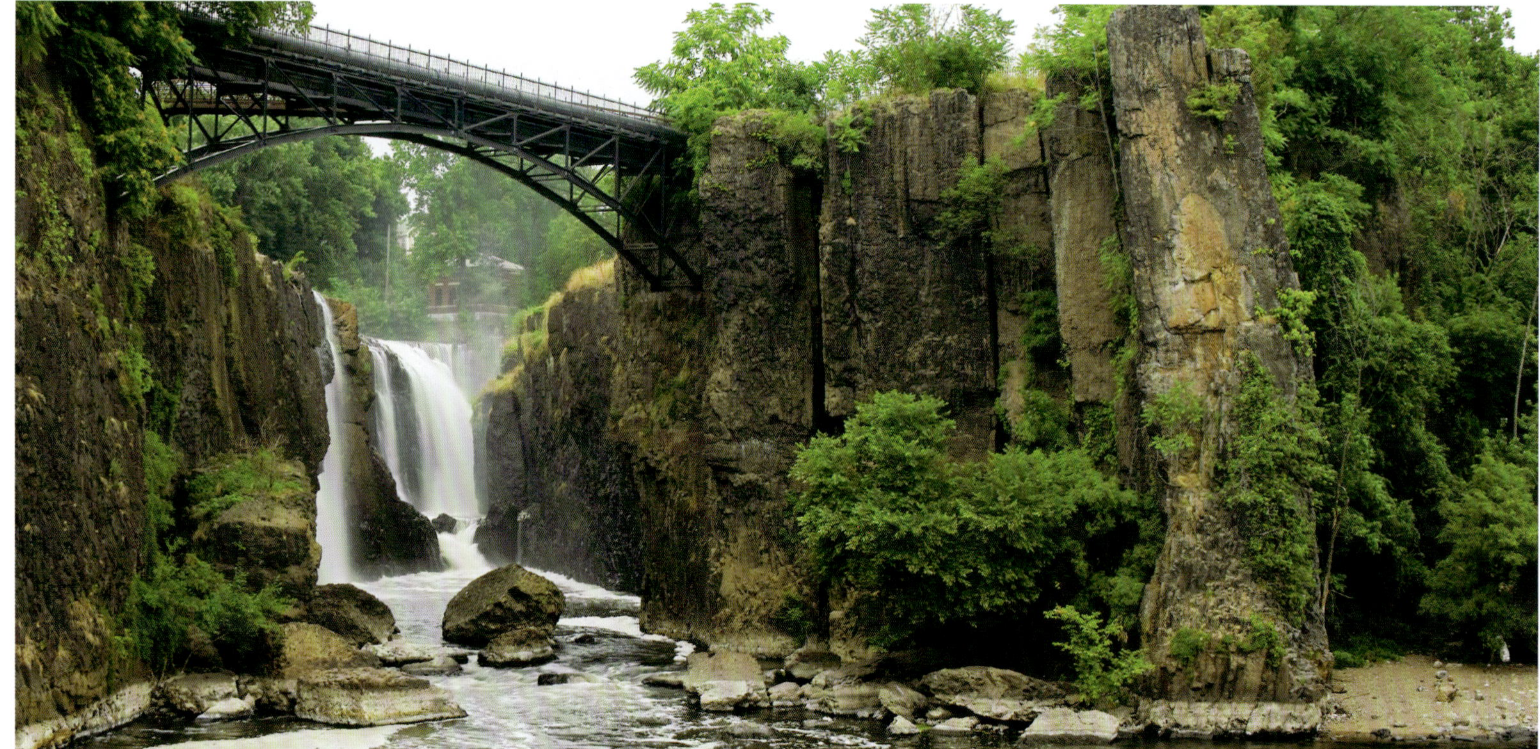

Thomas Edison National Historical Park

Located in West Orange, New Jersey, Thomas Edison National Historical Park preserves the home *(see below)* and laboratory of Thomas Edison, one of America's greatest inventors. The site offers a glimpse into Edison's work and life, showcasing his innovations and contributions to modern technology.

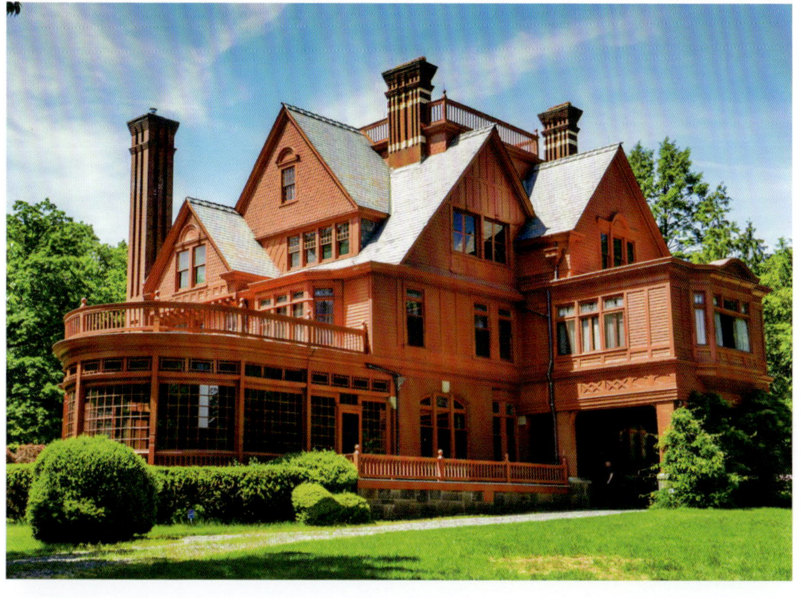

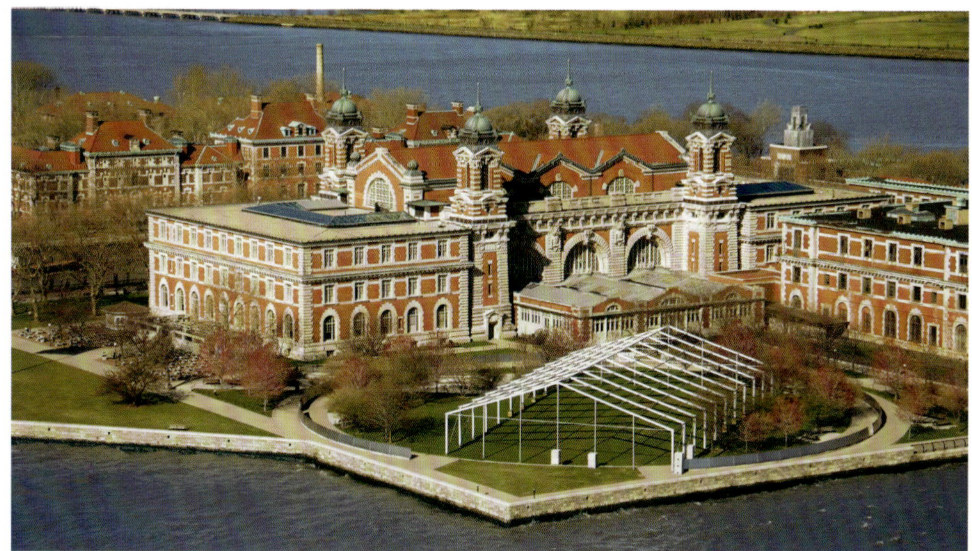

Ellis Island

Ellis Island, part of the Statue of Liberty National Monument, is a historic site located in New York Harbor. It served as the nation's busiest immigration station from 1892 to 1954, processing over 12 million immigrants seeking a new life in America. Today, it's a powerful symbol of the American immigrant experience, and a place for reflection and learning. Most of the island is in Jersey City, NJ, but a small section is an exclave of New York City.

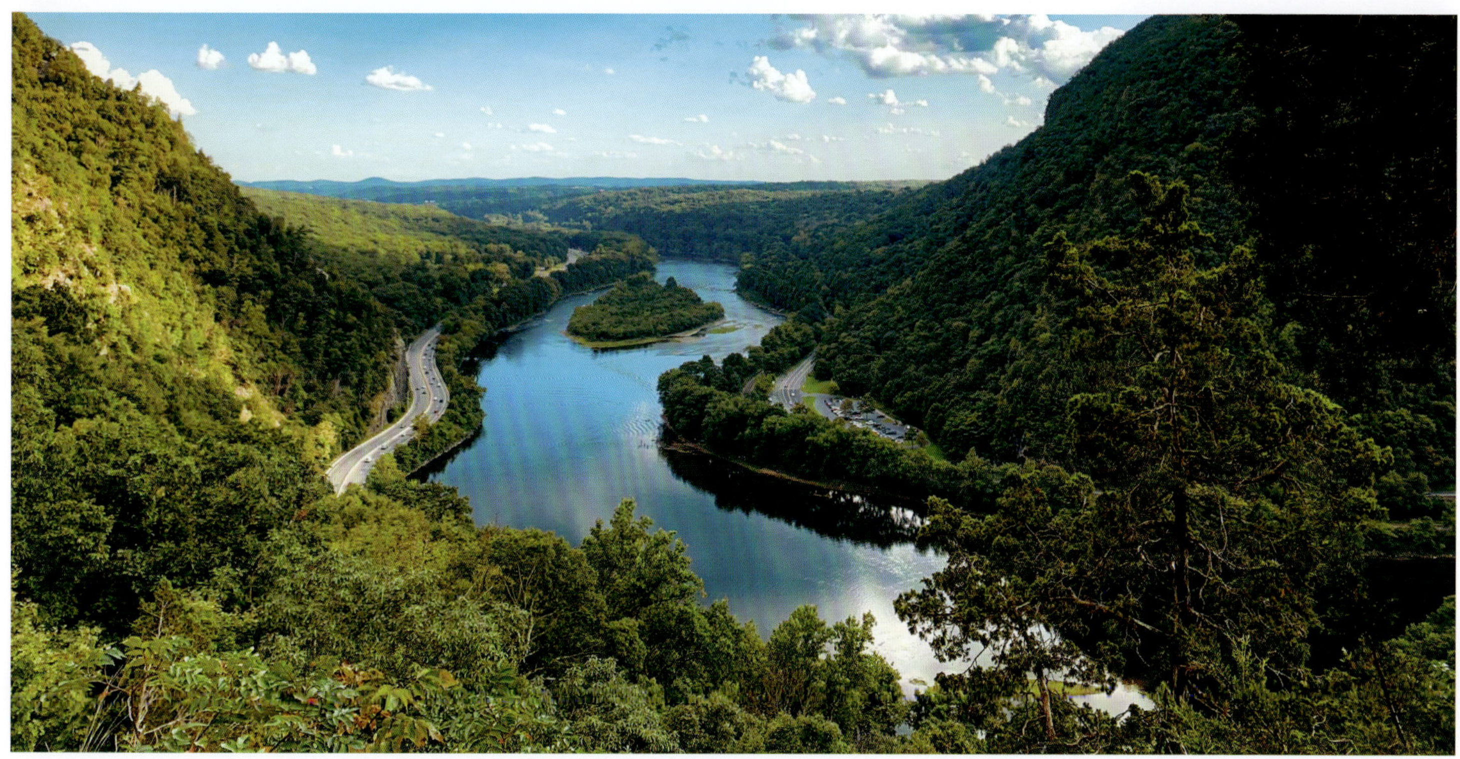

Delaware Water Gap National Recreation Area

Delaware Water Gap National Recreation Area spans over 70,000 acres along the Delaware River in Pennsylvania and New Jersey. It's a haven for outdoor enthusiasts, offering stunning natural landscapes, abundant wildlife, and opportunities for recreation and relaxation. The area is centered around the Delaware Water Gap, a dramatic geological feature where the river cuts through the Kittatinny Ridge.

Gateway National Recreation Area

Gateway National Recreation Area is a 27,000-acre park spanning parts of New York City and New Jersey. Managed by the National Park Service, it offers a mix of natural beauty, outdoor recreation, and historic sites. It includes beaches, wetlands, historic military installations, and wildlife habitats, making it a unique urban escape.

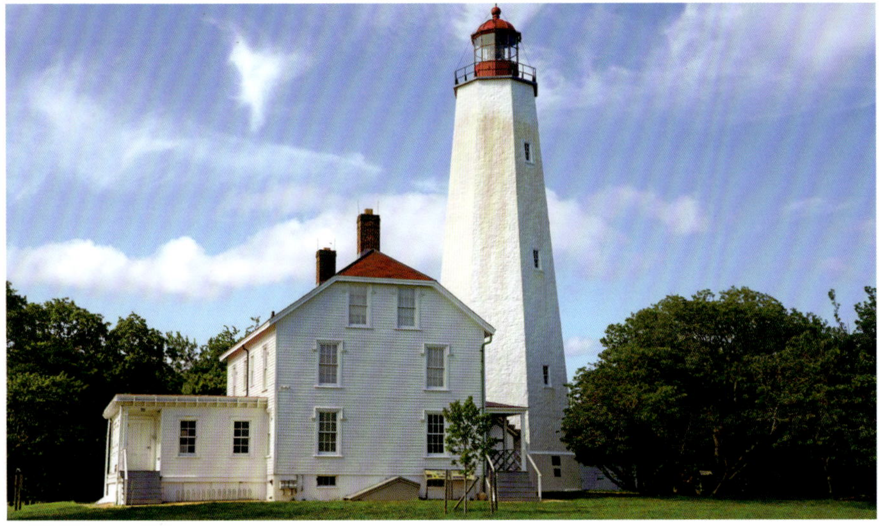

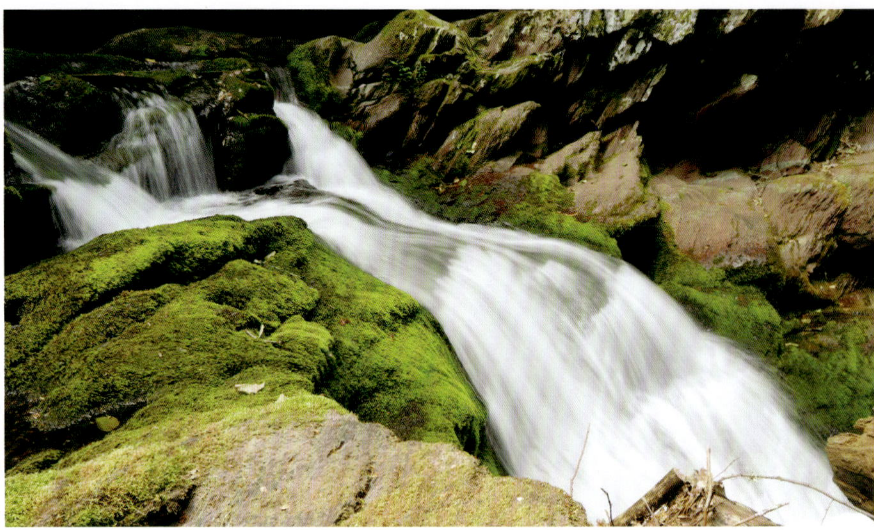

Lower Delaware National Wild and Scenic River

The Lower Delaware National Wild and Scenic River spans portions of Pennsylvania and New Jersey, preserving a 67-mile stretch of the Delaware River and its tributaries. This section of the river is notable for its ecological, historical, and recreational significance, offering visitors a peaceful and scenic retreat.

Great Egg Harbor River

The Great Egg Harbor River, located in southern New Jersey, is a designated National Wild and Scenic River known for its natural beauty, recreational opportunities, and ecological significance. Spanning over 55 miles, the river flows from its headwaters in the Pinelands National Reserve to the Great Egg Harbor Bay, eventually emptying into the Atlantic Ocean.

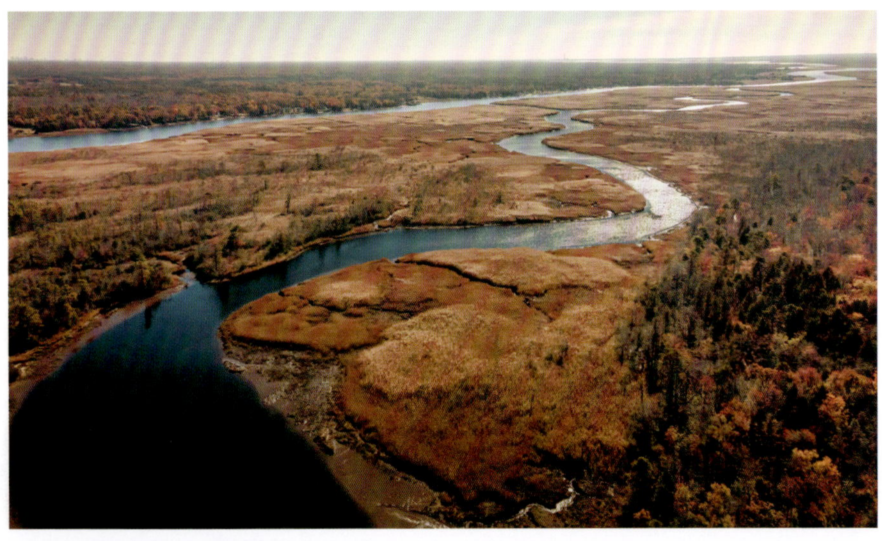

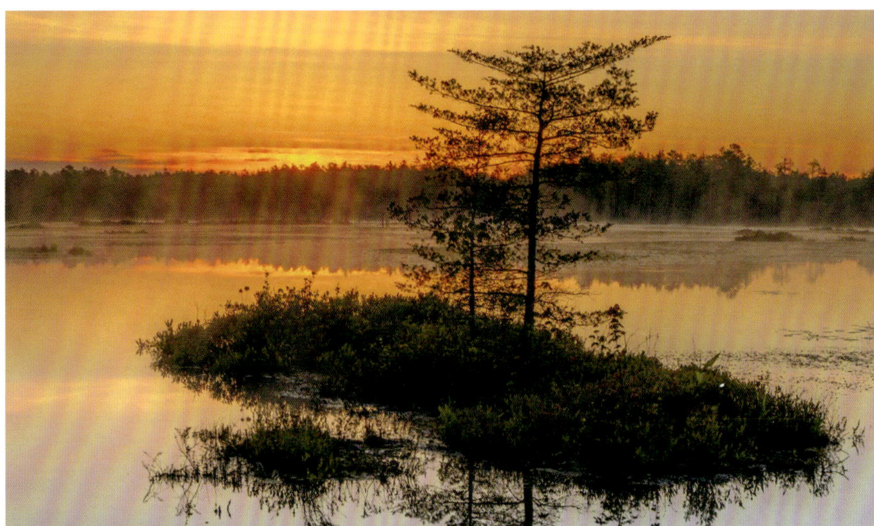

New Jersey Pinelands National Reserve

Also known as the Pine Barrens, New Jersey Pinelands National Reserve is a vast natural area covering over 1.1 million acres in southern New Jersey. Designated in 1978 as the nation's first National Reserve, it protects a unique ecosystem, cultural heritage, and diverse wildlife. This area is part of the larger Atlantic Coast Pine Barrens ecosystem.

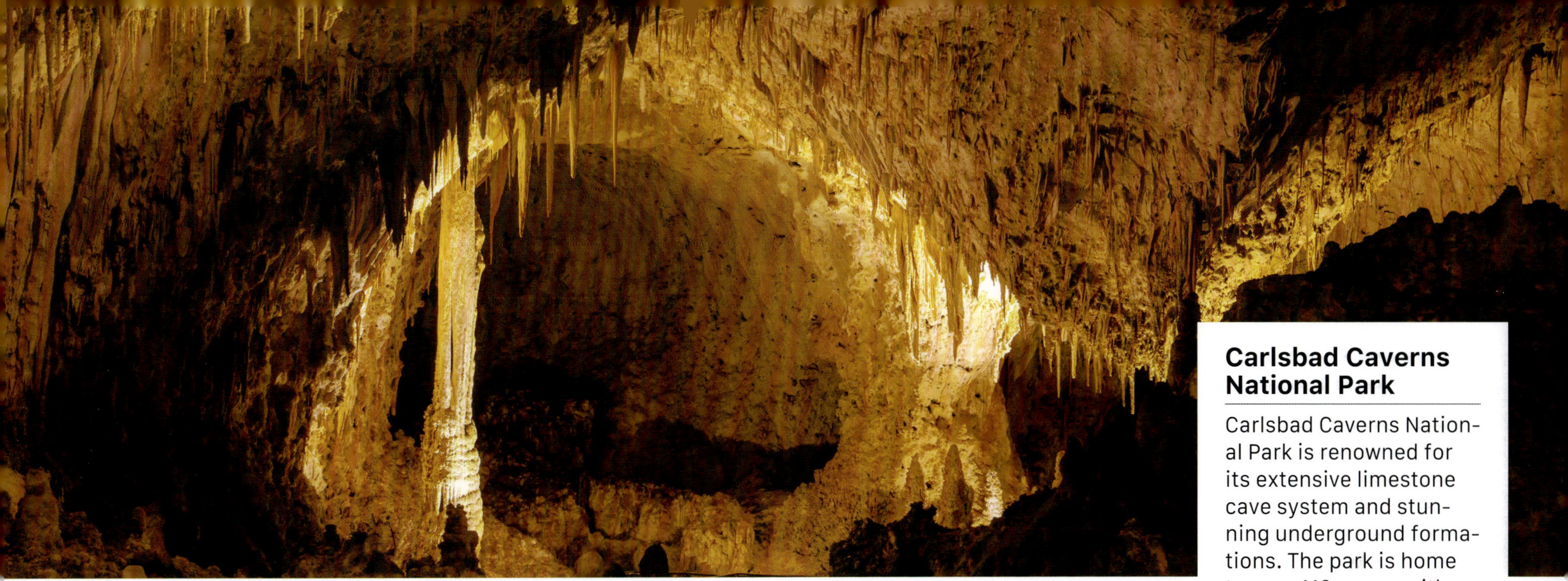

Carlsbad Caverns National Park

Carlsbad Caverns National Park is renowned for its extensive limestone cave system and stunning underground formations. The park is home to over 119 caves, with the Big Room being the largest single cave chamber in North America.

NEW MEXICO

Chaco Culture National Historical Park

Chaco Culture National Historical Park preserves some of the most significant archeological sites in North America. The park was a major center of Puebloan culture between 850 and 1250 CE, featuring massive multi-story stone buildings, ceremonial kivas, and an extensive network of roads connecting to other Puebloan sites.

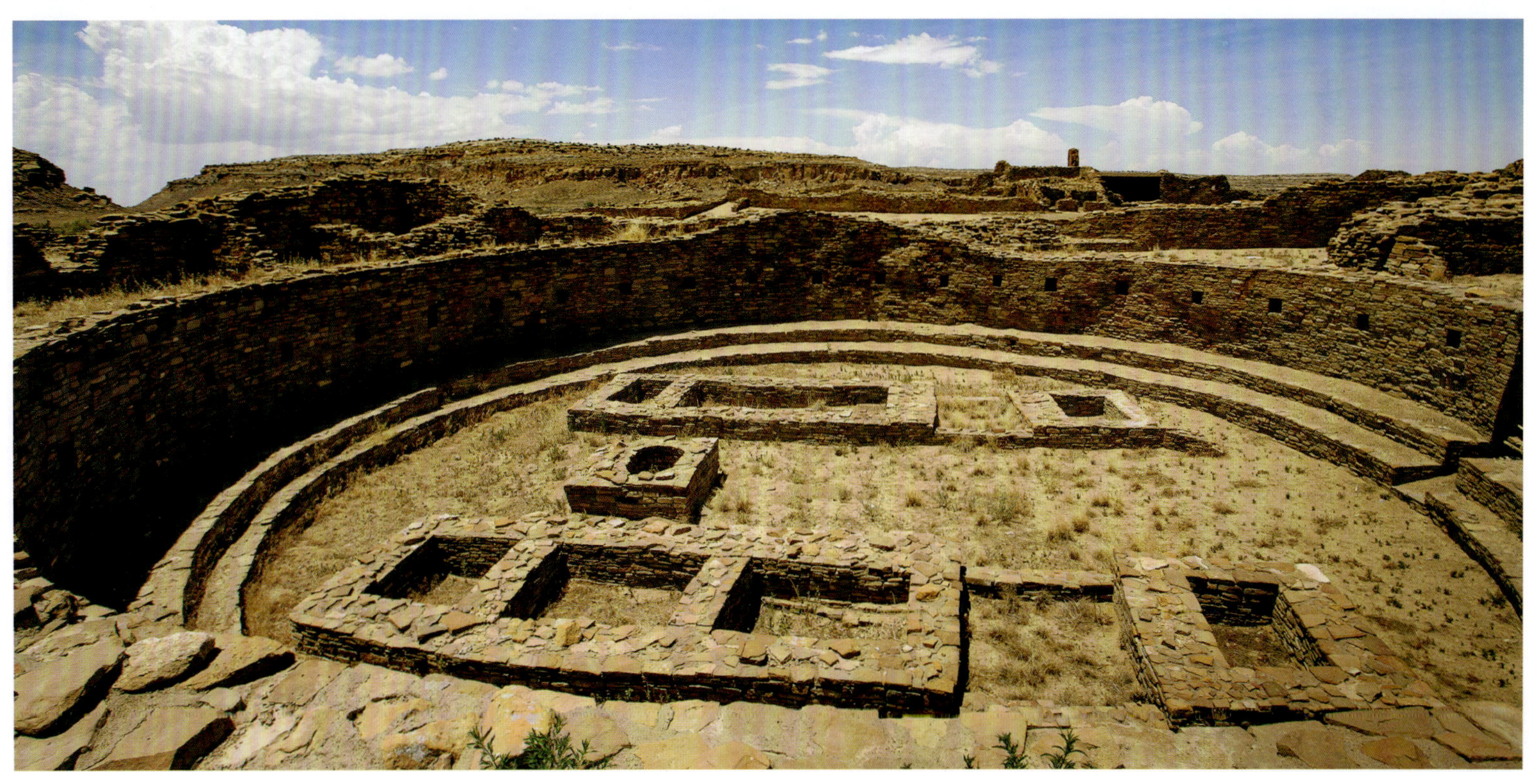

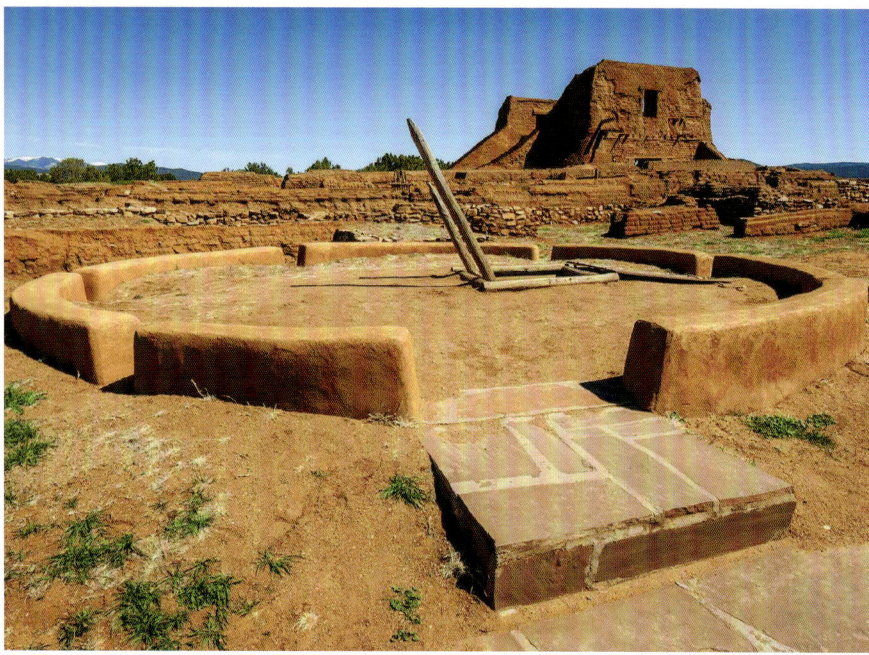

Pecos National Historical Park

Pecos National Historical Park preserves centuries of cultural history, blending Native American, Spanish, and English influences. The park is centered around the Pecos Pueblo, which was a thriving trading hub for Puebloan peoples from around 1100 to the 1600s. The site also includes the remains of a 17th-century Spanish mission church, reflecting the region's colonial history.

White Sands National Park

White Sands National Park is a stunning natural wonder featuring the world's largest gypsum dunefield. Spanning over 275 square miles in the Tularosa Basin, the park is known for its dazzling white dunes that create a surreal and ever-changing landscape.

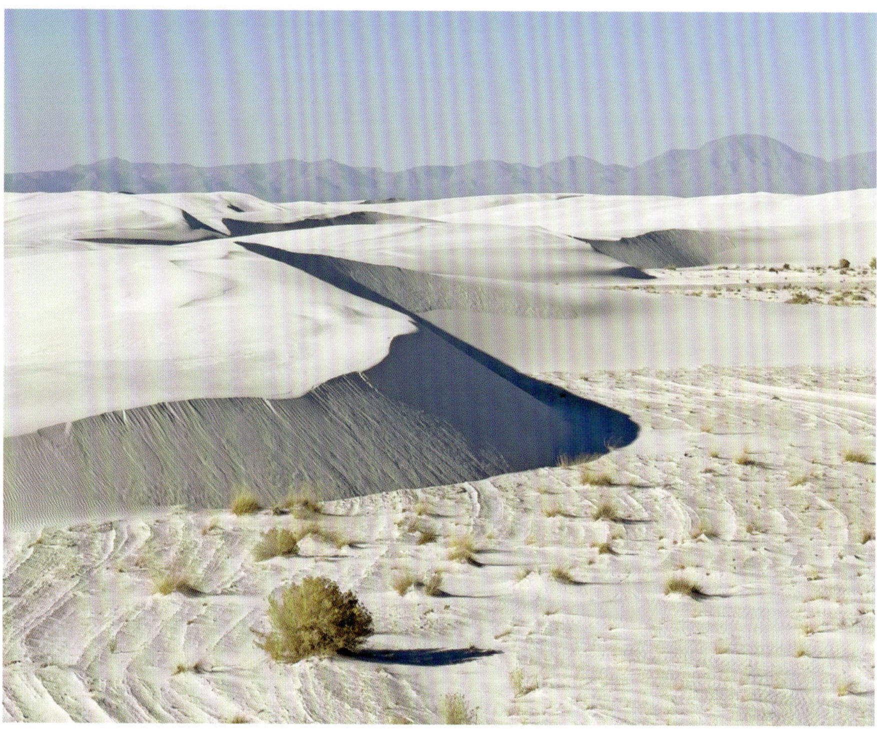

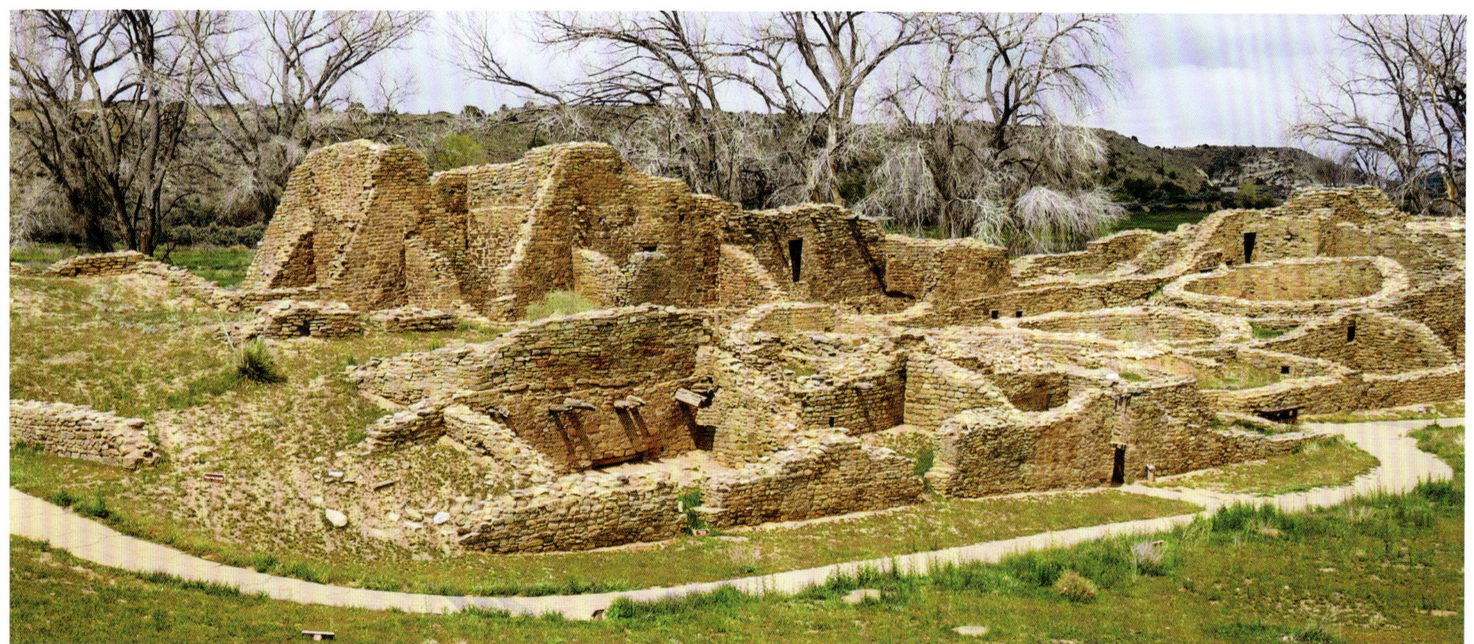

Aztec Ruins National Monument

Aztec Ruins National Monument preserves the well-kept remains of a 12th and 13th-century Ancestral Puebloan community. Despite its name, the site is not associated with the Aztecs, but was mistakenly named by early explorers. The monument offers a fascinating glimpse into the ingenuity, culture, and architecture of the ancestral Puebloan people.

Capulin Volcano National Monument

Capulin Volcano National Monument is a well-preserved cinder cone volcano that offers visitors the chance to explore the remnants of ancient volcanic activity. Rising more than 1,300 feet above the surrounding plains, the volcano provides picturesque panoramic views and a unique geological experience.

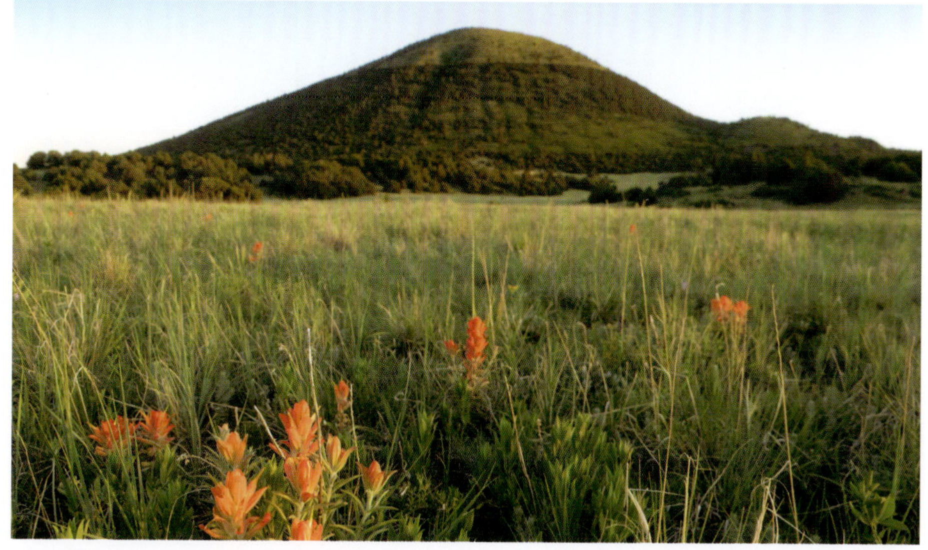

El Camino Real de Tierra Adentro National Historic Trail

El Camino Real de Tierra Adentro National Historic Trail is a 1,590-mile route that follows one of the oldest and most important trade and cultural roads in the Americas. Established in the late 16th century, "the Royal Road of the Interior Land" stretches from Mexico City to San Juan Pueblo, passing through present-day Mexico, Texas, and New Mexico. The Bridge of Ojuelos, along with 59 other sites on the route, was declared a UNESCO World Heritage Site.

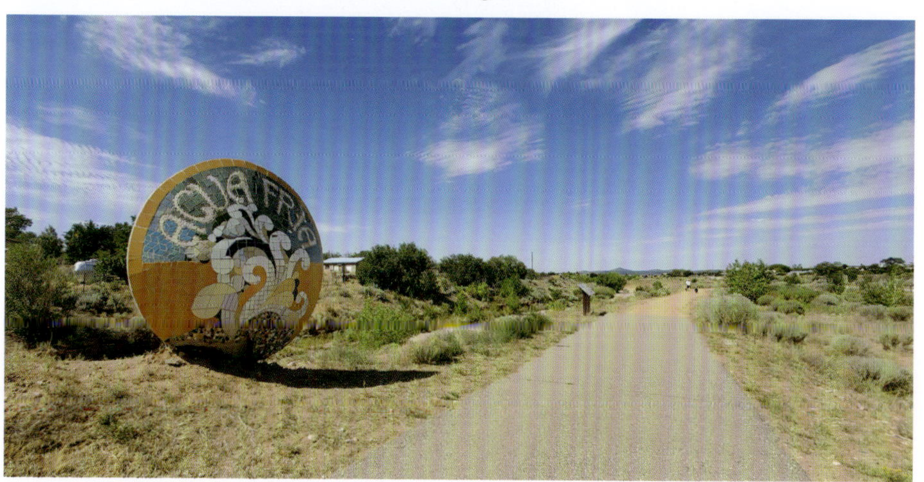

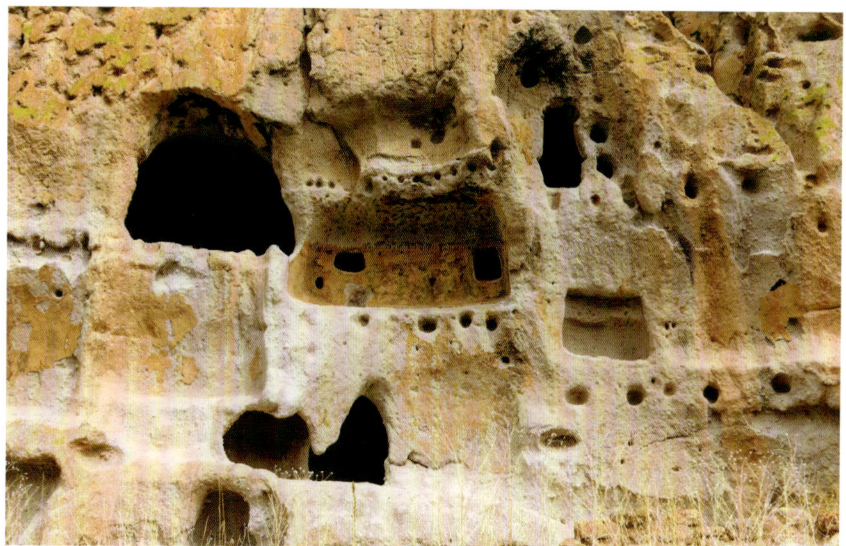

Bandelier National Monument

Bandelier National Monument preserves ancient Puebloan cliff dwellings and cultural sites dating back over 11,000 years. The monument spans more than 33,000 acres of rugged canyons, mesas, and archaeological sites, offering a unique glimpse into the lives of the Indigenous people who once inhabited the area.

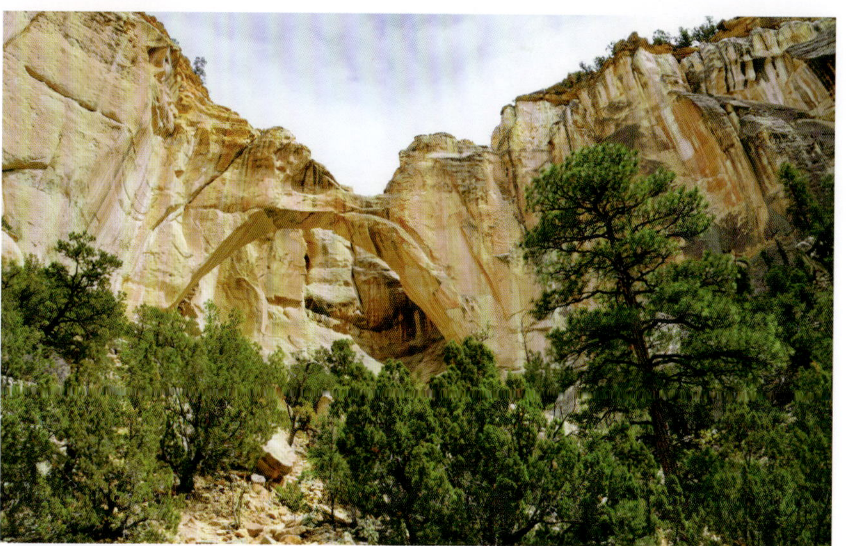

El Malpais National Monument

El Malpais National Monument is a fascinating landscape formed by volcanic activity, showcasing diverse geological features like lava flows, cinder cones, and volcanic craters. The monument spans over 114,000 acres and offers a unique mix of natural beauty, cultural history, and outdoor recreation.

El Morro National Monument

El Morro National Monument is famous for its towering sandstone bluff known as Inscription Rock *(see below)*, which bears carvings and petroglyphs left by ancient Indigenous peoples, Spanish explorers, and later settlers. The site has been a crucial landmark for travelers for centuries, providing a natural water source and serving as a cultural crossroads.

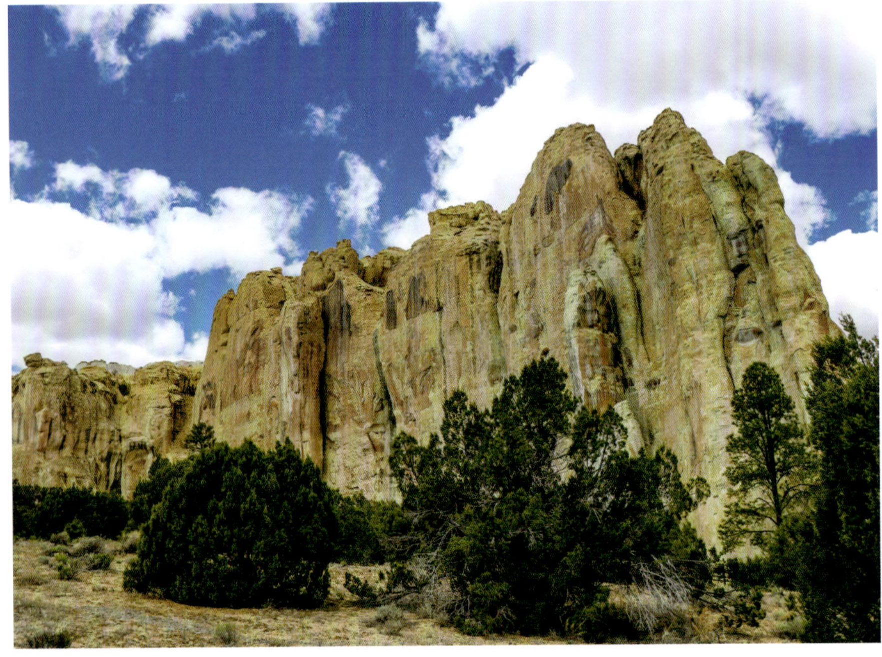

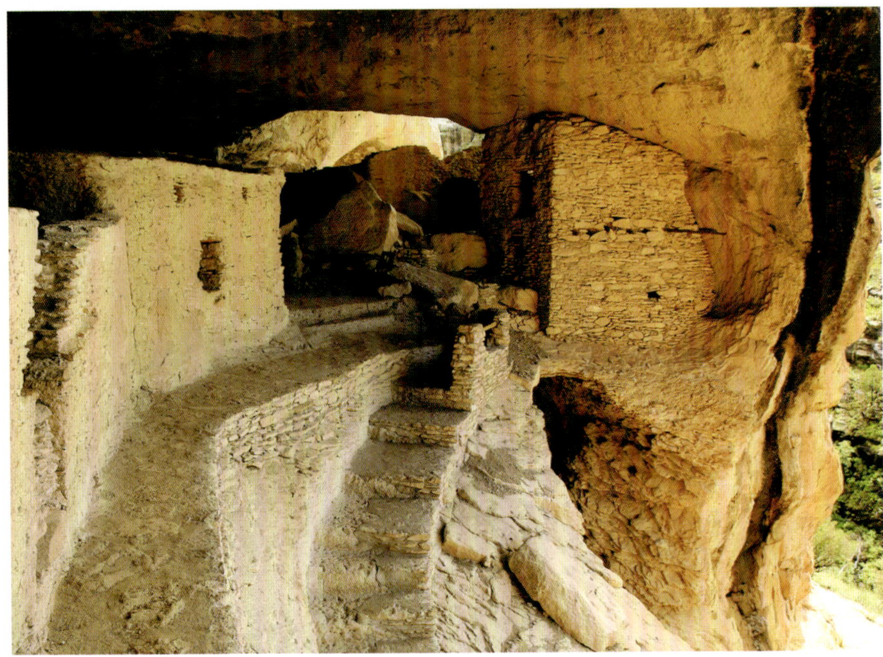

Gila Cliff Dwellings National Monument

Gila Cliff Dwellings National Monument preserves the ancient cliff dwellings of the Mogollon people, who lived in the area between the 13th and early 14th centuries. The monument features a series of well-preserved cliff dwellings built into natural caves along the Gila River, offering a glimpse into the lives of these early Native American inhabitants.

Fort Union National Monument

Located in northeastern New Mexico, Fort Union National Monument preserves the ruins of a significant military fort that played a crucial role in the development and protection of the American frontier during the mid-19th century. Established in 1851, the fort was strategically positioned along the Santa Fe Trail, serving as a military post to protect travelers, trade routes, and U.S. interests in the region.

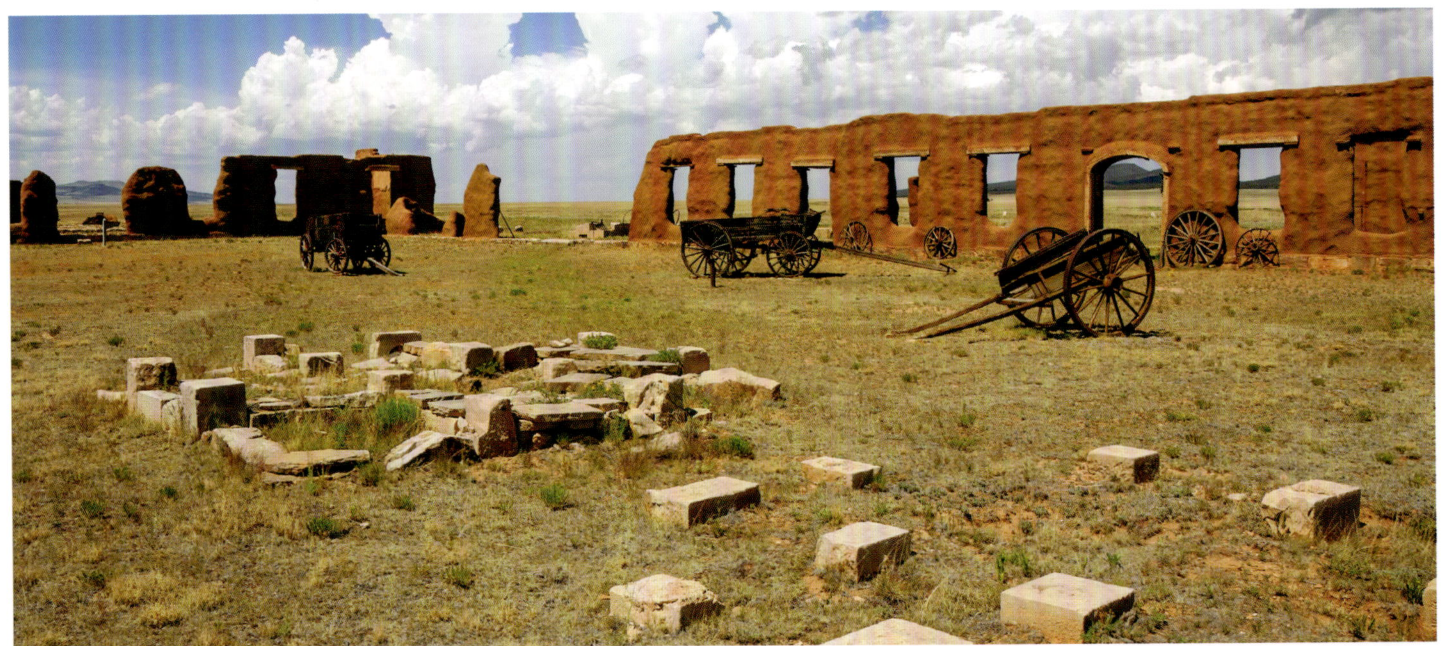

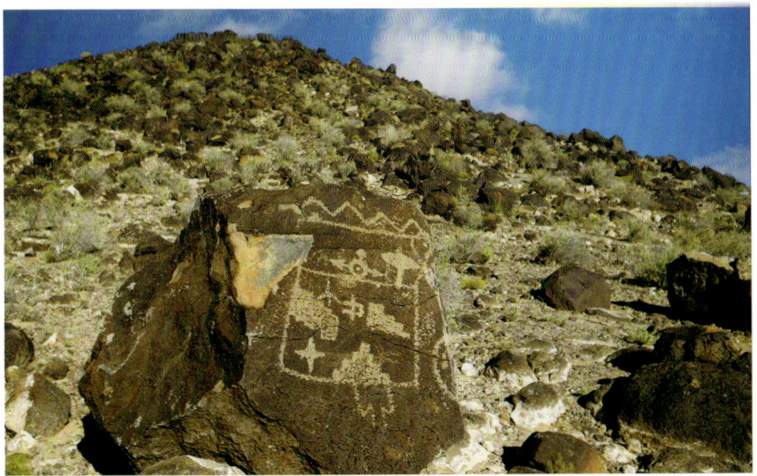

Petroglyph National Monument

Located in Albuquerque, NM, Petroglyph National Monument preserves one of the largest collections of petroglyphs in North America. The monument features over 20,000 images carved into volcanic rocks by Native American and Spanish settlers over the past 700 years. The petroglyphs provide valuable insight into the cultural and spiritual practices of the region's Indigenous peoples.

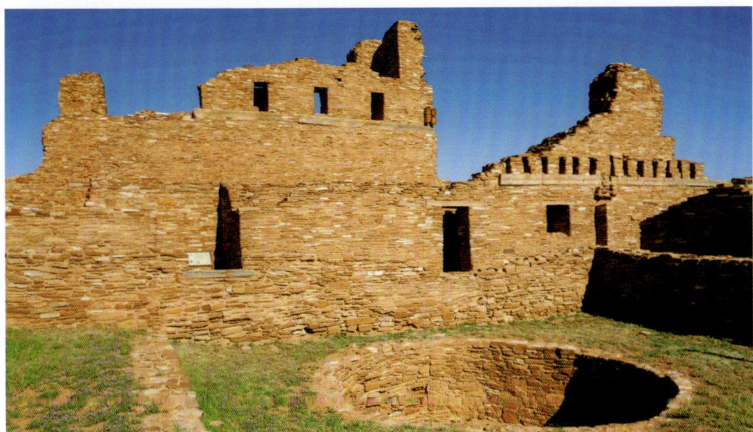

Salinas Pueblo Missions National Monument

Salinas Pueblo Missions National Monument preserves the remains of three historic Spanish colonial missions and several Puebloan villages. The site showcases the intersection of Native American and Spanish cultures in the late 17th and early 18th centuries. The Abó, Gran Quivira, and Quarai missions were built by Spanish settlers and missionaries to convert and assimilate the local Pueblo peoples.

Santa Fe National Historic Trail

The Santa Fe National Historic Trail is a significant route that spans approximately 1,200 miles across five states—Missouri, Kansas, Colorado, Oklahoma, and New Mexico. It was a vital 19th-century commercial and cultural link between the United States and Mexico, serving as a trade corridor from 1821 to 1880. The trail highlights historic landscapes, trading posts, wagon ruts, and cultural sites that tell the story of pioneers, traders, Native Americans, and settlers who traversed this path.

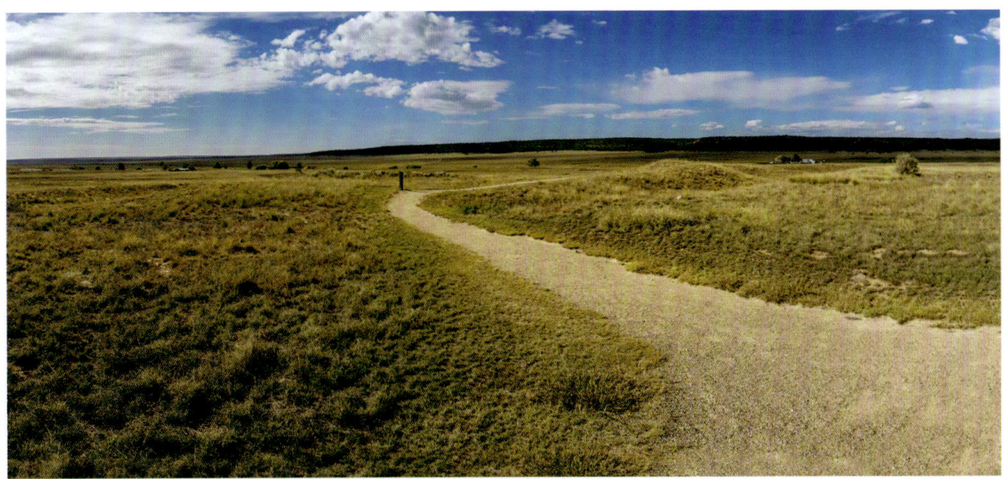

Valles Caldera National Preserve

Located in northern New Mexico, Valles Caldera National Preserve is a stunning geologic area within the Jemez Mountains. It preserves the massive Valles Caldera, a volcanic crater formed about 1.25 million years ago, which spans 13.7 miles in diameter. The caldera is a beautiful and ecologically diverse area with lush meadows, forests, hot springs, and wildlife.

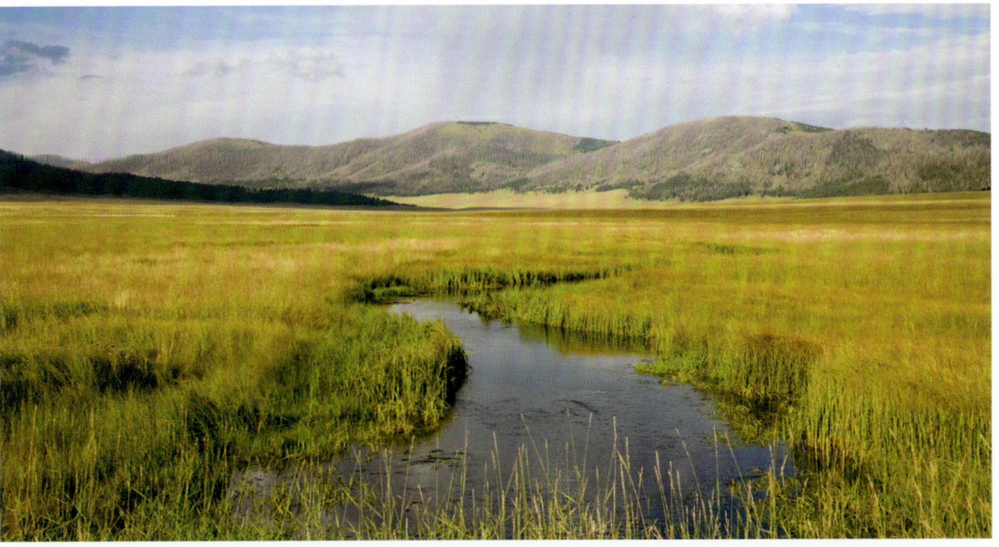

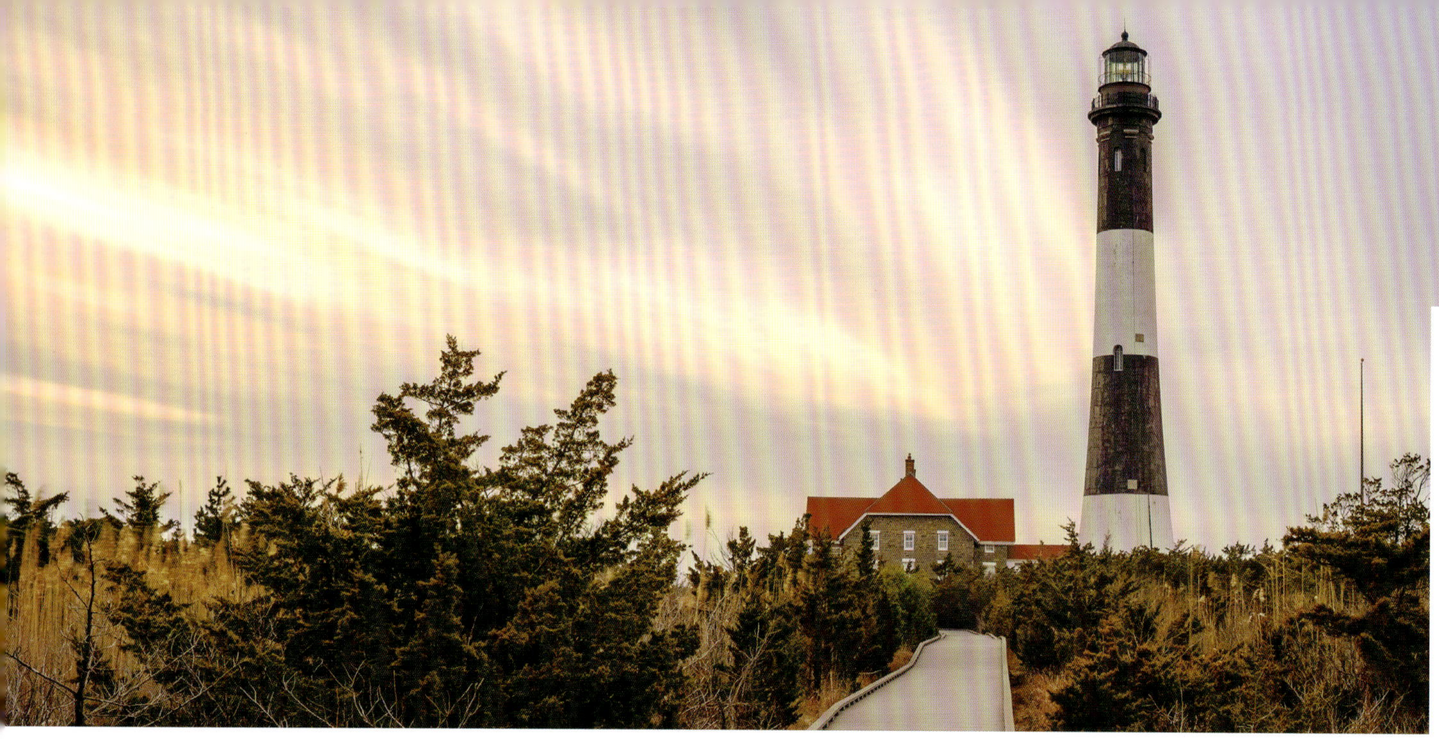

Fire Island National Seashore

Fire Island National Seashore is a stunning barrier island located off the southern coast of Long Island, NY. Spanning 26 miles, the park is home to maritime forests, salt marshes, and dunes, providing habitat for various wildlife. Notable landmarks include the beautiful Fire Island Lighthouse *(see left)*, and the historic William Floyd Estate, the home of a Declaration of Independence signer.

NEW YORK

Harriet Tubman National Historical Park

Harriet Tubman National Historical Park preserves the legacy of Harriet Tubman, a renowned abolitionist, Underground Railroad conductor, and humanitarian. The park encompasses key sites associated with her life, including her residence *(see right)*, the Harriet Tubman Home for the Aged, and the Thompson Memorial African Methodist Episcopal Zion Church, where she worshipped.

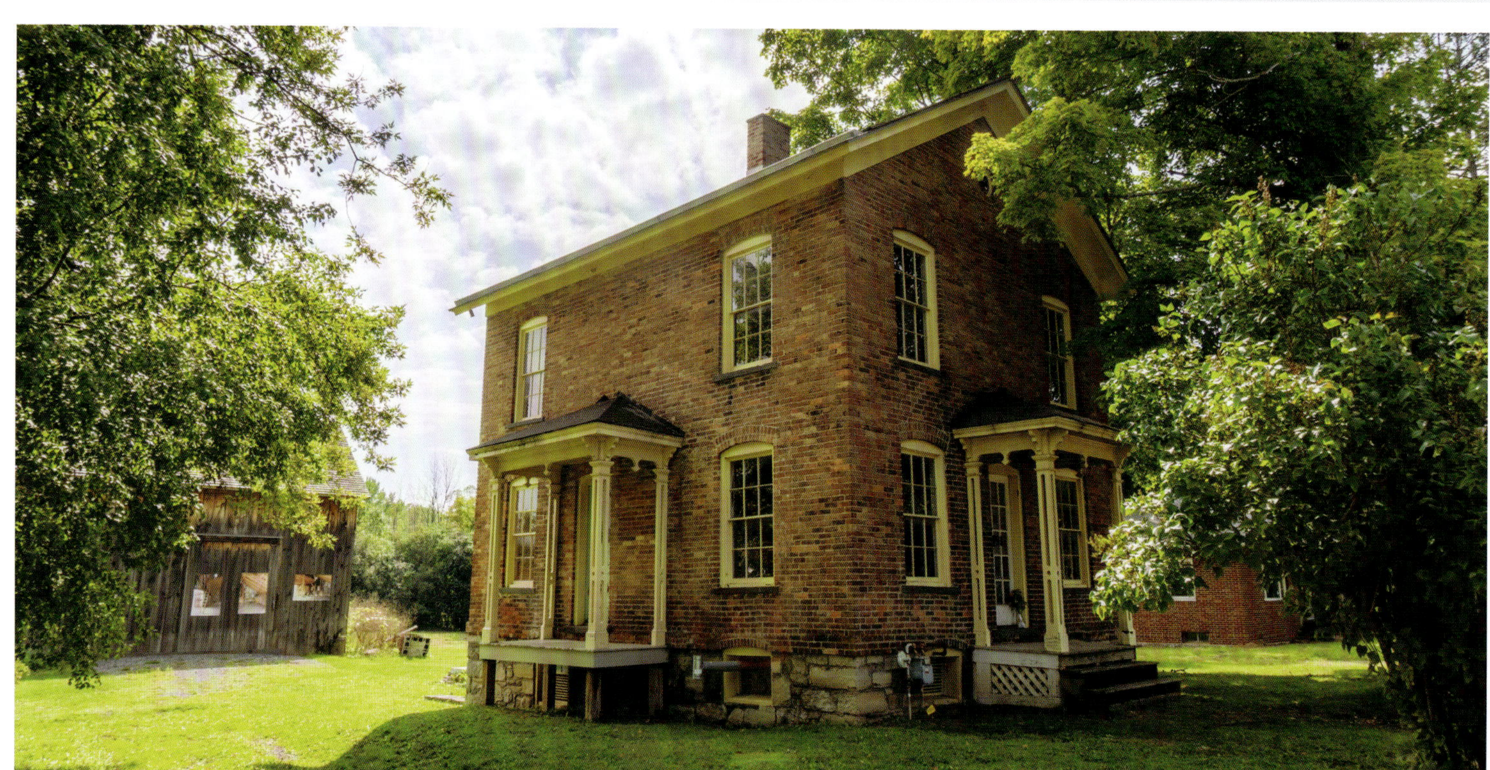

National Parks of New York Harbor

National Parks of New York Harbor is a collection of 11 national park sites located in and around New York City, showcasing the region's rich history, culture, and natural beauty. Managed by the National Park Service, these sites include iconic landmarks like the Statue of Liberty, Ellis Island, and Castle Clinton, which celebrate the nation's immigrant heritage and ideals of freedom.

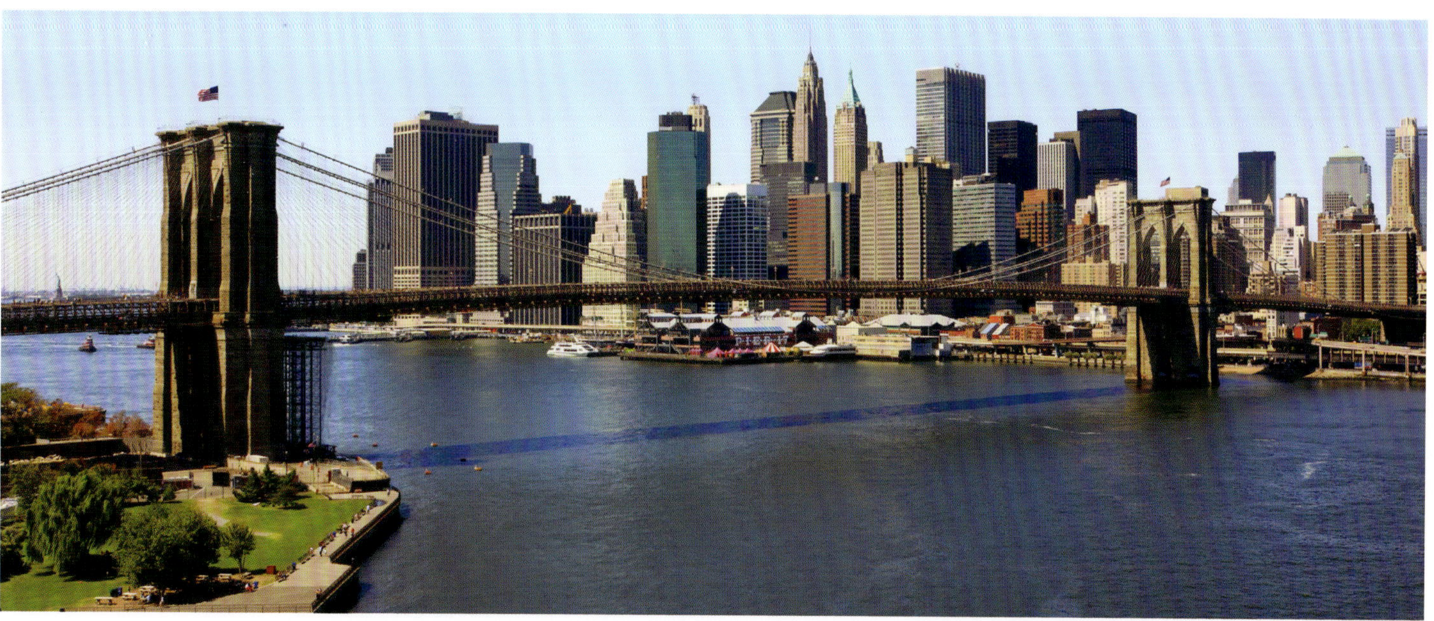

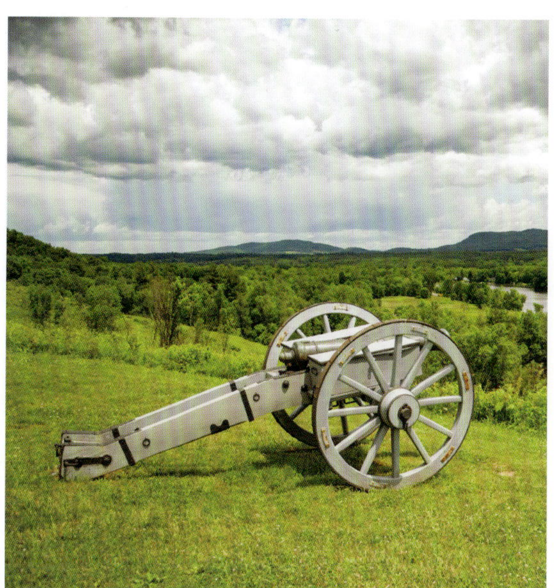

Women's Rights National Historical Park

Women's Rights National Historical Park honors the birthplace of the women's rights movement in the U.S. The park preserves and interprets sites associated with the first Women's Rights Convention, held in Seneca Falls in 1848, where activists like Elizabeth Cady Stanton and Frederick Douglass advocated for gender equality and women's suffrage. The park consists of four major historical properties: Wesleyan Methodist Church, the Elizabeth Cady Stanton House, the M'Clintock House, and the Richard Hunt House.

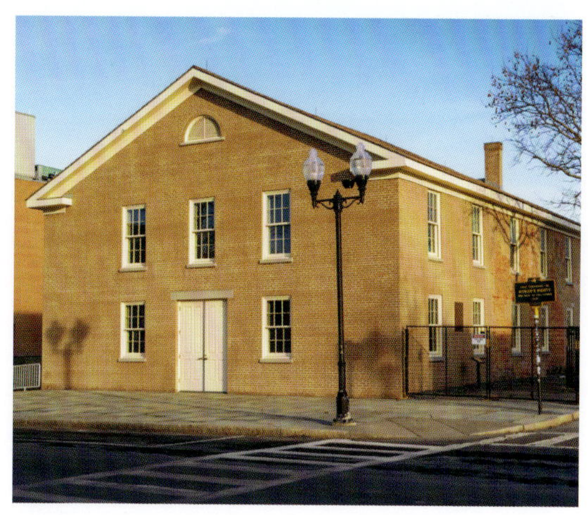

Saratoga National Historical Park

Saratoga National Historical Park commemorates the site of the Battles of Saratoga, a pivotal turning point in the American Revolutionary War. Fought in 1777, these battles resulted in a decisive victory for the Continental Army, leading to the surrender of British General John Burgoyne and securing French support for the American cause.

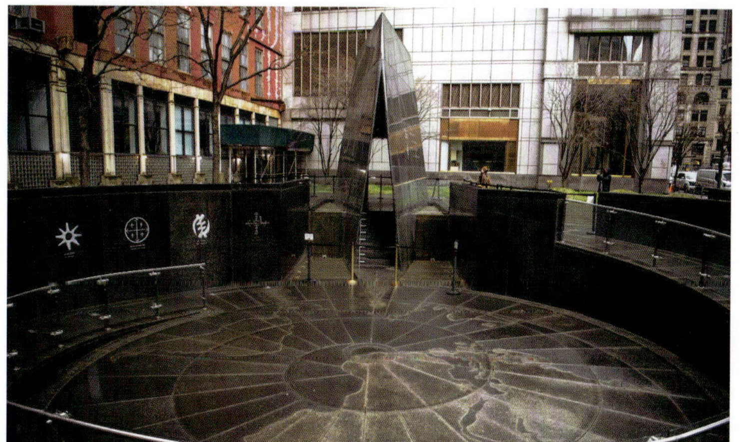

African Burial Ground National Monument

African Burial Ground National Monument preserves the site of a historic cemetery where over 15,000 free and enslaved Africans were buried during the 17th and 18th centuries. Rediscovered in the 1990s, the site is a powerful reminder of the contributions and struggles of African Americans in early New York City.

Castle Clinton National Monument

Castle Clinton National Monument is a historic fortification that has played a significant role in American history. Constructed between 1808 and 1811 as part of a series of coastal defenses, it was originally known as West Battery. In the mid-19th century, it became America's first immigration station, processing over 8 million immigrants before the opening of Ellis Island in 1892. Today, Castle Clinton serves as a visitor center, offering exhibits and historical insights into its multifaceted past.

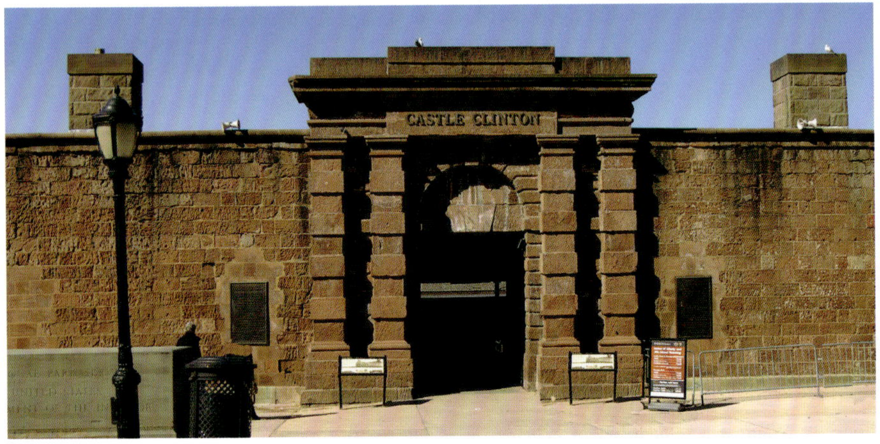

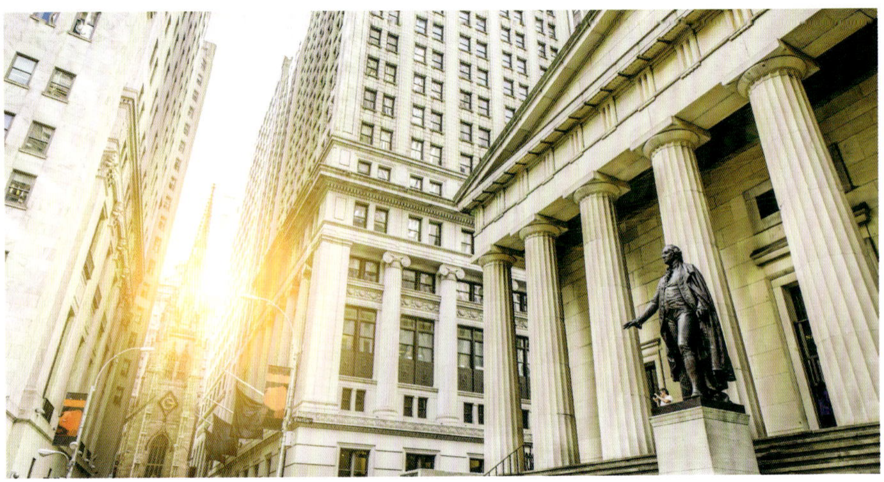

Federal Hall National Memorial

Located on Wall Street in New York City, Federal Hall National Monument is a historic site that played a key role in the early history of the U.S. The original building, constructed in 1703, served as New York's City Hall and later as the nation's first capitol under the Constitution. It was here that George Washington took the oath of office as the first President of the U.S. in 1789 and where the Bill of Rights was introduced to Congress.

Eleanor Roosevelt National Historic Site

Eleanor Roosevelt National Historic Site preserves Val-Kill, the beloved home of Eleanor Roosevelt, one of America's most influential first ladies. Val-Kill served as her personal retreat, workspace, and a center for humanitarian efforts. Visitors can explore the house, which contains many of her personal belongings, as well as the surrounding grounds, which include gardens and walking trails.

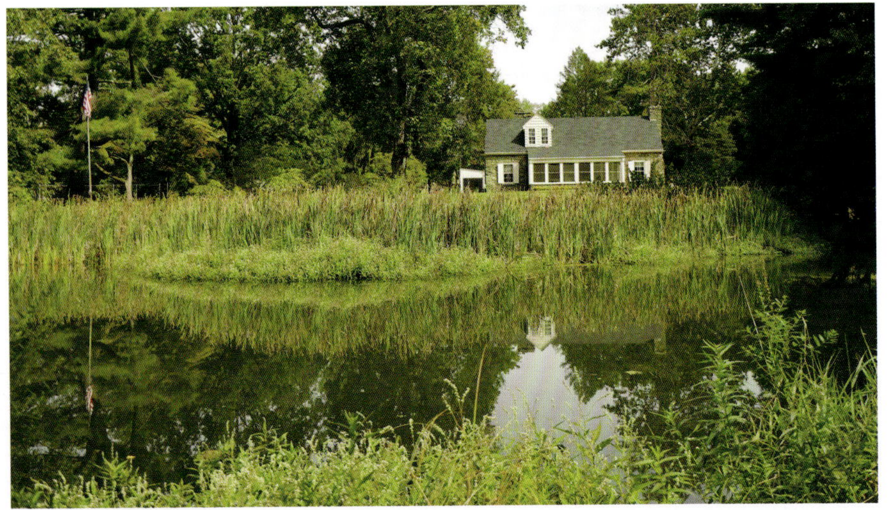

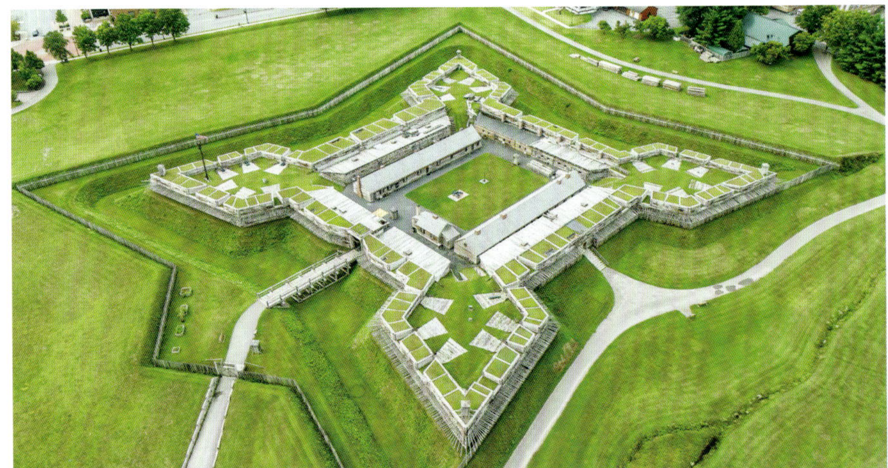

Fort Stanwix National Monument

Fort Stanwix National Monument commemorates the historic fort that played a crucial role during the American Revolutionary War. It became a key defensive site in the Mohawk Valley and is best known for withstanding a British siege during the 1777 Battle of Oriskany. The reconstructed fort now serves as a monument, offering visitors a chance to explore its structures and learn about its strategic importance.

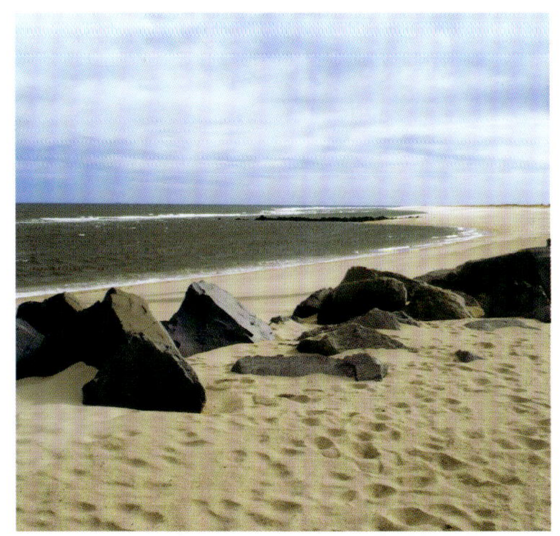

Gateway National Recreation Area

Gateway National Recreation Area is a sprawling nature and historic preserve spanning over 26,000 acres across New York and New Jersey. Established in 1972, the park offers a mix of beaches, marshlands, historic sites, and recreational opportunities. The area is home to diverse wildlife, making it a haven for birders and nature enthusiasts, while its beaches and trails attract visitors for swimming, hiking, and biking.

General Grant National Memorial

General Grant National Memorial, also known as Grant's Tomb, is located in Riverside Park in New York City. It's the final resting place of Ulysses S. Grant, the 18th President of the United States and commanding general of the Union Army during the Civil War, and his wife, Julia Dent Grant. The memorial is the largest mausoleum in North America and features neoclassical architecture with a domed roof and grand interior.

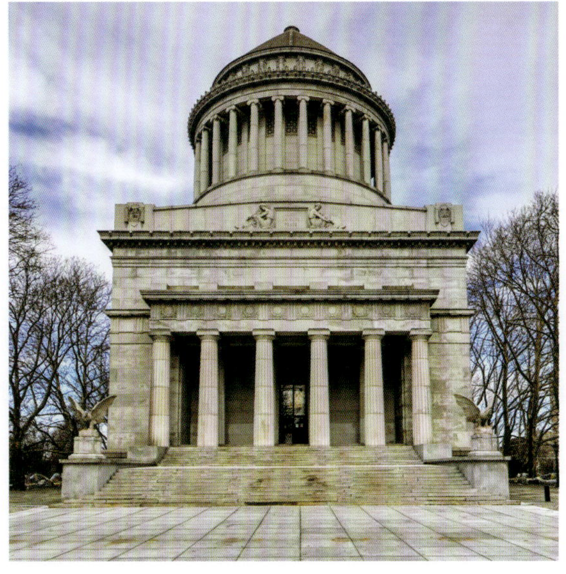

Home of Franklin D. Roosevelt National Historic Site

Home of Franklin D. Roosevelt National Historic Site preserves the lifelong home and estate of Franklin Delano Roosevelt, the 32nd President of the United States. Known as "Springwood," this site served as Roosevelt's family residence, personal retreat, and the place where many significant decisions were made during his presidency.

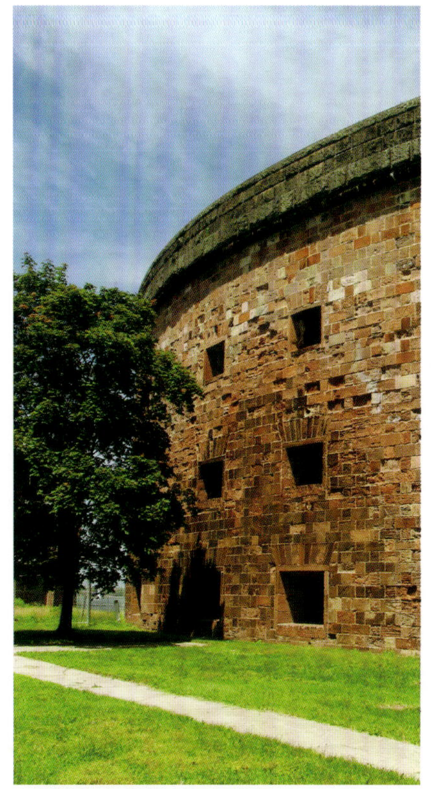

Governors Island National Monument

Located in New York Harbor, Governors Island National Monument preserves two historic fortifications: Fort Jay and Castle Williams. These structures were built in the early 19th century to defend New York City from naval attacks—they played a key role in the harbor's coastal defense system. Today, the site offers visitors guided tours, exhibits, and scenic views of New York Harbor.

Hamilton Grange National Memorial

Hamilton Grange National Memorial preserves the home of Alexander Hamilton, one of the Founding Fathers of the United States. Built in 1802, the Federal-style house was Hamilton's retreat and the only home he ever owned. The memorial offers visitors a glimpse into Hamilton's life through exhibits, guided tours, and restored interiors reflecting his era.

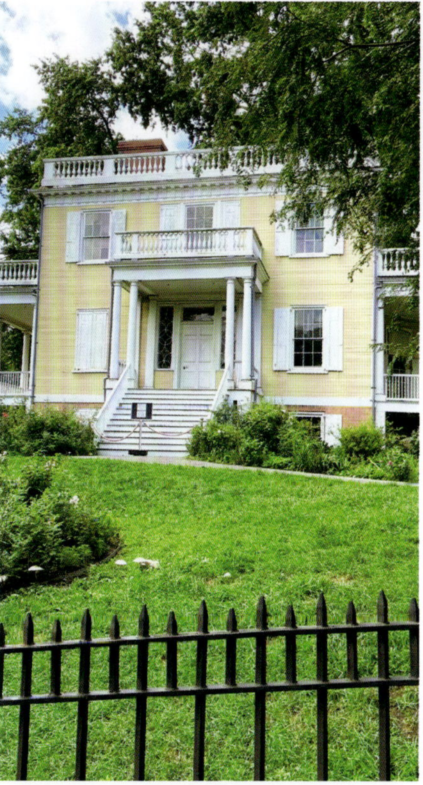

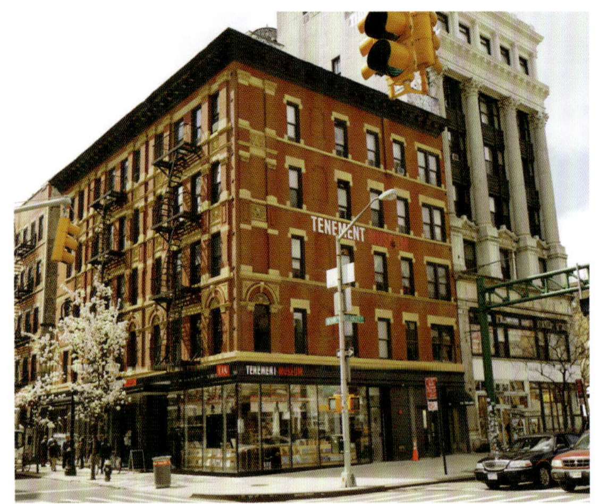

Lower East Side Tenement Museum

Lower East Side Tenement Museum preserves and interprets the history of immigrant life in American during the 19th and 20th centuries. Through guided tours of recreated apartments and businesses, as well as exhibits and storytelling programs, visitors gain a vivid understanding of the challenges and triumphs faced by immigrant families.

Martin Van Buren National Historic Site

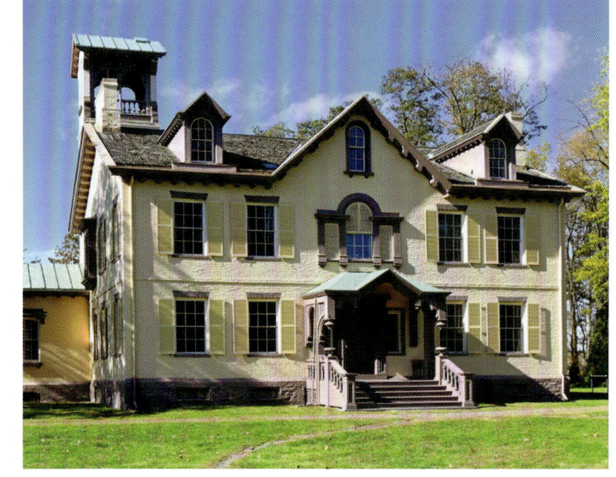

Located in Kinderhook, New York, Martin Van Buren National Historic Site preserves Lindenwald, the home and farm of Martin Van Buren, the 8th President of the United States. The site features the restored mansion, which reflects Van Buren's life, political career, and the social and economic changes of the 19th century.

Sagamore Hill National Historic Site

Sagamore Hill National Historic Site preserves the home of Theodore Roosevelt, the 26th President of the United States. Known as the "Summer White House" during his presidency, Sagamore Hill served as Roosevelt's family residence and a place where he hosted political leaders and dignitaries. Visitors can explore the house, walk the scenic grounds, and learn about Roosevelt's legacy as a conservationist, reformer, and statesman.

Saint Paul's Church National Historic Site

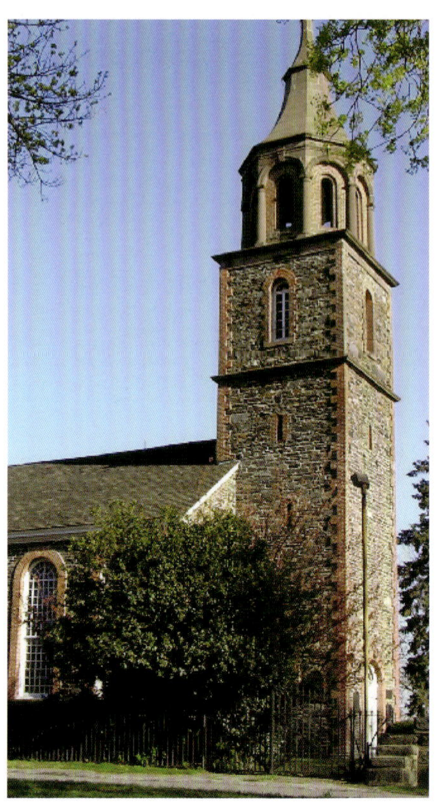

Saint Paul's Church National Historic Site preserves a historic church that dates back to 1763. The church played a significant role during the American Revolution, serving as a refuge for both British and American forces at different times. The site includes the church, the surrounding cemetery, and the interpretive exhibits that highlight the church's role in American history.

Statue of Liberty National Monument

Located on Liberty Island in New York Harbor, Statue of Liberty National Monument is one of the most iconic symbols of freedom and democracy in the U.S. The monument includes the Statue of Liberty, a gift from France in 1886, which stands as a welcoming beacon to immigrants arriving by sea and represents the enduring values of liberty, hope, and independence.

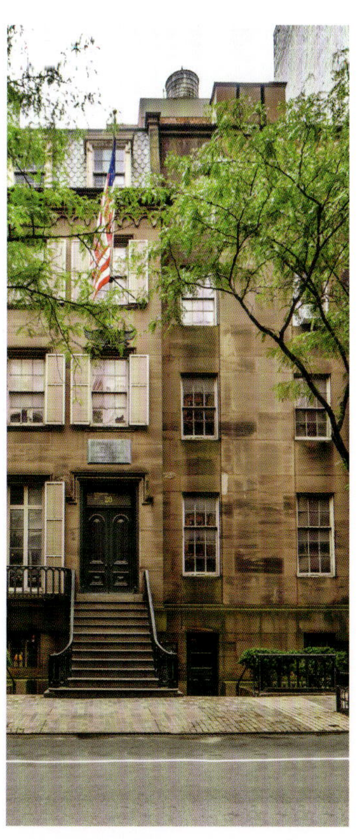

Theodore Roosevelt Birthplace National Historic Site

Theodore Roosevelt Birthplace National Historic Site preserves the reconstructed childhood home of Theodore Roosevelt, the 26th President of the United States. Originally built in 1848, the house was where Roosevelt was born in 1858 and spent his formative years. The site features period furnishings, personal artifacts, and exhibits that highlight Roosevelt's early life, family, and the influences that shaped his dynamic career.

Theodore Roosevelt Inaugural National Historic Site

Theodore Roosevelt Inaugural National Historic Site commemorates the location where Theodore Roosevelt was sworn in as the 26th President of the United States on September 14, 1901. The site offers exhibits, interactive displays, and guided tours that explore Roosevelt's sudden rise to the presidency, his progressive policies, and his impact on American history.

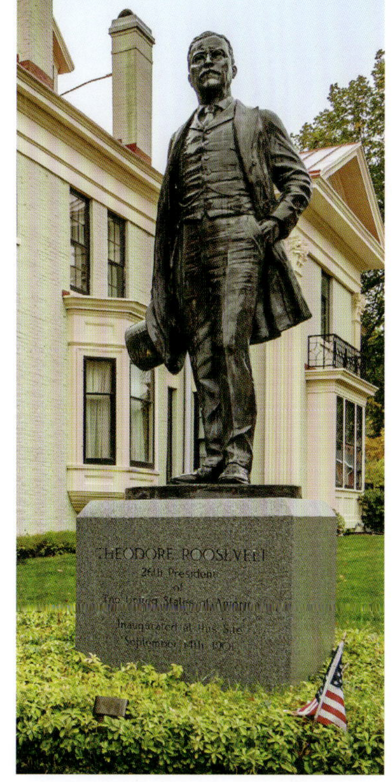

Stonewall National Monument

Located in the Greenwich Village neighborhood of New York City, Stonewall National Monument commemorates the Stonewall Uprising of June 1969, a pivotal event in the LGBTQ+ rights movement. As the first national monument dedicated to LGBTQ+ history, it serves as a powerful symbol of resilience, and the ongoing struggle for inclusion and justice. Visitors can reflect on the events of the uprising, explore the surrounding area, and learn about the contributions of activists.

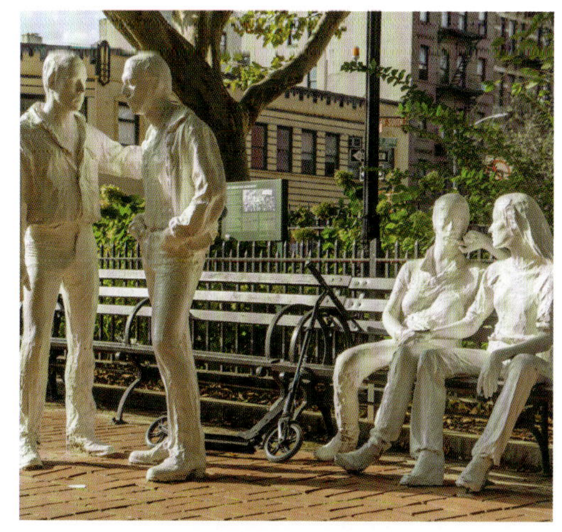

Thomas Cole National Historic Site

Thomas Cole National Historic Site preserves the home and studio of Thomas Cole, the founder of the Hudson River School style of American art. Established as a historic site in 1999, it celebrates Cole's life, work, and his role in shaping American landscape painting during the 19th century. The site includes Cole's restored home, studios, and grounds, which inspired many of his masterpieces.

Vanderbilt Mansion National Historic Site

Vanderbilt Mansion National Historic Site preserves the opulent Gilded Age home of Frederick and Louise Vanderbilt. Built between 1896 and 1899, the 54-room Beaux-Arts mansion reflects the wealth and lifestyle of one of America's most prominent families. Visitors can explore the mansion's lavish interiors, filled with period furnishings and artwork, as well as the surrounding estate designed by renowned architects and landscape planners.

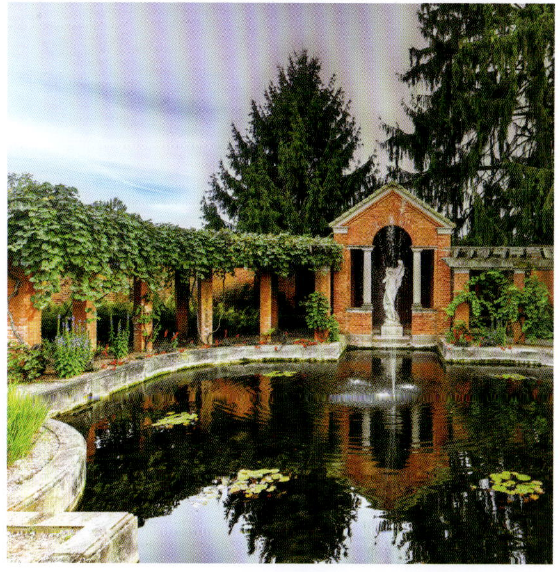

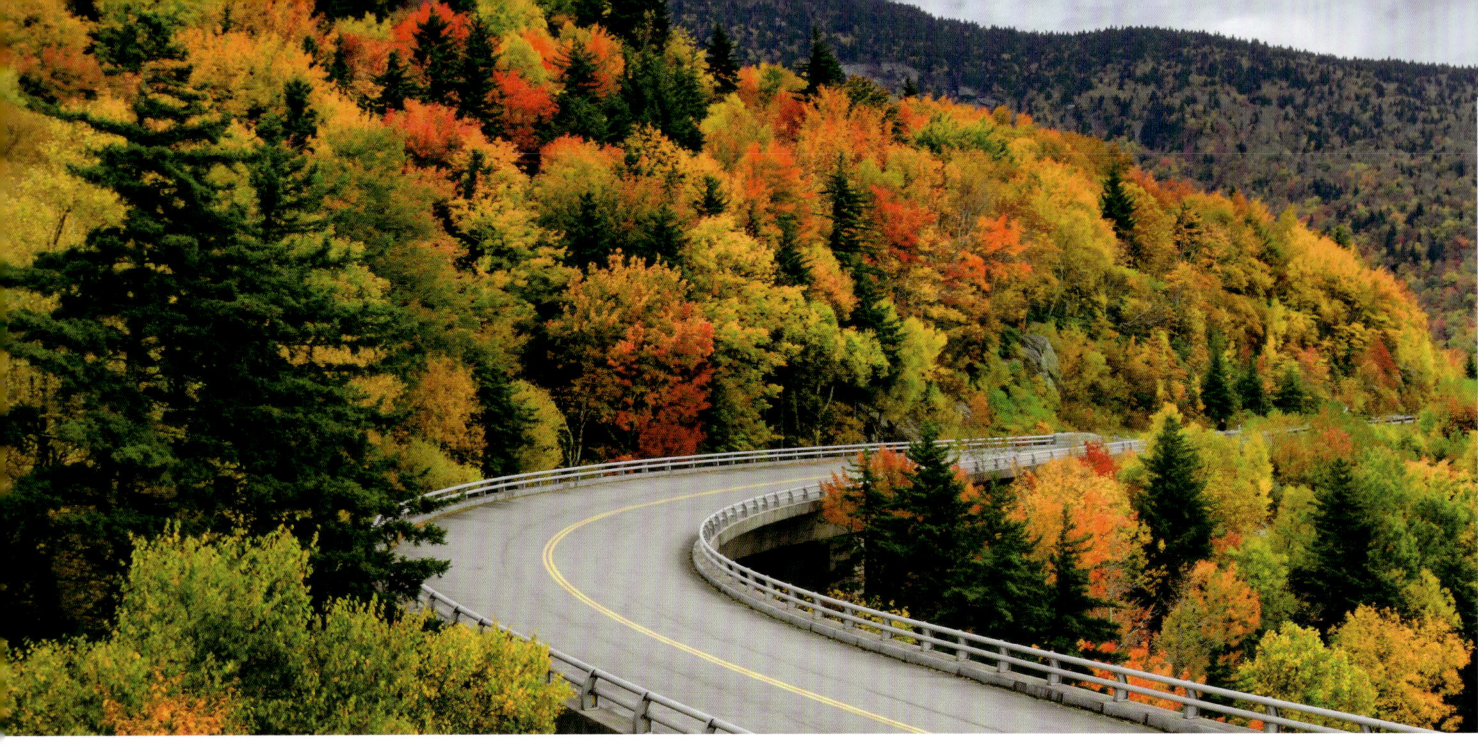

Blue Ridge Parkway

Often called "America's Favorite Drive," Blue Ridge Parkway is a scenic roadway stretching 469 miles through the Appalachian Mountains in Virginia and North Carolina. Managed by the National Park Service, it connects Shenandoah National Park to Great Smoky Mountains National Park, offering breathtaking views, rich biodiversity, and cultural heritage along the way. The parkway features numerous overlooks, hiking trails, and visitor centers, including iconic sites like Mabry Mill, Linville Falls, and Mount Mitchell.

NORTH CAROLINA

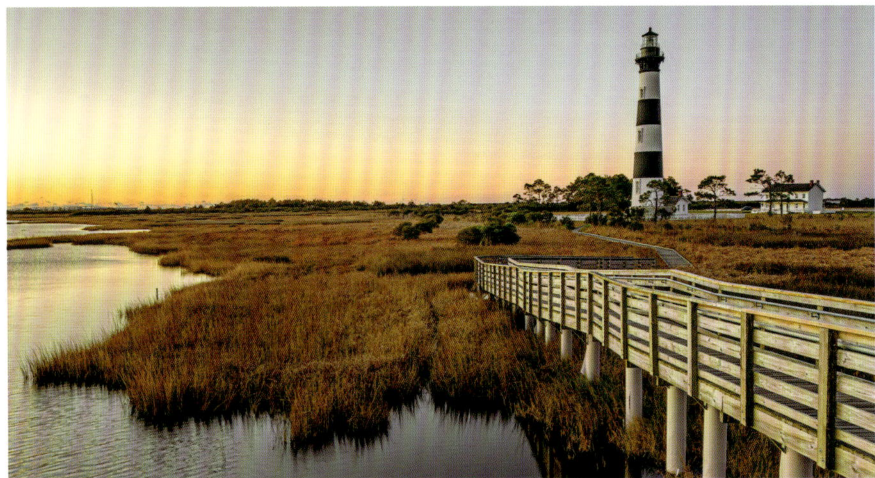

Cape Hatteras National Seashore

Located on North Carolina's Outer Banks, Cape Hatteras National Seashore is the nation's first national seashore, preserving over 70 miles of pristine coastline along the Atlantic Ocean. The seashore is known for its unspoiled beaches, dynamic barrier islands, and rich history, and offers opportunities for swimming, fishing, surfing, and birding.

Cape Lookout National Seashore

Cape Lookout National Seashore, located along the southern Outer Banks of North Carolina, preserves 56 miles of undeveloped barrier islands known for their natural beauty and rich history. Accessible only by boat, the seashore offers untouched beaches, wild dunes, salt marshes, and opportunities for outdoor activities like swimming, fishing, kayaking, and shell collecting.

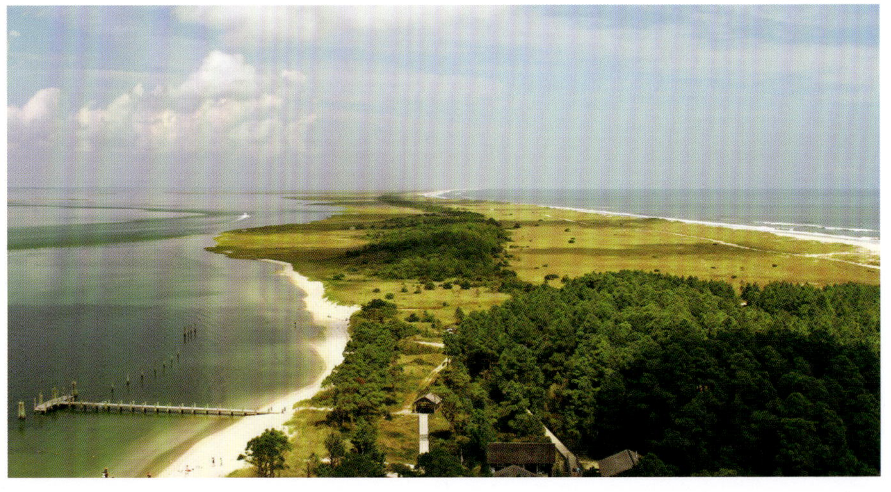

Great Smoky Mountains National Park

Straddling the border between North Carolina and Tennessee, Great Smoky Mountains National Park is the most visited national park in the U.S. Renowned for its mist-covered mountains, diverse ecosystems, and rich cultural history, the park spans over 500,000 acres and offers stunning landscapes of forests, waterfalls, and wildflower meadows.

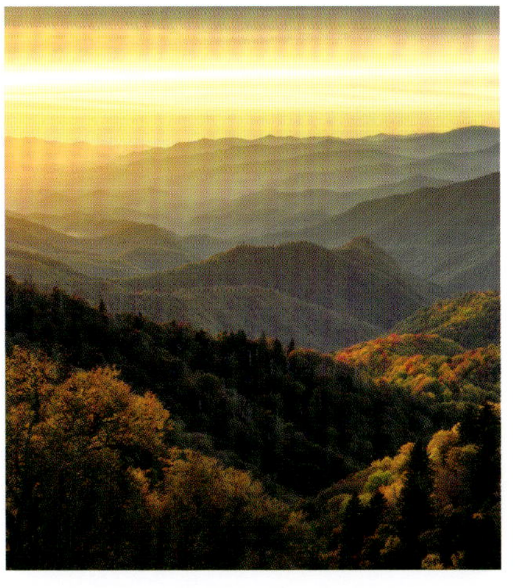

Guilford Courthouse National Military Park

Guilford Courthouse National Military Park commemorates the Battle of Guilford Courthouse, a pivotal engagement during the American Revolutionary War. Fought on March 15, 1781, the battle was a tactical victory for the British, but came at a high cost, weakening their forces and contributing to their ultimate defeat at Yorktown later that year. The park features battlefields, monuments, and interpretive trails that provide insight into the strategies and sacrifices of the soldiers.

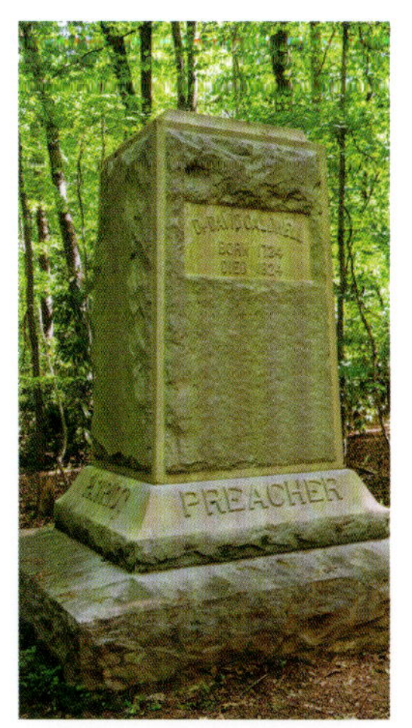

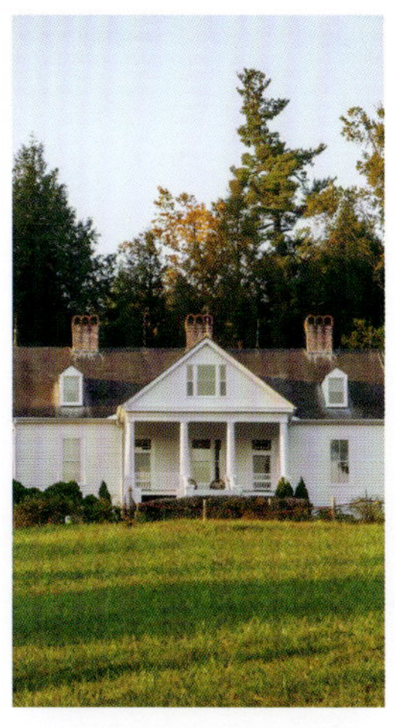

Carl Sandburg Home National Historic Site

Carl Sandburg Home National Historic Site preserves the home and legacy of Carl Sandburg, a Pulitzer Prize-winning poet, author, and social activist. Known as "Connemara," the estate served as Sandburg's residence for the final 22 years of his life, where he wrote and contributed significantly to American literature. The site includes Sandburg's house, which holds his extensive library, and the surrounding 264-acre property, featuring hiking trails, ponds, and pastures.

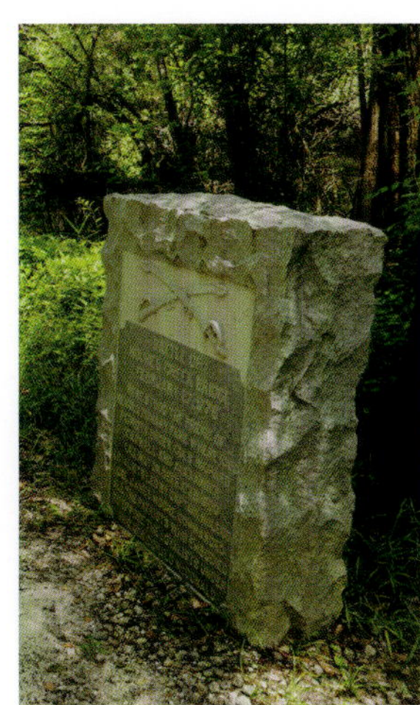

Moores Creek National Battlefield

Moores Creek National Battlefield commemorates the Battle of Moores Creek Bridge, a pivotal Revolutionary War engagement fought on February 27, 1776. The battle resulted in a decisive Patriot victory over Loyalist forces, marking a significant early step toward independence in the Southern colonies and boosting support for the Revolutionary cause. The site features a restored battlefield, a reconstructed bridge, and interpretive trails that immerse visitors in the history of the conflict.

Fort Raleigh National Historic Site

Located on Roanoke Island in North Carolina, Fort Raleigh National Historic Site preserves the site of England's first attempts to establish a colony in the New World. Established in the late 16th century, the Roanoke Colony is famous for the mysterious disappearance of its settlers, often referred to as the "Lost Colony." The site includes reconstructed earthworks, exhibits, and interpretive programs that explore the history of the colony, its interactions with the Indigenous peoples, and the enduring mystery of its fate.

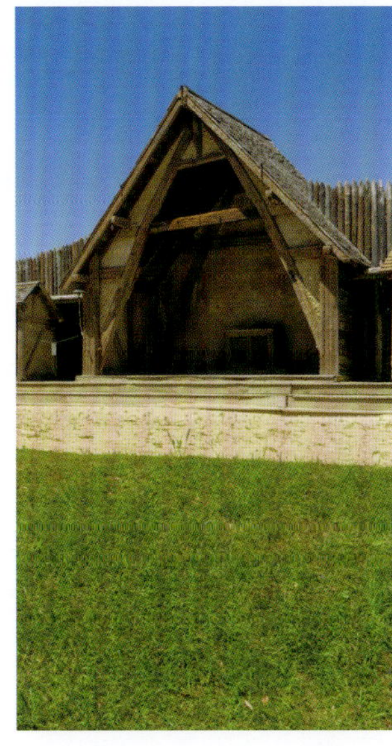

Wright Brothers National Memorial

Wright Brothers National Memorial celebrates the achievements of Orville and Wilbur Wright, who successfully conducted the first powered flight on December 17, 1903. This historic event, taking place on the sandy dunes of the Outer Banks, marked the birth of modern aviation. The site features a visitor center with exhibits on the Wright brothers' lives, their experiments, and the development of their aircraft. Visitors can also explore the reconstructed 1903 hangar and workshop, climb to the top of the hill where the Wright Brothers Monument stands *(see right)*, and more.

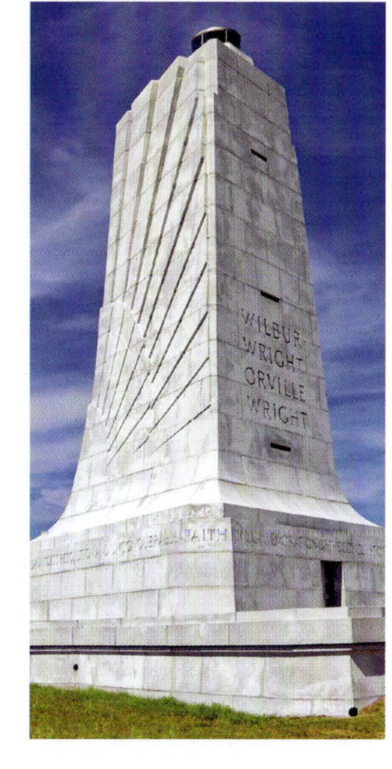

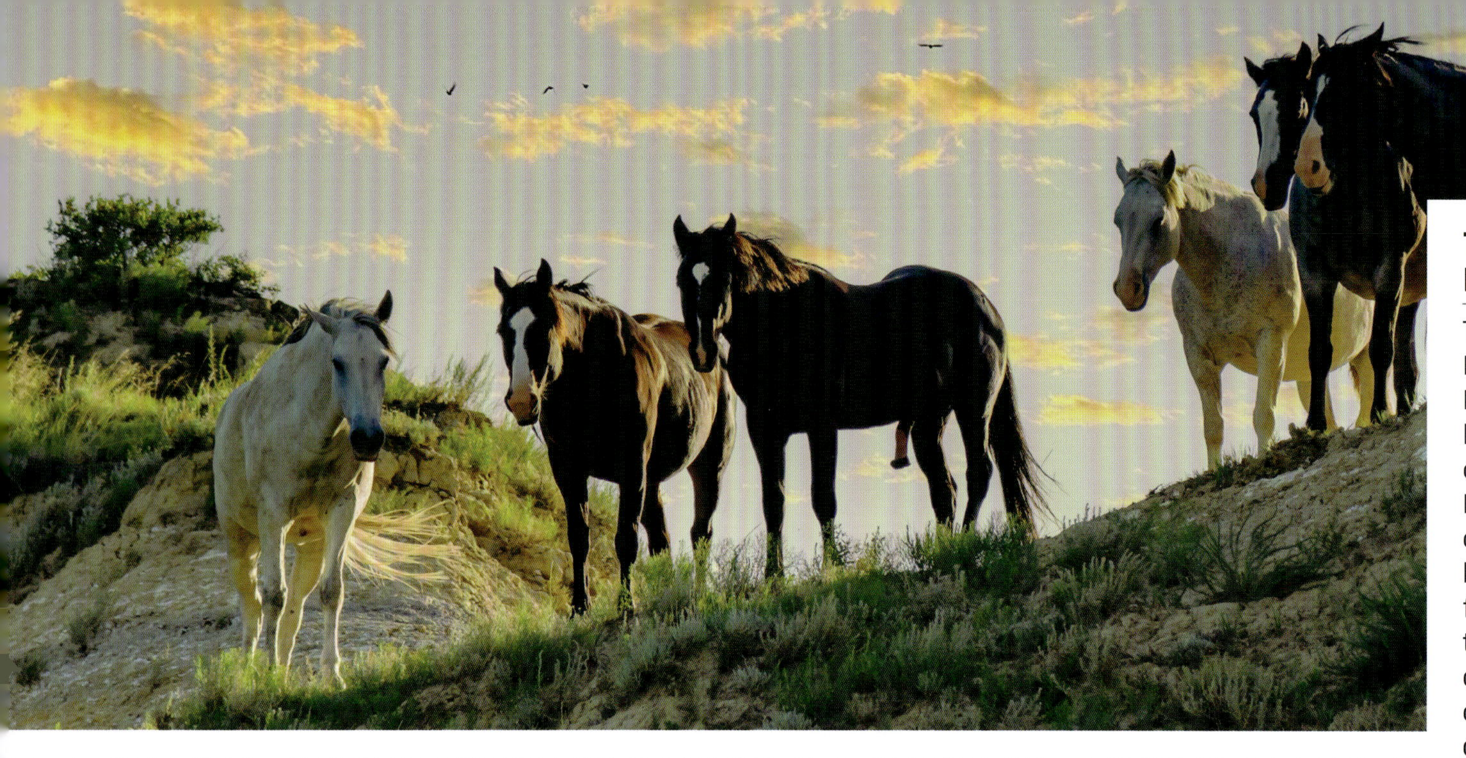

Theodore Roosevelt National Park

Theodore Roosevelt National Park, located in western North Dakota, preserves the rugged landscapes and diverse wildlife of the North Dakota Badlands. Named after the 26th President of the United States, the park is known for its dramatic scenery, featuring layered rock formations, wide-open prairies, and canyons. Visitors can explore over 70 miles of hiking trails, drive the scenic South Unit Loop Road, and observe a variety of wildlife, including bison elk, wild horses, and prairie dogs.

NORTH DAKOTA

Knife River Indian Villages National Historic Site

Knife River Indian Villages National Historic Site preserves the remains of several Native American villages that were part of the Northern Plains' Mandan, Hidatsa, and Arikara tribes. The site offers insight into the culture, history, and traditions of these tribes, showcasing their dwellings, agricultural practices, and the environment they thrived in. Visitors can explore the reconstructed earth lodges, walk interpretive trails, and drop by the visitor center to learn about the history of the tribes, their interactions with European explorers, and the impact of the Lewis and Clark expedition.

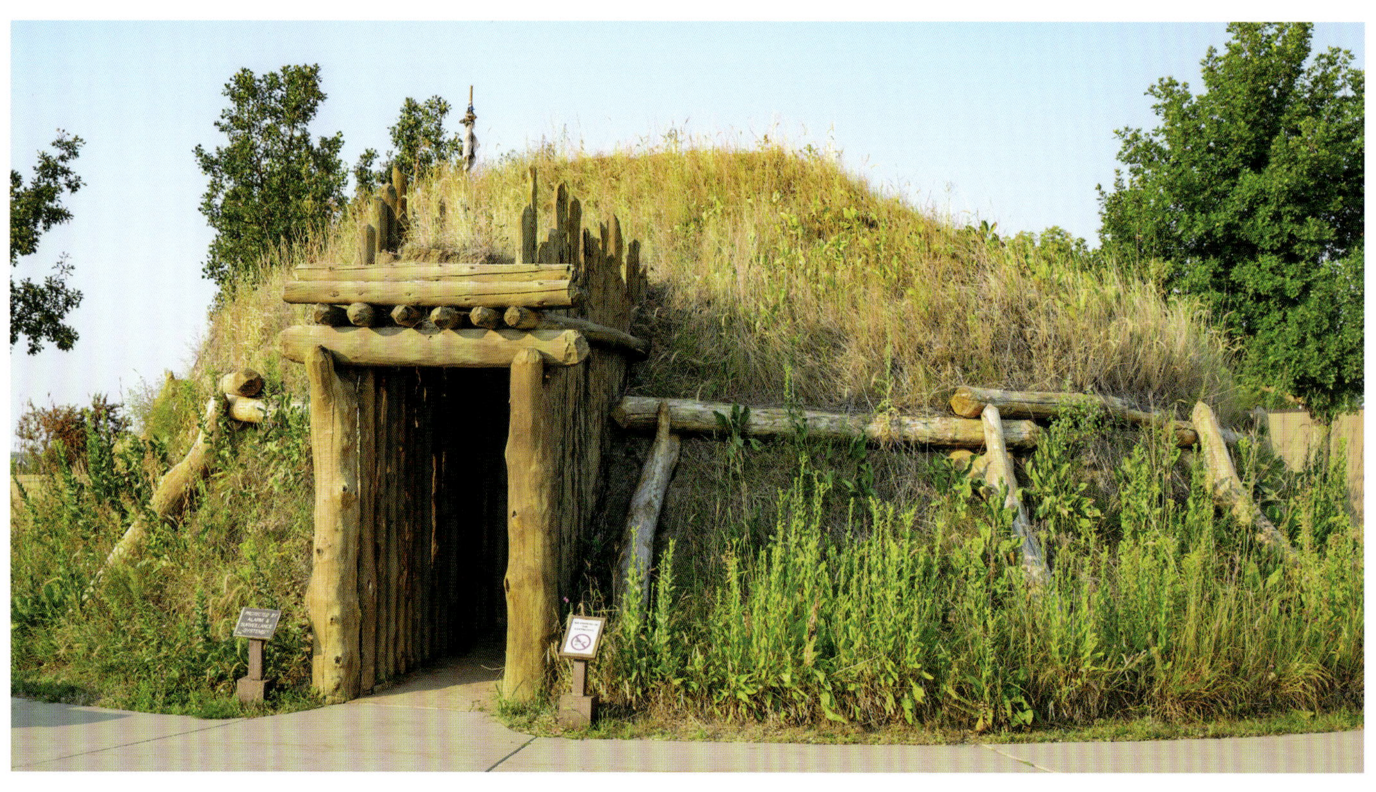

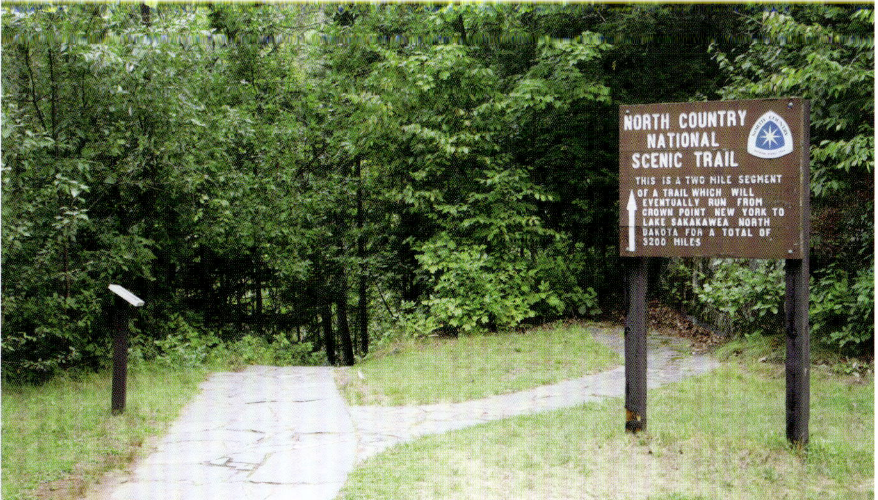

North Country National Scenic Trail

The North Country National Scenic Trail is a long-distance hiking trail that stretches over 4,600 miles across seven states, from New York to North Dakota. It traverses a wide variety of landscapes, including forests, prairies, wetlands, and hills, providing hikers with a varied and scenic view of the American wilderness.

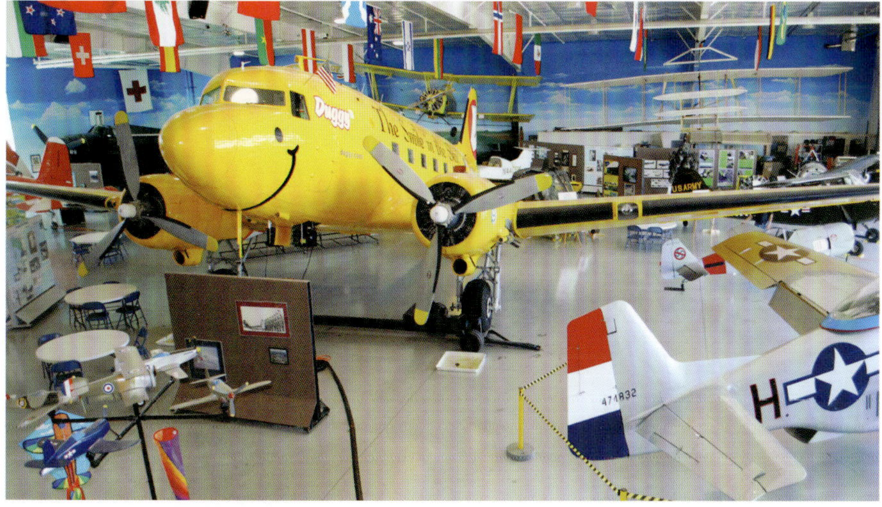

Fargo Air Museum

Fargo Air Museum is dedicated to preserving and showcasing the history of aviation through exhibits, aircraft, and memorabilia. The museum features a collection of historic aircraft, ranging from World War II planes to more modern aircraft, as well as artifacts and displays highlighting the evolution of aviation. Visitors can explore the museum's exhibits, including aircraft restoration projects, interactive displays, and aviation-related historical documents.

International Peace Garden

International Peace Garden, located on the border between the United States and Canada, spans 2,339 acres near Dunseith, North Dakota, and Boissevain, Manitoba. The garden is a symbol of peace and cooperation between the two nations, dedicated to fostering goodwill and celebrating the shared values of peace, unity, and friendship. The park features beautifully landscaped gardens, scenic walking paths, and monuments, including the iconic International Peace Garden Tower and a peace chapel.

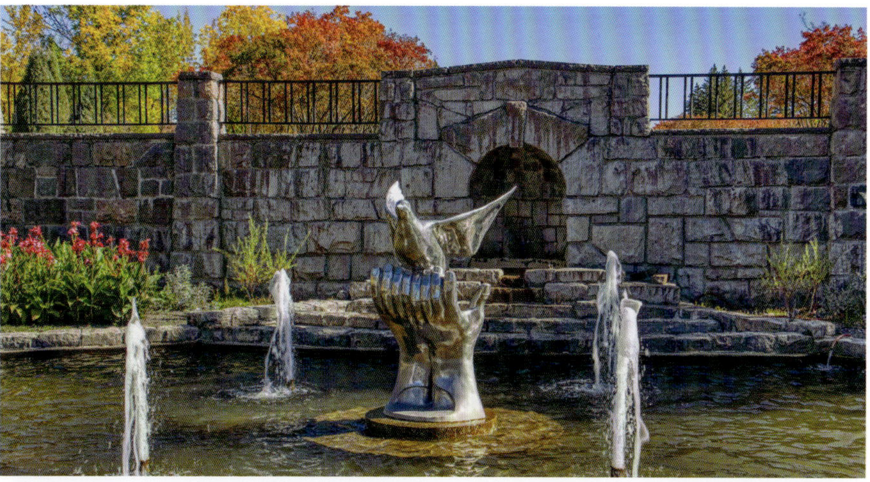

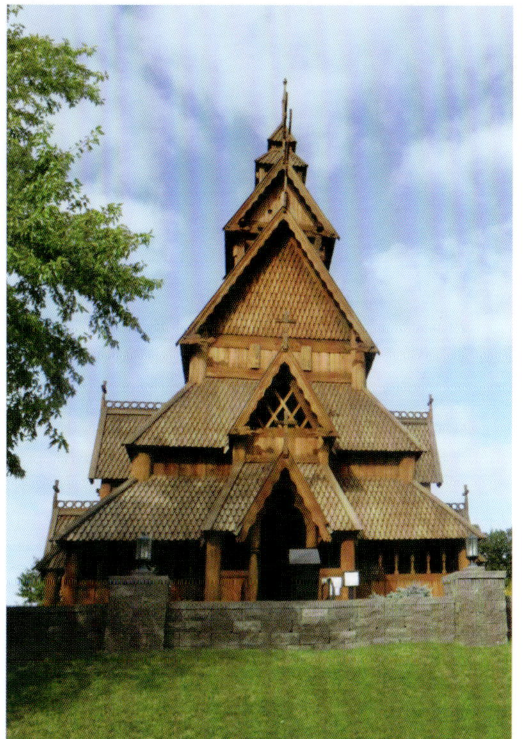

Scandinavian Heritage Park

Located in Minot, ND, Scandinavian Heritage Park celebrates the cultural contributions of Scandinavian immigrants to the region. The park features a variety of sculptures, monuments, and buildings representing the heritage of Denmark, Finland, Iceland, Norway, and Sweden. Highlights of the park include a traditional Finnish sauna, a replica of a Norwegian Stave Church, and a beautiful 15-foot-tall Dala horse, a symbol of Swedish culture.

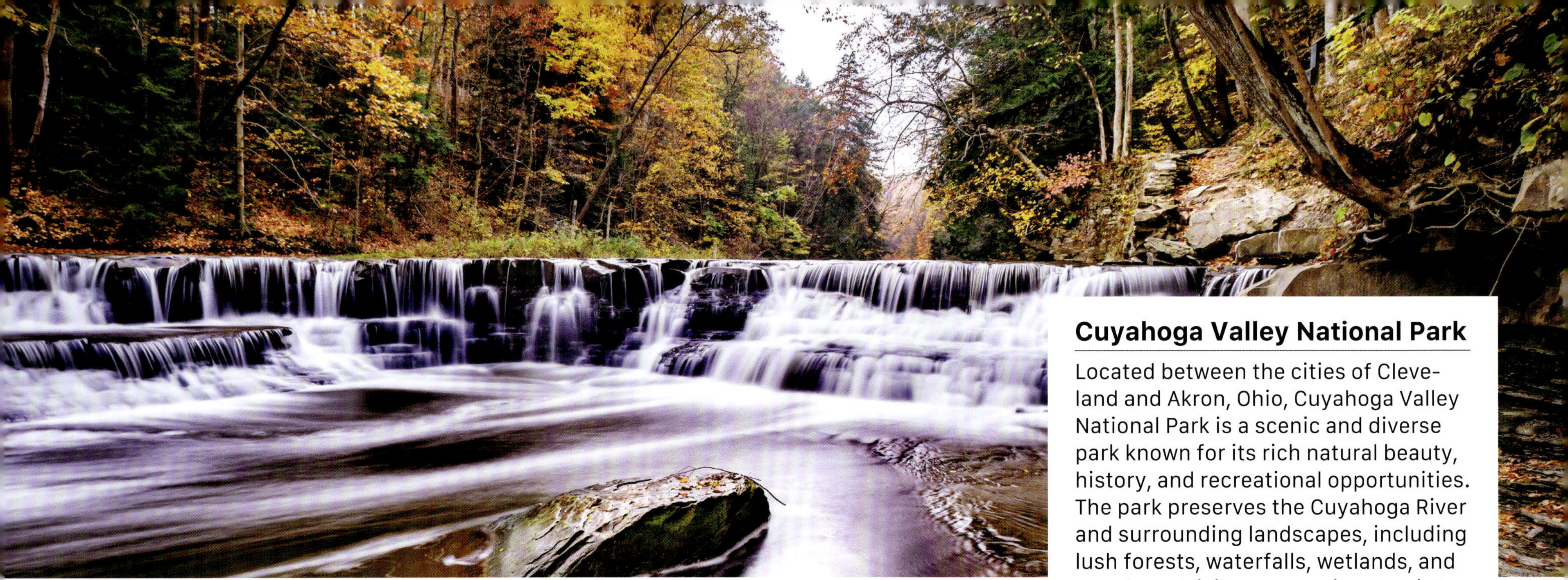

OHIO

Cuyahoga Valley National Park

Located between the cities of Cleveland and Akron, Ohio, Cuyahoga Valley National Park is a scenic and diverse park known for its rich natural beauty, history, and recreational opportunities. The park preserves the Cuyahoga River and surrounding landscapes, including lush forests, waterfalls, wetlands, and meadows. Visitors can enjoy a variety of activities, such as hiking, biking, birding, and scenic train rides on the Cuyahoga Valley Scenic Railroad.

Dayton Aviation Heritage National Historical Park

Dayton Aviation Heritage National Historical Park commemorates the birthplace of powered flight and honors the legacy of the Wright brothers, Orville and Wilbur Wright. The site also honors famous Dayton poet and novelist Paul Laurence Dunbar, and American aviation pioneers. The park is spread across multiple sites, including the Wright Brothers' home and the Wright Brothers' aviation factory.

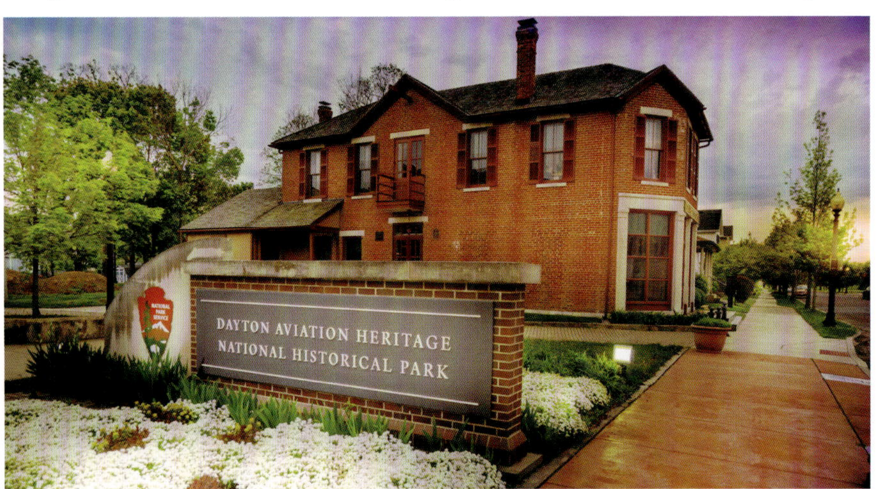

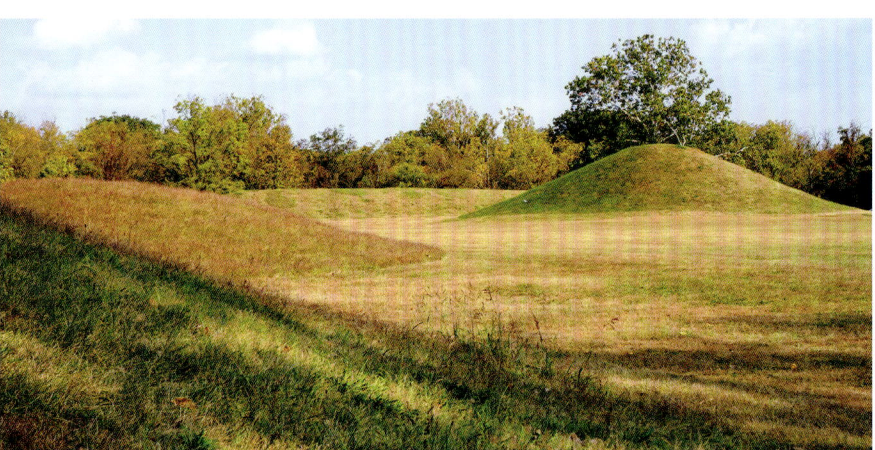

Hopewell Culture National Historical Park

Hopewell Culture National Historical Park preserves the earthworks and burial mounds built by the Hopewell people, a Native American culture that thrived from 200 BCE to 500 CE. The park includes several sites, such as Mound City Group, Seip Earthworks, and Hopeton Earthworks, where visitors can explore the geometric mounds and learn about the Hopewell's advanced trade networks, artistry, and spiritual beliefs.

Charles Young Buffalo Soldiers National Monument

Charles Young Buffalo Soldiers National Monument honors the life and legacy of Colonel Charles Young, a distinguished military leader, educator, and civil rights advocate. The site includes Young's home, which serves as a center for learning about his achievements, and the history of the Buffalo Soldiers.

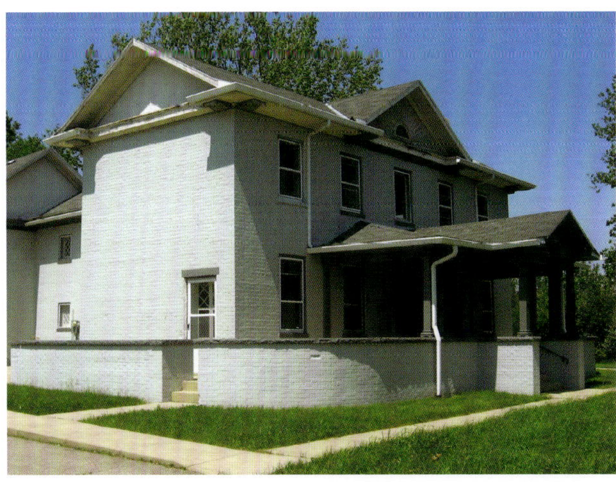

First Ladies National Historic Site

First Ladies National Historic Site honors the lives and contributions of America's first ladies and their impact on the nation's history. The site includes the restored home of Ida Saxton McKinley, wife of President William McKinley, as well as an education and research center housed in a nearby historic bank building. Visitors can enjoy exhibits and guided tours that showcase the personal stories, accomplishments, and public roles of the first ladies, as well as their influence on social and political issues throughout U.S. history.

James A. Garfield National Historic Site

James A. Garfield National Historic Site preserves the home and estate of James Abram Garfield, the 20th President of the United States. Known as "Lawnfield," the site served as Garfield's family residence and the location of his successful 1880 front-porch campaign, where he campaigned from his home instead of traveling around the country. The site includes the restored Victorian home, outbuildings, and a visitor center with exhibits about Garfield's life, career, and presidency.

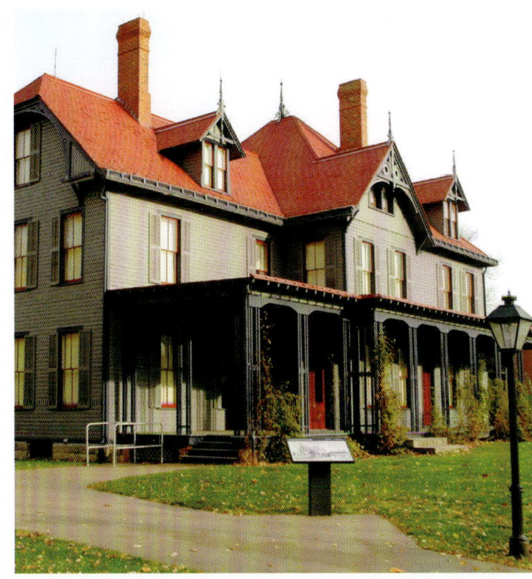

Perry's Victory and International Peace Memorial

Located on South Bass Island in Lake Erie, near Put-In-Bay, OH, Perry's Victory and International Peace Memorial commemorates the Battle of Lake Erie during the War of 1812, and celebrates the lasting peace between the U.S., Canada, and Great Britain. The centerpiece of the site is a 352-foot Doric column, one of the tallest monuments in the U.S., offering stunning views of the surrounding lake and islands from its observation deck.

William Howard Taft National Historic Site

William Howard Taft National Historic Site preserves the birthplace and boyhood home of William Howard Taft, the 27th President of the U.S. and the 10th Chief Justice of the Supreme Court—the only person to have served as both in U.S. history. Visitors can tour the restored 19th-century Greek Revival house, which features period furnishings, family artifacts, and exhibits detailing Taft's life, career, and contributions to American law and governance.

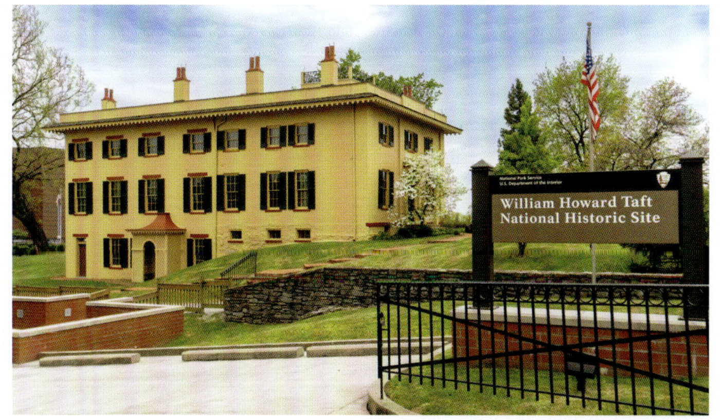

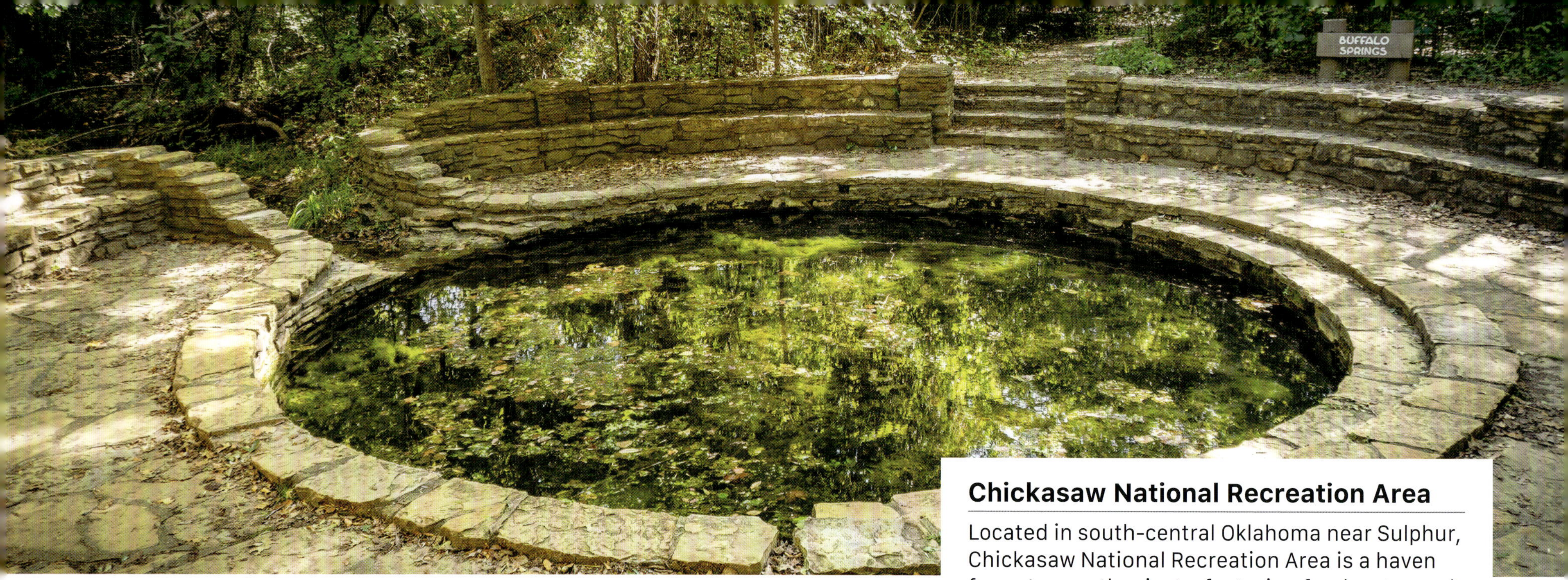

OKLAHOMA

Chickasaw National Recreation Area

Located in south-central Oklahoma near Sulphur, Chickasaw National Recreation Area is a haven for nature enthusiasts, featuring freshwater and mineral water springs *(see above)*, scenic hiking trails, and lakes—such as Lake of the Arbuckles—perfect for fishing, boating, and swimming.

Fort Smith National Historic Site

Fort Smith National Historic Site preserves the rich history of the frontier era, law enforcement, and the westward expansion of the U.S. The site includes the remains of two frontier forts built in 1817 and 1838, as well as the historic federal courthouse used by Judge Isaac C. Parker. Visitors can explore the reconstructed gallows, the courtroom, and exhibits that highlight the stories of soldiers, settlers, and Native Americans.

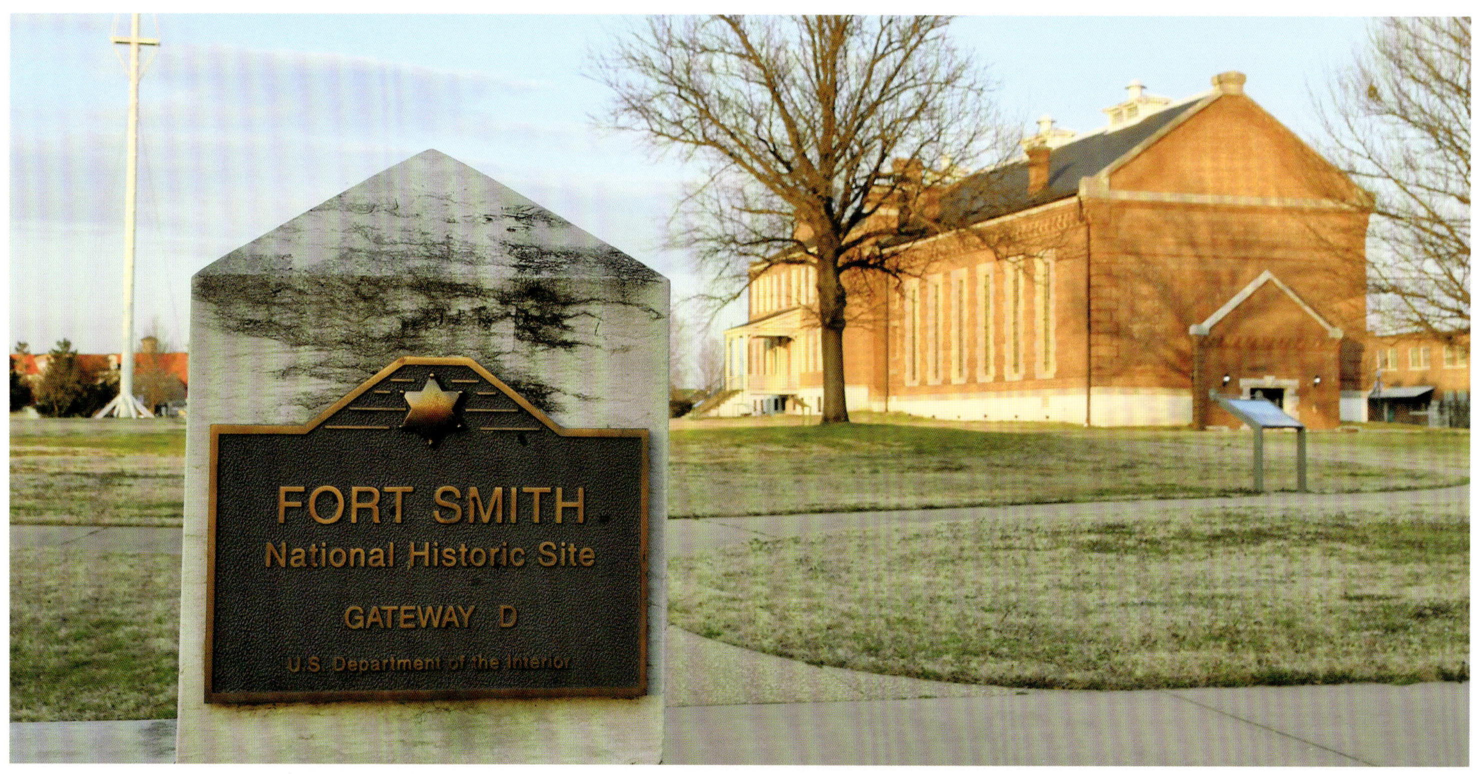

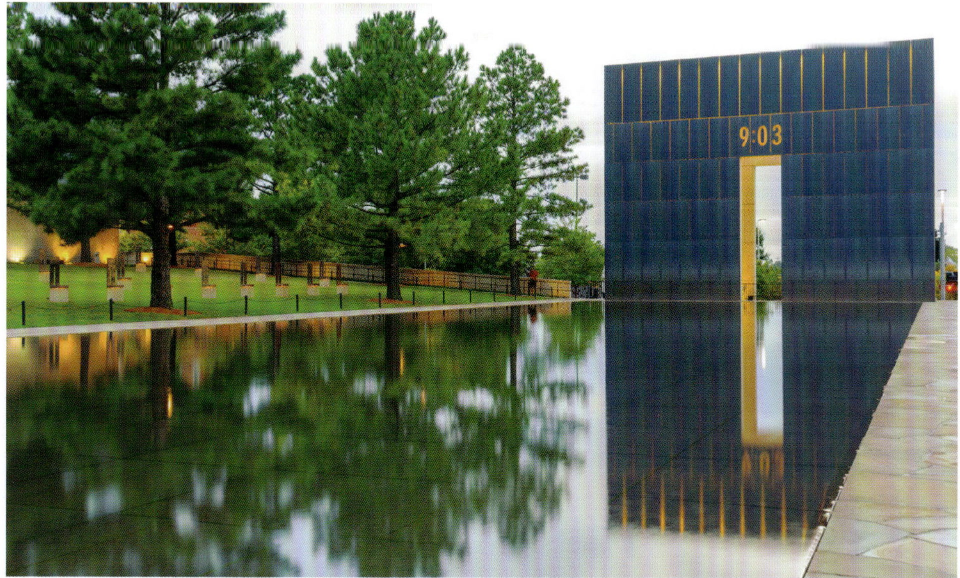

Oklahoma City National Memorial

Oklahoma City National Memorial honors the victors, survivors, and rescuers affected by the April 19, 1995, bombing of the Alfred P. Murrah Federal Building. This tragic act of domestic terrorism claimed 168 lives and left a lasting impact on the nation. The memorial features the Outdoor Symbolic Memorial *(see above)*, which includes the Field of Empty Chairs, each representing a life lost, the Reflecting Pool, and the Survivor Tree.

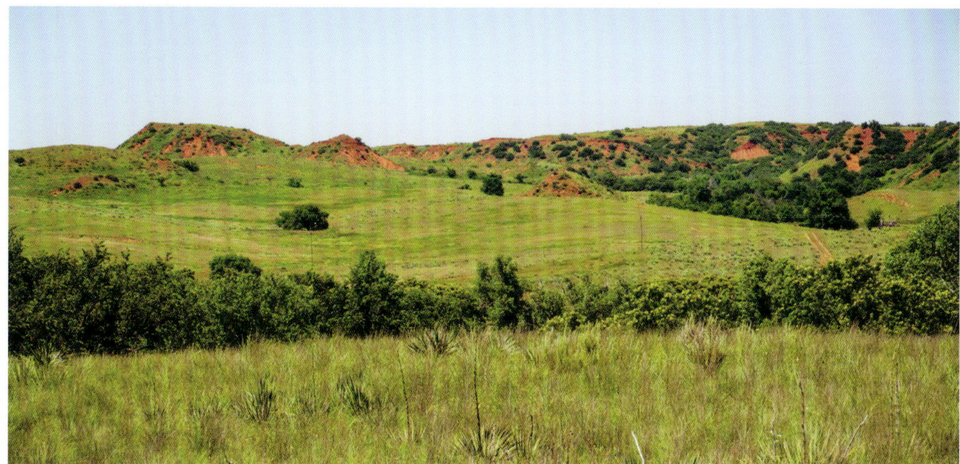

Washita Battlefield National Historic Site

Washita Battlefield National Historic Site preserves the site of the Battle of Washita, a significant and tragic event in American history. The site includes interpretive trails, exhibits, and a visitor center that provides historical context about the battle, its impact on the Cheyenne people, and the broad conflicts between Indigenous nations and the U.S. government.

Trail of Tears National Historic Trail

The Trail of Tears National Historic Trail commemorates the tragic chapter in U.S. history where Native American tribes—including the Cherokee, Creek, Choctaw, Chickasaw, and Seminole—were forcibly removed from their ancestral homelands to designated Indian Territory, resulting in an estimated 13,200–16,700 deaths. The trail spans nine states, tracing the routes traveled by the tribes on foot, by wagon, and by boat. Visitors can explore historic sites, interpretive centers, and museums that preserve the stories of resilience, cultural loss, and survival.

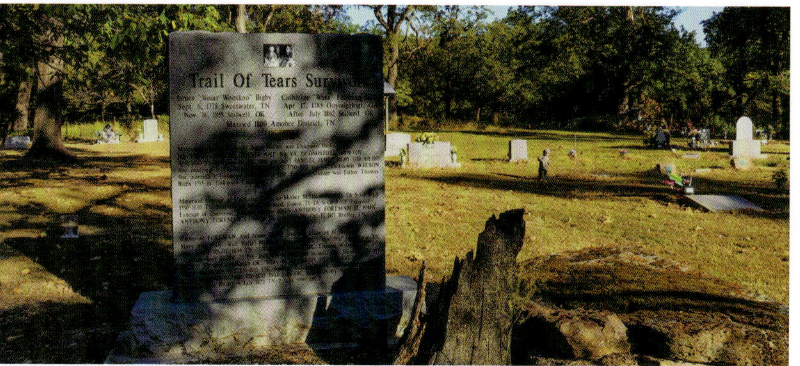

Henry Overholser Mansion

Henry Overholser Mansion is a beautifully preserved historic home that offers a glimpse into the city's early days and its rise during the late 19th and early 20th centuries. Built in 1903 by Henry Overholser, known as the "Father of Oklahoma City," the mansion is an exquisite example of Victorian architecture with ornate details and period furnishings. Visitors can take guided tours to learn about the Overholser family, their contributions to the city's development, and the history of the region.

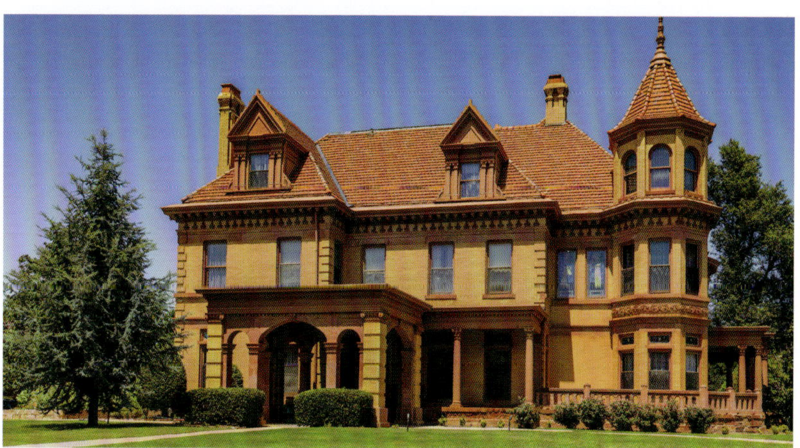

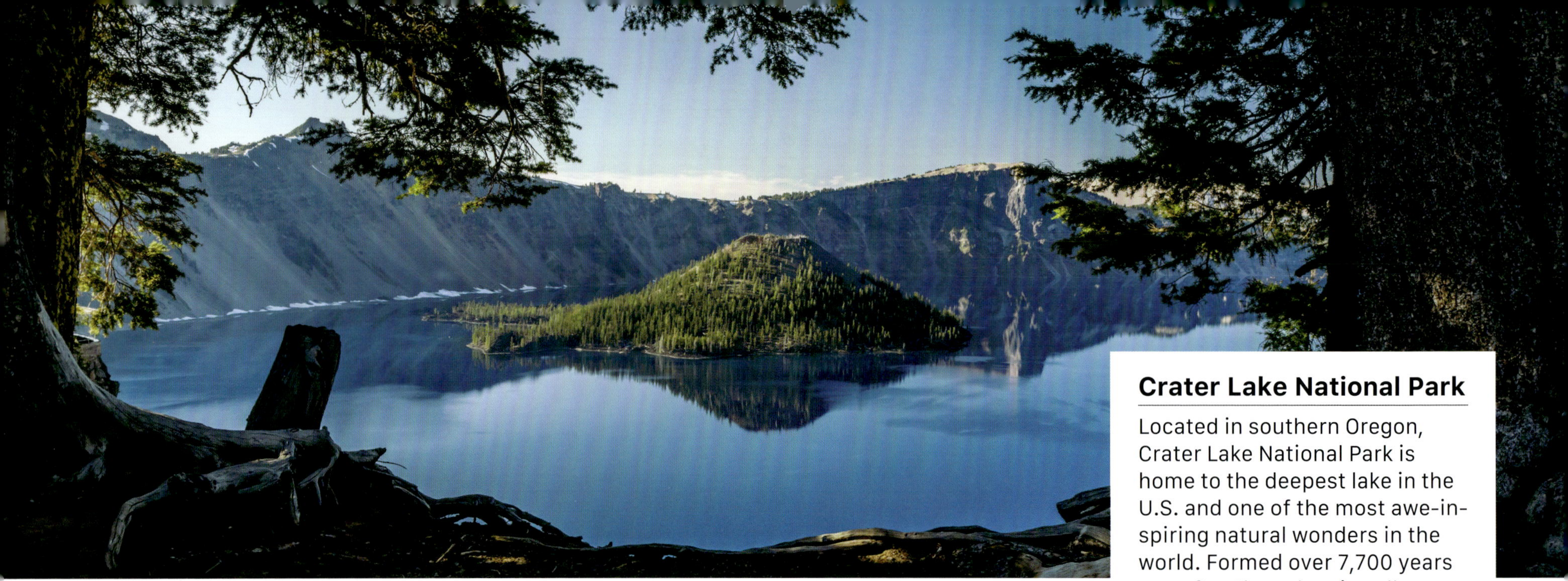

Crater Lake National Park

Located in southern Oregon, Crater Lake National Park is home to the deepest lake in the U.S. and one of the most awe-inspiring natural wonders in the world. Formed over 7,700 years ago after the volcanic collapse of Mount Mazama, Crater Lake is renowned for its brilliant blue water and remarkable clarity.

OREGON

Lewis and Clark National Historical Park

Lewis and Clark National Historical Park, located along the Columbia river in Oregon and Washington, commemorates the historic 1804–1806 expedition led by Meriwether Lewis and William Clark. The park includes Fort Clatsop, where the expedition wintered in 1805–1806, as well as other key sites along the Pacific Coast. Visitors can explore reconstructed structures, interpretive trails, and exhibits that provide insight into the expedition's challenges, achievements, and interactions with Indigenous peoples.

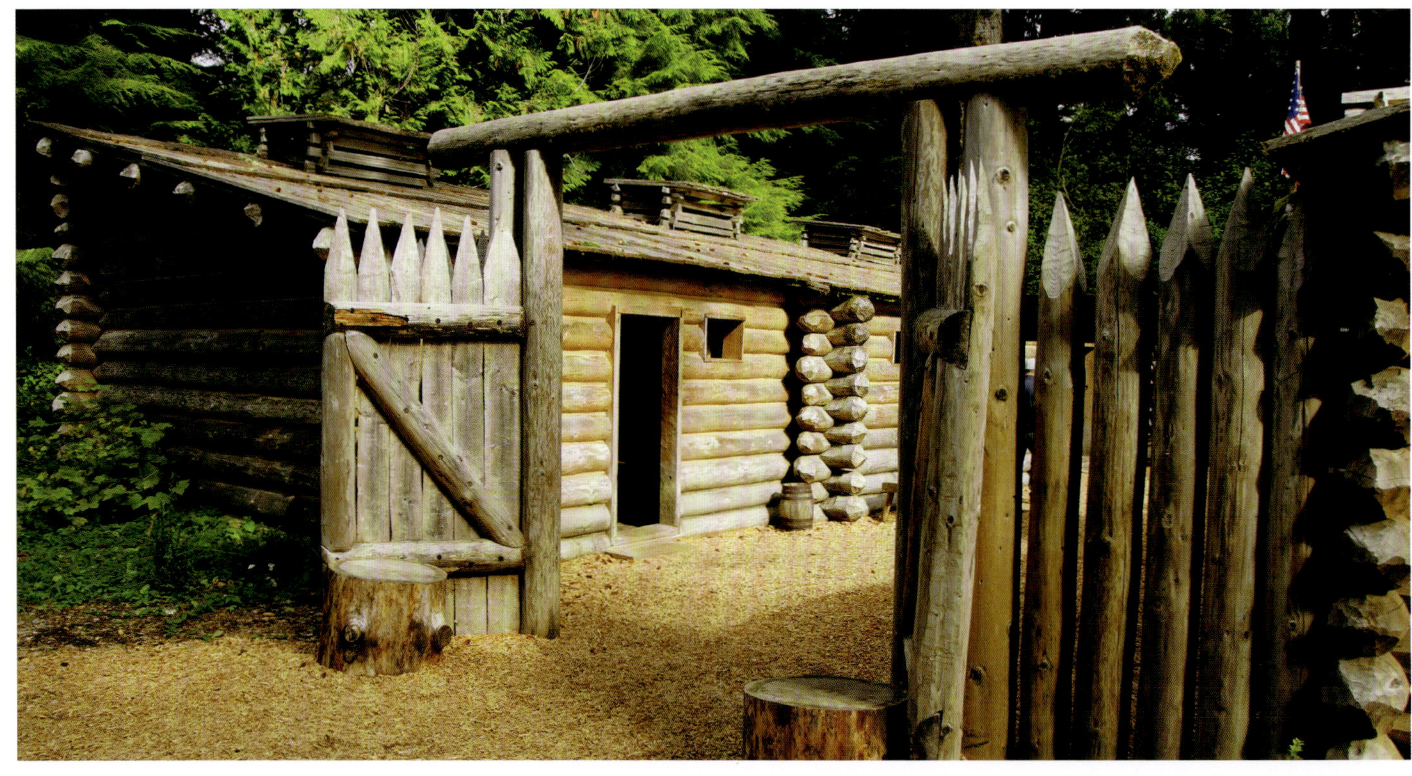

Oregon Caves National Monument and Preserve

Located in the Siskiyou Mountains of southern Oregon, Oregon Caves National Monument and Preserve is a unique natural wonder featuring a network of marble caves formed over hundreds of thousands of years. Known as the "Marble Halls of Oregon," the caves are famous for their intricate formations, including stalactites, stalagmites, and flowstones.

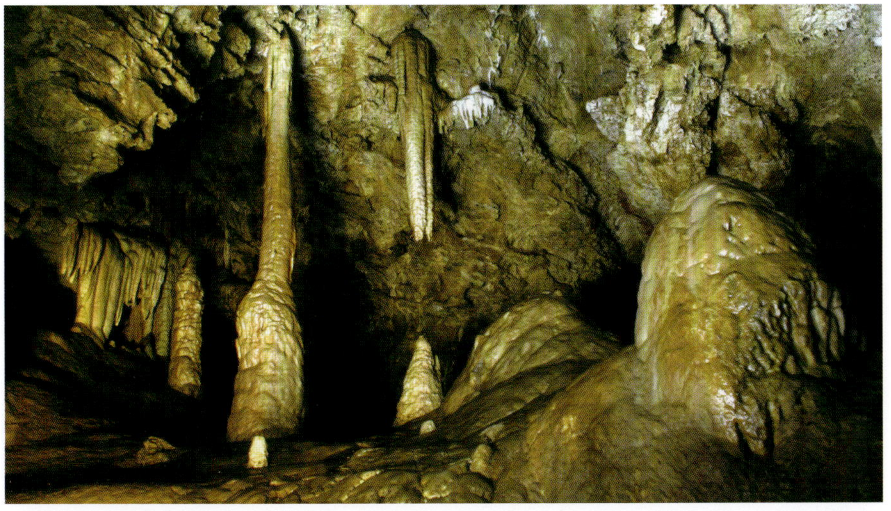

John Day Fossil Beds National Monument

Located in central Oregon, John Day Fossil Beds National Monument is a treasure trove of paleontological and geological history. Spanning three units—Sheep Rock, Painted Hills, and Clarno—this monument preserves a stunning record of plant and animal evolution over the past 40 million years, as well as colorful landscapes shaped by volcanic activity and erosion.

Fort Vancouver National Historic Site

Fort Vancouver National Historic Site, located in Washington and Oregon, preserves the history of the Pacific Northwest as a hub of trade, military presence, and cultural exchange during the 19th century. The site includes a reconstructed fort, historical buildings, and gardens, as well as the Pearson Air Museum, which highlights early aviation history. Visitors can explore exhibits, attend living history demonstrations, and learn about the interactions between Indigenous peoples, traders, settlers, and the military.

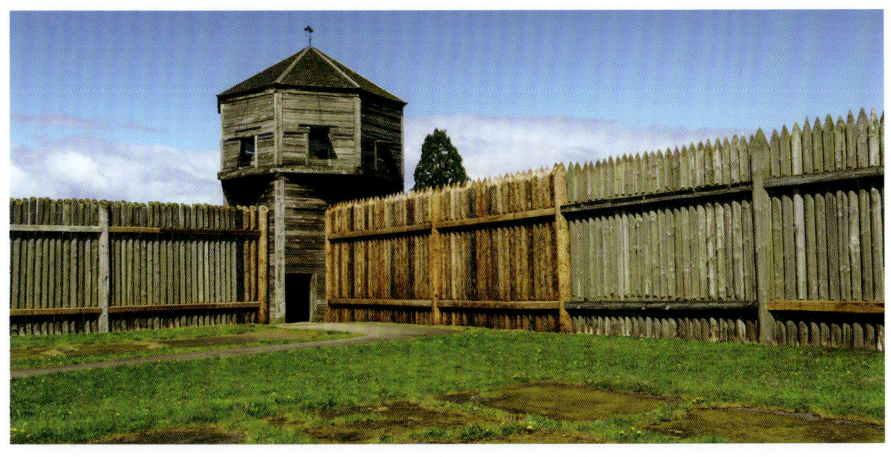

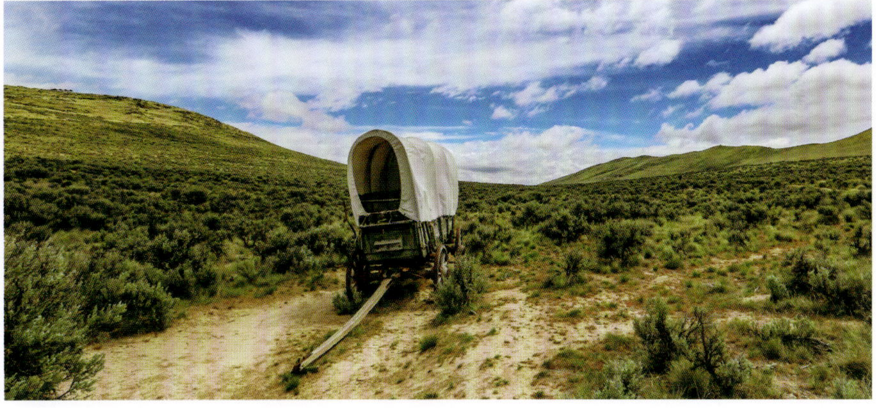

Oregon National Historic Trail

The Oregon National Historic Trail commemorates the historic route used by pioneers in the mid-1800s to migrate westward to Oregon's fertile Willamette Valley. Spanning approximately 2,170 miles across six states—Missouri, Kansas, Nebraska, Wyoming, Idaho, and Oregon—the trail follows the footsteps of thousands who traveled by wagon in search of new opportunities. Visitors can explore landmarks, interpretive centers, and historic sites that preserve the legacy of this epic journey, including wagon ruts, pioneer graves, and reconstructed forts.

PENNSYLVANIA

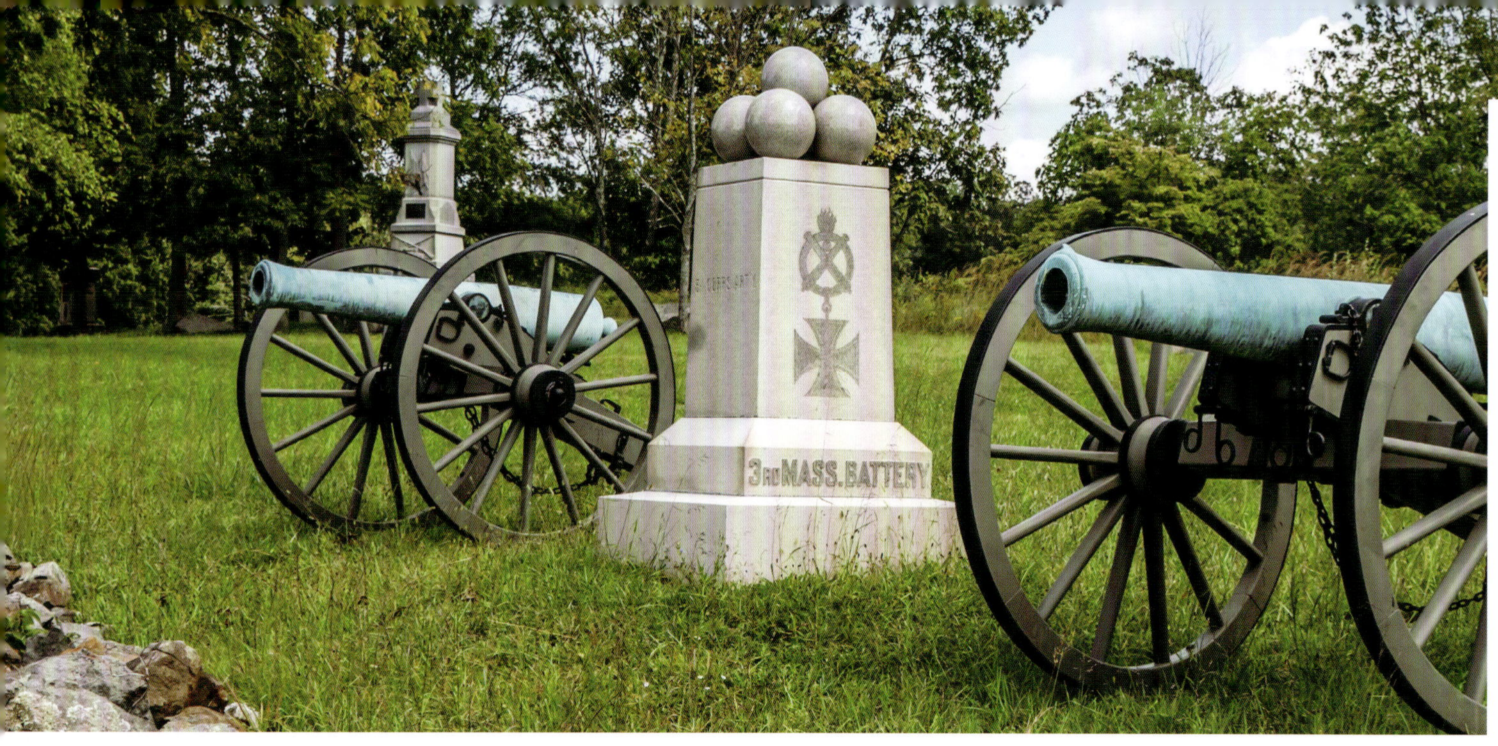

Gettysburg National Military Park

Gettysburg National Military Park preserves the site of the Battle of Gettysburg, a pivotal clash during the American Civil War. This battle marked a turning point in the war, resulting in a decisive Union victory and leading to President Lincoln's famous Gettysburg Address. Visitors can explore the battlefield through guided tours, walking trails, and the Gettysburg Museum and Visitor Center, which features artifacts, exhibits, and a massive cyclorama painting depicting the battle.

Independence National Historical Park

Independence National Historical Park is a key site for understanding the birth of the United States. Known as the "birthplace of American democracy," it includes several important landmarks, most notably Independence Hall, where the Declaration of Independence was adopted in 1776 and the U.S. Constitution was signed in 1787. The park also includes the Liberty Bell *(see right)*, a symbol of American freedom, and numerous other historic buildings, such as the Congress Hall and the Old City Hall.

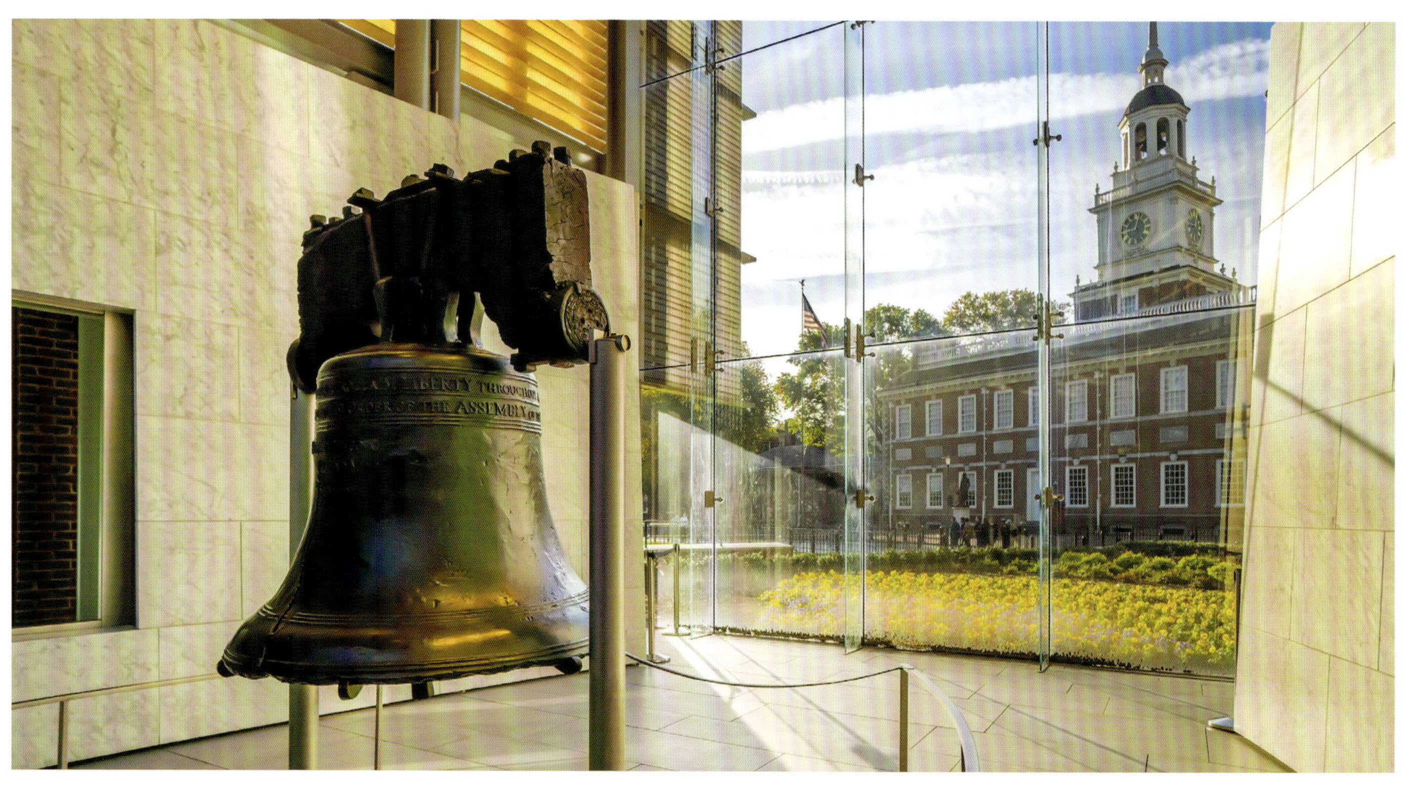

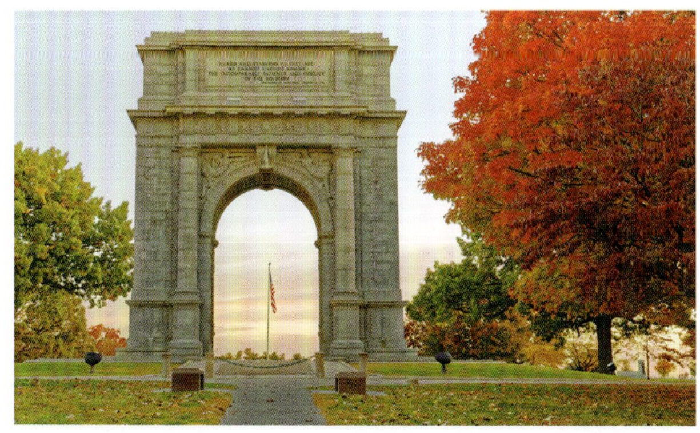

Valley Forge National Historical Park

Valley Forge National Historical Park preserves the site of the Continental Army's winter encampment during the American Revolution from December 1777 to June 1778. The park spans over 3,500 acres and includes historic structures, monuments, and memorials, as well as walking and biking trails. Key sites include Washington's Headquarters, the Muhlenberg Brigade Huts, and the National Memorial Arch *(see above)*.

Edgar Allan Poe National Historic Site

Edgar Allan Poe National Historic Site preserves the home where famed American writer Edgar Allan Poe lived from 1843 to 1844. Poe, known for his dark and macabre stories and poems, such as "The Tell-Tale Heart" and *The Raven*, wrote several important works during his time in this house. The site offers visitors a glimpse into Poe's life and work, showcasing his living conditions, personal artifacts, and the literary environment that influenced his writing.

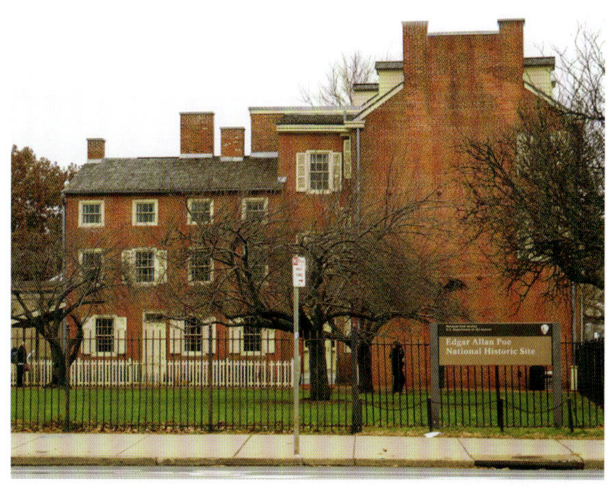

Eisenhower National Historic Site

Eisenhower National Historic Site preserves the home and farm of Dwight D. Eisenhower, the 34th President of the United States, and a key military leader during World War II. The property includes his residence, where he and his wife Mamie lived from 1950 under his death in 1969, as well as the farm where Eisenhower enjoyed his retirement and reflected on his presidency. The site offers visitors a chance to explore the Eisenhowers' personal lives, their contributions to American history, and the home's role as a meeting place for leaders during the Cold War.

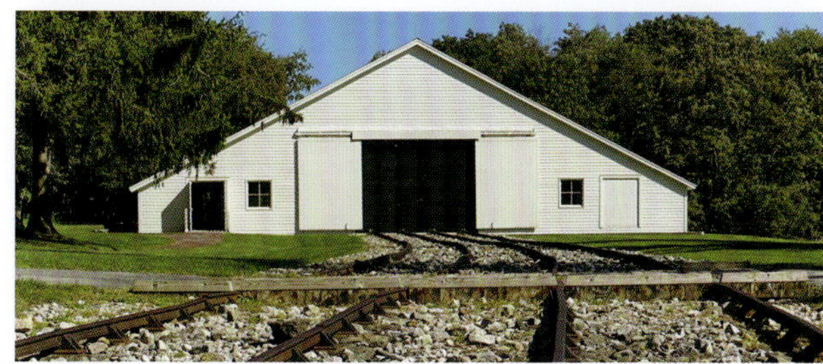

Allegheny Portage Railroad National Historic Site

Located in western Pennsylvania, Allegheny Portage Railroad National Historic Site preserves the remains of the first railroad to successfully cross the Allegheny Mountains. The site includes the reconstructed engine house, a portion of the track, and the iconic incline planes where canal boats were lifted over the steep mountain ridges. Visitors can explore exhibits, hike along the trails, and learn about the challenges of constructing the railroad, and its significance in advancing transportation and industry in early America.

Flight 93 National Memorial

Flight 93 National Memorial honors the passengers and crew of United Airlines Flight 93, who heroically thwarted a hijacking attempt on September 11, 2001. The plane, headed for a target in Washington D.C., crashed into a field near Shanksville after passengers and crew members fought the hijackers, preventing a greater tragedy. The memorial site includes the Wall of Names, which lists the names of the 40 victims, and the Flight Path Walkway, which marks the flight's trajectory before it crashed.

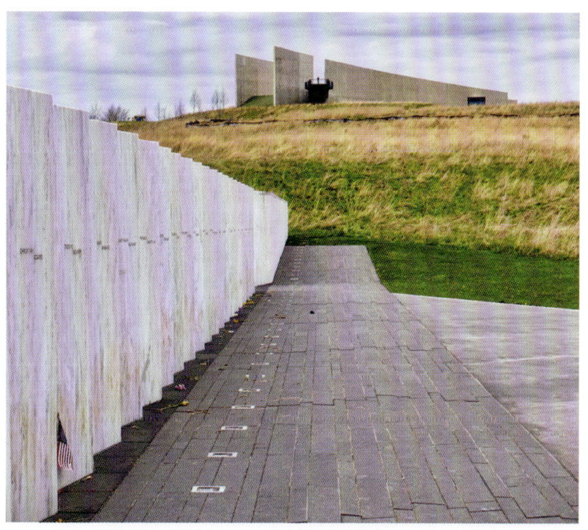

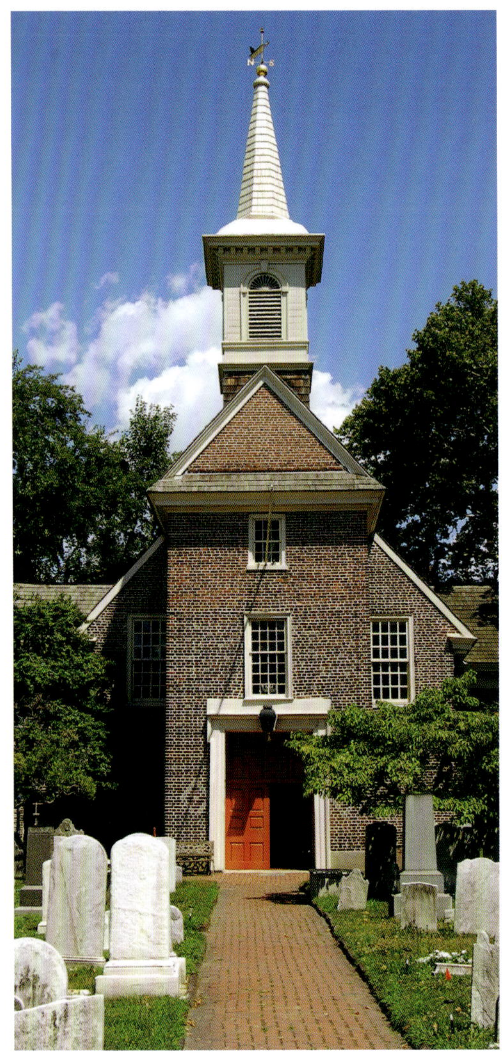

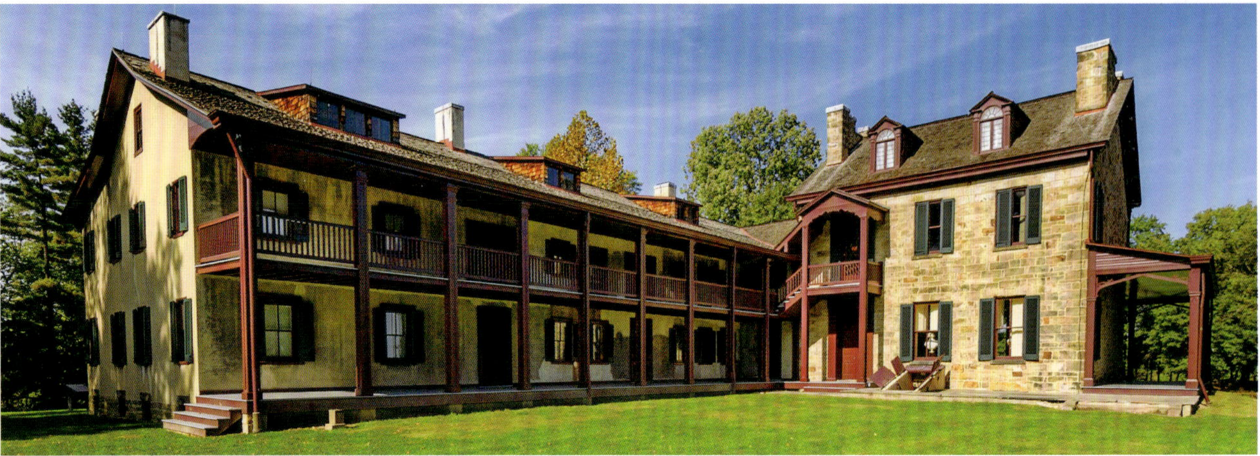

Friendship Hill National Historic Site

Friendship Hill National Historic Site preserves the country estate of Albert Gallatin, a prominent early American statesman, diplomat, and Secretary of the Treasury under Presidents Thomas Jefferson and James Madison. The site includes Gallatin's restored home, and the surrounding 661 acres of scenic grounds overlooking the Monongahela River. Visitors can explore exhibits about Gallatin's life, his contributions to the young nation, and the history of the estate.

Gloria Dei Church National Historic Site

Known locally as "Old Swedes'," Gloria Dei Church National Historic Site is the oldest church in Pennsylvania, built between 1698 and 1700 by Swedish settlers who established the New Sweden colony. The church features colonial-era architecture, historic furnishings, and a cemetery with graves dating back to the 17th century. Visitors can explore the church's role in early American history, including its connection to the Swedish and Finnish settlers who contributed to the region's development.

Hopewell Furnace National Historic Site

Hopewell Furnace National Historic Site preserves a restored 19th-century iron-making community that played a significant role in early American industry. The site features a charcoal-fueled blast furnace, the ironmaster's mansion, worker homes, and other historic buildings, providing a glimpse into life in an industrial village. Visitors can view exhibits, watch demonstrations of traditional iron-making techniques, and learn about the contributions of the diverse workforce, including immigrants, enslaved people, and free laborers.

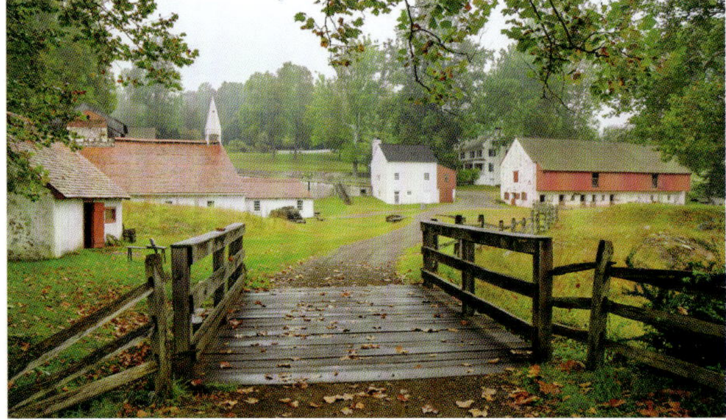

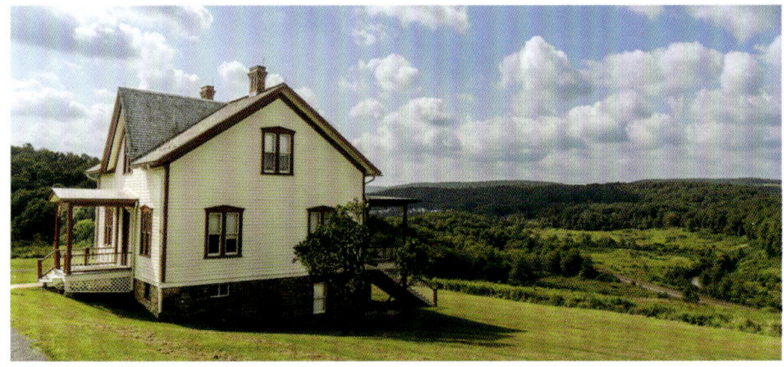

Johnstown Flood National Memorial

Located in southwestern Pennsylvania, Johnstown Flood National Memorial commemorates the devastating Johnstown Flood of May 31, 1889. The disaster occurred when the South Fork Dam, holding back Lake Conemaugh, failed after days of heavy rain. The resulting flood released 20 million tons of water, destroying the town of Johnstown and killing over 2,200 people, making it one of the deadliest disasters in U.S. history. The memorial preserves the remnants of the dam and the former lakebed, offering exhibits, films, and guided tours at the visitor center to tell the story of the flood, its causes, and its aftermath.

Potomac Heritage National Scenic Trail

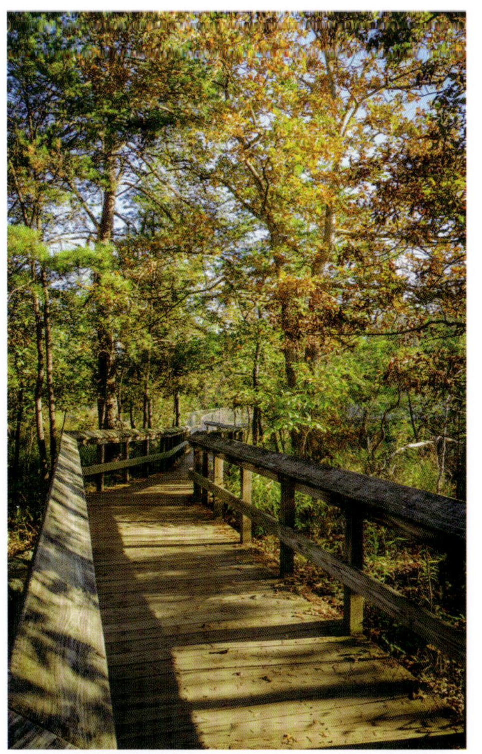

Potomac Heritage National Scenic Trail is a network of trails that spans over 700 miles through the mid-Atlantic region, connecting the landscapes and history of the Potomac River watershed. Stretching through Pennsylvania, Maryland, Virginia, and Washington, D.C., the trail system links natural areas, historic sites, and cultural landmarks. The trail network includes sections such as the Chesapeake and Ohio Canal Towpath, the Mount Vernon Trail, and parts of the Appalachian Trail, offering opportunities for hiking, biking, and paddling.

Steamtown National Historic Site

Steamtown National Historic Site preserves the history of steam railroading in America. Centered around a 19th-century railroad yard, the site features vintage locomotives, railcars, and equipment that illustrate the vital role of railroads in the nation's industrial and economic development. Visitors can view exhibits in the museum, watch demonstrations of locomotive maintenance in the roundhouse, and even take seasonal train excursions on restored steam and diesel trains.

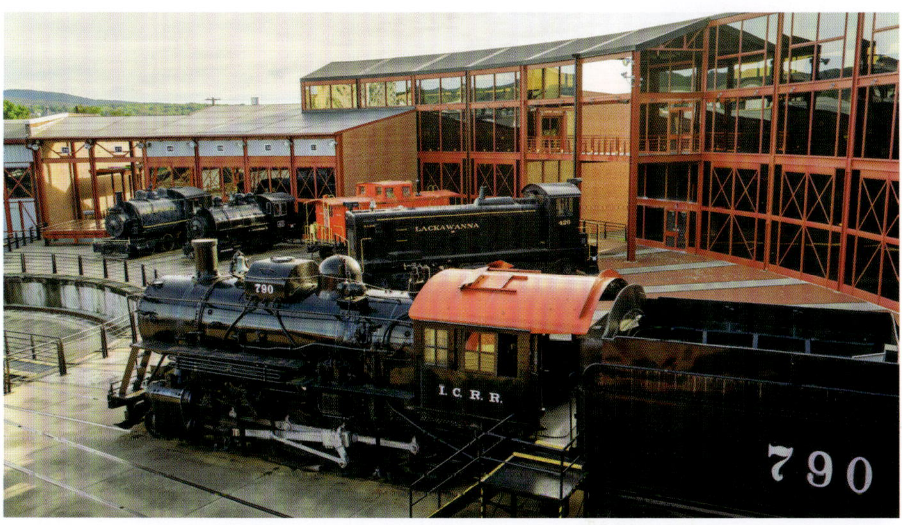

Lewis and Clark National Historic Trail

The Lewis and Clark National Historic Trail follows the historic route taken by the Lewis and Clark Expedition from 1804 to 1806, a journey commissioned by President Thomas Jefferson to explore the newly acquired Louisiana Territory and find a water route to the Pacific Ocean. Spanning over 4,900 miles through 16 states, the trail begins near St. Louis, MO, and ends at the Pacific Coast in Oregon. The trail passes through varied landscapes, including rivers, prairies, mountains, and forests, showcasing the natural beauty and cultural history of the U.S.

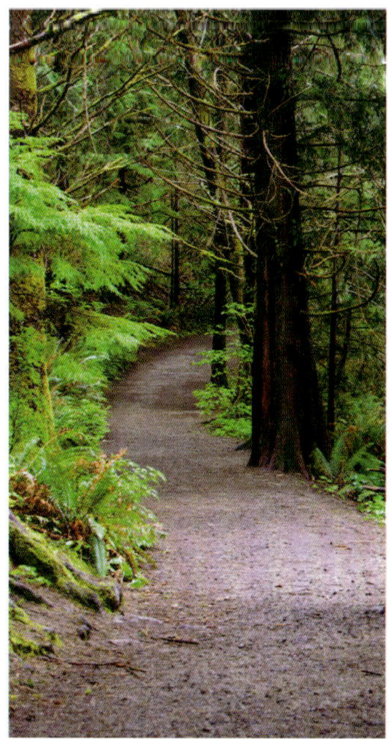

Thaddeus Kosciuszko National Memorial

Thaddeus Kosciuszko National Memorial honors the life and legacy of Thaddeus Kosciuszko, a Polish Lithuanian military engineer and American Revolutionary War hero. The memorial is housed in a historic townhouse where Kosciuszko lived in 1797 during his brief return to the U.S. Inside, exhibits and displays highlight his life, military achievements, and advocacy for freedom and equality.

Other Pennsylvania National Sites

- Carlisle Federal Indian Boarding School National Monument
- Fort Necessity National Battlefield
- Upper Delaware Scenic and Recreational River
- Fallingwater
- Reading Terminal Market

RHODE ISLAND

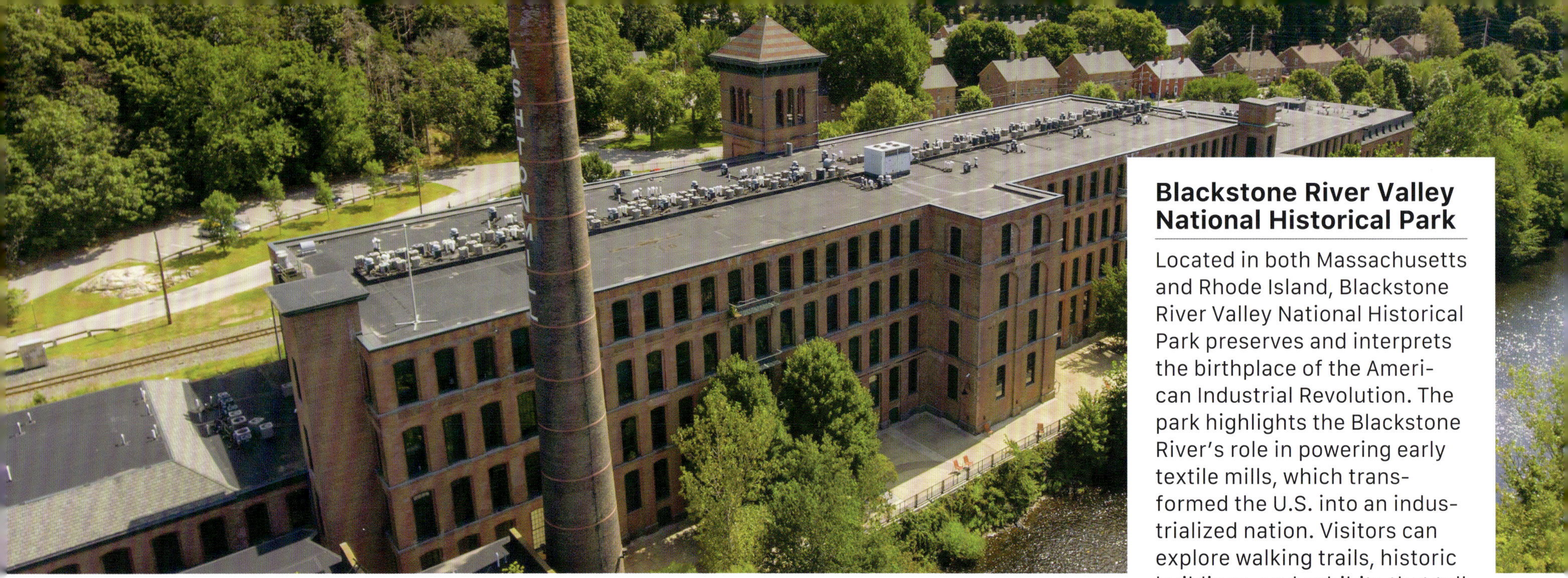

Blackstone River Valley National Historical Park

Located in both Massachusetts and Rhode Island, Blackstone River Valley National Historical Park preserves and interprets the birthplace of the American Industrial Revolution. The park highlights the Blackstone River's role in powering early textile mills, which transformed the U.S. into an industrialized nation. Visitors can explore walking trails, historic buildings, and exhibits that tell the story of innovation, labor, and the environmental impact of industrialization.

Roger Williams National Memorial

Roger Williams National Memorial honors Roger Williams, the founder of Rhode Island and a pioneer of religious freedom and separation of church and state. The 4.5-acre park features landscaped grounds, interpretive exhibits, and a visitor center where guests can learn about Williams's advocacy for individual liberty, his relationships with Indigenous peoples, and his role in shaping American ideals of tolerance and freedom.

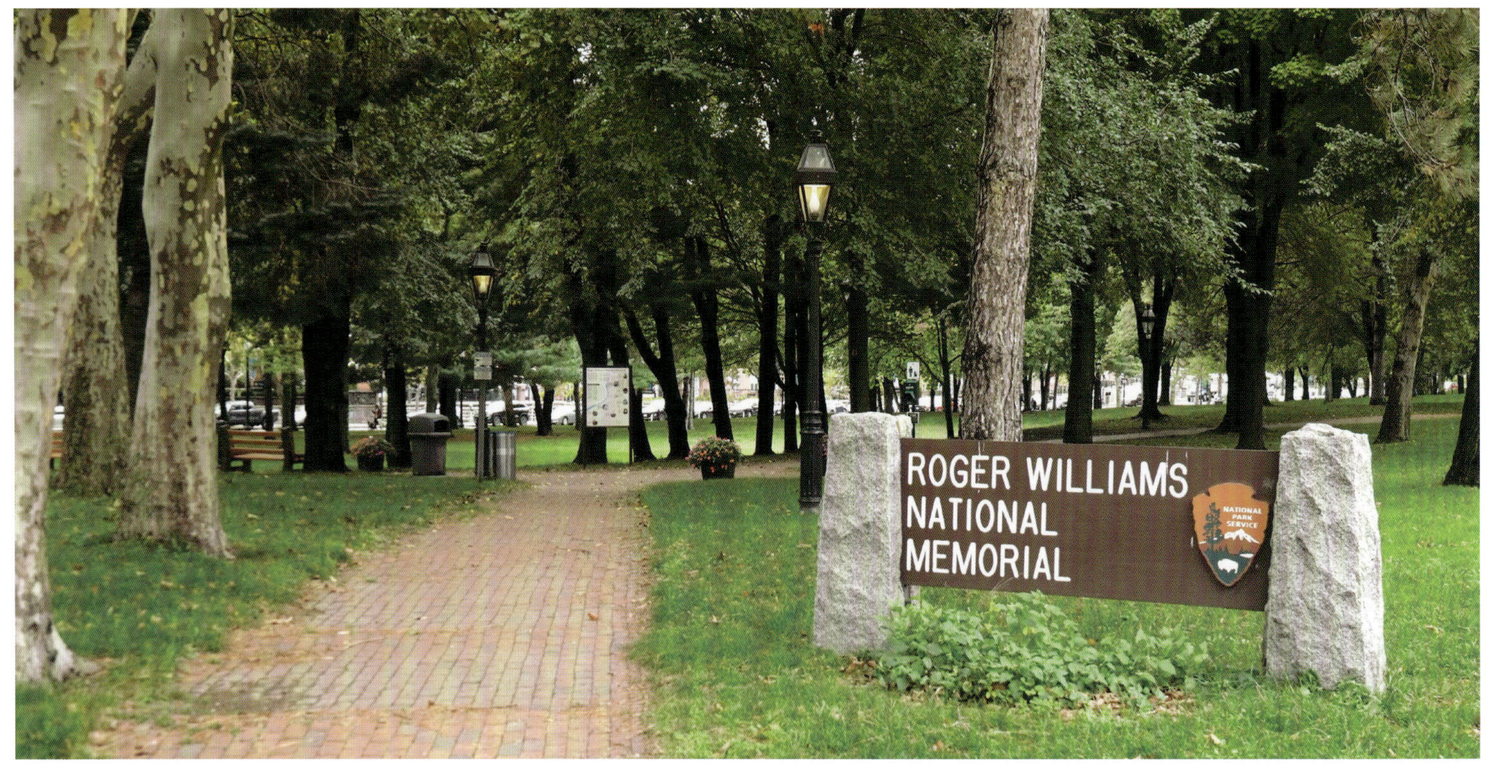

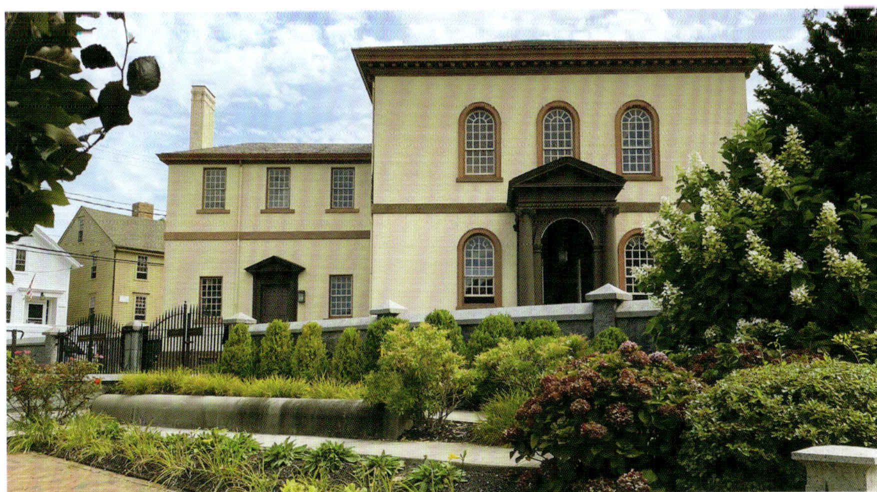

Touro Synagogue National Historic Site

Touro Synagogue National Historic Site is the oldest surviving synagogue building in the U.S. The site commemorates the Jewish community's contributions to early American history, and the principle of religious liberty—famously underscored in a 1790 letter from President George Washington, affirming the nation's commitment to tolerance. Visitors can tour the beautifully preserved synagogue, learn about its history through guided tours, and gain insight into the experiences of Jewish settlers in colonial America.

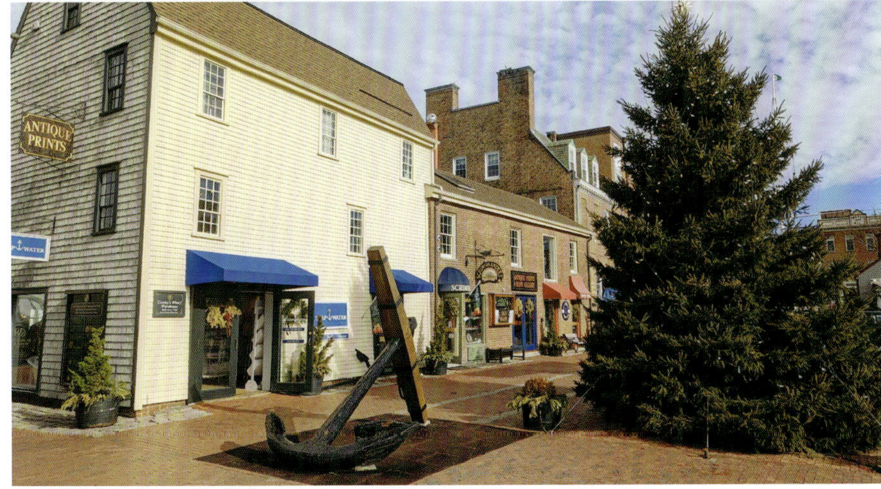

Bowen's Wharf

Known as the "Anchor of Newport," Bowen's Wharf is a historic waterfront destination that blends maritime heritage with modern-day charm. Visitors can enjoy strolling along the cobblestone streets, admiring historic architecture, or embarking on boat tours and sailing excursions to explore Newport Harbor and Narragansett Bay.

The Breakers Mansion

The Breakers is a grand Gilded Age mansion and National Historic Landmark. Built in 1895 as a summer home of Cornelius Vanderbilt II, the 70-room mansion exemplifies opulence and architectural grandeur. The Breakers offers guided and self-guided tours, allowing visitors to explore its lavish rooms and learn about the Vanderbilt family, their lifestyle, and the cultural history of the Gilded Age.

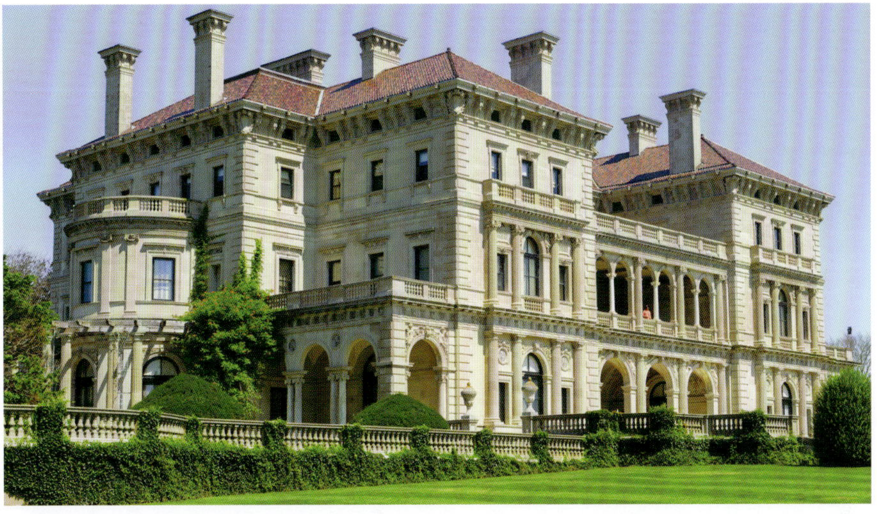

Green Animals Topiary Garden

Green Animals Topiary Garden is the oldest and most famous topiary garden in the U.S. Part of the Preservation Society of Newport County, the seven-acre estate features over 80 topiaries sculpted into whimsical shapes, including animals, birds, and geometric designs, all created from meticulously-trimmed trees and shrubs.

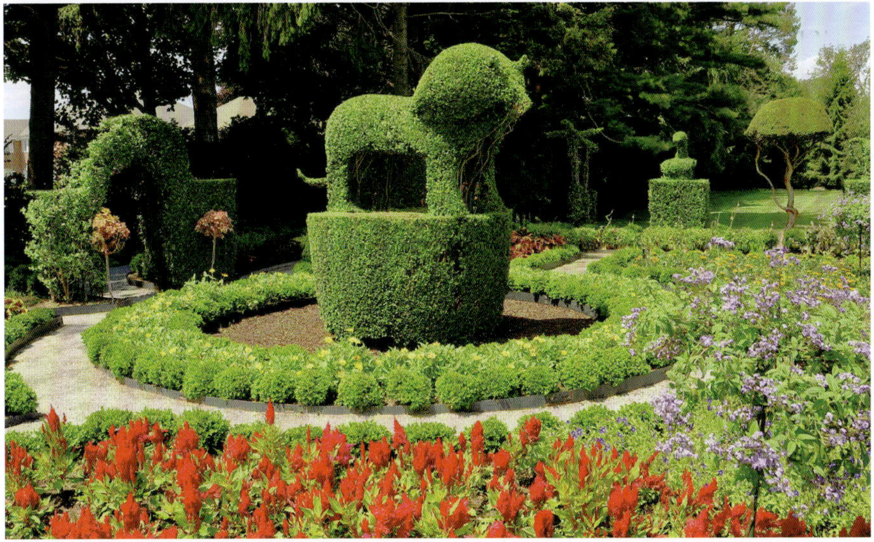

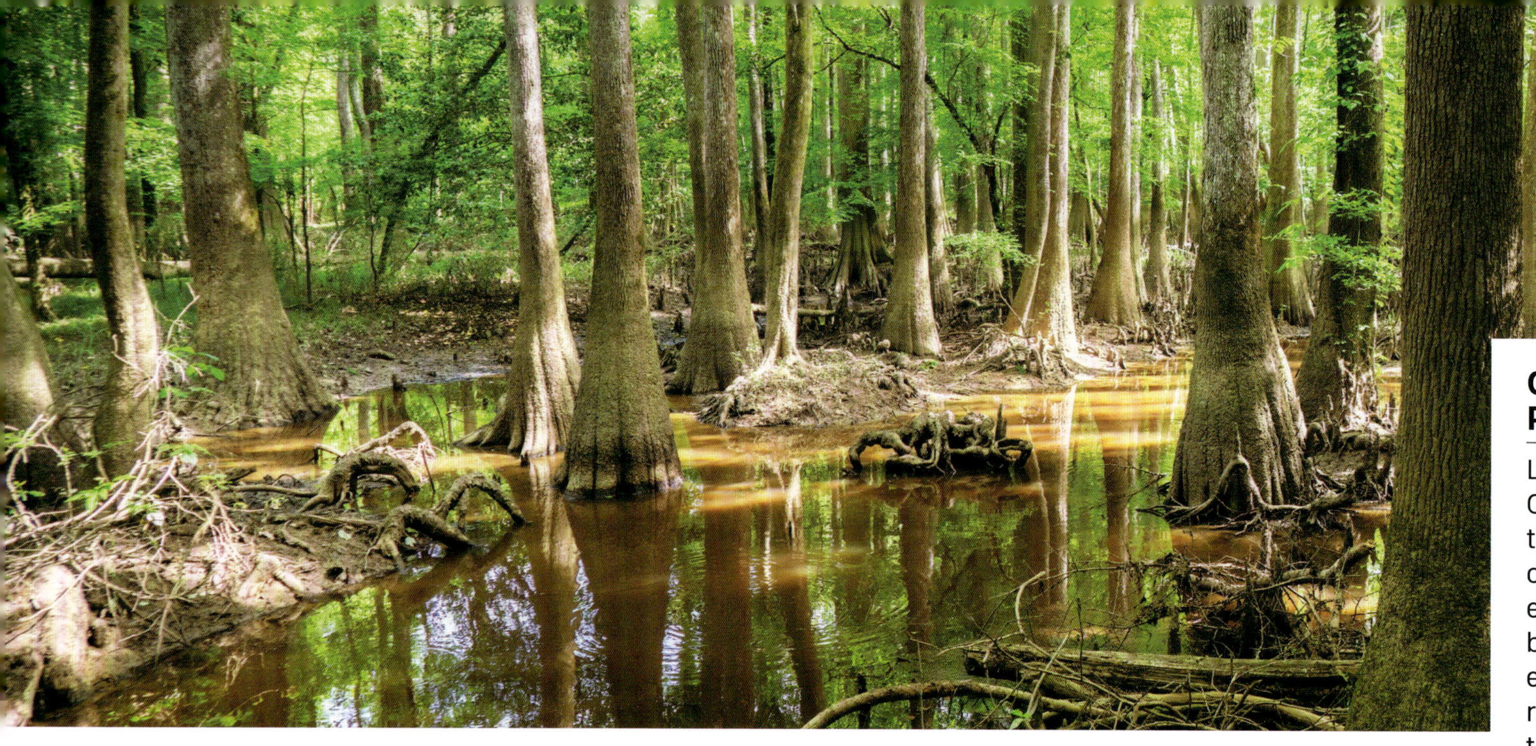

Congaree National Park

Located in central South Carolina, Congaree National Park preserves one of the largest intact expanses of old-growth bottomland hardwood forest in the U.S. The park is renowned for its towering trees, biodiversity, and the unique floodplain ecosystem created by the Congaree and Wateree Rivers.

SOUTH CAROLINA

Fort Sumter and Fort Moultrie National Historical Park

Fort Sumter and Fort Moultrie National Historical Park preserves sites significant to American military history and the Civil War. Visitors can explore exhibits, walk through the fortifications, and learn about the strategic importance of Charleston Harbor.

Kings Mountain National Military Park

Located in South Carolina near the North Carolina border, Kings Mountain National Military Park commemorates the pivotal Battle of Kings Mountain during the American Revolutionary War. The park features a visitor center with exhibits, a battlefield trail, and monuments honoring those who fought and died in the battle.

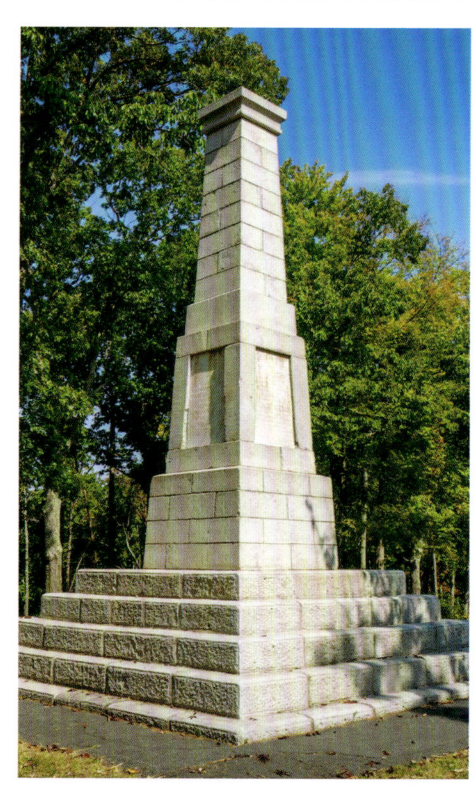

Reconstruction Era National Historical Park

Reconstruction Era National Historical Park preserves sites that were central to the Reconstruction period following the Civil War. Key sites include the historic Old Beaufort Firehouse *(see right)*, and the Penn Center, one of the first schools for formally-enslaved African Americans.

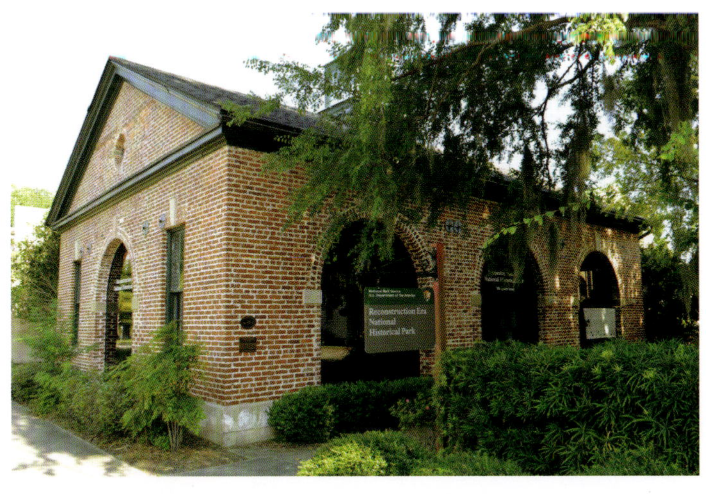

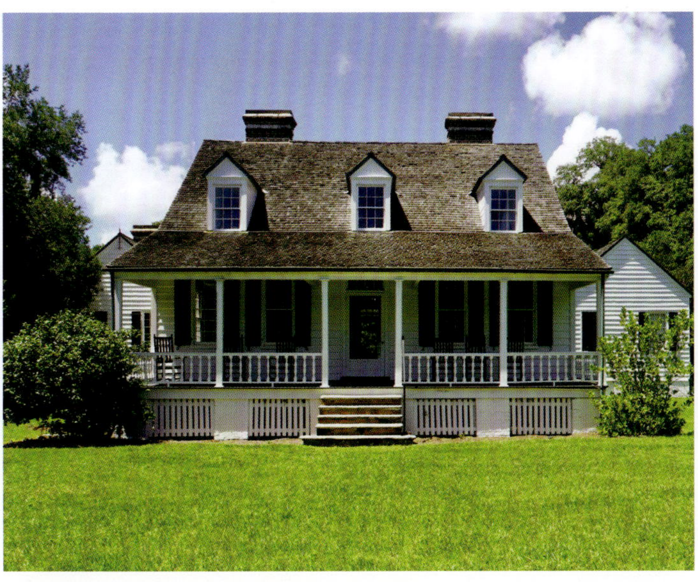

Charles Pinckney National Historic Site

Charles Pinckney National Historic Site preserves the birthplace and former plantation of Charles Pinckney, a Founding Father and signer of the U.S. Constitution. Visitors can explore the preserved ruins of the Pinckney plantation, including the main house, outbuildings, and the surrounding grounds, which reflect the agricultural and social history of the era.

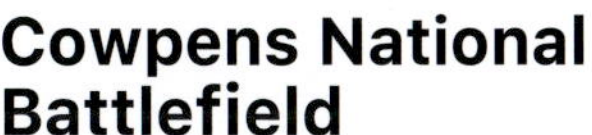

Cowpens National Battlefield

Cowpens National Battlefield preserves the site of the Battle of Cowpens, a decisive American victory during the Revolutionary War. The park features a visitor center with exhibits about the battle and the broader context of the Southern theater of the war, historic structures, and the battlefield trail that allows visitors to walk the historic site and see key locations of the battle.

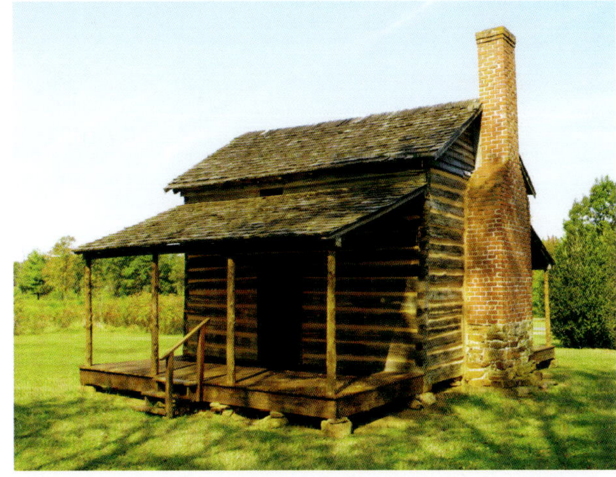

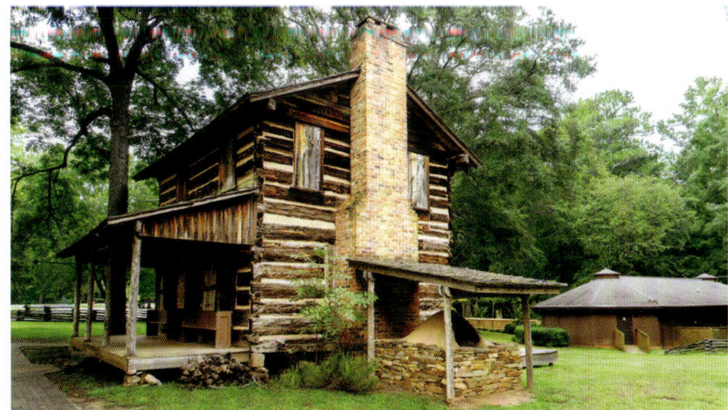

Ninety Six National Historic Site

Also known as Old Ninety Six and Star Fort, Ninety Six National Historic Site preserves the site of the significant 1781 Siege of Ninety Six during the American Revolution. The site features the remains of the star-shaped fortifications, a visitor center with exhibits, and walking trails that guide visitors through the history of the siege, the settlement, and the surrounding area.

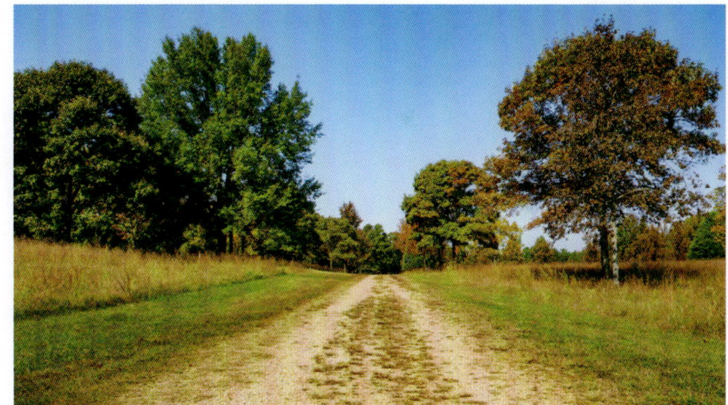

Overmountain Victory National Historic Trail

Overmountain Victory National Historic Trail commemorates the route taken by Patriot militia from the Appalachian Mountains who traveled to the Battle of Kings Mountain during the American Revolution. The 330-mile trail spans multiple states—Virginia, Tennessee, North Carolina, and South Carolina—and includes key battlefields, historic sites, and landmarks that were part of the Patriots' journey. Visitors can explore various segments of the trail through interpretive programs, hiking, and visiting historic sites.

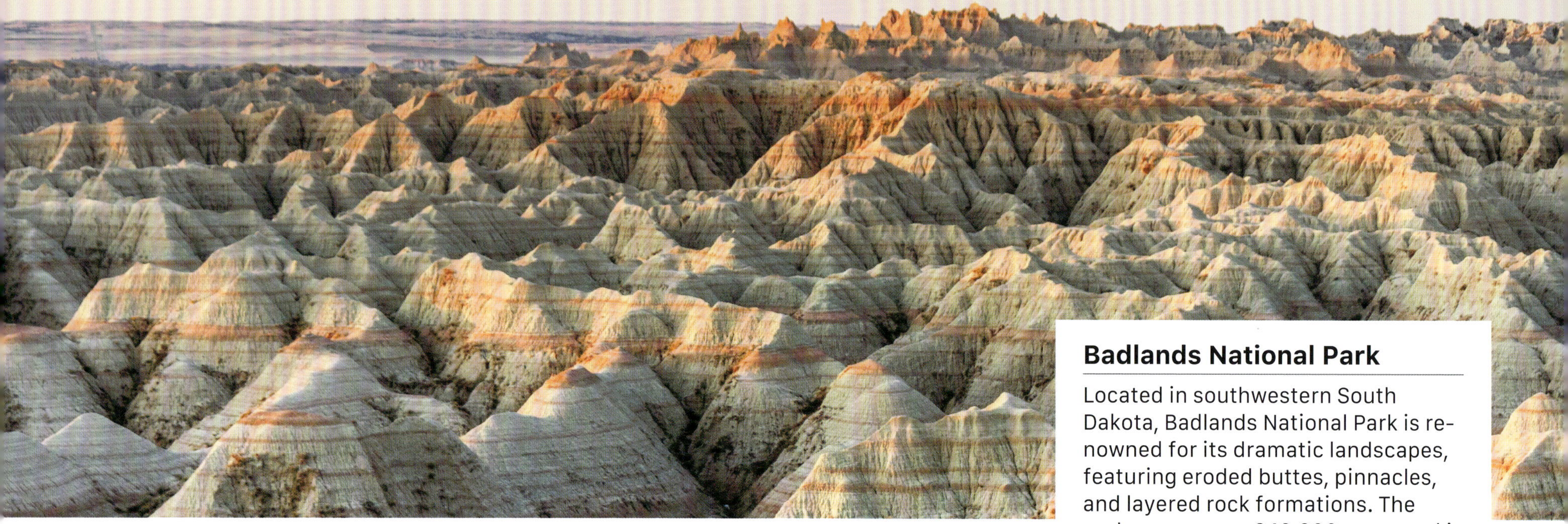

SOUTH DAKOTA

Badlands National Park

Located in southwestern South Dakota, Badlands National Park is renowned for its dramatic landscapes, featuring eroded buttes, pinnacles, and layered rock formations. The park covers over 240,000 acres and is part of the larger Great Plains, offering visitors a striking contrast of geological features and diverse wildlife.

Wind Cave National Park

Located in the Black Hills of South Dakota, Wind Cave National Park is one of the oldest and most unique national parks in the U.S. It's famous for its intricate and extensive cave system, particularly its well-formed boxwork—thin blades of calcite that project from cave walls and ceilings, forming a honeycomb pattern. The cave has more than 160 miles of mapped passageways, making it one of the longest caves in the world.

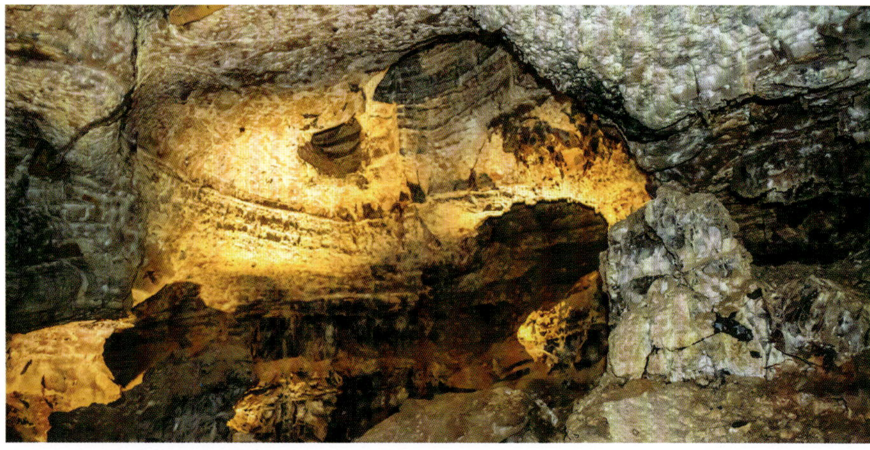

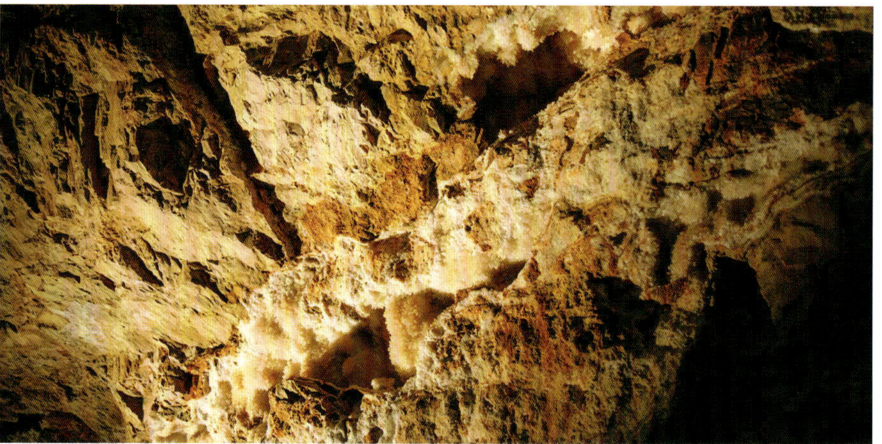

Jewel Cave National Monument

Jewel Cave National Monument is home to one of the longest caves in the world, with over 200 miles of explore passages. Located in the Black Hills of South Dakota, the cave is notable for its stunning formations, including sparkling calcite crystals, which give the cave its "jewel" name. Visitors can take guided tours to explore these underground wonders and learn about the cave's geology, history, and discovery.

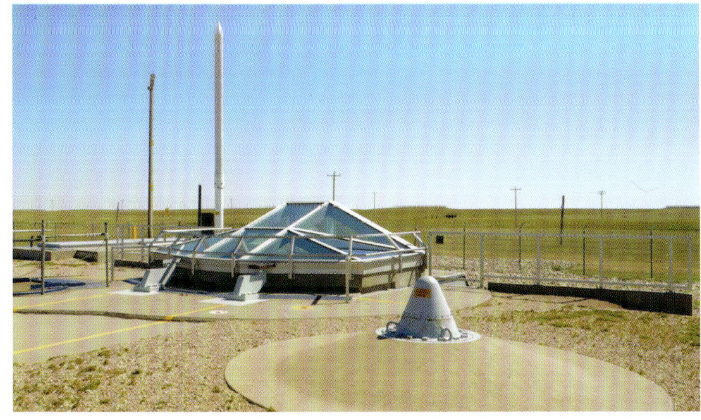

Minuteman Missile National Historic Site

Minuteman Missile National Historic Site preserves the history of the Cold War-era Minuteman missile system, which was a key component of the U.S.'s nuclear defense strategy. The site includes several missile silo facilities, a launch control center, and exhibits that provide insight into the role of nuclear deterrence during the Cold War.

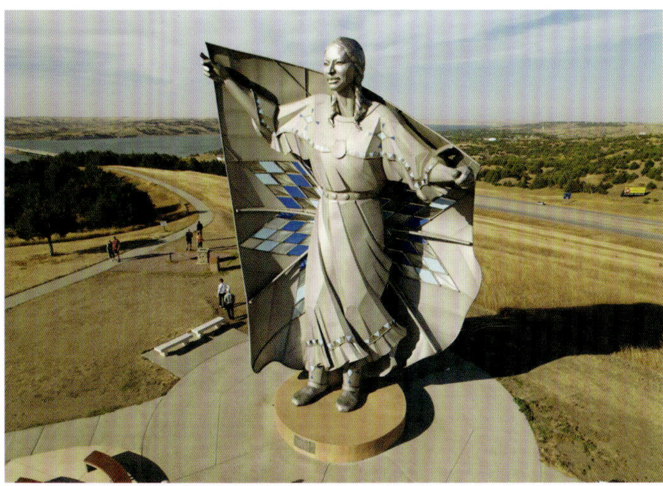

Dignity of Earth and Sky

Dignity of Earth and Sky is a large-scale public art sculpture in Chamberlain, SD, along the Missouri River. Created by artist Dale Claude Lamphere, the sculpture features a 50-foot-tall Indigenous woman in Plains-style dress holding a star quilt, symbolizing the strength, dignity, and resilience of Indigenous peoples. The artwork is designed to honor the Lakota and Dakota peoples, as well as to celebrate the beauty and power of the natural world.

Mount Rushmore National Memorial

Located in the Black Hills of South Dakota, Mount Rushmore National Memorial is a monumental sculpture carved into what was formerly the "Six Grandfathers," a mountain sacred to the Indigenous peoples of the Great Plains. Featuring the faces of four U.S. presidents—George Washington, Thomas Jefferson, Theodore Roosevelt, and Abraham Lincoln—the sculpture symbolizes the nation's history, leadership, and ideals.

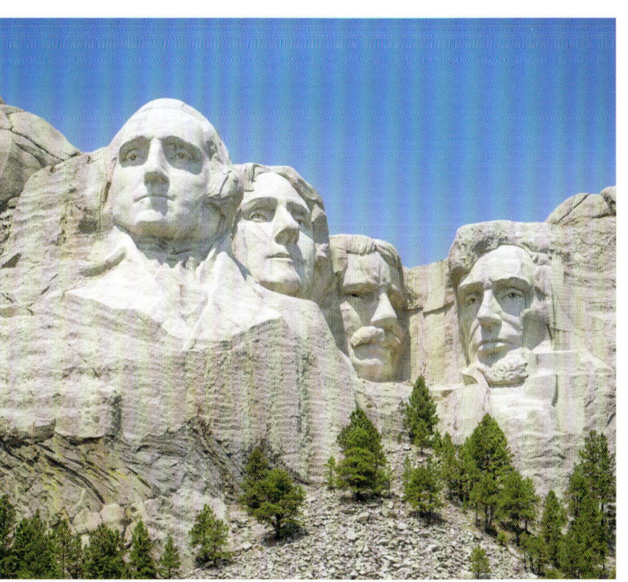

Falls Park

Falls Park is a beautiful urban park centered around the awe-inspiring Sioux Falls, a series of cascading waterfalls on the Big Sioux River. The park covers over 123 acres and offers visitors picturesque views, walking trails, and the opportunity to explore the falls up close. In addition to the natural beauty, Falls Park features a visitor center with exhibits on the history of the falls and city's founding, a restored 19th-century mill, and observation decks that provide panoramic views of the falls.

The Mammoth Site

The Mammoth Site is an active paleontological dig site and museum that preserves the remains of 61 mammoths, primarily from the Pleistocene Epoch. Discovered in 1974, the site is one of the largest concentrations of mammoth fossils in the world. Visitors can tour the site, viewing the fossils in their original positions and observing ongoing excavation work.

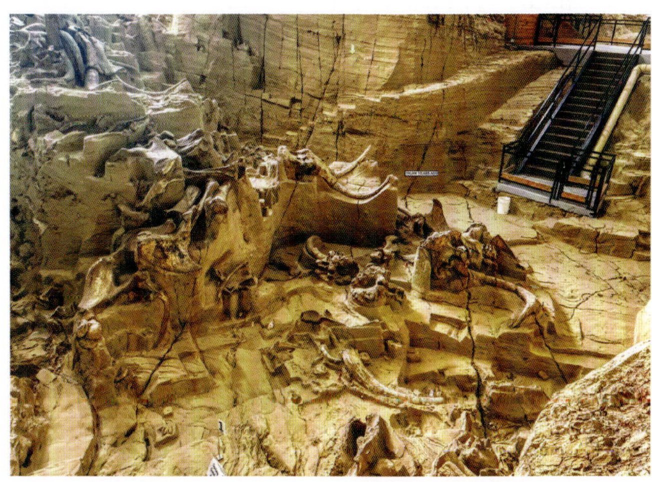

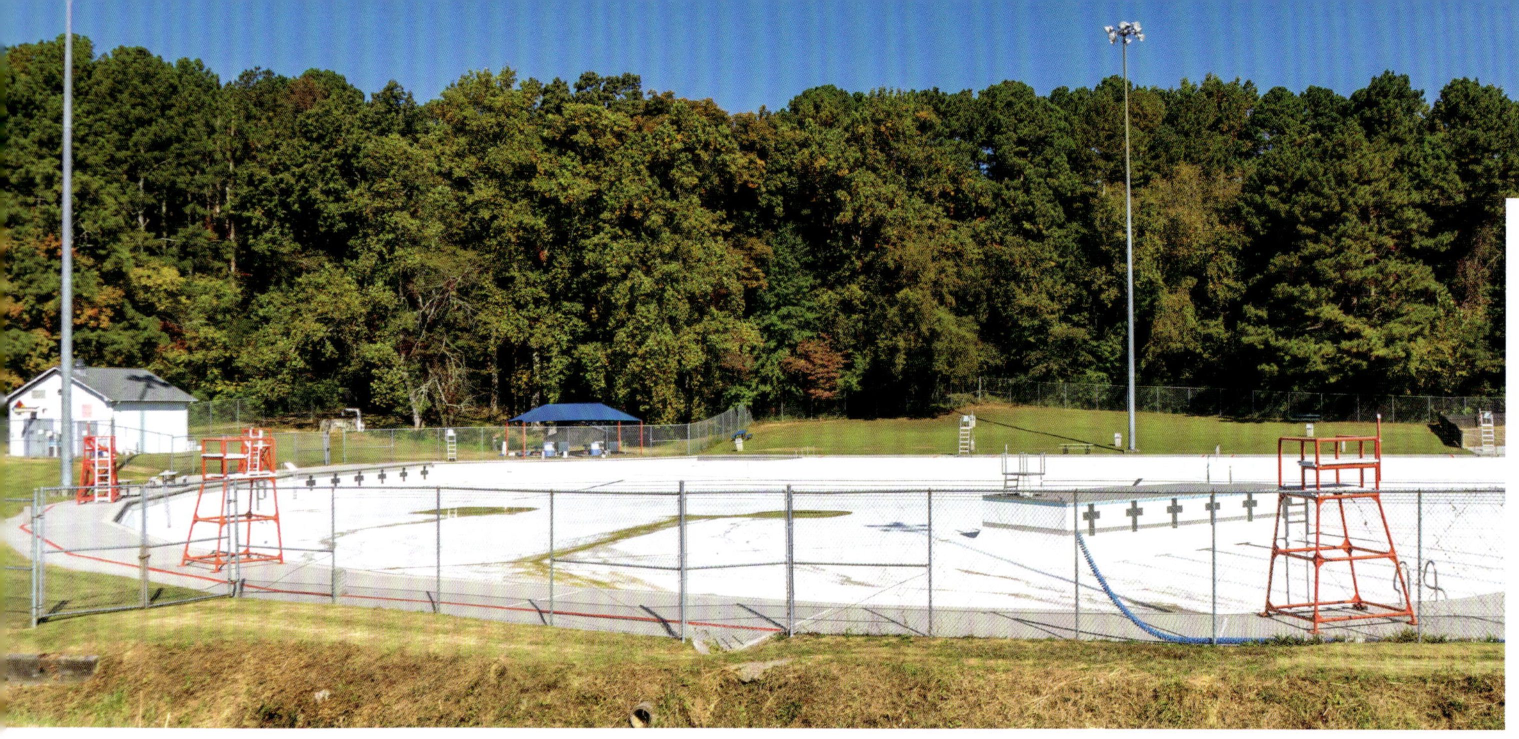

Manhattan Project National Historical Park

Manhattan Project National Historical Park commemorates the groundbreaking scientific and military efforts that led to the creation of the first atomic bombs during World War II. The park spans three sites: Los Alamos, New Mexico; Oak Ridge, Tennessee; and Hanford, Washington, each of which played a critical role in the Manhattan Project.

TENNESSEE

Andrew Johnson National Historic Site

Andrew Johnson National Historic Site preserves the home and legacy of Andrew Johnson, the 17th President of the United States. The site includes Johnson's former residence where he lived before and after his presidency, as well as his tailor shop, where he worked as a young man. The park offers visitors a chance to learn about Johnson's presidency, his Reconstruction policies, and his post-presidential years, providing historical context to his role in shaping American history.

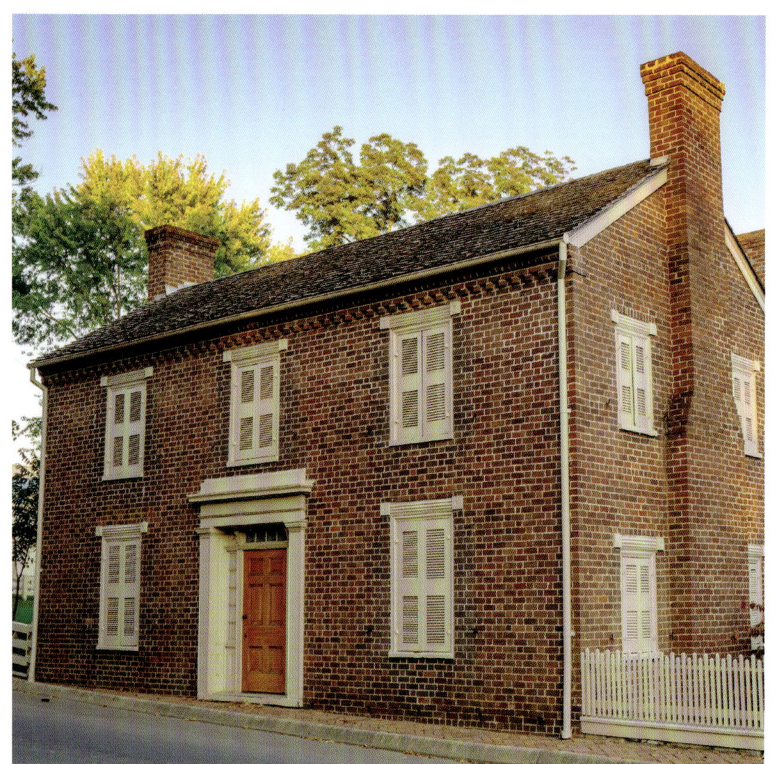

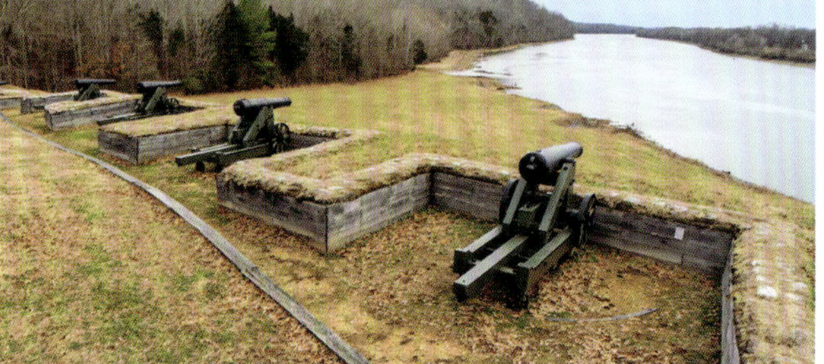

Fort Donelson National Battlefield

Fort Donelson National Battlefield preserves the site of the first major Union victory during the American Civil War. The park includes the remains of the Confederate fort, earthworks, and historic cannons, as well as the Dover Hotel, where Confederate forces officially surrendered. Visitors can view the battlefield through driving tours, walking trails, and exhibits at the visitor center, which provide insight into the battle and its significance.

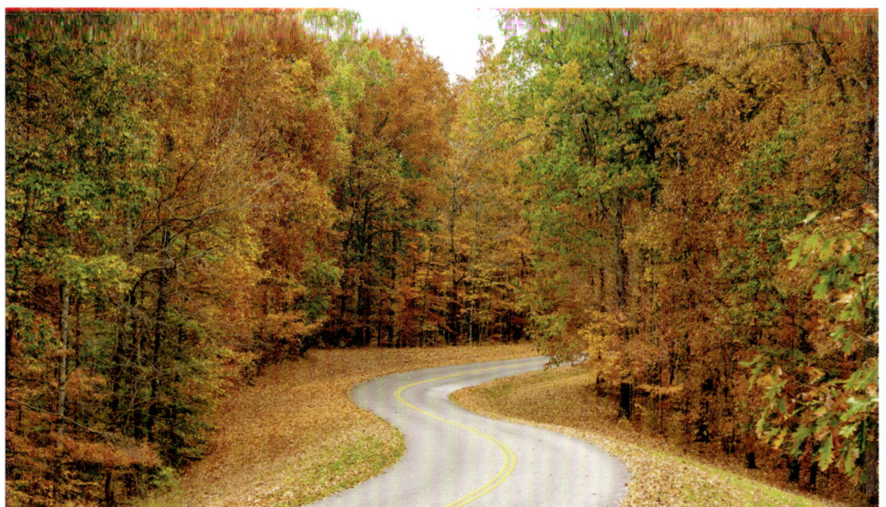

Natchez Trace Parkway and National Scenic Trail

The Natchez Trace Parkway and National Scenic Trail are a protected route that follows the historic Natchez Trace, a path used by Native Americans, European settlers, and traders for centuries. The parkway stretches 444 miles from Natchez, Mississippi, to Nashville, Tennessee, offering scenic views, historic sites, and recreational opportunities along the way.

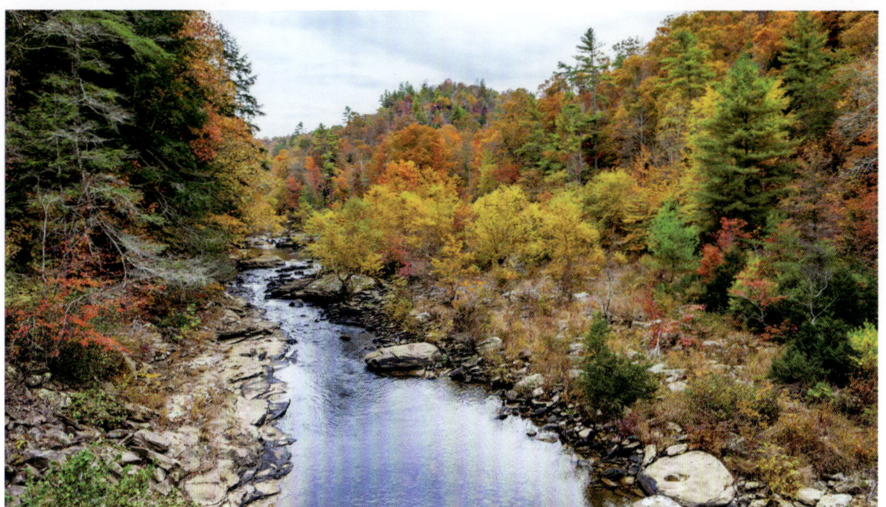

Obed Wild and Scenic River

Obed Wild and Scenic River protects a free-flowing river system that has carved deep gorges through the Cumberland Plateau. The area is known for its dramatic cliffs, rugged terrain, and diverse wildlife, making it a popular destination for outdoor activities like hiking, rock climbing, paddling, and fishing. The river features challenging whitewater rapids, attracting kayakers and canoeists seeking adventure.

Shiloh National Military Park

Located in southwestern Tennessee and northeastern Mississippi, Shiloh National Military Park preserves the site of the Battle of Shiloh, a pivotal engagement during the American Civil War. One of the war's bloodiest, this battle resulted in over 23,000 casualties and marked a critical Union victory, securing control of the Mississippi Valley. The park includes the Shiloh Battlefield and the Corinth Civil War Interpretive Center, which highlights the strategic significance of nearby Corinth, MS, as a transportation hub.

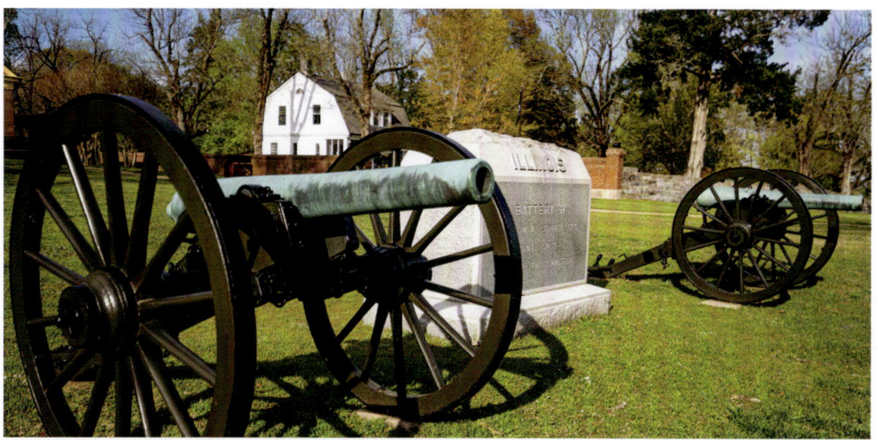

Stones River National Battlefield

Stones River National Battlefield preserves the site of the Battle of Stones River, a significant Civil War clash fought from December 31, 1862, to January 2, 1863. This Union victory boosted Northern morale and helped secure middle Tennessee under federal control. The battlefield includes key landmarks such as the Slaughter Pen, Hell's Half Acre, and Fortress Rosecrans, a massive Union supply base. The part also features a national cemetery where many of the fallen soldiers are buried.

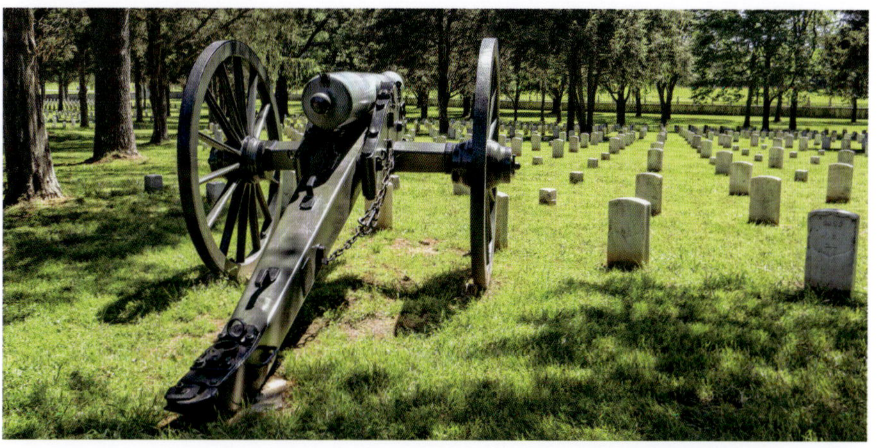

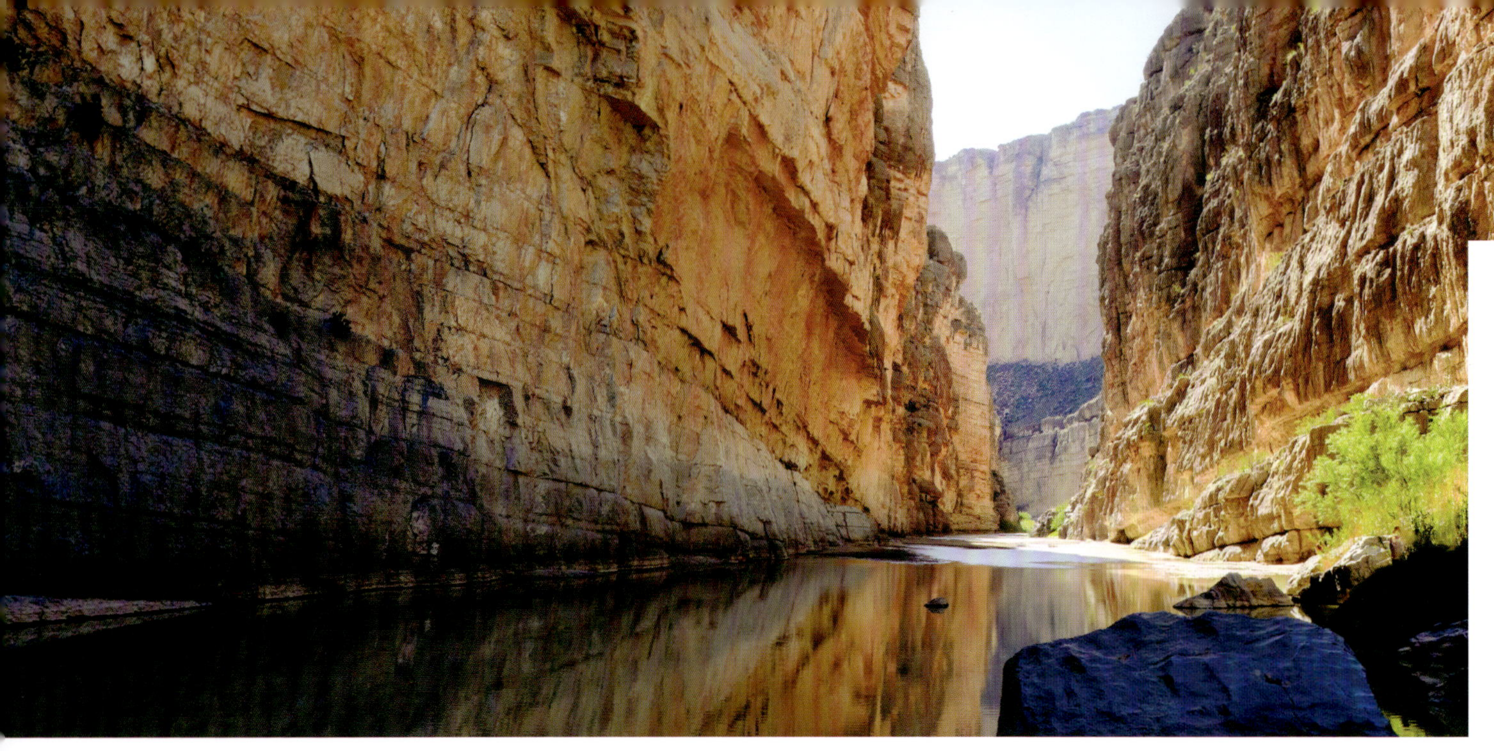

Big Bend National Park

Located in southwestern Texas along the Rio Grande, Big Bend National Park is significant for its vast desert landscapes, rugged mountains, and deep river canyons. The park offers a variety of outdoor activities, including hiking, camping, birding, stargazing, and rafting through dramatic canyons like Santa Elena *(see left)*. It's also home to a plethora of wildlife, such as javelinas, black bears, and over 450 bird species.

TEXAS

Big Thicket National Preserve

Big Thicket National Preserve, located in southeast Texas, is a unique and biodiverse area that protects a wide variety of ecosystems, including forests, swamps, savannas, and prairies. The preserve serves as a meeting point for several ecosystems, including piney woods, hardwood forests, and coastal prairies, supporting species like orchids, carnivorous plants, river otters, alligators, and a variety of bird species.

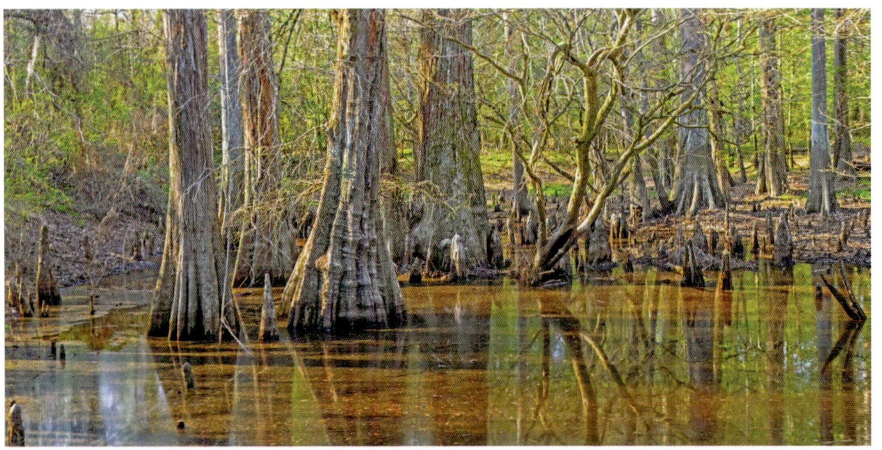

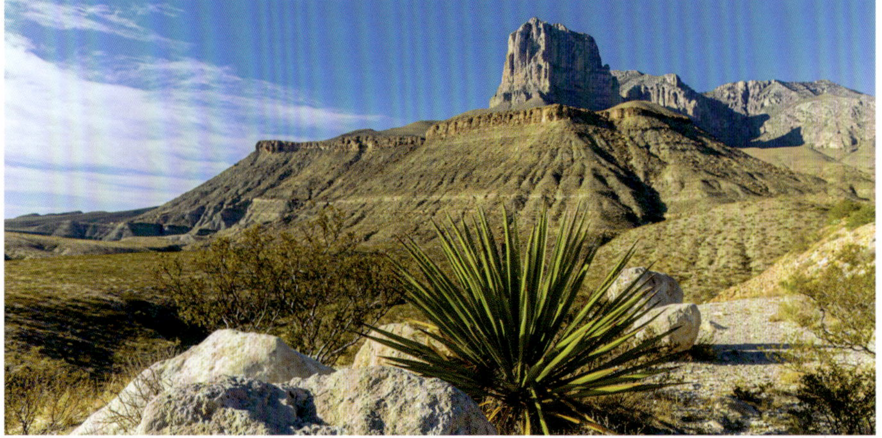

Guadalupe Mountains National Park

Located in west Texas near the New Mexico border, Guadalupe Mountains National Park is home to the rugged Guadalupe mountain range, which includes the striking El Capitan, and Guadalupe Peak—the highest point in Texas at 8,751 feet. The park features dramatic limestone cliffs, vast canyons, and rare alpine forests. It's also a fossil-rich region, showcasing remnants of the Permian Reef, a 260-million-year-old marine formation.

Lyndon B. Johnson National Historical Park

Lyndon B. Johnson National Historical Park commemorates the life and legacy of Lyndon B. Johnson, the 36th President of the United States. The park consists of two main areas: the Johnson City District, where Johnson's boyhood home, his grandparents' log cabin settlement, and the visitor center are; and the LBJ Ranch District, where Johnson's personal ranch—known as the Texas White House—and retreat are.

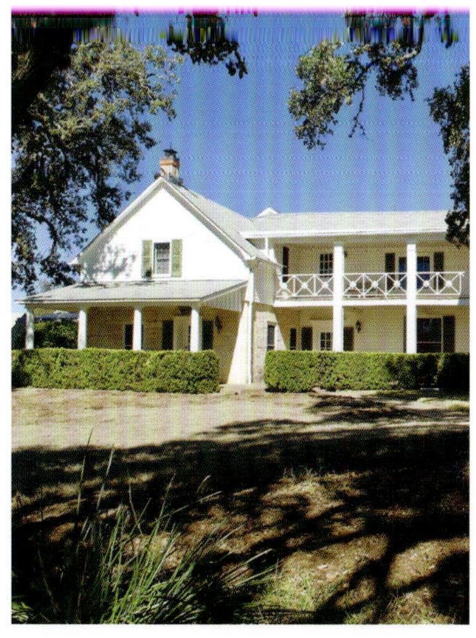

San Antonio Missions National Historical Park

San Antonio Missions National Historical Park preserves four of the five Spanish colonial missions established in San Antonio, TX, in the 18th century: Mission Concepción, Mission San José, Mission San Juan Capistrano, and Mission Espada. The park showcases the missions' impressive architecture, including churches, aqueducts, and irrigation systems, which reflect the ingenuity and cooperation of Spanish settlers and Indigenous communities. Visitors can explore the history of the missions through guided tours, exhibits, and interpretive programs.

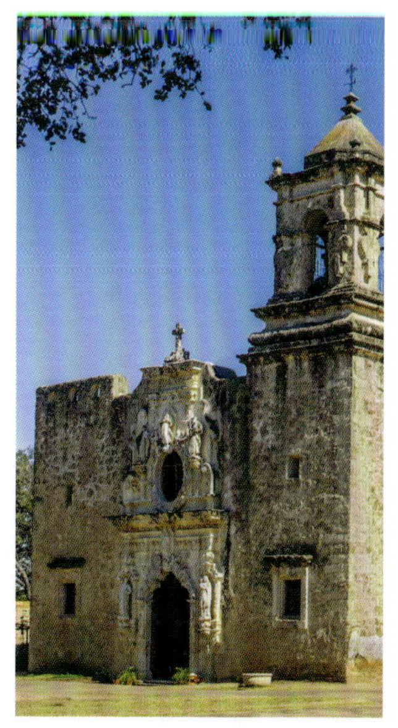

Padre Island National Seashore

Located along the gulf coast of Texas, Padre Island National Seashore is a protected barrier island spanning 70 miles. It's the longest stretch of undeveloped barrier island in the world and offers a pristine environment of sandy beaches, dunes, grasslands, and tidal flats. The park is renowned for its varied wildlife, including migratory birds and sea turtles, particularly the endangered Kemp's ridley sea turtle. The island's Laguna Madre, one of the saltiest bodies of water in the world, is a haven for windsurfing and fishing.

Alibates Flint Quarries National Monument

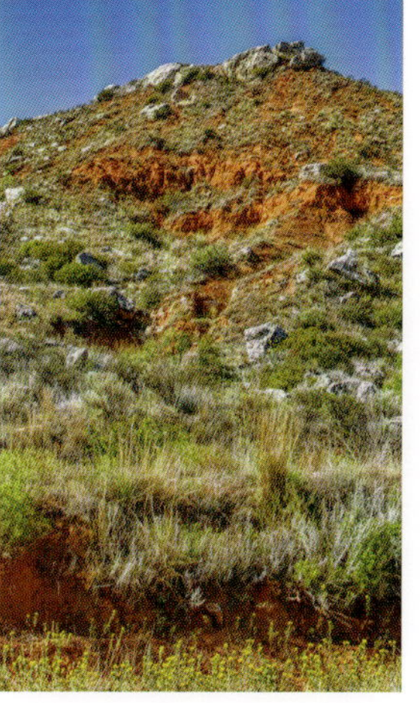

Located in the Texas Panhandle near Amarillo, Alibates Flint Quarries National Monument preserves an important archaeological and geological site where Native Americans quarried flint for tools and weapons for thousands of years. The monument protects more than 700 quarry pits, showcasing the ingenuity and resourcefulness of ancient peoples. Visitors can learn about the site's history through guided tours, hiking trails, and educational programs.

Palo Alto Battlefield National Historical Park

Palo Alto Battlefield National Historical Park preserves the site of the first major battle of the Mexican-American War. This pivotal conflict marked the start of a war that significantly shaped the borders of the U.S. and Mexico. The park offers visitors the opportunity to explore the battlefield through walking trails, interpretive signs, and a visitor center with exhibits detailing the causes, events, and consequences of the war. It also highlights the perspectives of both nations, and the soldiers and civilians affected by this conflict.

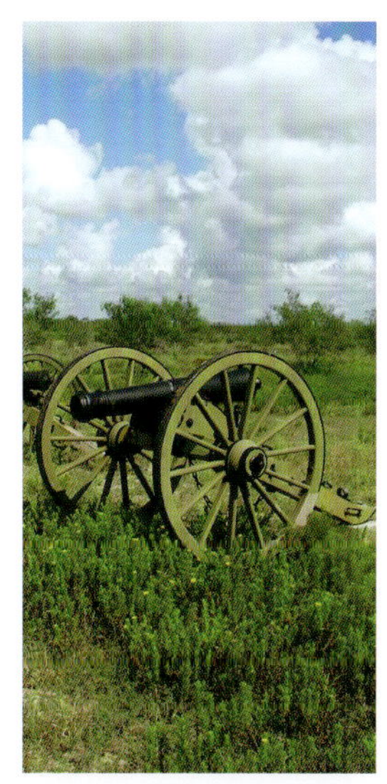

Amistad National Recreation Area

Amistad National Recreation Area is centered around Amistad Reservoir in southwest Texas, a large lake formed by the Amistad Dam on the Rio Grande. Known for its scenic beauty, the area offers opportunities for outdoor recreation, including boating, fishing, swimming, camping, and hiking.

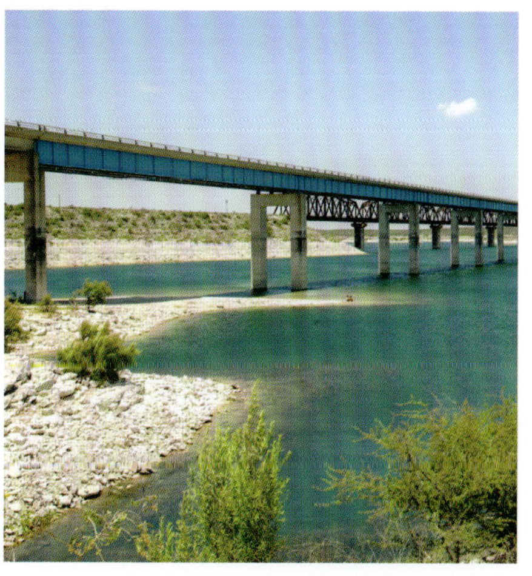

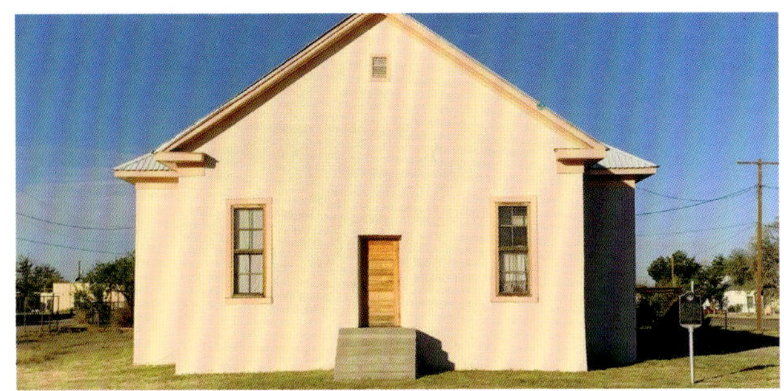

Blackwell School National Historic Site

Blackwell School National Historic Site preserves the historic Blackwell School, a segregated school that served Mexican American students from 1909 to 1965. The site highlights the experiences of students who attended during the era of "separate but equal" education, and sheds light on the challenges and resilience of the Mexican American community.

Chamizal National Memorial

Chamizal National Memorial commemorates the peaceful resolution of a century-long border dispute between the United States and Mexico over land shifted by changes in the Rio Grande. The site features cultural exhibits, a theater, and outdoor spaces that celebrate the shared heritage of the U.S. and Mexico.

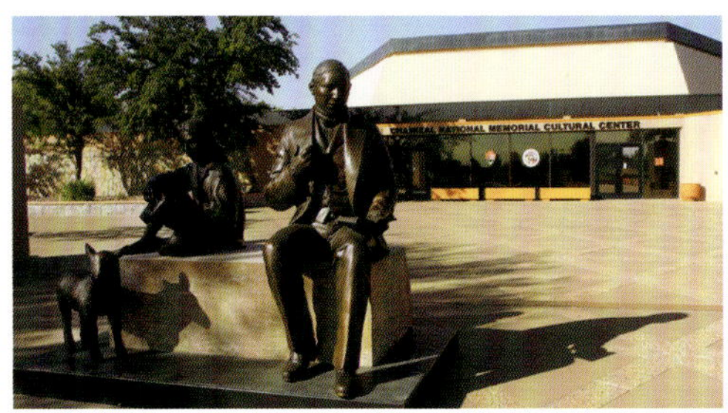

El Camino Real de los Tejas National Historic Trail

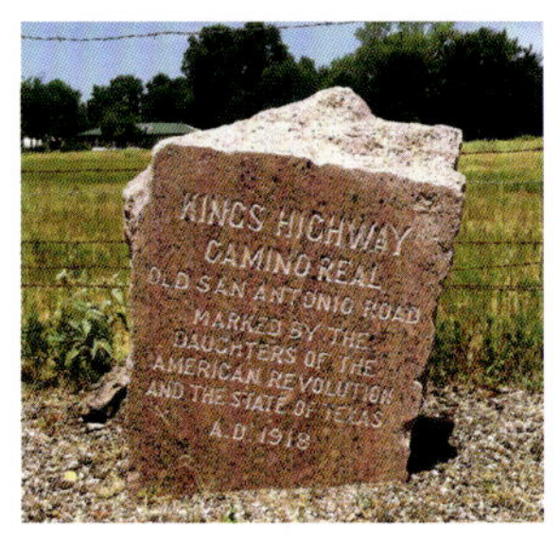

Spanning across Texas and into Louisiana, El Camino Real de los Tejas National Historic Trail marks a historic route that dates back over 300 years. It played a vital role in trade, cultural exchange, and the settlement of the region by connecting Mexico to Spanish missions, settlements, and forts in what is now Texas and Louisiana. Today, the trail is celebrated for its historical significance and the multiple cultures it brought together, including Indigenous peoples, Spanish colonists, and later settlers.

Fort Davis National Historic Site

Fort Davis National Historic Site preserves one of the best-restored frontier military posts in the U.S. Visitors can explore restored buildings, museum exhibits, and walking trails that provide insight into 19th-century military life, frontier history, and the diverse people who lived and worked at the fort.

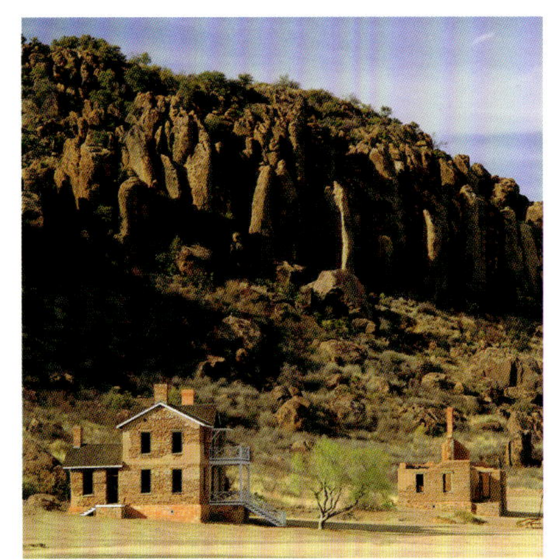

Rio Grande Wild and Scenic River

Rio Grande Wild and Scenic River protects over 196 miles of the Rio Grande as it flows through breathtaking desert landscapes, including the Chihuahuan Desert and the rugged canyons of Big Bend National Park. Visitors can enjoy activities such as rafting, kayaking, fishing, and hiking along the river's remote stretches, including the famous Santa Elena, Mariscal, and Boquillas Canyons.

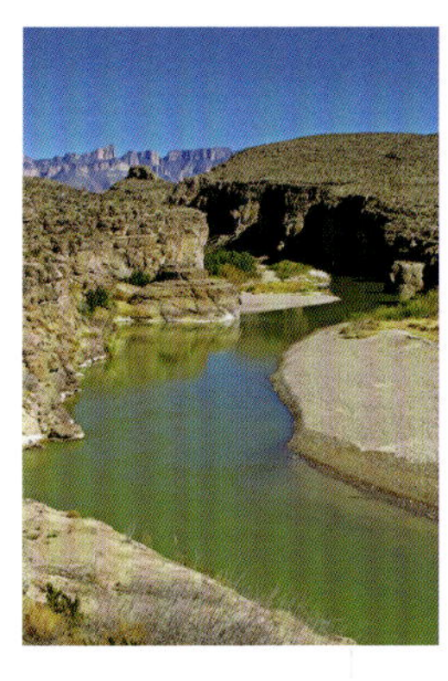

Lake Meredith National Recreation Area

Lake Meredith National Recreation Area is a scenic destination centered around Lake Meredith, a reservoir formed by Sanford Dam on the Canadian River. The area offers a variety of outdoor recreational activities, including boating, fishing, swimming, camping, hiking, and wildlife viewing.

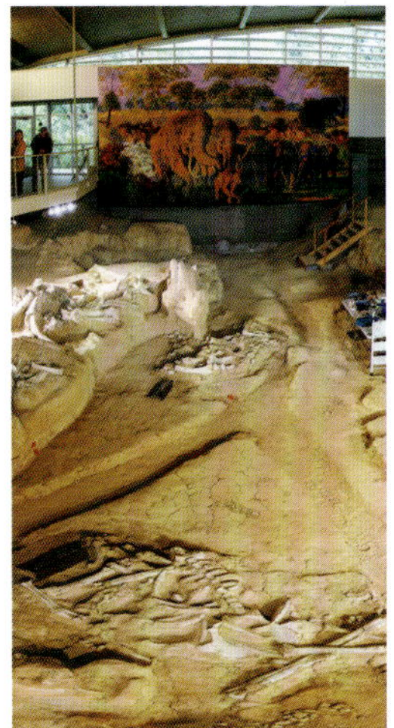

Waco Mammoth National Monument

Waco Mammoth National Monument is a paleontological site preserving the fossilized remains of a herd of Columbian mammoths that lived approximately 67,000 years ago. Discovered in 1978, the site provides a rare glimpse into the Ice Age, and the life of these massive creatures, with many fossils still in the position where they were discovered. Visitors can explore the dig shelter, which protects the fossils, and learn about the history and significance of the site through guided tours and interactive exhibits.

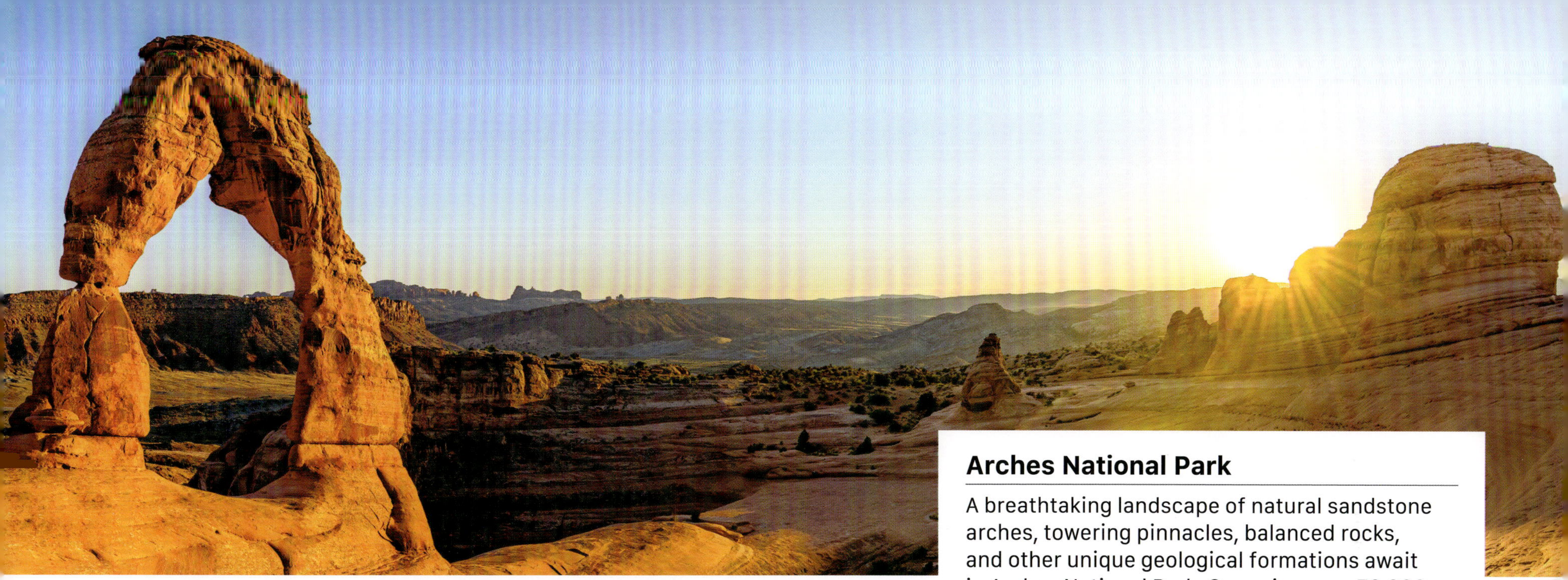

Arches National Park

A breathtaking landscape of natural sandstone arches, towering pinnacles, balanced rocks, and other unique geological formations await in Arches National Park. Spanning over 76,000 acres, it's home to more than 2,000 natural arches, including the iconic Delicate Arch *(see above)* and Landscape Arch.

UTAH

Bryce Canyon National Park

Bryce Canyon National Park is famous for its striking landscape of natural amphitheaters filled with red, orange, and white rock formations known as hoodoos. These unique spire-shaped formations were sculpted by erosion over millions of years, creating one of the most visually stunning geological wonders in the world.

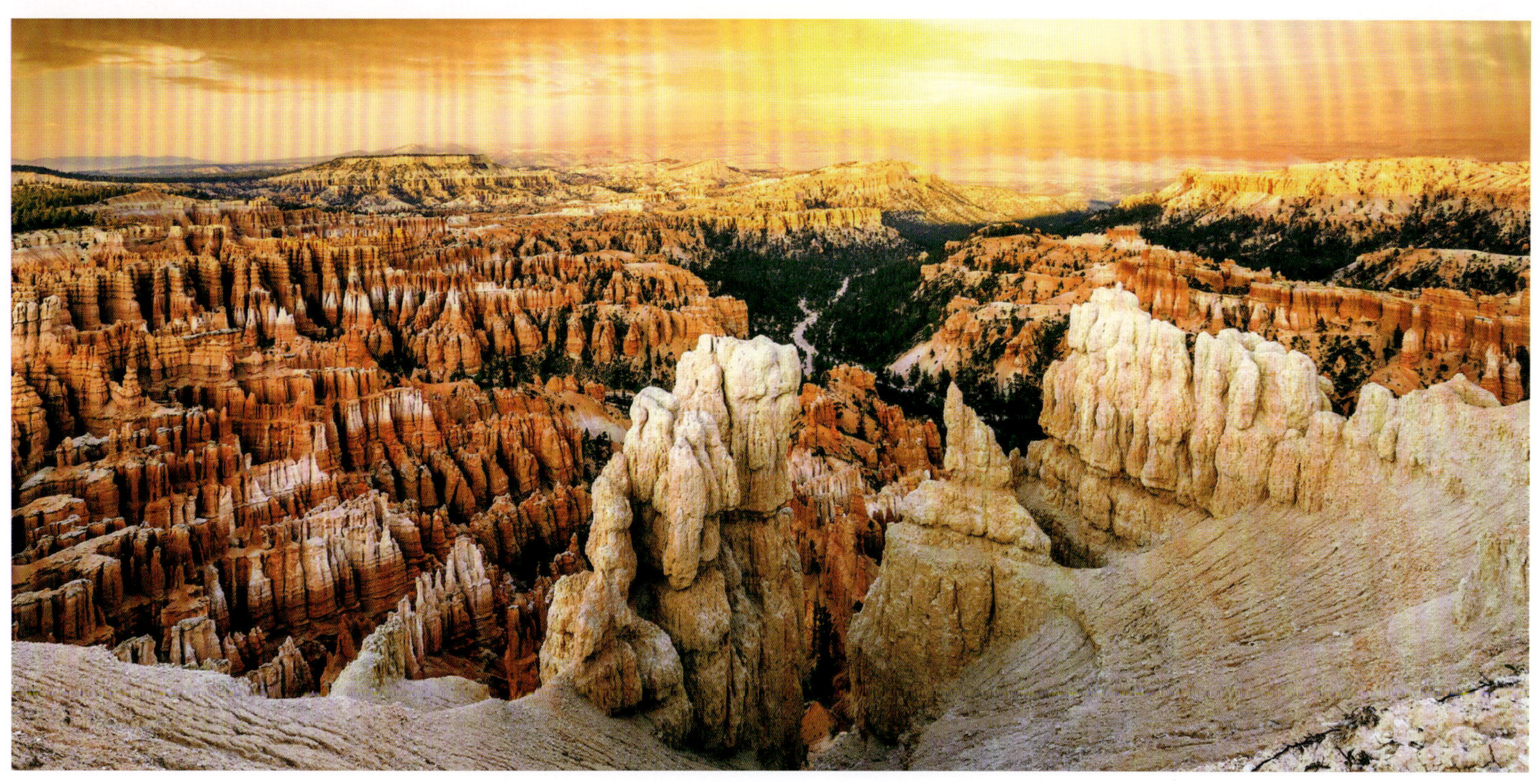

Canyonlands National Park

Canyonlands National Park is a vast and rugged wilderness known for its stunning desert landscapes, deep canyons, towering mesas, and dramatic rock formations. Divided into four districts—Island in the Sky, the Needles, the Maze, and the Colorado and Green Rivers—the park offers a plethora of experiences and breathtaking scenery.

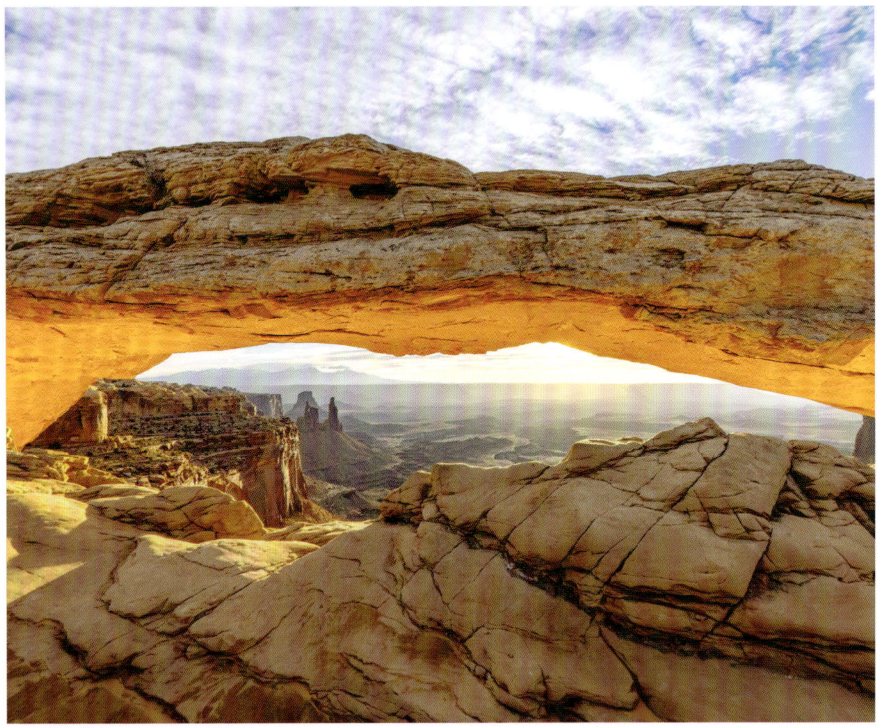

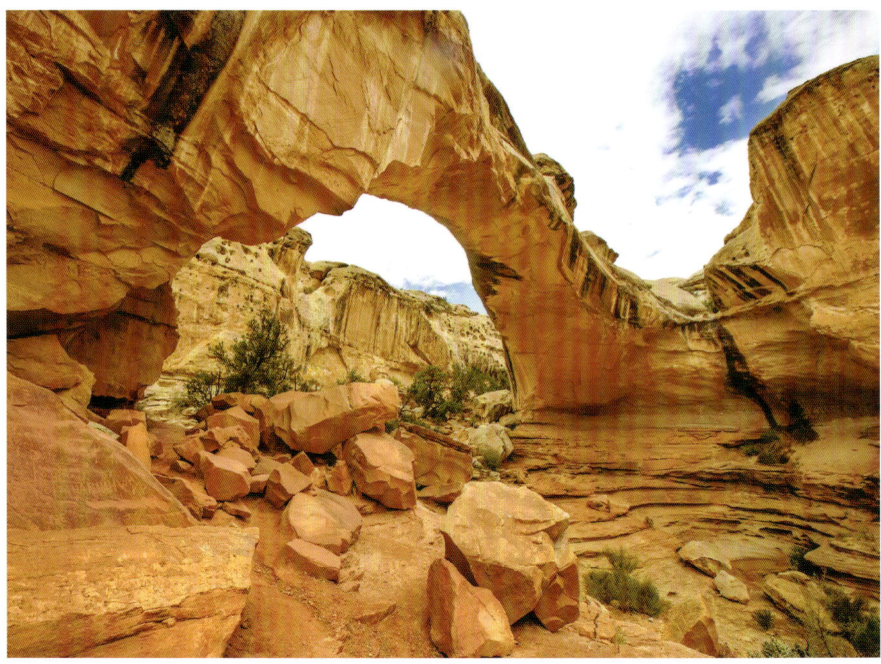

Capitol Reef National Park

Located in south-central Utah, Capitol Reef National Park is a hidden gem known for its colorful canyon, towering cliffs, and unique geological features. The park's centerpiece in the Waterpocket Fold, a nearly 100-mile-long warp in the Earth's crust that showcases millions of years of geological history. The park also features domes, arches, and striking rock formations that resemble a coral reef, inspiring its name.

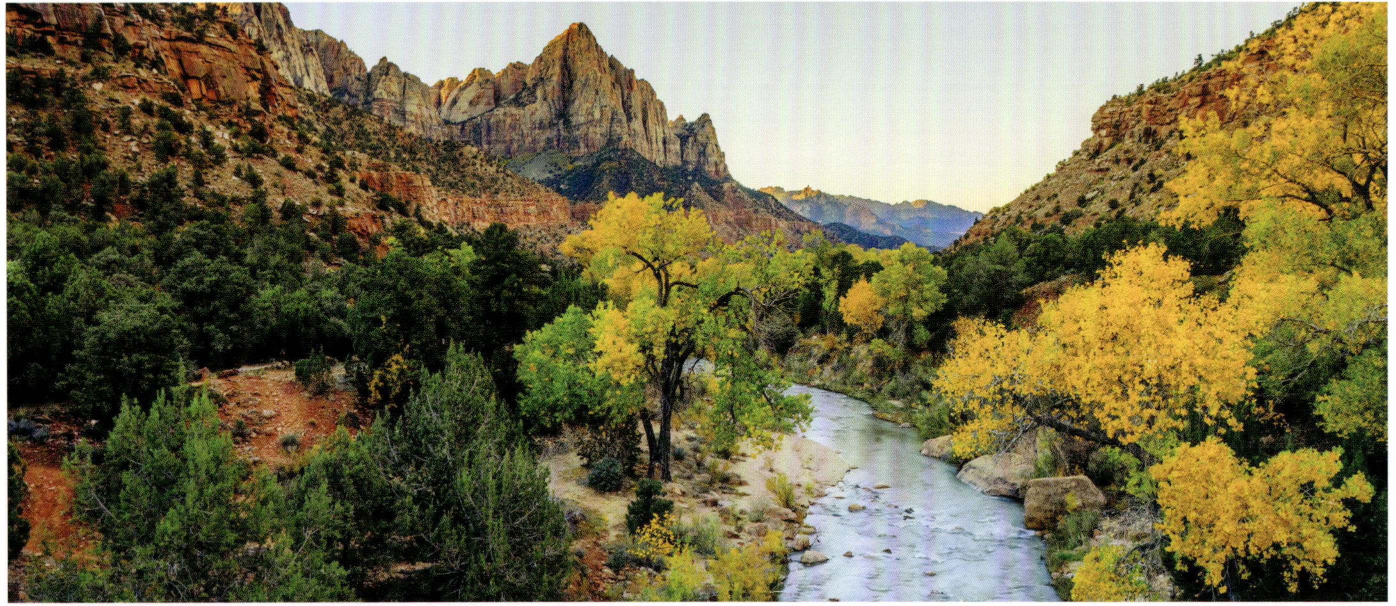

Zion National Park

Renowned for its dramatic sandstone cliffs, deep canyons, and picturesque desert landscapes, Zion National Park in southern Utah has countless activities for the nature-lover and outdoor enthusiast. The park's centerpiece is Zion Canyon, carved by the Virgin River, with towering red and orange cliffs that rise thousands of feet. Zion's unique geography supports diverse ecosystems, featuring lush greenery alongside arid desert terrain.

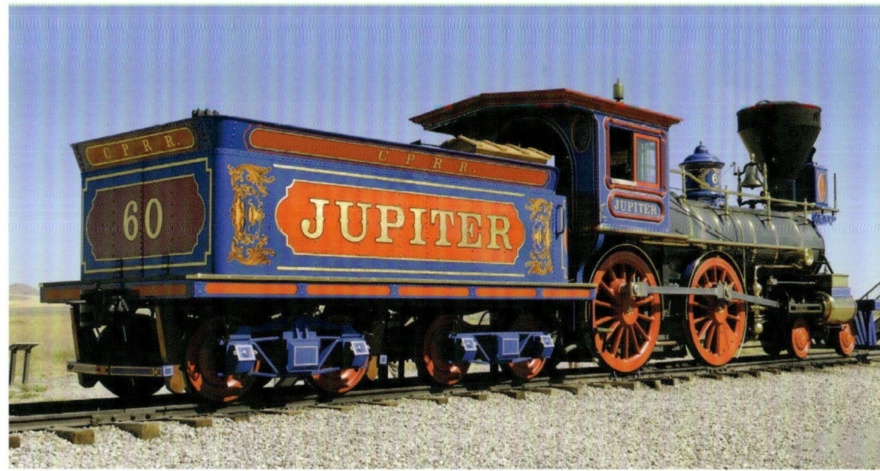

Golden Spike National Historical Park

Golden Spike National Historical Park commemorates the completion of the first transcontinental railroad on May 10, 1869. The site marks where the Union Pacific and Central Pacific Railroads met at Promontory Summit, symbolizing the joining of the east and west coasts of the U.S. Visitors can explore the historic site, see replicas of the original steam locomotives—the Jupiter *(see above)* and No. 119—and watch reenactments of the "Golden Spike" ceremony.

Glen Canyon National Recreation Area

Spanning parts of Utah and Arizona, Glen Canyon National Recreation Area is a vast and beautiful landscape centered around Lake Powell, a reservoir formed by the Glen Canyon Dam on the Colorado River. The area features dramatic red rock canyons, clear blue waters, and scenic vistas, offering unparalleled opportunities for outdoor recreation and exploration.

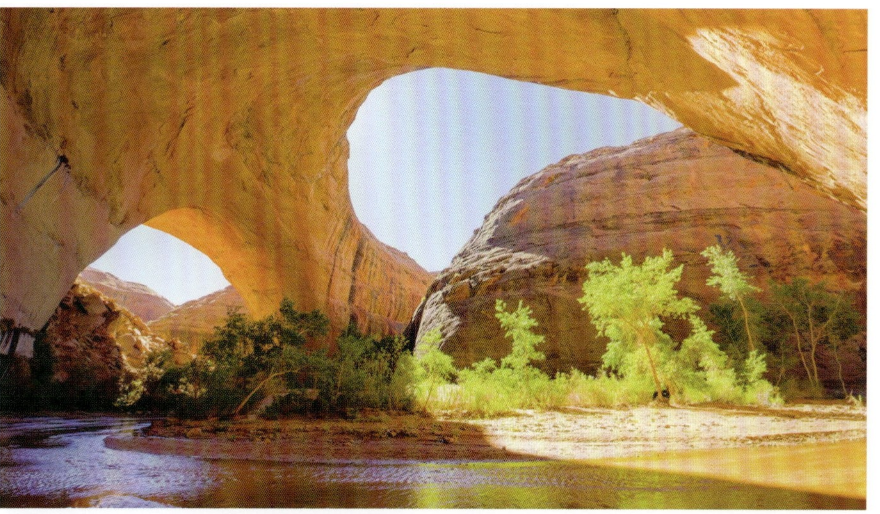

Cedar Breaks National Monument

Cedar Breaks National Monument is a natural amphitheater spanning over three miles and plunging 2,000 feet deep. The monument is distinguished for its colorful rock formations, shaped by millions of years of erosion, featuring vibrant red, orange, and purple hues. The surrounding forests and meadows are home to various wildlife and beautiful wildflower displays in summer, while the winter months provide opportunities for snowshoeing and cross-country skiing.

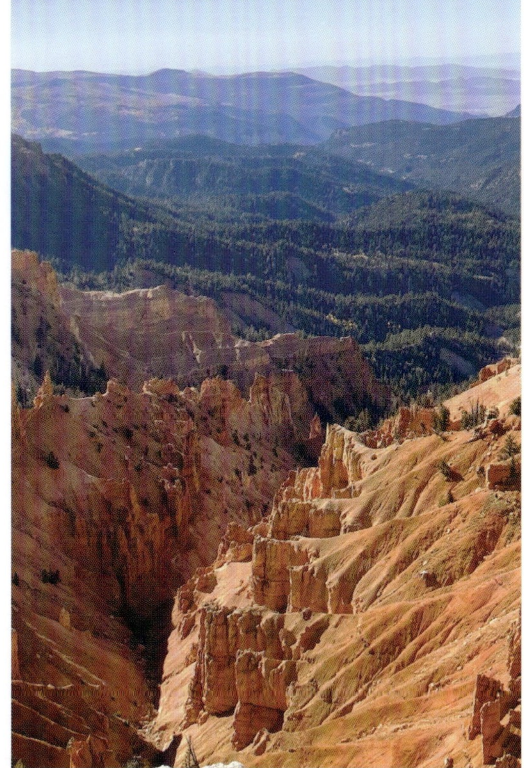

Hovenweep National Monument

Located on the Utah-Colorado border, Hovenweep National Monument preserves six groups of ancient Ancestral Puebloan villages dating back to 1200–1300 CE. The monument is best known for its well-preserved stone towers, including square, circular, and D-shaped structures, which were built on canyon rims and boulders.

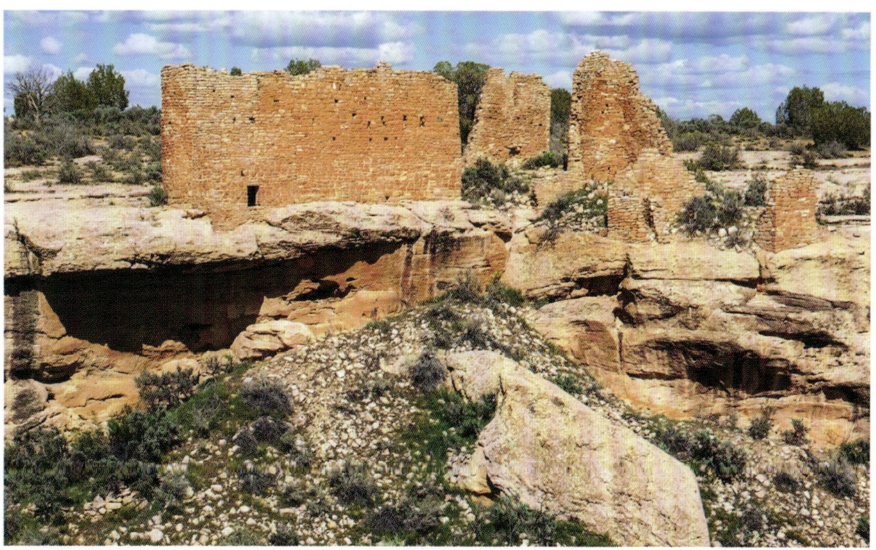

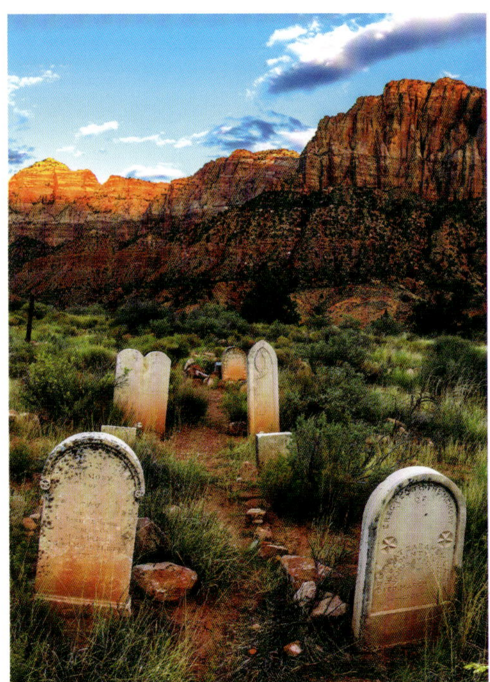

Mormon Pioneer Trail National Historic Trail

The Mormon Pioneer Trail National Historic Trail stretches over 1,300 miles across the American West, following the path traveled by thousands of Mormon pioneers from Nauvoo, Illinois, to the Great Salt Lake—what is now Salt Lake City—in Utah between 1846 and 1869. The trail passes through diverse landscapes, including prairies, deserts, and mountains, with numerous landmarks, including forts, cemeteries *(see left)*, and historic sites.

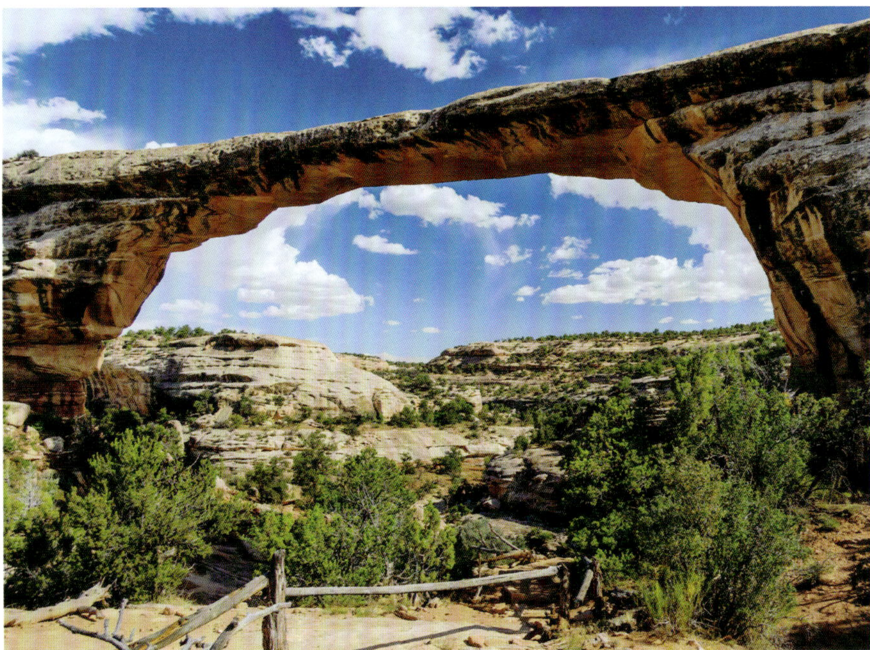

Natural Bridges National Monument

Natural Bridges National Monument is renowned for its impressive natural rock bridges, which were carved by the forces of water and time. The park is home to three massive sandstone bridges—Sipapu, Kachina, and Owachomo—each with its own unique size, shape, and history.

Rainbow Bridge National Monument

Rainbow Bridge National Monument is home to one of the world's largest natural bridges, spanning 290 feet in height and 275 feet in length. This stunning sandstone arch, formed by the forces of erosion, is a sacred site for several Native American tribes, including the Navajo, Hopi, and White Mesa Ute; it's considered one of the most iconic natural formations in the American Southwest.

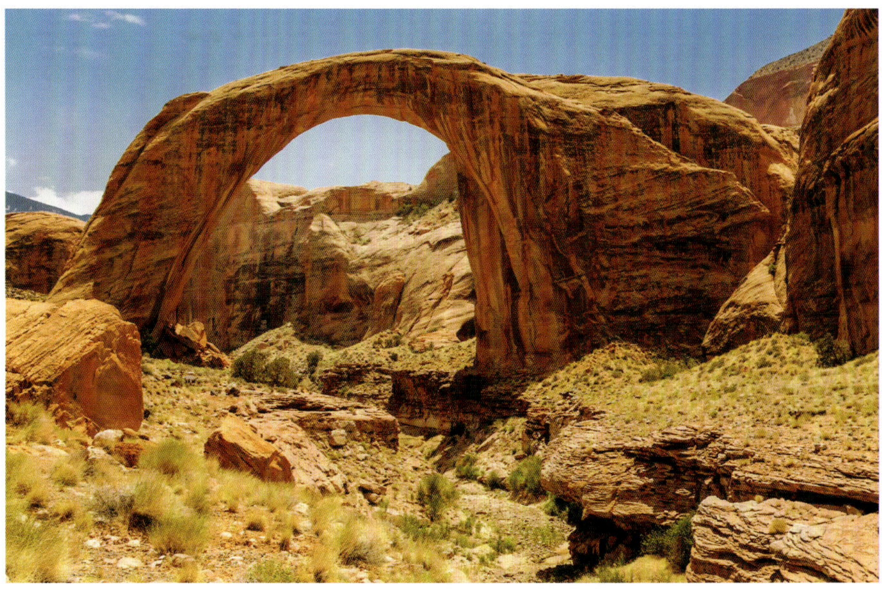

Timpanogos Cave National Monument

Located in Utah's Wasatch Mountains, Timpanogos Cave National Monument is known for its amazing underground cave system—a series of limestone caves, including the Timpanogos Cave, which is decorated with intricate formations such as helictites, stalactites, stalagmites, and flowstones. Adventurous visitors can explore the cave system through guided tours, which take them on a steep, scenic hike up the mountain.

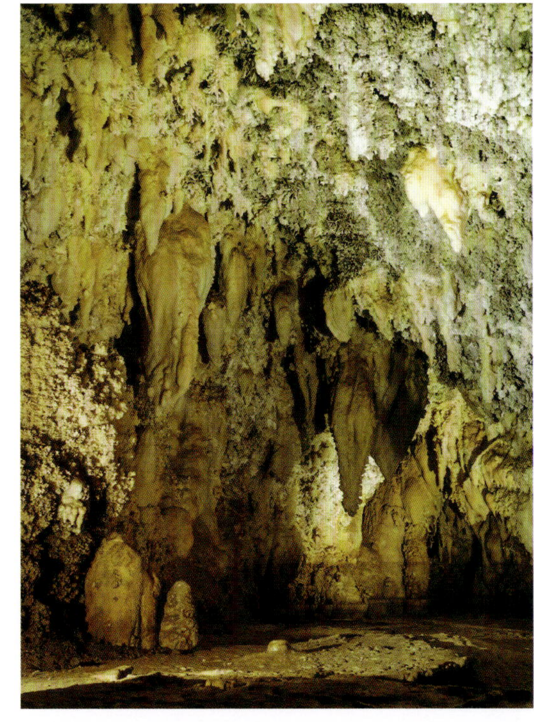

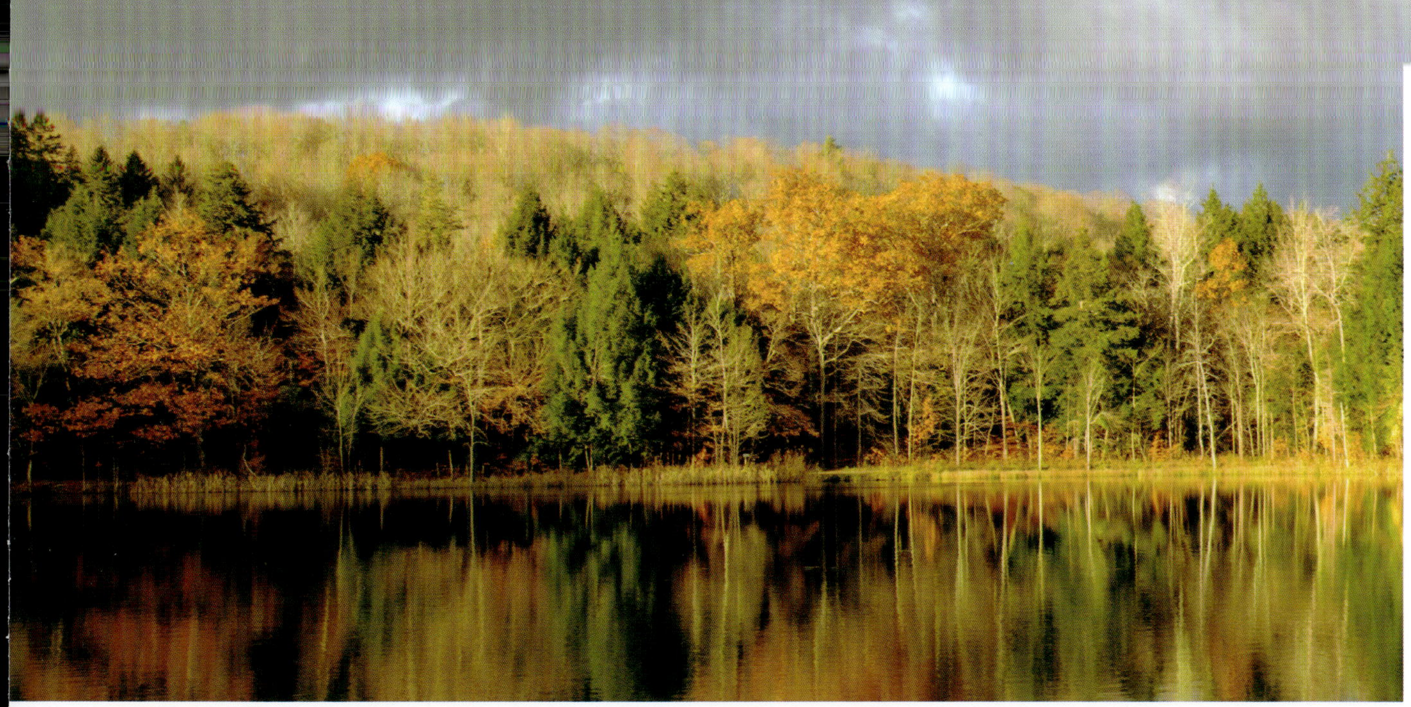

Marsh-Billings-Rockefeller National Historical Park

Marsh-Billings-Rockefeller National Historical Park preserves the legacy of conservation in America through the stories of three influential families. The park includes the Marsh-Billings-Rockefeller Mansion, which was first the boyhood home of George Perkins Marsh—one of America's first environmentalists—before later becoming the estate of Frederick Billings, a conservationist and entrepreneur, and then Mary and Laurance Rockefeller. Visitors can tour the historic mansion, gardens, and the managed forest, which demonstrates sustainable land-use practices.

VERMONT

Quechee Gorge

Known as "Vermont's Little Grand Canyon," Quechee Gorge is one of the state's most beautiful natural attractions. Carved by the Ottauquechee River over thousands of years, the gorge plunges approximately 165 feet, making it the deepest gorge in Vermont. Visitors can enjoy breathtaking views from the U.S. Route 4 bridge or explore hiking trails that run along the gorge and down to the river.

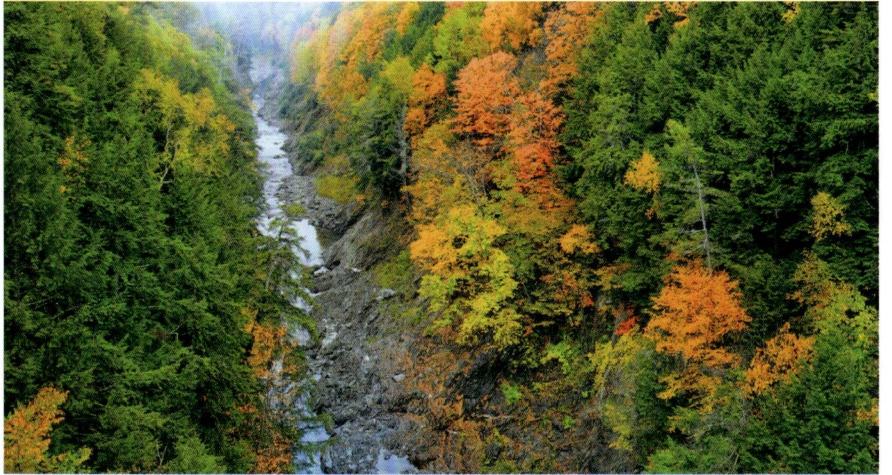

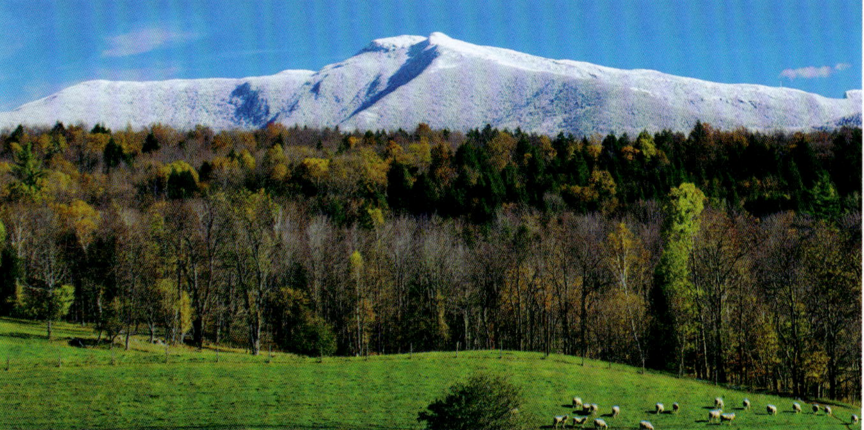

Mount Mansfield

Located in northern Vermont, Mount Mansfield is the state's highest peak at 4,395 feet. Known for its distinctive ridgeline resembling a human profile, the mountain offers some of the best hiking and outdoor experiences in New England. Visitors can explore the mountain through various trails, including sections of the Long Trail, which runs along the summit ridge. The mountain is also a popular destination for skiing and snowboarding in the winter.

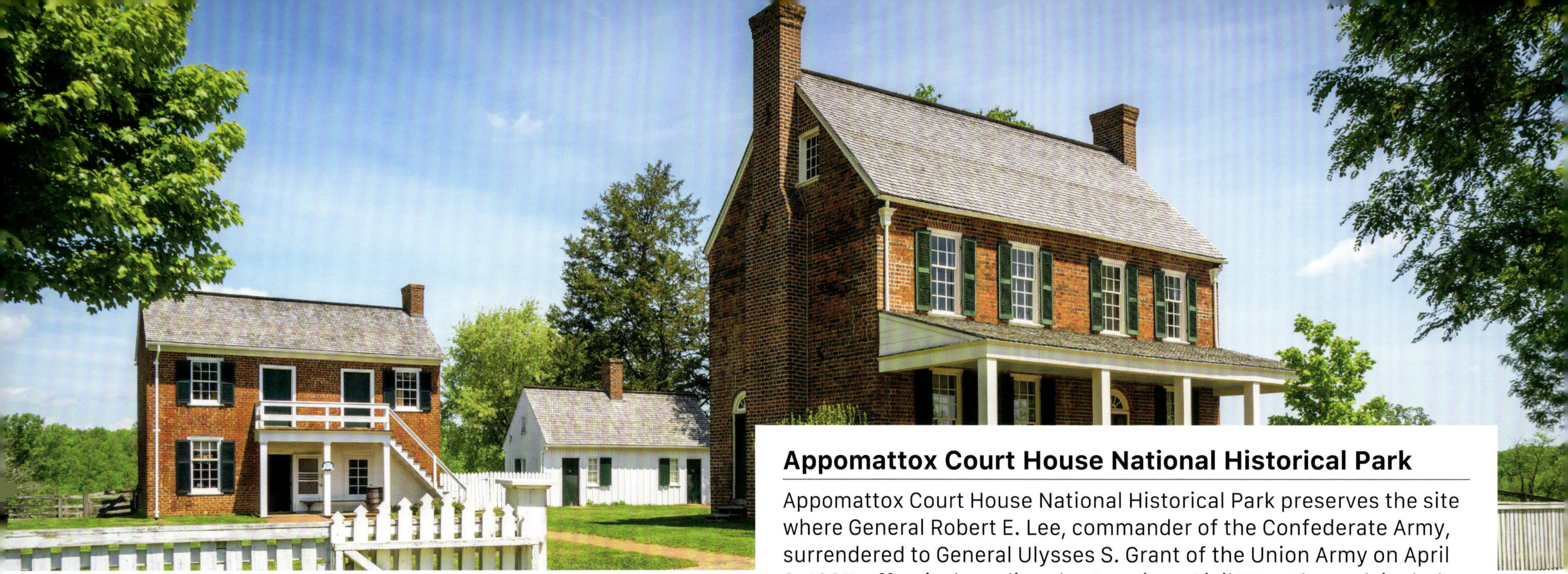

VIRGINIA

Appomattox Court House National Historical Park

Appomattox Court House National Historical Park preserves the site where General Robert E. Lee, commander of the Confederate Army, surrendered to General Ulysses S. Grant of the Union Army on April 9, 1865, effectively ending the American Civil War. The park includes the restored Appomattox Court House where the historic surrender took place, along with other buildings, such as the McLean House and the courthouse, which played key roles in the events of that day.

Assateague Island National Seashore

Located along the coasts of Maryland and Virginia, Assateague Island National Seashore is a protected barrier island known for its pristine beaches, salt marshes, and diverse wildlife. The island is famous for its wild horses, known as the Assateague ponies, which roam freely throughout the area.

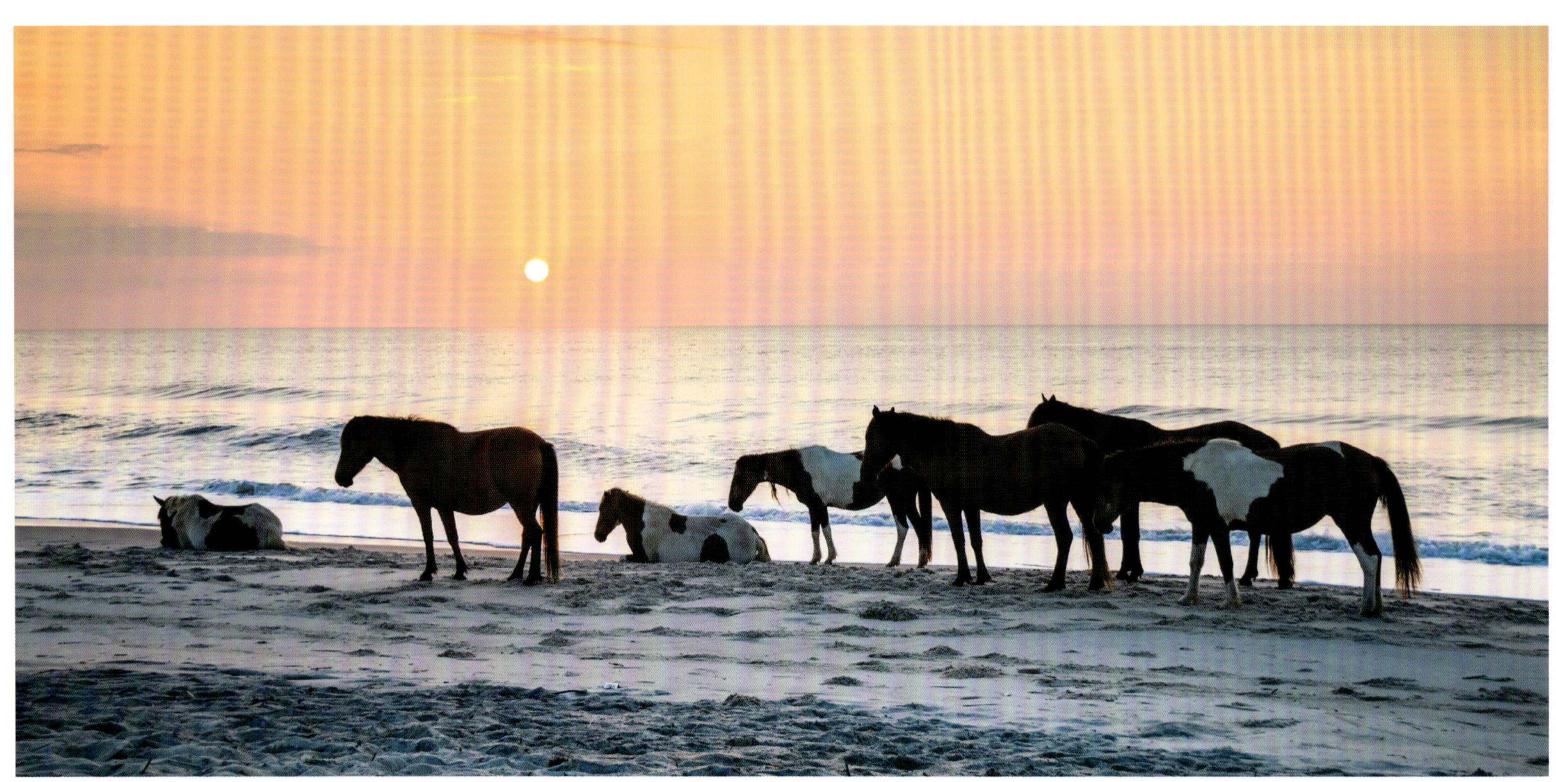

Cape Henry Memorial

Cape Henry Memorial commemorates the site where English colonists first landed in 1607, marking the beginning of the English settlement in America. Part of the Colonial National Historical Park, the memorial honors the early English explorers and settlers who played a pivotal role in shaping the history of the United States.

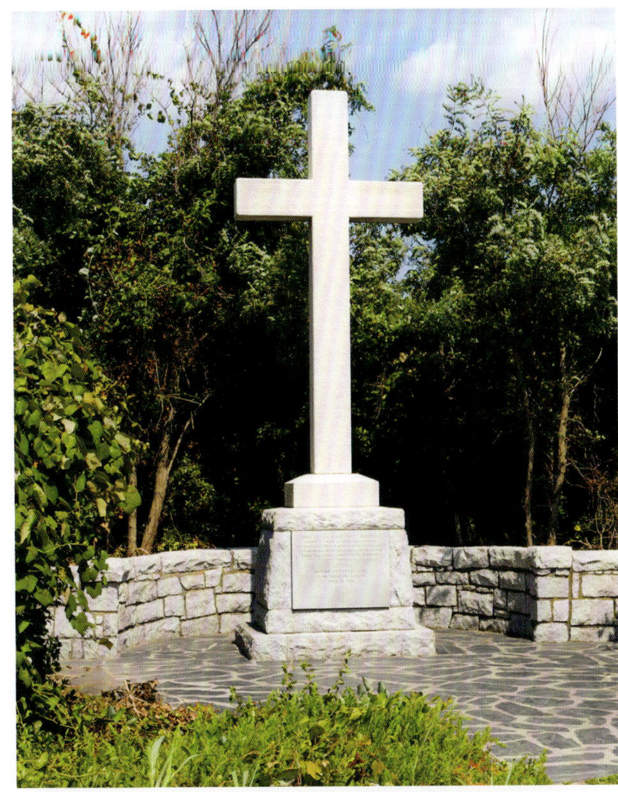

Colonial National Historical Park

Colonial National Historical Park preserves and interprets key sites from early American history, particularly during the Colonial and Revolutionary War periods. The park is home to several significant historical locations, including the Jamestown Settlement, the site of the first permanent English colony in America, and the Yorktown Battlefield. The park also includes the Colonial Parkway, a scenic route connecting these historic sites.

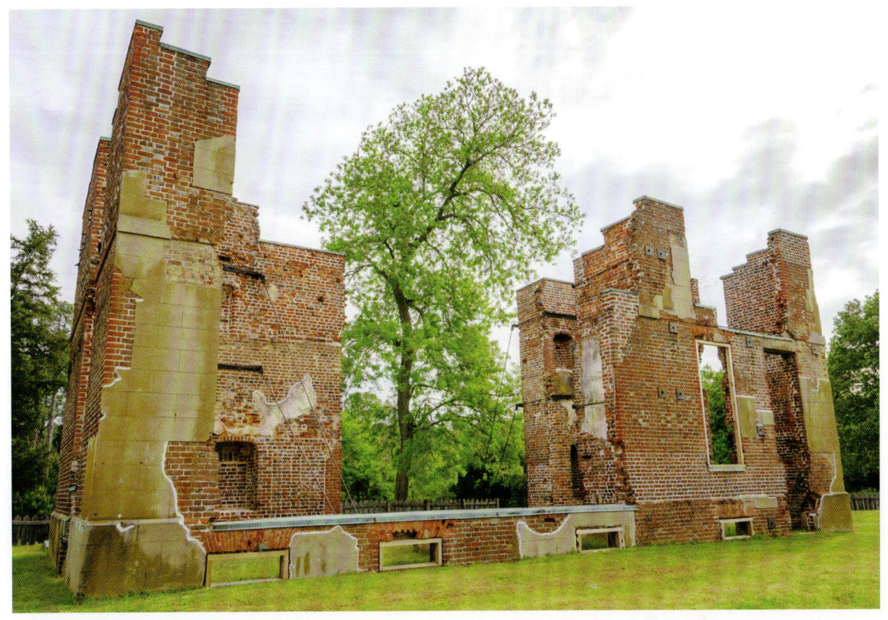

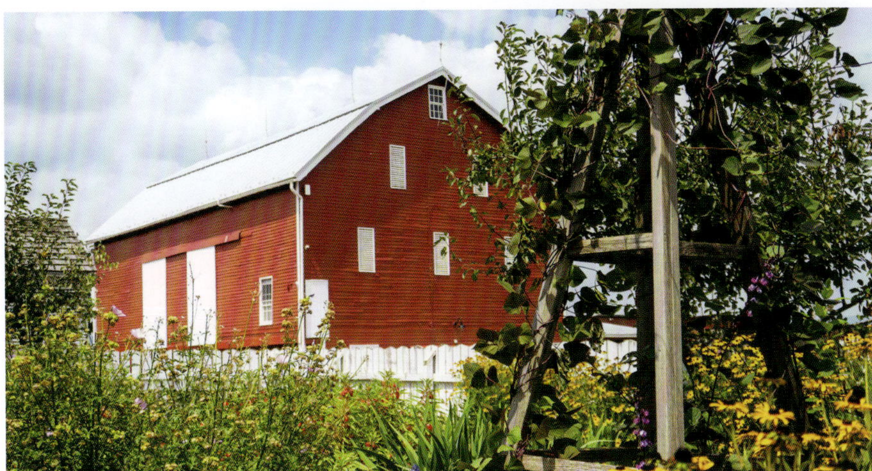

Cedar Creek & Belle Grove National Historical Park

Cedar Creek & Belle Grove National Historical Park, located in Virginia's Shenandoah Valley, preserves the site of the Battle of Cedar Creek, a significant Civil War battle. The park includes Belle Grove Plantation, which was home of the Hite family and served as a strategic location during the battle. The plantation house is now a museum, offering exhibits on the battle, the history of the plantation, and the experiences of both Union and Confederate soldiers.

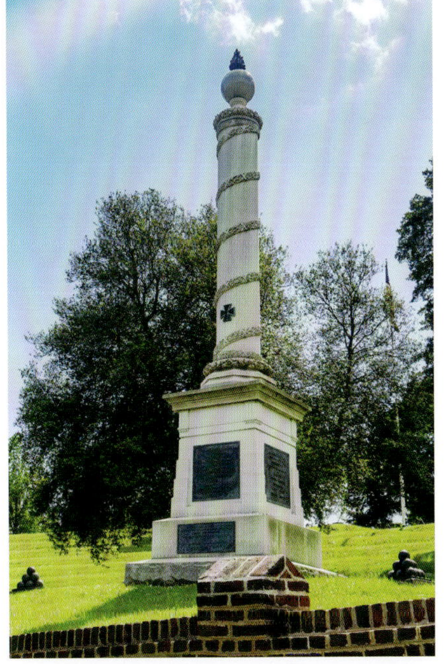

Fredericksburg and Spotsylvania National Military Park

Fredericksburg and Spotsylvania National Military Park preserves four major Civil War battlefields: Fredericksburg, Chancellorsville, the Wilderness, and Spotsylvania Court House. The park includes preserved battlefields, historic structures, and monuments that honor the soldiers and their sacrifices. Visitors can tour the battlefields, explore the visitor centers, and view exhibits that provide insights into the strategies, hardships, and impact of the battles.

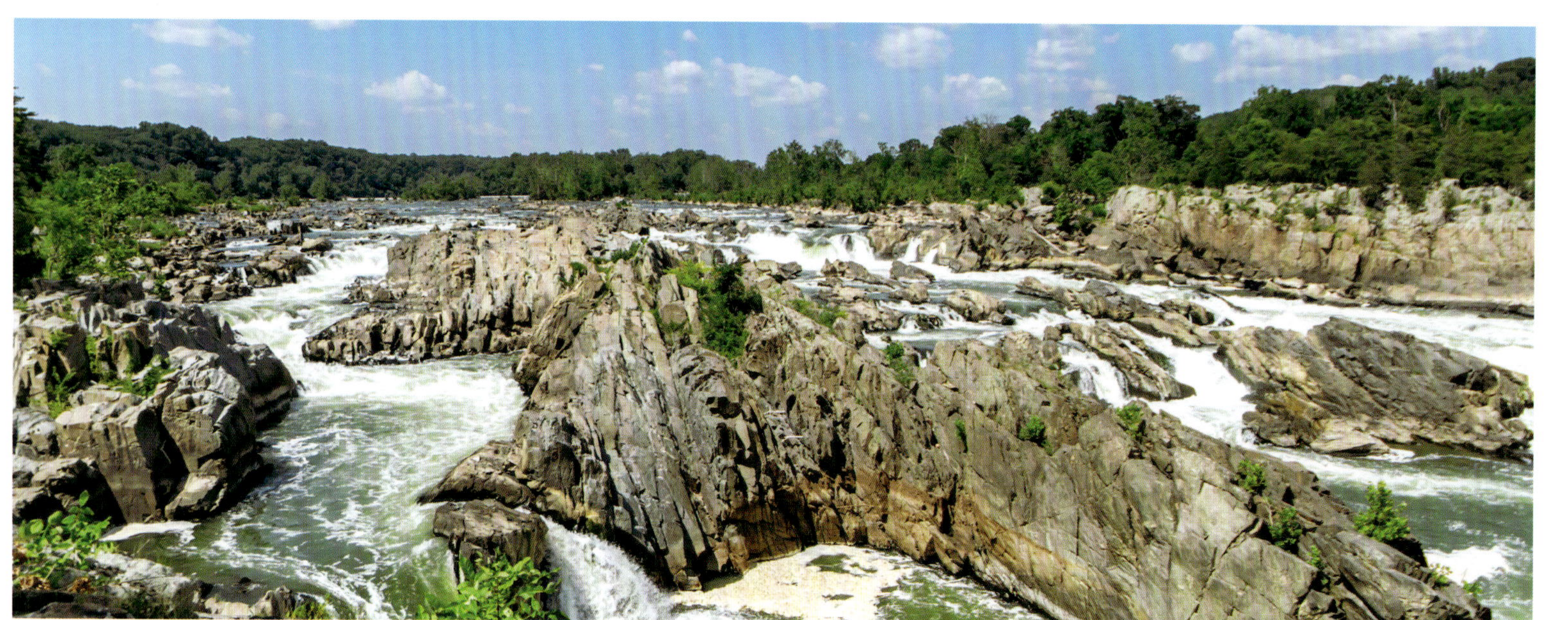

Great Falls Park

Great Falls Park is a scenic and natural area along the Potomac River, known for its astonishing waterfalls and rugged landscapes. The park features the Great Falls of the Potomac, where the river cascades over a series of steep rapids and cliffs, creating a dramatic display of nature's power.

Historic Jamestowne

Historic Jamestowne is a cultural heritage site that was the location of the first permanent English settlement in America. As part of the Colonial National Historical Park, visitors can tour the preserved archaeological sites, view exhibits at the visitor center, and learn about the challenges faced by the settlers, including their interactions with Indigenous peoples, the survival struggles, and the eventual growth of the colony. Key sites include the ruins of the Jamestown church, the grave sites of early settlers, and the archeological findings.

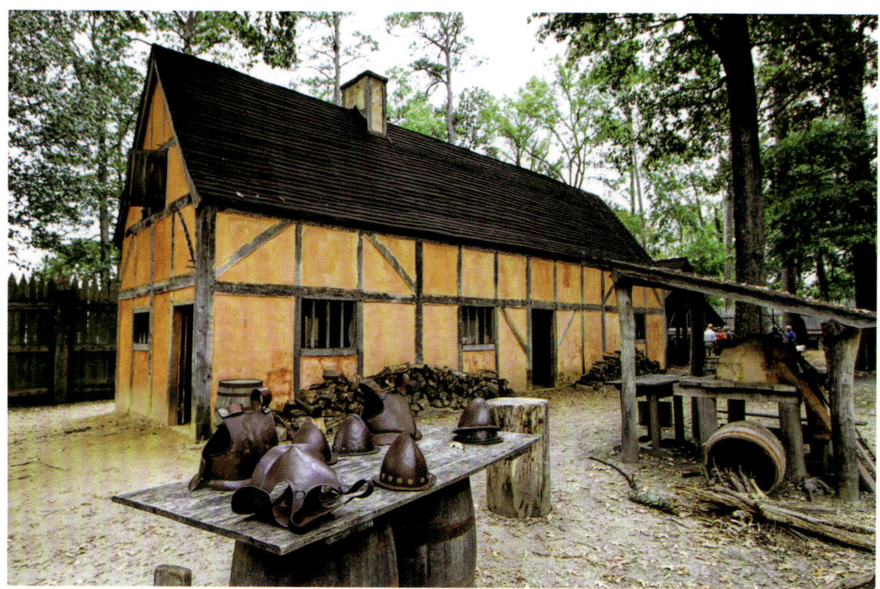

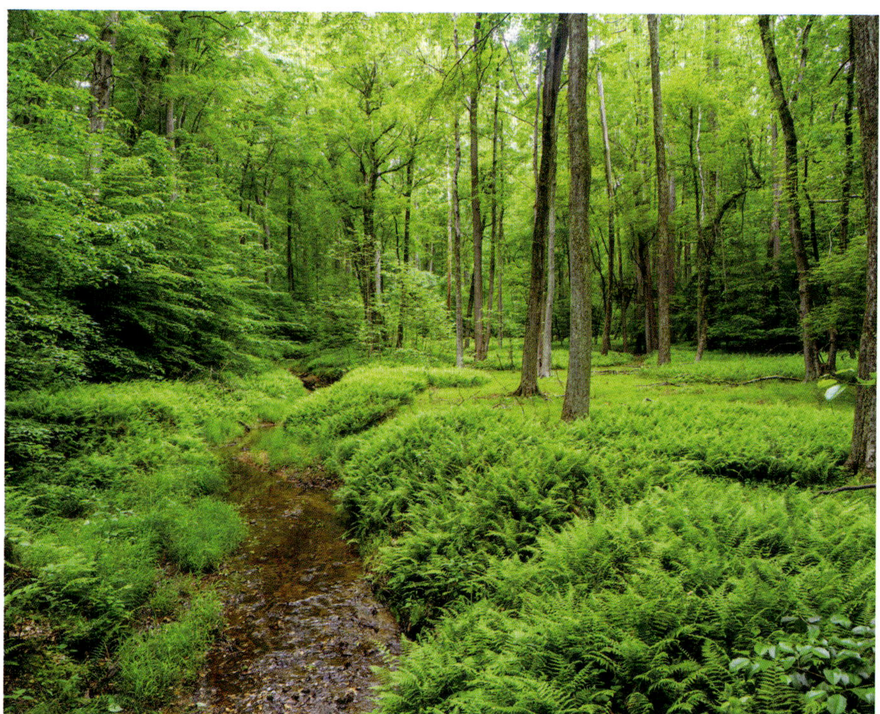

Prince William Forest Park

Prince William Forest Park is a large, scenic national park offering a peaceful retreat just outside Washington, D.C. The park spans over 15,000 acres of diverse ecosystems, and it has more than 37 miles of trails, ranging from easy walks to more challenging hikes, providing opportunities to explore its rich natural beauty.

Shenandoah National Park

Located in the Blue Ridge Mountains of Virginia, Shenandoah National Park offers breathtaking views, distinctive wildlife, and over 200,000 acres of protected wilderness. The park is renowned for its scenic Skyline Drive, which runs the length of the park and provides stunning vistas of the valley below. It also features more than 200 miles of hiking trails, including a portion of the famous Appalachian Trail.

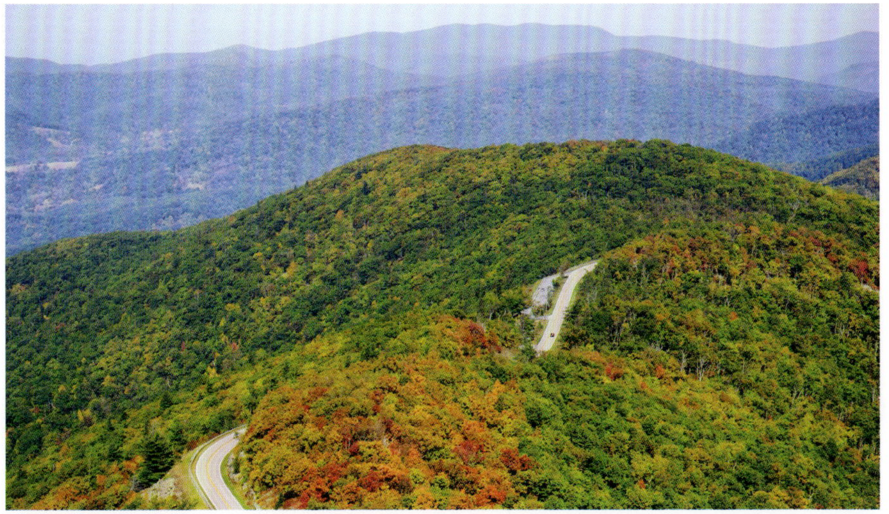

Yorktown Battlefield

Yorktown Battlefield is part of the Colonial National Historical Park and preserves the site where the Union Army won the American Revolutionary War. The visitor center features exhibits, artifacts, and presentations about the battle's significance. Visitors can also explore the battlefield itself, view historic fortifications, view the Yorktown Victory Monument, and tour the Moore House, where surrender negotiations took place.

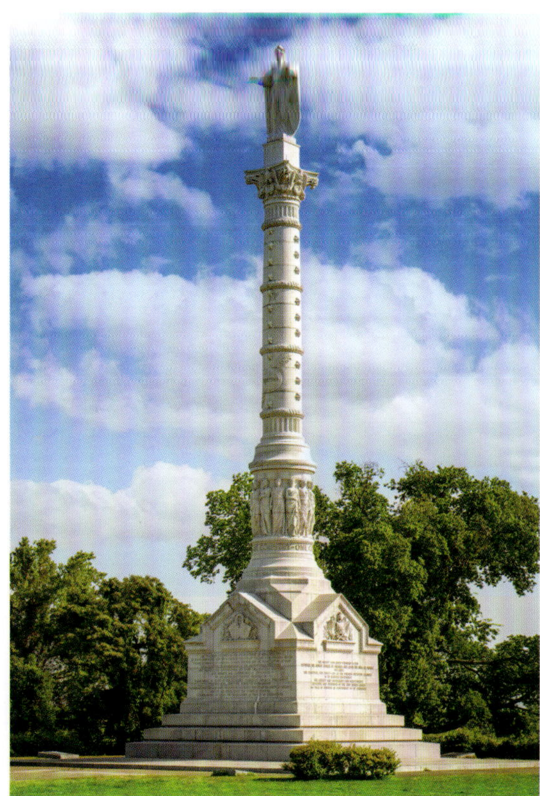

Wolf Trap National Park for the Performing Arts

Originally known as the Wolf Trap Farm Park for the Performing Arts, this park is unique for blending outdoor natural beauty with world-class cultural performances. It's home to the Wolf Trap Opera House, an open-air venue that hosts a variety of performances, including concerts, theater, dance, and opera, from both local and international artists.

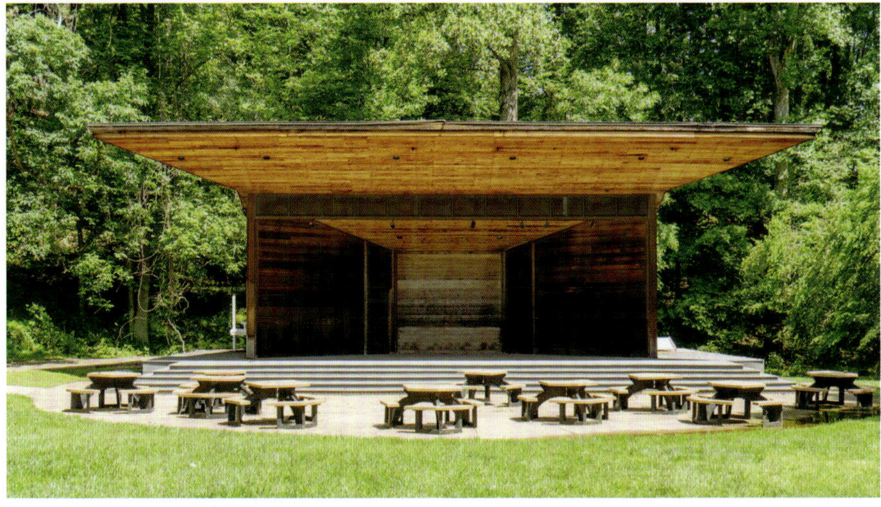

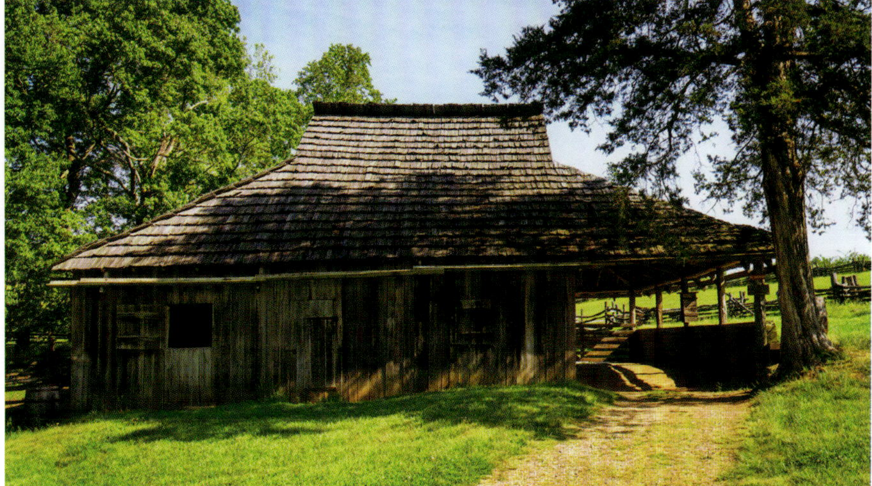

Booker T. Washington National Monument

Booker T. Washington National Monument preserves the birthplace and early home of Booker T. Washington, a prominent African American educator, author, and leader. The site features a reconstructed 19th-century tobacco farm, interpretive exhibits, walking trails, and educational programs that highlight Washington's early life, his journey to freedom, and his lasting impact on American society.

Fort Monroe National Monument

Fort Monroe National Monument is a former military installation with a rich and complex history. Known as the "Gibraltar of the Chesapeake," the fort was completed in 1834 and served a strategic coastal defense site. The monument includes the massive stone fort, historic buildings, and Casemate Museum, which features exhibits on the fort's military history, the Civil War, and its role in advancing freedom.

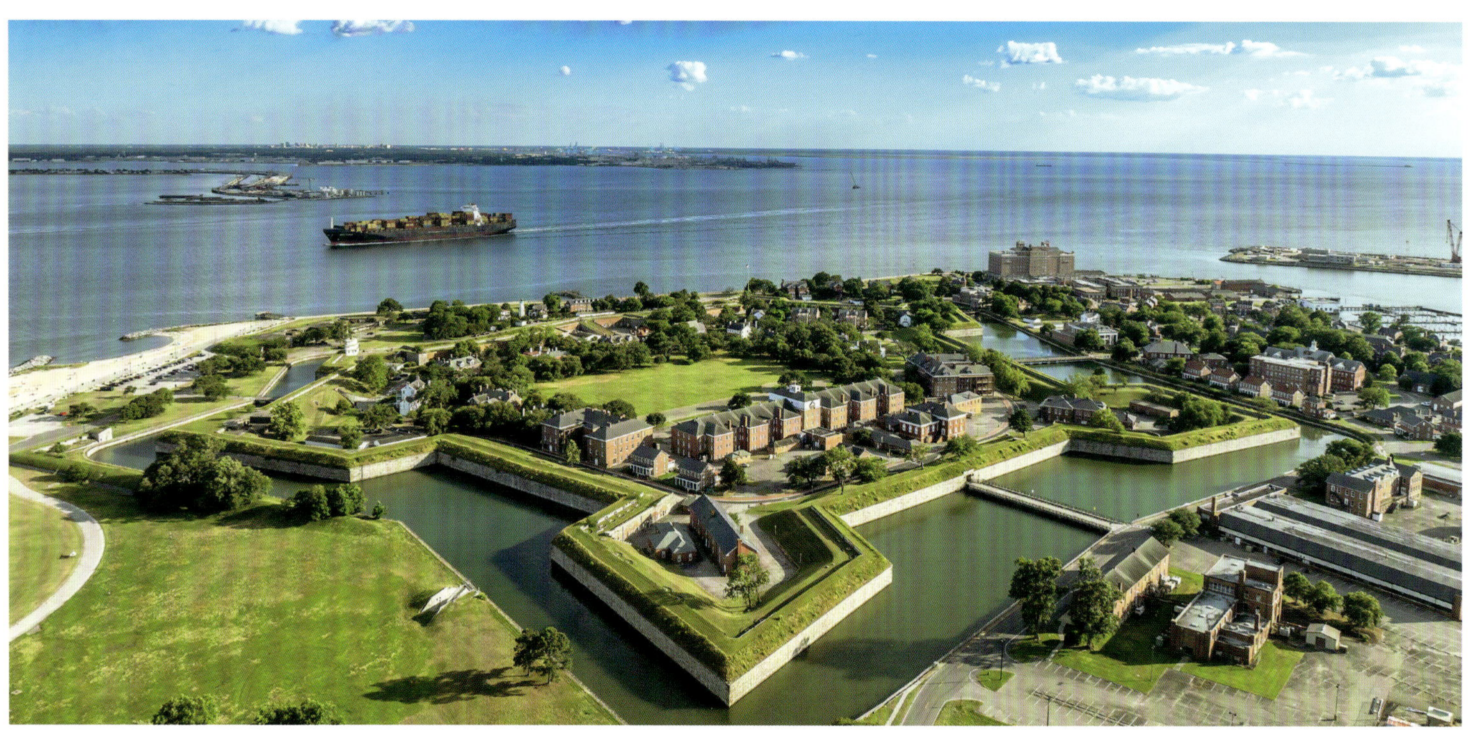

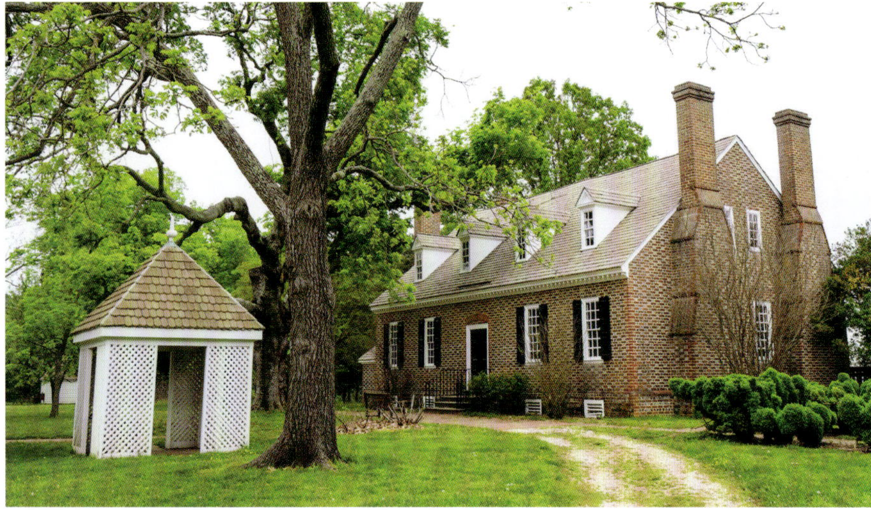

George Washington Birthplace National Monument

George Washington Birthplace National Monument preserves the site where George Washington, the first President of the United States, was born in 1732. The park features a reconstructed Colonial-era plantation, including a Memorial House, gardens, outbuildings, and a working farm. Visitors can explore the historic grounds, enjoy interpretive exhibits, and learn about Washington's early life, his family, and the environment that shaped him. The park also includes trails and scenic views of the Potomac River.

Green Springs National Historic Landmark District

Green Springs National Historic Landmark District is a well-preserved rural area in Louisa County, VA, known for its historic architecture, agricultural heritage, and scenic landscapes. The district encompasses over 14,000 acres, featuring rolling farmland, and historic homes and structures—such as Boswell's Tavern *(see below)*—dating back to the 18th and 19th centuries.

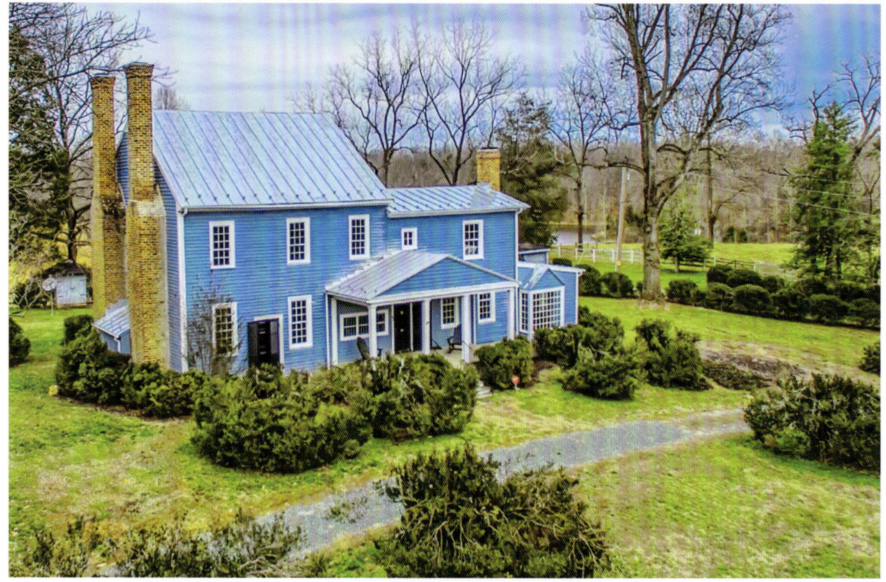

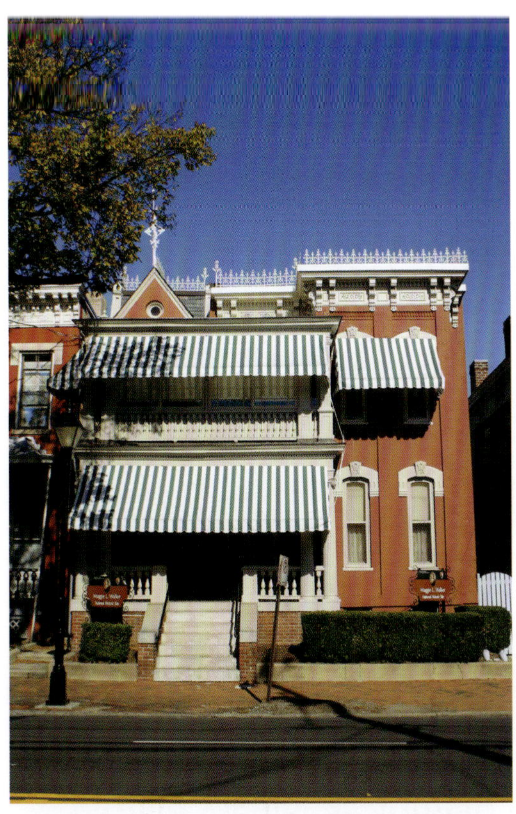

Maggie L. Walker National Historic Site

Maggie L. Walker National Historic Site offers the life and legacy of Maggie Lena Walker, a trailblazing African American businesswoman, educator, and civil rights leader. The site includes her restored historic home, which is preserved to reflect its appearance during her lifetime. Visitors can tour the home, view exhibits about Walker's life and achievements, and learn about her role in advancing opportunities for African Americans during the Jim Crow era.

Petersburg National Battlefield

Petersburg National Battlefield commemorates the site of the Siege of Petersburg, a pivotal Civil War campaign that lasted from June 1864 to April 1865. The park spans multiple units, including battlefields, forts, and trench systems. Key sites include the Crater, where a massive Union mine explosion failed to break Confederate lines, and Fort Stedman, a location of fierce fighting near the end of the siege.

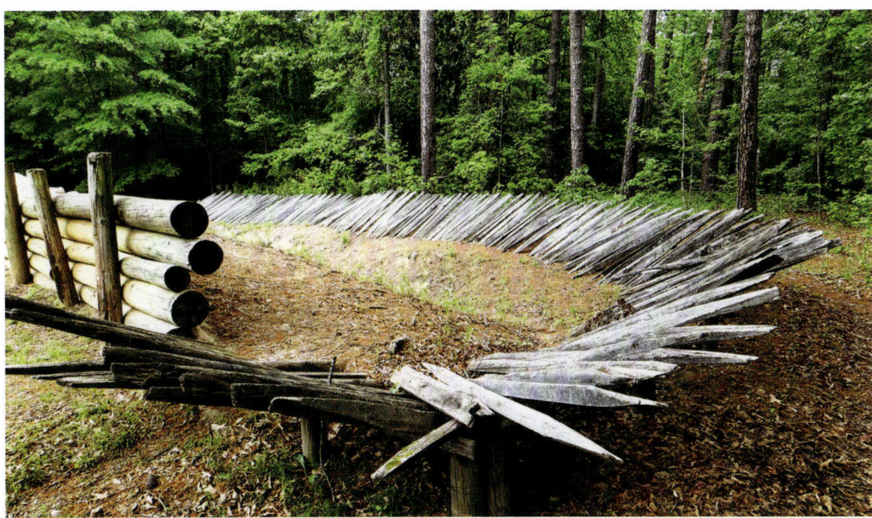

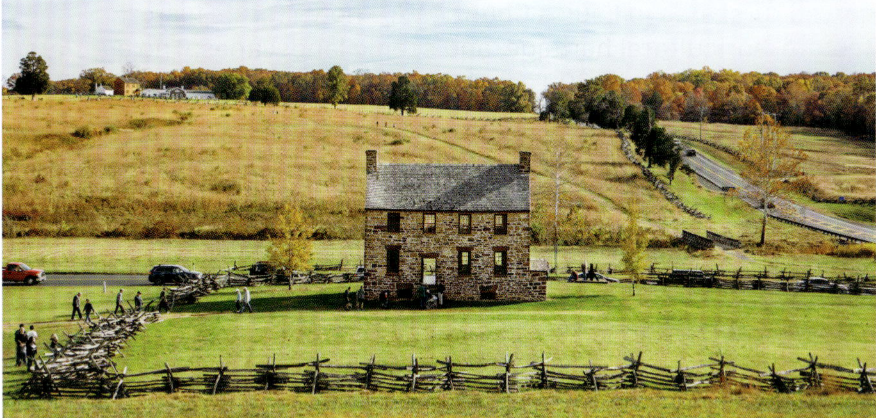

Manassas National Battlefield Park

Located in northern Virginia, Manassas National Battlefield Park preserves the site of two significant Civil War battles: the First and Second Battles of Bull Run, fought in 1861 and 1862, respectively. The park spans over 5,000 acres and includes key battlefield locations, historic structures, and monuments. Visitors can explore walking trails, view interpretive exhibits at the Henry Hill Visitor Center, and attend ranger-led tours to learn about the strategies, soldiers, and impact of the battles.

Richmond National Battlefield Park

Richmond National Battlefield Park preserves multiple sites associated with key Civil War battles found to defend or capture the Confederate capital. The park spans nearly 3,000 acres over 13 units, encompassing battlefields, fortifications, and historic structures tied to pivotal campaigns. Site that can be visited include Gaines' Mill, Cold Harbor, and Drewry's Bluff—each offering interpretive trails, exhibits, and detailed accounts of the battles and strategies—and the Tredegar Iron Works *(see right)*.

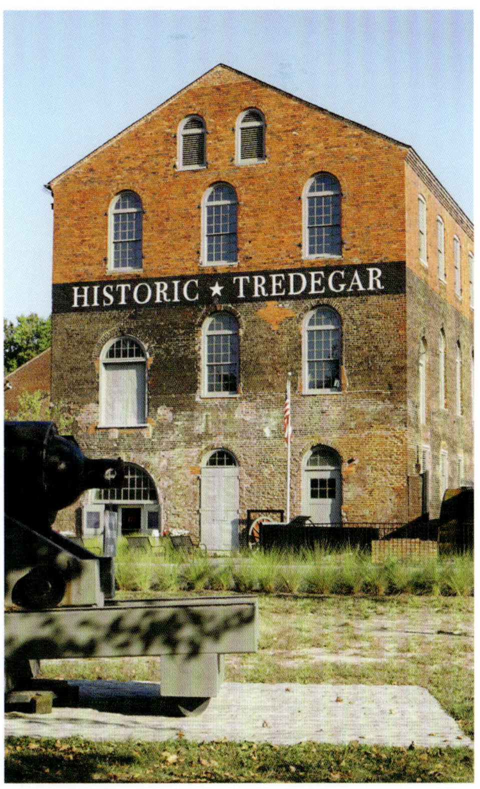

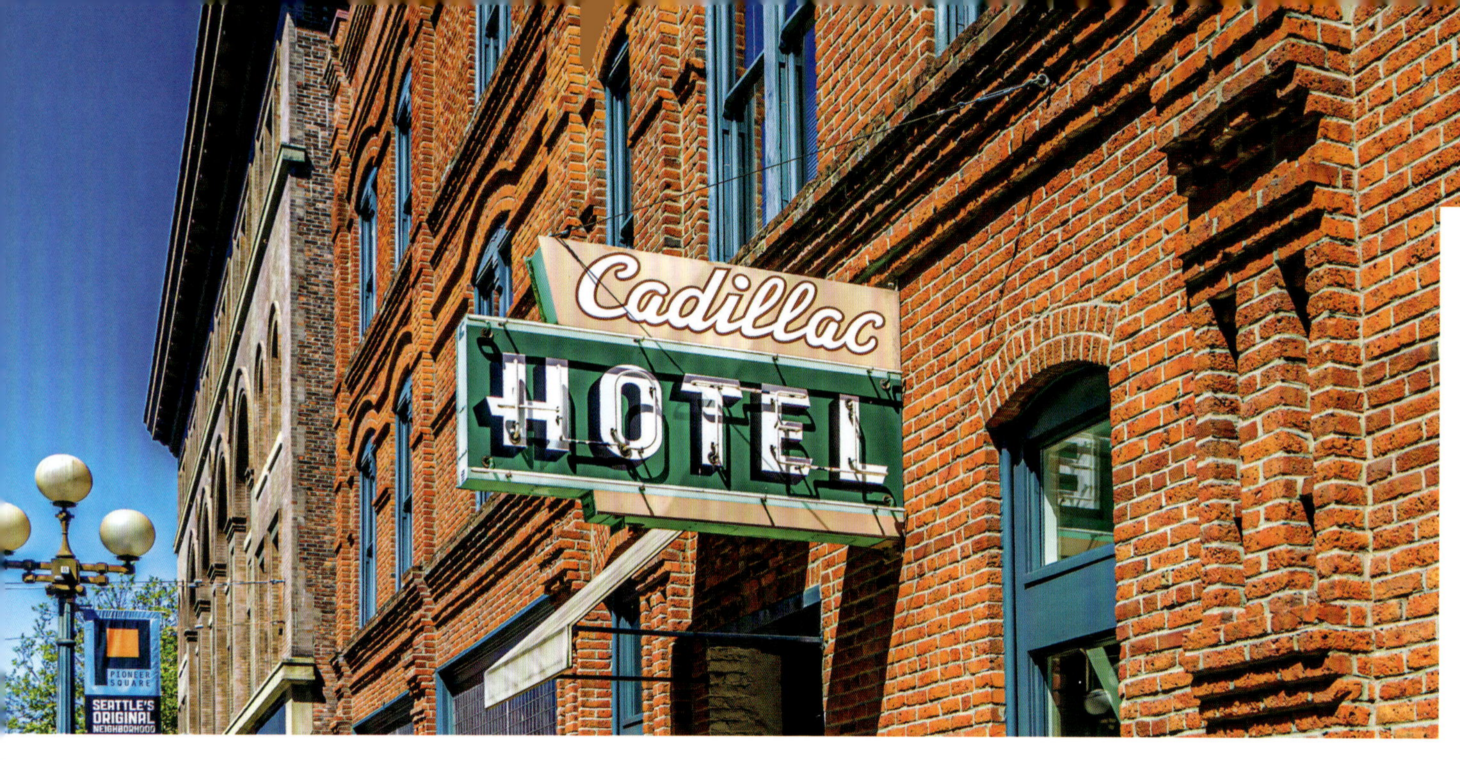

Klondike Gold Rush National Historical Park – Seattle Unit

The Seattle Unit of Klondike Gold Rush National Historical Park commemorates the city's role as a gateway to the Klondike Gold Rush of 1897–1898. Housed in the historic Cadillac Hotel *(see left)*, the park's visitor center features exhibits, films, and interactive displays that highlight the stories of prospectors, the challenges of the journey, and Seattle's transformation into a bustling supply hub during the gold rush.

WASHINGTON

Mount Rainier National Park

Mount Rainier National Park protects the iconic Mount Rainier, a 14,410-foot active stratovolcano, and the tallest peak in the Cascade Range. The park encompasses over 236,000 acres, featuring lush old-growth forests, subalpine meadows, glaciers, and waterfalls. Popular activities include hiking on over 260 miles of trails, climbing the summit, and exploring the famous Wonderland Trail, a 93-mile loop around the mountain.

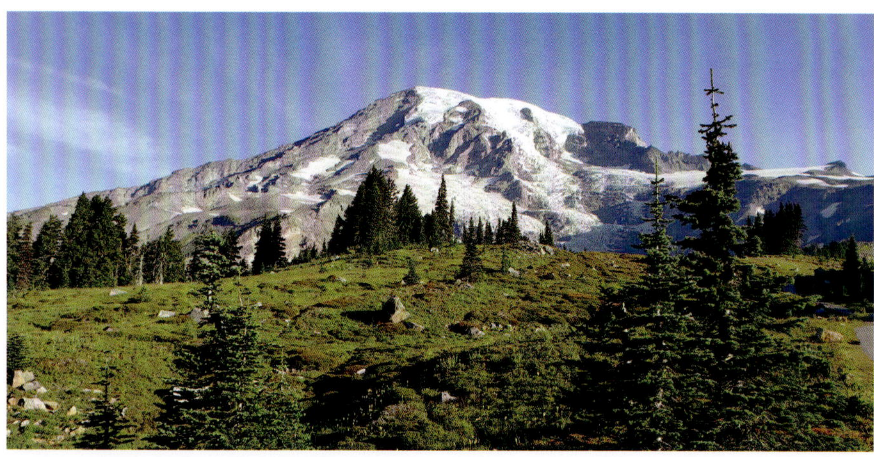

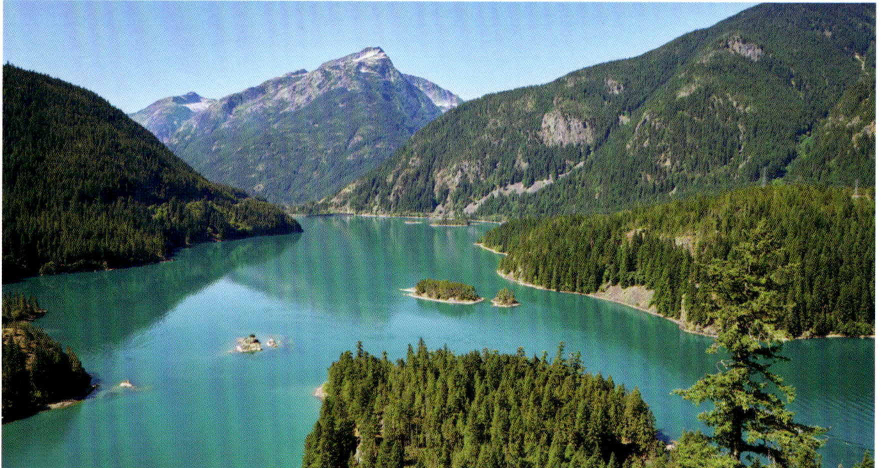

North Cascades National Park

Located in northern Washington state, North Cascades National Park is renowned for its rugged mountain peaks, over 300 glaciers, and pristine wilderness. Popular activities include hiking on over 400 miles of trails, backcountry camping, mountaineering, and wildlife viewing, with species like black bears, mountain goats, and bald eagles inhabiting the area.

Olympic National Park

Olympic National Park, located on the Olympic Peninsula in Washington state, is noted for its incredible diversity of ecosystems and landscapes. Covering nearly one million acres, the park includes lush, temperate rainforests, rugged coastlines, alpine peaks, and glaciated valleys. Visitors can explore the scenic Hoh Rainforest; walk along dramatic beaches like Rialto Beach and Ruby Beach; and hike through the Olympic Mountains, including Mount Olympus.

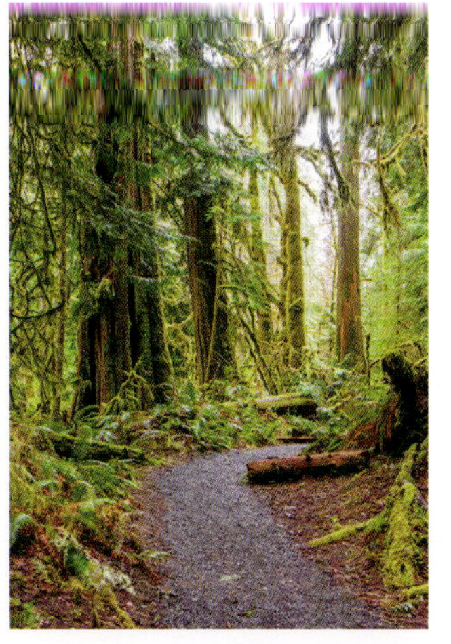

Lake Roosevelt National Recreation Area

Lake Roosevelt National Recreation Area, located in northeastern Washington state, surrounds the 130-mile-long reservoir created by the Grand Coulee Dam on the Columbia River. Named after President Franklin D. Roosevelt, who championed the dam's construction, the area offers diverse recreational opportunities amid scenic landscapes. Visitors can enjoy boating, fishing, swimming, and camping along the reservoir's extensive shoreline.

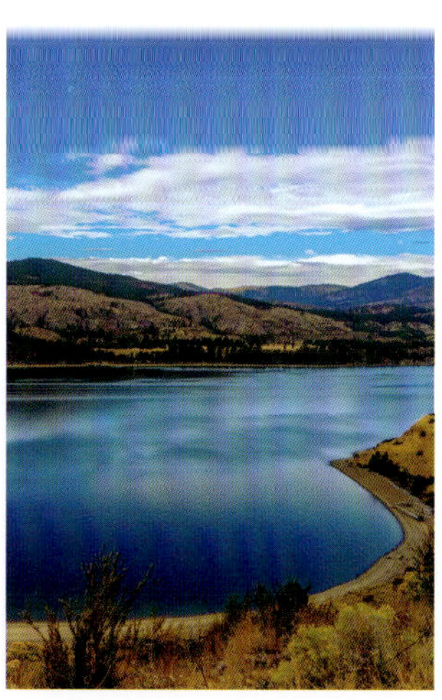

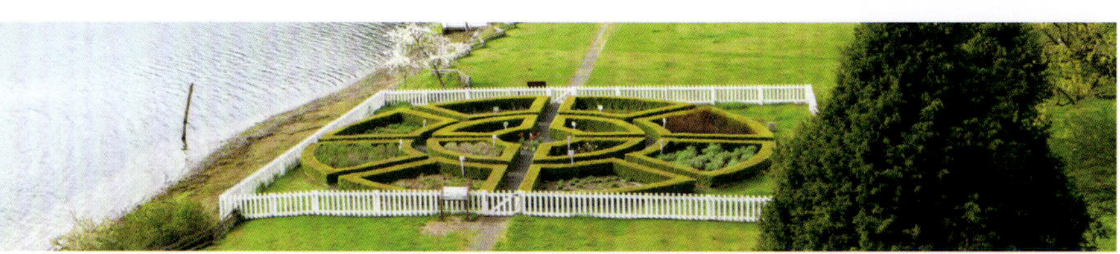

San Juan Island National Historical Park

San Juan Island National Historical Park commemorates the peaceful resolution of the Pig War, a boundary dispute between the U.S. and Britain in 1859. The park consists of two main units: American Camp and English Camp, representing the military encampments of each nation during the conflict. Visitors can explore historic buildings, scenic landscapes, and interpretive exhibits at both sites: American camp features sweeping coastal views, prairies, and opportunities for wildlife viewing, while English Camp *(see above)* is nestled in a sheltered bay with lush forests and historic gardens.

Whitman Mission National Historic Site

Located near Walla Walla, WA, Whitman Mission National Historic Site commemorates the tragic story of Marcus and Narcissa Whitman—missionaries who established a mission among the Cayuse people in 1836, with the aim to introduce Christianity and Western agricultural practices to the Cayuse, but instead faced cultural misunderstandings and tensions with them. The site preserves the mission grounds, a cemetery, and a monument to the Whitmans. Visitors can explore trails, exhibits, and programs that provide insight into the cultural conflicts and legacies of this chapter in American history.

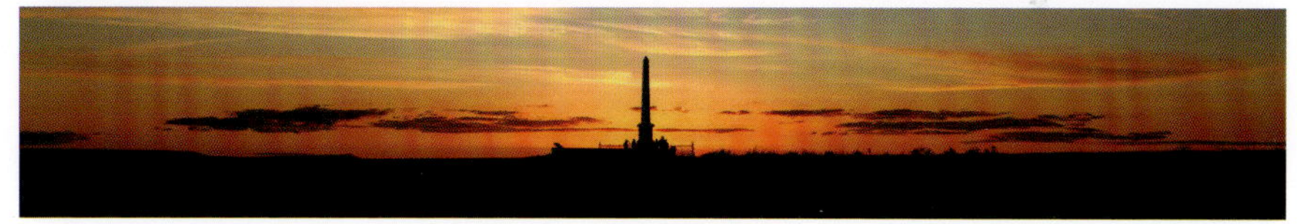

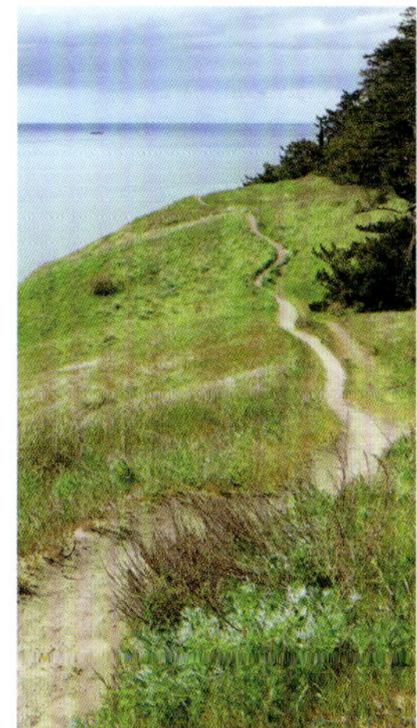

Ebey's Landing National Historical Reserve

Located on Whidbey Island in Washington state, Ebey's Landing National Historical Reserve preserves the cultural and natural heritage of Puget Sound. The reserve protects historic farms, Victorian-era homes, and the 19th-century town of Coupeville, showcasing the area's rich history of Native American culture, European settlement, and maritime trade. It also includes stunning coastal bluffs, forests, and prairies, offering opportunities for hiking, birding, and photography.

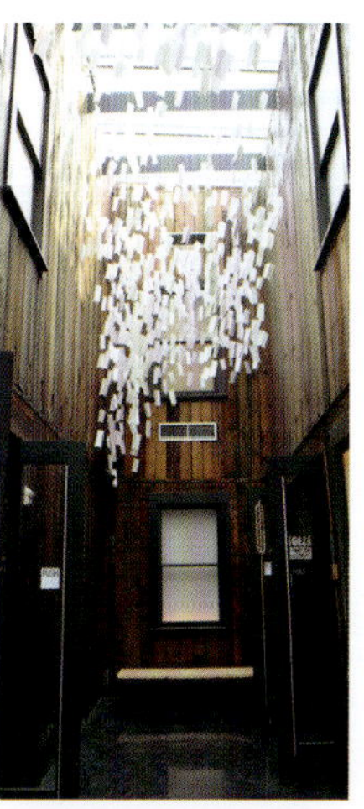

Wing Luke Museum Affiliated Area

Wing Luke Museum is dedicated to preserving and sharing the history, culture, and experiences of Asian American, Native Hawaiian, and Pacific Islander (AANHPI) communities. Named after Wing Luke, the first Asian American elected to public office in the Pacific Northwest, the museum is housed in a historic building in the Chinatown-International District of Seattle. Through exhibits, guided tours, and cultural programs, this Smithsonian Institution affiliate highlights stories of immigration, resilience, and contributions of AANHPI individuals and communities.

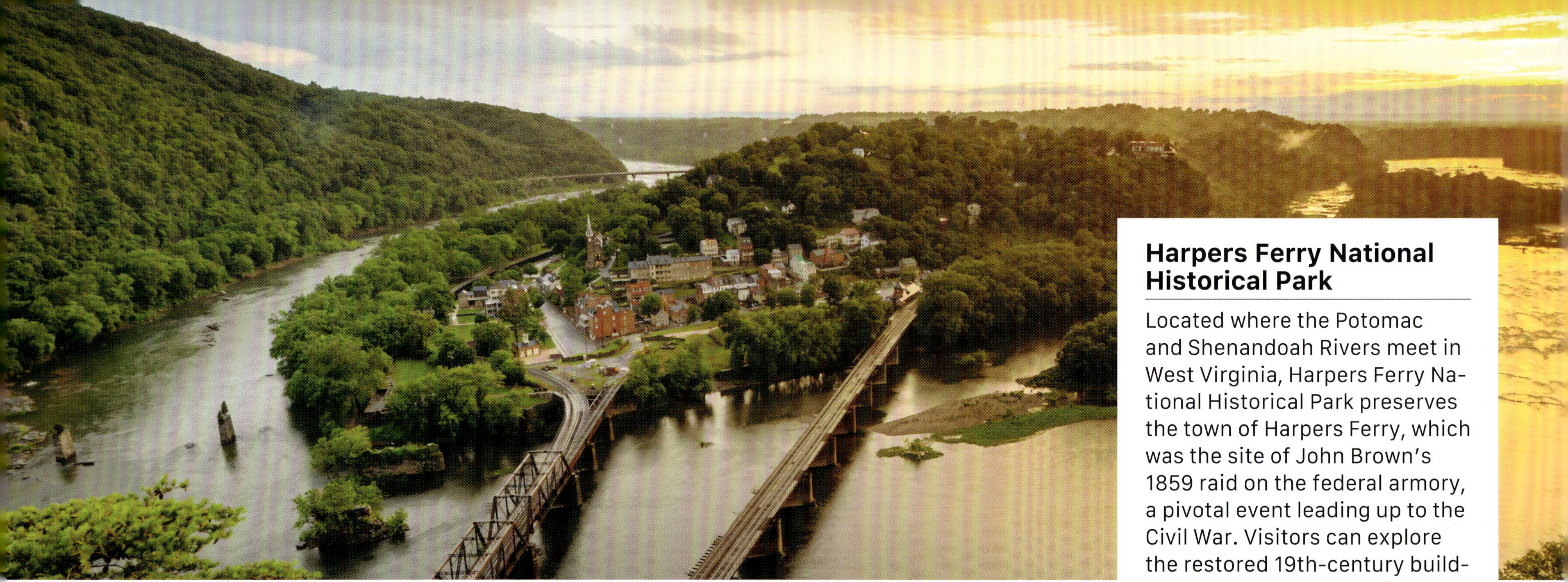

WEST VIRGINIA

Harpers Ferry National Historical Park

Located where the Potomac and Shenandoah Rivers meet in West Virginia, Harpers Ferry National Historical Park preserves the town of Harpers Ferry, which was the site of John Brown's 1859 raid on the federal armory, a pivotal event leading up to the Civil War. Visitors can explore the restored 19th-century buildings, museums, and exhibits that highlight the town's role in industry, transportation, and the abolitionist movement.

New River Gorge National Park and Preserve

New River Gorge National Park and Preserve protects over 70,000 acres of rugged landscapes surrounding the New River, one of the oldest rivers in North America. Known for its dramatic sandstone cliffs, lush forests, and diverse wildlife, the park is a haven for outdoor enthusiasts. The park is famous for the New River Gorge Bridge, an engineering marvel and one of the longest steel-arch bridges in the world.

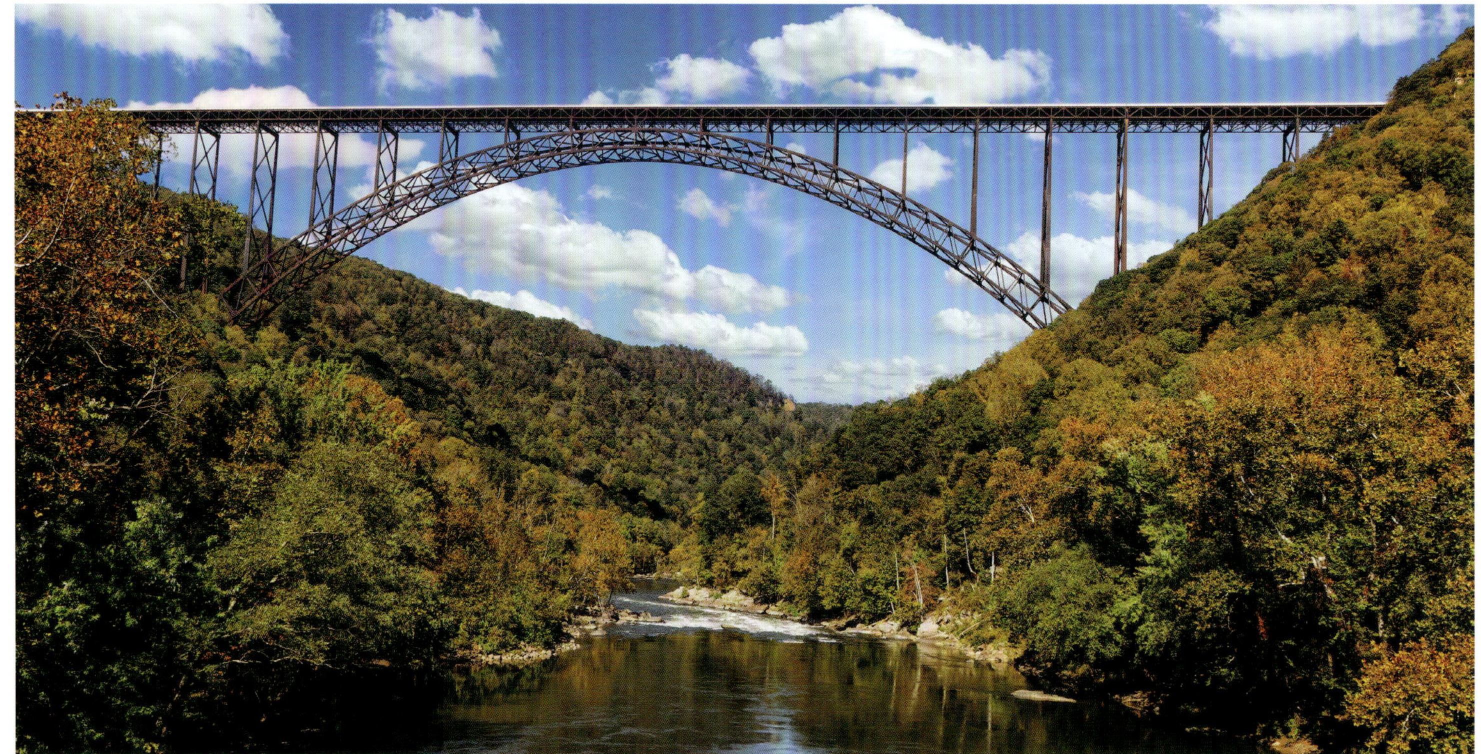

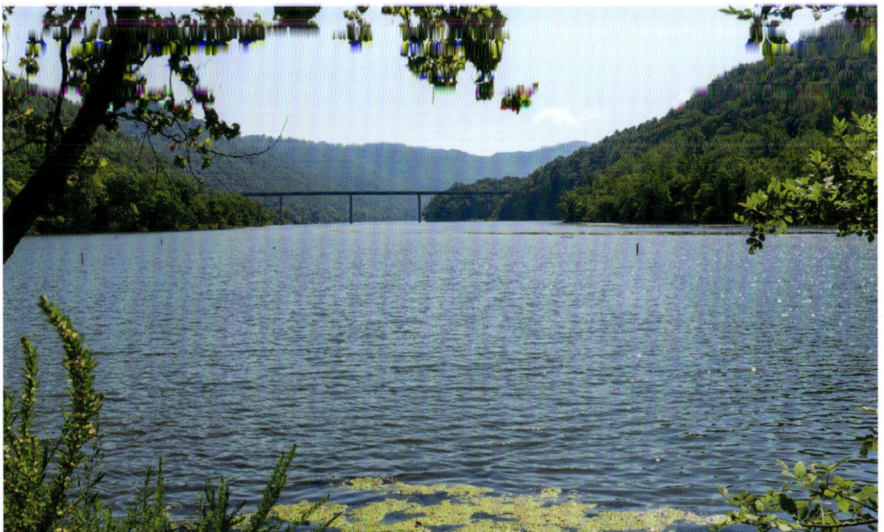

Bluestone National Scenic River

Bluestone National Scenic River preserves a 10.5-mile stretch of the free-flowing Bluestone River, a tributary of the New River. Known for its unspoiled natural beauty, the river flows through a tranquil gorge surrounded by lush forests and a variety of wildlife, offering a pristine environment for outdoor recreation and exploration.

Gauley River National Recreation Area

Gauley River National Recreation Area protects 25 miles of the Gauley River and six miles of the Meadow River. The area is renowned for its world-class whitewater rafting and kayaking, particularly during the fall "Gauley Season" when dam releases create intense rapids, including Class V rapids.

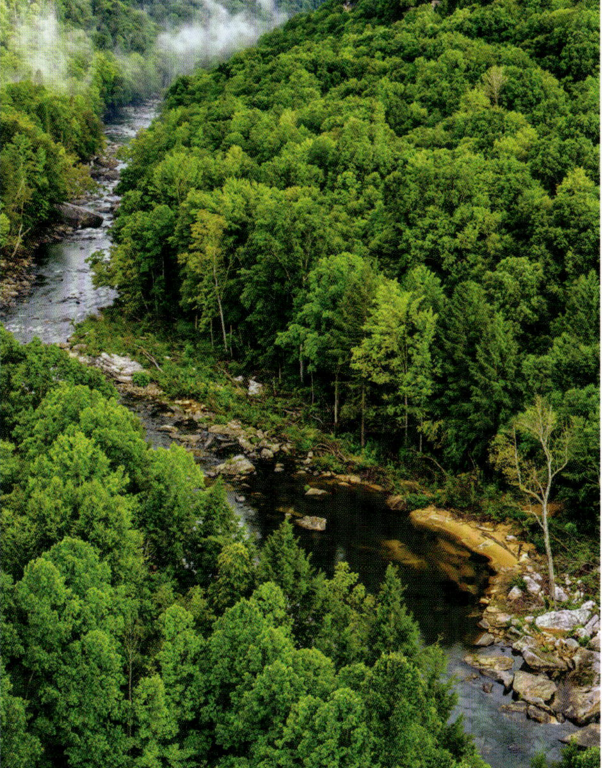

Spruce Knob–Seneca Rocks National Recreation Area

Located in the Monongahela National Forest in West Virginia, Spruce Knob–Seneca Rocks National Recreation Area is a stunning destination that encompasses three iconic landmarks: Spruce Knob, the highest point in West Virginia at 4,863 feet; Seneca Rocks, a dramatic quartzite cliff popular among climbers and hikers; and Smoke Hole Canyon, a canyon along the South Branch Potomac River.

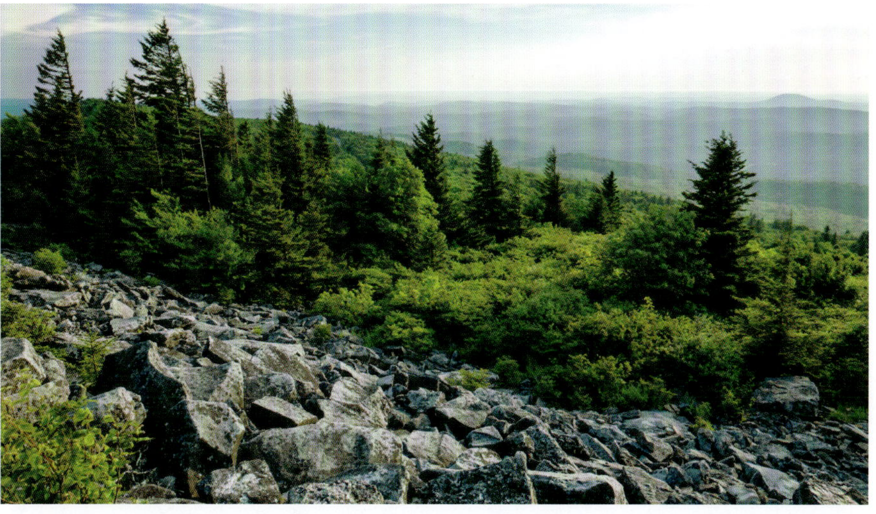

Weston State Hospital

Weston State Hospital is a historic psychiatric hospital known for its massive Gothic Revival architecture. Originally constructed between 1858 and 1881, the hospital—also called the Trans-Allegheny Lunatic Asylum—was designated to accommodate 250 patients but became severely overcrowded in the 20th century, housing thousands at its peak. The hospital closed in 1994, but it now offers guided tours focused on its history, architecture, and the evolution of mental health care.

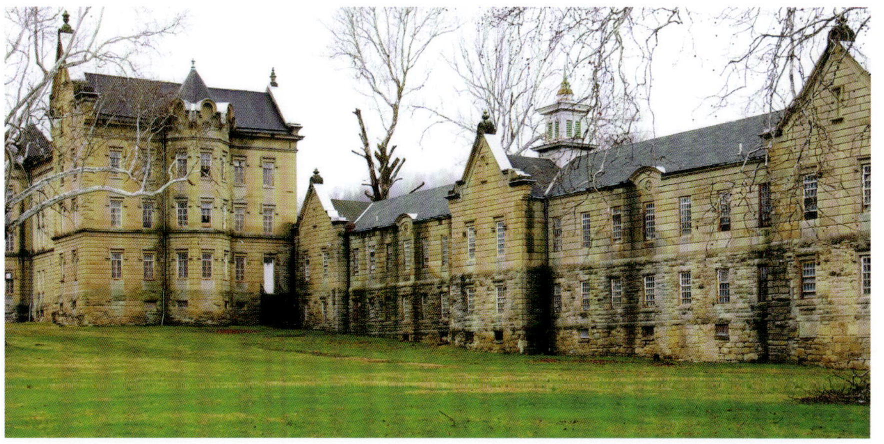

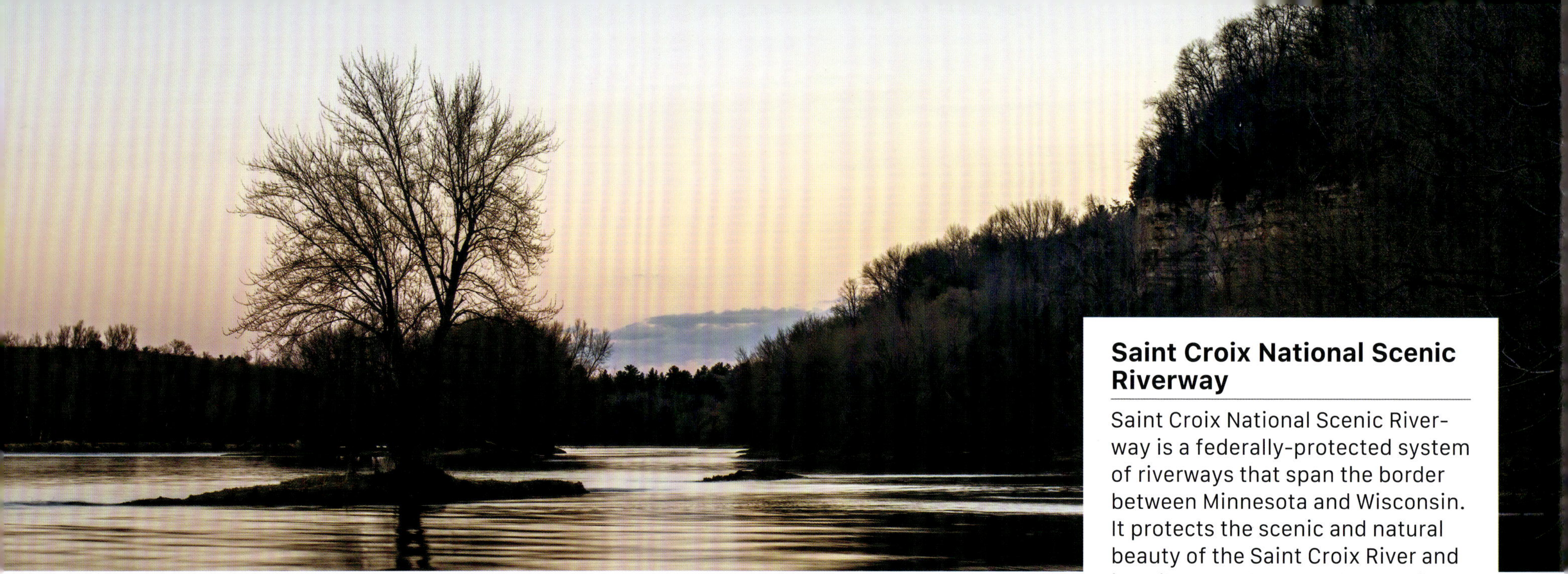

WISCONSIN

Saint Croix National Scenic Riverway

Saint Croix National Scenic Riverway is a federally-protected system of riverways that span the border between Minnesota and Wisconsin. It protects the scenic and natural beauty of the Saint Croix River and its tributary, the Namekagon River, and offers a range of recreational and educational opportunities along its 252-mile stretch.

Apostle Islands National Lakeshore

Located in northern Wisconsin on the shores of Lake Superior, Apostle Islands National Lakeshore is a breathtaking collection of 21 islands and 12 miles of mainland coastline. Known for its rugged beauty, the area features pristine beaches, sea caves, old-growth forests, and historic lighthouses. Visitors can explore the islands by boat, kayak, or ferry, with activities such as hiking, camping, fishing, and birding. The sea caves are particularly popular, transforming into stunning ice caves during winter *(see right)*.

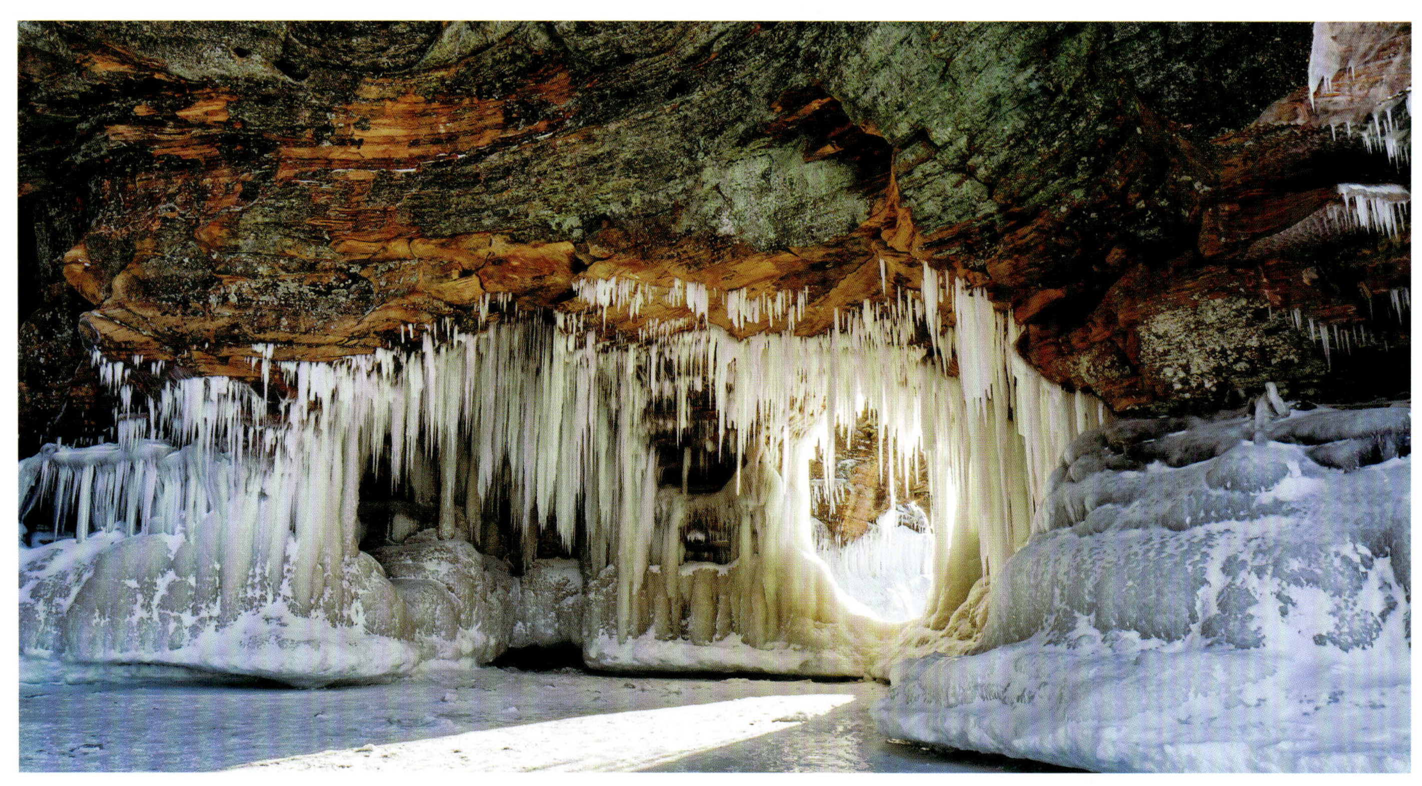

Ice Age National Scenic Trail

Lying entirely within Wisconsin, the Ice Age National Scenic Trail is a 1,200-mile footpath that traces the edge of the last glacial retreat in North America. The trail winds through diverse landscapes shaped by glaciers, including rolling hills, rugged ridges, glacial lakes, and picturesque valleys. Visitors can explore sections of the trail ranging from easy walks to challenging treks, with opportunities to observe unique geological features, such as kettles, eskers, and moraines.

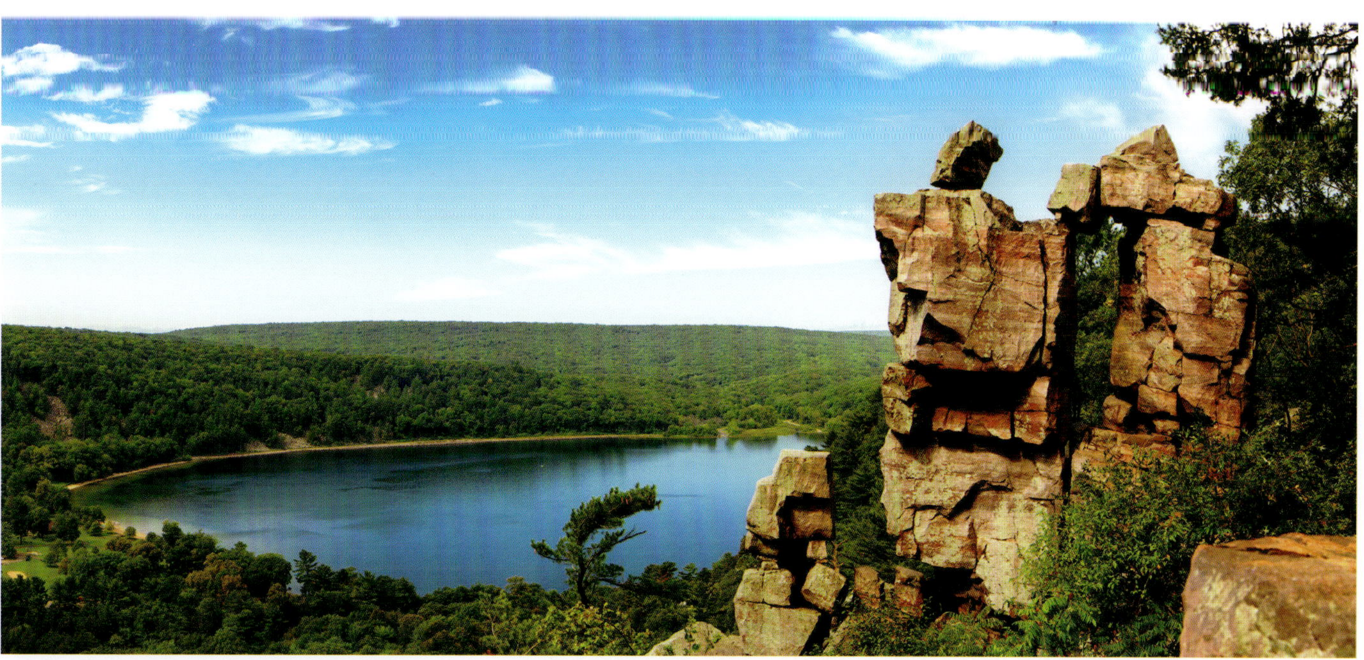

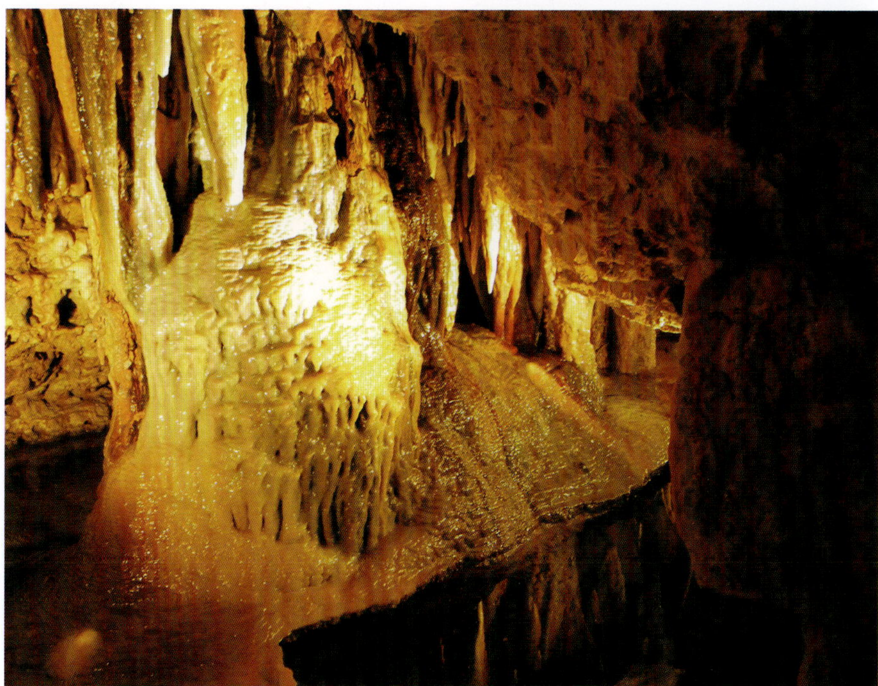

Cave of the Mounds

Cave of the Mounds is a breathtaking natural limestone cave, often called the "jewel box" of America's caves due to its colorful crystal formations. Discovered in 1939, the cave features intricate stalactites, stalagmites, flowstones, and other formations created over millions of years by mineral-rich water seeping through the rock.

Pabst Mansion

Pabst Mansion is a historic Milwaukee home built in 1892 as the residence of Captain Frederick Pabst, founding of the Pabst Brewing Company. This Flemish Renaissance Revival-style mansion is renowned for its attractive architecture, intricate woodwork, stained glass windows, and period furnishings. Visitors can enjoy guided tours that showcase the Pabst family's history, Milwaukee's brewing heritage, and the cultural significance of the area.

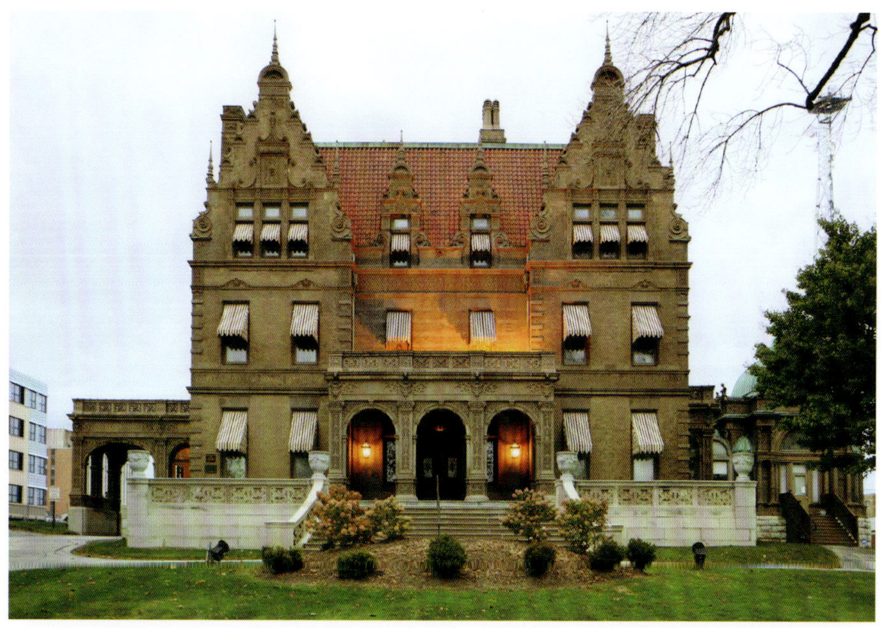

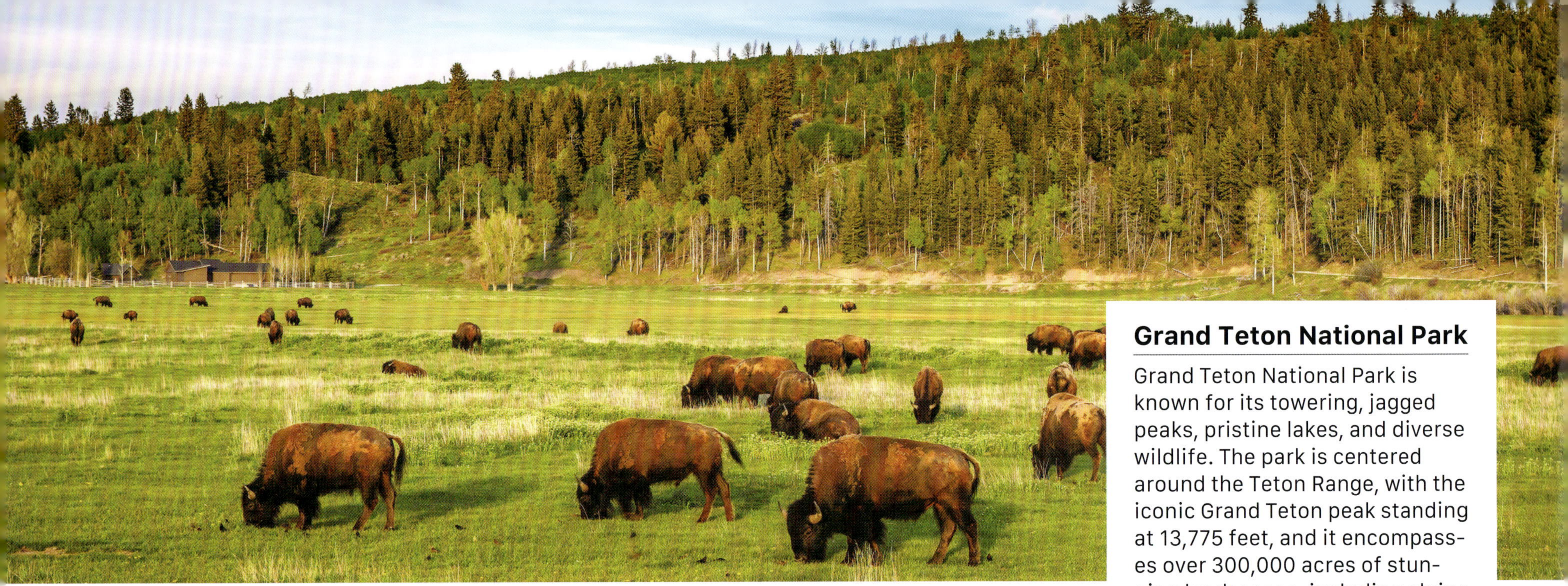

WYOMING

Grand Teton National Park

Grand Teton National Park is known for its towering, jagged peaks, pristine lakes, and diverse wildlife. The park is centered around the Teton Range, with the iconic Grand Teton peak standing at 13,775 feet, and it encompasses over 300,000 acres of stunning landscapes, including alpine meadows, forests, and the Snake River, which winds through the valley below the mountains.

Bighorn Canyon-National Recreation Area

Bighorn Canyon National Recreation Area is split into two districts: the North District in Montana and the South District in Wyoming. The South District of the Bighorn Canyon National Recreation Area is located in Wyoming. It offers opportunities for outdoor recreation, such as hiking, boating, fishing, camping, and wildlife viewing. The Bighorn Lake, created by the Yellowtail Dam, provides a scenic setting for water activities, while the surrounding cliffs and ridges offer breathtaking views.

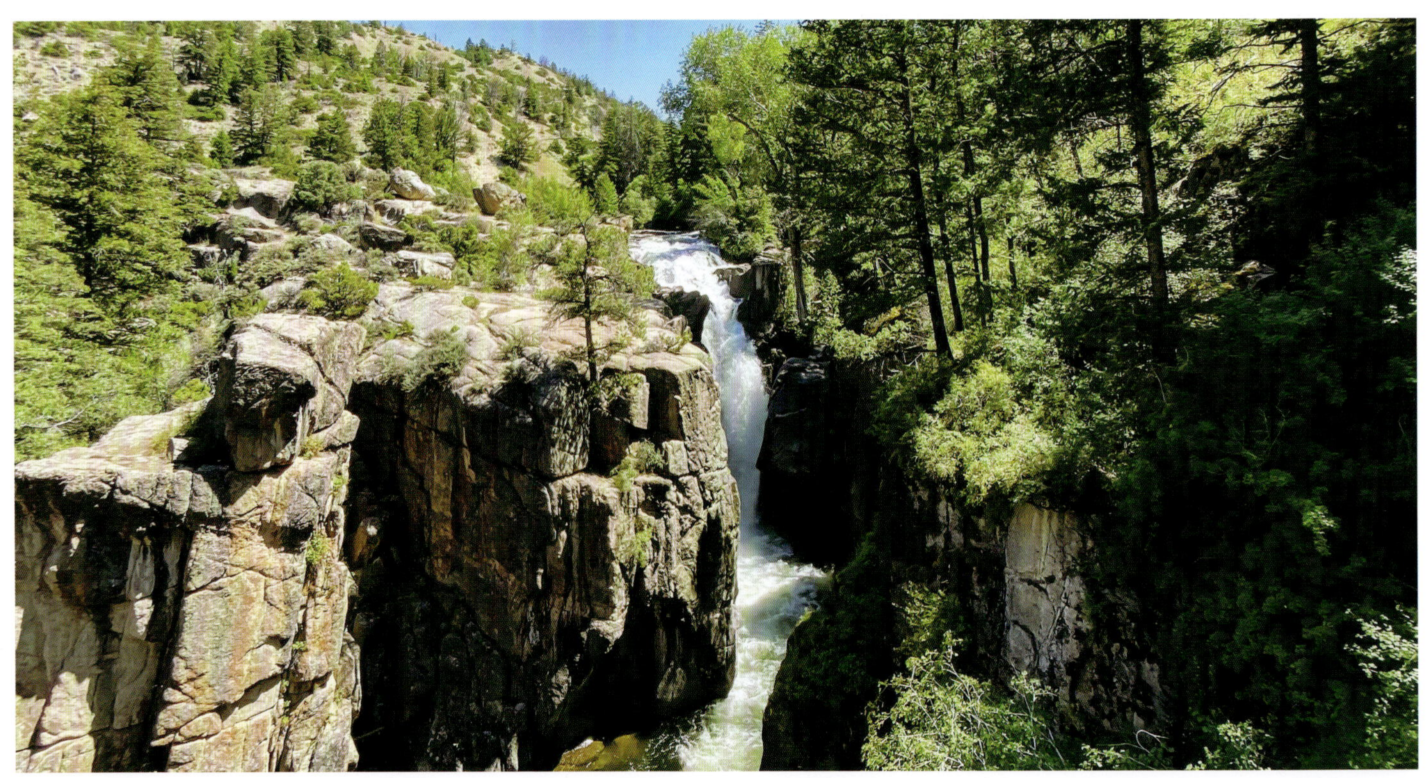

Devils Tower National Monument

Also known as Bear Lodge, Devils Tower is a striking geological formation, and the first U.S. national monument, established in 1906. The tower rises 1,267 feet above the surrounding landscape, with its distinctive vertical columns of rock formed by an ancient volcanic eruption millions of years ago. Visitors can explore the area by hiking around the base or taking the 1.3-mile Tower Trail, which offers close-up views of the tower and the surrounding area, and experienced rock climbers can enjoy challenging routes. The site is considered sacred by several Native American tribes.

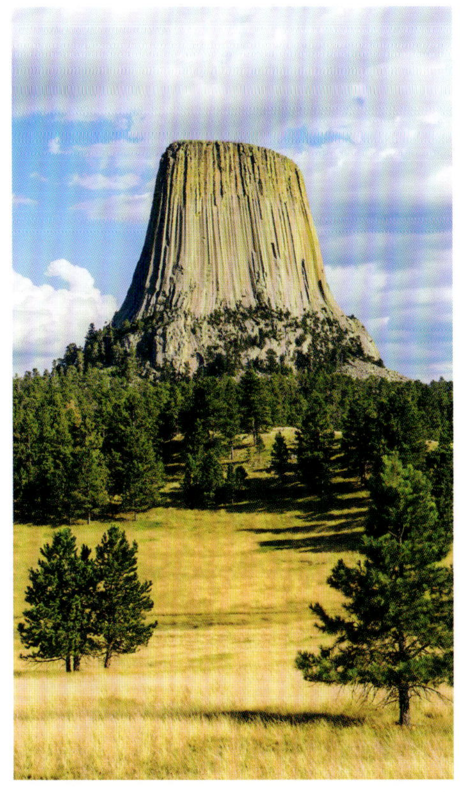

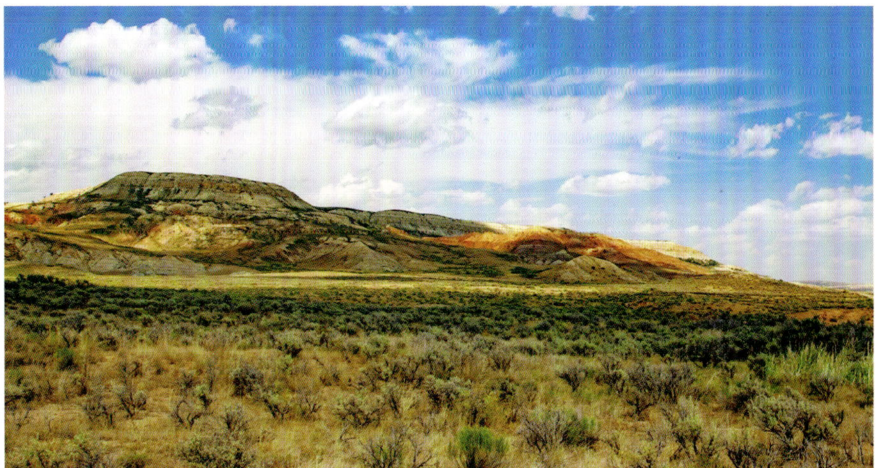

Fossil Butte National Monument

Fossil Butte National Monument is a renowned site for paleontological research and fossil preservation. The monument is home to one of the richest deposits of ancient fossils, dating back to the Eocene Epoch—around 50 million years ago. Fossils of fish, plants, insects, and other animals from a prehistoric lake ecosystem are beautifully preserved in the region's sedimentary layers.

Fort Laramie National Historic Site

Fort Laramie National Historic Site preserves the historic military outpost that played a key role in the westward expansion of the U.S. during the 19th century. Established in 1834 as a trading post and later expanded into a U.S. Army fort, Fort Laramie was an important site for travelers on the Oregon, California, and Mormon Trails, as well as a strategic military post during the Indian Wars. Visitors to the site can view restored buildings, including the fort's officers' quarters, barracks, and the commander's quarters.

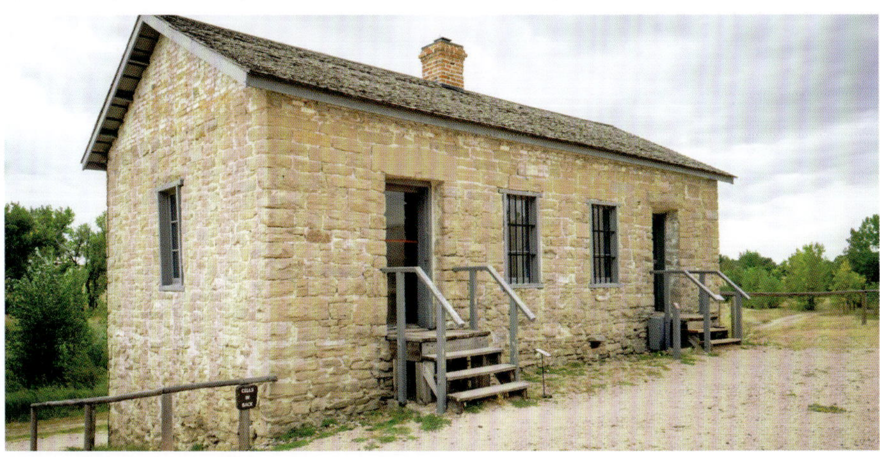

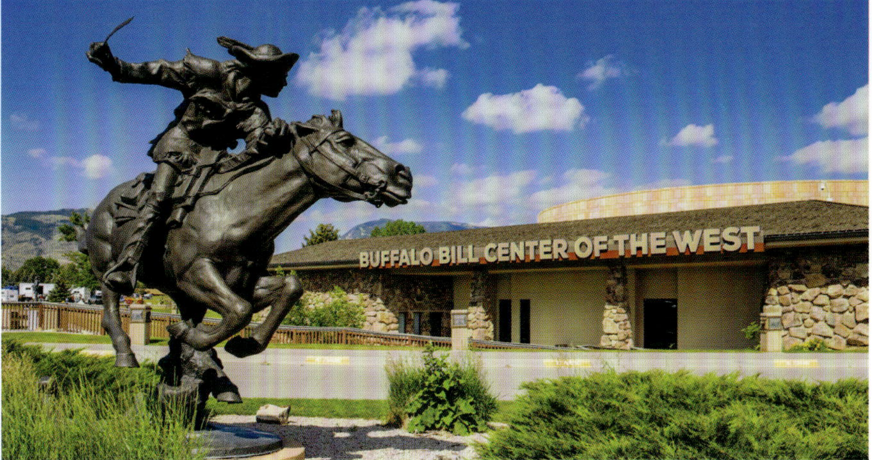

Buffalo Bill Center of the West

Formerly known as the Buffalo Bill Historical Center, Buffalo Bill Center of the West is a complex of five museums dedicated to the history and culture of the American West. The center's collections cover a broad range of topics, from Native American art and artifacts, to the life and legacy of Buffalo Bill Cody. The five museums include: The Buffalo Bill Museum, the Cody Firearms Museum, the Plains Indian Museum, the Whitney Western Art Museum, and the Draper Natural History Museum.

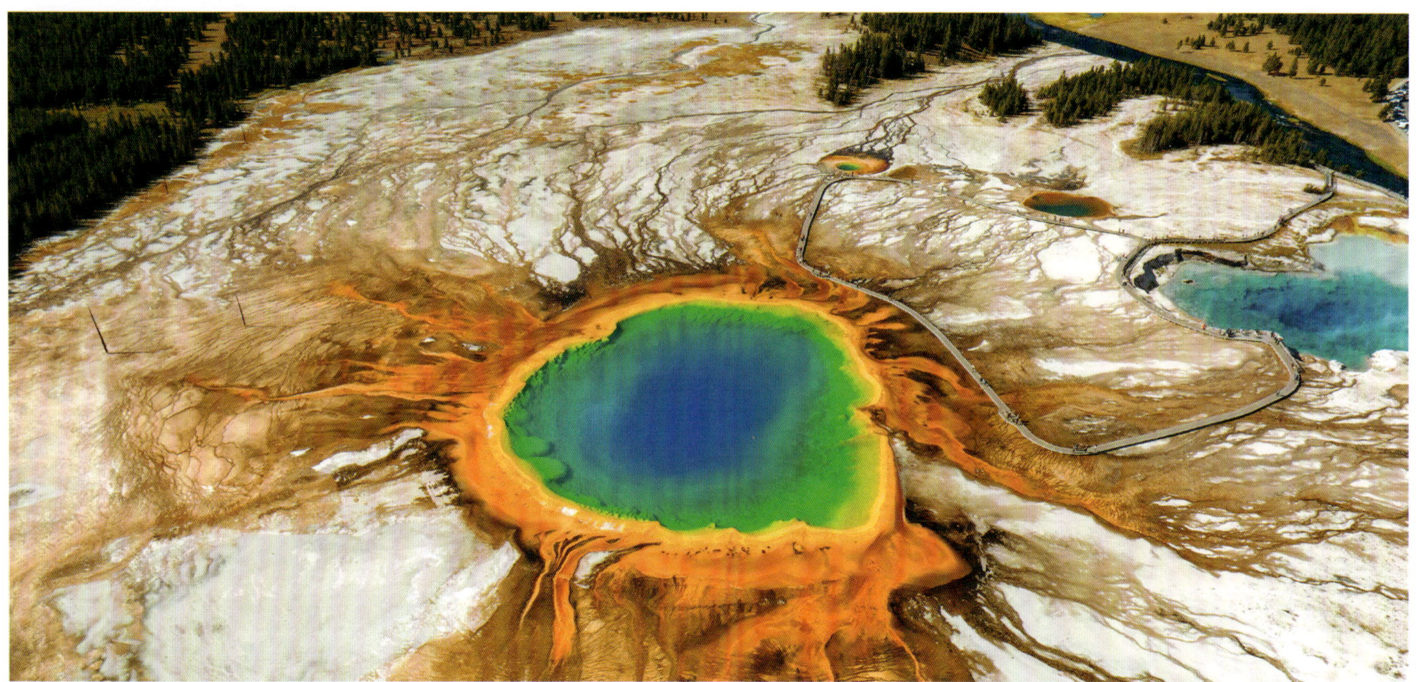

Grand Prismatic Spring

Located in Yellowstone National Park in Wyoming, Grand Prismatic Spring is the largest hot spring in the United States, and the third-largest in the world. Known for its striking colors, the spring's vibrant blue center is surrounded by concentric rings of orange, yellow, and green, created by heat-loving microorganisms that thrive in the different temperatures of the spring. The surrounding area features boardwalks and a viewpoint that offers a spectacular aerial view of the spring.

Old Faithful

Old Faithful, located in the Wyoming part of Yellowstone National Park, is one of the world's most famous geysers. It erupts approximately every 60 to 110 minutes, shooting a column of hot water and steam up to 185 feet into the air, creating a spectacular natural display. The geyser's predictable eruptions make it a popular attraction for visitors, who can watch the event from nearby boardwalks and observation areas.

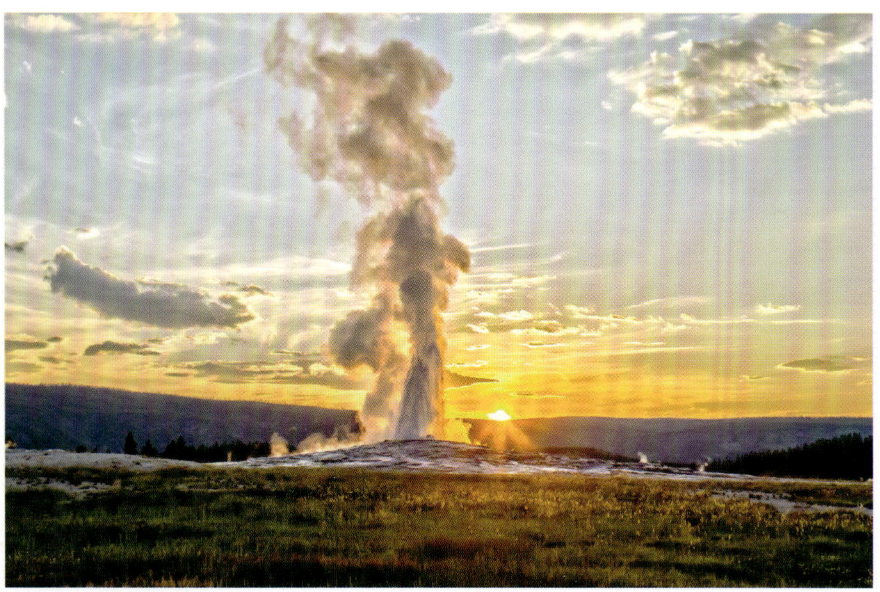

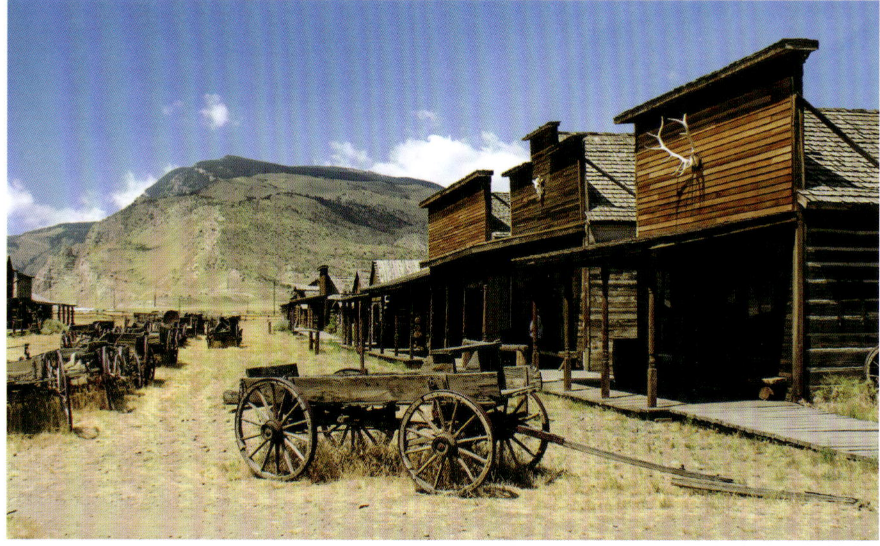

Old Trail Town and Museum of the Old West

Located in Cody, WY, Old Trail Town and Museum of the Old West is a historical attraction that offers visitors a glimpse into the life and culture of the American Old West. The museum features a collection of authentic frontier buildings, including cabins, saloons, and a stagecoach, many of which were moved to the site from nearby areas. The exhibits highlight the history of early settlers, Native American tribes, and legendary figures like Buffalo Bill Cody, with displays of artifacts, tools, clothing, and weapons from the period.